Internationales Jahrbuch des Deutschen Idealismus

International Yearbook of German Idealism

Internationales Jahrbuch des Deutschen Idealismus
International Yearbook of German Idealism

9 · 2011 **Freiheit** / *Freedom*

Herausgegeben von/*edited by*
Fred Rush (Notre Dame) und/*and* Jürgen Stolzenberg (Halle/S.)
Redaktion/*Associate editors*
Paul Franks (Toronto) und/*and* Lars-Thade Ulrichs (Halle/S.)

De Gruyter

Online-Zugang für Subskribenten/*Online access for subscribers:*
http://www.degruyter.de/journals/ijbdi

ISSN 1613-0472

ISBN 978-3-11-028029-6 (Br.)
ISBN 978-3-11-028374-7 (online)
ISBN 978-3-11-028375-4 (Br./online)

Bibliografische Information Der Deutschen Nationalbibliothek

Die Deutsche Nationalbibliothek verzeichnet diese Publikation in der Deutschen National-
bibliografie; detaillierte bibliografische Daten sind im Internet über <http://dnb.d-nb.de>
abrufbar.

© 2013 Walter de Gruyter GmbH, Berlin/Boston
Datenkonvertierung/Satz: Werksatz Schmidt & Schulz GmbH, Gräfenhainichen
∞ Gedruckt auf säurefreiem Papier, das die US-ANSI-Norm über Haltbarkeit erfüllt.

Printed in Germany

www.degruyter.com

In memoriam Konrad Cramer
(1933–2013)

Inhalt

II. Rezensionen

In memoriam Konrad Cramer
(1933–2013)

Am 12. Februar 2013 ist der Philosoph Konrad Cramer in Göttingen gestorben. Konrad Cramer, Sohn des Philosophen Wolfgang Cramer, wurde 1967 in Heidelberg bei Hans-Georg Gadamer und Dieter Henrich mit einer Arbeit zur theoretischen Philosophie Kants promoviert. Die Habilitation erfolgte 1975. Im Jahre 1977 nahm er einen Ruf an die Pädagogische Hochschule Westfalen-Lippe, Abteilung Münster an und wechselte 1980 als ordentlicher Professor der Philosophie an die Universität Münster. Seit 1982 war Cramer bis zu seiner Emeritierung Inhaber des Lehrstuhls für Philosophie an der Georg-August-Universität Göttingen.

Konrad Cramer war Ordentliches Mitglied der Akademie der Wissenschaften zu Göttingen, Vorsitzender der Leitungskommission für die Akademieausgabe der Schriften Kants und Mitglied des Wissenschaftlichen Beirats der Internationalen Schleiermacher-Gesellschaft sowie Mitherausgeber der Historisch-kritischen Ausgabe der Werke F.D.E. Schleiermachers und Ehrendoktor der Theologischen Fakultät der Martin-Luther-Universität Halle-Wittenberg.

Seine international hoch geschätzten Forschungen zu zentralen Positionen des klassischen Rationalismus, zur Philosophie Kants, des deutschen Idealismus und der neuzeitlichen Theorie der Subjektivität sind von der Absicht geleitet, das theoretische Potential einer philosophischen Theorie von den interpretativen Verstellungen, denen sie im Laufe der Zeit unterworfen ist, zu befreien, die in ihr entwickelten Argumente freizulegen und ihre Überzeugungskraft zu prüfen. Aufgrund ihrer analytischen Tiefenschärfe haben sie Maßstäbe für die philosophische Forschung gesetzt.

Seine intellektuelle Brisanz, seine argumentative Präsenz und die Kraft seiner Persönlichkeit waren faszinierend.

Dem Idealismus-Jahrbuch war Konrad Cramer als Mitglied des Beirats verbunden.

In memoriam Konrad Cramer
(1933–2013)

The philosopher Konrad Cramer died on February 12, 2013 in Göttingen. The son of the philosopher Wolfgang Cramer, Konrad Cramer received his Ph.D. in 1967 at Heidelberg with a dissertation on Kant's theoretical philosophy under the direction of Hans-Georg Gadamer and Dieter Henrich. His habilitation followed in 1975. In 1977 he took a position at the Pädagogische Hochschule Westfalen-Lippe, Münster Division and, in 1980, was appointed Professor of Philosophy at the Universität Münster. From 1982 until his retirement, Cramer held the Chair of Philosophy at the Georg-August-Universität, Göttingen.

Cramer was a member of the Göttingen Academy of Sciences, chairman of the Oversight Commission for the Akademie-Ausgabe of Kant's writings, a member of the Scientific Advisory Board of the International Schleiermacher Society, as well as a co-editor of the historical-critical edition of Schleiermacher's works. He received an honorary doctorate from the theology faculty of the Martin-Luther-Universität, Halle-Wittenberg.

Cramer's research in central areas of classical rationalism, Kant's philosophy, German idealism, and in the modern theory of subjectivity is an object of international admiration. His work is guided by the intent to liberate the theoretical potential of a given philosophical theory from the interpretative obstructions to which it is submitted over time, to lay bare the arguments developed within it, and to assess its persuasiveness. The analytic depth and focus of Cramer's work established a benchmark for philosophical research.

His fiery intellect, argumentative presence, and power of personality were fascinating.

Konrad Cramer was a member of the Editorial Board of the International Yearbook of German Idealism.

Vorwort

Freiheit ist ohne Zweifel eines der zentralen Themen der klassischen deutschen Philosophie. Für Kant ist *Freiheit* nicht nur der Grundbegriff der praktischen Philosophie, sondern auch der „Schlußstein von dem ganzen Gebäude eines Systems der reinen Vernunft". Mit Blick auf die Französische Revolution nannte Fichte seine Wissenschaftslehre „das erste System der Freiheit". In der Nachfolge Fichtes ist dem frühen Schelling die Freiheit „das A und O aller Philosophie", während der spätere Schelling die Theorie der Freiheit mit der Frage nach der Herkunft des Bösen verbindet. Hegel schließlich begreift Freiheit als die „Substanz und das Wesen des Geistes", dessen Konkretionen in Kunst, Religion und der Weltgeschichte die Philosophie darzustellen habe.

Die im vorliegenden 9. Band des *Internationalen Jahrbuchs des Deutschen Idealismus/International Yearbook of German Idealism* versammelten Beiträge nehmen aus unterschiedlichen Perspektiven zu der Vielfalt der Bedeutung und der systematischen Funktion Stellung, die den Begriff der Freiheit in der klassischen deutschen Philosophie auszeichnet. Hierbei werden auch die polemischen Bezüge berücksichtigt, in denen die unterschiedlichen Konzeptionen entwickelt worden sind. Darüber hinaus wird deutlich, wie sehr diese Debatten in der gegenwärtigen Diskussion über Freiheit wirksam sind.

Das lässt sich u. a. mit Bezug auf das Verhältnis gegenwärtiger Konzeptionen von Autonomie im Sinne von Selbstdenken und selbstverantworteter Lebensführung und der kantischen Idee der Autonomie als Selbstgesetzgebung der Vernunft zeigen. In kantkritischer Absicht kontrastiert *Charles Larmore* diese Idee Kants mit einem Konzept von Vernunft, demzufolge die Funktion der Vernunft allein darin besteht, sich auf schon existierende Gründe zu beziehen und diese sich zu eigen zu machen. Wie sehr zentrale Begriffe der praktischen Philosophie Kants wie die der Freiheit des Willens und der Freiheit der Willkür (*libertas indifferentiae*) bis heute interpretationsbedürftig geblieben sind, zeigt der Beitrag von *Heiner F. Klemme*. Von einem systematischen Interesse am Problem der Willensfreiheit geleitet, zeigt Klemme, wie Kants Leugnung der Position eines moralischen Indifferentismus mit der von Kant nicht geleugneten Tatsache einer Entscheidung gegen das moralische Gesetz vereinbar ist. Die Aufklärung des alltäglichen Verantwortungsbewusstseins durch die Ideen der Tugend und der Freiheit und deren normative Funktion ist *Pierre Keller* zufolge die Aufgabe der kritischen Moralphilosophie Kants. Dies erscheint zugleich als kritischer Maßstab gegenüber der Philosophie Hegels, die Freiheit zum konstitutiven Prinzip eines Systems aller Begriffe macht. So interpretationsbedürftig die Bedeutung zentraler Begriffe der praktischen Philosophie Kants nach wie vor ist, so dunkel ist das Theoriestück der Deduktion des kategorischen Imperativs in der *Grundlegung zur Metaphysik der Sitten* bis heute geblieben. Hier sucht der Beitrag von *Rocco Porcheddu* einen Schritt weiter zu kommen. Porcheddu plädiert für eine Rekonstruktion des Arguments der Deduktion aus dem Begriff der theoretischen Freiheit, die, ohne einen Rekurs auf die faktische Selbstgewissheit des sittlichen Bewusstseins zu benötigen, eine geschlossene Beweisführung von der Zuschreibung der Urteilsfähigkeit bis zur Geltung des kategorischen Imperativs erlaubt. Als aufklärungsbedürftig erweist sich auch das viel zitierte Wort Fichtes von der Wissenschaftslehre als dem „ersten System der Freiheit". Dem geht der Beitrag von *Allen Wood* nach. In einer gewissen Nähe zu Kants Argument für die Geltung des kategorischen Imperativs im Ausgang von der theoretischen Freiheit ist das Argument Fichtes zu sehen, dass Freiheit eine notwendige Voraussetzung für die theoretischen Funktionen des Verstehens, Begreifens und Urteilens ist, deren Leugnung nicht nur auf einem falschen Begriff von unseren kognitiven Leistungen, sondern auch der Kompetenz, moralisch zu urteilen, beruht. Als eine immer noch unabgegoltene Streitsache ist die Auseinandersetzung zwischen Fichte und Schelling um die Begründung des Projekts einer Philosophie der Natur anzusehen. Der Beitrag von *Christian Klotz* zeigt dies anhand der weiteren Entwicklung Fichtes und Schellings, die zu einer je verschiedenen Philosophie des Absoluten und seiner Offenbarung im Menschen führen, der ein unterschiedlicher Begriff von Freiheit entspricht: Freiheit als prävolitive Selbstbestimmung auf der einen Seite (Fichte), Freiheit als Fähigkeit zum Guten und Bösen auf der anderen Seite (Schelling). Der Beitrag von *Michelle Kosch* untersucht einen der zentralen Aspekte der Freiheitstheorie Fichtes, der mit dem Konzept der von Fichte sog. „formalen Freiheit" bezeichnet ist und der für moralisches Handeln, und das heißt, für die Zuschreibung von Verantwortung und die Adressierung moralischer Imperative erforderlich ist. *Sebastian Schwenzfeuer* untersucht Schellings Metaphysik der Freiheit, der zufolge die menschliche Freiheit als Vermögen des Guten und Bösen von einem ontologischen Freiheitsbegriff abzuleiten ist, sowohl vor dem Hintergrund seiner Natur- und Identitätsphilosophie als auch im Kontrast zu den Freiheitskonzeptionen Kants und Fichtes. Eine Anwendung der von der nachkantischen praktischen Philosophie bereitgestellten begrifflichen Mittel, insbesondere Fichtes und Hegels, auf spezifische Probleme der englischen Gesetzgebung zur psychischen Gesundheit bietet der Beitrag von *Wayne Martin*. Mit Blick auf die neueren Hegelinterpretationen, die von John McDowell und Robert Brandom vorgelegt worden sind, untersucht *Franz Knappik* Brandoms Überlegungen zu Hegels metaphysischer Voraussetzung von Freiheit, die von dem Konzept eines „rational constraint" ausgehen, das seinerseits eine Theorie der ontologischen Homogenität und der begrifflichen Strukturiertheit von Geist und Welt voraussetzt. Anhand einer Kritik Brandoms entwickelt der Beitrag eine alternative Version des „rational-constraint-Arguments" und des ihm entsprechenden Freiheitsbegriffs. Im Ausgang von systematischen Problemen, die sich aus Schopenhauers Theorie der Verneinung des Willens und der ästhetischen Erfahrung mit Blick auf seinen Determinismus ergeben, suchen *Alex Neill* und *Sandy Shapshay* zu einer Klärung im Rückgriff auf Schopenhauers Begriff transzendentaler Freiheit beizutragen. Ein engagiertes Plädoyer für Hegels Freiheitsbegriff und seine Funktion, die Sphäre des Rechts zu begründen, bietet auf dem Wege einer begriffanalytischen Klärung und in Auseinandersetzung mit Ulrich Pothasts Konzept von Freiheit als lebendiger Vernünftigkeit der Beitrag von *Hans Friedrich Fulda*.

Allen Beiträgern danken wir für ihre engagierte Mitwirkung. Ein besonderer Dank gilt der Bereitschaft der Beiträger, dem Anliegen des Jahrbuchs, systematische Fragestellungen nicht nur auf einen Autor fixiert, sondern in vergleichender Perspektive und im Blick auf die aktuellen Diskussionen zu behandeln, Rechnung zu tragen. Dem Verlag de Gruyter gilt wie stets unser Dank für die vertrauensvolle Betreuung des Jahrbuchs. Christiane Straub, Tomas Cabi, Jordan Rodgers und Jordan Corwin ist für die Hilfe bei der Einrichtung der Manuskripte für den Druck sehr herzlich zu danken. Der 10. Band wird dem Thema *Geschichte* gewidmet sein.

Fred Rush   Jürgen Stolzenberg
Notre Dame   Halle (Saale)

Preface

Freedom is doubtless one of the central themes of classical German philosophy. For Kant *freedom* is not only the grounding concept of practical philosophy, but the "keystone of the entire edifice of a system of pure reason." With the French Revolution in mind, Fichte called his Science of Knowledge "the first system of freedom." In the wake of Fichte, freedom is "the alpha and omega of all philosophy" to the early Schelling, while the later Schelling joins the theory of freedom with the question of the origin of evil. Finally, Hegel conceives freedom as the "substance and the essence of spirit," whose concrete forms in art, religion, and world history it is the task of philosophy to portray.

The essays collected in this ninth volume of the *International Yearbook of German Idealism/Internationales Jahrbuch des Deutschen Idealismus* offer views from different perspectives on the diverse significance and systematic function distinctive of the concept of freedom in classical German philosophy. In this connection the polemical contexts in which the different conceptions were developed are also considered. Moreover, it is made clear just how much impact these debates have on the current discussion of freedom.

This is apparent *inter alia* in the relationship of current conceptions of autonomy as thinking for oneself and of leading life in a self-responsible manner and the Kantian idea of autonomy as self-legislation of reason. In his critique of Kant *Charles Larmore* contrasts this idea of Kant's with a concept of reason according to which the function of reason consists only in referring to and appropriating already existing reasons. The contribution of *Heiner F. Klemme* shows how central concepts of Kant's practical philosophy, such as those of freedom of *Wille* and freedom of *Willkür* (*libertas indifferentiae*), remain in need of interpretation. Guided by a systematic interest in the problem of free will, Klemme shows how Kant's denial of the position of moral indifferentism is consistent with the fact, not denied by Kant, that one may decide contrary to the moral law. According to *Pierre Keller*, the task of Kant's critical moral philosophy is the clarification of the everyday sense of responsibility through the ideas of virtue and freedom and their normative function. This figures likewise as the critical standard vis-à-vis the philosophy of Hegel, which takes freedom to be the constitutive principle of a system of all concepts. As much as the significance of these central concepts of Kant's practical philosophy still requires interpretation, so is the deduction of the categorical imperative in the *Groundwork for the Metaphysics of Morals* obscure. The essay by *Rocco Porcheddu* seeks to make progress here. Porcheddu advocates a reconstruction of the argument of the deduction on the basis of the concept of theoretical freedom, which, without requiring recourse to the actual self-certainty of moral consciousness, provides a sound argument from the attribution of the capacity to judge to the validity of the categorical imperative. Fichte's much-cited dictum that the Science of Knowledge is the "first system of freedom" also requires clarification, and *Allen Wood*'s essay pursues this. Fichte's argument that freedom is a necessary condition for the theoretical functions of understanding, conception, and judging, the renunciation of which rests not only upon a false conception of our cognitive powers but also of our competence to judge morally, is to be seen in proximity with Kant's argument for the validity of the categorical imperative out of theoretical freedom. The confrontation of Fichte and Schelling on the question of grounding the project of a philosophy of nature is a dispute yet to be settled. The contribution of *Christian Klotz* illustrates this by taking into account the development of Fichte's and Schelling's thought, a development that leads each to a different philosophy of the absolute and of its disclosure in humankind, corresponding to a different concept of freedom: freedom as pre-volitional self-determination, on the one side (Fichte), and freedom as capacity for good and evil, on the other (Schelling). *Michelle Kosch*'s essay investigates one of the central aspects of Fichte's theory of freedom, denoted by his concept of "formal freedom," which is necessary for moral action and, that means, for the ascription of responsibility and address of moral imperatives. *Sebastian Schwenzfeuer* investigates Schelling's metaphysics of freedom, according to which human freedom, as the capacity for good and evil, is to be derived from an ontological concept of freedom against the background of his philosophy of nature and identity philosophy and in contrast to Kant's and Fichte's conceptions of freedom. The contribution by *Wayne Martin* applies the conceptual resources provided by post-Kantian practical philosophy, particularly that of Fichte and Hegel, to specific problems of consent in English mental health law. Taking up the newer interpretations of Hegel put forward by John McDowell and Robert Brandom, *Franz Knappik* investigates Brandom's reflections on Hegel's metaphysical supposition of freedom that proceed from the concept of a "rational constraint," which presupposes a theory of the ontological homogeneity of a conceptually-structured mind and world. By means of a critique of Brandom the essay develops an alternative version of the "rational constraint argument" and of the corresponding concept of freedom. Proceeding from systematic problems that arise out of Schopenhauer's theory of denial of the will and of aesthetic experience in view of his determinism, *Alex Neill* and *Sandy Shapshay* offer a clarification by retrenching in a corrected understanding of Schopenhauer's concept of transcendental freedom. The essay by *Hans Friedrich Fulda*, by way of a conceptual-analytic clarification and in debate with Ulrich Pothast's concept of freedom as living rationality, offers a lively brief for Hegel's concept of freedom and its function in grounding the sphere of right.

We thank all contributors for their dedicated participation. Special thanks are due for the readiness of the contributors to take into account the request of the *Yearbook*, to treat systematic questions not simply fixing on one author but comparatively and in light of current discussions. Our thanks are due, as always, to the publisher, de Gruyter, for its confidence in and support of the *Yearbook*. The editors are also grateful to Christiane Straub, Tomas Cabi, Jordan Rodgers, and Jordan Corwin for preparing the manuscripts for press. The tenth volume of the *Yearbook* will be dedicated to the topic: *History*.

Fred Rush   Jürgen Stolzenberg
Notre Dame   Halle (Saale)

I. Beiträge

Charles Larmore

Kant and the Meanings of Autonomy

Mit Kant wurde „Autonomie" zu einem Schlüsselbegriff der Philosophie. Man irrt sich aber, wenn man denkt, dass alles, was wir gemeinhin unter „Autonomie" verstehen, in einer notwendigen Beziehung zu Kants eigenem Begriff davon steht. Heutzutage gelten Menschen als „autonom", wenn sie für sich selbst denken oder ohne Rücksicht auf Lohn und Drohung das Richtige tun. Diesen Einstellungen des Selbstdenkens und der „Selbstführung" schrieb Kant zwar eine wichtige Rolle in seiner Moralphilosophie zu, bezeichnete sie aber nie als „Autonomie". Er hatte seine guten Gründe dafür. In solchen Fällen handelt es sich nämlich um unsere Beziehung als denkende und handelnde Wesen zu anderen Menschen, während Kant den Ausdruck „Autonomie" für eine Beziehung reservierte, in der wir selbst zu den Prinzipien unseres Denkens und Handelns stehen: Nach ihm besteht nämlich der Geltungsgrund nicht nur moralischer, sondern aller Prinzipien des Denkens und Handelns in einer Selbstgesetzgebung der Vernunft, die daher als die Urheberin der Gültigkeit dieser Prinzipien anzusehen ist. In diesem Aufsatz analysiere ich entsprechend das Verhältnis zwischen der kantischen Auffassung der Autonomie und den Einstellungen des Selbstdenkens und „Selbstführens" und erprobe, inwieweit Kants eigene Auffassung stichhaltig ist.

"Autonomy" is a philosophical notion that people continually invoke without hesitation, as though everyone agreed that what it signifies is a good thing. That, in my view, is a sign that they do not know exactly what they mean by the term, or that different people mean different things by it. Indeed, the term has a number of distinct, established meanings. With Kant, "autonomy" became a key concept of philosophy. But it would be a mistake to assume that everything we understand today by "autonomy" stands in a necessary relation to Kant's own concept of it. According to Kant's idea of autonomy, the ground of validity for not only moral, but also for all principles of thought and action, consists in the self-legislation of reason, which is therefore to be considered the source of their validity. As Kant said of the moral law:

> The will is not merely subject to the law but subject to it in such a way that it must be viewed as also giving the law to itself and just because of this as first subject to the law (of which it can regard itself as the author) (GMS, p. 431/GMM, p. 39).[1]

In the following, I will contrast the Kantian conception of autonomy as self-legislation with other meanings of the word and consider to what extent that conception itself is coherent.

---

[1]   I sometimes modify cited English translations from the German.

I. Political and legal pre-history

As is well known, the word "autonomy" had a long history before Kant took it over in his *Grundlegung zur Metaphysik der Sitten* of 1785.[2] Two things about this pre-history are interesting. First, the term "autonomy" was used almost exclusively in political or legal contexts without being extended to the domain of moral philosophy and without being applied to the general philosophical question of how rational beings are related to the principles of their thought and action. Second, neither the political nor the legal meaning of the word provided a precise or even suggestive model for the way in which Kant would develop the concept of autonomy in these other and broader contexts.

The Greeks did not use "*autonomia*" with reference to individuals but only with reference to political communities, and in particular to those that do not stand under the rule of foreign powers or a tyrant. Such communities are autonomous insofar as they live according to their own laws, that is, by the laws that they have chosen to regulate their common life. Now, that does not mean that they base the authority of these laws solely on their own will or their own legislation. Even if the laws become legally binding by having been decided upon by the appropriate procedures, it could be and often is the case – not only in antiquity – that the community has imposed those laws on itself because it (or, more precisely, its representatives) is convinced of their antecedent moral validity. This shows that a system of positive law does not in general offer a model of what Kant understands by "autonomy", and not only because his concept of autonomy refers to individual rational beings and not to communities. Even more significant is the fact that law rests ultimately, as I indicated, on an already existing and presumably valid system of norms, namely on morality. Kant's concept of autonomy, by contrast, is supposed to explain the nature of morality itself and thus not only the binding force or obligatory character of moral rules, but also their very validity or correctness.[3]

In the early modern period, "autonomy" continued to be used in this political sense. At the same time, however, a new, legal meaning emerged. The term "autonomy" came to designate the authority for self-legislation or for legal self-determination that a municipality, an organization, or even an individual (for example, a member of the nobility or a property owner) enjoyed within the framework of a given, overarching legal order. Such a public or private legal authority is exercised when, for instance, a city council passes a law or a citizen sells his house. In these cases, the validity of the ordinance or the sale of the real

---

[2]   On the history of the concept, see above all Pohlmann, 1971.

[3]   In Kant this distinction consists in the fact that the morally correct thing becomes obligatory for rational beings like us who may be inclined to act otherwise and who are therefore required to subordinate our inclinations to what is morally correct.

estate depends upon the decisions of the responsible city officials or of the owner. But this kind of autonomy is obviously a local phenomenon, which is defined and limited by an already existing legal order. It could therefore hardly serve as a model for the Kantian conception, according to which autonomy not only applies to the realm of morality and even more generally to the nature of reason itself, but is supposed to explain the validity of all the laws and principles they involve.

This was the situation up until Kant. "Autonomous" in the political sense were communities that live by their own laws, that is, laws that they themselves have approved. "Autonomous" in the legal sense were municipalities or individuals that are authorized by an overarching legal system to pass laws or to engage in legal transactions. Nothing in this context would have prepared us for the radical and quite general claim with which Kant expressly introduces the word "autonomy" to designate the fundamental nature of every rational being as such: "Autonomy of the will is the quality of the will wherein the will is a law to itself (independently of any quality of the objects of the will)" (GMS, p. 440/ GMM, p. 47). One can understand why Kant chose the term "autonomy" for his doctrine of the self-legislation of reason, but his reasons stemmed more from etymological considerations than from established linguistic usage. Christian Wolff, whose writings shaped not only substantively but also terminologically the German philosophical landscape of the time, used the expression only in its political meaning.

Moreover, Kant did not begin talking about "autonomy" at all until quite late, for the first time in fact in the *Groundwork* of 1785, and there he used the concept exclusively in the meaning he was introducing. In the lectures on moral philosophy that he regularly held in the mid-1770s, not only is the word missing, but the concept as well, if we are able to trust the transcripts. There Kant already presents the laws of morality as universal, categorically necessary rules of action that, in the case of human beings, who can be inclined otherwise, become categorically binding obligations. However, he asserts as well that we can grasp not only their validity, but also their obligatory character or (as I shall also say) their bindingness through our understanding alone, without reference to the will of God and – there is no mention of this at all – without reference to any self-legislating activity on our part.[4]

Since Kant's concept of autonomy seems untenable to me, I am tempted to say: too bad he did not remain with this conception. For the only significant

---

[4]   VM, pp. 55–73, 79. This recent edition is based on the "Kaehler" transcript of 1773–1775. For an English translation based on similar transcripts, see KLE, pp. 65–73, 76. When Kant writes in these lectures, "All obligation is either external or internal" (VM, p. 49/KLE, p. 62), he is not referring to the bindingness itself of a moral law, but rather to the "motivating grounds" (*Bewegungsgründe*) (VM, p. 50/KLE, p. 62) – one's own will (*Willkür*) or someone else's – by which a person is moved to comply with the law.

weakness of the lectures on moral philosophy of the 1770s is Kant's assumption that the understanding itself cannot provide a sufficient motive for action.[5] If the understanding were actually motivationally inert, then it also could not move us to revise existing convictions or to draw conclusions. Since that is obviously false, it cannot be, as Kant supposes, excluded from the outset that the understanding is also capable of moving us to perform those actions whose correctness it indicates to us. According to the Kant of these lectures, however, carrying out, if not recognizing, a moral law can only take place (legal coercion and social pressure aside) through "moral feeling" as it has been formed by habituation or through an anticipation of God's rewards and punishments (VM, pp. 67–69, 61–62/KLE, pp. 71, 68–69). Or, to be more exact: that is his general position. In another passage Kant concedes that the understanding does possess "a moving force" (*bewegende Kraft*) insofar as it resists "immoral actions [...] because they run counter to the use of its rule". But then he adds that this motivational force of the understanding is not in fact sufficient to prevail over the opposing impulses (*elateres*) of sensuality (VM, pp. 70–1/KLE, p. 72). Kant's concession is on the right track. But the added qualification is not because, among other things, moral feeling and reverence for God only gain the upper hand by pointing to reasons for not giving in to those impulses and thus they themselves involve an exercise of the understanding. Naturally, one can be driven by temptations to act against one's better judgment, and good habits, which involve proper feelings, are the best protection against such temptations. But phenomena of this sort cannot be well understood by means of a crude dichotomy between understanding and feeling.

Later, in the *Groundwork*, Kant came to the conclusion that moral feeling and the fear of God are inappropriate motives for moral action. But this change did not lead him to question the assumption of the motivational inertness of the understanding. (In section IV, I will return to the continuing role of this assumption in Kant.) Instead, the "critical philosophy" that comes to expression in the *Groundwork* has left behind the conceptual framework of the earlier lectures on ethics. The understanding is no longer credited with the capacity of comprehending the bindingness of moral rules since their bindingness, like the bindingness and indeed the validity of all the principles of our thought and action, has now ceased to be regarded as strictly speaking an object of knowledge, but instead as a product of self-legislating reason. That, of course, is Kant's doctrine of autonomy. All in all, with the reservations mentioned, I myself prefer the standpoint of the lectures on ethics.

---

[5]   Cf. VM, pp. 68–69/KLE, p. 71: "If I judge by the understanding that the action is morally good, then I am still very far from doing this action of which I have so judged. [...] To be sure, the understanding can judge, but to give this judgment of the understanding a force so that it becomes a motive to impel the will to carry out the action, that is the philosophers' stone".

As I will explain later, Kant's concept of autonomy implicitly underlies his conception of theoretical reason as well, although the term itself does not appear in either edition of the *Critique of Pure Reason* (1781, 1787). However, it is interesting to note for which attitudes of mind Kant never used the word, even though they too consist in an exercise of reason, even though he also treated them extensively, and even though we ourselves tend to speak of them as paradigm forms of autonomy (so that careless commentators sometimes refer to his treatment of them as "Kant's doctrine of autonomy"). We commonly call people "autonomous" who think for themselves or who do what is right regardless of reward or threat. It is completely different in Kant, who did indeed ascribe an important role in his moral philosophy to these capacities of thinking for oneself and of governing oneself, but who never designated them as "autonomy". There is a good reason for this. Such cases have to do with the relation that we in our thinking and acting have to other people, whereas Kant reserved the term "autonomy" or "self-legislation" for a relation in which we can stand to the principles or laws themselves of thought and action. Yet that does not mean, as we will see, that he did not think of trying to explain these attitudes of mind by means of his concept of autonomy. On the contrary, he claimed that only on this basis are they explicable.

I will now examine more closely both phenomena – thinking for oneself and self-governance – in order to show to what extent Kant correctly analyzes them without appealing to his concept of autonomy and how he then goes astray when he attempts to found them on this concept after all.

II. Thinking for oneself

The text in which Kant directly takes up the phenomenon of thinking for oneself is his essay of 1784, "An Answer to the Question: What is Enlightenment?", in which he summons his readers: "*Sapere aude*! Have the courage to make use of your own understanding!" (WIA, p. 35/KPP, p. 17) He explains the nature of this attitude of mind primarily through a discussion of its opposite, the immaturity that consists in letting others tell us what we should think. Clearly, Kant does not mean to assert that someone who thinks independently never relies on the knowledge of experts or on the reports of eyewitnesses. Rather, what is decisive is that one trusts the statements of others only when one sees good reasons oneself for believing in their reliability (though not, of course, in their infallibility).

For Kant, then, the essence of the Enlightenment is the determination to think for oneself without guidance from another. Unfortunately, he offers no other explanation of the general absence of this attitude of mind until his own time apart from one that is ultimately psychological: It is a "self-imposed immaturity", to which most people have surrendered out of "laziness and cowardice". Insofar as political and religious powers have succeeded in preventing the development of independent thinking in order to further their own goals, they have only exploited, according to this explanation, the lapses for which these people have themselves been responsible. Kant underestimates the role of the various social, intellectual and even religious movements that have produced and encouraged, to cite his own words, "the spirit of a rational valuing of one's own worth and of each individual's calling to think for himself" (WIA, p. 36/ KPP, p. 18).

However, what I would like to call attention to is that Kant does not use the word "autonomy" a single time in this essay, either to designate thinking for oneself or to explain the conditions of its possibility, and this, it will be recalled, only one year before the publication of the *Groundwork of the Metaphysics of Morals*. The concept does not occur implicitly, either. In a passage concerned with the question whether one age may take it upon itself to limit through certain agreements the right to think for oneself in a subsequent age, Kant does remark that "the touchstone of whatever can be decided upon as law for a people lies in the question: whether a people could impose such a law upon itself?" (WIA, p. 39/KPP, p. 20) But this statement invokes the political concept of autonomy, which, as I mentioned, leaves open the ultimate basis of the self-imposed law: a people can subject itself to a law and thereby make it legally binding because it is convinced that this law is in itself already morally valid.

It should not really be surprising that Kant's essay on enlightenment does not use the word "autonomy" or even rely on his own concept of it. Thinking for oneself – an attitude of mind that we ourselves habitually refer to as "autonomy" – and autonomy in the Kantian sense are two entirely different things. The former concerns our relation to other people, the latter our relation to the principles of our thought and action. Kant proceeds in this essay as if he could adequately analyze the capacity of thinking for oneself without going into the nature of the validity and bindingness of the principles in accord with which we exercise this capacity. That assumption is correct, and indeed so much so that everything he says there about independence of thought remains untouched even if – as I believe necessary – we completely reject his account of the latter subject, namely his doctrine of autonomy.

What by contrast we ought to find striking, if not quite surprising, is the way in which Kant two years later takes up again the theme of thinking for oneself. Toward the end of his essay "What Is Orientation in Thinking?" (1786), he seeks to distinguish three meanings of the expression "freedom of thought", which is another name for "thinking for oneself". This freedom, he claims, consists not only in not being prevented by the "civil coercion" of the state or by social pressure (through the "coercion of conscience") from following one's own thinking wherever it leads. It must, thirdly, be understood as the "subjection of reason to no other laws than those which it gives to itself". That is a clear allusion to the autonomy of reason as defined in the *Groundwork* one year before:

> Hence the will is not merely subject to the law but subject to it in such a way that it must be viewed as also giving the law to itself and just because of this as first subject to the law (of which it can regard itself as the author [*Urheber*]) (GMS, p. 431/GMM, p. 39).

And it is a statement in which Kant, without using the term itself, extends his idea of "autonomy" from morality to the domain of theoretical reason. In a footnote, he goes so far as to characterize thinking for oneself by way of a formulation that directly recalls the first formula of the moral law from the *Groundwork*:

> To make use of one's own reason means no more than to ask oneself concerning everything one is supposed to accept: whether one finds it possible to make the reasons why one accepts something or the rule that follows from what one accepts a universal principle for the use of one's reason (O, pp. 146–7/KPW, p. 249).

Self-legislation as the commitment to operate only by universalizable rules or maxims applies, says Kant, as much to theoretical as to practical reason – since, as he asserts at the beginning of the *Groundwork*, "there can, in the end, be only one and the same reason, which must be distinguished merely in its application" (GMS, p. 391/GMM, p. 5) – and thus constitutes the essence of thinking for oneself as the correct exercise of one's own reason.

Why is there such a departure from the more modest approach of "What is Enlightenment?" Why does Kant now consider it necessary to bring in his conception of autonomy, if not the word itself, and to claim that thinking for oneself is possible only when reason gives itself its own laws? The answer lies no doubt in the fact that this concept was introduced formally for the first time in the *Groundwork*, that is, one year after the essay on enlightenment, but only one year before the essay on orientation in thinking. 1785 is indeed a crucial year in Kant's development, one in which he achieved through the formulation of the concept of autonomy a much deeper understanding of the foundations of his philosophical project.

In "Orientation", Kant explains the necessity of appealing to this concept by claiming that freedom of thought in the two other senses mentioned – which roughly correspond to the understanding of thinking for oneself in the essay on Enlightenment – can only be guaranteed through the self-legislation of reason. "If reason", Kant writes, "does not want to be subject to the law that it gives to itself, it must bow under the yoke of laws which another gives it" (O, p. 145/ KPW, p. 248).

That is, however, an astonishingly bad argument. It is first of all poor because it relies on a confusing contrast between "reason", which is a faculty, but which Kant treats here (as elsewhere) as though it were an agent in itself, and "another" (*ein Anderer*), which manifestly can only be a human being. This sort of confusion is good evidence that Kant has run together the two distinct problematics of reason's relation to its principles, on the one hand, and a rational being's relation to other such beings, on the other.

Second, the argument presupposes that we cannot be subject to any law of thought without it having been imposed on us – if not by ourselves (through our own reason), then by someone else. But why such an implausible presupposition? Kant is clearly appealing to the principle "no law without a legislator", a principle that is as questionable as it is familiar. For who imposed on us, for instance, the logical law of non-contradiction? It makes no sense to speak of the imposition of a law of this kind since, among other things, any reason one might see for such an imposition or for the acceptance of such an imposition would have to presuppose the validity of the law in question. Why can this example not serve as a model for other, more complicated cases? The fundamental laws of thought would then be laws that exist in their own right and that, therefore, we have simply to acknowledge – a conception that I consider in fact to be correct (see below sections IV–V).

The essay "What is Enlightenment?" offers, therefore, a far better account of the nature of thinking for oneself. Precisely because Kant does not even pose there the question about the relation in which we stand to the principles of our thinking, this essay heeds the point that I have made repeatedly: thinking for oneself is a disposition that has to do with our relation as rational beings to other such beings, and not with our relation as rational beings to the principles guiding our thought and action or to reasons in general and to the basis of their validity and bindingness. We are ourselves used to describing the ability to think for oneself without the tutelage of political, religious or other authorities as "the autonomy of the individual". There is nothing wrong with this, so long as we do not confuse this ability with what Kant himself terms "autonomy". And so long as we (unlike Kant) recognize that these two relations – that of the individual to other individuals and that of reason to its principles – can be treated in relative independence from one other. There have been attempts, of course, to explain the validity of certain principles on which we rely by the fact that we belong to some tradition and thus to base the latter relation on the former, precisely with the aim of calling into question the claims of individual autonomy. The latter goal is understandable; thinking for oneself is not a value immune to criticism. It is, however, a mistake to pursue that goal in this manner. It would be better to regard tradition as the necessary vehicle of principles whose validity itself exists independently of their having been passed down through tradition.[6] For surely it would be odd to believe that a principle, quite apart from its content, is binding on us solely because earlier generations happened to have observed it.

---

[6]   Cf. Larmore, 2008, chap. 1.

In any case, it is clear that autonomy, as Kant understands it, does not – contrary to his essay on orientation – represent an essential presupposition of the capacity to think for oneself. Escaping the tutelage of others in order to think and act by one's own lights is quite compatible with the belief that the principles by which one then proceeds have an antecedent validity that reason does not establish, but instead must acknowledge. There is, as I will explain later, the additional fact that Kant's opposing view is fundamentally incoherent.

III. Self-governance

I turn now to the second attitude of mind which we often call "autonomy", but which Kant never does, although he discusses it extensively and even attempts, as in the case of thinking for oneself, to explain its possibility by means of the concept of autonomy he introduced. It is the readiness to do what is right without consideration of any threats or rewards by a higher power, divine or human. Following J. B. Schneewind, I will refer to this disposition as "self-governance", which is not to be confused with "self-legislation" or "autonomy" in the Kantian sense.[7]

St. Paul, in his *Letter to the Romans*, has such a disposition in mind when he writes:

> When the Gentiles, who have not the law, do by nature the things contained in the law, these, having not the law, are a law unto themselves; who show the work of the law written in their hearts, their conscience also bearing witness, and between themselves their thoughts accusing or else excusing one another (2:14–15).

By the expression "the law" those commandments are meant through which God has instructed us how we should treat one another morally. Although the Gentiles did not receive such a law from God, they nevertheless are, Paul is saying, capable of behaving as God's commandments demand when they follow their conscience (*syneidesis*). Thus they are "a law unto themselves" (*heautois eisin nomos*), by which Paul certainly does not mean that the Gentiles view their own reason as the author of the distinction between right and wrong, but rather that they turn their conscience, which bears witness (*symmaturein*) to this distinction, into the law of their conduct. Self-governance is thus the ability to follow one's sense of right and wrong without the need of any higher authority. It not only presupposes that one can distinguish oneself between right and wrong, but also and especially that one can find in oneself the motives for doing what is right.

In our day, a capacity of this kind is often described as "autonomy". There is nothing wrong about doing so. It makes sense to say that autonomy consists in what Paul terms "being a law unto oneself" (*heautoi einai nomos*). Self-gov-

---

[7]   See Schneewind, 1998.

ernance, together with thinking for oneself, is indeed one of the unproblematic things that can be called "autonomy" in the individual realm. One should simply be aware that it is not what Kant understood by "autonomy" and that it cannot be explained by his conception. Someone who can act on the basis of his sense of right and wrong without further incentives does not need to assume that the standards he invokes receive their validity or bindingness somehow through his reason instead of assuming that his reason is what enables him to grasp these standards as the objective truths they are. Self-governance is a capacity of mind that has to do solely with the motivation, not with the principles, of moral action.

Kant, however, was of a different opinion: not in the lectures on moral philosophy of the 1770s, in which he neglected the phenomenon of self-governance and mentioned only moral feeling and reverence for God as internal motives for moral action,[8] but in the *Groundwork* of 1785. There he places the ability to do what is right for its own sake at the center of his account of moral action and goes on to insist that this ability is possible solely through the self-legislation of reason he calls "autonomy". Let us look more closely at these two aspects of his position in the *Groundwork*.

As is well known, Kant in this work draws a fundamental distinction between acting "in conformity with duty" (*pflichtmäßig*) and acting "out of duty" (*aus Pflicht*). One can act in conformity with one's duty for any number of motives: out of self-interest, out of sympathy for others, out of fear of legal sanctions, out of hope for God's reward. But only then, Kant claims, does one act morally, when one acts out of duty, that is, out of the intention to do what is right simply and solely because it is right, independently even of one's changing feelings of sympathy. Kant calls this attitude "respect for the law", defining respect as "the consciousness of the subordination of my will to a law without the intervention of other influences on my mind", a subordination in the sense of a self-subordination under the moral law, since respect is described as a "self-effected feeling" (*selbstgewirktes Gefühl*) (GMS, p. 401n/GMM, p. 14n). This is a conception of what I have called "self-governance", and indeed a rather strict one, inasmuch as it excludes all feelings of sympathy and compassion. Moreover, Kant does not at this point in the book connect this "self-effected feeling" of respect for the law with the idea of self-legislation, which he only later in the *Groundwork* introduces under the name of "autonomy".

It is true that in the same passage in which he brings up the concept of respect he offers the following clarification: "The *object* of respect is therefore simply the *law*, and indeed the law that we impose upon *ourselves* and yet as necessary in itself" (GMS, p. 401n/GMM, p. 14n). Yet the self-imposition of the

---

⁸ Oddly, he cites there in passing (VM, p. 62/KLE, p. 68) the passage from St. Paul, apparently without perceiving its implications.

law that he is talking about here – at least if we limit ourselves to what the statement literally says – is not the self-legislation of autonomy, which according to a later passage in the *Groundwork* supposedly consists in the will being "not merely subject to the law but subject to it in such a way that it must be viewed as also giving the law to itself and just because of this as first subject to the law (of which it can regard itself as the author [*Urheber*])" (GMS, p. 431/GMM, p. 39). For what Kant means in this earlier passage is the self-subordination or subordination of one's own conduct under a law that, as he remarks, is viewed as "necessary in itself" (*an sich notwendig*), that is, as in itself unconditionally valid and binding. Nothing is said here about the origin of its validity and bindingness; nothing is said, for instance, to suggest that one is only subject to the law because, as the later passage says, one is its author. Up to this point, Kant is speaking solely of a motivational structure that can be characterized quite appropriately as "self-governance" (and that one could even call "self-legislation" as well, albeit in a very different sense from the one Kant preferred and that implies authorship).

But Kant did not of course let matters rest there. When he turns to explaining how this attitude of respect is possible, Kant reaches for his concept of autonomy. In order to be able to act solely out of respect for the moral law, without ulterior motives (or "interest", as he says) and not on the basis of our essentially variable feelings of sympathy, we have to view ourselves, says Kant, as the authors of this law, and indeed of its very validity and bindingness, as – to repeat the passage in which he introduces the concept of autonomy – "not merely subject to the law but subject to it in such a way that it [our will] must be viewed as also giving the law to itself and just because of this as first subject to the law (of which it can regard itself as the author)" (ibid.). Yet, the claim that respect can be explained only through autonomy is not one that Kant demonstrates convincingly.

His main argument, which I must cite at length, goes as follows:

If we look back upon all previous efforts that have ever been made to discover the principle of morality, we need not wonder now why all of them had to fail. It was seen that the human being is bound to laws by his duty, but it never occurred to them that he is subject *only to laws given by himself but still universal.* [...] For, if one thought of him only as subject to a law (whatever it may be), this law had to carry with it some interest by way of attraction or constraint, since it did not as a law arise from *his* will; in order to conform with the law, his will had instead to be constrained by *something else* to act in a certain way. By this quite necessary consequence, however, all the labor to find a supreme ground of duty was irretrievably lost. For, one never arrived at duty but instead at the necessity of an action from a certain interest. This might be one's own or another's interest. But then the imperatives had to turn out always conditional and could not be fit for a moral command. I will therefore call this basic principle the principle of the *autonomy* of the will in contrast with every other, which I accordingly count as *heteronomy* (GMS, pp. 432–433/GMM, pp. 40–41).

To put the argument more succinctly: for Kant, it is supposedly a "necessary consequence" (*notwendige Folgerung*) that, if one thinks of oneself as subject to a moral law without simultaneously considering oneself as (through one's reason) its author, an action out of respect for this law becomes impossible, since one then can act in accord with this law only on the condition that one believes one is thereby satisfying or advancing some interest. Kant is even of the opinion that one can more generally, in whatever realm, only then guide oneself by reason when this reason institutes its own principles. Later in the *Groundwork* he says precisely that, in a generalization of his doctrine of autonomy that is apparently meant to hold no less for theoretical than for practical reason:

> Now, one cannot possibly think of a reason that would consciously receive direction from any other quarter with respect to its judgments, since the subject would then attribute the determination of his judgment not to his reason but to an impulse. Reason must regard itself as the author (*Urheberin*) of its principles independently of alien influences; consequently, as practical reason or as the will of a rational being it must be regarded of itself as free (GMS, p. 448/GMM, p. 54).

These two passages do not offer a very good argument, however. Let me sketch here why I believe so; a more detailed account will follow in the next section.

It is not true that we can in general only regard a reason for thinking or doing something as valid (and as binding) if we either consider ourselves the author of its validity or appeal to some given interest that would be satisfied or furthered if we were to think or act in that way.[9] For in any case where we bestowed on some consideration the status of being an unconditional reason for thought or action, we would have to see reasons to give it that authority, and since these reasons could not themselves rest on any of our given interests, they would have to be viewed as valid in their own right, independently of our authorship as well as of our interests. If there would then have to be reasons of this sort, why could not moral reasons figure among them? The "necessary consequence" of which Kant speaks does not exist. Acting out of respect for moral principles, which constitutes Kant's conception of self-governance and which we ourselves may call "autonomy", is entirely possible without autonomy in the Kantian sense.

Let me summarize what has been said thus far. "Autonomy" can mean many different things. Before Kant, the word had a political meaning – the ability of a community to live by its own laws – as well as a legal meaning – the authority to

---

9   If this argument is supposed to be compatible with the argument of "Orientation" – namely, that thinking for oneself presupposes autonomy, since a law to which one is subject but which one has not given oneself must be a law that someone else has imposed – then Kant must have presumed that a law that one views as binding solely on the basis of an interest is either a law that one imposes on oneself, though only on this conditional basis, or else is a law imposed by someone else whom it is in one's interest to obey.

proceed self-legislatively within an overarching legal order – both of which could not have been especially influential for Kant's definition of the concept. These days we often designate as autonomy in the individual realm the ability to think without the guidance of another or to do what is right without regard to reward or punishment. But thinking for oneself and self-governance are not what Kant himself understood by "autonomy", namely, a self-legislation that establishes the very validity and bindingness of the principles of our thought and action, even though Kant was also of the view that thinking for oneself and respect for the moral law are themselves only possible on the basis of an autonomy of this sort. In that, as I have indicated, he was mistaken.

IV. Kant's Concept of Autonomy

But what about Kant's concept of autonomy itself? Up to this point, I have tried to show that thinking for oneself and self-governance do not depend on autonomy in the Kantian sense. Both are dispositions of mind that, however exactly we may wish to analyze them, are essentially coherent, if not to say invaluable. In both these senses, there is indeed what we may call "autonomy". But autonomy as Kant understood it is another matter. I have already on several occasions indicated in passing that the autonomy of reason, in which reason is understood as the author of the validity of the principles of our thought and action, is in my view a questionable and even contradictory concept. This point I now want to argue more closely.

Since the question concerns the very coherence of Kant's idea of autonomy, it is good to remind ourselves of its actual scope and of its deepest motivations. Although the term "autonomy" appears for the first time in the *Groundwork*, the concept itself underlies not only his moral philosophy, but also his "critical philosophy" as a whole. I quoted above the passage from the *Groundwork* in which theoretical reason, no less than practical reason, is called the "author (*Urheberin*) of its principles". Even in writings such as the *Critique of Pure Reason* where the word does not occur, the concept is clearly at work. One need only think of the famous passage in the Preface to the second edition of the *Critique*, which declares that "reason has insight only into that which it produces after a plan of its own" (KrV, B XIII). For Kant, reason gives itself its own laws in every sphere of its employment, and it does so in a way that makes it the author of their authority.

The fundamental concern that led him to this position is easy to comprehend. Ever since the scientific revolution of the seventeenth century, a naturalistic picture of the world as a realm of value-neutral facts has become increasingly dominant, with the result that all norms of thought and action, all distinctions between justified and unjustified, good and evil, right and wrong, have seemed to be ultimately intelligible (leaving God aside) only as something of our own creation. One way to meet this challenge found in the eighteenth century paradigmatic expression in the philosophy of David Hume: all such distinctions ultimately arise from given feelings and desires, so that reason can only be the "slave of the passions". Kant was too much of a rationalist to be attracted to this approach for very long, although for a while he partially embraced it in the realm of moral philosophy.[10] This temporary temptation comes out in his lectures on moral philosophy of the 1770s, particularly in the thesis, previously discussed, that the understanding, although capable of comprehending the bindingness of moral principles, is unable to move us to act accordingly except on the basis of some affective state such as, for instance, a "moral feeling". Kant could not long remain satisfied with this thesis, which was a jumble of rationalistic and sensualistic elements, not only because of his doubts about the supposedly necessary role of feelings in the motivation of moral action, but also because the idea that the understanding can grasp the bindingness of certain principles was a remnant of an older rationalism that no longer appeared compatible with the new naturalistic world-picture. What could present itself to the understanding as the bindingness of principles or even their validity in the world of Newtonian physics from which everything normative has disappeared?

As a result, Kant saw himself obliged to place rationalism on a new foundation. In his "critical philosophy", the bindingness, like the validity, of principles is no longer perceived by the understanding as an object of knowledge, but rather is produced by self-legislating reason, in some cases with regard to given interests, in others independently of them and categorically. Kant's concept of autonomy was thus supposed to provide the solution to a problem that had become pressing with the development of modern science: What can it mean to live according to reason when the world itself no longer contains any directives that we could grasp in order to know how to think or act? The answer was to see in reason the source and author of its own principles. That this conception of reason fits so well into the naturalistic view of the world, which has come to be ever more widely accepted (whether rightly so is a question to which I shall return), explains why, despite some rather obvious objections. It has exercised so great an influence for more than two centuries. This conception had in Kant's eyes the further advantage that reason – now conceived as a self-legislating faculty in contrast to the understanding, which was still deemed a motivationally inert, because merely perceptual, faculty – could count in virtue of its self-activity as able to motivate action without the aid of any given feelings and, thereby, to become "practical".

The difficulty is that, on closer examination, talk of the self-legislation of reason does not appear to make much sense. The claim that the authority of

---

[10]   Cf. Henrich, 1963.

principles is our own work is contradictory, even when one adds that we do not establish them arbitrarily but rather through the exercise of our reason. Insofar as one can speak meaningfully at all about imposing a principle on ourselves that would otherwise not be valid and binding, such self-legislation can take place only on the condition that we *see reasons* to adopt this principle. These reasons themselves have to possess then an authority that cannot be explained by the supposed autonomy of reason. Their validity can only be *acknowledged*, and that means by a faculty of reason that has to be understood as essentially receptive, not as self-legislating.

In order to appreciate the contradictoriness of the Kantian conception, let us examine a few cases in which it is indisputable that rules acquire their validity through self-legislation. Consider, for instance, the rules that govern the release of new drugs or that regulate traffic on the road. Not only are there reasons for adopting such rules, reasons that show that it is appropriate or corresponds to our interests to set them up. Equally obvious is the fact that the authority of these reasons – their ability to justify the establishment of such rules – is not something created by the exercise of our reason. These reasons are valid independently of our doing, and we employ our reason in order to recognize their validity, not in order to institute it. That means in turn that even the authority of a self-imposed rule cannot depend completely on the exercise of our reason, since it rests on the recognized authority of the reasons justifying the institution of that rule. Thus, I can, for example, in view of my tendency to promise too much, give myself the rule not to make in the future any important promise without drawing up a list of everything that I have already promised, and a necessary condition for my being bound by this rule is that I have imposed it upon myself. But that is of course not a sufficient condition for its bindingness, which also derives from the underlying principle that I am aiming to honor – namely, that promises are to be kept or maybe that a good reputation is to be maintained.

In the end, there must always be reasons, whether principles or not, whose independent validity we simply acknowledge. That is how it is with most of the principles by which we think and act, in contrast to the special rules I have been mentioning: when it does appear necessary to adduce reasons for these principles, they are reasons to believe that the principles are valid, not reasons to decide that they are to be established as valid.

V. Reason and World

Thus it becomes evident what the nature of reason really is. Reason cannot be essentially self-legislating since it must always draw its bearings from reasons that prescribe to it how it is to proceed. Reason is rather to be understood as a faculty whose exercise basically consists in *responding to reasons*. According to

Kant, "[reason] has to view itself as the author of its principles, independently of alien influences (*unabhängig von fremden Einflüssen*)" (GMS, p. 448/GMM, p. 54).[11] It should now be clear how false this assertion is. To the extent that reason guides itself by reasons whose authority it presupposes, it is very far from being "dependent on alien influences", as the second half of Kant's statement would entail. The implicit opposition between "instituting one's own principles" and "being subject to alien influences" is a false dichotomy. For reasons are hardly foreign bodies with respect to reason. They are precisely that to which we must respond, if we are to be able to exercise our reason at all.[12] Guiding oneself by reasons means, furthermore, grasping reasons in such a way that one is moved to think or act accordingly. Reason is thus at one and the same time cognitive and motivating, a combination that Kant ridiculed already in his lectures on moral philosophy of the 1770s as a "philosophers' stone" (*Stein des Weisen*) and that he continued to dismiss, though without justification, as impossible to the end (VM, p. 69/KLE, p. 71).[13]

The objection I have raised against Kant's concept of autonomy is not completely unknown, and adherents of the Kantian tradition have devised various strategies to escape it. I cannot discuss all of them here, but I would like to say a few words about the approach of Christine Korsgaard. The particular interest of her reformulation of the Kantian idea of autonomy lies in the fact that she dispenses with the terms "giving" and "imposing" in order to avoid the implication that a law that one gives oneself has to be a law that one could also *not* give oneself and that one thus requires a reason for imposing. According to Korsgaard, the fundamental principles of our thought and action are to be understood as "constitutive" of them.[14] They guide, she says, these activities by virtue of making up their very essence, similarly to the way the rules of chess determine what is and is not a valid move in chess. In this sense, we would ourselves, insofar as we think or act, be the authors of these principles, yet without having the choice of imposing them on ourselves or not. For, not to adhere to them would mean no longer to think or do anything intelligible (just as moving a rook diagonally is not to make a foolish move, but to make no move at all in the game of chess).

---

[11]   In this passage (quoted above, near the end of section III), Kant claims that if reason "would consciously receive direction from any other quarter with respect to its judgments", it would not then be reason but rather some "impulse" (*Antrieb*) that ultimately determines one's judgment. That Kant does not even mention the possibility of reason receiving direction from reasons stems from his (naturalistic) assumption that the world, with which reason deals, cannot contain anything normative.

[12]   Cf. Seel, 2002, p. 285: "Self-determination, correctly understood, is the ability to allow oneself to be determined".

[13]   See note 5 above.

[14]   See Korsgaard, 2009, pp. 32, 67, 81. See also Korsgaard, 1996, pp. 235–236.

Now, Korsgaard is right that some of the fundamental principles she mentions – for instance, the principle of non-contradiction or the principle that to will an end is to will the corresponding means (though not, I think, any moral principles) – are "constitutive" in the sense indicated: they represent the conditions of possibility of coherent thought and action. But that does not yield a justification of the idea of autonomy. For what is it that makes a particular principle constitutive? The recognition that in assenting to a contradiction we are failing to think anything meaningful consists in seeing that the rule of avoiding all contradiction has a validity that we must respect in order to think coherently at all. It is thus the completely unrestricted validity of the principle that explains its being constitutive and not the other way around. Only in virtue of possessing an unconditional authority for all possible thought does it become a constitutive principle of coherent thinking. For only so can we explain to ourselves why we cannot conceive of any meaningful thought at odds with this principle and why we are thus not thinking anything at all, if we violate it. Someone who says to himself, "I attempt to abide by the principle of contradiction because otherwise I would not be thinking anything intelligible", would, if he were to think the matter through to the end, understand by that: "I attempt to abide by the principle of contradiction because its unconditional authority makes it the principle of all intelligible thought". The concept of autonomy can thus not be saved by the fact that some principles are so close to us that we are not free to accept them or not. On the contrary, this phenomenon makes clear to what extent our innermost being is constituted by its relation to a normative order of reasons of whose authority we are not the author.

I observed before how Kant's concept of autonomy and the naturalistic worldview seem made for one other. If reason, however, is no longer to be understood as self-legislating, but instead as responding to reasons that already exist, then we must develop another view of the world that corresponds to this conception of reason. That is no small task, and I will in closing make only a few brief remarks to sketch what is in my view the correct route to take.

First, we should remember that naturalism is a metaphysics and not a theorem of the modern natural sciences. If we want to work out another view of the world that makes comprehensible how something like reasons can exist to which reason must respond, then it would not be to put somehow into question the truth of modern science, but instead to understand better what it means that their claim to truth is well-founded. The task is thus to develop another metaphysics according to which reasons belong to the structure of reality or to the world itself, to the world – if I may adopt Wittgenstein's phrase – in the sense of everything that is the case, independently of whatever opinions we might have about it.

Second, we should note concerning the essence of reasons themselves that they cannot be equated with either physical or psychological phenomena. Reasons have obviously a normative character: to have a reason to do X means that one *ought* to do X, if nothing else counts against it. At the same time, however, reasons always depend on the physical and psychological facts that are relevant for our thought and action. To have a reason to do X means that something in the circumstances in which one finds oneself counts in favor of doing X. Reasons consist in a certain kind of relation, the normative relation of counting-in-favor-of, in which phenomena of the natural world, physical or psychological facts, stand to our possibilities of thought and action. Reasons have thus a *relational* character, although they are not thereby any less objective, since relations too can form part of reality. In particular, the reasons that exist do so independently of our opinions about them. Their relational character reflects the obvious fact that reasons exist only insofar as there are beings like us that have such possibilities. But which reasons exist to do this or that is something that we have to discover.

Elsewhere, I have called this view of the world a kind of "Platonism", since reasons resemble Plato's forms in that they constitute a third, essentially normative dimension of the world that differs both from nature as well as from mind.[15] The conception of reason that I have set forth in opposition to Kant's idea of autonomy could also be regarded as an older ("pre-critical") style of "rationalism". But the important thing, of course, is that we use traditional models merely as guides in order to do greater justice to the subject itself.

(Translated from the German by Robert Norton and revised by the author.)

References

Henrich, Dieter (1963): "Über Kants früheste Ethik", in: *Kant-Studien*, 54(4), pp. 404–431.

Kant, Immanuel (1902 ff.): *Kants gesammelte Schriften*, ed. Königlich Preußische Akademie der Wissenschaften, Berlin [= AA].

- *Kritik der reinen Vernunft*, in: *AA*, vols. 3–4 [= KrV].
- *Grundlegung zur Metaphysik der Sitten*, in: *AA*, vol. 4, pp. 385–464 [= GMS].
- "Beantwortung der Frage: Was ist Aufklärung?", in: *AA*, vol. 8, pp. 35–42 [= WIA].
- "Was heißt: Sich im Denken orientieren?", in: *AA*, vol. 8, pp. 133–147 [= O].
- (1991): *Political Writings*, ed. H. Reiss, Cambridge [= KPW].
- (1996): *Practical Philosophy*, ed. M. Gregor, Cambridge [= KPP].
- (1997): *Lectures on Ethics*, ed. P. Heath and J.B. Schneewind, Cambridge [= KLE].
- (1998): *Groundwork of the Metaphysics of Morals*, trans. M. Gregor, Cambridge [= GMM].
- (2004): *Vorlesung zur Moralphilosophie*, ed. W. Stark, Berlin [= VM].

Korsgaard, Christine (1996): *The Sources of Normativity*, Cambridge.

- (2009): *Self-Constitution: Agency, Identity, and Integrity*, Oxford.

---

[15]   See Larmore, 2008, chap. 5, §§ 6–8, and Larmore 2012, in which I develop this theory of reasons and reason much more fully.

Larmore, Charles (2008): *The Autonomy of Morality*, Cambridge.
– (2012): *Vernunft und Subjektivität*, Berlin.
Pohlmann, Rosemarie (1971): "Autonomie", in: *Historisches Wörterbuch der Philoso-phie*, ed. J. Ritter, vol. 1, Darmstadt, pp. 701–719.
Schneewind, J.B. (1998): *The Invention of Autonomy*, Cambridge.
Seel, Martin (2002): *Sich bestimmen lassen*, Frankfurt a. M.

Heiner F. Klemme

Kants Erörterung der „libertas indifferentiae" in der *Metaphysik der Sitten* und ihre philosophische Bedeutung[1]

In the "Introduction" to his Metaphysics of Morals *Kant argues that "freedom of choice [Freiheit der Willkür] cannot be defined – as some have tried to define it – as the ability to make a choice [Wahl] for or against the law* (libertas indifferentiae), *even though choice [Willkür] as a* phaenomenon *provides frequent examples of this in experience". This contribution will discuss the concepts of will and the power of choice mainly in the context of the Doctrines of Right and Virtue. I will refer to the reasons by which Kant was caused to develop this seemingly paradoxical conception of our freedom of choice. Kant's considerations are philosophically significant because he tries to substantiate why there are conceptual reasons that let all attempts to explain our decisions for or against our moral obligations fail.*

1. Einleitung

Es gehört zu den verwirrenden Aspekten von Kants praktischer Philosophie, dass er ihre wichtigsten Begriffe, nicht selten in ein und derselben Schrift, in verschiedenen Bedeutungen gebraucht, ohne sie klar voneinander abzugrenzen. Und wendet er sich diesen Begriffen dann doch in definitorischer Absicht zu, will dem Leser nicht immer die Pointe seiner Bemühungen einleuchten. Hierfür mag es verschiedene Erklärungen geben: Ein *Autor*, der sich nicht die Zeit nehmen will, die Bedeutung seiner Begriffe vollumfänglich zu erläutern; ein *Leser*, der über den Kontext von Kants Philosophie nur unzureichend aufgeklärt ist und Erläuterungen erwartet, die einem Zeitgenossen des Königsberger Philosophen selbstverständlich sind; eine *philosophische Problematik*, die von Autor wie Leser nur schwer zu durchschauen und begrifflich zu fixieren ist. Dies alles trifft sicherlich auf Kants Ausführungen zu den Begriffen des Willens und der Willkür zu, deren Relevanz für seine praktische Philosophie außer Frage steht. Kant vertritt die Ansicht, dass sich das Begehrungsvermögen prinzipiell vom (im engeren Sinne so zu verstehenden) Erkenntnisvermögen und vom Vermö-

---

[1] Für kritische und weiterführende Kommentare zu früheren Fassungen des vorliegenden Beitrags danke ich Reinhard Brandt (Marburg), Bernd Ludwig (Göttingen), Gabriel Rivero (Mainz) und Falk Wunderlich (Mainz) sowie den Teilnehmern meines Mainzer Oberseminars über die Philosophie der Neuzeit. – Vereinzelt greife ich auf Passagen aus früheren Aufsätzen zurück (Klemme, 2006, 2008, 2008 a und 2008 b).

gen der Lust und Unlust unterscheidet. Die Auffassung von Christian Wolff und seinen Anhängern, nach der sich alle Vermögen auf eine einzige „Grund-kraft"[2] zurückführen lassen, ist falsch. Allein im Gebrauch dieser drei Grund-kräfte stiften wir nach Kant eine Beziehung zwischen ihnen. So handelt es sich bei unserem Begehrungsvermögen um ein „Begehrungsvermögen nach Begrif-fen" (AA VI, S. 213), weil wir uns durch die Vorstellung von Begriffen und Ge-setzen zum Handeln bestimmen können. Wir sind als Vernunftwesen in der Lage, uns durch die Vorstellung eines Gesetzes zum Handeln zu bestimmen, das wir uns selbst gegeben haben. Wir können dies tun, müssen es aber nicht, wie Kant durch die Unterscheidung einerseits zwischen dem Moralgesetz (Kau-salität aus Freiheit) und dem Naturgesetz (Naturkausalität) und andererseits zwischen dem oberen und dem unteren Begehrungsvermögen anzeigt.[3] Auch wenn Kants Texte gelegentlich einen anderen Eindruck vermitteln mögen, ist es wichtig zu sehen, dass diese Vermögen nicht substantiell sondern primär funk-tional zu differenzieren sind: Wir schließen von den verschiedenen Funktionen im Urteil auf verschiedene Vermögen des Subjekts, nicht aber von der vorgängi-gen Erkenntnis der Vermögen auf entsprechende Funktionen. So zeigt sich, dass wir uns einerseits durch die Vorstellung des Moralgesetzes zum Handeln bestimmen können und dann autonom handeln. Wir können uns andererseits aber auch durch unsere Sinnlichkeit bestimmen lassen und handeln dann heteronom, weil wir uns durch diesen Aktus den Gesetzen der Natur unterwer-fen.[4] Wir wählen, uns selbst zu bestimmen oder uns als ein Objekt der Natur bestimmen zu lassen.

Das Verhältnis von unterem und oberem Begehrungsvermögen verweist in einer von Kant nie eindeutig geklärten Weise auf die Unterscheidung zwischen dem Willen (als dem Ursprung der Gesetze der Freiheit) und der Willkür (als dem Ursprung der Maximen unseres Handelns). Mit dieser Unterscheidung ist das Problem der begrifflichen Fixierung unserer Fähigkeit verbunden, uns für oder gegen das Moralgesetz zu entscheiden: Obwohl wir dem Moralgesetz nur

---

2   „*Wolff* nimmt Eine Grundkraft an und sagt: Die Seele selbst ist eine Grundkraft, die sich das Universum vorstellt. Es ist schon falsch, wenn man sagt: die Seele ist eine Grundkraft. [...] Wir finden demnach, daß wir verschiedene Grundkräfte annehmen müssen, und nicht Einer als phänomena der Seele erklären können; denn wer wollte sich wohl bemühen, den Verstand aus den Sinnen herzuleiten? *Demnach sind das Erkenntnisvermögen, das Vermögen der Lust und Unlust, und das Begehrungs-Ver-mögen, Grundkräfte.*" (AA XXVIII, S. 261–262)

3   Vgl. AA V, S. 22–25.

4   Bereits Alexander Gottlieb Baumgarten trifft eine funktional begründete Unterschei-dung zwischen dem unteren und dem oberen Begehrungsvermögen (facultas appeti-tiva inferior und superior): „Da das BEGEHRUNGSVERMÖGEN dem Erkenntnis-vermögen folgt [sequitur] [...], wird es entweder dem unteren folgen und ist dann das UNTERE BEGEHRUNGSVERMÖGEN [...], oder dem oberen" (2011, § 676, vgl. § 689).

deshalb unterworfen sind, weil wir es uns selbst (als Vernunftwesen) geben (vgl. AA IV, S. 435–436), befolgen wir es nicht immer. Der kategorische Imperativ kann ein zugleich vernünftiges und sinnliches Wesen wie den Menschen nur deshalb praktisch nötigen, nach Maximen zu handeln, die sich zu einer allgemeinen Gesetzgebung qualifizieren, weil die Befolgung des moralischen Gesetzes für zugleich freie und reine Vernunftwesen eine „praktische Nothwendigkeit"[5] zum Ausdruck bringt. Der Begriff der (moralischen) Nötigung zeigt an, dass wir gerade nicht (wie reine Vernunftwesen) praktisch notwendig nach dem Moralgesetz handeln *müssen*, sondern entsprechend handeln *sollen*. Wir unterliegen einer Verbindlichkeit, nach dem Moralgesetz zu handeln, weil wir zwar erstens im Gegensatz zu reinen Vernunftwesen auch über subjektive, auf unsere Glückseligkeit und die Befriedigung unserer Neigungen zielende Gründe der praktischen Selbstbestimmung verfügen, aber zweitens unser zur intelligiblen Welt gehörender Willen (so das Argument der *Grundlegung zur Metaphysik der Sitten*) unser „eigentliches Selbst" (AA IV, S. 458; vgl. S. 457) darstellt. Denken wir uns als praktisch, nehmen wir den Standpunkt der „Verstandeswelt" (AA IV, S. 458) ein und verstehen uns als Urheber unserer Handlungen. Unser Bewusstsein des kategorischen Imperativs ist aber nicht allein das Bewusstsein einer Verbindlichkeit, dem Moralgesetz folgen zu sollen, weil wir uns als Vernunftwesen mittels des moralischen Gesetzes selbst (als Menschen) verpflichten, uns im Gebrauche unserer Vernunft als Vernunftwesen zu erhalten (bzw. zu realisieren). Dieses Bewusstsein ist zugleich das Bewusstsein einer kausal weder durch das Moralgesetz noch durch die Naturgesetze bestimmbaren (objektivierbaren und damit erkennbaren) Spontaneität, sich für oder gegen unsere moralischen Pflichten zu entscheiden. Auf diese Spontaneität (Freiheit) beziehen sich Philosophen von alters her unter anderem mit den Begriffen „libertas indifferentiae" und „aequilibrium arbitrii"[6]. Es ist wichtig zu sehen, dass Kant

---

[5]   AA VI, S. 223. Kant diskutiert die Unterscheidung zwischen praktischer Notwendigkeit (des Gesetzes), Verbindlichkeit (obligatio), Pflicht (officium) und Nötigung in der „Einleitung in die Metaphysik der Sitten" (AA VI, S. 222–223). In der *Grundlegung* schreibt er: „Die Abhängigkeit eines nicht schlechterdings guten Willens vom Prinzip der Autonomie (die moralische Nötigung) ist *Verbindlichkeit*. Diese kann also auf kein heiliges Wesen gezogen werden. Die objektive Notwendigkeit einer Handlung aus Verbindlichkeit heißt *Pflicht*." (AA IV, S. 439) Achenwall und Pütter schreiben zum Begriff der Verbindlichkeit: „Wer zu einer freien Handlung verbindet, bestimmt den Willen durch den Begriff eines Guts oder Übels, also durch ein Motiv […]. Daher wird die Verbindung eines Motivs mit einer freien Handlung *moralische Verbindlichkeit* genannt." (Achenwall/Pütter, 1995, § 82)

[6]   Siehe z. B. Crusius (1744, S. 61, § 50: „libertas indifferentiae oder aequilibrii") sowie den Artikel „Freyheit des Willens" in Walch (1775). Zu den historischen Quellen von Kants Begriff der Willkür siehe die informativen Studien von Kawamura (1996) und Schwaiger (2011, S. 79–95). Kawamura weist u.a. auf die Bedeutung von Friedrich Wagners Schrift *Versuch Einer gründlichen Untersuchung, Welches Der wahre Begriff von der Freyheit des Willens sey?* (Berlin, 1730) (s. Kawamura, 1996, S. 22 u. ö.) hin.

dieser kausal unbestimmten, indifferenten Freiheit, von Crusius die „vollkommene Freiheit" (1744, S. 61, § 50), von Schelling „die Pest aller Moral" (2008, S. 111) und von Hegel eine Vorstellung genannt, die „nur für gänzlichen Mangel an Bildung des Gedankens genommen werden" (1970, S. 66, § 15) kann, eine spezielle Bedeutung gibt, wenn er sie in der *Metaphysik der Sitten* (1797) nicht etwa als das Vermögen versteht, Beliebiges zu wollen. Vielmehr handelt es sich nach Kant um das Vermögen, sich im Gebrauche der Willkür für oder gegen eine durch den kategorischen Imperativ ausgedrückte moralische *Verbindlichkeit* zu entscheiden. Ob wir dieser subjektiv als Nötigung empfundenen Verbindlichkeit praktisch folgen wollen, müssen wir selbst entscheiden. Wir können und müssen uns entscheiden, ob wir aus Achtung vor dem Moralgesetz unsere Pflichten erfüllen wollen oder nicht.

Unter den für das Verständnis dieses Aspekts menschlichen Wollens einschlägigen Passagen in Kants kritischen Schriften ragt der Abschnitt über die *„Vorbegriffe zur Metaphysik der Sitten* (Philosophia practica universalis)" (AA VI, S. 221) in der „Einleitung" in die *Metaphysik der Sitten* auch deshalb heraus, weil Kant sich nur in ihm ausführlich[7] mit dem Begriff der „libertas indifferentiae" beschäftigt. In dieser Passage stellt er fest, dass die „Freiheit der Willkür [...] nicht durch das Vermögen der Wahl, für oder wider das Gesetz zu handeln (libertas indifferentiae), definiert werden [kann] – wie wohl es einige[8]

---

[7]   Siehe u. a. auch KrV, A 802/B 830 („Eine Willkür nämlich ist bloß *tierisch* (arbitrium brutum), die nicht anders als durch sinnliche Antriebe, d. i. *pathologisch* bestimmt werden kann. Diejenige aber, welche unabhängig von sinnlichen Antrieben, mithin durch Bewegursachen, welche nur von der Vernunft vorgestellet werden, bestimmet werden kann, heißt die *freie Willkür* (arbitrium liberum), und alles, was mit dieser, es sei als Grund oder Folge, zusammenhängt, wird *Praktisch* genannt."). Zu weiterer (vorkritischen) Ausführungen zum Begriff der Willkür und der Freiheit siehe Klemme (1996 a, S. 82–95) und Schönecker (2005).

[8]   Diese Position hat bekanntlich Carl Leonhard Reinhold vertreten: Die „Freyheit des Willens" ist „im positiven Sinne [...] das Vermögen der Selbstbestimmung durch Willkühr für oder gegen das praktische Gesetz" (Reinhold, 1791, S. 272; vgl. Allison, 1990, S. 133, Bojanowski, 2006, S. 237, Bojanowski, 2007, S. 222 ff., und Baum, 2012). Bereits 1791 definiert Karl Heinrich Heydenreich im zweiten Band seiner *Betrachtungen über die Philosophie der Natürlichen Religion* (Leipzig) die „[m]oralische Freiheit" als „das Vermögen, den vollständigen Grund von Handlungen zu enthalten und wirksam zu machen, welche dem Sittengesetz der Vernunft angemessen oder zuwider sind, ohne zu einem von beyden weder durch Einflüsse fremder Kräfte, noch durch seine eignen Vorstellungen nothwendig bestimmt werden zu können. Dies ist der strenge, und, wie ich glaube, allein wahre Begriff der *moralischen Freiheit. Das moralisch freye Wesen ist ihm zu Folge durch sich selbst, und ohne alle Bedingung, gleich vermögend für contradictorisch entgegengesetzte Handlungen,* kann entweder sittlich gut, oder sittlich böse handeln, ohne eines von beyden *müssen* zu können" (1791, S. 63–64). Siehe den Hinweis auf Heydenreich bei Bondeli (2012, S. 143, Anm. 53). – Zur Debatte über den ‚Indifferentismus' von Reinhold auf der einen Seite und Carl Christian Erhard Schmids ‚Fatalismus' (wir bilden uns das Gefühl der Freiheit nur ein) auf der anderen Seite, siehe Creuzer (1793) sowie Tafani (1999). – Kant ist sich selbstverständ-

versucht haben, – obzwar die Willkür als *Phänomen* davon in der Erfahrung häufige Beispiele gibt"[9]. Diese Aussage stellt den Leser vor ein Rätsel: Auf der einen Seite bezieht Kant Stellung gegen die Auffassung des moralischen Indifferentismus, wonach wir uns frei für oder gegen unsere moralischen Pflichten entscheiden können. Denn nur dann, wenn wir die „Freiheit der Willkür" als Freiheit definieren könnten, uns für oder gegen unsere moralischen Pflichten zu

lich der langen Tradition dieser Debatte bewusst, wie bereits aus seinen Ausführungen in der *Nova Dilucidatio* (1755) deutlich wird (vgl. AA I, S. 397 u. 401 ff.). – Eine besonders prägnante Darstellung der Alternative zwischen der Position der „Fatalisten" und der Position derjenigen, „welche die Freyheit der Gleichgültigkeit annehmen" (Garve, 1772, S. 295), findet sich in Christian Garves „Anmerkungen" zu seiner 1772 erschienenen Übersetzung von Adam Fergusons Schrift über die *Grundsätze der Moralphilosophie*. Garve ist aus Gründen der Selbstbeobachtung davon überzeugt, dass beide Positionen zutreffen, sieht sich aber nicht in der Lage, eine Theorie zu entwickeln, die erklärt, wie ich auf der einen Seite eine Empfindung von der Bestimmtheit meines Wollens durch Vorstellungen und auf der anderen Seite eine Empfindung davon haben kann, „selbst der Urheber meiner Handlungen" (Garve, 1772, S. 295) zu sein. Bemerkenswert ist vor allem Garves Überzeugung, dass unser Glaube an die Tugend nicht dadurch erschüttert werden kann, dass wir die ihr zugrunde liegende Freiheit nicht erklären können: „[…] lassen sie uns keine unsrer Empfindungen leugnen, weil wir sie nicht zu erklären wissen; aber vor allen Dingen, lassen sie uns keine unsrer Mitbrüder verdammen, weil sie unter zwey Empfindungen, die sich in der Theorie nicht vereinigen lassen, einer andern als wir den Vorzug geben. Es giebt einen Punkt der Vereinigung, der gewiß, und unschätzbar ist. Wir allen glauben das Daseyn der Tugend. Dieser Glaube ist früher als alle Systeme." (Garve, 1772, S. 296) An anderer Stelle fasst Garve seine Auffassung mit folgenden Worten zusammen: „Ich weiß nicht wie ich frey bin, aber ich weiß, wie ich vollkommen seyn soll." (Garve, 1772, S. 298) In gewisser Weise kann Kants Konzeption transzendentaler und praktischer Freiheit in der *Kritik der reinen Vernunft* als Antwort auf Garve Exposition eines quasi-antinomischen Verhältnissesn von Freiheit und Fatalismus verstanden werden: Diese Schrift zeigt erstens, dass die „Kausalität aus Freiheit" der Naturkausalität *„nicht widerstreitet"* (KrV A 558/B 586; vgl. auch Kants berühmten Brief an Garve vom 21.09.1798, AA XII, S. 255). Im spekulativen Gebrauch der Vernunft wird keine der beiden Positionen „begünstigt" (KrV, A 776/B 804). Und sie zeigt zweitens, dass die Vernunft in ihrem praktischen Gebrauch „ein Recht habe, etwas anzunehmen, was sie auf keine Weise im Felde der bloßen Spekulation, ohne hinreichende Beweisgründe, vorauszusetzen befugt wäre; […]. Dort ist sie im Besitze, dessen Rechtmäßigkeit sie nicht beweisen darf [sic. muss, H. K.], und wovon sie in der Tat den Beweis auch nicht führen könnte. Der Gegner soll also beweisen." (KrV, A 776-777/B 804–805; vgl. AA IV, S. 457 sowie AA VIII, S. 13 u. AA VIII, S. 284 Anm.) Dem Gegner wird es aber nicht gelingen, die Nichtexistenz der praktischen Freiheit mit den Mitteln des spekulativen oder theoretischen Vernunftgebrauchs zu beweisen: „Die Frage wegen der transzendentalen Freiheit betrifft bloß das spekulative Wissen, welches wir als ganz gleichgültig bei Seite setzen können, wenn es um das Praktische zu tun ist, und worüber in der Antinomie der reinen Vernunft schon hinreichende Erörterung zu finden ist." (KrV, A 803–804/B 831–832).

9   AA VI, S. 226. Zwei wichtige Vorarbeiten zu dieser Textpassage finden sich in AA XXIII (S. 248–249) und in AA IX (S. 470–472) von Kants *Gesammelten Schriften* (Kant, 1900 ff.); siehe dazu zuletzt Baum (2012).

entscheiden, wäre der Indifferentismus wahr. Auf der anderen Seite betont Kant aber, wir wüssten aus „Erfahrung", dass wir „dem Gesetze nicht allein *gemäß*, sondern auch *zuwider* zu wählen" (AA VI, S. 226) vermögend sind. Doch obwohl die Erfahrung oft genug beweist, dass wir uns für oder gegen die Gebote des Moralgesetzes entscheiden können, beweist sie nicht, dass die Freiheit „darin gesetzt werden kann, daß das vernünftige Subject auch eine wider seine (gesetzgebende) Vernunft streitende Wahl treffen kann" (AA VI, S. 226).

Was ist der tiefere Sinn dieser paradox[10] anmutenden Argumentation? Warum spricht Kant dem Menschen als einem „vernünftigen Subject" und „*intelligiblen Wesen*" ein Vermögen ab, das er ihm „als *Sinnenwesen* der Erfahrung" (AA VI, S. 226) zuspricht? Aus welchem Grund behauptet er diese – von ihm nicht so bezeichnete – Antinomie im Begriff des Wollens? Warum weist er nicht entweder die These oder die Antithese als falsch zurück? In den nachfolgenden Überlegungen wird davon ausgegangen, dass Kant nicht bloß ein epistemologisches (erkenntniskritisches) Argument gegen die Möglichkeit einer *Definition* anführt, obwohl er sich gegen diese Möglichkeit sicherlich auch wendet: Wir können den positiven Begriff der Freiheit „theoretisch gar nicht darstellen [...], weil Erscheinungen kein übersinnliches Object (dergleichen doch die freie Willkür ist) verständlich machen können"[11]. Das Problem sitzt tiefer. Kant benötigt einen Begriff des menschlichen Wollens, der einerseits einen notwendigen Zusammenhang zwischen Freiheit und Moralgesetz herzustellen erlaubt, ohne andererseits unsere Wahlfreiheit als Menschen aufzuheben. Wenn die „Freiheit nimmermehr darin gesetzt werden kann, daß das vernünftige Subject auch eine wider seine (gesetzgebende) Vernunft streitende Wahl treffen kann" (AA VI, S. 226), dann kann die „freie Willkür" nicht einmal provisorisch als das Vermögen bestimmt werden, für oder gegen das Moralgesetz zu handeln.[12] Wäre dies der einzig legitime Begriff der Willkür, gäbe es jedoch keine moralisch schlechte, einem Menschen zurechenbare Handlung. Wenn die conditio sine qua non der Zurechenbarkeit meines Handelns darin besteht, dass *ich* die moralisch schlechte Handlung vollzogen habe, müssen wir über einen entsprechenden Begriff der Willkür verfügen. In einem Satz: Kant benötigt eine Konzeption der *einen* Willkür, die zugleich frei und nicht frei ist, sich für oder gegen das moralische

---

10   „Paradox" ist hier im Sinne einer unseren Erwartungen widersprechenden, ‚widersinnigen' Begriffsklärung oder Argumentation zu verstehen. Kant nimmt in seinen Schriften auf diesen weiten Begriff des Paradoxen oft Bezug (s. Klemme, 2007).

11   AA VI, S. 226; vgl. XXIII, S. 248 („Das wäre ein Hinüberziehen der Sinnlichkeit in das Feld des reinen Vernunftvermögens.").

12   In einer Vorarbeit zur „Einleitung" in die *Metaphysik der Sitten* schreibt Kant: „Die freye Willkühr kann nicht durch ein Object der Lust als ihre Materie bestimt werden denn sonst wäre die bestimmende Ursache in der Natur. Also nur durch die Form des Gesetzes der eigenen Causalität des Subjects" (AA XXIII, S. 245).

Gesetz zu entscheiden.[13] Es ist eine Willkür, die zum einen als „freie Willkür"
ein „übersinnliches Object" ist, zum anderen aber als sinnlich bestimmte Willkür der Phänomenwelt angehört. Die Klärung dieses Begriffs muss demnach im
Kontext der Lehre vom transzendentalen Idealismus erfolgen. Kant muss deutlich machen, wie die Willkür einerseits als Phänomen eine Eigenschaft aufweisen kann, die wir ihr andererseits jedoch als unter der Legislative der reinen Vernunft bzw. des reinen Willens stehend absprechen müssen. Ob das gelingen
kann?

2. Die „Freiheit der Willkür" ist keine „libertas indifferentiae"

Grundlegend für die Beantwortung der Frage nach einer Wahlmöglichkeit zwischen dem moralischen Guten und Schlechten ist, wie angedeutet, die Unterscheidung zwischen dem Willen und der Willkür, die Kant in dem Absatz erläutert, der seinen Ausführungen zur „libertas indifferentiae" in der *Metaphysik
der Sitten* vorangeht: „Von dem Willen gehen die Gesetze aus; von der Willkür
die Maximen. Die letztere ist im Menschen eine freie Willkür; der Wille, der auf
nichts Anderes, als bloß auf Gesetz geht, kann weder frei noch unfrei genannt
werden, weil er nicht auf Handlungen, sondern unmittelbar auf die Gesetzgebung für die Maxime der Handlungen (also die praktische Vernunft selbst) geht,
daher auch schlechterdings nothwendig und selbst keiner Nötigung *fähig* ist.
Nur die *Willkür* kann also *frei* genannt werden"[14]. Kant identifiziert in diesem
Zitat den Willen mit der praktischen Vernunft und nennt ihn an anderer Stelle

---

[13]   Diese Entscheidung erübrigt sich bei einem reinen Vernunftwesen, weil dessen Maxi-
       men objektiv dem Moralgesetz entsprechen. So schreibt Kant in der *Kritik der prakti-
       schen Vernunft*: Beim Menschen ist das moralische Gesetz ein kategorischer Imperat-
       iv, „weil eine pathologisch afficirte (obgleich dadurch nicht bestimmte, mithin auch
       immer freie) Willkür einen Wunsch bei sich führt, der aus subjectiven Ursachen ent-
       springt, daher auch dem reinen objectiven Bestimmungsgrunde oft entgegen sein kann
       und also eines Widerstandes der practischen Vernunft, der ein innerer, aber intellec-
       tueller Zwang genannt werden kann, als moralischer Nöthigung bedarf" (AA V, S. 32;
       vgl. AA V, S. 65–66).
[14]   AA VI, S. 226. In einer der beiden Vorarbeiten schreibt Kant: „Der Wille des Men-
       schen muß von der Willkühr unterschieden werden. Nur die letztere kann frey ge-
       nannt werden und geht blos auf Erscheinungen d. i. auf actus die in der Sinnenwelt
       bestimmt sind. – Denn der Wille ist nicht unter dem Gesetz sondern er ist selbst der
       Gesetzgeber für die Willkühr und ist absolute praktische Spontaneität in Bestimmung
       der Willkühr. Eben darum ist er auch in allen Menschen Gut und es giebt kein gesetz-
       wiedriges wollen. Die Maximen der Willkühr aber weil sie auf Handlungen als Er-
       scheinungen in der Sinnenwelt gehen können böse seyn und die Willkühr als Natur-
       vermögen ist in Ansehung jenes Gesetze (des Pflichtbegriffes) frey durch die sie
       eigentlich nicht unmittelbar bestimmbar ist sondern nur vermittelst der Maximen sie
       jenem gemäs oder zuwieder zunehmen" (AA XXIII, S. 248).

auch „einen reinen Willen" (AA VI, S. 221). Der reine Wille ist die Quelle bzw. der „Ursprung" (AA VI, S. 221) der Gesetze. Da wir uns im Abschnitt über die „*Vorbegriffe zur Metaphysik der Sitten*" befinden, in dem Kant diejenigen Begriffe bestimmt, die „ihren beiden Theilen" (also der *Rechtslehre* und der *Tugendlehre*) „gemein" (AA VI, S. 222) sind, darf unterstellt werden, dass es sich um Gesetze sowohl des inneren als auch des äußeren Freiheitsgebrauchs handelt. Zwar spricht Kant vom „obersten Grundsatz der Sittenlehre" („handle nach einer Maxime, die zugleich als allgemeines Gesetz gelten kann") und weist darauf hin, dass jede Maxime, die diesem Grundsatz widerspricht, „der Moral zuwider" (AA VI, S. 226) ist. Doch weil alle Rechtspflichten auch ethische Pflichten sind, d.h. die innere Gesetzgebung der Ethik die äußere Gesetzgebung des Rechts einschließt, muss es möglich sein, die Begriffe des Willens und der Willkür auch auf das Recht zu beziehen (vgl. AA VI, S. 390). Für den Begriff der Willkür[15] ist dies offenkundig, definiert Kant das Recht doch als den „Inbegriff der Bedingungen, unter denen die Willkür des einen mit der Willkür des anderen nach einem allgemeinen Gesetze der Freiheit zusammen vereinigt werden kann" (AA VI, S. 230).

In welchem Sinne des Wortes ist die Willkür frei? Zunächst weist Kant darauf hin, dass die Willkür der Ursprung der Maximen ist. Eine Maxime ist „das *subjective* Prinzip zu handeln, was sich das Subject selbst zur Regel macht (wie es nämlich handeln will)"[16]. Eine erste Möglichkeit, die Freiheit der Willkür zu verstehen, besteht darin, sie auf das Handeln oder Nichthandeln nach einer Maxime zu beziehen. Muss sich ein Mensch subjektive Regeln zur Bestimmung seiner Willkür[17] bilden, wenn er handeln will, oder kann er auch ohne Maximen[18] tätig werden? Die Antwort auf diese Frage kann hier offen bleiben,

---

[15] Der Bezug zum Willen wird implizit über den Begriff des „*moralischen Imperativs*" (AA VI, S. 239) hergestellt. Allerdings soll an dieser Stelle nicht verschwiegen werden, dass das Verhältnis des Rechts zur Ethik und damit der Status des Willens im Recht höchst umstritten ist. Zu dieser Debatte siehe u.a. Kersting (1993, S. 136 ff.), Geismann (2010, S. 25 ff.) und Klemme (2013 a).

[16] AA VI, S. 225. In der *Kritik der praktischen Vernunft* nennt Kant Maximen „*Willensmeinungen* des Individuums" (AA V, S. 66); in der *Religionsschrift* definiert er sie als „Regel, die die Willkür sich selbst für den Gebrauch ihrer Freiheit macht" (AA VI, S. 21).

[17] Dies scheint die Position der Religionsschrift zu sein: „[…] die Freiheit der Willkür ist von so ganz eigenthümlicher Beschaffenheit, daß sie durch keine Triebfeder zu einer Handlung bestimmt werden kann, *als nur sofern der Mensch sie in seine Maxime aufgenommen hat* (es sich zur allgemeinen Regel gemacht hat, nach der es sich verhalten will); so allein kann eine Triebfeder, welche es auch sei, mit der absoluten Spontaneität der Willkür (der Freiheit) zusammen bestehen" (AA VI, S. 23–24).

[18] In der *Anthropologie-Menschenkunde* (1781/82) findet sich der Hinweis, dass der Mensch entweder „nach Instinkt oder nach Grundsätzen" (AA XXV, S. 1150) handelt. „Wenn er nach Instinckt handelt, so hat er sich bis zur Thierheit erniedrigt, und wenn er nach maximen handelt, so soll er nicht die Instinckte schwächen, sondern ihnen nur durch die Vernunft Zweckmäßigkeit geben" (AA XXV, S. 1150). An anderer Stelle

weil Kant diese Thematik in der „Einleitung in die Metaphysik der Sitten" nicht aufgreift.

Eine zweite Interpretation der Freiheit der Willkür bezieht sich auf den Inhalt der Maximen. Ich kann es mir zur Regel machen, jeden Morgen vor 8 Uhr aufzustehen. Ich kann es mir aber auch zur Regel machen, erst nach 8 Uhr aufzustehen. Welche Maxime ich mir bilde, hängt von meinen Interessen und Vorlieben, meinen Begierden und Neigungen ab. Meine Freiheit besteht also darin, meinen Maximen einen bestimmten Inhalt (eine Materie) zu geben. Obwohl nicht von der Hand zu weisen ist, dass der Inhalt meiner Maxime für die Bedeutung meiner freien Willkür relevant ist und sich meine Freiheit gerade darin zeigt, beliebige Maximen bilden zu können, scheint an dieser Bestimmung der Freiheit noch etwas Entscheidendes zu fehlen. Maximen haben nach Kant nicht nur einen Inhalt. Sie haben auch eine Form. Und es ist diese Form, die für ihre moralische Beurteilung von zentraler Bedeutung ist. An der Form der Maxime können wir erkennen, ob ihr Inhalt moralisch erlaubt, verboten oder gefordert ist.[19] Erst wenn wir die Maxime aus der Perspektive ihrer Form (d. h. ihrer möglichen Gesetzesförmigkeit) betrachten, nehmen wir eine *moralische* Perspektive auf sie ein, die nicht allein durch unsere Begierden und Neigungen, sondern wesentlich durch den kategorischen Imperativ geprägt wird. Ganz in diesem Sinne heißt es in einer Vorarbeit zu der „Einleitung" in die *Metaphysik der Sitten*: „[...] die Willkühr als Naturvermögen ist in Ansehung jener Gesetze (des Pflichtbegriffes) frey durch die sie eigentlich nicht unmittelbar bestimmbar ist sondern nur vermittelst der Maximen sie jenem gemäs oder zuwider zu nehmen" (AA XXIII, S. 248). Die Freiheit der Willkür scheint sich also ihrem Vermögen zu verdanken, ihren Maximen einen bestimmten Inhalt zu geben, der dem Moralgesetz entweder gemäß oder zuwider ist. Dies entspricht Kants These, dass uns unsere Freiheit „durchs moralische Gesetz allererst kundbar wird" (AA VI, S. 226). Würden wir uns des moralischen Gesetzes nicht bewusst sein, wären wir auch nicht berechtigt, uns als frei wollende Subjekte zu begreifen. Das Bewusstsein des Moralgesetzes, das der Freiheit und das der Nötigung durch das Gesetz verweisen begrifflich aufeinander. Wollen wir verstehen, inwiefern die Willkür frei genannt werden kann, müssen wir also die Beziehung verstehen, die zwischen dem „obersten Grundsatz der Sittenlehre" auf der einen Seite und unserer Will-

---

lesen wir: „Wer kein Interesse an der Sittlichkeit hat, der kann kein guter Mensch seyn. Wenn die Menschen in Umstände kommen, wo sie bei der Tugend Gefahr laufen, so sieht man, daß Maximen fehlen. Gespräche über Sittlichkeit haben viel Vorzügliches, seine Maximen festzusetzen und sie bei Gelegenheit zu zeigen. Wer also an keinem moralischen Gespräche Geschmack findet, der hat keine bestimmten Maximen gefasst" (AA XXV, S. 1107). Es ist nach Kant also eine *empirische* Frage, ob Menschen faktisch nach Maximen handeln, und zwar eine solche, die negativ zu beantworten ist; vgl. dagegen zuletzt Schadow (2012, S. 140 ff.) und die dort angegebene Literatur.

[19]   „Welche Form in der Maxime sich zur allgemeinen Gesetzgebung schicke, welche nicht, das kann der gemeinste Verstand ohne Unterweisung unterscheiden" (AA V, S. 27).

kür auf der andere Seite besteht. In dieser Absicht soll zunächst der Begriff des Willens als der Grund praktischer Gesetze thematisiert werden.

Warum kann der Wille weder frei noch unfrei genannt werden? Der Wille ist weder frei noch unfrei, „weil er nicht auf Handlungen, sondern unmittelbar auf die Gesetzgebung für die Maxime der Handlungen (also die praktische Vernunft selbst) geht" (AA VI, S. 226). Demnach gehört es zum Begriff des Willens, gesetzgebend zu sein. Der Wille hat nicht die Wahl, nicht das Gesetz zu geben, nach dem ein reines Vernunftwesen sein Begehrungsvermögen gebraucht.[20] Formulieren wir dieses Zitat um und setzen für den Willen mit umgekehrten Vorzeichen die Willkür ein: ‚Die Willkür ist frei, weil sie auf Handlungen und auf die Maxime der Handlungen geht‘. Mit dieser Formulierung sind wir auf ein für das Verständnis der *Metaphysik der Sitten* zentrales Problem gestoßen: Ist die Willkür frei, weil sie sich unmittelbar auf Handlungen oder weil sie sich auf „Maxime[n] der Handlungen" bezieht? Was auf den ersten Blick wie eine unklare Bestimmung der freien Willkür aussieht[21], nämlich die Alternative zwischen unmittelbarem Handlungsbezug und Maximenbezug (oder Gesetzgebung), könnte sich auf den zweiten Blick als eine ingeniöse Unklarheit entpuppen, die in gedrängter Form den unterschiedlichen normativen Erfordernissen der *Rechtslehre* und der *Tugendlehre* Rechnung zu tragen erlaubt.

Beginnen wir mit der *Rechtslehre*. Kommt es in ihr auf den unmittelbaren Bezug der freien Willkür auf die Handlung oder auf die „Maxime der Handlungen" an? Dass es auf *beide* – und zwar aus unterschiedlichen Gründen – ankommt, wird aus dem allgemeinen Rechtsprinzip deutlich: „‚Eine jede Handlung ist recht, die oder nach deren Maxime die Freiheit der Willkür eines jeden mit jedermanns Freiheit nach einem allgemeinen Gesetze zusammen bestehen kann‘" (AA VI, S. 230). Das Rechtsprinzip trifft eine Aussage über eine Handlung, die nach einem allgemeinen Gesetz mit jedermanns Freiheit „zusammen bestehen kann". Aber es trifft diese Aussage unter Einbezug des Begriffs einer Maxime. Um die Relevanz dieses Einbezugs angemessen bewerten zu können, ist darauf zu achten, dass Kant den Maximenbegriff im allgemeinen Rechtsprinzip in einem speziellen Sinne verwendet. Er hat hier eine andere Bedeutung als der Begriff der Maxime in der *Tugendlehre*. Dies wird aus der „Einleitung" in

---

[20] In der Vorarbeit notiert Kant: „Der Mensch als Noumen ist sich selbst so wohl theoretisch als praktisch gesetzgebend für die Objecte der Willkühr und so fern frey aber ohne Wahl" (AA XXIII, S. 248; vgl. AA IV, S. 412, 414).

[21] Diese Unklarheit begegnet auch in einer der beiden Vorarbeiten: Einerseits behauptet Kant, dass die Willkür frei ist, weil die „Maximen der Willkühr", die „auf Handlungen als Erscheinungen in der Sinnenwelt gehen können", böse sein können. Andererseits scheint er die „Freyheit der Willkür" direkt auf Handlungen beziehen zu wollen: „Die Freyheit der Willkühr in Ansehung der Handlungen des Menschen als Phänomen besteht allerdings in dem Vermögen unter zwey entgegengesetzten (der gesetzmäßigen und gesetzwiedrigen) zu wählen und nach dieser betrachtet sich der Mensch selbst als Phänomen" (AA XXIII, S. 248).

die „Metaphysischen Anfangsgründe der Tugendlehre" deutlich, in der Kant feststellt, dass das Verhältnis von Zweck und Maxime in zwei verschiedenen Richtungen interpretiert werden kann: Erstens wird es in der *Rechtslehre* „jedermanns freier Willkür überlassen, welchen Zweck er sich für seine Handlung setzen wolle. Die Maxime derselben aber ist a priori bestimmt: daß nämlich die Freiheit des Handelnden mit Jedes anderen Freiheit nach einem allgemeinen Gesetz zusammen bestehen könne" (AA VI, S. 382). In rechtlicher Hinsicht zeichnet sich die freie Willkür also dadurch aus, dass wir aufgrund dieses Vermögens beliebige Zwecke mit unseren Handlungen verbinden können. Frei ist die Willkür genau deshalb, weil wir aufgrund dieses Vermögens das tun *können*, was wir zu tun beabsichtigen. Die Maxime der Handlung bezeichnet nun eine zusätzliche *normative* (vernunftrechtliche, obligationstheoretische) Perspektive, die wir nach dem „allgemeinen Rechtsgesetz" („handle äußerlich so, daß der freie Gebrauch deiner Willkür mit der Freiheit von jedermann nach einem allgemeinen Gesetze zusammen bestehen könne"; AA VI, S. 231) auf unser Wollen und Handeln einnehmen *sollen*. Unangesehen der Frage, welchen Zweck ich mit der Handlung verfolgen will, kann ich an der Maxime meiner Handlung feststellen, ob sich meine Handlung in ihrem äußeren Verlauf zu einer allgemeinen Gesetzgebung qualifiziert, durch die „die Freiheit des Handelnden mit Jedes anderen Freiheit nach einem allgemeinen Gesetz zusammen bestehen" kann (AA VI, S. 382). Frei ist unsere Willkür insofern, als wir im Rahmen des allgemeinen Rechtsprinzips zu tun *befugt* sind (tun *dürfen*), was wir zu tun beabsichtigen. Im Gegensatz zum tugendethischen Maximenbegriff ist es für den rechtlichen Maximenbegriff irrelevant, welchen Zweck ich mit meiner Handlung verbinde bzw. welches das Motiv (die Triebfeder, der Bewegungsgrund) meiner Handlung ist. Insbesondere erweist es sich für die rechtliche Bewertung der Handlung als irrelevant, ob ich die Handlung aus Achtung vor dem Moralgesetz oder aus Neigung vollziehe. Denn im Recht kann ich sogar dann rechtlich handeln (meine Rechtspflicht erfüllen), wenn ich mir meiner Maxime nicht bewusst bin. Aus diesem Grunde ist es wichtig, im Rechtsbereich zwischen der Handlung und ihrer Maxime zu unterscheiden. Die rechtliche Qualität meiner Handlung bemisst sich an ihrer Maxime, der ich mir nicht bewusst sein muss, um meine Rechtspflicht zu erfüllen oder gegen diese Pflicht zu verstoßen.

Wir können festhalten, dass die Willkür im Rechtsbereich frei ist, weil wir mittels ihrer innerhalb der Grenzen des allgemeinen Rechtsgesetzes äußere Handlungen vollziehen und mit ihnen beliebige Zwecke zu verbinden befugt sind. Wenn die freie Willkür das Vermögen bezeichnet, beliebige Zwecke mit meinen Handlungen zu verbinden, dann schließt sie selbstverständlich das Vermögen ein, bestimmte Handlungen bloß deshalb zu verfolgen oder zu unterlassen, weil sie nach dem Rechtsgesetz verboten oder gefordert sind. Das Recht interessiert sich nicht für meine Zwecke, oder besser: Es interessiert sich für diese nur dann und insofern, als sich diese Zwecke in konkreten Handlungen äußern, die unter dem Rechtsgesetz stehen.

In der Ethik wird das Verhältnis von Zweck und Maxime gegenüber ihrer rechtlichen Bestimmung verkehrt. Während es mir das Recht freistellt, welchen Zweck ich mit meiner Handlung verfolge, solange dieser Zweck nicht gegen „die Maxime der pflichtgemäßen Handlungen" (AA VI, S. 382) verstößt, schreibt mir im Bereich der Ethik die Pflicht (d. h. der kategorische Imperativ) den Zweck vor, aus dem die Maxime folgt, nach der ich handeln soll. Die Ethik „kann nicht von den Zwecken ausgehen, die der Mensch sich setzen mag, und darnach über seine zu nehmende Maximen, d. i. über seine Pflicht, verfügen; denn das wären empirische Gründe der Maximen, die keinen Pflichtbegriff abgeben, als welcher (das kategorische Sollen) in der reinen Vernunft allein seine Wurzel hat; wie denn auch, wenn die Maximen nach jenen Zwecken (welche alle selbstsüchtig sind) genommen werden sollten, vom Pflichtbegriff eigentlich gar nicht die Rede sein könnte. – Also wird in der Ethik der *Pflichtbegriff* auf Zwecke leiten und die *Maximen* in Ansehung der Zwecke, die wir uns setzen *sollen*, nach moralischen Grundsätzen begründen müssen" (AA VI, S. 382). Die Ethik macht es mir aus Gründen, die für unsere Thematik unerheblich sind, zur Pflicht, die eigene Vollkommenheit und die fremde Glückseligkeit als letzte oder oberste Zwecke meines Handelns zu befördern (vgl. AA VI, S. 391–394).

Um die ethische Dimension der Willkürfreiheit zu verstehen, ist Kants These zu beachten, dass die rechtlichen Pflichten von enger, die ethischen Pflichten aber von weiter Verbindlichkeit sind. Eine weite Verbindlichkeit liegt genau dann vor, wenn das Gesetz zwar die Maximen, aber nicht (wie das Recht dies kann) unmittelbar die Handlungen gebietet: „Dieser Satz ist eine Folge aus dem vorigen; denn wenn das Gesetz nur die Maxime der Handlungen, nicht die Handlungen selbst gebieten kann, so ists ein Zeichen, daß es der Befolgung (Observanz) einen Spielraum (latitudo) für die freie Willkür überlasse, d. i. nicht bestimmt angeben könne, wie und wie viel durch die Handlung zu dem Zweck, der zugleich Pflicht ist, gewirkt werden solle" (AA VI, S. 390). Mit anderen Worten: Über eine freie Willkür im Bereich der Tugendethik zu verfügen, bedeutet, die Befugnis zu haben, die eine „Pflichtmaxime" durch eine andere „Pflichtmaxime" (AA VI, S. 390). einzuschränken: „Es wird aber unter einer weiten Pflicht nicht die Erlaubniß zu Ausnahmen von der Maxime der Handlungen, sondern nur die der Einschränkung einer Pflichtmaxime durch die andere (z. B. die allgemeine Nächstenliebe durch die Elternliebe) verstanden, wodurch in der That das Feld für die Tugendpraxis erweitert wird" (AA VI, S. 390). Unsere Willkür ist in tugendethischer Hinsicht frei, weil wir die Befugnis haben, verschiedene ethisch gebotene Maximen gegeneinander abzuwägen und uns für eine von ihnen zu entscheiden.[22] Es ist eine Freiheit, von der wir

---

[22] Dies entspricht dem Begriff *„Freyheit nur zum Guten"*, der sich bei Crusius findet. In seiner *Anweisung vernünftig zu leben* unterscheidet Crusius drei Arten von Freiheit: „[...] 1) eine *Freyheit nur zum Guten*, welche nur unter den möglichen guten Thaten

innerhalb der Grenzen des Moralgesetzes Gebrauch machen können und aus Gründen der „Tugendpraxis" Gebrauch machen müssen. Diese Freiheit widerspricht dem Moralgesetz nicht, sondern fällt mit dem Begriff der unter dem Gesetz stehenden Freiheit zusammen. Dieser Freiheit werden wir uns „durchs moralische Gesetz" bewusst. Dass die freie Willkür in tugendethischer Hinsicht darin bestehen könnte, meiner Maxime auch einen pflichtwidrigen Inhalt zu geben, davon ist in diesem Zusammenhang bei Kant nicht die Rede.

Damit sind wir argumentationslogisch an der Stelle angelangt, von der wir ausgegangen sind: „Die Freiheit der Willkür [...] kann nicht durch das Vermögen der Wahl, für oder wider das Gesetz zu handeln, (libertas indifferentiae) definirt werden" (AA VI, S. 226). Warum negiert Kant dies? Wie kann ich eine moralisch schlechte Handlung vollziehen, wenn ich nicht die Freiheit habe, mich gegen das Moralgesetz zu entscheiden?

Bevor wir diese Frage zu beantworten versuchen, mag es hilfreich sein, nach dem Grund unserer Verpflichtung zu fragen und damit unsere Frage nach dem Verhältnis von Wille und Willkür aufzunehmen. Kant weist darauf hin, dass der „Grundsatz, welcher gewisse Handlungen zur Pflicht macht, [...] ein praktisches Gesetz ist". Dass wir nach Maximen handeln sollen, die sich zu einem allgemeinen Gesetz qualifizieren, stellt eine „Verbindlichkeit" dar, die im kategorischen Imperativ ausgesagt wird: „handle nach einer Maxime, welche zugleich als ein allgemeines Gesetz gelten kann!"(AA VI, S. 225) Würden wir keine Maximen bilden, könnten wir auch nicht feststellen, ob sie sich zu einem allgemeinen Gesetz qualifizieren. Dies würde für das Recht zwar subjektiv betrachtet eine Situation kognitiver Unsicherheit mit Beziehung auf unsere Rechtspflichten bedeuten, aber wir könnten doch zufälligerweise immer noch unsere Rechtspflichten erfüllen. Im Bereich der Tugendpflichten würde es uns jedoch verwehrt sein, Handlungen zu vollziehen, die aufgrund ihrer Maximen einen inneren moralischen Wert haben, weil das moralische Gesetz (die reine Vernunft) uns verpflichtet, aus Achtung vor diesem Gesetz[23] zu handeln. Wir wären zwar zur (ethischen) Legalität, aber nicht zur Moralität in der Lage. In

eine frey erwehlen kan, 2) eine *Freyheit nur zum Bösen*, welche nur unter den möglichen bösen Thaten eine frey erwehlen kan, 3) eine *Freiheit zum Guten und Bösen*, welche sich sowohl zu guten als bösen Thaten determiniren kan, weil ihr beyde möglich sind. In den Stand der letztern muß ein endlicher Geist, wenn er einer wahren moralischen Tugend fähig seyn soll, irgend einmal gesetzt werden. [...] Demnach ist die Freyheit nicht nothwendig eine Kraft, nach den besten Vorstellungen des Verstandes zu handeln, sondern da, wo unter den vorgestellten Handlungen wircklich eine die beste ist, da *soll* sie nur eine Kraft seyn, das beste erwehlen zu können, und nach der göttlichen Absicht *soll* sie zu der wircklichen Ergreiffung desselben angewendet werden" (Crusius, 1744, § 52, S. 64–65).

[23]   Nur wenn wir aus dem Gefühl der Achtung vor dem Moralgesetz handeln, erfüllen wir dieses Gesetz im vollen Umfange. Diese Ansicht erinnert an Römer 13, 10: „So ist nun die Liebe des Gesetzes Erfüllung."

jedem Fall verweist Kant auf die Vernunft, die den subjektiven Grundsatz meines Wollens „der Probe unterwirft", ob ich mich „durch denselben [...] zugleich als allgemein gesetzgebend" (AA VI, S. 225) denken kann. Wenn Kant den Willen als Ursprung der Gesetze begreift, versteht er ihn als Grund einer objektiven Notwendigkeit, der sich die freie Willkür als Ursprung der Maximen unterwerfen soll. Der Wille steht zur Willkür in einem Verhältnis der Nötigung (Verbindlichkeit, obligatio), die im kategorischen Imperativ ausgedrückt wird. Voraussetzung dieser Nötigung ist eine Willkür, die auf der einen Seite durch Sinnlichkeit affiziert wird, die auf der anderen Seite aber unter dem Willen und seiner Gesetzgebung steht: Weil unsere „Willkür sinnlich afficirt [ist] und so dem reinen Willen nicht von selbst angemessen, sondern oft widerstrebend ist"[24], sind die objektiven praktischen Gesetze der Freiheit für uns kategorische „Imperative (Gebote oder Verbote)" (AA VI, S. 221). Dementsprechend definiert Kant die „*Verbindlichkeit*" als „die Nothwendigkeit einer freien Handlung unter einem kategorischen Imperativ der Vernunft" (AA VI, S. 222). Das Gebot der Vernunft, eine Handlung zu vollziehen, die unter das Moralgesetz fällt, wird subjektiv als Nötigung begriffen. Dies bedeutet, dass ein Wille zwar der Ursprung von objektiven Gesetzen der Freiheit ist, selbst aber nicht genötigt werden kann. Die Nötigung bezieht sich allein auf ein Begehrungsvermögen, das Kant „sinnliche Willkür" (AA VI, S. 226) nennt. Wenn die freie Willkür durch den kategorischen Imperativ genötigt wird, sich in bestimmter Weise zum Handeln zu bestimmen, wie kann es dann sein, dass diese Willkür nicht frei ist, „für oder wider das Gesetz zu handeln, (libertas indifferentiae)"?

Wenden wir uns Kants Begründung in der „Einleitung" für seine Aussage zu. Zunächst unterscheidet er zwischen dem negativen und dem positiven Freiheitsbegriff.[25] Beide Freiheitsbegriffe (Kant spricht von einer negativen und einer positiven „Eigenschaft" der einen Freiheit) werden durch ihren unterschiedlichen Bezug zum Begriff der Nötigung erläutert. Das Subjekt der Nöti-

---

24 AA VI, S. 221. Die Unterscheidung zwischen sinnlicher und freier Willkür findet sich (wenn auch im Kontext der empirischen Psychologie) zuerst – so Schwaiger (2011, S. 91) – bei Baumgarten: „Das Vermögen, nach seinen sinnlichen Begierden zu begehren oder zu verwerfen, ist SINNLICHE WILLKÜR [ARBITRIUM SENSITIVUM]), das Vermögen, nach seinem Belieben zu wollen oder nicht zu wollen ist (freie Willkür [liberum arbitrium]) FREIHEIT [LIBERTAS] [...] (sittliche Freiheit, Freiheit schlechthin [moralis, simpliciter sic dicta]). Die Freiheit, rein zu wollen oder nicht zu wollen, ist REINE FREIHEIT [LIBERTAS PURA]" (Baumgarten, 2011, § 719, S. 384/385). Siehe auch Kawamura (1996, S. 56–57).

25 Zum Verhältnis von negativer und positiver Freiheit s. a. AA IV, S. 446–447, 458 und AA V, S. 33: „Jene *Unabhängigkeit* aber ist Freiheit im *negativen*, diese *eigene Gesetzgebung* aber der reinen und als solche praktischen Vernunft ist Freiheit im *positiven* Verstande. Also drückt das moralische Gesetz nichts anders aus, als die *Autonomie* der reinen praktischen Vernunft, d. i. der Freiheit, und diese ist selbst die formale Bedingung aller Maximen, unter der sie allein mit dem obersten praktischen Gesetze zusammenstimmen können".

gung kann entweder die Sinnlichkeit oder die Vernunft sein. Dementsprechend besteht die *„negative* Eigenschaft" der Freiheit darin, nicht durch „sinnliche Bestimmungsgründe zum Handeln genöthigt" zu werden. Die positive Eigenschaft der Freiheit besteht darin, sich selbst als Intelligenz als dasjenige Subjekt zu betrachten, dass „in Ansehung der sinnlichen Willkür *nöthigend* ist"[26]. Betrachten wir uns als Intelligenz und damit als Grund der Geltung des kategorischen Imperativs in uns, gilt das, was Kant zuvor über den „reinen Willen" geschrieben hat, nämlich dass dieser nicht als frei betrachtet werden kann.

Wie aber verhalten sich „reiner Wille" und „freie Willkür" zueinander? Mit dieser Frage wenden wir uns dem Verhältnis von oberem und unterem Begehrungsvermögen zu. Kant benötigt, wie wir einleitend festgestellt haben, eine Konzeption des Wollens, in der Wille und freie Willkür als zwei Aspekte ein und desselben Begehrungsvermögens[27] begriffen werden können. So lautet das Erfordernis – und darin besteht das ganze Problem. Es kann nicht zwei verschiedene ‚Willen' oder ‚Willkürvermögen' geben, sondern nur verschiedene Perspektiven unserer praktischen Selbstbestimmung. Auf der einen Seite ist die reine Vernunft (oberes Begehrungsvermögen) praktisch und gibt uns das Gesetz (Wille). Auf der anderen Seite ist das Begehrungsvermögen (unteres Begehrungsvermögen) Grund von subjektiven Regeln des Handelns, die auf unserer Sinnlichkeit beruhen und ihrem Ursprung nach nichts mit der reinen praktischen Vernunft zu tun haben. Der Wille gibt das Gesetz, aber durch ihre Maxime wirkt die Willkür in der Welt. Das im „obersten Grundsatz der Sittenlehre" ausgesprochene Gebot, nach einer Maxime zu handeln, „die zugleich als allgemeines Gesetz gelten kann" (AA VI, S. 226), vereinigt in sich diese zwei Perspektiven: Die Perspektive der sinnlich affizierten Willkür, die unter den Gesetzen der Natur steht, und die Perspektive der freien Willkür, die unter dem Moralgesetz steht und sich bewusst ist, nicht durch die Sinnlichkeit auf ein bestimmtes Handeln festgelegt zu sein. Der positive Begriff der freien Willkür fällt mit dem Begriff des Willens als dem Ursprung des moralischen Gesetzes zusammen. Die freie Willkür gehört (wie der Wille) in den Bereich der intelligiblen Welt. Ihr kann keine sinnliche Anschauung adäquat sein. Je nachdem, ob wir uns als Intelligenz zur noumenalen Welt oder zur Sinnenwelt zählen, nehmen wir eine der beiden Perspektiven auf unser Wollen ein (vgl. AA VI, S. 417). Im Bewusstsein einer moralischen Nötigung sind wir uns zugleich als Autor und Adressat dieser praktischen Nötigung präsent.[28] Aus diesem Grunde kann

---

[26]   AA VI, S. 226. Weil wir gerne tun, was uns gefällt (was wir begehren), kann die sinnliche Willkür nicht der Grund einer Nötigung sein.

[27]   Zu dieser Beziehung von Wille und Willkür s. auch Willaschek (1992, S. 51–52).

[28]   Diese Form des Selbstverhältnisses wird in der *Grundlegung* viel klarer, in der Kant noch nicht zwischen Wille und Willkür unterscheidet: „Der Wille wird als ein Vermögen gedacht, *der Vorstellung gewisser Gesetze* gemäß sich selbst zum Handeln zu bestimmen" (AA IV, S. 427).

weder der reine Wille als Ursprung des Gesetzes frei oder unfrei genannt werden, noch darf die freie Willkür als ein Vermögen begriffen werden, sich gegen das Moralgesetz zu entscheiden. Wenn ich als reines Vernunftwesen das Vermögen hätte, mich gegen das Moralgesetz zu entscheiden, würde dies alle Verbindlichkeit aufheben. Wäre der Mensch als intelligibles Wesen dazu befähigt, sich gegen das Moralgesetz zu entscheiden, hätte er – wie es in der Vorarbeit heißt – einen „bösen Willen" (AA XXIII, S. 248): „(Wir können die Freyheit der Willkühr nicht so definieren daß sie ein Vermögen sey dem Gesetz gemäs oder auch zuwieder zu handeln denn das wäre eine völlige subjective Gesetzlosigkeit derselben (*indifferentia arbitrii*) Unabhängigkeit von allen Bestimmungsgründen derselben woraus gar keine Handlung entspringen kann.)"[29]. Kants These also, dass die „Freiheit der Willkür" nicht als das Vermögen der Wahl definiert werden kann, für oder gegen das Gesetz zu handeln, bezieht sich auf die Mitgliedschaft der Willkür in der intelligiblen Welt.[30] Als ein vernünftiges Subjekt kann ich nicht wollen, gegen das Moralgesetz zu verstoßen. Ich habe nicht einmal die Wahl, mich positiv für das Moralgesetz zu entscheiden, weil meine freie Willkür notwendig an das Gesetz gebunden ist.

Diese Überlegungen werden durch Kants Ausführungen zum Begehrungsvermögen in der „Einleitung" in die *Metaphysik der Sitten* bestätigt, auch wenn er durch einige seiner Formulierungen den Eindruck erweckt, als ob Wille (reine Vernunft) und Willkür in substantieller Hinsicht betrachtet zwei verschiedene Vermögen darstellten. Zunächst zum Begriff des Willens: „Der Wille ist also das Begehrungsvermögen, nicht sowohl (wie die Willkür) in Beziehung auf die Handlung, als vielmehr auf den Bestimmungsgrund der Willkür zur

---

[29] AA XXI, S. 470. Kant hat diese Ansicht bereits in der Religionsschrift vertreten: Der Mensch ist kein *„teuflisches* Wesen" (AA VI, S. 35), das dem Moralgesetz „rebellischerweise" (AA VI, S. 36) seinen Gehorsam aufkündigt.

[30] Kants These, dass der Wille und die freie Willkür nicht den Bestimmungen von Raum und Zeit unterliegen, ist keine regulative Idee, wie Allison (1990, S. 140) meint, sondern eine (im Sinne der *kritischen* Philosophie) ‚ontologische' These. Anders als Allison bin ich der Auffassung, dass nach Kant unsere moralischen Entscheidungen keine Ereignisse in Raum und Zeit sind, auch wenn sie zugleich als derartige Ereignisse erkannt werden können (vgl. u. a. KrV, A 551–553/B 579–581). Stände unser Vermögen, uns zum Handeln zu bestimmen (von Kant Wille oder Willkür genannt), unter den Bedingungen der Zeit, wäre sein Gebrauch durch die Gesetze der Natur bestimmt. In diesem Falle könnten wir uns selbst unmöglich durch die Vorstellung eines Gesetzes zum Handeln bestimmen, das einen rein begrifflichen (intelligiblen) Charakter hat. Der Akt unserer Bestimmung zum Handeln ist somit der Differenz zwischen Natur (Kausalität der Natur) und Freiheit (Kausalität aus Freiheit) vorgeordnet. Erst nach dem Vollzug der Selbstbestimmung ist die Willkür sowohl moralisch bewertbar wie empirisch erkennbar. Würde unser (oberes) Begehrungsvermögen nur im Sinne einer regulativen Idee den Bedingungen von Raum und Zeit nicht unterliegen, wäre übrigens schwer nachvollziehbar, wieso unsere moralischen Verbindlichkeiten nicht ebenfalls einen bloß regulativen Charakter haben sollten.

Handlung betrachtet, und hat selber vor sich eigentlich keinen Bestimmungsgrund, sondern ist, sofern sie die Willkür bestimmen kann, die praktische Vernunft selbst" (AA VI, S. 213). Kant weist nun darauf hin, dass die „Willkür, die durch *reine Vernunft* bestimmt werden kann," die „freie Willkür" genannt wird. Würde dagegen die Willkür „nur durch Neigung (sinnlichen Antrieb, stimulus) bestimmbar", würde sie eine „thierische Willkür (arbitrium brutum) sein" (AA VI, S. 213). Weil die „menschliche Willkür" zwar durch Neigungen „*afficirt*, aber nicht *bestimmt* wird", handelt es sich bei ihr um eine „freie Willkür" (AA VI, S. 213). Wir werden nicht durch „sinnliche Antriebe" bestimmt (negativer Begriff der Freiheit), sondern haben das Vermögen, unsere Willkür durch reine Vernunft zu bestimmen (positiver Begriff der Freiheit). Dies ist genau dann der Fall, wenn wir unsere Maximen dem Moralgesetz unterwerfen. Mit anderen Worten: Bestimmen wir unsere unter dem Moralgesetz stehende Willkür tatsächlich durch dieses Gesetz, ist die reine Vernunft in unserem Handeln praktisch geworden. Wir haben dem Willen bzw. der reinen Vernunft subjektive Realität gegeben. Wille und Willkür, die objektive und die subjektive Seite unseres „Begehrungsvermögens nach Begriffen", fallen zusammen. Bestimmt die praktische Vernunft die Willkür in Beziehung auf eine Handlung, ist die Willkür praktische Vernunft.

3. Die „Willkür *als Phänomen*" belegt die Existenz der „libertas indifferentiae"

Wenn die „Freiheit der Willkür" nicht als Freiheit verstanden werden kann, für oder gegen das Moralgesetz zu handeln, wie können wir dann erklären, „daß der Mensch als *Sinnenwesen* der Erfahrung[31] nach ein Vermögen zeigt dem Gesetze nicht allein *gemäß*, sondern auch *zuwider* zu wählen" (AA VI, S. 226) befähigt ist? Kant steht es offenbar nicht frei, diese „Erfahrung" als illusorisch abzutun. Denn wenn der Mensch nicht die Freiheit besäße, im Wissen um das

---

[31] Worin besteht diese Erfahrung? Vielleicht denkt Kant an unsere moralischen Urteile über Handlungen, die hätten geschehen sollen, aber nicht geschehen sind, weil wir uns anders entschieden haben: „Es ist niemand, selbst der ärgste Bösewicht, wenn er nur sonst Vernunft zu brauchen gewohnt ist, der nicht, wenn man ihm Beispiele der Redlichkeit in Absichten […] nicht wünschte, daß er auch so gesinnt sein möchte. Er kann es aber nur wegen seiner Neigungen und Antriebe nicht wohl in sich zu Stande bringen, wobei er dennoch zugleich wünscht, von solchen ihm selbst lästigen Neigungen frei zu sein. Er beweiset hiedurch also, daß er mit einem Willen, der von Antrieben der Sinnlichkeit frei ist, sich in Gedanken in eine ganz andere Ordnung der Dinge versetze, als die seiner Begierden im Felde der Sinnlichkeit" (AA IV, S. 454). Wenig später heißt es entsprechend: „Alle Menschen denken sich dem Willen nach frei. Daher kommen alle Urteile über Handlungen als solche, die *hätten geschehen sollen*, ob sie gleich *nicht geschehen sind*" (AA IV, S. 455)

moralische Gesetz das Schlechte zu tun, gäbe es vor dem Hintergrund seiner strikten Trennung von Sinnlichkeit und Verstand kein moralisches Sollen, dessen er sich bewusst ist. Der Begriff der Nötigung durch die reine Vernunft würde keinen Sinn ergeben. Schließlich setzt der kategorische Imperativ voraus, dass wir als sinnliche Wesen etwas wollen, was wir als „vernünftige Naturwesen" (AA VI, S. 237) nicht wollen *sollten*. Gäbe Kant die Antithese auf, würde er auf die konsequent rationalistische Position von Gottfried Wilhem Leibniz und Christian Wolff[32] zurückfallen. Moralische Schlechtigkeit würde auf einem Mangel an Erkenntnis beruhen, keinesfalls aber wäre sie (wie schon Crusius[33] argumentierte) allein im *Wollen* begründet.

Wenn Kant weder die These noch die Antithese negieren kann, weil dies entweder die Negation seiner Konzeption der Autonomie oder des im kategorischen Imperativ zum Ausdruck gebrachten moralischen Sollens bedeutete, fragt sich, warum er nicht expressis verbis eingesteht, eine Antinomie der praktischen Vernunft entdeckt zu haben. Meines Erachtens gibt es hierfür einen guten Grund. Im Unterschied zu den in den drei Kritiken vorgetragenen Antinomien zeichnet sich die Antinomie von 1797 durch eine Besonderheit aus: Es gibt keine Möglichkeit, sie durch den Rekurs auf den transzendentalen Idealismus aufzulösen. Vielmehr beruht die Wahrheit von These und Antithese auf dem transzendentalen Idealismus. Und die Wahrheit der Antithese setzt die Wahrheit der These voraus, denn ohne die Kausalität der reinen praktischen Vernunft gäbe es kein Bewusstsein des moralischen Sollens und damit kein Bewusstsein unserer Freiheit (vgl. KrV, A 547/B 575). Weil Kant die Antinomie der reinen praktischen Vernunft nicht durch den Rückgriff auf seinen transzendentalen Idealismus auflösen kann, wird er gezögert haben, den (scheinbaren) Widerspruch zwischen der Negation des intelligiblen und der Behauptung eines (wie ich ihn nennen möchte) phänomenalen Indifferentismus eine Antinomie zu nennen.

---

[32]   Siehe u. a. Klemme (2008 a u. 2008 b). Diese Position wird von zahlreichen Autoren vertreten, unter anderem von Achenwall und Pütter in den *Elementa iuris naturae* (1750): Der Wille ist allgemein das Bestreben, „welches aus dem entsteht, was wir für ein Gut oder ein Übel halten. Im besonderen wird Wille verstanden für das Begehren, welches aus dem entsteht, was wir für ein Gut halten, und insofern wird ihm das Nichtwollen entgegengesetzt, das ist die Abneigung, welche aus dem entsteht, was wir für ein Übel halten" (1750, § 43, S. 29). Und an anderer Stelle heißt es: „Die menschliche Seele hat die Fähigkeit das auszuwählen, was dem Verstand als das Beste erscheint, welche Fähigkeit man *Freiheit des Geistes* nennt" (1750, § 55, S. 33).

[33]   In der *Nova Diludicatio* (1755) schreibt Kant: „Der berühmte Crusius glaubt allerdings, manches Dasein werde durch seine eigene Wirklichkeit so bestimmt, daß er es für eitel hält, etwas darüber hinaus zu fordern. Titius handelt aus freiem Wollen; ich frage: warum er dies lieber getan als nicht getan habe; er antwortet: weil er gewollt hat [quia voluit]. Warum aber hat er gewollt? Dies zu fragen, behauptet er, sei ungereimt. Wenn man fragt: warum hat er nicht lieber etwas anderes getan? Antwortet er: weil er dies schon tut" (AA I, S. 397; zitiert nach der deutschen Übersetzung in Kant, 1968, S. 441).

Wenn die Lehre vom Transzendentalen Idealismus der tiefere Grund für die Wahrheit von Thesis und Antithesis ist, dann kann diese Lehre auch nicht in Anspruch genommen werden, um den Widerspruch einerseits zwischen dem Begriff eines gesetzgebenden Willens und andererseits unserer Erfahrung aufzuheben, die bestätigt, was ersterer negiert, nämlich dass wir uns für oder wider die Gebote des moralischen Gesetzes entscheiden können. Mit den Bordmitteln der kantischen Philosophie kann es keine die beiden Behauptungen versöhnende *dogmatische* Lehre geben. Wie unsere durch die Erfahrung bestätigte Fähigkeit, uns im Wissen um das Gute für das Böse zu entscheiden, möglich ist, hält Kant für unerklärlich.[34] Das ist die zentrale These, die er in der „Einleitung" in die *Metaphysik der Sitten* vertritt: Wir können unser Vermögen, eine pflichtwidrige Handlung zu vollziehen, zwar nicht durch den Verweis auf die intelligible Natur des Menschen erklären, aber wir können dieses Vermögen auch nicht negieren.[35] Trotz des guten Willens können (so Kant in einer zweiten Vorarbeit zur „Einleitung") „böse Handlungen und Maximen entspringen", die „als phaenomen nicht aus dem intelligiblen Substract des freyen Willens erklärt werden"[36] können.

Obwohl wir die Möglichkeit eines gesetzwidrigen Wollens nicht zu erklären vermögen, können wir den Modus angeben, unter dem unsere Wahl steht. Kant

---

[34]   Siehe AA VI, S. 226 u. KrV, A 556 f./B 584 f. Dies entspricht durchaus der Position der *Religion innerhalb der Grenzen der bloßen Vernunft*: Der Grund des Bösen liegt in einer Maxime, die auf einem subjektiven Grund beruht. „Dieser subjective Grund muß aber immer wiederum selbst ein Actus der Freiheit sein (denn sonst könnte der Gebrauch oder Missbrauch der Willkür des Menschen in Ansehung des sittlichen Gesetzes ihm nicht zugerechnet werden und das Gute oder Böse in ihm nicht moralisch heißen). Mithin kann in keinem die Willkür durch Neigung *bestimmenden* Objecte, in keinem Naturtriebe, sondern nur in einer Regel, die die Willkür sich selbst für den Gebrauch ihrer Freiheit macht, d.i. in einer Maxime, der Grund des Bösen liegen. Von dieser muß nicht weiter gefragt werden können, was der subjective Grund ihrer Annehmung und nicht vielmehr der entgegengesetzten Maxime im Menschen sei. Denn wenn dieser Grund zuletzt selbst keine Maxime mehr, sondern ein bloßer Naturtrieb wäre, so würde der Gebrauch der Freiheit ganz auf Bestimmung durch Naturursachen zurückgeführt werden können: welches ihr widerspricht" (AA VI, S. 21). Zum Beweisziel der Religionsschrift, auf die hier nicht näher eingegangen werden kann, vgl. u.a. Klemme (1999).

[35]   Brandt vertritt dagegen die Ansicht, dass die „Willkür eine Hilfskonstruktion ist, die in den zwei Welten von Natur und Freiheit keinen Ort hat" (2010, S. 79).

[36]   Das ganze Zitat aus der Vorarbeit lautet: „Worauf es nun beruhe daß dieses Vermögen nicht immer die Bestimmung der Willkühr zum Guten zur Folge hat sondern des guten Willens ungeachtet des bösen Handlungen und Maximen entspringen kan als phaenomenon nicht aus dem intelligibelen Substract des freyen Willens erklärt werden. Sowie warum wir was außer uns ist im Raum u. was in uns ist in der Zeit vorstellen und nicht vielmehr umgekehrt kein Grund angegeben werden kann denn das betrifft die sinnliche Form der Gegenstände so ist es hier mit der der Handlungen die wir wenn sie böse sind nur mechanisch nie aber warum ein solcher Mechanism in uns angetroffen wird uns erklären können" (AA XXIII, S. 249).

erläutert diesen Modus in der *Kritik der praktischen Vernunft*: Unsere Natur ist so beschaffen, „daß die Materie des Begehrungsvermögens (Gegenstände der Neigung, es sei der Hoffnung, oder Furcht) sich zuerst aufdringt, und unser pathologisch bestimmbares Selbst [...] gleich als ob es unser ganzes Selbst ausmachte, seine Ansprüche vorher und als die ersten und ursprünglichen geltend zu machen bestrebt sei" (AA V, S. 74). Weil sich unsere pathologische Natur unserem Selbst „zuerst aufdringt", unsere Willkür also sinnlich affiziert wird, müssen wir uns anstrengen, die „Hindernisse" (AA IV, S. 201, 449; AA V, S. 267 u. ö.), die sie uns in den Weg legt, zu überwinden, wenn wir aus Achtung vor dem Moralgesetz handeln wollen (vgl. AA V, S. 151 ff.). Unsere Willkür ist frei, weil sie unter dem Moralgesetz steht, das von uns verlangt, unsere Maximen so zu wählen, dass sie sich zu einer allgemeinen Gesetzgebung qualifizieren. Weil das „Abweichen vom Gesetz [...] kein übersinnliches Vermögen" (AA VI, S. 248) ist, kann die freie Willkür nicht als ein Vermögen definiert werden, vom Gesetz abzuweichen. Diese Wahlmöglichkeit begreift Kant als ein „Unvermögen": „Die Freiheit in Beziehung auf die innere Gesetzgebung der Vernunft ist eigentlich allein ein Vermögen; die Möglichkeit von dieser abzuweichen ein Unvermögen"[37]. Wie jedoch das eine aus dem anderen abgeleitet werden kann, erklärt Kant für unerklärlich, weil wir die Bedeutung eines intelligiblen Begriffs nicht durch Erfahrung erklären können: „Es ist eine Definition, die über den praktischen Begriff noch die *Ausübung* derselben, wie sie die Erfahrung lehrt, hinzuthut, eine *Bastarderklärung* (definitio hybrida), welche den Begriff im falschen Lichte darstellt" (AA VI, S. 227).

Die Differenz zwischen „Vermögen" und „Unvermögen", die gerade nicht belegen soll, dass das Unvermögen eine unfreie Handlung[38] impliziert, kann

---

[37]   AA VI, S. 227. „In dem Begriffe der Freyheit einer Willkühr denkt man sich zugleich ein Vermögen allen Gesetzwiedrigen Neigungen zum Trotz doch dem Gesetz zu folgen, die Moglichkeit davon abgeleitet zu werden ist ein Unvermögen welches nicht von der Erfahrung gelehrt sondern daraus geschlossen wird" (AA XXI, S. 472). Bereits in der *Grundlegung* scheint Kant die Position zu vertreten, dass die moralisch verwerfliche Maxime (subjektiv betrachtet) nicht als Widerstreit gegen das Moralgesetz interpretiert werden darf: „Wenn wir nun auf uns selbst bei jeder Übertretung einer Pflicht Acht haben, so finden wir, daß wir wirklich nicht wollen, es solle unsere Maxime ein allgemeines Gesetz werden, denn das ist uns unmöglich, sondern das Gegenteil derselben soll vielmehr allgemein ein Gesetz bleiben; nur nehmen wir uns die Freiheit, für uns oder (auch nur für diesesmal) zum Vorteil unserer Neigung davon eine *Ausnahme* zu machen. [...] Da wir aber einmal unsere Handlungen aus dem Gesichtspunkte eines ganz der Vernunft gemäßen, dann aber auch eben dieselbe Handlung aus dem Gesichtspunkte eines durch Neigung afficierten Willens betrachten, so ist wirklich hier kein Widerspruch, wohl aber ein Widerstand der Neigung gegen die Vorschrift der Vernunft (antagonismus), wodurch die Allgemeinheit des Prinzips (universalitas) in eine bloße Gemeingültigkeit (generalitias) verwandelt wird, dadurch das praktische Vernunftprincip mit der Maxime auf dem halben Wege zusammenkommen soll" (AA IV, S. 424).
[38]   So zutreffend Bojanowski (2007, S. 223) gegen Prauss (1983, S. 111–115).

vielleicht am besten durch den Begriff der *Anstrengung* (Kant spricht u.a. von „Kraftanwendung"[39]) erklärt werden. Obwohl wir uns gegen unsere Pflichterfüllung entschieden haben, hätten wir uns auch anders entscheiden können, wenn wir nur willens gewesen wären, eine Anstrengung auf uns zu nehmen. Und obwohl wir uns entschieden haben, unsere Pflicht zu erfüllen, hätten wir uns auch dafür entscheiden können, keine Anstrengung auf uns zu nehmen. Warum wir uns aber entschieden haben, die Anstrengung nicht auf uns zu nehmen, ist für uns völlig unerklärlich. In jedem Fall ist es eine Entscheidung, die unsere Handlungsmaxime betrifft, und unsere Handlung kann uns zugerechnet werden, weil wir uns anders hätten entscheiden können.

Kants Position kann durch Ausführungen zum Begriff einer moralischen Handlung erläutert werden, die sich in Georg Friedrich Meiers *Allgemeine practische Weltweisheit* (1764) finden. Auch wenn für den Wolffianer Meier die für die kantische Handlungstheorie typische Unterscheidung zwischen Form (der Vernunft) und Materie (der Sinnlichkeit) nicht akzeptabel wäre, vermittelt seine Unterscheidung zwischen einer ‚unmittelbar' und einer ‚mittelbar freien' Handlung zumindest einen guten Eindruck von der Problemstellung, an der sich Jahrzehnte später noch Kant abarbeitet. Selbst wenn wir uns (in Kants Terminologie) den Gesetzen der Natur überlassen, handeln wir nach Meier in einem bestimmten Sinne des Wortes frei: „Gesetzt, ein Reisender kommt an einen Scheideweg; wenn er sich nun umsieht, und die Merkmale des rechten Weges überlegt, und alsdenn sich entschließt, den einen unter beyden zu wählen: so handelt er in der That frey, indem er bey diesem seinen Entschlusse, seine Vernunft und seinen freyen Willen, würklich gebraucht hat. Alsdenn ist seine Handlung eine unmittelbar freye Handlung, weil sie eine Würkung der Geschäftigkeit seines freyen Willens ist. Allein gesetzt, daß er, wenn er an einen Scheideweg[40] kommt, eben in tiefen Gedanken gehe, an den Weg nicht gedenke, und vollkommen in seinem Gemüthe zerstreuet sey: so wird er, ohne Bewußtseyn, entweder den rechten oder unrechten Weg gehen. Demohnerachtet handelt er in beyden Fällen frey, weil es ihm möglich gewesen ist, die Zerstreuung

---

[39] AA V, S. 24; VI, S. 50; VII, S. 147. Diese Position ist prinzipiell nicht originell und wird in ähnlicher Form im 18. Jahrhundert unter anderem vom Naturrechtler Heineccius (1738, § 49, S. 51) sowie im 20. Jahrhundert von G.E. Moore (Moore, 1975, S. 119–132) und Ernst Tugendhat (1992, S. 334–351) vertreten. Siehe weiterführend Klemme (1996).

[40] In der *Grundlegung zur Metaphysik der Sitten* nimmt Kant die Metapher vom Scheideweg auf: Der Wert des Willens liegt in dem Prinzip, nach dem er handelt, „denn der Wille ist mitten inne zwischen seinem Princip a priori, welches formell ist, und zwischen seiner Triebfeder a posteriori, welche materiell ist, gleichsam auf einem Scheidewege, und da er doch irgend wodurch muß bestimmt werden, so wird er durch das formelle Princip des Wollens überhaupt bestimmt werden müssen, wenn eine Handlung aus Pflicht geschieht, da ihm alles materielle Princip entzogen worden" (AA IV, S. 400; vgl. AA VI, S. 380).

des Gemüths zu verhüten, an den Weg zu gedenken, und nach Ueberlegung seine Reise fortzusetzen. In diesem Falle ist, die Handlung, nur mittelbarer Weise frey. Der freye Wille ist in diesem Augenblicke unthätig bey dieser Handlung, und sie ist keine Würkung des freyen Willens selbst. Weil es aber dem Menschen möglich gewesen wäre, seinen freyen Willen in diesem Augenblick zu gebrauchen, und den Weg nach Einsichten und Ueberlegungen zu wählen: so wird diese Handlung mit Recht, unter die freyen Handlungen, gerechnet" (1764, § 33, S. 70–71).

Dass Kant seine These, dass die „Freiheit der Willkür [...] nicht durch das Vermögen der Wahl, für oder wider das Gesetz zu handeln," nicht so verstanden wissen wollte, dass wir als Menschen nicht die Wahl hätten, gegen das moralische Gesetz zu verstoßen, wird nicht nur aus dem Text der „Einleitung" in die *Metaphysik der Sitten* und den beiden Vorarbeiten deutlich. Kant hat diese These bereits zu dem Zeitpunkt seiner Abfassung der *Grundlegung zur Metaphysik der Sitten* (allerdings in einer anderen Terminologie) vertreten. In der aus dem Sommer 1784 stammenden Nachschrift seines Kollegs über Naturrecht (*Naturrecht-Feyerabend*) lesen wir: „Der Mensch kann das Gute und Böse wählen, also ist der gute Wille bei dem Menschen ein zufälliger Wille. Bei Gott ist sein guter Wille nicht zufällig; daher findet auch bei ihm kein imperatives Gesetz statt, um ihn zum guten Willen zu nöthigen. [...] Die objective praktische Nothwendigkeit ist bei Gott auch subjective praktische Nothwendigkeit. Zwang ist Nöthigung zur ungernen Handlung. Demnach muß ich da eine Triebfeder zum Gegentheile haben. – Die praktischen Gesetze können daher auch Zwang seyn, auch wenn der Mensch ungern etwas thut; so muß ers doch tun. Ich soll das thun, heißt eine durch mich nothwendige Handlung würde gut seyn. Daraus folgt noch nicht, daß ich es thun werde: denn ich habe auch subjective Gegengründe. Ich stelle mir jene daher als nothwendig vor. Gebothe sind also für einen unvollkommnen Willen. Praktische Gesetze, als neceßitirende Gründe der Handlung heißen Imperative" (Kant, 2007, S. 11–12).

Klar erkennbar in diesem Zitat ist der (wie wir ihn nennen können) Dualismus unserer Handlungsgründe. Den subjektiven Gründen unserer Sinnlichkeit, denen wir nur zu gerne folgen, weil sie angenehm und reizvoll sind, stehen die objektiven und notwendigen Gründe unserer Vernunft gegenüber. Zwischen beiden Arten von Gründen findet kein gradueller Übergang statt. Sie sind der Art nach verschieden, weil ihr Ursprung entweder in der Vernunft oder in der Sinnlichkeit liegt. Dass wir Menschen diese Wahlfreiheit haben, betont Kant ausweislich der Nachschrift des Kollegs über Naturrecht mit großem Nachdruck. Wie diese Wahlfreiheit zu erklären ist, bleibt aber auch in dieser Nachschrift offen. Das kann nicht wirklich überraschen. Alle Erklärungen von Ereignissen nehmen auf ein Gesetz der Kausalität Bezug. Alle Gesetze sind solche der Natur und der Freiheit. Weil wir erklären wollen, warum wir eher nach der einen als nach der anderen Art der Kausalität handeln, würde dies bedeuten, dass wir entweder auf die Kausalität der Freiheit oder die Kausalität der Natur zurückgreifen müssten. Damit würde das Problem zum Verschwinden gebracht, aber zum Preis der Negation des Phänomens dieser Wahlfreiheit. Wenn Kant nicht nur in der Einleitung in die *Metaphysik der Sitten* sondern auch im *Naturrecht-Feyerabend* die Wahl mit unserem intelligiblen Vermögen des Wollens in Zusammenhang bringt, kann es nicht überraschen, dass Kant in der *Grundlegung* an einer berühmten Stelle behaupten kann, dass „ein freier Wille und ein Wille unter sittlichen Gesetzen einerlei" (AA IV, S. 447) ist, ohne diese Wahlmöglichkeit damit negieren zu wollen. Ganz im Gegenteil ist die Identifikation des Willens mit dem Moralgesetz die Voraussetzung dafür, dass eine sinnlich affizierte Willkür sich zum Guten entscheiden kann.

4. Überlegungen zur philosophischen Bedeutung von Kants Position

Das Problem der Verhältnisbestimmung von Wille und Willkür begleitet die Entwicklungsgeschichte der kantischen Ethik von Anfang an. Weil Kant davon überzeugt ist, dass uns das moralische Gesetz nur deshalb verbindet, weil wir es uns selbst geben, muss unser Wollen einen gesetzgebenden (legislativen) und einen ausführenden (exekutiven) Aspekt umfassen, wobei wir als ausübende Gewalt die Chance haben, uns gegen unsere eigene Gesetzgebung zu entscheiden. Es ist diese durch und durch paradoxe Problemsituation, auf die Kant auch mit seinen Ausführungen zur „libertas indifferentiae" 1797 reagiert. Wille und Willkür sind funktional zu differenzieren, dürfen aber nicht als zwei substantiell verschiedene Vermögen[41] begriffen werden. Autor und Adressat des Gesetzes müssen identisch sein, aber eben nicht so, dass nicht noch Raum bliebe für ein Wollen, das sich für oder gegen das moralische Gesetz entscheiden kann. Auf der einen Seite ist die Willkür frei, weil sie „unter dem Gesetz"[42] steht, das der Wille gibt. Die Willkür ist damit der Wille bzw. die reine praktische Vernunft. Sie gibt dem Gesetz, das sich die Vernunft selbst gibt, im Handeln eine objektive Realität. Auf der anderen Seite ist die Willkür frei, weil wir uns nach dem Zeugnis unserer Erfahrung für oder gegen unsere Pflichterfüllung entscheiden können, ohne die Geltung des Moralgesetzes grundsätzlich zu bezweifeln.

---

41   „Vermögen" meint zum einen „facultas", zum anderen aber den Gebrauch, den wir von der „facultas" machen. Hierauf weist Henry Allison hin: „Kant uses the terms *Wille* and *Willkür* to characterize respectively the legislative and executive functions of a unified faculty of volition, which he likewise refers to as *Wille*. Accordingly, *Wille* has both a broad sense in which it connotes the faculty of volition or will as a whole and a narrow sense in which it connotes one function of that faculty" (1990, S. 129).

42   AA IV, S. 433; vgl. AA V, S. 4 Anm.

Mit seinen spröden Ausführungen in der „Einleitung" in die *Metaphysik der Sitten* unternimmt Kant einen letzten Versuch, den ethischen Voluntarismus[43] in seine Schranken zu weisen, ohne die Idee des moralischen Sollens und damit der Freiheit des Menschen zum moralisch Guten und Schlechten aufzuheben. Kant versucht im Rahmen seines transzendentalen Idealismus das scheinbar Unmögliche: Die Notwendigkeit des moralischen Gebotes mit der Zufälligkeit unser handlungsrelevanten Entscheidung, die freie Willkür mit der sinnlichen Willkür begrifflich zu vereinigen. Theoriegeschichtlich betrachtet kann dieser Vermittlungsversuch zwischen (grob gesprochen) Leibniz und Wolff auf der einen und Joachim Lange und Crusius auf der anderen Seite jedoch nur zum Preis einer Auffassung menschlichen Wollens gelingen, die einen strikten Dualismus von Sinnlichkeit und Vernunft, phänomenalem Indifferentismus und intelligibler Vernunftnotwendigkeit zur Voraussetzung hat. Das diesen Dualismus vereinigende Prinzip muss aus erkenntniskritischen Gründen unbekannt bleiben. Demnach lautet Kants These: So wenig plausibel es ist, das Phänomen der „libertas indifferentiae" zu leugnen, so wenig plausibel sind alle Versuche, dieses Phänomen mit unserem Begriff einer durch das Moralgesetz geprägten praktischen Rationalität zu vereinigen. Die Lösung dieses Problems überschreitet die Grenzen unserer Vernunft.[44]

Blicken wir auf Kants Überlegungen zur „libertas indifferentiae" von 1797 aus der Perspektive eines modernen Lesers, der ein systematisches Interesse am Problem der Willensfreiheit (verstanden als unser Vermögen, uns für oder gegen unsere moralischen Pflichten zu entscheiden) und der praktischen Rationalität nimmt, stechen einige Besonderheiten hervor, die zumindest kursorisch hervorgehoben werden sollen:

(1) Es gibt nach Kant *keine kontextfreie* und damit *voraussetzungsfreie Konzeption* der Willensfreiheit. Schon die Unterscheidung zwischen sinnlicher und freier Willkür verdankt sich einer These über praktische Vermögen und Funktionen, die vor einem normativen Hintergrund entwickelt wird. Im Bewusstsein des Moralgesetzes sind wir uns nicht nur eines Gesetzes der Freiheit bewusst, wir sind uns auch bewusst, nicht durch „sinnliche Bestimmungsgründe zum Handeln genöthigt zu werden" (AA VI, S. 26).

(2) Willensfreiheit drückt eine *Weise der praktischen Selbstbeziehung* und *Selbstbestimmung* aus, die zwischen dem Willen als gesetzgebender und der Willkür als ausübende Gewalt besteht. Wir sind zugleich (als intelligibles Subjekt) Autor und (als Mensch) Adressat des Gesetzes. Bestimmen wir uns zum Handeln, nehmen wir unweigerlich auf uns selbst Bezug, müssen wir uns zu unserer rationalen und sinnlichen Natur praktisch verhalten.

---

[43]   Siehe beispielsweise Descartes (1915, S. 580–581).

[44]   Kants Überlegungen zur Unterscheidung zwischen Wille und Willkür mögen „hardly models of philosophical lucidity" (Allison, 1990, S. 135) sein, aber unsere Ausführungen zu dieser Unterscheidung haben vielleicht deutlich gemacht, worin die Dunkelheit sachlich begründet ist.

(3) Mit dem Begriff der „Freiheit der Willkür" stellt Kant fest, dass Indeterminiertheit nicht unsere Freiheit ermöglicht, sondern dass unser Bewusstsein der Indeterminiertheit vielmehr unser Freiheitsbewusstsein voraussetzt. Unser Vermögen, uns gegen das moralische Gesetz zu entscheiden, setzt voraus, dass ein reines Vernunftwesen mit Notwendigkeit nach dem Moralgesetz handelt. Nur weil wir durch die „Freyheit eines intelligiblen Wesens" (AA XXI, S. 471) (rational) genötigt werden, können wir als Menschen wählen, ob wir so handeln wollen, wie wir vernünftigerweise, d. h. nach dem Gesetz der Freiheit, handeln sollen.

(4) Kant ist, was unser Wollen anbetrifft, kein *reiner* Rationalitätstheoretiker. Sicherlich gibt es eine Bedeutung von Freiheit bei Kant – nämlich Freiheit als potentielle und als reale Autonomie –, nach der der Begriff der Freiheit mit dem Begriff der Vernunft zusammenfällt. Aber es gibt eben auch eine Bedeutung von Freiheit, nach der wir uns sehr wohl zum Schlechten entscheiden können. Jede plausible Konzeption praktischen Rationalität muss ihre eigenen Grenzen benennen können. Sie muss erklären, warum wir unsere Wahlfreiheit nicht erklären können.

(5) Unsere Entscheidung für oder gegen das Moralgesetz kann kausal nicht erklärt werden. Aber dies bedeutet nicht, dass wir keine Gründe für unsere Wahl angeben können. Wenn wir uns für die Befolgung unserer moralischen Gründe entscheiden, nennen wir moralische Gründe; entscheiden wir uns gegen sie, verweisen wir, wenn wir denn rational sind, auf unser Glück als obersten Handlungszweck. Weil die Kosten des moralischen Handelns zu hoch waren, habe ich mich dafür entschieden, eine eigeninteressierte Handlung zu wählen. So willkürlich ist unsere Willkürfreiheit also dann doch nicht. Wir befinden uns nicht in der Situation von Buridans Esel, der sich zwischen zwei gleich großen und gleich weit entfernten Heuhaufen nicht entscheiden kann. Nachdem wir uns entschieden haben, können wir auch einen Grund angeben, warum wir uns so entschieden haben. Weil Kant dem Menschen nicht zutrauen möchte, dass er dem Moralgesetz „rebellischerweise" (AA VI, S. 36) seinen Gehorsam aufkündigt, erklärt er unsere Entscheidung zugunsten unserer Gründe der Sinnlichkeit entweder mit einem subjektiven Unvermögen, die Begierde zu überwinden (was objektiv die Tat aber nicht rechtfertigt), oder damit, dass wir Ausnahmen von der strikten Geltung des Moralgesetzes für uns selbst zu begründen versuchen (vgl. AA IV, S. 424).

(6) Die philosophisch wichtigste Einsicht, die wir Kants Diskussion der „libertas indifferentiae" verdanken, betrifft vielleicht das Verhältnis von praktischer Rechtfertigung und Skepsis. Kant ist davon überzeugt, dass wir bestimmten Phänomenen unsere praktische Anerkennung nicht versagen können. Wir sind uns der Geltung des kategorischen Imperativs bewusst[45], und wir sind uns

---

[45]   Kants These in der *Grundlegung* (die ich der Faktum-Lehre der *Kritik der praktischen Vernunft* für überlegen ansehe) besagt, dass wir berechtigt sind, als unter der Idee der

bewusst, gegen unsere Pflichten bloß deshalb verstoßen zu können, weil wir es wollen. Das Bewusstsein des Moralgesetzes ist die Quelle der Rechtfertigung unserer in der 1. Person Singular geäußerten Urteile über das moralisch Gute und Schlechte. Wir sind gerechtfertigt, uns und andere für unsere Entscheidungen im Einzugsbereich moralischer Gründe zu kritisieren, obwohl wir in theoretischer Perspektive nicht erklären können, wie die Entscheidung möglich ist. Wir scheitern bei der Erklärung des praktischen Begriffs der Wahlfreiheit, so wie wir theoretisch den Begriff der Freiheit nicht anschaulich machen können. Aber so wie wir berechtigt sind, unter der Idee der Freiheit zu handeln, obwohl wir diese Idee mit den Mitteln der theoretischen Philosophie nicht erkennen oder rechtfertigen können, sind wir berechtigt, uns als Autoren unserer Maximen und Handlungen zu begreifen. Nach Kant handeln nicht die Motive oder Begierden[46], sondern Menschen, die über einen eigenen Willen verfügen. Unser Unwissen darüber, warum wir uns in letzter Instanz für oder gegen das moralische Gesetz entscheiden, berechtigt uns in praktischer Hinsicht nicht zur Skepsis gegenüber der Geltung dieses Gesetzes. Dieses verlangt unter den Bedingungen, unter denen wir Menschen existieren, eine Form der Willkürfreiheit, die sich zum Guten wie zum Bösen entscheiden kann.

Die Lehre vom „Gleichgewicht der Willkür" ist also nach Kant gerade nicht „die Pest aller Moral" (Schelling), sondern steht im Mittelpunkt einer Ethik für endliche, mundane Subjekte, die den Grund der Verbindlichkeit in der eigenen, sich selbst und aus sich selbst zum Handelnden bestimmenden Vernunft finden. Weil wir keine kausale Erklärung für unsere unter der „Idee der Freiheit" vollzogene Selbstbestimmung geben können, müssen wir uns gewissermaßen über uns selbst wundern. Nach welchen Gründen wir gehandelt haben, wird uns (wenn überhaupt) erst post festum bewusst. Der Zufall, die Kontingenz, gehört zu unserem praktischen Selbstverständnis als Personen. In moralischer Hinsicht bleiben wir uns ein Rätsel. Und wenn wir dieses Rätsel durch kausale Erklärungen zum Verschwinden bringen würden, hätten wir uns selbst als freie Subjekte negiert. Wir könnten uns nur noch als ein „Stück der Natur" (AA IV, S. 456) begreifen. Womöglich ist das die kaum hervorgehobene Pointe der kantischen Philosophie der Freiheit: Wir sind in praktischer Hinsicht unerforschliche Wesen, weil wir unsere Freiheit theoretisch nicht darstellen können und prak-

---

Freiheit handelnde Subjekte bestimmte Geltungsansprüche zu erheben, obwohl diese nicht im Rahmen einer (modern gesprochen) naturalistischen Bedeutungstheorie reformuliert werden können. Die theoretische Philosophie kann die Unmöglichkeit der Freiheitsidee nicht beweisen (vgl. AA IV, S. 455 ff.). Der Anspruch, unter der Idee der Freiheit zu handeln (und damit auch das Bewusstsein des moralischen Sollens), hat keinen empirischen Status, sondern ist im Begriff praktischer Vernunft enthalten (vgl. dagegen Merkel, 2008, S. 60–61).

46 Das ist die Position von Achenwall und Pütter in den *Elementa iuris naturae* (1750): „Das Motiv lenkt den Willen". („Motivum flectit voluntatem.") (Achenwall/Pütter, 1750, S. 40, § 86).

tisch nicht aufgeben wollen. Die Kontingenz unserer moralischen Selbstbestimmung begleitet unser Handeln wie das Licht den Tag. Wir können, wenn wir wollen, gut sein. Aber *ob* wir gut sein wollen, hängt davon ab, ob wir gewillt sind, eine Anstrengung auf uns zu nehmen, um uns aus Achtung vor dem Moralgesetz zum Handeln zu bestimmen. Ist es uns jedoch physisch (empirisch) unmöglich, die moralisch geforderte Anstrengung auf uns zu nehmen, bedeutet dies, dass wir subjektiv nicht im Gebrauche unserer Freiheit und somit für unser Handeln nicht verantwortlich sind. Mehr gibt es dazu nach Kant nicht zu sagen.

Literatur

Achenwall, Gottfried/Pütter, Johann Stephan (1995): *Elementa iuris naturae* (1750)/ *Anfangsgründe des Naturrechts*, hrsg. und übersetzt von Jan Schröder, Frankfurt a. M./Leipzig.

Allison, Henry E. (1990): *Kant's theory of freedom*, Cambridge.

Baum, Manfred (2012): „Kants Replik auf Reinhold", in: Bondeli, Martin/Heinz, Marion/Stolz, Violetta (Hrsg.): *Wille, Willkür, Freiheit. Reinholds Freiheitskonzeption im Kontext der Philosophie des 18. Jahrhunderts* (= Studia Reinholdiana, Bd. 2), Berlin/New York, S. 153–163.

Baumgarten, Alexander Gottlieb (2011): *Metaphysica / Metaphysik*, 4. Aufl. (Halle im Magdeburgischen, 1757), historisch-kritische Ausgabe, hrsg. Gawlick, Günter/ Kreimendahl, Lothar, Stuttgart-Bad Cannstatt.

Bojanowski, Jochen (2006): *Kants Theorie der Freiheit*, Berlin.

Bojanowski, Jochen (2007): „Kant und das Problem der Zurechenbarkeit", in: *Zeitschrift für philosophische Forschung* 61, S. 207–228.

Bondeli, Martin (2012): „Zu Reinholds Auffassung von Willensfreiheit in den *Briefen II*", in: Bondeli, Martin/Heinz, Marion/Stolz, Violetta (Hrsg.): *Wille, Willkür, Freiheit. Reinholds Freiheitskonzeption im Kontext der Philosophie des 18. Jahrhunderts* (= Studia Reinholdiana, Bd. 2), Berlin/New York, S. 125–152.

Brandt, Reinhard (2010): *Immanuel Kant – Was bleibt?*, Hamburg.

Creuzer, Leonhard (1793): *Skeptische Betrachtungen über die Freyheit des Willens, mit Hinsicht auf die neuesten Theorien über dieselbe*, Gießen (Nachdruck Hildesheim 1978).

Crusius, Christian August (1744): *Anweisung vernünftig zu leben, Darinnen nach Erklärung der Natur des menschlichen Willens die natürlichen Pflichten und allgemeinen Klugheitslehren im richtigen Zusammenhange vorgetragen werden*, Leipzig (= Crusius, *Die philosophischen Hauptwerke*, hrsg. Giorgio Tonelli, Band I, Hildesheim 1969).

Descartes, René (1915): *Meditationen über die Grundlagen der Philosophie*, hrsg. Arthur Buchenau, Hamburg (Nachdruck 1995).

Ferguson, Adam (1772): *Grundsätze der Moralphilosophie*, uebersetzt und mit einigen Anmerkungen versehen von Christian Garve, Leipzig (Nachdruck: *Reception of the Scottish Enlightenment in Germany*, edited and introduced by Heiner F. Klemme, vol. 6, Bristol, 2000).

Geismann, Georg (2010): *Kant und kein Ende. Band 2: Studien zur Rechtsphilosophie*, Würzburg.

Hegel, G. W. F.: *Grundlinien der Philosophie des Rechts* (= *Werke in zwanzig Bänden*, 7), hrsg. Eva Moldenhauer und Karl Markus Michel, Frankfurt a. M. 1979 u. ö.

Heineccius, Johann Gottlieb (1738): *Grundlagen des Natur- und Völkerrechts* (= *Elementa ivris naturae et gentium*, 1738), hrsg. Christian Bergfeld, Frankfurt a. M. 1994.

Heydenreich, Karl Heinrich (1791): *Betrachtungen über die Philosophie der Natürlichen Religion*, 2. Band, Leipzig.

Kant, Immanuel (1900 ff.): *Gesammelte Schriften*, hrsg. Preussische Akademie der Wissenschaften u. a., Berlin (= Akademie-Ausgabe). (Zitiert mit „AA" und unter Angabe des Bandes.)

Kant, Immanuel (1968): *Die Religion innerhalb der Grenzen der bloßen Vernunft*, in: *Gesammelte Schriften Bd. VI*, hrsg. Preussische Akademie der Wissenschaften, Berlin (Nachdruck der Ausgabe 1907/14).

Kant, Immanuel (1968): *Grundlegung zur Metaphysik der Sitten*, in: *Gesammelte Schriften Bd. IV*, hrsg. Preussische Akademie der Wissenschaften, Berlin (Nachdruck der Ausgabe 1903/11).

Kant, Immanuel (1968): *Kritik der praktischen Vernunft*, in: *Gesammelte Schriften Bd. V*, hrsg. Preussische Akademie der Wissenschaften, Berlin (Nachdruck der Ausgabe 1908/13).

Kant, Immanuel (1968a): *Werkausgabe in 12 Bänden*, hrsg. Wilhelm Weischedel, Frankfurt a. M.

Kant, Immanuel (1998): *Kritik der reinen Vernunft*, hrsg. Jens Timmermann, Hamburg 1998. (Zitiert mit „KrV" und nach den Originalausgaben A und B.)

Kant, Immanuel (1968): *Metaphysik der Sitten*, in: *Gesammelte Schriften Bd. VI*, hrsg. Preussische Akademie der Wissenschaften, Berlin (Nachdruck der Ausgabe 1907/14).

Kant, Immanuel (2007): *„Naturrecht-Feyerabend" (Einleitung)*, in: *Rivista internazionale di filosofia del diritto* LXXXIV, S. 237–281 (auch in: Kant, *Gesammelte Schriften*, Band XXVII). (Zitiert nach der Originalpaginierung.)

Kawamura, Katsutoshi (1996): *Spontaneität und Willkür. Der Freiheitsbegriff in Kants Antinomienlehre und seine historischen Wurzeln*, Stuttgart-Bad Cannstatt.

Kersting, Wolfgang (1993): *Wohlgeordnete Freiheit. Immanuel Kants Rechts- und Staatsphilosophie*, Frankfurt a. M.

Klemme, Heiner F. (2013): „Zweckmäßigkeit mit Endzweck. Über den Übergang vom Natur- zum Freiheitsbegriff in Kants *Kritik der Urteilskraft*", in: Bacin, Stefano u. a. (Hrsg.): *Akten des XI. Internationalen Kant-Kongresses, Pisa 2010*, Berlin/Boston (im Druck).

Klemme, Heiner F. (2013a): „Der Transzendentale Idealismus und die *Rechtslehre*. Überlegungen zum Zusammenhang von Pflicht, Recht und Ethik bei Kant", in: *Kants Rechtslehre*, hrsg. Werner Euler und Burkhard Tuschling, Berlin (im Druck).

Klemme, Heiner F. (2008): „Moralisches Sollen, Autonomie und Achtung. Kants Konzeption der ‚libertas indifferentiae' zwischen Wolff und Crusius", in: Rohden, Valerio u. a. (Hrsg.): *Recht und Frieden in der Philosophie Kants, Akten des X. Internationalen Kant-Kongresses*, Band 5, Berlin/New York, S. 215–227.

Klemme, Heiner F. (2008a): „A discreta antinomia da razão pura prática de Kant na *Metafísica dos costumes*", in: *Cadernos de filosofia alemã* XI, S. 11–31.

Klemme, Heiner F. (2008 b): „Necessità pratica e indifferenza del volere. Considerazioni sulla ‚libertas indifferentiae'", in: Fonnesu, Luca (Hrsg.): *Etica e mondo in Kant*, Bologna, S. 57–73.

Klemme, Heiner F. (2007): „Kant und die Paradoxien der Kritischen Philosophie", in: *Kant-Studien* 98, S. 40–56.

Klemme, Heiner F. (2006): „Praktische Gründe und moralische Motivation. Eine deontologische Perspektive", in: Klemme, Heiner F./Kühn, Manfred/Schönecker, Dieter (Hrsg.): *Moralische Motivation. Kant und die Alternativen*, Hamburg, S. 113–153.

Klemme, Heiner F. (2006 a): *Kants Philosophie des Subjekts. Systematische und entwicklungsgeschichtliche Untersuchungen zum Verhältnis von Selbstbewußtsein und Selbsterkenntnis*, Hamburg.

Klemme, Heiner F. (1999): „Die Freiheit der Willkür und die Herrschaft des Bösen. Kants Lehre vom radikalen Bösen zwischen Moral, Religion und Recht", in: Klemme, Heiner F./Ludwig, Bernd/Pauen, Michael/Stark, Werner (Hrsg.): *Aufklärung und Interpretation. Studien zur Philosophie Kants und ihrem Umkreis*, Würzburg, S. 125–151.

Meier, Georg Friedrich (1764): *Allgemeine practische Weltweisheit*, Halle im Magdeburgischen (= Christian Wolff, *Gesammelte Werke, Materialien und Dokumente*, Band 107, Hildesheim, Zürich, New York, 2006).

Merkel, Reinhard (2008): *Willensfreiheit und rechtliche Schuld. Eine strafrechtsphilosophische Untersuchung*, Baden-Baden.

Moore, G. E. (1975): *Grundprobleme der Ethik* (= *Ethics*, 1912), München.

Prauss, Gerold (1983): *Kant über Freiheit als Autonomie*, Frankfurt a. M.

Reinhold, Carl Leonhard (1792): *Briefe über die Kantische Philosophie*, Zweyter Band, Leipzig.

Schadow, Steffi (2012): *Achtung für das Gesetz. Moral und Motivation bei Kant*, Berlin/Boston.

Schelling, F. W. J. (2008): *Über das Wesen der menschlichen Freiheit*, hrsg. von Horst Fuhrmans, Stuttgart.

Schönecker, Dieter (2005): *Kants Begriff transzendentaler und praktischer Freiheit. Eine entwicklungsgeschichtliche Studie*, Berlin/New York.

Schwaiger, Clemens (2011): *Alexander Gottlieb Baumgarten – Ein intellektuelles Porträt. Studien zur Metaphysik und Ethik von Kants Literatur*, Stuttgart-Bad Cannstatt.

Tafani, Daniela (1999): *Christoph Leonhard Creuzer. La Discussione della dottrina morale di Kant alla fine del Settecento*, Genova.

Tugendhat, Ernst (1992): „Der Begriff der Willensfreiheit", in: Tugendhat, Ernst: *Philosophische Aufsätze*, Frankfurt a. M., S. 334–351.

Walch, Johann Georg (1775): „Freyheit des Willens", in: Walch, Johann Georg, *Philosophisches Lexicon* [...], Vierte Auflage in zween Theilen, 1. Teil, Leipzig, Sp. 1402–1424.

Willaschek, Marcus (1992): *Praktische Vernunft. Handlungstheorie und Moralbegründung bei Kant*, Stuttgart/Weimar.

Pierre Keller

Ideas, Freedom, and the Ends of Architectonic

In diesem Aufsatz wird gezeigt, dass bei Kant und generell in der Tradition des deutschen Idealismus Ideen die Grundlage aller Normativität und Freiheit sind. Ideen erfüllen diese normative Rolle als Interpretationen platonischer Ideen. Die kritische Aneignung der platonischen Ideenlehre ist von zentraler Bedeutung sowohl für die negative wie auch für die positive Seite des Projekts einer Kritik der reinen Vernunft. Negativ wird die „Hypostasierung" von Ideen in der platonischen Tradition als Ausdruck eines transzendentalen Scheins und damit als metaphysischer Grundirrtum moniert. Diese falsche Vergegenständlichung betrifft die Seele, den Kosmos und Gott und damit die spezielle Metaphysik der Leibniz-Wolffschen Schule. Diese Trias wird in der platonischen Tradition – aber nicht von Platon selber – als Ideen bezeichnet. Als positives Fazit der Ideenlehre gelten die Ideen als normative Grundlage aller Seelenfunktionen und damit aller Vorstellungen, insbesondere aber aller Begriffe. Ideen werden als Quelle aller Zwecke, die der Mensch sich setzen kann, und sogar aller Zwecke überhaupt begriffen. Sowohl Kants positive wie auch seine negative Interpretation platonischer Ideen wird von Hegel in seiner Lehre vom Begriff in veränderter Form aufgenommen. Kant wie auch Hegel haben ein teleologisch funktionales Verständnis von Seelenaktivität. Diese Seelenaktaktivität wird von Maßstäben geleitet, die ihre vollkommene Erfüllung und ihr normatives Ziel in Ideen haben. Diese teleologisch-funktionale Konzeption der Seele geht auf Platons Politeia zurück. Kant interpretiert solche Funktionen der Seele und die ihnen zugrunde liegenden Ideen allerdings in Bezug auf ihre Einheitsfunktion bei Ich-Gedanken. Diese kopernikanische Wende in der Konzeption der Ideen wird von Hegel übernommen. Kant bringt alles in der teleologisch-funktionalen Einheit einer umfassenden metaphysischen Wissenschaft zusammen. In diesem System haben alle besonderen Wissenschaften und ihre Erkenntnisse eine genau spezifizierte Leistung und Funktion. Diese Auffassung wird bei Hegel zum Ausgangspunkt seiner philosophischen Enzyklopädie (als System aller Begriffe) genommen. Die Philosophie ist laut Kant ihrem Wesen nach architektonisch. Sie setzt alle Erkenntnis in eine streng bestimmbare Beziehung zu den wesentlichen Zwecken des Menschen. Die Metaphysik und die Erkenntnislehre sind für Kant zuerst aus der Sicht der professionellen Schulphilosophie zu verstehen. Am Ende sind sie aber nur pragmatisch auf die wesentlichen Zwecke der Menschheit ausgerichtet. So ist die Freiheit der „Schlussstein" des gesamten Gebäudes, weil der Mensch in der Freiheit seiner Handlung Quelle der Zwecke ist, ohne die der Zweck der Erkenntnis und damit die Erkenntnis selbst insgesamt als Aktivität von Menschen unbegreiflich ist. Während Hegel und der deutsche Idealismus diese Idee der Freiheit philosophisch auf den Begriff bringen wollen, sieht Kant im Versuch, unseren alltäglichen praktischen Verpflichtungen eine metaphysische Deutung zu geben, die das alltägliche Verständnis der Verantwortung übersteigt, die Quelle aller metaphysischen Irrtümer. Das alltägliche Verantwortungsbewusstsein setzt die Ideen der Tugend und Freiheit als Handlungsmuster voraus.

Die kritische Aufgabe der Philosophie ist es, das Alltagsbewusstsein gegen Missverständnisse in Schutz zu nehmen. Die kritische Philosophie zeigt die wahre Bedeutung der Ideen, die dem Alltagsbewusstsein zugrunde liegen, indem sie zeigt, wann diese wahre Bedeutung entweder unterboten oder überboten wird.

Human beings, but especially modern individuals, are characterized by Hegel in his *Lectures on Aesthetics* as amphibians that live in two different worlds, the world of sense and nature, and the world of intellect and norms (VÄ, pp. 80–81). As natural creatures we are subject to the vicissitudes of nature. We suffer from the forces of nature that compel us and the natural drives that impel us. As creatures of intellect we raise ourselves to "eternal ideas" and "freedom". We repay nature's violence against us with our own violence against her, beginning with the abstractions of natural science and the interventions of experiment and technology to which we subject the natural world. This long-standing opposition in culture between two worlds is brought to a head in modernity in Kant's philosophy and especially in his notion of moral autonomy. Moral autonomy involves not only action according to the idea of morality, but moral responsibility for such action, which itself involves the idea that we can do what we ought to do. Morality and the moral obligations we impose on ourselves as free agents thus stand juxtaposed, on the one hand, to the natural inclinations that impel us and, on the other, to nature as a context of causal forces in which we find ourselves exhaustively determined by causal laws.

Kant's philosophy brings the fundamental oppositions in culture into their sharpest relief by juxtaposing the standpoints that we take on ourselves as denizens of the world of nature and as free agents who guide ourselves by the standards that we set for ourselves on the basis of the intellectual world of ideas. In principle, Kant has the resources for resolving the fundamental opposition between nature and our free agency. If Hegel argues that Kant has brought the fundamental divisions in human self-conception to a head, he has also provided the tools for articulating and resolving those fundamental oppositions:

> It is the Kantian philosophy that has not only felt the need for this point of unification [between "nature and spirit (in a contrastive sense)"], but has also clearly recognized it and brought it before our minds. In general, as the foundation alike of intelligence and will, Kant took self-related rationality, freedom, self-consciousness finding and knowing itself as inherently infinite. This recognition of the absoluteness of reason in itself, that has occasioned philosophy's turning point in modern times, must be recognized, and, even if we pronounce Kant's philosophy to be inadequate, this feature is not to be refuted (VÄ, pp. 83–84).[1]

---

[1]   Hegel's notes to his lectures on the philosophy of art are lost, but in the earliest extant students notes that we have of these lectures – given in Berlin, 1821 – we find independent evidence for the claim attributed to Hegel by Hotho in his edition: "What is this final standpoint? How is the divine, the eternal to be grasped? The Kantian philos-

Kant has a conception of self-consciousness that systematically connects different items within a normative context of significance and also connects one normative context of significance (e.g., that of theoretical intellect) to another (e.g., that of the will and moral agency). Each normative context is constituted by a comprehensive standard governing the norms in that context. These different normative contexts are systematically connected in a comprehensive whole that exists only as their relationship to the standpoint of an agent. The possibility of such ends-directed action is implicit in the spontaneity of a self-conscious subject (KrV, B 132). It is implicit in the agent's ability to connect one representation with other possible and actual representations according to a standard that it establishes for itself. This independence from sense is most apparent in the comprehensive context of significance that is instituted when a self-conscious agent relates different things together in what is not only salient for that individual, but might also be salient for that individual. This systematic relatedness that things have to the standpoint of self-conscious agents with different kinds of possible ends is what Hegel refers to as "self-related rationality"; such self-related rationality is inherently infinite because it involves an infinite number of possible things that one might do, including an infinite number of conceptual distinctions that can be drawn. It is free because these distinctions have their significance for self-consciousness only in their systematic articulation of distinctive differences that are grounded in the ways in which we are self-conscious of different possible ends that we might have and different possible means for their achievement.

Hegel argues that Kant retains the fundamental opposition between nature and free agency. Kant in a certain sense dissolves the fundamental opposition between nature and free agency both in self-consciousness in general and in his account of the normative role of ideas in agency in particular. Nature is to some extent understood as something that is both independent of our ends as agents and as conforming to those very ends. However, Kant does not take the "dissolved opposition" as the "actually true" one, but rather as one that we merely represent to ourselves in thought (Hegel, 2005, p. 59).

I. Ideas, Conceptual Function, and Representational Holism

One of the important developments in German idealism is its move away from the kind of semantic molecularism and atomism of mental ideas characteristic of British empiricism to a meaning and justification holism that gives up eventually on the primacy of propositions and mental representations in favor of em-

---

ophy says: This ultimate final end is the rationality that relates to itself, self-consciousness that knows itself, that is free in itself and absolutely rational" (Hegel, 1995, p. 25).

bedding thought in a wider comprehensive engagement with the world. It is hard to miss the fact that Kant's position involves justification holism, but Kant seems to hold on to the primacy of mental representations. Kant's conception of judgment might be thought to require semantic molecularism in virtue of his distinction between analytic and synthetic judgments. Analytic judgments involve truths that depend only on what is contained in a certain concept. This suggests that the concepts involved in analytic judgments have no relation to anything outside of them. But on Kant's view even analytic judgments have concepts that arise synthetically. Any particular concept has its distinctive significance only if it can be grasped in comparison with and in contrast to other concepts, and with respect to the things that are normatively to be represented by that concept. This is displayed both in the position that a concept occupies in a Porphyry tree of distinct concepts with generic and specific differences and by the set of objects that are recognized by a certain concept. Both of these notions are in the end implicitly holistic. This betrays their source in Plato's synoptic conception of dialectic, synthesis and division (*dihairesis*).

The synthesis of perceptual representations and of concepts in judgments in the first *Critique* is often interpreted in an atomistic way. This atomism is sometimes juxtaposed to the inherently unified and interpretation-demanding presentation of experience in terms of ideas in the third *Critique* and the *Opus postumum*. Rudolf Makkreel speaks of an "essential shift away from the essentially atomistic psychological assumptions of the first *Critique*" (Makkreel, 1990, pp. 196–197). The atomistic reading of the first *Critique* fails to recognize that perceptual synthesis as well as the synthesis of concepts in judgment has a unity that is for Kant the qualitative unity of "a theme in a play, a speech or fable" (KrV, B 131; see also B 114). This qualitative unity in turn has its source in the comprehensive original synthetic unity of apperception that allows any possible representation to be connected in a systematically distinctive way with any other (KrV, B 131–4). This idea is not new to the second edition of the first *Critique* – the A Deduction is based on the idea that cognition is "a whole of compared and connected representations" (KrV, A 97) that has its basis in pure apperception (KrV, A 116–117). Without the comprehensive background unity of possible connection provided by the original synthetic unity of apperception, nothing can meaningfully be distinguished or connected. Any representation that is to have cognitive content must be a representation that I can systematically connect together with other possible and actual representations and be aware of as a representation that I might at least have had. The totality of such possible and actual representations are grasped together in a normative maximal whole of significant connectedness which Kant calls an "idea".

It goes against the received view of concepts for Kant to take the use of concepts to presuppose ideas that provide a comprehensive context in which they may be used. This presupposition is, however, implicit in his conception of the way in which concepts are grounded in the distinctive cognitive function of thought. Hölderlin remarks in a letter to Schiller, dated August 1797, that the "idea is prior to the concept" and that "I regard reason as the beginning of the understanding" (HSW VI, 1, p. 249). Following the received view that concepts of the understanding always come before ideas of reason in Kant, Eckart Förster argues that by taking ideas of reason to come before concepts of the understanding, Hölderlin reverses Kant's position in the first *Critique* (though paradoxically Kant is supposed to have reversed himself later in the *Opus postumum*).[2] Reason depends for its articulated concepts on the concepts and categories of the understanding. Since ideas of reason are concepts of the totality of conditions, they are in a sense only concepts of the understanding extended to what is unconditioned in syllogistic inference. But this extension is only possible because there is in a certain sense an unconditioned basis for concepts in the very idea of the understanding.

There is a sense in which Kant derives concepts of reason from pure concepts of the understanding. We articulate concepts of reason in comprehending the totality of conditions that are presupposed in the use of concepts of the understanding. But pure concepts of the understanding themselves "spring pure and unmixed from the understanding as absolute unity" (KrV, A 67/B 92). The absolute unity from which the concepts of the pure understanding spring is itself the idea of the pure understanding, so concepts of the pure understanding (i.e., the categories) in a sense have their source in the comprehensive significance that is an idea. (Kant identifies absolute unity of representation with the idea in the *Critique of Judgment* – KU, p. 377.)[3] Kant's argument in the Transcen-

---

2   Förster, 2000, pp. 148–150. Förster argues that when Kant writes in the *Opus postumum* (OP, p. 15) that "reason precedes, with the projection of its forms" he has changed his view (op. cit., p. 150). But this precisely corresponds to the position developed by Kant in the Appendix to the Transcendental Dialectic: "reason thus prepares the field for the understanding" with its principles of sameness of kind, variety of what is the same in kind under lower kinds and systematic affinity or relatedness of all conceptual form (KrV, A 657/B 685). These principles are indeed presupposed for all concepts, but especially for any effort to fully articulate the concepts and principles of the pure understanding. The proof of the completeness of the table of categories depends on the fact that these concepts "fill out the whole field of the pure understanding" (KrV, A 64/B 89); for this purpose one has to have some grasp of that field of conceptual relations.

3   A reading of the Metaphysical and Transcendental Deductions that has them hinge on the original synthetic unity of self-consciousness and even derives the logical functions of judgment from the objective unity of apperception is to be found in Reich, 1992 [original, 1936]. Reich relies on an abstract definition of judgment that cannot provide the foundational role for Kant that Reich assigns to it. Reich's dependence on Kant's *Reflexionen* for his main argument is also problematic. Brandt 1991 offers a reconstruction of Kant's completeness argument on the basis of the structure of judgment and is closer to the text of the *Critique*, which repudiates the Reich view. Brandt sidesteps Kant's own statement of the basis for his argument – the origin of the pure concepts of the understanding in the absolute unity of the understanding – by arguing that taking this *ratio essendi* as a *ratio cognoscendi* would make the table of judgments

dental Logic for the completeness of the functions of judgment, categories and principles depends on transcendental philosophy's commitment to seek its concepts according to a principle. The "Clue for the Discovery of the Pure Concepts of the Understanding", to which Kant refers in the second edition as the "Metaphysical Deduction of the Categories", is based on this idea that concepts are "connected among themselves by means of a concept or idea [...] [that] provides a rule" for completely articulating those concepts (KrV, A 67/B 92). It is only through our grasp of the systematic unity of what we can understand that we are able to articulate specific concepts, judgments, and their forms. The whole of cognition, including the different possible concepts and judgments, can only be provided by an idea of reason, and the proof of completeness will have to consist in a proof that the set of a priori concepts articulated exhausts the field of the understanding, but for this one must have a sense of the filed of the understanding as a whole. This grip on the field of the understanding is provided by the idea of the understanding.[4]

Understanding or thought has a distinctive interpretative function in cognition as opposed to the presentational function of intuition (KrV, A 51/B 75). Each of these functions makes its distinctive contribution to the end of cognition. Kant follows Leibniz in thinking of cognition, and indeed of all human activity, as a complex interconnected whole of function directed at our ends. The end is defined by and defines function. Function itself involves an essential reference to agency, in its Latin root (*fungor*). Leibniz introduces the notion of function and Kant's takes over that usage with a clear conception of the connection of function with action.[5] Concepts depend on the interpretative function of

---

superfluous and is not available to humans (Brandt, 1991, p. 48). In the process Brandt fails to see the way in which the argument for the completeness of forms of judgment itself depends on the premise of the absolute unity or idea of the understanding. Brandt seems ultimately to rely on the idea that the functions are visually displayed in their systematic form in the table of logical functions. This is correct so far as the text is concerned, but it is not satisfactory as an argument. A proper understanding of the role of the idea in Kant's argument undermines Brandt's objections to the view that the logical form of judgment is grounded in the objective unity of apperception. On these points I find myself in agreement with Wolff 1995, esp. pp. 137–138, 177, 187– 189. But for Wolff, the idea of the understanding is the inferred concept of a discursive understanding as a faculty of judgment (Wolff, 1995, pp. 137, 177). In this way, his reconstruction is different from that of Brandt in detail rather than in fundamental conception.

4   "Hence the sum total of its [the pure understanding's] cognition will constitute a system that is to be grasped and determined under one idea, the completeness and articulation of which system can at the same time yield a touchstone of the correctness and genuineness of all the components of cognition fitting into it" (KrV, A 65/B 90; cf. A 645/B 673).

5   The concept of a function is introduced by Plato at the end of the first book of the *Republic* and frames his discussion of the human soul and of the identity of things; things are for Plato the way they truly are when they best perform their proper function. It is then that they most approximate to the idea that is the standard for that

thought. The interpretative function of thought is expressed in the most general terms in the logical function of judgment. This logical function is the normative unity of the action of subordinating concepts under each other in judgment. Each concept or term is a discrete unity of action and function that relates differentially to the unitary function of thought in general and to objects by means of the category corresponding to a certain unitary function of thought. The comprehensive set of such relations is expressed in Kantian terms as the dependence of concepts on the idea.

Kant calls the "original synthetic unity of apperception" (KrV, B 131) the standpoint of possible self-consciousness from which we are able to connect or distinguish different representations. In connecting and distinguishing different representations according to concepts, we purport to do so in a way that is right for different standpoints; concepts thus have normative import. They capture what objects are in a certain systematically distinctive way. The unity that objects have from the standpoint of a self-consciousness that can represent itself in the same way from different standpoints is just what provides the basis for the normative commitments of concepts and judgments. This original synthetic unity connects the different functions of cognition together in the necessary end of cognition by providing the idea that is the normative whole in which concepts have their significance. This normative whole is involved when reason "considers its objects merely according to ideas and in accordance with them

---

function. Plato argues that the human being and the city-state are organic unities of function that ought to be directed at a task defined by their distinctive good and do so the more that they approximate to the idea of functional excellence or virtue (justice) that governs them as a whole. Kant's conception of the idea that governs the overall operation of human faculties and functions takes up this idea. The modern, structural notion of function is first introduced by Leibniz, in its mathematical as well as in its more general significance. However, it turns out that this structural notion of function is conceived and understood by Leibniz and Kant in terms of its relation to goal-directed agency. Leibniz's aim is to appropriate the Platonic and Aristotelian sense of function, but show how it can become the basis for a mechanistic mathematical-physical account of events. Each physical state, as well as each mental state, is regarded as a function of the overall goal-directed activity of a substance. Kant and Hegel accept a methodological version of this conception and make it their own in their own versions of teleological functionalism. The teleological conception of function as action carries over to Leibniz's conception of logical and a mathematical function, as it does for Kant and Hegel. Like his contemporaries, Leibniz thinks of curves as prior to equations. Curves are taken to be the result of geometric actions; an equation is thought of as the normative rule that relates pairs of coordinates resulting from geometric actions. The reference to geometric action is reflected in the way in which Leibniz first introduces the word "function" in 1673. The term is introduced as a line doing something in a given figure. A function is thus a magnitude that performs a special duty, which performs a "mathematical job". Leibniz uses "functions" to denote the various "offices" that a straight line may fulfill in relation to a curve, viz., its tangent, normal, etc. (GM III, p. 316).

determines the understanding, which then makes an empirical use of its own concepts (even the pure ones)" (KrV, A 547/B 575). In a certain sense, there is a single self-conscious point of view that is the condition for the possibility of all distinctive contexts in Kant. But this single comprehensive point of view manifests the context of global significance that it institutes in different systematic ways according to different ideas and functions, all of which are in turn systematically related to the one comprehensive context of significance. Any distinctions that can meaningfully be drawn between items are contrasts within a systematic pattern. This systematic pattern is organized according to the possibility that each and all of us have to compare and contrast those items for ourselves. Further, we can only draw these distinctions for ourselves, in ways that are also intelligible to others. The comprehensive context of possibilities instituted by the original synthetic unity of apperception constitutes what Kant regards as the condition for the possibility of all concepts, of all thought, and of logic itself (KrV, B 133–134 & n). We grasp this unity in and through the idea of the understanding.

II. Kant's Copernican Revolution and the Architectonic of Ideas and Ends

Kant's use of the term "idea" is intended to revert to the manner in which it is used and introduced by Plato as a technical term. Ideas are for Kant ideal standards or archetypes for comprehension and are as such intrinsically normative. Kant calls them archetypes, following neo-Platonic terminology for the role of ideas as models, and sees their significance especially with respect to anything concerning freedom and practice (KrV, A 313/B 370). Ideas are always maximal models that cannot have sensible instances that fully exemplify them: "as the concept of a maximum they [ideas] can never be given in a way that is congruent with the concrete" (KrV, A 327/B 384). This prevents ideas from being sensible objects and indeed prevents them in the end from being any kind of object for Kant at all. This, however, does not prevent us from using ideas as rules and norms, for in a normative context the idea is partially given, if to a "limited and deficient" extent, in the concrete through "the rule" that is obeyed (KrV, A 328/B 385). It is in the very nature of rules and norms that we are responsive to them, even as we inevitably fall short of fully realizing them.

Kant's *Critique of Pure Reason*, in fact his whole critical project, is framed by a Janus-faced stance to, on the one hand, Plato and the Platonic tradition and, on the other, Epicurus and the empiricist tradition. Kant thinks that the Platonic tradition emphasized reason as a source of cognition to the ultimate exclusion of sense and the empiricist tradition emphasized sense against reason. Both traditions, however, assumed that there was an ultimate way of grasping things in terms of ideas that put us directly in cognitive contact with ultimate reality.[6] The *Critique* is both a profound defense of Platonism and also has the Platonic conception of metaphysics as its chief target (the metaphysics of empiricism is also an important target). The Platonic tradition and the rationalism

6   Kant rejects the empiricist account of ideas, according to which sense qualities such as red count as "ideas", as an "unbearable" use of language (KrV, A 320/B 377). Kant's sympathy is with Plato on ideas. He aims to understand Plato better than Plato understood himself on the nature of ideas by showing that one can understand ideas without treating them as objects, without "hypostasizing" them (KrV, A 313–4n/B 370–1n). Understanding ideas without making them into objects also provides a place for what empiricists call "ideas". The first *Critique* steers a middle way between empiricism and Platonism-rationalism; as such, the *Critique* is the inevitable historical development out of two competing tendencies in "the self-development of reason" according to its underlying (architectonic) idea (KrV, A 835/B 863). When we use our sense and our reason we must use them cooperatively and not to the exclusion of one another, because we cannot ever understand things except discursively and interpretatively: we cannot know things through direct acquaintance either with sensible or non-sensible simple ideas (KrV, A 853/B 881–882). Empiricism and Platonism-rationalism share what is for Kant an illusory account of cognition according to which we can be directly acquainted with the ultimate constituents of the universe in a way that involves no interpretation. Kant sees the *Critique* as part of the historical and intellectual process by which this necessary illusion is exposed and ideas are better understood in their true role in thought.

     For Kant, both empiricism and Platonism-rationalism tend to offer an ultimately very important, but also illusory account of how things are. (Kant's "history of pure reason", KrV, A 852–855/B 880–883, anticipates in this way the conception of the idea and its role in the history of philosophy in German idealism.) While Platonism is better positioned to understand the place of human freedom in the grand scheme of things than is empiricism, it too fails to avoid error by virtue of its metaphysical over-reach. The Platonist-rationalist conception is good at seeing how reason is involved in what we do; the empiricist conception is good at tracing causal influences in our experience. Neither has a sufficient appreciation of its inherent limitations. Kant sees the Antinomy that arises between these two positions, and the ability of the *Critique* to resolve it, as a good experimental test for the coherence and adequacy of the *Critique* and of his Copernican Revolution (KrV, B XVII–XIX). Kant had already juxtaposed Platonism (and rationalism) to Epicureanism (and empiricism) with respect to ideas in 1770 (AA II, pp. 395) as he does in the Antinomy in the first *Critique* (KrV, A 462/B 490 ff., but esp. A 471/B 499). Kant's formulation of the antinomy of reason in 1769 had something to do with his recognition of the competing strengths of the Platonic-rationalist and Epicurean-empiricist conceptions of metaphysics. Kant's sympathy with the role of the senses and experience in theoretical cognition is to be contrasted with his rejection of the Epicurean principle of pleasure in respect to morals (*De mundi*, p. 396). In 1770, Kant appeals to the idea of virtue as well as to the idea of cognitive perfection as a maximum of perfection that Plato calls idea: "the maximum of perfection is called ideal, but idea in Plato (like his idea of a Republic)" (*De mundi*, p. 396). Kant takes us in *De mundi* to have theoretical knowledge of God, so he recognizes a theoretical maximum (of rationality and goodness) in the idea of God alongside the notion of a moral standard of perfection. Rousseau's influence transforms the way in which Kant sees the Platonic notion of idea in an important respect (Reich, 2001). It grounds our grasp of ideas in our everyday understanding of our moral com-

that it inspires takes us to understand things best by kicking the ladder of sensible experience away and thinking of things purely in terms of ideas. Kant is critical of Plato's doctrine that ideas are objects of pure thought (noumena). The introduction to the first *Critique* offers the memorable comparison of Plato's flight to ideas with the flight of a dove. The dove succumbs to the illusion that because the thin, ethereal air offers less resistance to its flight and thus seems to allow it to fly better, it would fly even better in airless space: "Likewise, Plato abandoned the world of senses because it set such narrow limits for the understanding, and dared to go beyond it on the wings of ideas, in the empty space of the understanding" (KrV, A 5/B 8).

In the Transcendental Aesthetic and Analytic, Kant argues that we neither have an intellectual intuition (*noesis*) of the kind that the Platonic tradition ascribes to us, nor can we know things from the vantage point of an intuitive intellect (*nous*). Our knowledge is limited to experience. The Transcendental Dialectic is an important critique of the systematic metaphysical illusions to

---

mitments rather than in a distinctive kind of cognition available only to philosophers; this is reflected in Kant's view that the thesis side of the Antinomy, which defends a Platonist conception of ideas, has popularity, commonsense, and morality on its side (KrV, A 467/B 495). This common sense account of the meaning of moral ideas allows Kant to reject in the position of the thesis, and in Plato and Leibniz, metaphysical or transcendental realism about ideas. The transcendental ideas of self, freedom, and God do offer theoretical support for moral ideas. But the transcendental ideas support moral ideas by showing that they are not theoretically impossible. Kant rejects any need to provide a theoretical account of ideas of the kind that the metaphysical or transcendental realist demands. Along with transcendental realism about ideas, Kant also rejects the notion of an intellectual intuition (*noesis*) of ideas as objects of theoretical contemplation that we can know independently of the normative commitments of common sense. This again allows Kant to attack both the position of Plato and Leibniz. Leibniz's account of ideas is often almost nominalist, since it always seems to locate ideas in the mind. There is, however, also a sense for him in which God's very existence is necessitated by the coherence of the idea of a most perfect being; thus, the idea of a most perfect being may exist in the mind, but it must have an extra-mental significance if it is to have the metaphysical implications that the ontological argument for the existence of God gives to it. Kant's interpretation of Leibniz's conception of divine perfection in terms of the metaphysical primacy of the Platonic idea of the good is not as implausible as it at first appears to be, especially when the idea of the good is given a neo-Platonic Augustinian interpretation. While Leibniz's simple substances are more Aristotelian than Platonic in inspiration, the simple and logically mutually independent ideas that make up God's mind are themselves more allied to the conception of ideas as simple unities from Plato's *Phaedo*. Leibniz is sympathetic to Plato's account of explanation there and views the Platonic doctrine of the recollection of ideas as an anticipation of his own views. Leibniz attempts in early work to prove that God's existence is possible by appeal to the compatibility of simple ideas (GP VII, p. 261 [1676]). Leibniz takes it to be necessary to show God's existence to be possible in order to show that God's existence follows from God's possibility.

which Plato and the Platonist tradition are supposed to succumb.[7] Kant argues that the Platonic-rationalist conception of soul, of cosmos (as something grounded in supersensible ideas), and of the idea of the good as the supreme explanatory principle for why everything must be the way it is (the transcendental ideal) are illusory metaphysical objects. Platonism is the main target of Kant's critique of the claims of pure theoretical reason.

But such Platonic ideas are crucial both to making sense of our practice and to the overall architectonic unity of reason (KpV, A 474–475/B 502–503). Plato's ascent to the good shows how individuals can become free from the illusory normative standards and desires provided by experience and view things according to maximally comprehensive standards based on reason. The idea of a community based on mutual regard for each other's free agency according to ideal, experience-independent standards of virtue and moral perfection thus becomes conceivable. This is how Kant can see Plato's ideal state as the idea of a constitution that would allow "the greatest human freedom" under laws (KpV, A 315 ff./B 371 ff.). There is thus something importantly right for Kant in the kind of ascent to the idea of the good that Plato sketches in the *Republic* as the basis for an understanding of what the ideal state ought to be:

> If we abstract from its exaggerated expression, then the philosopher's spiritual flight, which considers the physical copies in the world order, and then ascends to their architectonic connection according to ends, i.e., ideas, is an endeavor that deserves respect and imitation; but in respect of that which pertains to principles of morality, legislation and religion where the ideas first make the experience (of the good) itself possible, even if they can never be fully expressed in experience, they perform a wholly unique service (KrV, A 318/B 375).[8]

---

[7]   Kant reads Leibniz as a Platonist: "He, adhering to the Platonic school, assumed innate, pure intellectual intuitions, called ideas, which are encountered in the human mind, though now only obscurely" (ApH, p. 141n).

[8]   When Kant praises Plato for his ascent from copies to the architectonic connection of things according to ends and ideas, he has as much Leibniz as Plato's ascent to the idea of the good in mind. Kant derives the term "architectonic" from Leibniz. Leibniz uses the term to refer to those principles of "things themselves" according to which God forms those things for the best (GP VII, p. 278 [1676]). Architectonic principles do not involve absolute or logical necessity but are based on the principle of the "best choice" (by God, but also in a methodological sense). So like Plato, Leibniz thinks that we cannot understand things unless we understand why they are best the way they are. Architectonic principles constitute the teleological underpinnings of the mechanical causal relations between well-founded phenomena in nature. Like Leibniz, Kant wants to preserve the idea of mechanism as a model for scientific explanation. But like Leibniz, Kant takes the conception of the best to be important to the overall context of scientific explanation because it allows one to understand coherence in the much richer terms provided by the idea and its normativity. The principle of the best involved in architectonic gives the systematic conceptions of the different sciences a distinctive organic functional unity of coherence by relating them together in terms of an idea of optimal function in a functional whole (KrV, A 832–3/B 860–1).

The *Critique* emulates Plato's ascent in its trajectory to the idea of the highest good. But it does so on the basis of Kant's own distinctive, metaphysically deflationary reading of ideas and in his own distinctive way of connecting ideas together in the normative commitments of self-conscious agents. In the first *Critique*, Kant initially seems to envision two different systematic orders of nature, constituted by ideas of reason: one according to a systematic set of causal laws of nature, and one according to a systematic set of norms that apply to us as free agents. These two systematic orders of nature in the end have to be brought together from the moral point of view in the higher systematic unity of the idea of the highest good: "The world must be represented as having arisen out of an idea if it is to be in agreement with that use of reason without which we would hold ourselves unworthy of reason, namely the moral use, which depends throughout on the idea of the highest good. All research into nature is thereby directed toward the form of a system of ends. [...]" (KrV, A 815–816/ B 843–844). This system of ends is also in the end relevant even to our use of our understanding: "What sort of use can we make of our understanding, even in regard to experience, if we do not set ends for ourselves?" (KrV, A 816/B 844). In the end the notion of a systematic order of nature makes sense only relative to a determinate conception of rationality and the good. The very notion of a systematic order turns out to depend on what is amenable to our rational ends and in this sense to depend on the set of ends that we can set ourselves as rational beings. Cognitive functions are themselves to be understood in terms of the contribution that they make first to the end of human cognition and then less

---

"From this point of view philosophy is the science of the relation of all cognition to the essential ends of human reason (*teleologia rationis humanae* [teleology of human reason]), and the philosopher is not an artist of reason, but the legislator of human reason" (KrV, A 839/B 867). It is this standpoint of legislator of human reason looking to how everything can be brought together in a conception of the best that Kant takes Plato to be occupying in the *Republic*. This is an ideal or "archetype" of the philosopher that Kant thinks is worthy of emulation. This does not mean of course that Kant endorses the idea of the good as an ultimate principle of reality. There is an architectonic interest of reason in being able to understand things in terms of comprehensive normative ideas rather than merely in terms of a chain of causes: "human reason is architectonic in its nature, that is, it looks at all cognitions as belonging to a possible system [...]" (KrV, A 474/B 502). Kant objects to the position of empiricism (expressed in the antithesis of the Antinomy) that empiricism makes such a systematic unity of cognition "totally impossible" because it does not allow for a complete conception of the edifice of cognition (KrV, A 474–5/B 502–3). He also objects "that mere empiricism seems to strip both [reason and religion] of all support and influence" since empiricism cannot do justice to the normative commitments of agency; "thus also moral ideas and principles lose all their validity and fall with the transcendental ideas that are their theoretical support" (KrV, A 468/B 496). But this does not mean that Kant takes the transcendental ideas of self, world (including the cosmological idea of freedom), and God as any the less illusory when construed as objects of theoretical insight.

directly to other human ends. The fundamental distinction between sensibility and understanding ultimately gets its significance in relation to the end of (theoretical) cognition. Cognition is for Kant an activity whose significance *as an activity* depends on it being something that we do. This gives cognition an implicit and inherent relation to the action of pursuing the end of cognition. This normative role of ends in cognition explains why Kant introduces the distinction between intuition and concepts in the Transcendental Aesthetic by characterizing concepts as means to the cognitive end of interpreting objects immediately presented by intuition (KrV, A 19/B 33).

Ideas provide a standard of perfect or complete coherence relative to which the correct exercise and operation of the different faculties or capacities of human agents make sense. Each of the capacities that Kant distinguishes is related to the others through its own distinctive and ineliminable functional role or purpose ("as an organ") in presenting us with and distinguishing a comprehensive set of possible objects (KrV, B XXIII). This functional role makes sense only in relation to a norm provided by the idea. The set of possible objects is in turn the differential object of the comprehensive set of tasks that comprise a system of ends. For Kant, the comprehensive system of ends includes not only our epistemic end of interpreting experience, but also the more encompassing practical end of integrating such cognition into a worthwhile life. The final end of human life is also the end relative to which all of the other essential ends of reason have their systematic unity; this is the "entire vocation of human beings" addressed by moral philosophy (KrV, A 839/B 867). Thus, for Kant the ends we set ourselves are subordinate to a successful life under the guise of the moral good as the ultimate end of human activity. This is why Kant insists that the whole of pure reason is given only through the final end of reason. This final encompassing end of reason, the practical, concerns what we ought to do (KrV, B XXXVII ff.; A 839/B 867).[9] The architectonic and systematic structure of the different sciences depends on their indirect relation to the ultimate end of human agency.

---

[9]   Kant's account of representation is grounded in a teleological-functional account of the capacities of the self that he takes over from Plato, Aristotle, and Leibniz. Kant accepts the Platonic-Aristotelian conception that excellence of function for the soul is grounded in ideas that provide ideal standards of function. So, surprising as it may seem, Kant has a conception of intellectual and moral perfection and thus of intellectual and moral virtues with a basis that is largely shared with Plato and Aristotle: intellectual and moral perfection is excellence of function according to an optimum set by an idea. A life lived well is one in which one's capacities are optimally developed and exercised and also harmonize with the full exercise of their capacities by other persons. This conception is in the background in Kant's work, in part because he wishes to reject the metaphysically realist interpretation of this conception that he ascribes to Plato and Aristotle, to the scholastic tradition, and to Leibniz and Wolff.

Metaphysics can become a science, since metaphysics depends on knowledge by pure reason, and the nature of reason, as Kant understands it, has the systematicity that is at the basis of all science; it is "in the nature of pure speculative reason that it has a true limb structure [*Gliederbau*], in which everything is an organ, namely everything is for the sake of one and every individual for the sake of all, so that every insufficiency, be it a mistake (error) or deficiency, must unavoidably give itself away" (KrV, B XXXVII–XXXVIII). Reason has a unity that is displayed in the idea of reason; this is "the idea in the whole" that provides for the "limb structure of the system, as a unity" (KrV, B XLIV). However, the whole of pure reason is not available to us in theoretical reason alone, but is "given in its own right through the final end that reason has in the practical" (ibid.). Our ability to represent objects through intuition and then concepts requires the Copernican Revolution of taking objects to be given only on the basis of a comprehensive context of invariant conditions to which we ourselves are subject. But metaphysics becomes possible as a science through the "experiment of the equivalence of the result" (KrV, B XXXVIII) that one gets as one proceeds from the different elements of cognition up to the whole of pure reason, and back again to those different elements. Since pure reason as a whole is only given in an encompassing good to be achieved by practical reason, Kant's Copernican Revolution ultimately makes the agent's stance central to metaphysics. The agent's stance in turn presupposes the idea that one is free to bring about ends and hence the good; this is why the idea of freedom is the "keystone" of Kant's whole critical edifice (KpV, 3–4). So it is only insofar as our different cognitive activities and their function in cognition cohere with the overall role of the end of cognition in the ends of a worthwhile life that they can be taken to be functioning appropriately. We can return to the particular elements of cognition from the whole provided by practical cognition to determine whether we have missed out on any cognitive function or have had that function misfire. Then we will see that the "attempt [*Versuch*, viz., experiment] to change even the smallest part immediately leads to contradictions not only in the system but also in general human reason" (ibid.). There is an inherent connection between the nature of science and the kind of comprehensive functional-teleological systematicity provided by the idea. A science is only a science if each element of the science makes a systematic contribution to the end that defines the whole of the science: "The scientific concept of reason contains the end and the form of the whole that is congruent to it [the end]. The unity of the end to which and through which all parts also relate to each other makes every part one that can be missed when one knows the rest. [...] The whole is therefore articulated into members (*articulatio*) and not piled up (*coacervatio*)" (KrV, A 832/B 860). Each science "is not only articulated into members according to an idea, but each is in turn purposively unified as members of a whole allowing an architectonic of all human cognition" (KrV, A 835/B 863). Kant thinks of all cognition, the whole edifice of human culture, as having a systematic structure that differentially contributes to the ends that we set and must set for ourselves as human beings. The very systematicity of standpoint-invariant conditions that makes for the identity of objects for us according to Kant's Copernican Revolution is ultimately sunk into and gets its significance from what we can do (this insight is passed on to German idealism by Fichte, who puts it front and center in all of his thought).

In reasoning in general, but in acting in particular, we cannot help but commit ourselves to a comprehensive systematic order in which our actions have consequences and those actions are taken to spring from our choices. So we form for ourselves a conception of the comprehensive order to which those actions must belong and "with complete spontaneity [...] [our reason] makes its own order according to ideas" (KrV, A 548/B 576). Our knowledge of the actual causal order of things is not only inherently incomplete, but that order of spatio-temporal objects is an inherently contextual one that we have to regiment as a totality of causal conditions by the use of ideas. There is thus never a question of whether reason ought to "expect its ideas to have effects in experience" (KrV, A 548/B 576). The very order that our reason articulates for us with ideas has a significance that cannot be detached from the intrinsically normative significance of such ideas. Thus Kant takes the view that "ideas first make the experience (of the good) itself possible, even if they can never be fully expressed in experience [...]" (KrV, A 318/B 375).

In giving us access to a comprehensive context of moral significance, moral ideas also provide us with standards according to which we ought to act: "we have the true originals in our mind alone. [...] [I]t is only by means of this idea that any judgment of moral worth or lack of worth is possible" (KrV, A 315/ B 375). To say that moral ideas are causes, as Plato says and Kant wants to say (KrV, A 317/B 374), is just to say that insofar as we reason about things in the context of moral evaluation, we cannot but regard moral ideas as consequential for what we do. This claim also lies behind Kant's thesis in the Preface to the *Critique of Practical Reason* that the reality of freedom displayed by our moral commitments is the keystone of the whole critical edifice (KpV, p. 4). In our ability to set ends for ourselves, we show ourselves to be ultimate sources of significance that then give significance to all other things. If our end-setting ability is to be responsive to absolute obligations that we impose on ourselves, then it cannot be understood in terms of anything that determines us from outside of that very autonomy. But from the vantage point of that end-setting we form a conception of the world that conforms to our general capacity to set ends for ourselves. Such end-setting belongs to a comprehensive conception of the good when it allows us to satisfy our desires in a manner that conforms to our moral obligations. Since Kant regards only those norms as binding that we can also act on, our normative commitments bring with them a systematic commitment to being free to act on the norms to which we are committed.

It is important to the pragmatism implicit in Kant's position that our commitments as agents are best understood in the way that they are understood in everyday life: "the highest philosophy can get no further in respect to the essential ends of human nature than the direction that nature has awarded to the most common understanding" (KrV, A 831/B 860; cf. B XXXIII). Kant thinks that the problem with the Platonist or other metaphysical interpretations of the commitments of our everyday conception of ourselves is that they do not add genuine illumination to those commitments. Philosophers do not have the privilege of insight into the nature of things that Plato ascribes to them (KrV, A 831/B 860). We lose nothing to the "interest of human beings" when we do away with the claims of technical-philosophical metaphysics; the loss is only to the "monopoly of the schools" (KrV, B XXXII).

Kant takes the idea of freedom to be centrally affected by his rejection of the pretensions of school metaphysics. It can easily seem as if the Platonic-Aristotelian conception of ourselves as beings who are guided by the normative significance of ideas in what we do, requires a theoretical metaphysics of ideas. But Kant's position is that there is a fundamental illusion in taking ourselves to know in a theoretical sense that we belong to the realm of ideas; the function of the theoretical metaphysical conception of ideas is only to show that there is nothing logically incoherent in the idea of agency guided by ideas (KrV, B XXIX). From there on out, the idea of freedom is not a theoretical one: it is not a cosmological, but a practical idea. Our practice of holding ourselves accountable for what we do regardless of the force of incentives to do otherwise establishes the real possibility of practical freedom. In this sense, we have a kind of performative proof of the real possibility of practical freedom through the activity of practical reason: "if as pure reason it is really practical, it proves its reality and that of its concepts by its deed" (KpV, p. 3). The authority of the moral law presents us with the idea that we are able to be motivated to act by principles of reason alone (i.e., pure practical reason). This is not a proof that we are able to act freely from the standpoint of theoretical reason. But it does give us a basis for thinking of our action as unconditioned by antecedent events, since we are supposed to be doing what we are doing because it is the right thing to do rather than for some reason tied to our psychological history. So long as the notion of unconditioned action is not logically contradictory, then the commitments of pure practical reason give theoretical (i.e., speculative) reason an action that could be unconditioned by antecedent events.

Causal determinism is not a threat to our responsibility for what we do, since it consists in the idea that guides us of a comprehensive explanation of events. But exhaustive causal determination must be compatible with our being able to articulate that possibility to ourselves and to others in intelligible terms. To take experience and the explanatory order of nature to have a being that is independent of our ability to give significance to that explanatory order would pose a threat to what we can do. But this is not really an intelligible claim. The explanatory order of events in which we work can only have the significance that we can give to it. This is not a proof that freedom in the cosmological sense is really possible as a datum in the actual world. But it is a proof that one cannot demonstrate freedom to be theoretically impossible. The proof for such a claim would have to presuppose that the framework of causal explanation itself has a significance that can never be accounted for except in terms of some further causal story (KrV, A 558/B 586). This leaves open the logical possibility for practical action that is free. It is in this sense that Kant thinks that "freedom as a pure transcendental idea", "the idea of a spontaneity that could start to act from itself, without needing to be preceded by any other cause that in turn determines it to action according to the law of causal connection" is needed in order to constitute an "absolute totality in causal conditions" (KrV, A 533/B 556). The role of the cosmological idea of freedom is in leaving open the logical possibility of free agency. The commitments of the agent's stance do all the rest. Platonism is for Kant the illusion that we can accomplish more than this with the resources of theoretical reason.

III. Kant's Teleological-Functional Architectonic and Hegel's Idea

Kant's idea of architectonic as the comprehensive, teleological-functional whole in terms of which we are able in principle systematically to articulate everything becomes the basis for Hegel's conception of the Idea, and allows Hegel in his philosophy of nature and his philosophy of spirit to bring together Kant's and Aristotle's conceptions of nature, the mind, and thought.

Hegel's conception of logic is an analysis of the conceptual conditions of thought – in effect the analysis of what Kant calls the idea of the pure understanding. It is an effort exhaustively to articulate the idea of logical possibility. Despite the fact that Hegel organizes his *Logic* along the lines set out by Kant in his tables of the functions of judgment, the categories, and the concepts of reflection, Hegel generally criticizes Kant for simply adopting the forms of judgment and categories from logical practice, and hence from experience. But he has a better grasp of Kant's proof intentions than he generally reveals.[10]

---

[10] Discussion of Hegel's criticism that Kant's way of deriving the forms of judgment and categories is too dependent on experience may be found in Longuenesse, 2005, esp. pp. 107 ff. Longuenesse emphasizes the "leading thread" role of judgment in Kant's own argument, but does not highlight the significance of ideas or of the idea of the understanding in Kant's argument. I take the idea of the understanding to provide the leading thread. *R.* 5240 (HNM, p. 125) offers "formula, model, paradigm, original standard and idea" as glosses on "clue" or "leading thread" ("*Leitfaden*"), so this is by no means implausible. The idea provides the contextual significance that guides us in

Hegel displays a sophisticated understanding of the role of the idea in Kant's completeness proof in a remark he makes on the insufficiencies of Kant's derivation of the forms of judgment and categories in his *Encyclopedia*. In a *Zusatz* to § 171, Hegel praises Kant for grasping the different forms of judgment not just as an empirical multiplicity. Kant is also said to have grasped those forms as a "totality determined by thought" so that "the universal forms of the logical idea itself are that through which these forms [of judgment] are determined" (EPWI, p. 322, Zusatz). While Hegel is disposed to criticize Kant for his "empiricism" and his overemphasis on the understanding (conceived in contrast to reason), Hegel sees that there is another side to Kant's approach. Kant's conception of apperception is the key to Hegel's own conception of a concept: "It belongs to the deepest and most correct insights to be found in the Critique of Reason that the unity that is the essence of the concept, is recognized as the original-synthetic unity of apperception, as the unity of the 'I think' or of self-consciousness. – This proposition constitutes the so-called transcendental deduction of the categories. [...]" (WLII, p. 253).[11] Hegel places such weight on

---

inquiry, contemplation, or action. Judgment relates terms to possible objects. This requires both the idea of a comprehensive systematic whole of conceptual distinctions and of a corresponding whole of objects.

[11]   Robert Pippin offers an interpretation of Hegel's idealism that emphasizes the connection to Kant's original synthetic unity of apperception (Pippin, 1989, pp. 8 ff.). But he does not link apperception to purposive activity in the way that I take to be basic. Each concept has a teleological-functional significance that culminates in the comprehensive end of exhaustive articulation that is the process of the idea. Pippin also reads the connection to the possibility of self-consciousness to commit Hegel to claims to self-knowledge about how things are in "our conceptual scheme", as if there could be another that Hegel would reject as non-contrastive and hence meaningless. Pippin takes Hegel's departure from Kant to be about the status of intuition. I do not think that Hegel has a problem with Kant's theory of intuition, or even with the idea that intuition gives us mere appearances; for Hegel thinks that finite things are inherently appearances (EPWI, p. 122).

Brandom, 2002 also makes the synthetic unity of apperception central to Hegel's conception of concepts and helpfully ties Hegel's conception of concepts to what one can do. Brandom takes Hegel to be committed to a kind of conceptual pragmatism and non-psychological functionalism that takes meaning to be a function of position in a systematic structure. Brandom also takes knowledge to involve implicitly knowing how to do something. I am sympathetic to this aspect of Brandom's understanding of Hegel's project, but Brandom's effort to build pragmatic considerations into semantics makes sense only if one operates with a conception of concepts that is much more abstract and proposition-based than Hegel is willing to accept. Brandom's starting point is the activity of inference; he takes the standpoint of syntax and pragmatics to be basic to understanding the incompatibilities between propositions that show up in inferences. Hegel's use of terms such as "concept", "proposition", "judgment" and "inference" is much more expansive in its meaning than the Carnap- and Sellars-influenced conception with which Brandom works and is intended to show that the kind of significance that can show up in language, in sentences, and in inferences can only be understood in terms of our comprehensive engagement with the world as agents.

the role of apperception in constituting the significance of concepts, and of objects (as what are grasped by concepts), that he takes the principle of unifiability in a single possible comprehensive self-consciousness to be the very deduction itself. Hegel sees that Kant's Transcendental Deduction is based on the defense of the idea of the understanding (concept, for Hegel) and its logical functions and their applications that Kant develops in the Metaphysical Deduction. This defense is based on the manner in which Kant's conception of the

Moreover, my reading of Hegel's metaphysics does not fit in to the set of alternatives suggested by Beiser, 2005, pp. 56–57, which attributes a kind of Spinozist realism to Hegel. This is the way in which he understands Hegel's view that freedom and causal necessity are compatible; Hegel's reconciliation of the self with the world seems for Beiser rather a form of resignation to fate (ibid., pp. 75–76). Beiser's Spinozism fails to do justice to the fact that Hegel regards the dependence of substance, causation, and interaction on his conception of the concept as a refutation of Spinozism. I am also skeptical of Beiser's effort to shoe-horn Hegel into traditional realist categories. I do not think Hegel is committed to the independent existence of universals, nor to nominalism, nor to Beiser's own "Aristotelian" view that "universals exist only in things", unless Beiser uses "thing" very differently from the way Hegel uses the term. Universals are abstractions for Hegel. But so are things that exist only in a context of spatial and temporal relations to other things. I would reject Beiser's dismissal of "universals existing beyond the historical and natural world" (ibid., p. 57). I take Hegelian concepts to be the basis for, and in this sense independent of, the vagaries of the historical and natural world. They are not what is real in that world, but whatever is actual in that world. Concepts are concrete, not abstract, universals (or abstract particulars); they are as such inherently universal, but also particular and individual (this is for Hegel an inherently contextual difference). The view I attribute to Hegel is neither realist nor idealist in the traditional senses of those words, since there is no contrast available to the framework of intelligibility that is the idea. Beiser would probably regard my reading as a version of the super-subject view he criticizes in Pippin, but it is immune to his objections (ibid., pp. 70–71). I need not accept the charge of subjectivism, nor do I accept the validity of his claim that the subject is substance in the beginning (in the beginning all you have is being, and substance belongs to the logic of essence). This betrays a misunderstanding of the priority relation between the idea and substance; the beginning, whether in being or later in substance, is an abstraction from the idea. Again, this seems to me to depend on reconstructing Hegel's views along what amounts to a false dichotomy: either those views are comfortably "subjective-idealist" or "realist".

My own interpretation is perhaps closest to that of Herbert Marcuse, whose early work emphasizes the importance of Kant's unity of apperception and of its manifestation in the productive imagination for Hegel's thought (Marcuse, 1989, pp. 18, 30 ff.) and for Hegel's notion of concept and ontology (pp. 119 ff.). Marcuse's emphasis on the "process" (*Bewegtheit*) involved in the unpacking of concepts links his account of Hegelian concepts to his teacher Heidegger's appropriation of Aristotle's teleological-functional account of agency. Marcuse directly ties process, taken as the nature of being and of concepts, to Hegel's appropriation of Aristotle's conception of being as actuality. Marcuse notes that Hegel identifies "actuality" (*Wirklichkeit*) with the *energeia* in which the inner fully manifests and expresses itself in the outer (EPWI, p. 280, Zusatz; see esp. Marcuse, 1989, pp. 103 ff.).

original synthetic unity of apperception grounds both concepts, functions of judgment and objects by unifying them in the idea of the understanding. Hegel rightly reads Kant's conception of concepts as rooted in the systematicity implicit in the very idea of understanding things in both an identical and a systematically contrastive manner from a shared normative point of view. An impersonal normative point of view for correct interpretation of objects is preserved in the concept insofar as it represents things in the same systematically distinctive way for different agents (VÄ, p. 148; cf. also WLII, pp. 249 ff.).

Hegel's fundamental dispute with Kant concerns whether we should regard the comprehensive whole in terms of which we think about things as what is true, or only regard as true what belongs to the context of experience and what we can explain in terms of causal laws. Hegel's gripe with Kant is over whether truth is strictly speaking to be found in appearances, intuition and experience, let alone limited to appearances in intuition. Kant maintains against Plato's view that "in the senses there is nothing but semblance, and [...] only the understanding cognizes what is true" (KrV, A 854/B 882). Hegel's point is that the normativity of the idea of truth that we must always presuppose as agents prevents us from identifying truth with the limited context of spatio-temporal appearances. Plato must in this sense be right, although this does not mean for Hegel that the Platonic notion of the idea has any truth or significance that is completely independent of its normative role in guiding our agency. For Kant, the systematicity of ideas is presupposed as a criterion of truth, but involves the necessary illusion of an unconditioned totality that goes beyond whatever could appear to us in experience. Thus illusion is for Kant in theoretical (transcendental) ideas, and the truth in appearances (PM, p. 374). By contrast, with respect to the moral ideas and the practical idea of freedom "experience is (unfortunately!) the mother of illusion" (KrV, A 318–319/B 375). Hegel argues that we cannot do without the Platonic idea of the good in making sense of our experience as a whole. Since we need the kind of coherence of optimal systematic function of things in an organic, structured whole that only the idea of the good can ground, we cannot take the idea of the good to be mere illusion even if we can take Platonic objects to be illusory. Platonic ideas exist for Hegel only in and through their normative contribution to the way in which we relate to our world as agents.[12] This reflects Kant's view that ideas guide our action as norms.

---

[12]   Hegel radicalizes Kant's rejection of the charge that Plato's Republic is an empty pipe dream (PR, p. 24; KrV, A 316/B 372). Hegel asserts not only that "only the idea is actual" (PR p. 25), he also claims that not just the rationality but also the actuality (*Wirklichkeit*) of the state lies in its idea (PR, p. 24). Here he draws on the Aristotelian conception according to which the idea exists in its function and this is to be in function or in actuality (*energeia*); the idea is, as such, something more than what ought to be brought about or actualized by us. The idea is what is ultimately actual, but not as a super-agent; instead it is actual through the activity in which we as agents mutually

There is a necessary illusion involved in our temptation to take these normative standards for ultimately real objects of theory. This illusion is at its strongest when it comes to the cosmological idea of freedom. Hegel returns to the Platonic conception in which truth is in ideas and illusion in objects as they must appear to us in experience. He thus rejects that aspect of Kant's critique of Platonic or "enthusiastic" idealism (PM, p. 374). Hegel's conception of things is closer to Kant's insofar as they are taken from the idea of the unity of the theoretical and practical points of view; his main complaint against things as viewed from the unity of the theoretical and practical points of view is that Kant takes this to be merely a comprehensive standpoint rather than what is ultimately true.

Hegel develops the implications of Kant's conception of the systematic architectonic role of ideas and of his appropriation of the Kantian theory of ideas when he presents his *Encyclopedia* as a system of all philosophy consisting in a "circle of circles", in which each opens on to the next (EPWI, p. 60; WLII,

---

recognize each other according to norms. This is the sense in which institutions are nothing but the manifestation of the idea in a particular context. This is also the sense in which "the actual is rational and the rational is actual" (PR, p. 24). This does not mean for Hegel that what is now real is actual or rational. The real is at best the fleeting appearance of the actual. The difference between Plato and Aristotle is not over the truth of the idea, but whether the idea is merely potentiality (*dynamis*), as it is for Plato according to Aristotle, and as it is for Kant according to Hegel. For Hegel and Aristotle, the idea is actuality "essentially as ἐνέργεια, that is, of the inner which is absolutely outer, with that the unity of the inner and the outer or actuality in the emphatic sense" (EPWI, p. 281, Zusatz). The idea is that which must find expression in what we do, albeit never adequately, since it is the truth that always eludes the local context of experience. Hegel's conception of the actuality of the state as it manifests itself in a context allows him to point up the difference between Plato's *kallipolis* and the modern Kantian-Hegelian conception of the state. Plato's *kallipolis* expresses the "nature of Greek ethical life" (PR, p. 24) against a new principle of subjective freedom that was to be its destruction. Thus, Plato's *Republic* grasps the actuality of Greek ethical life in a manner that, like all philosophy, is retrospective. "[O]nly in the maturity of actuality does the ideal appear opposite the real and that reality build the world in its substance in the form of an intellectual kingdom" (PR, p. 28). Plato's *Republic* is an attempt to "grasp its time in thought" (PR, p. 26) and to arrest in at least the ideal world the passage of the actuality of Greek ethical life and the *polis*'s less inclusive and less sophisticated conception of freedom, a social conception of freedom that is grounded in the political freedom of its male citizens and threatened by their pursuit of their interests as private individuals. Plato's conception "in the deepest way violates the free infinite personality" (PR, p. 24), championed by Kant in his interpretation of the significance of Plato's ideal city-state. Hegel takes over Kant's critique of ideas as separate Platonic objects and also follows Kant in taking the objectification of ideas to be an inevitable result of the historical process of human activity. When we look at ideas as norms to which we aspire in a particular context without seeing their wider significance in what we do, they seem to take on an illusory life of their own as "an intellectual kingdom".

pp. 570–571). The idea that philosophy must be taught as a process of working from one conceptual circle of systematically connected differences to the next is conveyed by the title of the work. The comprehensive circle is what Hegel calls the idea. The subsystems of the idea are what Hegel calls "concepts". Concepts are for him articulations of things in a comprehensive context in which a totality of differences and possible distinctions are systematically connected according to a certain general principle. The significance of the concept itself changes as it articulates the full specificity of that context. As the significance of concepts unpacks, that significance is transformed. As that significance develops, the sophistication of the resources of articulation increases and the extent to which the concept can articulate its context comprehensively and fully increases as well. Understood completely comprehensively and such that reality fully accords with the standards they set for things, concepts taken together constitute a single encompassing absolute idea. Each concept has a relative independence from every other concept, but each is ultimately defined by its teleological-functional role in relation to the ultimate end of the comprehensive systematic comprehension of everything. Hegel sees that Kant's account of the architectonic structure of reason implies that all ideas are systematically related in a comprehensive teleological-functional whole. He realizes that the organizing principle of this whole is the original synthetic unity of apperception, but that the complex organic unity of teleological-functional structure characteristic of this architectonic structure cannot be accounted for purely on the basis of the abstract conception of self-consciousness.

In criticizing Kant, Hegel tends to play off the articulated teleological-functional whole of the concept and idea against the empty notion of universality that seems to be characteristic of the I or ego in the abstract.[13] But it is a mis-

---

[13]   Kant's presentation of his position encourages one to think of it as a kind of faculty psychology based on representations, or as a kind of transcendental psychology based on "facts of consciousness". This transcendental-psychological reading has been widely accepted from Kant's time to the present day. The German idealist alternative interpretation of Kant has its roots in the teleological-functional account of the human soul and society that underlies the narrative of Plato's *Republic* and is then appropriated by Aristotle in the foundations of his ethics in *EN Nicomachean Ethics* I.6 and in his psychology and theory of cognition in *De Anima* II. This teleological-functional interpretation of Kant underlies not only the interpretation of Kant provided by Fichte, but especially of Schelling and Hegel, and also underlies the position of Husserl, Cassirer, and less consistently of Heidegger. For an extended defense of this kind of reading of Kant's "functionalism" against the psychologistic reading of Kant, see Keller, 2001b. In Husserl, 1983, § 86, p. 176, Husserl insists that the "teleological functional" standpoint is the most important for phenomenology because in it intentionality and objects of thought (*noemata*) are constituted. Heidegger discovers the Aristotelian basis of this conception of intentionality. He takes intentionality and function to be grounded in truth on the basis of his reading of Aristotle's account of function, or rather of work (*ergon*), and its relation to truth (*aletheia*) in *Meta.*IX.10.

understanding to take Kant's conception of a priori structure to be purely abstract and formal. In all domains, there is an articulated structure of the idea that substantively defines the domain in question and systematically distinguishes it from other domains by virtue of its distinctive relation to the ends that we have as human beings.

By focusing on how things are from a local standpoint within space and time and addressing questions of explanation at this local level, viz., at the level of the understanding, the systematic context of the idea seems to present itself simply as the empty notion of complete comprehensiveness or of something absolutely unconditioned. This seems to leave us with no criteria of significance beyond "the *abstract identity of the understanding*" (EPWI, p. 121, Zusatz; cf. VHP, p. 353). This seems to me to be a fair objection to the received conception of Kant's ideas. But I have endeavored to show that the Kantian conception of architectonic is a conception of a systematic set of laws for all domains. These laws may be thought of as legislated by an ideal legislator who systematically

See Heidegger, 2002, p. 61. For discussion see Keller, 2001a. Cassirer explicitly subordinates mathematical function as symbolic form to the teleological conception of work (*ergon*) that defines man's nature functionally and not substantially. "It is this work, it is the system of human activities, which defines and determines the circle of 'humanity' and gives the different symbolic functions of human beings the character of an 'organic whole'" (Cassirer, 1962, p. 93). Ernst Cassirer's Davos controversy with Heidegger turns on the significance of ideas and of architectonic within the Kantian corpus (cf. the appendices on the Davos controversy in Heidegger, 1992, pp. 180–217). Ideas are connected together for us in the ultimate end of human agency; this gives human activities the character of an organic whole *of function* that Cassirer identifies with symbolic form. Cassirer thus defends Hegel's reading that, in its ideas, human reason has a kind of absoluteness and infinity in itself. Heidegger argues by contrast that, because understanding is finite and ideas of reason are only a "transgression of the understanding," significance in human beings is ultimately finite (Heidegger, 2002, pp. 145–146). This is a fundamental misunderstanding of Kant, and as a result, Heidegger's Kant interpretation must seek an ultimate single source of thought and experience in the imagination and temporality. Given Kant's own conception of architectonic significance and of the role of ideas in thought and sensibility, this fundamentally distorts Kant's position. Nevertheless, Kant's conception of the architectonic basis of a science of metaphysics is closer to Heidegger's conception of fundamental ontology than even Heidegger realizes. Kant's conception grounds all of metaphysics and distinctive meanings of being in the standpoint that an agent must take in relating to the world; against the philosophical tradition, Kant insists on a fundamental difference in what it is to be an agent from what it is to be an object that can ultimately be understood in theoretical terms. Heidegger chastises Kant for assimilating the problem of practical freedom to that of causation and determinism by locating the nexus of freedom in the cosmological idea (Heidegger, 2002, p. 166). In consequence, he misses the ultimate and very different significance of the cosmological idea (of theoretical reason) and of the idea of practical freedom in Kant's work. Far from running the practical idea of freedom together with the theoretical idea of freedom embodied in the cosmological idea, it is central to Kant's whole conception that their significance is fundamentally different.

distinguishes and connects different domains with different distinctive laws, all of which are supposed to contribute to the necessary and ultimate ends of human beings.

Hegel's worry about the abstractness of Kant's conception of the idea has general application. It is at the root of his worry about the emptiness of the categorical imperative of morality. The concern that the categorical imperative is empty is rooted in interpreting it as a procedure that operates independently of the systematic teleological-functional context of normative significance provided by the idea of morality. The procedure is rather the attempt to articulate that significance in its relevance to a particular context and cannot be applied without reference to human ends. The up-front presentation of the matter in the *Groundwork of the Metaphysics of Morals* (1783), in which Kant first developed the notion of a normative order of ends into an explicit conception of autonomy, can make the worry about empty formalism seem compelling by suggesting that situations of moral choice are to be met by appeal to an abstract, context-free test for the universalizability of a principle of action. The isolated principle of an action would be understood in terms of its capacity to be made into an isolated law. But the context of moral ideas with which the first *Critique* operates continues to be in place. The idea of duty and morality continues to be the "true original that lies in reason" (GMS, p. 409). This, the paradigm of the good ("das Urbild des Guten" GMS, p. 408), the original standard of the good, is the Platonic standard against which we measure the rightness or wrongness of our actions. One might still take reason to be operating only locally, but this would be inconsistent with the connection Kant argues holds between autonomy and the idea of freedom. The idea of freedom is embedded in the notion of autonomy and provides the context in which we are able to hold ourselves accountable in what we do to standards that we set for ourselves with our reason. To regard ourselves as autonomous is to regard ourselves as giving principles to ourselves independently of any commitment extrinsic to our reasoning about what is the right thing to do. The laws that we legislate to ourselves as moral agents are intrinsically motivating because we take them to express the demands made on us by our true or authentic selves, and thus to reflect our true interests (GMS, pp. 457–458, 461). We can only give laws to ourselves to which we hold our actions and those of other reasoning beings accountable because we have a standard of systematic normativity implicitly before our eyes as self-conscious reasoning creatures to which we hold ourselves accountable. This principle is implicit in the universal law formulation of the categorical imperative, and is fully explicit in the "kingdom of ends" formulation. The categorical imperative procedure of attempting to universalize a principle of action that we are considering tests the principle against the general context of moral significance.

The difference between Kant and Hegel is extremely subtle according to my reading. Kant takes norm- (i.e., idea-) guided, goal-directed, agency to be basic to the functional whole of our engagements, with ourselves and with the world.

But Kant also argues that such goal-directed agency cannot show up in its true character as practical idea as conceptualized by theory. This means that what shows up in the world as we understand it theoretically can never controvert or establish the idea of (practical) freedom that we have as agents. Our free agency can only be threatened if we take practical freedom to be embedded in a meta-physically (i.e., transcendentally) realist conception of the universe that demands an exhaustive theoretical conception of causal determination.[14]

Once we have made the Copernican turn, freedom will only show up as a practical notion (KrV, A 803/B 831; cf. KrV, B XXI). Hegel pushes this Copernican Revolution past Kant's conclusion. He takes freedom to be guaranteed by the manner in which concepts (Kantian ideas) establish the causal relations and interactions between substances that make up our world. A concept is the "totality" of the actual process in which things, their states and their relations are constituted. In this process dependency is overcome because each part is also the whole process in which things and their actions become intelligible (EPWI, pp. 305–308). This goes beyond what Kant allows, but only by developing the teleological relationship implicit in the very idea of freedom to which Kant thinks that we are committed in our action. Moreover, the ultimate significance of the contrast between the practical and the absolute idea is, for Hegel, something that can only be appreciated in its full unpacking. Since this is an open-ended process, the difference will not ever be completely fixed.[15] A non-contextual understanding of things and standards is the chief impediment to seeing that we are most free when we are guided by shared norms grounded in concepts that we impose on ourselves. Like Kant, Hegel takes these norms to display themselves in and through the very activity in which we engage with each other and with the world as agents. Hegel follows Kant in taking being, including that of Platonic ideas, which is not understood contextually, to be illusory. Being in

---

[14] It is tempting to interpret freedom as a cosmological idea of theoretical explanation involving ideas as unconditioned causes. This conception then seems to stand opposed to the idea of an exhaustive empirical causal explanation of action. However, both of these concepts are ideas of a complete whole of causal conditions that regiment experience and go beyond possible experience. This means that an account of free agency in terms of the causal power of ideas is at least logically possible and is not in conflict with experience (KrV, A 557 ff./B 585 ff.). When we think of causes in theoretical terms, then it looks like a conflict between free agency and causal explanation is inevitable. Kant faults both empiricism and Platonism-rationalism for approaching the problem of the compatibility of causal explanation and practical freedom in this way.

[15] While I agree with Neuhouser, 2000) that Hegel's theory of freedom is based on participation in an organically functional whole, I take this to have its source and model in Kant's account of the idea of agency and its role in architectonic rather than in Kant's account of biological organisms (cf. ibid., p. 308). It is because organisms have some of the self-determining characteristics of agents that they are relatively independent of their environments, rather than the other way around.

this sense is the semblance through which the process of articulation that is essence, concepts and the idea expresses itself (WLII, p. 16). Hegel's dialectic, like that of Kant, is the systematic exposure of the illusion of independent objects as one places things in an ever more encompassing context. But it is the very activity of making sense of things that generates the illusion of non-contextual being that we must continually combat in everything that we do.

The hidden significance of Kant's notion of architectonic and of his Copernican turn is that the different contexts of significance and being that are relevant to the metaphysical commitments we have in those different contexts are all systematically connected together by the relevance that they have for us as agents. As such, they are connected together by the idea of our practical agency, by the idea of practical freedom. This is the idea that what we do is something that we do for a reason, which we can share in principle also with others. Depending on the context, each of which is constituted as such by a normative idea of it as a whole, different metaphysical realist illusions await us. When we view ourselves from the point of view of ideas and norms, we are inclined to see ourselves in terms of the Platonic illusion that we are denizens of an intelligible world. When we view ourselves in terms of experience, we are inclined to the empiricist illusion that we are nothing but atoms or sensations. These two standpoints generate the theoretical illusion that we either possess or fail to possess a kind of metaphysical freedom that Kant calls cosmological freedom. Hegel thought that Kant had not taken his own insight seriously enough in reserving truth for appearances rather than for the ideas that make truth possible. However Hegel is also deeply Kantian in seeing freedom as our comprehensive emancipation from the local identification with a particular context that generates the illusions that it is the systematic task of philosophy to articulate and expose. While Kant and Hegel think that Plato paved the way for this emancipation by showing us that we could understand our behavior in terms of norms that emancipate us from our beliefs and desires, they also think that he could not avoid falling victim to a version of the very illusions from which he wanted to emancipate us.[16]

References

Beiser, Frederick (2005): *Hegel*, New York.
Brandom, Robert (2002): *Tales of the Mighty Dead*, Cambridge, MA.
Brandt, Reinhard (1991): *The Table of Judgments: Critique of Pure Reason A 67–76; B 92–101*, North American Kant Society Studies in Philosophy, vol. 4, Atascadero.

---

[16]   I would like to thank Fred Rush and my wife Edith Keller for all of their help and insightful comments.

Cassirer, Ernst (1960): *An Essay on Man: An Introduction to a Philosophy of Human Culture*, New Haven.

Förster, Eckart (2000): *Kant's Final Synthesis: An Essay on the Opus Postumum*, Cambridge.

Hegel, G. W. F. (1970): *Werke*, ed. E. Moldenhauer and K. M. Michel, Frankfurt a. M. [= HW].

– *Enzyklopädie der philosophischen Wissenschaften I*, in: HW, vol. 8 [= EPWI].

– *Grundlinien der Philosophie des Rechts*, in: HW, vol. 7 [= PR].

– *Philosophische Propädeutik*, in: HW, vol. 4 [= PP].

– *Vorlesungen über die Ästhetik I*, in: HW, vol. 13 [= VÄ].

– *Vorlesungen über die Geschichte der Philosophie III*, in: HW, vol. 20 [= VHP].

– *Wissenschaft der Logik II*, in: HW, vol. 6 [= WLII].

– (1995): *Vorlesung über Ästhetik, Berlin 1820/21*, ed. H. Schneider, Frankfurt.

– (2005): *Philosophie der Kunst: Vorlesung von 1926*, ed. A. Gethmann-Siefert, J.-I. Kwon, and K. Berr, Frankfurt a. M.

Heidegger, Martin (1992): *Kant and the Problem of Metaphysics*, tr. R. Taft, Indianapolis.

– (2002): *The Essence of Human Freedom*, tr. T. Sadler, London.

Hölderlin, Friedrich (1943 ff.): *Sämtliche Werke. Grosser Stuttgarter Ausgabe*, ed. F. Beisser, Stuttgart [=HSW].

Husserl, Edmund (1983): *Ideas Pertaining to a Pure Phenomenology and to Phenomenological Philosophy: First Book: General Introduction to a Pure Phenomenology*, tr. F. Kerstin, Dordrecht.

Kant, Immanuel (1902 ff.): *Kants gesammelte Schriften*, ed. Königlich Preussischen Akademie der Wissenschaften, Berlin [=AA].

– *Anthropologie in pragmatischer Hinsicht*, in: AA, vol. 7, pp. 119–333 [= ApH].

– *De mundi sensibilis atque intelligibilis forma et principiis*, in: AA, vol. 2 [= *De mundi*].

– *Grundlegung zur Metaphysik der Sitten*, in: AA, vol. 4, pp. 385–464 [= GMS].

– *Handschriftlicher Nachlaß. Metaphysik*, in: AA, vol. 18 [= HNM].

– *Kritik der praktischen Vernunft*, in: AA, vol. 5, pp. 1–164 [= KpV].

– *Kritik der reinen Vernunft*, in: AA, vols. 3–4 [= KrV].

– *Kritik der Urtheilskraft*, in: AA, vol. 5, pp. 165–486 [= KU].

– *Opus postumum I*, in: AA, vol. 21 [= OP].

– *Prolegomena zu einer jeden künftigen Metaphysik, die als Wissenschaft wird auftreten können*, in AA: vol. 4, pp. 255–383 [= PM].

Keller, Pierre (2001a): *Husserl, Heidegger and Human Experience*, New York.

– (2001 b): *Kant and the Demands of Self-Consciousness*, New York.

Leibniz, G. W. (1960): *Mathematische Schriften*, ed. C. I. Gerhard, Hildesheim [= GM].

– (1960): *Philosophische Schriften*, ed. C. I. Gerhard, Hildesheim [= GP].

Longuenesse, Béatrice (2005): *Kant and the Human Standpoint*, New York.

Makkreel, Rudolf (1990): *Imagination and Interpretation in Kant*, Chicago.

Marcuse, Herbert (1989): *Hegel's Ontology and the Theory of Historicity*, tr. S. Benhabib, Cambridge, MA.

Neuhouser, Frederick (2000): *Foundations of Hegel's Social Theory: Actualizing Freedom*, Cambridge, MA.

Pippin, Robert (1989): *Hegel's Idealism: The Satisfactions of Self-Consciousness*, New York.

Reich, Klaus (1992): *The Completeness of Kant's Table of Judgments*, tr. J. Kneller and M. Losonsky, Palo Alto.
– (2001): "Die Tugend in der Idee", in: *Gesammelte Schriften*, ed. M. Baum, Hamburg, pp. 306–313.
Wolff, Michael (1995): *Die Vollständigkeit der kantischen Urteilstafel: mit einem Essay über Freges Begriffschrift*, Frankfurt a. M.

Rocco Porcheddu

Das Verhältnis von theoretischer und praktischer Freiheit in der Deduktion des kategorischen Imperativs

This paper presents a strong reading of the deduction of the categorical imperative in Kant's Groundwork for the Metaphysics of Morals. *My central thesis is that the deduction has to be read as intending a complete* chain of proof *leading to the validity of the categorical imperative. Central to this argumentation is the developing of practical freedom out of what can be called epistemic spontaneity and which later in Kant's view is a logical implication of our ability to judge. This epistemic spontaneity finds its genuine expression in Kant's transcendental ideas. The systematic consistency of this ideas in its turn claims (among other things) a kind of freedom that contains more than the epistemic one and under which the free will (as* practical *and* transcendental freedom) *is to be subsumed. Since the developing of this latter freedom out of epistemic spontaneity implies the central and concluding argument for the validity of the categorical imperative (as I will show), in my interpretation the deduction intends a complete chain of evidence, starting from the ability to judge to the validity of the categorical imperative.*

Vorbemerkung

Dieter Henrich behauptet in seinem Aufsatz *Die Deduktion des Sittengesetzes*, Kant habe in der Deduktion des kategorischen Imperativs in der *Grundlegung zur Metaphysik der Sitten* gezeigt, „daß die Annahme der Realität der Freiheit nicht willkürlich geschieht. Sie ergibt sich aus der Natur des Verstandes, wenn auch unter der Voraussetzung, dass man sich einen Willen zuspricht. [...] Mehr als die Hypothese einer Idee kann und muß Freiheit aber im praktischen Gebrauch der Vernunft nicht sein" (Henrich, 1975, S. 83). Wenig später behauptet Henrich weiter, dass „alle Deduktion auch der *Grundlegung* am Ende auf die faktische Selbstgewißheit des sittlichen Wesens angewiesen ist" (ebd., S. 86).

Ich möchte in diesem Aufsatz zeigen, dass eine solche schwache Lesart die Leistung oder doch den Anspruch der Deduktion unterschätzt. Erstens kommt Willensfreiheit in der Deduktion nicht bloß der Status einer ‚hypothetischen Idee' zu, vielmehr ist sie eine notwendige Folge aus ihrerseits notwendig anzunehmenden epistemischen Grundannahmen. Zweitens trifft dies auch auf die Geltung des kategorischen Imperativs zu: Seine Geltung ist dem Anspruch der Deduktion in der GMS nach gerade *nicht* „am Ende auf die faktische Selbstgewißheit des sittlichen Wesens angewiesen", sondern ergibt sich letztlich ebenfalls aus einer unabweisbaren, zunächst in der Episteme der Vernunft liegende grundlegenden Welt- und Selbstsicht. Anders also als Henrich meint, hat Kant m. E. in der Entwicklung der Deduktion des kategorischen Imperativs in der *Grundlegung* einen veritablen Beweisgang vor Augen, wobei im Zentrum dieses Beweisgangs Kants Entwicklung der praktisch-transzendentalen Freiheit aus der epistemisch-theoretischen steht.

Das Hauptanliegen dieses Aufsatzes besteht somit im Nachzeichnen des Begründungsgangs von der theoretischen zur praktischen Freiheit. Dieser Weg wird uns u. a. in die Dialektik der *Kritik der reinen Vernunft* führen. Dann soll, in gebotener Kürze, danach gefragt werden, was diese Entwicklung von theoretischer zu praktischer Freiheit für die Geltung des kategorischen Imperativs austrägt.

I. Der Beweis epistemischer Freiheit in GMS III

Ein Beweis der notwendigen Selbstzuschreibung des Menschen von dem, was man epistemische oder theoretische Freiheit nennen kann, findet sich in der Sektion 2 des Deduktionskapitels der *Grundlegung* (GMS, S. 447 f.). Die Überschrift dieser Sektion lautet: „Freiheit muß als Eigenschaft des Willens aller vernünftigen Wesen vorausgesetzt werden". Sie bezeichnet eine Konsequenz aus der zu Anfang des Deduktionskapitels von Kant entwickelten Analytizitätsthese von Freiheit und sittlicher Autonomie. Bekanntlich besagt die Analytizitätsthese, dass Sittlichkeit der positive Begriff von Freiheit sei, wobei Kant Freiheit negativ als Eigenschaft des Willens bestimmt, „unabhängig von fremden [...] bestimmenden Ursachen" (GMS, S. 446) wirkend sein zu können. Es lässt sich in diesem Sinne hinzufügen, dass die Analytizitätsthese behauptet, das Sittengesetz sei notwendig die Regel praktisch-transzendental freier Handlungen. Weil das Sittengesetz nun in Kants Sicht ein Gesetz im strengen Sinne ist, also für alle (denkbaren) vernünftigen Wesen a priori gelten muss, und weil es ein *praktisches* Gesetz ist, muss es „(völlig a priori) schon mit dem Begriff des Willens eines vernünftigen Wesens überhaupt verbunden sein" (GMS, S. 426). Soll also das praktische Gesetz überhaupt gelten, muss es (a) für den Willen eines jeden vernünftigen Wesens gelten und muss (b) aufgrund der Analytizitätsthese „Freiheit [...] als Eigenschaft des Willens aller vernünftigen Wesen vorausgesetzt werden".

Der Beweis der genannten theoretisch-epistemischen Freiheit findet sich im folgenden Passus der zweiten Sektion:

> „Nun kann man sich unmöglich eine Vernunft denken, die mit ihrem eigenen Bewußtsein in Ansehung ihrer Urtheile anderwärts her eine Lenkung empfinge, denn alsdann würde das Subject nicht seiner Vernunft, sondern einem Antriebe die Bestimmung der Urtheilskraft zuschreiben. Sie muß sich selbst als Urheberin ihrer Principien ansehen unabhängig von fremden Einflüssen, folglich muß sie als praktische Vernunft, oder als Wille eines vernünftigen Wesens von ihr selbst als frei angesehen werden [...]" (GMS, S. 448).

Vernunft muss in Hinblick auf ihre Eigenschaft als Vermögen der Genese von Urteilen in der Sicht Kants also als ein spontanes Vermögen gedacht werden bzw. sie muss sich selbst als ein solches denken. Denn ein Urteil kann dem ihm inhärenten Wahrheits- bzw. Geltungsanspruch nur genügen, wenn es als ein Vollzug der Vernunft gedacht wird, dessen Vollzugsgründe und -prinzipien in der Vernunft selbst ihren Ursprung haben. Kant versteht hier Vernunft als das gesamte spontane Erkenntnisvermögen, bezieht sich in der Sache aber wohl vornehmlich auf Funktionen, die er in der KrV dem Verstand zuschreibt. Das ist insofern unproblematisch, als Kant öfter nicht deutlich zwischen Verstand und Vernunft als spontanen Erkenntnisvermögen unterscheidet.[1] Die Prinzipien, die Kant hier vor Augen hat, sind damit offenbar die Prinzipien des Denkens und Urteilens, also insgesamt alle erkenntnis- und geltungskonstituierenden apriorischen Regeln. Damit bezieht sich Kant offenbar auf seine Zwei-Stämme-Lehre der Erkenntnis, in welcher dem Verstand die Funktion der spontanen Synthesis des Mannigfaltigen des sinnlich Gegebenen zukommt. Der Verstand ist das Vermögen der „Spontaneität der Begriffe". Die reinen Verstandesbegriffe oder Kategorien sind „Begriffe vom Gegenstande überhaupt, dadurch dessen Anschauungen in Ansehung der logischen Functionen […] als bestimmt angesehen werden" (KrV, B 128). Kategorien konstituieren damit allererst mögliche Objekte und sind zugleich nichts anderes als auf mögliche Erfahrung bezogene, logische Urteilsfunktionen. An einer Stelle definiert Kant nun Wahrheit ganz traditionell als „Übereinstimmung der Erkenntnis mit ihrem Gegenstande" (KrV, A 58/B 82). Ist Objektkonstitution wesentlich spontane Leistung des Verstandes, setzen objektive Urteile die Spontaneität des Verstandes in Hinsicht auf die allgemeinsten Urteils- und Objektkonstitutionsregeln voraus. Bezogen auf das Freiheitsargument der Sektion 2 kann damit das Folgende festgehalten werden: Dass wir objektiv gültige Urteile fällen können, setzt voraus, dass die Prinzipien der Urteile apodiktisch sind. Apodiktisch, also in unserer Sicht nicht zufällig, können diese Regeln nur dann sein, wenn sie zum einen die eigene Subjektivität und zum anderen das Objekt konstituieren. Nichts anderes stellen die Kategorien als Formen der Urteile und der Synthesis des sinnlich Gegebenen dar. Denn die Synthesisleistung des Verstandes konstituiert nicht nur Objekte, sondern hat die Vereinigung in einem Bewusstsein, also Subjektivität zur Voraussetzung, die in der Sicht Kants in nichts anderem als in dieser Synthesisleistung besteht. Damit ist Vernunft in Hinsicht auf Urteile als ein spontan-autonomes Vermögen angesprochen.

Ist der Wille praktische, also kausal wirksame *Vernunft*, muss er, weil Vernunft, zunächst in ihrem epistemischen Gebrauch als Vermögen der Autogenese der eigenen Vollzugsgründe und -prinzipien gedacht wird, diese Eigenschaft ebenfalls aufweisen. Das ist auch mit Blick auf die zentrale erste Willensdefini-

---

[1]   Vgl. Refl. 5619, Refl. 5413, Refl. 5441.

tion in ihrem Kontext in GMS II konsequent gedacht.[2] So bestimmt Kant dort den Willen als das Vermögen der Ableitung der Handlungsvorstellung und der Handlung aus Gesetzen der Vernunft, und diese Ableitung ist nichts anderes als eine Erkenntnis und damit ein Urteil über kausale Zusammenhänge, das selbst zur kausalen Ursache wird.[3] Es ist also die zunächst als Episteme in den Blick tretende Vernunft, welcher in einem zweiten Schritt die Eigenschaft zugesprochen wird, Kausalität auf die empirische Welt auszuüben. Damit ist es offenbar diese Episteme, welche die Freiheit der Vernunft ursprünglich konstituiert und dann im Handeln ihre Anwendung findet.

Ein Hinweis ist im Kontext des Erweises dieser epistemischen Freiheit schließlich noch wichtig: Die Willensfreiheit wird in der zweiten Sektion, wie Kant selbst wenig später schreibt, „als etwas Wirkliches *nicht* […] in […] der menschlichen Natur" (GMS, S. 448, m. H.) bewiesen. Die Sektion 2 hat also *nicht* die Aufgabe, die menschliche Willensfreiheit zu beweisen. Vielmehr geht es in dieser, allgemein gesprochen, darum, die begrifflichen Verhältnisse zu explizieren, auf deren Boden ein Erweis der Willensfreiheit allererst erfolgen kann. Den Erweis der menschlichen Willensfreiheit selbst entwickelt Kant erst in der Sektion 3 des Deduktionskapitels. Es wurde behauptet, Kant habe in der zweiten Sektion noch viel weniger gezeigt und meine, an dieser Stelle des Deduktionsgangs nicht einmal behaupten zu können, dass der Mensch ein vernünftiges Wesen sei. Das zeige Kant erst durch den Hinweis auf die Vernunft-

---

2   Der Passus lautet bekanntlich: „Ein jedes Ding der Natur wirkt nach Gesetzen. Nur ein vernünftiges Wesen hat das Vermögen, *nach der Vorstellung* der Gesetze, d. i. nach Principien, zu handeln, oder einen *Willen*. Da zur Ableitung der Handlungen von Gesetzen *Vernunft* erfordert wird, so ist der Wille nichts anderes als praktische Vernunft" (GMS, S. 412 f.).

3   Kant schreibt unmittelbar nach der ersten Willensdefinition in GMS II und der Bestimmung des Willens als praktische Vernunft (GMS, S. 412 f.) weiter: „Wenn die Vernunft den Willen unausbleiblich bestimmt, so sind die Handlungen eines solchen Wesens, die als objectiv nothwendig erkannt werden, auch subjectiv nothwendig, d. i. der Wille ist ein Vermögen, nur *dasjenige* zu wählen, was die Vernunft unabhängig von der Neigung als praktisch nothwendig, d. i. als gut erkennt" (ebd.). Die Wendung „als objectiv nothwendig *erkannt*" (m. H.) steht für die Funktion der *kognitiven* Ableitung der Handlung. Denn der Gegenstand einer Erkenntnis ist ein intersubjektiv zugänglicher Sachverhalt, bzw. eine durch Vernunft in ihrer Geltung intersubjektiv einsehbare und überprüfbare Regel. Und auf diese durch Vernunft gestiftete intersubjektive Zugänglichkeit verweist das Adjektiv „objectiv". Eine Erkenntnis ist nun in dem hier leitenden Sinne nicht als kausaler Vollzug, sondern vielmehr als rein kognitiver Prozess zu verstehen. Die ‚als notwendig erkannte Handlung' ist damit eine bloß kognitiv antizipierte. Objektiv ist also dasjenige, was vernünftigerweise willensbestimmend sein *sollte*. „Subjectiv" wäre dann das konative Moment derselben Vorstellung. Von einem Willensakt ist also dann die Rede, wenn die „als nothwendig erkannte" Handlung das wollende Subjekt tatsächlich zu einer entsprechenden Handlung veranlasst, also „subjectiv" bestimmend ist und damit Ursache eines tatsächlichen Kausalvollzuges wird.

ideen und damit an späterer Stelle im Deduktionsgang.[4] Ich denke, dass Kant umgekehrt die Vernünftigkeit qua Urteilsfähigkeit des Menschen voraussetzt, um überhaupt die beschriebene theoretisch-epistemische Freiheit begründen zu können, welche ihrerseits die Basis für den Erweis der denkmöglichen praktisch-transzendentalen Freiheit darstellt, aus der wiederum die Geltung des kategorischen Imperativs folgt. Wie Kant hier genau verfährt, soll in den folgenden Abschnitten eingehend nachgezeichnet werden.

II. Der Zirkel von Freiheit und Sittlichkeit

Kant formuliert in der nun thematischen dritten Sektion des Deduktionskapitels (GMS, S. 448–453) „eine Art von Cirkel": „Wir nehmen uns in der Ordnung der wirkenden Ursachen als frei an, um uns in der Ordnung der Zwecke unter sittlichen Gesetzen zu denken, und wir denken uns nachher als diesen Gesetzen unterworfen, weil wir uns die Freiheit des Willens beigelegt haben" (GMS, S. 450). Sowohl die Form als auch der Inhalt des Zirkels werden nach wie vor kontrovers diskutiert, und das zu Recht. Denn dieser „Cirkel" stellt in verschiedenen Hinsichten eine Gelenkstelle im Begründungsgang der Deduktion dar. Zum einen befindet sich hier, wie u. a. Reinhard Brandt (vgl. Brandt, 1988, S. 186) völlig zutreffend formuliert, der „Übergang von der Metaphysik der Sitten zur Kritik der reinen praktischen Vernunft", der dem gesamten Deduktionskapitel bekanntlich den Titel gibt. Zum anderen befindet sich im Zirkel auch eine Gelenkstelle im Argumentationsgang von der epistemischen zur praktisch-transzendentalen Freiheit. Bevor diese zentralen Funktionen des Zirkels verstanden werden können, muss zunächst ein wenig Vorarbeit geleistet werden.

Im Passus der Sektion 3, der zur ersten Zirkelformulierung führt (es gibt zwei Formulierungen), finden sich einige Aussagen, in deren Licht der Zirkel erst adäquat interpretiert werden kann. Im ersten Satz der dritten Sektion betont Kant, wie gesehen, dass Kant im vorhergehenden Begründungsgang der Deduktion, also auch in der Sektion 2, Willensfreiheit „als etwas Wirkliches nicht [...] in uns selbst und der menschlichen Natur beweisen" (GMS, S. 448 f.) konnte. Nachdem Kant im Anschluss nochmals die Analytizitätsthese komprimiert wiederholt, nun mit dem Fokus auf der analytischen Verbindung von Freiheit und *kategorischem Imperativ*, liest man eine im zur Analyse stehenden Kontext bemerkenswerte Frage: „Warum aber soll ich mich denn diesem Princip unterwerfen [...]?" (GMS, S. 449), wobei mit dem „Princip" der katego-

---

[4]   Schönecker vertritt die Ansicht, erst mit dem Nachweis, dass der Mensch über Ideen verfügt, sei seine Vernünftigkeit gezeigt, also erst mit dem neunten Absatz der dritten Sektion in GMS III (vgl. Schönecker, 1999, S. 319).

rische Imperativ gemeint ist. Zunächst ist diese Frage bemerkenswert, weil sie sich prima facie aus dem bisherigen Begründungsgang der dritten Sektion gar nicht ergibt. Und in der Tat ist sie wohl eher als Hinleitung zu der nun folgenden Behandlung des moralischen Interesses zu deuten: „Ich will einräumen, daß mich hiezu kein Interesse treibt, denn das würde keinen kategorischen Imperativ geben; aber ich muß doch hieran nothwendig ein Interesse nehmen und einsehen, wie das zugeht" (ebd.). Dass der Mensch ein moralisches Interesse nehmen muss, kann auch so ausgedrückt werden, dass es objektiv zwingende Gründe gibt, aus denen er nicht umhin kann, moralisch zu wollen. Und dieses anzunehmende notwendige moralische Interesse folgt aus dem Begriff des kategorischen Imperativs, wie jeder Imperativ seine Geltung aus einem bestehenden Interesse gewinnt (vgl. GMS, S. 413 f.; GMS, S. 414 Anm.). Der nächste, für unser Thema relevante Satz dieses Passus lautet: „Es scheint also, als setzten wir in der Idee der Freiheit eigentlich das moralische Gesetz [...] nur voraus und könnten seine Realität und objective Nothwendigkeit nicht für sich beweisen" (ebd.). Das, was in diesem Satz einiges Kopfzerbrechen bereitet, ist das eine zusammenfassende Schlussfolgerung anzeigende „also" („Es scheint *also* [...]" m. H.). Denn es ist zunächst alles andere als einleuchtend, weshalb gerade *das*, also dass wir in der Idee der Freiheit das moralische Gesetz bloß voraussetzen, oder zumindest der entsprechende Verdacht, aus dem vorhergehenden Begründungsgang geschlussfolgert werden sollte.

Machen wir uns deshalb den Hauptbegründungsgang der ersten vier Sätze nochmals klar: Der erste Satz betont, dass Freiheit des Willens bisher noch nicht erwiesen wurde. Satz 2 wiederholt die Analytizitätsthese. Satz 3 kann als Einleitung zur These verstanden werden, die in Satz 4 formuliert wird: das Sollen ist Ausdruck des rein vernünftigen Interesses sinnlich-vernünftiger Wesen. Die Aussagen 2–4 folgen nun aus der Analytizitätsthese, dem Begriff von Moralität, demjenigen eines Imperativs überhaupt und dem kantischen Begriff des Interesses und stehen bereits vor der zweiten Sektion fest und nach dieser ist für Kant, wie er selbst es formuliert, die menschliche Willensfreiheit noch *nicht* erwiesen. Nehmen wir noch die in der zweiten Sektion formulierte Implikation der Begriffe *Wille* und *Freiheit* hinzu, dann scheint Kant darauf verweisen zu wollen, dass auf dem bloßen Wege der Explikation eben solcher begrifflicher Implikationen ein Beweis der menschlichen Freiheit nicht zu führen ist. Kurzum: Der „Übergang von der Metaphysik der Sitten zur Kritik der reinen praktischen Vernunft" wurde noch nicht vollzogen. Denn die „Metaphysik der Sitten" ist der Teil der „bloße[n] Zergliederung der Begriffe der Sittlichkeit" (GMS, S. 440) in der *Grundlegung*. Weil Kant also zu Anfang der dritten Sektion betont, dass die Freiheit des menschlichen Willens (und damit ein menschlicher Wille überhaupt) noch nicht erwiesen sei, und weil er in den folgenden drei Sätzen nichts anderes tut als bereits erreichte Ergebnisse über begriffliche Implikationen nochmals auszuführen, scheint es *also* in der Tat, „als setzten wir [...] das moralische Gesetz [...] nur voraus und könnten seine Realität [...] nicht für sich beweisen [...]". Dieser Befund verweist direkt auf den Zirkel und wird durch ihn gestützt.

Im „Cirkel" erweitert Kant seine Behauptung der Unzulänglichkeit des bisherigen begriffsanalytischen Begründungsgangs um einen weiteren Aspekt. Hier zunächst nochmals die erste Formulierung des Zirkels: „Es zeigt sich hier [...] eine Art von Cirkel, aus dem, wie es scheint, nicht heraus zu kommen ist. Wir nehmen uns in der Ordnung der wirkenden Ursachen als frei an, *um* [also zum *Zwecke*] uns in der Ordnung der Zwecke unter sittlichen Gesetzen zu denken" (GMS, S. 450, m. H.). Im Zirkel wird also der Verdacht formuliert, der Zweck der Annahme der menschlichen Willensfreiheit sei es, sich „unter sittlichen Gesetzen zu denken". Von hieraus lässt sich auch der argumentationsstrategische Sinn des Zirkels einsehen, der auf ähnliche Weise von Reinhard Brandt vorgestellt wurde.[5] Betrachtet man bloß die „Metaphysik der Sitten", und nicht die auf sie folgende „Kritik der reinen praktischen Vernunft", könnte einem aufmerksamen Leser der Verdacht kommen, alle relevanten Begriffe, allen voran der Begriff des Willens und der Freiheit, seien so definiert, wie Kant dies tut, *damit* Sittlichkeit aus dem Begriff eines Willens überhaupt folge, wie dies in der zweiten Sektion von GMS III vorgeführt wird. Der (annähernd) gesamte begriffliche Apparat der *Grundlegung* sei also so konstruiert, dass er zwangsläufig auf die Analytizität von Freiheit und Sittlichkeit und diejenige von Willen und Freiheit hinauslaufe. Dies würde erklären, weshalb Kant im Zirkel den Verdacht formuliert, die Freiheitsannahme geschehe, *um, also zu dem Zwecke*, uns unter sittliche Gesetze denken zu können. Ein Ausweg aus dem Zirkel muss also zeigen, dass es andere Gründe für die Annahme der mensch-

---

5   Vgl. Brand, 1988, S 186: „Man versuche, so der kantische Gedankengang, eben dies [die Realität des Sittengesetzes für den Menschen] aus den Begriffen herzuleiten, die bisher analysiert wurden – der Versuch gerät in einen Zirkel". Allerdings paraphrasiert Brandt die Zirkelformulierung Kants nicht ganz zutreffend: „Wir sind frei, weil wir dem Gesetz unterworfen sind, und: wir sind dem Gesetz unterworfen, weil wir frei sind". Es scheint auch, als bürde Brandt dem Zirkel eine zu große argumentationsstrategische Last auf, indem dieser zeigen soll, dass eine Moraltheorie überhaupt, die den Überschritt zu einer „Kritik der reinen praktischen Vernunft" nicht macht, sich zwangsläufig in Aporien verfange (vgl. ebd.). Beiden Positionen, meiner und Brandts, gemein ist die Annahme, dass der Zirkel die Aufgabe hat, die Notwendigkeit des Übergangs zur „Kritik der reinen praktischen Vernunft" deutlich zu machen. Vgl. auch Henrich, 1975, S. 70 f.: „Kant erläutert den Zirkelverdacht auf eine Weise, welche die Lösung, die er anstrebt, schon vorbereitet: Es wäre ganz offensichtlich, daß wir die Realität der Freiheit bloß wegen der ‚schon vorausgesetzten Wichtigkeit moralischer Gesetze' annehmen, wenn wir ausschließlich zu dem Zwecke, sittliche Gesetze für real halten zu können, zwei Ordnungen und dann zwei Welten voneinander unterscheiden würden". Henrich gibt hier den Begründungsgang nicht ganz zutreffend wieder, denn Kant schreibt in seiner ersten Nennung der Lehre der zwei Standpunkte in der dritten Sektion, (genauer zu Anfang der „Auskunft"), die Funktion zu, einen *Ausweg* aus dem Zirkel zu liefern, diese wird *im* Zirkel gar nicht erwähnt.

lichen Willensfreiheit gibt als den bloßen Wunsch, uns unter moralischen Gesetzen denken zu können. Diese Gründe müssen damit zwangsläufig *nicht-moralischer* Natur sein.[6]

III. Die „Auskunft" und Kants Ideenlehre

Der Ausweg aus dem Zirkel, von Kant „Auskunft" genannt, besteht zentral aus der angekündigten Entwicklung der menschlichen Willensfreiheit aus der theoretisch-epistemischen. Die „Auskunft" stellt weitgehend nichts anderes als eine komprimierte Version der Auflösung der dritten Antinomie in der *Ersten Kritik*

---

[6]   Allison gibt den Sinn des Zirkels ganz im Sinne der geleisteten Interpretation wieder, wenn er schreibt: „Thus, the [...] inference to which Kant refers is from the presupposition of freedom to standing under moral laws and the problem is that there is no independent grounding for this presupposition, not that this grounding is provided by the presumption that rational beings stand under moral laws". Entsprechend schreibt er zur logischen Form des Zirkels zutreffend „that the fallacy to which Kant is alluding is a petition prinzipii rather than a circulus in probando (a circular argument)" (Allison, 2011, S. 314).
Es wurde in den bisherigen Erläuterungen deutlich, dass der Zirkelverdacht sich auf den Begründungsgang der ersten beiden Sektionen vom GMS III bezieht, wenn nicht sogar auch auf weite Teile des zweiten Abschnitts der Schrift. Rekapituliert man den Hauptstrang der Argumentation der ersten beiden Sektionen des dritten Abschnitts, wird recht schnell deutlich, welche Art von Zirkel Kant höchst wahrscheinlich meint. Denn in Sektion 1 wird von der Freiheit als kausalem Vermögen, also aus Freiheit „in der Ordnung der wirkenden Ursachen" über Autonomie auf Sittlichkeit geschlossen, welchen Schluss den Gedanken der Analytizitätsthese darstellt. In der zweiten Sektion wird nun ein Freiheitsbeweis geführt, den man für einen Beweis der menschlichen Freiheit halten könnte, nämlich dann, wenn man die praktische Vernünftigkeit des Menschen schon voraussetzt. Wir haben es also in den ersten beiden Sektionen von GMS III im ersten Schritt mit einem Schluss von kausaler Freiheit auf Sittlichkeit und im zweiten Schritt mit einem – vermeintlichen – Beweis der menschlichen Willensfreiheit zu tun. Wie geschildert, deutet Kant dies zu dem Verdacht um, der Freiheitsbegriff könnte so entwickelt worden sein, wie es geschehen ist, *damit* Sittlichkeit aus diesem folge. Handelte es sich um einen *circulus in probando*, müsste – wie auch immer – ein Schluss von praktisch-transzendentaler Freiheit auf Sittlichkeit erfolgen und dann der umgekehrte Weg eingeschlagen werden, nämlich der ‚Erweis' der Freiheit aus dem sittlichen Vermögen des Menschen. Der zweite Schritt findet sich aber nicht. Stattdessen betont Kant unmittelbar im Anschluss an die zweite Sektion, dass wir Freiheit „als etwas Wirkliches nicht einmal in uns und in der menschlichen Natur beweisen" (GMS, S. 448 f.) konnten. Es kann sich folglich nicht um einen *circulus in probando* handeln, sondern muss sich vielmehr, eine dritte Alternative ausschließend, um eine *petitio principii* handeln. Ziehen wir Meiers Definition einer *petitio principii* heran, die Kant in seiner Logik-Vorlesung zugrundegelegt hat, wird auch deutlich, welches Prinzip „erbeten" ist: Denn Freiheit bzw. die Behauptung ihrer Realität ist der ‚Vordersatz [...] welcher ebenso ungewiss ist', wie die Behauptung der Geltung des Sittengesetzes für den Menschen. Die „erbettelten Beweisthümer" betreffen damit die Freiheit und diese ist das erbetene Prinzip (vgl. Meier, 1752, S. 774).

dar. Die dritte Antinomie nebst ihrer Auflösung wird weiter unten noch ausführlicher besprochen. Doch zunächst soll der Argumentationsgang der „Auskunft" skizziert werden, der mit folgendem Satz beginnt: „Eine Auskunft bleibt uns aber noch übrig, nämlich zu suchen: ob wir, wenn wir uns durch Freiheit als a priori wirkende Ursache denken, nicht einen anderen Standpunkt einnehmen, als wenn wir uns selbst nach unseren Handlungen als Wirkungen, die wir vor unseren Augen sehen, uns vorstellen" (GMS, S. 450). Die Rede vom „anderen Standpunkt" verweist auf das in Sektion drei entwickelte Theorem der Verstandes- oder intelligiblen Welt im Unterschied zur Sinnenwelt. Ganz allgemein gesprochen ist Kant der Auffassung, dass zur Erklärung der Gegenstände in Raum und Zeit sowie der raumzeitlichen Ordnung selbst zwei Arten von Kausalität und der durch sie verknüpften Dinge gedacht werden müssen: Einmal ist es die naturkausale Ordnung, und dann ist es die Kausalität auf Freiheit und die durch diese konstituierte Ordnung. Kant nennt diese beiden Ordnungen auch die „Sinnenwelt" und die „Verstandeswelt" bzw. „intelligible Welt". Es wird sich zeigen, dass der Erweis der menschlichen Willensfreiheit zentral in der Übertragung der Lehre der zwei Welten bzw. zwei Standpunkte auf das menschliche Handeln besteht.

Der Weg dorthin und damit die „Auskunft" beginnt damit, dass Kant seine berühmte Unterscheidung von Ding an sich und Erscheinung – und damit implizit diejenige von noumenaler und phänomenaler Ordnung – an die jeweiligen epistemischen Vermögen der Spontaneität und Sinnlichkeit bindet: Die sinnlich-passiven Vorstellungen ergeben nur „Erscheinungen", und wir gelangen durch diese „niemals" zur Erkenntnis „der Dinge an sich selbst" (GMS, S. 451), welche die Elemente der Verstandeswelt bzw. noumenalen Ordnung bilden.[7] Im nächsten Schritt wird diese Unterscheidung der verschiedenen Ordnungen (und der beigeordneten epistemischen Vermögen) auf die menschliche Subjektivität angewendet.[8] Auch bei uns selbst liefert unsere „innere Empfin-

<hr>

[7]   Vgl. GMS, S. 450 f.: „Es ist eine Bemerkung, welche anzustellen [...] kein subtiles Nachdenken erfordert [...]: daß alle Vorstellungen, die uns ohne unsere Willkür kommen (wie die der Sinne), uns die Gegenstände nicht anders zu erkennen geben, als sie uns afficiren[...] mithin, daß [...] wir dadurch [...] bloß zur Erkenntnis der *Erscheinungen*, niemals der *Dinge an sich selbst* gelangen können. Sobald dieser Unterschied [...] ([...] zwischen den Vorstellungen, die uns anders woher gegeben werden, [...] von denen, die wir lediglich aus uns selbst hervorbringen, und dabei wir unsere Thätigkeit beweisen) einmal gemacht ist, so folgt von selbst, daß man hinter den Erscheinungen doch noch etwas anderes, was nicht Erscheinung ist, nämlich die Dinge an sich, einräumen [...] müsse, ob wir gleich [...] was sie an sich sind, niemals wissen können".

[8]   Vgl. GMS, S. 451: „Sogar sich selbst [...] nach der Kenntniß, die der Mensch durch innere Empfindung von sich hat, darf er sich nicht anmaßen zu erkennen, wie er an sich selbst sei. [...] [I]ndessen er doch nothwendiger Weise über diese aus lauter Erscheinungen zusammengesetze Beschaffenheit seines eigenen Subjects noch etwas anderes zum Grunde Liegendes, nämlich sein Ich, so wie es an sich selbst beschaffen sein mag, annehmen und sich also [...] in Ansehung dessen [...], was in ihm reine

dung" nur eine „aus lauter Erscheinungen zusammengesetzte Beschaffenheit" des „eigenen Subjects", also das empirische Selbst, und somit kein „Ich, so wie es an sich selbst beschaffen sein mag" (ebd.). Dann wird der Nachweis geführt, dass der Mensch tatsächlich über (rein) spontan-apperzeptive Vorstellungen verfügt, die Vernunftideen. Das geschieht im neunten Absatz der dritten Sektion und wird unten ausführlich behandelt. Nun folgen zwei Schritte, die von Kant nicht hinreichend kenntlich gemacht werden, die sich aber aus dem Begründungsgang und der Textgrundlage ergeben: Die Vernunft ist genötigt, sowohl eine phänomenale als auch noumenale Ordnung anzunehmen, um sich selbst in ihrer epistemischen Spontaneität konsistent denken zu können, wobei in der Sicht Kants die Entwicklung dieser konsistenten Selbstsicht das „vornehmste Geschäft" (KrV, A XI) der Vernunft ausmacht. Im letzten Schritt wird die Lehre der zwei Standpunkte auf das menschliche Handeln übertragen: Aufgrund der in den Vernunftideen sich ausdrückenden Spontaneität und um willen der konsistenten Selbstsicht der Vernunft ist der Mensch berechtig und sogar genötigt, sich „zwei Standpunkte, daraus es sich selbst betrachten und Gesetze des Gebrauchs seiner Kräfte, folglich aller seiner Handlungen erkennen kann", (GMS, S. 452) zuzuschreiben. Wie angekündigt, kann die soeben skizzierte „Auskunft" nur mit Rekurs auf die Antinomienlehre der *Kritik der reinen Vernunft* verstanden werden.

Kants Ideenlehre in der Kritik der reinen Vernunft

In der transzendentalen Dialektik werden nicht bloß die Ideen der Vernunft aus ihrer Verfahrensweise als Vermögen des Schlussfolgerns entwickelt. Zugleich ist die transzendentale Dialektik – deswegen auch der Titel „Logik des Scheins" – der Ort, an dem die Illusionen der speziellen Metaphysik, namentlich der rationalen Psychologie, Kosmologie und Theologie als *notwendige* Illusionen aus der Konstitution der epistemischen Vernunft selbst entwickelt werden. Bevor wir zur Rolle der Zwei-Welten-Lehre im Zusammenhang mit den Ideen kommen, soll zunächst zumindest grob geklärt werden, wie diese Ideen aus der Vernunft als Schussfolgerungsvermögen entwickelt werden. Vernunft wird von Kant als „Vermögen der Principien" bezeichnet, genauer als Vermögen der „Erkenntnis aus Principien, [...] da ich das Besondere im Allgemeinen durch Begriffe erkenne" (KrV, A 300/B 357). Die Subsumtion des Untersatzes (Minor), der besonderen Erkenntnis, unter die allgemeine Regel (Major) geschieht nicht durch die Vernunft im engeren Sinne (als Urteilsvermögen), sondern durch die Urteilskraft. Ist aber diese Subsumtion gegeben, so formuliert die Vernunft aufgrund bloßer

---

Thätigkeit sein mag, (dessen, was gar nicht durch Afficirung der Sinne, sondern unmittelbar zum Bewußtsein gelangt) sich zur *intellektuellen Welt* zählen muß, die er doch nicht weiter kennt".

begrifflicher Implikationen von Major und Minor die Conclusio. Kant nimmt bekanntlich drei Vernunftschlüsse an: Den *kategorischen Vernunftschluss*, den man durch folgendes Schema wiedergeben kann: „A ist (bzw. ist nicht) B". Den *hypothetische Vernunftschluss*, der sich durch die Form auszeichnet: „Wenn etwas gesetzt ist, so ist etwas anderes gesetzt und umgekehrt". Und schließlich den *disjunktiven Vernunftschluss*: „A ist entweder B oder C".

Ein Obersatz kann nun seinerseits als Konklusion eines höherstufigeren Syllogismus verstanden werden und der Vernunftschluss sucht nun zu diesem Besonderen das Allgemeine bzw. die allgemeine Regel. Hier verfährt die Vernunft, im Ausgang von durch den Verstand gegebenen Regeln, nach dem Grundsatz „zu dem bedingten Erkenntnisse des Verstandes das Unbedingte zu finden, womit die Einheit desselben vollendet wird" (KrV, A 307/B 364). Kant nennt diesen Grundsatz, nach den (letzten) Bedingungen des gegebenen Bedingten zu suchen, die „logische Maxime" (ebd.). Diese sich aus dem rein logischen Gebrauch der Vernunft ergebende Maxime wird nun zu einem *synthetischen* Grundsatz durch die Annahme: „[W]enn das Bedingte gegeben ist, so sei auch die ganze Reihe einander untergeordneter Bedingungen, die mithin selbst unbedingt ist, gegeben" (ebd.). Diese Annahme des Gegebenseins der Totalität der gesamten Reihe der Bedingungen ist deswegen synthetisch, weil zwar „das Bedingte [...] sich analytisch [...] auf irgend eine Bedingung, aber *nicht* aufs Unbedingte" (KrV, A 308/B 364, m. H.) bezieht. *Dass* es also die letzte, unbedingte Bedingung zu gegebenem Bedingten bzw. die gesamte Reihe der Bedingungen gibt, folgt nicht analytisch aus der Vorstellung eines Bedingten überhaupt.

Der dialektische Schein und die unzulässige Erweiterung des Vernunftgebrauchs über die Erfahrungsgrenzen hinaus ergibt sich nun weiter aus der so zu nennenden ‚Ontologisierung' des von der Vernunft in synthetischem Gebrauch geforderten Unbedingten. Das, was zunächst bloß eine Forderung der Vernunft in ihrem logischen Gebrauch ist, erhält nun den Status einer Realität. Die Idee der Vernunft ist eben dieser mit einer Existenzbehauptung verbundene „Begriff des Unbedingten, so fern er einen Grund der Synthesis des Bedingten enthält" (KrV, A 322/B 379). Auf der Basis des jeweiligen Vernunftschlusses (kategorisch, hypothetisch, disjunktiv) ergeben sich die jeweiligen transzendentalen Ideen, die ihrerseits nichts anderes als transzendent gedachte Kategorien sind: „die absolute [...] Einheit des denkenden Subjects [Seele]", „die absolute Einheit der Reihe der Bedingungen der Erscheinungen [Welt]", „die absolute Einheit der Bedingungen aller Gegenstände des Denkens überhaupt [Gott]" (KrV, A 334/B 391).

Die dritte kosmologische Idee und ihre Antinomie

Im Abschnitt „System der kosmologischen Ideen" (KrV, A 408–421/B 435–448) schält Kant, unter der Kautele, dass die Ideen eine Totalität der *zeitlich* voraus liegenden Bedingungen zu einem gegebenen Bedingten darstellen sollen, aus den vier Kategorienklassen die kosmologischen Ideen heraus.[9] Diese sind in der Tafel der kosmologischen Ideen festgehalten.[10] Wie bereits erwähnt, sind die transzendentalen Ideen nichts anderes als „über die Grenzen des Empirischen" (KrV, A 409/B 435) hinaus erweiterte Kategorien. Kant präzisiert im Abschnitt „System der kosmologischen Ideen" diesen Gedanken:

> „Um nun diese [kosmologischen] Ideen nach einem Princip mit systematischer Präcision aufzählen zu können, müssen wir Erstlich bemerken, daß nur der Verstand es sei, aus welchem reine und transscendentale Begriffe entspringen können, daß die Vernunft eigentlich gar keine Begriffe erzeuge, sondern allenfalls nur den Verstandesbegriff [...] über die Grenzen des Empirischen [...] zu erweitern suche. Dieses geschieht dadurch, daß sie zu einem gegebenen Bedingten auf der Seite der Bedingungen (unter denen der Verstand alle Erscheinungen der synthetischen Einheit unterwirft) absolute Totalität fordert und dadurch die Kategorie zu transscendentalen Idee macht, um der empirischen Synthesis durch die Fortsetzung derselben bis zum Unbedingten [...] absolute Vollständigkeit zu geben" (KrV, A 408 f./ B 435 f.).

So wird aus der Kategorie der Kausalität, „welche eine Reihe der Ursachen zu einer gegebenen Wirkung darbietet", im Lichte der geforderten „absoluten Totalität" (KrV, A 414/B 441 f.) der Bedingungen die dritte kosmologische Idee: „Die absolute Vollständigkeit der Entstehung einer Erscheinung überhaupt" (KrV, A 415/B 443). Die Vernunft zeigt „unter dem Namen der Ideen" also eine „reine Selbstthätigkeit", die „über den Verstand erhoben" (GMS, S. 452) ist, weil die Ideen zwar ursprünglich Verstandesbegriffe sind, die Vernunft aber, im Unterschied zum Verstand, der vermittels der Anschauungen seine Regeln anwendet, in den Ideen Vorstellungen generiert, denen kein möglicher empirischer Sachverhalt mehr korrespondiert.

Bekanntlich ist die dritte kosmologische Idee samt ihrer Antinomie für die Moralphilosophie Kants von besonderer Bedeutung, wird in ihrer Auflösung doch die Denkmöglichkeit von praktisch-transzendentaler Freiheit eröffnet. Eine Antinomie besteht aus zwei sich widersprechenden Sätzen (Thesis und Antithesis), für die sich in der Sicht Kants jeweils konsistente Beweise führen lassen. Es seien nun die Thesis und Antithesis der dritten Antinomie genannt und ganz komprimiert ihr jeweiliger Beweis: *Thesis*: „Die Causalität nach Gesetzen der Natur ist nicht die einzige, aus welcher die Erscheinungen der

---

9   Im Falle der „Synthesis der mannigfaltigen Theile des Raumes" (KrV, A 412/B 439), bezogen auf die Sukzession der „Synthesis [...], wodurch wir ihn apprehendiren" (ebd.).

10 Diese sind: „Die Zusammensetzung des gegebenen Ganzen aller Erscheinungen", die „Vollständigkeit der Theilung eines gegebenen Ganzen in der Erscheinung", die „absolute Vollständigkeit der Entstehung einer Erscheinung überhaupt", die „absolute Vollständigkeit der Abhängigkeit des Daseins des Veränderlichen in der Erscheinung" (KrV, A 415/B 443).

Welt insgesammt abgeleitet werden können. Es ist noch eine Causalität durch Freiheit zu Erklärung derselben anzunehmen nothwendig" (KrV, A 444/B 472).

Der *Beweis* kann folgendermaßen zusammengefasst werden: Falls es nur Naturkausalität gibt, ist die naturkausale Reihe nie abgeschlossen, und es gibt also keinen hinreichenden Grund für die gesamte Reihe. Denn jeder Zustand der Ursache ist seinerseits gewirkt und in Hinsicht auf seine Wirkung kein für sich hinreichender Grund. Das Naturgesetz verlangt aber, „daß ohne hinreichend a priori bestimmte Ursache nichts geschehe" (KrV, A 446/B 474). Somit widerspricht das Naturgesetz als alleiniges Kausalgesetz sich selbst und verweist auf eine erste hinreichende Ursache der gesamten Kausalreihe, die ihrerseits nicht bewirkt ist.

Antithesis: „Es ist keine Freiheit, sondern alles in der Welt geschieht lediglich nach Gesetzen der Natur" (KrV, A 445/B 473). Der *Beweis* der Antithesis lässt sich folgendermaßen wiedergeben: Freiheit als „ein Vermögen, einen Zustand […] schlechthin anzufangen", wird von Kant im Beweis der Antithesis dahingehend interpretiert, dass „die Causalität, […] schlechthin anfangen [muss], so daß nichts vorhergeht, wodurch diese geschehende Handlung [der freien Ursache] nach beständigen Gesetzen bestimmt sei" (ebd.). Dass etwas, wenn es frei ist, Ursache ist, kann in keiner Weise aus Vorhergehendem mit Rekurs auf eine gesetzliche Regel erklärt werden. Das gilt natürlich nur unter der Voraussetzung, dass Kausalität identisch mit *Natur*kausalität ist. Und hierin liegt auch die Pointe des Beweises der Antithesis: Ist eine gesetzlose Kausalität nicht denkbar und ist das Naturgesetz das einzig zur Verfügung stehende Kausalgesetz, widerspricht der Begriff einer Kausalität aus Freiheit sich selbst.[11]

Die Antinomie besteht also darin, so könnte man sagen, dass um die Widersprüchlichkeit einer rein naturkausalen Erklärung der Erscheinungen zu vermeiden, etwas gefordert ist, das seinerseits, auf der Basis bloßer Geltung des Gesetzes der Naturkausalität, widersprüchlich oder gar sinnlos ist – eine Kausalität aus Freiheit.

Der bereits in der Analytik der KrV entwickelte transzendentale Idealismus, das heißt die Lehre von der Idealität von Raum und Zeit und die sich hieraus ergebende Annahme, „daß alles, was im Raume oder der Zeit angeschauet wird, mithin alle Gegenstände einer uns möglichen Erfahrung nichts als Erscheinung, d. i. bloße Vorstellungen, sind" (KrV, A 490 f./B 518 f.), soll die Antinomie bekanntlich überwinden. Denn seine theoretische Folge bildet die Annahme einer

---

[11] In diesem Sinne schreibt Kant wenig später: „Also ist die transscendentale Freiheit dem Causalgesetze entgegen und eine solche Verbindung der sucessiven Zustände wirkender Ursachen, nach welchen keine Einheit der Erfahrung möglich ist, […] mithin ein leeres Gedankending […]. Die Freiheit (Unabhängigkeit) von den Gesetzen der Natur ist […] eine Befreiung vom […] Leitfaden aller Regeln, […]. Natur also und transscendentale Freiheit unterscheiden sich wie Gesetzmäßigkeit und Gesetzlosigkeit" (KrV, A 445 f./B 473).

(intellektuellen) Kausalität einer noumenalen Ordnung auf die phänomenale. Hierdurch ist es möglich, die Einheit der Naturkausalität zu wahren und trotzdem die These zur Geltung zu bringen, wonach Naturkausalität zur Erklärung der Erscheinungen insgesamt nicht hinreicht, sondern eine Kausalität aus Freiheit fordert. Somit kann eine Kausalität aus Freiheit in Ansatz gebracht werden, ohne dass aus dieser Gegenstände *in der Zeit* erklärt werden müssen – und könnten. Sind nämlich alle Erscheinungen in Raum und Zeit bloße Vorstellungen, dann fordern die Erscheinungen überhaupt einen „transscendentale[n] Gegenstand" (KrV, A 538/B 566), der sie als Vorstellungen bestimmt. Innerhalb dieser Ordnung der Erscheinungen ist die Geltung des ‚Verstandesgesetzes der Naturkausalität' damit ungebrochen. Doch diese gesamte naturkausale Ordnung der Erscheinungen bedarf ihrerseits – als Ordnung bloßer Vorstellungen – einer Begründung. Das entscheidende Argument gegen die Thesis, dass durch das Ansetzen eine Kausalität aus Freiheit Erscheinungen nicht mehr erklärt werden könnten, ist somit außer Kraft.

Bereits im Abschnitt „Der transscendentale Idealismus als der Schlüssel zu Auflösung der kosmologischen Dialektik" (KrV, A 490–497/B 518–525) überträgt Kant die Lehre des transzendentalen Idealismus auf die menschliche Subjektivität: „Jener Raum selber aber sammt dieser Zeit und zugleich mit beiden alle Erscheinungen sind doch an sich keine Dinge, sondern nichts als Vorstellungen [...]; und selbst ist die innere und sinnliche Anschauung unseres Gemüths [...] auch nicht das eigentliche Selbst, so wie es an sich existirt" (KrV, A 492/B 520). In diesem Abschnitt findet sich auch schon die Zuordnung der (passiven) Rezeptivität der Sinnlichkeit zu den Erscheinungen. Im Abschnitt „Erläuterung der cosmologischen Idee einer Freiheit in Verbindung mit der allgemeinen Naturnothwendigkeit" (KrV, A 542–557/B 570–586) schließlich formuliert Kant die Zuordnung rein spontaner Vernunftvollzüge zur noumenalen Subjektivität und die These des reinen spontanen Ursprungs der Vernunftideen.

> „Allein der Mensch, der die ganze Natur sonst lediglich nur durch Sinne kennt, erkennt sich selbst auch durch bloße Apperception und zwar in Handlungen und inneren Bestimmungen, die er gar nicht zum Eindrucke der Sinne zählen kann, und ist sich selbst freilich eines Theils Phänomen, andern Theils aber, nämlich in Ansehung gewisser Vermögen, ein bloß intelligibler Gegenstand, weil die Handlung desselben gar nicht zur Receptivität der Sinnlichkeit gezählt werden kann. Wir nennen diese Vermögen Verstand und Vernunft; vornehmlich wird die letztere ganz eigentlich und vorzüglicher Weise von allen empirisch bedingten Kräften unterschieden, da sie ihre Gegenstände bloß nach Ideen erwägt und den Verstand darnach bestimmt, der denn von seinen (zwar auch reinen) Begriffen einen empirischen Gebrauch macht" (KrV, A 546 f./B 574 f.).

Nimmt man alles zusammen – die durch den transzendentalen Idealismus gedachte ontologische Fundierung der phänomenalen durch die noumenale Ordnung, die Übertragung dieses Ordnungsverhältnisses auf die menschliche Subjektivität und schließlich die Zuordnung der spontan-apperzeptiven Vollzüge der Vernunft zur noumenalen, der rezeptiv-passiven zur phänomenalen Subjektivität –, dann kann die sich vom sechsten bis zum einschließlich elften Absatz erstreckende „Auskunft" der dritten Sektion (GMS III) weitgehend als eine Zusammenfassung der Hauptgedanken der Auflösung der dritten Antinomie gelesen werden. Da die Antinomie von Kant als „Veruneinigung" der Vernunft „mit sich selbst" (KrV, A 464/B 492) gesehen wird, die in einem vorkritischen Stadium unvermeidbar ist, und da einzig der transzendentale Idealismus und die aus ihm folgende Zwei-Welten-Lehre den Ausweg aus diesem aporetischen Zustand der Vernunft selbst weist, kann das Antinomienkapitel als das Zentrum des gesamten kritischen Geschäfts der Vernunft angesehen werden.

Die Spontaneität der Vernunft und ihr „vornehmstes Geschäft"

Es sollte nun möglich sein, die letzten Schritte der Auskunft und damit Kants Übergang von der theoretischen zur praktisch-transzendentalen Freiheit nachvollziehen zu können. Hierzu sei zunächst der neunte Absatz der dritten Sektion in toto zitiert:

> „Nun findet der Mensch in sich wirklich ein Vermögen, dadurch er sich von allen andern Dingen, ja von sich selbst, so fern er durch Gegenstände afficirt wird, unterscheidet, und das ist die *Vernunft*. Diese, als reine Selbstthätigkeit, ist sogar darin noch über den *Verstand* erhoben: daß, obgleich dieser auch Selbstthätigkeit ist und nicht wie der Sinn bloß Vorstellungen enthält, die nur entspringen, wenn man von Dingen afficirt (mithin leidend) ist, er dennoch aus seiner Thätigkeit keine andere[n] Begriffe hervorbringen kann als die, so bloß dazu dienen, um die *sinnlichen Vorstellungen unter Regeln zu bringen* und sie dadurch in einem Bewußtsein zu vereinigen, ohne welchen Gebrauch der Sinnlichkeit er gar nichts denken würde, da hingegen die Vernunft unter dem Namen der Ideen eine so große Spontaneität zeigt, dass er dadurch weit über alles, was ih[m] Sinnlichkeit nur liefern kann, hinausgeht und ihr vornehmstes Geschäft darin beweiset, Sinnenwelt und Verstandeswelt voneinander zu unterscheiden, dadurch aber dem Verstande selbst seine Schranken vorzuzeichnen" (GMS, S. 452).

Die Rede vom „Vermögen", durch welches sich der Mensch „von sich [...] selbst, so fern er durch Gegenstände afficirt wird, unterscheidet", ist das Vermögen der vorher thematischen „reinen Thätigkeit", die „gar nicht durch Afficirzung der Sinne, sondern unmittelbar zum Bewußtsein gelangt" (GMS, S. 451). Denn diese „reine Thätigkeit" wird dem „Ich, so wie es an sich selbst beschaffen sein mag" (ebd.), zugeordnet. Die ‚reine Thätigkeit' wird in Absatz 9 dann auch präzisierend ‚reine Selbstthätigkeit' und ‚reine Spontaneität' genannt.

Wie gesehen, sind die Ideen der Vernunft nichts anderes, als über den Erfahrungsgebrauch hinaus erweiterte Kategorien des Verstandes. Insofern ist es der *Verstand*, der „über alles, was ihm Sinnlichkeit nur liefern kann, hinausgeht". Die Vernunft, die „im Namen der Ideen" den Verstand über die Erfahrungsgrenzen hinaustreibt, ist zugleich diejenige, die ihm „seine Schranken" vorzeichnet, und zwar durch die Unterscheidung von Sinnen- und Verstandeswelt. Diese von Kant formulierte enge Verbindung von reinem Ausdruck der Spontaneität und der Beschränkung des Geltungsbereiches des Verstandes ist mit Blick auf die Antinomienlehre nun gut einsehbar. Die durch die Vernunft *rein spontan* hervorgebrachten Ideen führen im Falle der kosmologischen Ideen in eine Antinomie, deren Auflösung in der Sicht Kants einzig der transzendentale Idealismus und seine Folgetheoreme leisten können. Die Beschränkung des Verstandes, die bereits durch den Umstand geschieht, dass die Erweiterung seiner Begriffe über die Erfahrung hinaus eben in eine Dialektik bzw. Antinomie führt, wird, so könnte man sagen, durch die vermittels der Zwei-Welten-Lehre geleistete Auflösung zu Ende gedacht: Erst die Zwei-Welten-Lehre weist dem Verstand und seinem Gesetz der Naturkausalität endgültig seinen erkenntnistheoretischen Ort zu. Insofern kann Kant schreiben, dass durch die Unterscheidung von Sinnen- und Verstandeswelt dem *Verstand* seine Schranken vorgezeichnet werden. Somit hängen der reinste Ausdruck der Spontaneität der Vernunft, die Ideen, ihr ‚vornehmstes Geschäft' der Selbst- und Metaphysikkritik, das Einschränken der Verstandesbegriffe auf Erscheinungen, und schließlich die Eröffnung der Möglichkeit praktisch-transzendentaler Freiheit, direkt miteinander zusammen.[12]

Das wird gänzlich deutlich durch die Analyse desjenigen Passus von Sektion 3, in dem Kant die Zwei-Welten-Lehre auf das menschliche Handeln anwendet:

> „*Um deswillen* muß ein vernünftiges Wesen sich selbst als Intelligenz [...] zur Verstandeswelt gehörig [...] ansehen; mithin hat es zwei Standpunkte, daraus es sich selbst betrachten und Gesetze des Gebrauchs seiner Kräfte, folglich aller seiner Handlungen erkennen kann, einmal, sofern er zur Sinnenwelt gehört, unter Naturgesetzen (Heteronomie), zweitens, als zur intelligiblen Welt gehörig, unter Gesetzen, die, von der Natur unabhängig, nicht empirisch, sondern bloß in der Vernunft gegründet sind" (GMS, S. 452, m. H.).

Auffällig ist, dass der Satz mit „um deswillen" anfängt, was sogleich an den Zirkel denken lässt, in dessen erster Formulierung es heißt: „Wir nehmen uns in der Ordnung der wirkenden Ursachen als frei an, *um* uns in der Ordnung der Zwecke unter sittlichen Gesetze zu denken" (GMS, S. 450, m. H.). In der zwei-

---

[12] Vgl. zum Begriff des ‚vornehmsten Geschäfts' die Vorrede der A-Auflage der KrV, in der es heißt, dass „das beschwerlichste aller ihrer [der Vernunft] Geschäfte, [...] das der Selbsterkenntniß" der Vernunft sei, diese zugleich ein „Gerichtshof" und eben eine „Kritik der reinen Vernunft", also „eine Kritik [...] des Vernunftvermögens überhaupt in Ansehung aller Erkenntnisse, zu denen sie unabhängig von aller Erfahrung streben mag, mithin die Entscheidung der Möglichkeit oder Unmöglichkeit einer Metaphysik überhaupt und die Bestimmung sowohl der Quellen, als des Umfanges und der Gränzen derselben [...]" (KrV, A XI f.).

ten Formulierung lautet die entsprechende Stelle, der Verdacht (eines Zirkels) sei gehoben, „daß wir nämlich vielleicht die Idee der Freiheit nur *um* des sittlichen Gesetzes *willen* zum Grunde legten" (GMS, S. 453, m. H.). Auch der zitierte Absatz 10 fängt mit „um deswillen" an, was als Indiz dafür gedeutet werden mag, dass hier dezidiert auf den Zirkel rekurriert wird bzw. sich hier das für die Zirkellösung entscheidende Argument findet. Allerdings ist zunächst zu fragen, auf was sich „um deswillen" in Absatz 10 bezieht. Es wurde vermutet, dass es sich auf die „reine Spontaneität" des 9. Absatzes bezieht, und zwar gelesen im Sinne von „aus dem Grunde". Diese Lesart hat einiges für sich und eine entsprechende Paraphrase des ersten Satzes von Absatz 10 würde unter Berücksichtigung der gelieferten Interpretation des neunten Absatzes folgendermaßen lauten:

> ‚Aus dem Grunde bzw. wegen seiner epistemischen Spontaneität, muss sich das vernünftige Wesen als zur Verstandeswelt gehörig ansehen, mithin hat es zwei Standpunkte, daraus es sich selbst betrachten und die Gesetze des Gebrauchs seiner Kräfte, *folglich alle seine Handlungen*, erkennen kann …'.

Problematisch an dieser Interpretation ist die Lesart von „um-willen" im Sinne von „aus diesem Grunde", da man „um willen" viel eher im Sinne von „aus diesem Zwecke" lesen würde. Dies wiederum lässt es kaum zu, „reine Spontaneität" als Adressaten von „um deswillen" zu lesen. Denn was soll es bedeuten, dass der Mensch sich zum Zwecke seiner epistemischen Spontaneität zu zwei Welten gehörig zählen muss?

Wechseln wir aber einmal den Adressaten von „um willen" von der „reinen Spontaneität" zum „vornehmsten Geschäft" des neunten Absatzes: ‚Um willen' des kritischen Geschäfts der Vernunft, Verstandeswelt und Sinnenwelt zu unterscheiden und dadurch den Verstand in seine Schranken zu verweisen, müsste der Mensch dann genannte zwei Standpunkte einnehmen. Nun, diese Lesart passt sehr gut zu Ergebnissen aus dem Referat der Antinomienlehre der KrV. Denn die Lehre von den zwei Standpunkten als Folge des transzendentalen Idealismus stellt, wie gesehen, den Ausweg aus der Antinomie der Vernunft in Hinsicht auf die kosmologischen Ideen dar. Um willen also der durch das kritische Geschäft nur möglichen konsistenten Selbstsicht der epistemischen Vernunft, die ohne dieses ‚vornehmste Geschäft' „mit sich selbst entzweit" (Prol, S. 340) wäre, muss der Mensch bzw. das vernünftige Wesen sich selbst eine noumenale und phänomenale Seite zuschreiben und zwei Standpunkte einnehmen, „daraus es sich selbst betrachten und Gesetze des Gebrauchs seiner Kräfte, folglich aller seiner Handlungen erkennen kann".[13]

---

[13] Prauss sieht bereits in der „reinen Spontaneität" des neunten Absatzes (Sek. 3) eine Einheit aus theoretischer und praktischer Vernunft angesprochen und verfehlt damit den Begründungsgang der „Auskunft": Die – gesicherte – *theoretische* Vernunft zwingt um willen ihrer konsistenten Selbstsicht zu einer Form von Freiheit, die mehr umfasst als theoretische Spontaneität (vgl. Prauss, 1983, S. 255).

Diese Lesart hat auch in Hinblick auf die Interpretation des Zirkels besondere Vorteile. So wurde als ein Befund aus der Interpretation des Zirkels festgehalten, dass ein Ausweg aus diesem nicht-moralische Gründe für die Annahme der Freiheit eröffnen muss. Auf den präzisen Wortlaut beider Zirkelformulierungen eingehend, muss genauer die Freiheit, wenn sie nicht „um willen" der Moralität angenommen werden darf, „um willen" von etwas anderem angenommen werden. Dieses Andere ist die konsistente Selbstsicht der Vernunft in ihrem epistemischen Gebrauch. *Um willen ihrer konsistenten epistemischen Selbstsicht muss die Vernunft also eine Freiheit annehmen, die die Möglichkeit von Willensfreiheit einschließt.*

Halten wir uns nochmals die wichtigsten Etappen des Begründungsgangs von der epistemischen zur praktisch-transzendentalen Freiheit vor Augen: Kant schließt aus dem Vermögen zu urteilen auf eine Art epistemisch-theoretische Spontaneität. Diese epistemische Spontaneität generiert notwendig Vorstellungen – Kants Ideen – deren systematische Konsistenz ihrerseits u. a. praktisch-transzendentale Freiheit fordert. Umgekehrt heißt das: Die denkmögliche praktisch-transzendentale Freiheit bildet letztlich eine Bedingung der möglichen Zuschreibung von Urteilsfähigkeit.[14]

---

[14]   Allison fasst den Zusammenhang von theoretischer und praktisch-transzendentaler Freiheit folgendermaßen zusammen:
"1) Since it involves absolute spontaneity, my (self-certifying) consciousness of possessing theoretical reason requires me to conceive myself as a member of an intelligible world.
2) But in considering myself in this way, I cannot regard my agency or practical reason, which I am also conscious of having, as merely illusory, since, *ex hypothesis*, the factors that could render it illusory are absent when I consider myself in this way.
3) Therefore, insofar as I consider myself as a member of an intelligible world (as I am constrained to do by my possession of theoretical reason), I am entitled to presuppose that my reason has a practical capacity or, equivalently, that I have free will" (Allison, 2011, S. 329).
Allison verkennt hier m. E. die systematische Relevanz des Umstandes, dass die Lehre der zwei Standpunkte eine direkte Konsequenz aus der Auflösung der dritten Antinomie ist, in der die Denknotwendigkeit von praktisch-transzendentaler Freiheit erwiesen wird – zumindest dem Anspruch nach. Es ist eben nicht einfach so, dass meine theoretische Spontaneität mich als Intelligenz und damit als Glied der intelligiblen Welt auszeichnet – das ist klar. Vielmehr liegt das entscheidende Argument in dem Aufweis einer „Veruneinigung" der spontanen theoretischen Vernunft „mit sich selbst" (KrV, A 464/B 592) in Hinblick auf den genuinen Ausdruck ebendieser theoretischen Spontaneität – den Vernunftideen. Diese „Veruneinigung" nötigt uns zur Annahme einer Form von Freiheit, die mehr als die theoretische ist. Pointiert formuliert: Nicht weil ich theoretische Freiheit unabweisbar habe, darf ich mir in einer Art Analogieschluss *auch* praktisch-transzendentale Freiheit zusprechen. Ich muss mir eine Form praktisch-transzendentaler Freiheit zusprechen, weil meine theoretische Freiheit selbst über sich und auf diese hinausweist.

IV. Das abschließende Deduktionsargument

In der 4. Sektion des Deduktionskapitels mit der Überschrift „Wie sind kategorische Imperative möglich?" formuliert Kant das abschließende Deduktionsargument. Der hier entscheidende Passus lautet:

> „Das vernünftige Wesen zählt sich als Intelligenz zur Verstandeswelt, und bloß als eine zu dieser gehörige wirkende Ursache nennt es seine Causalität einen *Willen*. Von der anderen Seite ist es sich seiner doch auch als eines Stücks der Sinnenwelt bewußt, in welcher seine Handlungen [...] als bestimmt durch andere Erscheinungen, nämlich Begierden und Neigungen [...] eingesehen werden müssen. Als bloßen Gliedes der Verstandeswelt würden also alle meine Handlungen dem Princip der Autonomie des reinen Willens vollkommen gemäß sein; als bloßen Stücks der Sinnenwelt würden sie gänzlich dem Naturgesetz der Begierden und Neigungen [...] gemäß genommen werden müssen. [...] *Weil aber die Verstandeswelt den Grund der Sinnenwelt, mithin auch der Gesetze derselben enthält*, also in Ansehung meines Willens (der ganz zur Verstandeswelt gehört) unmittelbar gesetzgebend ist und also auch als solche gedacht werden muß, so werde ich mich als Intelligenz, obgleich andererseits wie ein zur Sinnenwelt gehöriges Wesen, dennoch dem Gesetze der ersteren, [...] und also der Autonomie des Willens unterworfen [...] ansehen müssen" (GMS, S. 453).

Der zentrale Gedanke dieser Passage kann folgendermaßen wiedergegeben werden: Weil die noumenale Ordnung, also die Verstandeswelt bzw. intelligible Welt und ihre Prinzipien, in einem fundierenden Verhältnis zur Sinnenwelt stehen, und weil der Wille des Menschen ganz zur Verstandeswelt gehört und auch vom Menschen so gedacht werden muss, gilt dieses ontologische Verhältnis auch für die Willensvollzüge bzw. das Handeln des Menschen als sinnlich-vernünftigem Wesen. Der kategorische Imperativ stellt das oder zumindest ein Gesetz der Verstandeswelt dar und ist zugleich ein Organisationsprinzip des menschlichen, empirischen Handelns. Insofern realisiert das Handeln nach dem kategorischen Imperativ dieses ontologische Fundierungsverhältnis von sinnlicher Ordnung durch die noumenale. Der Mensch kann sich also nur im Handeln nach dem kategorischen Imperativ in praktischer Hinsicht konsistent als das denken, was er ist, nämlich als sinnliches *und* vernünftiges Wesen.

Ein Aspekt der Auflösung der dritten Antinomie wurde bisher noch nicht thematisiert, er ist aber für das Verständnis des Beweiskraft der Deduktion von eminenter Bedeutung: Der transzendentale Idealismus, die Zwei-Welten- und Zwei-Standpunkte-Lehre, sowie ihre Anwendung auf die menschliche Subjektivität (sei es die epistemische oder praktische), haben als solche immer sowohl Phänomenalität *als auch* Nouomenalität im Blick. Besonders deutlich wird dies in Kants Definition des Begriffs des Intelligiblen in der KrV: „Ich nenne dasjenige an einem Gegenstand der Sinne, was selbst nicht Erscheinung ist, intelligibel" (KrV, A 538/B 566, m. H.). Die intelligible Welt ist also eine solche immer *in Verbindung* mit der Sinnenwelt. Es muss noch mehr gesagt werden: Der transzendentale Idealismus baut auf der Überlegung auf, dass die noumenale Ordnung die phänomenale Ordnung *fundiert*. Gehen wir, um dies näher zu erläutern, nochmals zur Antinomienlehre zurück. So findet sich bereits in der Definition des Begriffs des transzendentalen Idealismus dieses Fundierungsverhältnis angedeutet: „Wir haben in der transscendentalen Ästhetik hinreichend bewiesen: daß alles, was im Raume oder der Zeit angeschauet wird, mithin alle Gegenstände einer uns möglichen Erfahrung nichts als Erscheinungen, d. i. bloße Vorstellungen sind, die [...] keine *an sich gegründete* Existenz haben" (KrV, A 490/B 518 f., m. H.).

Ist die Existenz der Erscheinungen nicht „an sich gegründet", muss sie auf etwas anderem gründen, nämlich auf dem „Ding an sich" als ihrer „nichtsinnlichen Ursache" (KrV, A 494/B 522). Diese Feststellung, dass der transzendentale Idealismus und damit die Unterscheidung von Sinnen- und Verstandeswelt sozusagen von vornherein die ontologische Fundierung des Sinnlichen durch das Noumenale im Blick hat, ist in Hinsicht auf die Deduktion des kategorischen Imperativs von kaum zu überschätzender Relevanz. Denn das bedeutet, *dass der Beweis der menschlichen Freiheit durch die „Auskunft" gar nicht von der Annahme der ontologischen Superiorität der Verstandeswelt zu trennen ist.* Der Mensch muss mit dem Erweis seiner Freiheit also nicht bloß „zwei Standpunkte, daraus er sich selbst betrachtet und die Gesetzes des Gebrauchs seiner Kräfte, folglich aller seiner Handlungen" (GMS, S. 452) annehmen. Er muss auch zwangsläufig annehmen, dass seine noumenale Seite die empirische fundiert.

Damit aber folgt die Geltung des kategorischen Imperativs, der ja dieses Fundierungsverhältnis auf die Praxis überträgt, unmittelbar aus dem Erweis der denkbaren menschlichen Willensfreiheit, wie er in der Auflösung der dritten Antinomie und der „Auskunft" präsentiert wird. Ist die hier entwickelte Interpretation zutreffend, liefert Kant damit eine geschlossene Beweisführung von der Zuschreibung von Urteilsfähigkeit bis zur Geltung des kategorischen Imperativs. Dieter Henrich hat also Unrecht, wenn er behauptet, dass „alle Deduktion auch der *Grundlegung* am Ende auf die faktische Selbstgewißheit des sittlichen Wesens angewiesen ist" (Henrich, 1975, S. 86).

Literatur

Allison, Henry (2011): *Kant's Groundwork for the Metaphysics of Morals. A Commentary*, Oxford.

Brandt, Reinhard (1988): „Der Zirkel im dritten Abschnitt von Kants *Grundlegung zur Metaphysik der Sitten*", in: Oberer, Hariolf/Seel, Gehard (Hrsg.): *Kant. Analysen – Probleme – Kritik*, Würzburg, S. 169–191.

Henrich, Dieter (1975): „Die Deduktion des Sittengesetzes", in: Schwan, Alexander (Hrsg.): *Denken im Schatten des Nihilismus. Festschrift für Wilhelm Weischedel*, Darmstadt, S. 55–112.

Kant, Immanuel (1900 ff.): *Gesammelte Schriften*, Bde 1–22, hrsg. von der Preußische Akademie der Wissenschaften, Berlin, Bd. 23 Deutsche Akademie der Wissenschaften zu Berlin, ab Bd. 24 Akademie der Wissenschaften zu Göttingen.[15]

Meier, Georg Friedrich (1752): *Auszug aus der Vernunftlehre*, Halle.

Prauss, Gerold (1983): *Kant über Freiheit als Autonomie*, Frankfurt/M.

Schönecker, Dieter E. (1999): *Kant: Grundlegung III. Die Deduktion des kategorischen Imperativs*, Freiburg, München.

---

[15]   Siglenverzeichnis:
AA : Akademie-Ausgabe
GMS: Grundlegung zur Metaphysik der Sitten (AA 04)
KpV: Kritik der praktischen Vernunft (AA 05)
KrV: Kritik der reinen Vernunft (zitiert nach Originalpaginierung A/B)
KU: Kritik der Urteilskraft (AA 05)
Päd: Pädagogik (AA 09)
Prol: Prolegomena zu einer jeden künftigen Metaphysik (AA 04)
Refl: Reflexion (AA 14–19).

Allen Wood

Fichte's Absolute Freedom

J. G. Fichte beschrieb seine Konversion zum Kantianismus als eine Hinwendung zur Anerkennung des „Begriffs einer absoluten Freiheit" sowie sein eigenes Systems als „das erste System der Freiheit". Dieser Beitrag untersucht Bedeutung und Inhalt von Fichtes Konzept der „absoluten Freiheit" und die Gründe, deren wegen Fichte es als rational betrachtet, dass der menschliche Wille absolute Freiheit besitzt. Fichte setzt absolute Freiheit gleich mit volition, *welche verstanden wird als „ein freies Uebergehen von Unbestimmtheit zur Bestimmtheit, mit dem Bewusstseyn desselben". Dies erfordert zum einen, dass wir selbst die absolute Quelle unserer Handlungen sind, und zum anderen, dass uns eine Vielzahl möglicher Handlungen zur Verfügung steht. Die Grundlagen für unseren Freiheitsglauben bestehen erstens in einer Verpflichtung zur Sittlichkeit und zweitens darin, dass absolute Freiheit eine Voraussetzung für die theoretischen Haltungen des Verstehen, Begreifens und Überzeugens ist. Unter „Verpflichtung zur Sittlichkeit" versteht Fichte indes allein eine Handlung unter normativen Begriffen; ohne die Bedingungen moralischer Verantwortung oder Schuld. Fichte argumentiert, dass „Dogmatiker", welche ihre Metaphysik vielmehr auf kausale Prozesse der Dinge als auf freie Tätigkeit begründen, darauf festgelegt sind, eine für sie selbst undurchschaubare (und dadurch unaufrichtige) Beziehung zu ihrem eigenen Bewusstsein zu akzeptieren und ihr eigenes Moralvermögen abzustreiten.*

Johann Gottlieb Fichte's first publication, *Attempt at a Critique of All Revelation*, appeared rather late in his life – in spring, 1792, just before his thirtieth birthday. He had at that point been acquainted with the Kantian philosophy less than two years. Thus Fichte was in many respects already a thoroughly formed philosopher before his conversion to Kantianism, and he even thought of himself as already having a philosophical "system". As far as we can tell, this system was largely influenced by Spinoza, and involved necessitarianism about the will.[1] In Fichte's own view, the pivotal point of his conversion away from this system was "the concept of absolute freedom". As he reported in a letter of late summer, 1790 to F. A. Weisshuhn:

I have been living in a new world ever since reading the *Critique of Practical Reason*. Propositions which I thought could never be overturned have been overturned for me. Things have been proven to me which I thought never could be

---

[1] Our best direct textual evidence, scanty though it is, consists in the *Aphorisms on Religion and Deism* (1790), which apparently pre-date Fichte's acquaintance with Kant and were first published in 1845, as part of I. H. Fichte's comprehensive edition of his father's works (ARD, pp. 1–8).

proven – for example, the concept of absolute freedom, the concept of duty, etc. […].
Thus I was deceived by the apparent consistency of my previous system, and
thus are thousands of persons perhaps still deceived (FGA, III, no. 63; EW,
pp. 357–358).

A letter in November of the same year to H. N. Achelis likewise describes the
"revolution that has occurred in my way of thinking":

> I now believe wholeheartedly in human freedom and realize full well that duty,
> virtue and morality are all possible only if freedom is presupposed. I realized this
> truth very well before – perhaps I said as much to you – but I felt that the entire
> sequence of my inferences forced me to reject morality. It has, in addition, become
> quite obvious to me that very harmful consequences follow from the assumption
> that all human actions occur necessarily, and just as obvious that this is largely the
> source of the tremendous ethical corruption of the so-called 'better classes'"
> (FGA, II, no. 70a; EW, pp. 360–361).

As we see from this very last remark, Fichte identifies his commitment to
"absolute freedom" not only with the idea that duty, virtue and morality are not
illusions, but also with a *social* cause: human equality, the recognition of the
rights of the poorer classes (from which Fichte, son of an emancipated serf,
himself came) as against the unjust privileges of their corrupt oppressors, the
"so-called 'better classes'". Another noteworthy claim, present in the letter to
Weisshuhn, is that the denial of absolute freedom involves some kind of self-
inconsistency, incoherence, or even self-deception. We will see in due course
that this is by no means marginal to Fichte's conception of absolute freedom.
Absolute freedom was also to become the foundation of his Kantian philosophical system, after his rejection of the version put forward by Reinhold:
"Reinhold tries to make everything that happens in the human soul into a representation (*Vorstellung*). Anyone who does this can know nothing of freedom and the practical imperative" (Letter to H. Stephani, FGA, III, no. 171;
EW, p. 371). In spring, 1795, Fichte declares to Jens Baggesen: "My system is the
first system of freedom" (FGA, III, no. 282a; EW, p. 385).

What is absolute freedom?

Fichte saw his commitment to "absolute freedom" as a version of Kantianism;
at the same time, he saw his own system as the *first* "system of freedom". We
may therefore better understand the "absoluteness" of Fichte's absolute freedom if we compare, and yet also *contrast*, Fichte's concept of absolute freedom
with Kant's concept of transcendental freedom.

Kant and Fichte on freedom. For Kant, *transcendental* freedom is a certain kind
of causal power, namely, the power of beginning a state or an occurrence (or a
whole series of states and occurrences) spontaneously or "from itself" (*von*

selbst) (KrV, A 533/B 561). If the human being (or the human soul) is a transcendentally free cause in this sense (Kant thinks we cannot know either way whether it is), then it is a finite substance (corporeal or incorporeal – this is also unknowable), whose existence is causally dependent on other things. Substances in the natural world possess causal powers to begin a state or occurrence, but this power is itself the effect of other substances acting on it with similar causal powers – which powers are themselves the effects of other substantial causes, and so on indefinitely. The Third Antinomy of pure reason concerns the *idea* (the concept of reason, not capable of exhibition in experience) of a causal power that is not dependent in this way on other such powers, and this is what Kant means by the power to begin a state or occurrence "from itself". Kant holds that *practical* freedom, the capacity to act without the action being necessitated by a natural impulse, requires transcendental freedom, since any cause whose causal power results from the causal power of causes external to it (such as a natural impulse) would have its action thus necessitated (KrV, A 534/B 562; GMS, p. 446; KpV, p. 33). Since practical freedom is a kind of causality, and causality acts according to laws, there must also be a law for a *free* cause – the *moral law* or law of *autonomy* (GMS, pp. 446–447; KpV, pp. 29, 33).

Fichte accepts Kant's conception of freedom as the power to begin a state spontaneously – or, as he prefers to put it, "absolutely"; he regards the I as free in this sense (SL, p. 37). But Fichte does not identify the I with a *substance* or *thing* possessing this power. Instead, Fichte conceives the I as originally only as an *acting;* it is an act that is absolutely free in the sense that it is self-posited (GWL, pp. 96–97; ZE, pp. 462–463; GN, pp. 1–2, n; SL, pp. 3–4). As a transcendental condition of the I, its action must be directed to an external object (a not-I or corporeal world); therefore, the I's free act must also be ascribed to a body or corporeal substance (the I's material body) (ZE, p. 495; GN, pp. 56–62; SL, pp. 12, 110–112, 129–130). For Fichte, a disembodied or immaterial I would be impossible: "Apart from this connection with a body [the I] would not be a person at all, but would be something quite inconceivable (if one can refer to a thing that is not even conceivable as 'something')." (VBG, p. 295; cf. GN, p. 59)

Free will and the body. Here we ought to think not so much of Kant as of the more direct precursor of Fichte's doctrine: Spinoza's conception of the mind and body as the same thing conceived under two different attributes (S, *Ethics* II P7S, P13S). Or we might think of its direct successor: Schopenhauer's doctrine that the will is the body experienced directly as a thing in itself (Schopenhauer, 1958, p. 1: § 18). But we need to keep in mind that both Spinoza and Schopenhauer think of the mind or will as a *thing* (a *being*), whereas Fichte understands it as an absolutely self-positing *act*. The body for Fichte is part of nature, and must be conceived as a living organic whole (SL, pp. 112–122). This natural body is not, as such, the subject of action; nor is the power of acting the I ascribes to itself a causal power belonging to the body. The active, self-positing I is rather the *will*, and the power of acting is ascribed to the I as will (GN, pp. 20–23; SL, pp. 18–23). The will and the body are regarded by the I as the same, but viewed from different sides (SL, pp. 11–12, 130), just as in Spinoza the body and mind are the same *res*, conceived under two different attributes: extension and thinking. But as I (or subject), I can distinguish myself even from my body, and this is because the I is *not* a thing but an act. For Fichte, the only *thing* with which I can identify myself is the body, which, however, is not the I, but rather the vehicle of the *free volitional act* that is the I. The body is a cause in the realm of bodies, acting on other bodies and being acted upon by them (GWL, pp. 125–136; GN, pp. 56–61; SL, p. 11); but it is the I as will that is active, self-positing and free in the absolute sense.

The I as will, in order to be free, must be capable of absolutely free acts, hence something that "has to exist in advance of its nature", or to "be before it is determined" (SL, pp. 35–36). (Fichte never uses the famous Sartrean formula: *Existence precedes essence*, but he is obviously the original author of the idea it expresses.)[2] Fichte thus accepts Kant's conception of transcendental freedom, but only if it is regarded as belonging to an *act* of self-positing, not if it is conceived as the causal power belonging to a thing or substance. Further, however, there is a sense in which Fichte's "absolute" freedom is not the same as Kant's conception of a power to begin a state "from itself". Fichte also differs from Kant in that he does not regard the state that is begun absolutely as begun solely "from itself" in the sense that it is unconnected with something prior to it. For Fichte, to think of the I's free act as "connected to nothing at all" would be to identify freedom with mere contingency in the sense of "blind chance", and the indeterminacy of freedom with mere "not-determinacy=0" (SL, pp. 33–34, 137). Fichte consistently denies that freedom could be anything of that sort.

The "essence" or "original being" of the I. Fichte agrees with Kant, however, in denying that this connection is a causal connection to some prior *being*; but absolute freedom can also not be thought of (as Spinoza does) merely as causal origination within oneself. Instead, a free act is connected to something prior – not to a prior being or causal power but rather to a "thinking" or a "pure concept" (SL, pp. 35–37). The concept in question is simply that of the I's own self-positing, its "tendency to absolute self-activity" (SL, pp. 37–40), or a "drive for the entire I" (SL, pp. 40–42), which is identified also with "the concept of [the I's] self-sufficiency (*Selbständigkeit*)" (SL, pp. 59–60). This "tendency" or "drive" is identified with the I's "pure being", "true essence" (SL, p. 24), "essential character" or "original being" (SL, pp. 29–31).

---

[2]   This formula is best known from its repetition several times within a few pages early in Sartre's popular essay "Existentialism is a Humanism" (Sartre, 1956 b, pp. 289–291); but in *Being and Nothingness*, Sartre declares: "Consciousness is a being whose existence posits its essence" (Sartre, 1956 a, p. lxii; cf. p. 438; Heidegger, 1953, p. 42).

It is apt to be confusing when Fichte says, on the one hand, that the I, which is "an act and not a being" must "exist in advance of its nature" and "be before it is determined", yet then, on the other hand, speaks of the I's having a "pure being" or "true essence". The point of this latter talk, however, is *not* to identify the kind of nature or essence that could belong to a *thing* or *substance* – i.e., the kind of nature or essence that could figure in a causal explanation of what a thing does. Rather, Fichte is trying to characterize the *thinking* or *concept* that belongs to the I's self-positing and constitutes what is prior to its free acting. This could not be a pre-existing nature or essence, as might belong to a thing, but rather only a "necessary thinking (by the intellect) of self-sufficiency as a norm in accordance with which the intellect charges itself to determine itself freely" (SL, p. 52). In other words, the concept of what the I must "be before it is determined" is *normative*. We could put it this way: *An I (or a self) is whatever must regard itself as subject to a norm requiring it to be self-active and self-sufficient (or independent) entirely to itself.* In ascribing to itself the power to act according to a normative concept, the I thinks of itself as absolutely free.

One familiar determinist argument says that if actions are not causally necessitated, then they must be merely chance or random events – which would make them not only bizarre exceptions to the laws of nature but also unintelligible as free acts. The Fichtean reply to this argument is that the alternatives "causal determination" and "blind chance" present us with a false dilemma, and that this must be a false dilemma if we are even to entertain the concept of *action*. Action occurs only if the transition from indeterminacy to determinacy is effected not by a necessitating cause but by an act of self-determination which is governed (as Fichte puts it) by "concepts" (or norms). Acting grounded on a normative concept is diametrically opposed to something's happening "indeterministically" in the sense of its occurring merely from "blind chance" or at random. But a normative concept can be neither an *external* cause nor a *necessitating* cause: it has to be a ground of *self*-determination on the part of the agent that leaves the self-determining agent with the alternative possibilities of acting either in accord with the normative concept or contrary to it.

What is required for absolute freedom?

The norm of absolute freedom. Fichte's concept of absolute freedom is exceedingly abstract. It may be hard to see how it is supposed to apply to morality, or even to human action in general. We may wonder, for instance, what "norm" could be constituted merely by the "concept of self-sufficiency" or "independence" (*Selbständigkeit*). But to satisfy ourselves on that question would take us in a direction different from the one I propose for this inquiry. It would lead us, on the one hand, to explore Fichte's moral epistemology – his conception of conscience and the subjective conditions for acquiring moral conviction (§ 15 of SL, pp. 163–177). It would also require us to answer the thoughtful doubts raised by Frederick Neuhouser in his excellent study, *Fichte's Theory of Subjectivity*, about whether any determinate objective norm at all can be derived solely from the idea of freedom or self-determination (Neuhouser, 1990, pp. 131–166). (In a different context, this is an objection often raised about the existentialist ethics of Sartre and Beauvoir.) Though this is not the place for a thorough reply to it, a hint in this direction may still be helpful for our purposes.

I believe such worries are directly addressed by Fichte in § 18 of the *System of Ethics*, entitled: "Systematic elucidation of the conditions of I-hood in their relationship to the drive for absolute self-sufficiency". "Self-sufficiency" is identified by Fichte with wholeness or entirety, the drive for unity (SL, pp. 40–45; cf. VBG, pp. 296–299, 304–306). More specifically, it is addressed in Fichte's argument that the true norm for self-sufficiency lies in intersubjectivity, and our relation to others (SL, pp. 218–230). The self-sufficiency or wholeness here is the goal of a quest, through rational communication, to unify all rational beings through an end that they can share necessarily (SL, pp. 230–235). This leads to Fichte's conception of human society as church, state, and community of scholars (SL, pp. 235–253). In other words, the human vocation of absolute freedom turns out to be a *social* vocation: "A reciprocity (*Wechselwirkung*) through concepts, a purposeful community (*zweckmäßige Gemeinschaft*). [...] If all human beings could be perfect, they would be totally equal (*gleich*) to one another. [...] The ultimate and highest goal of society is the complete unity and unanimity of all its members." (VBG, pp. 305–306, 310) In other words, the ideals of freedom and community, properly understood, are not in tension but actually require each other.

Our present purposes, however, as I've already said, do not require us to understand the whole of Fichte's normative ethics and social philosophy. More to the point will be an exploration of the way Fichte understands the conditions of human action generally, as the expression of absolute freedom. The basic idea is that freedom is located in the gap between the absolute norm of reason as self-sufficiency and our own choice whether to comply with it. The Fichtean name for this gap is "will", which Fichte defines as "the absolutely free transition from indeterminacy to determinacy, accompanied by consciousness of this transition" (SL, p. 158). We are free because, and insofar as, we recognize ourselves as subject to a norm proceeding from our "pure being" or "true essence" – as an I which ought to make itself into a self-sufficient whole – and acknowledge in ourselves the power or faculty (*Vermögen*) to determine ourselves as this norm directs. According to this conception, a "will" is by its very concept *free*, and "an unfree will is an absurdity" (SL, p. 159).[3]

---

[3]   This doctrine was picked up by Hegel, who held that freedom is the very substance of the will, its *Bestimmung* ("determination": that is, its "nature" and also its "vocation"). See Hegel, 1991 § 4, A.

The I as will. Several things, according to Fichte, belong as such to the concept of the I as a free will. First, the I must think of itself as directed to something outside itself (a not-I or material world), toward which its power of freedom is directed (GN, pp. 23–29; SL, pp. 75–76). As we have already seen, the I is not a *thing* (whether material, spiritual, or of any other sort) but an *act*. But in being directed toward a material world, this act must belong also to something material: the body (GN, pp. 55–61). The I's material body, moreover, must be an organized (living) product of nature (SL, pp. 101–121).

Second, it follows from this that the I must be finite and situated, limited and also challenged by a world around it, to which the I is passive, that sets a boundary or limit to its efficacy (SL, pp. 97–98): "The determination to act presupposes stasis. [...] [The I] must already have been provided with its object, and must have received it passively. Hence self-determination to act necessarily presupposes a passive state." (GEW, pp. 372–373) The passivity of the I is "feeling", which is fundamental to all consciousness (GWL, pp. 289-322; GEW, pp. 365–372; SL, pp. 105–106). The world of the I is its own world: "My world [...] is determined through its opposition or contrast with me: that is, the world as I originally find it, the world that is supposed to exist without any assistance from me, is determined by its opposition to me, through its contrast with me as I necessarily find myself to be, not as I perhaps ought to make myself freely" (SL, pp. 72–73). Fichte is the originator of all the later existentialist ideas of "worldhood".[4]

Third, it follows that the I is free at all only if, and to the extent that, it *makes itself free*, by actually determining itself in accordance with the norm that constitutes its selfhood. The I "cannot ascribe to itself a power of freedom without finding in itself an actual exercise of this power, that is, an actual act of free willing" (SL, p. 83). I can choose to remain passive to my feelings, failing to determine myself freely at all, and thus choose to remain *unfree*; to those who make this choice, their own freedom cannot be proven, simply because they have not *made themselves* free. "I am what I am because this is what I willed to be. I could have let the wheels of necessity carry me away. I could have let my convictions be determined by the impressions received from nature, or by the tendency of my passions and inclinations, or by the opinions my con-

---

4   Heidegger's "being-in-the-world", *Befindlichkeit*, and "facticity" are also to be understood as the transcendental conditions of all more abstract conceptions that people may form of an "objective" world (for example, the world human beings cognize through natural science) (Heidegger, 1953, pp. 52–62, 130–140). Fichte is also the author of the Heideggerian conception of spatiality as distance or "de-severance" (*Entfernung*) (Heidegger, 1953, pp. 101–111). Spatiality, transcendentally considered, is first and foremost that which separates us from, or alternatively, connects us to, the changes in our world that we can bring about through our free agency. "'Object X lies at such and such a distance from me in space' means that in traversing the space from me to the object I must first apprehend and posit such and such other objects in order to be able to posit the object in question." (SL, p. 99)

temporaries wanted to impart to me. But this is not what I willed. I have torn myself free" (BEW, p. 348; cf. SL, pp. 32–33). It would be pointless to try to convince someone they have some property when they don't in fact have it. This is still pointless even if they could acquire the property if they chose to, and if they rationalize their refusal to make this choice by claiming self-deceptively that the choice is impossible for them. Fichte does not think he can convince anyone of their own freedom unless that person chooses to act freely, thereby putting themselves in a position to be convinced (EE, pp. 429–435; ZE, pp. 508–515; SL, pp. 25–26).

Finally, the I "cannot ascribe to itself the power of freedom without also thinking of several actual and determinate actions as possible through its freedom" (SL, p. 79). To be aware of ourselves as free is to be aware of our future as "open", and of the "arrow" of time as fundamentally the separation of the past, which is determined as the condition of my free action, from the future, which I may determine in one or another different ways that are open to me (SL, p. 97). "For us there must necessarily be a past. For only if there is a past can there be a present, and only if there is a present is consciousness possible. [...] Consciousness is possible only if the I posits a not-I in opposition to itself. Understandably, this is possible only if the I directs its ideal activity at the not-I. This is an activity of the I and not of the not-I only insofar as it is free activity, that is, only insofar as it could be directed at any other object instead of this one" (GEW, pp. 409–410). Consciousness is possible, therefore, only in time, and only for an imagination that hovers (*schwebt*) between alternative possibilities (GWL, pp. 216–217; SL, pp. 136–137).

The conditional analysis of "could have done otherwise". According to some compatibilists about freedom and determinism, to say that I could have done otherwise than I did requires no more for its truth than that it be true that if I had desired to do otherwise, then I would have done otherwise. This, they then point out, is compatible with its also being true that given my actual desires, I was causally determined to do as I have done in fact, and also compatible with my actual desires having been causally determined to be what they were. On this analysis, then, "I could have done otherwise" counts as true even if, given my actual desires, and the determinist assumptions that I have been causally necessitated to have them and causally necessitated by them to do as I in fact do, it is also causally necessitated that I will do as I in fact do. In other words, on the conditional analysis, "I could have done otherwise" might count as true even when it is precisely *not* true that I could have done otherwise.[5]

---

[5]   This is unfortunately by no means the only case where some philosophical analysis of a proposition everyone accepts as true makes a mockery of Alfred Tarski's "Convention T". Emotivist and expressivist metaethics is another rich source of such cases. For a good critical discussion of the conditional analysis, see Ginet, 1980.

Fichte's conception of absolute freedom is well suited to resisting the conditional analysis. Because the I must "be before it is", there is nothing that I am at the time of action which could be subject to causal necessitation determining what I do. Whether or not my desires might be causally determined, I could not be. Further, whatever actual desires I may have at a certain time, my formal freedom consists in the possibility of resisting them, not being determined by them in the choice of what I do. The I's "original being" is a "drive for the whole I" (SL, p. 40), but the result of this drive is not to a passively experienced desire or "feeling"; it is a "thought" or normative concept (SL, pp. 43–45). This norm is one that I may choose to obey or choose to violate. For these reasons, it is not only true that whatever I do, I could have done otherwise, but also that at the time of any action, there are several distinct, determinate actions possible to me. It follows that the truth of "I could have done otherwise", in the only sense in which this is (or ever could be) true, is *unconditional*. It is *not* true only relative to some felt desire of mine, and it involves the presence to me of a plurality of real possibilities whose practical availability to me is not conditional on any desire I might have. Whenever I make a *choice*, it must be *unconditionally* true at that time that I could have done otherwise.

Formal and material freedom. Fichte's absolute freedom can be understood only in terms of two distinct but related conceptions, which Fichte calls "formal freedom" and "material freedom" (SL, pp. 135–139). Formal freedom is the power or faculty of the I to determine itself in a variety of different ways (SL, pp. 50–52). "Originally, that is, apart from its own contribution (*Zutun*), it *is* absolutely nothing; through its own doing (*Tun*), it must make itself into what it is supposed to become – This proposition is not proven, nor can it be proven. It is purely and simply up to each rational being to find himself in this manner and grant the same" (SL, p. 50).

Without an act of self-determination, there is properly speaking no person, no I at all. Awareness of the I is awareness of a free action; but an act requires subjection to a norm, though not necessarily conformity to it. Such an act presupposes both a norm of material freedom and the power of acting according to this norm, which is formal freedom. A free will must be free in a formal sense in order to be self-positing, or a transition from indeterminacy to determinacy. Material freedom is the actual determination of oneself in conformity to the norm of self-sufficiency. Only a materially free action is free in an absolute sense, but formally free action is a necessary condition for materially free action. One might try to identify "formal freedom" with Kant's conception of "practical freedom in the negative sense", and "material freedom" with "practical freedom in the positive sense" (or autonomy of will). Fichte does equate material freedom with the Kantian moral law, "ought" or "categorical imperative" (SL, p. 55), but rejects the claim that there is a relation of reciprocal entailment between two *different* thoughts: freedom and the moral law (KpV, pp. 29–30). These are, he says, simply *the same thought* (SL, p. 53):

> In several passages, Kant derives our conviction concerning freedom from our consciousness of the moral law. This is to be understood as follows: the appearance of freedom is an immediate fact of consciousness and by no means a consequence of any other thought. And yet, as was previously pointed out, one might still wish to explain this appearance further and could thereby transform it into an illusion. There is no theoretical reason for not doing this, but there is a practical one: namely, the firm resolution to grant primacy to practical reason, to hold the moral law to be the true and ultimate determination of our essence, and not to transform it into an illusion by means of sophistical reasoning – which is certainly a possibility for the free imagination. If, however, one does not go beyond the moral law, then one also does not go beyond the appearance of freedom, which thereby becomes for us the truth, inasmuch as the proposition 'I am free; freedom is the sole true being and the ground of all other being' is quite different from the proposition 'I *appear* to myself to be free.' What can be derived from consciousness of the moral law, therefore, is [only] faith in the *objective validity* of this appearance (SL, pp. 53–54).

The conviction that we are free

This difficult passage may be taken not only as explaining Fichte's identification of our consciousness of freedom with our consciousness of the moral law, but also as an invitation to turn from Fichte's concept of absolute freedom to his account of the grounds for our conviction (which Fichte also calls our "faith") that we are absolutely free.

"Faith" in freedom: idealism vs. dogmatism. A certain kind of popular religious apologetics goes as follows: "Both religious belief and unbelief ultimately rest on *faith*: The believer accepts the Word of God, while the unbeliever accepts the authority of reason and science. Hence the unbelieving rationalist is just as guilty as the religious person of making an irrational leap of faith. Belief and unbelief are thus on a par: The only difference is that the believer is honest enough to admit the irrationality of his faith, whereas unbelievers try to pretend their faith is something it is not".

Those who engage in this sort of talk ought to be ashamed. Whether the believer's faith is rational or not, the acceptance of what is genuinely grounded on reason and evidence is not (could not be) irrational. The above apologetic rhetoric is nothing but a brazen attempt to represent self-deceptive irrationality as honesty and virtue, and intellectual integrity as if it were dishonesty and a vice. It is as shallow and transparent as it is disgraceful. Fichte was, after all, trained for the Lutheran ministry, and at times he appears to presents his defense of absolute freedom as if it were a version of this same absurd ploy: It appears to us, he says, that we are free, but those who think everything can be explained in terms of the causal relations among *things* (Fichte calls them 'dogmatists') propose to explain this appearance away as an illusion.

> If one nevertheless decides not to explain this appearance any further and decides to consider it absolutely inexplicable, i.e. to be the truth [...] and our entire philosophy is based on precisely this decision – then this is not because of any theoretical insight but because of a practical interest. I *will* to be self-sufficient, and therefore take myself to be so. Such an assent, however, is *faith*. Our philosophy therefore begins with an item of faith, and knows that it does so. Dogmatism too, which, if it is consistent makes the claim stated above, starts with faith (in the *thing in itself*); but it usually does not know this (SL, pp. 25–26; cf. EE, pp. 429–435).

A closer look, however, reveals that Fichte is not guilty of arguing in the manner of popular religious apologetics. In the course of avowing his faith in the divine government of the world, for instance, Fichte declares that faith "should not be represented as an arbitrary assumption one may adopt or not as one pleases, as a free decision to consider true whatever the heart wishes and to do so because this is what it wishes" (GGW, p. 179; IW, p. 144). Nor is the choice between "idealism" and the opponent "dogmatism" seen by Fichte as arbitrary, or a "leap" ungoverned by reasons. For one thing, this choice is as rooted in the kind of person one is, and Fichte decidedly refuses to portray the two kinds of people as in any sense on a par either morally or intellectually. The idealist's faith is more honest than the dogmatist's; but this is not (as the shabby religious apologetics would have it) because the idealist admits he believes without reasons, while the dogmatist does not admit this. The idealist is more honest because his entire self-orientation is direct and open, while dogmatists are necessarily in flight from themselves and dishonest with themselves.

The starting point of idealism is the self-positing act of self-consciousness, which alone makes possible the kind of consciousness we human beings have. There is in every human consciousness some awareness of the consequences of this act, and this awareness constitutes the "appearance of freedom", which can either be accepted for the truth that it is, or else subverted by being declared an illusion, and explained away as a product of the causal action of things. To do this, however, also makes it impossible to provide an adequate account of the difference between things and our representation of them in consciousness, which is grounded in the free act of self-positing (EE, pp. 435–438). The dogmatist must deny this act, and refuse to accept the distinction between things and our representation of them, even though it is on the latter that our possibility of knowing things at all necessarily depends (EE, pp. 438–439).

By accepting as true the appearance of freedom, idealists have an immediate belief in their own worth and dignity, and a consequent commitment to morality, as well as a commitment to the search for truth for its own sake. By contrast, the dogmatist "possesses only an indirect or mediated belief in his own dispersed self, which is conveyed to him only by objects" (EE, p. 433). Dogmatists are committed to saying (what they often do say), that the unavoidable appearance that we are free is an illusion.[6] This admission deprives them of any immediate trust in the truth of their own convictions, along with confidence in their own worth. They cannot unite their world-view with their own self-consciousness, so they have to see themselves as the victim of self-deceptive illusions, and they've become used to tolerating this dishonesty in themselves whenever they can't help noticing it. Dogmatists are, Fichte thinks, the sort of people who are at home in a social system of unjust privileges, justifying their privileges as "necessary" – if not absolutely, then at least to the existing world – as it must be, or to the status quo, represented as a social system that could claim the loyalty of people of good will. Their denial of freedom includes a cowardly, complacent unwillingness to imagine or hope for any other world or any better system.[7] "Someone whose character is morally slack or who has been enervated and twisted by spiritual servitude, scholarly self-indulgence and vanity, will never be able to raise himself to the level of idealism." (EE, p. 434) The dogmatist's stance is not confident or candid, Fichte thinks, but is characterized by passion and defensiveness: "When the dogmatist's system is attacked he is in real danger of losing his own self. Yet he is not well prepared to defend himself against such attacks, for there is something in his own inner self which agrees with his assailant. This is why he defends himself with so much vehemence and bitterness" (EE, p. 434).

On Fichte's account, then, this is not a case of one irrational "leap of faith" set over against another, after the fashion of popular religious apologetics. It is highly misleading – too charitable: not to idealism, but to dogmatism – for

---

[6]   Spinoza, for example, insists that there is in every human being an "innate" belief in their freedom of her will (Ep. 58, in S, p. 250). Spinoza explains this belief as a result of people's ignorance of the external causes of their actions, combined with the error of mistaking for their entire cause the partial cause of them of which they are conscious in themselves (S, *Ethics* II, P40S2a; cf. Ep. 58). Fichte thinks of Spinoza as the most consistent possible dogmatist (GWL, p. 120). He never represents Spinoza, however, as an example of moral slackness, corruption or self-deception, but always speaks of him with utmost respect.

[7]   "When one speaks of the technical and practical aspects of executing what is demanded by pure reason [...] the proposition, 'we are not able to do this,' always means the same thing. If, for example, what is demanded is a thorough improvement of the constitution of the state then the response is, 'these proposals cannot be carried out' – meaning, of course, they cannot be carried out if the old abuses are to remain in place" (SL, pp. 197–198). Compare: "Those who hide from total freedom [...] who try to show that their existence is necessary [...] – these I shall call *salauds*" (Sartre, 1956 b, p. 308). In the Mairet translation, *salauds* is rendered as "scum". It has also been translated as "swine", "shits", and "bastards", as it also is in Lloyd Alexander's translation of *Nausea* (Sartre, 1964, pp. 82–94). I leave it as an exercise for the reader to decide which similar words should apply to the wealthy and corporations in the U.S. who sustain the Republican party in order not merely to preserve, but in the last generation even aggressively to expand their obscene political power and economic privileges.

Fichte to imply that the relation between idealism and dogmatism is something like an intellectual standoff, where "faith" must resolve a question that cannot be decided by reason. The question *is* decided by reason, and the only sense in which the dispute between the idealist and dogmatist is not decided by reason is that the dogmatist is a dishonest and self-deceptive person who cannot bear to listen to reason.

We are as yet unclear, however, on the nature of the "proof" of freedom that Fichte thinks is available to the idealist, and also why despite this "proof" Fichte still regards faith in idealism as a "choice" made on practical grounds rather than a clear case of detached theoretical knowledge. One thing that should be clear by now is that Fichte is not basing his defense of freedom merely on the fact that we "appear" to ourselves to be free. He realizes that this fact is equally acknowledged by dogmatists, who declare it to be an illusion; Fichte concedes that the idealist cannot objectively demonstrate to the dogmatist that this appearance is not an illusion. The decisive reasons favoring idealism – those dishonestly evaded by dogmatists – do not consist in such an objective proof. Fichte does regard as one "advantage" idealism has over dogmatism "the fact that it is able to exhibit the presence within consciousness of the foundation it wishes to employ in its explanation of experience, viz. the freely acting intellect" (EE, p. 430). But the advantage afforded idealism by the appearance of freedom, or the presence in consciousness of the freely acting intellect, must somehow be exploited by argument in order to show the superiority of idealism over dogmatism. These reasons rather provide a rational ground for the idealist's *decision* to treat the appearance of freedom as the truth, in contrast the dogmatist's decision to regard this appearance as an illusion. Only in actually making this decision, subjecting ourselves to a norm of self-sufficiency, do we give ourselves reason to be convinced of our freedom. The decision in question, as Fichte presents it, is a *moral* one. The conviction of freedom depends on the act of committing ourselves to morality.

Freedom as a moral commitment

Don't think: "responsibility" or "blame". This commitment, however, is *not* for Fichte a commitment to freedom as a supposed condition for moral *responsibility* or *accountability*. This point is important to emphasize, because opponents of freedom of the will often depict its defenders as preoccupied with this issue – especially as seeking to rationalize what are now called the "reactive attitudes" of blame and indignation. In fact, the truth is just the reverse: It is the *determinists* who are more often morbidly obsessed with the issue of responsibility and blame. Compatibilist determinists, for example, often think they have solved the problem of freedom if they can give some plausible compatibilist account of "our" practices of holding people responsible, blaming and punishing them, and so forth. Proponents of the "conditional analysis" usually favor it because they think it gives us "enough" freedom to justify "our" judgments of moral responsibility and blame.[8] Determinists tend to be utterly oblivious to any issues regarding free agency other than those involving moral responsibility.

Fichte claims that absolute freedom is necessary for "duty, virtue and morality", but he never claims that it is required for moral *responsibility* (or even that morality requires this latter notion). Fichte's accounts of blame and punishment, which occur only in the context of right, are wholly anti-retributivist, oriented solely to the coercive prevention of acts that violate right and interfere with the external freedom of others (GN, pp. 260–285). They involve no appeal whatever to freedom of the will. They could be offered just as well by any compatibilist, or even by a hard determinist who views practices of blame and punishment solely as causal mechanisms for securing external compliance with legal requirements. I submit that Fichte retained – not totally, but still to a surprising extent – the Spinozist aversion to "reactive attitudes" even after his conversion to Kantianism. *For Fichte, the moral commitment to freedom is simply <u>not about</u> "moral responsibility" or the freedom we (supposedly) "need" in order to blame people or to justify our indignation at their actions.*[9]

---

[8]   They may even be right in thinking this – if "our" sick reactive attitudes are so out of control that we judge people responsible whenever they provoke our rancor or ire, without caring a whit whether they are actually free agents.

[9]   Fichte does argue on one occasion that the fact that we hold people accountable for an action shows we think they could have done otherwise, and therefore exhibits our commitment to regarding them as free. But the aim of this argument is very limited. It is *ad hominem* only, and addressed solely to those who might claim they have no awareness in themselves of the moral law whose content Fichte claims to be identical with material freedom. Fichte admits that some such people might be right, if they have not made themselves subject to the law through freely positing themselves as self-sufficient. But he appeals even in their case to judgments he imagines them making about *others* – "[when], for example, he does not become indignant toward and infuriated with the fire that engulfs his house, but is indignant and infuriated with the person who set that fire or who was careless. Would he not be a fool to be infuriated with this person if he did not suppose that he could also have acted otherwise and that he ought to have acted otherwise?" (SL, p. 62). Fichte's claim here is only that indignation toward a person presupposes that we think the person could have, and ought to have, acted otherwise. Since the argument is *ad hominem*, Fichte could concede that it cannot convince anyone of absolute freedom if (like Spinoza) the person thinks that since people cannot act otherwise than they do, fury and indignation toward them makes no more sense than fury and indignation toward lifeless objects. This is certainly not a general argument that absolute freedom must be presupposed because morality requires responsibility, blame, and indignation, and these make sense only on the assumption of freedom. To my knowledge, Fichte never offers any such argument.

Moral commitment means: materially free action. We begin to see why Fichte really regards idealism as based on moral "faith" when we realize that he is proposing to offer morally-motivated arguments for the conviction that we are free only to those who have already chosen to act on principles of moral self-sufficiency – in other words, only to those who already consciously acknowledge the kind of (Kantian or Fichtean) morality that requires absolute freedom as its presupposition. Fichte does think that the conviction of one's own absolute freedom is required for motivation to make materially free choices in obedience to one's conscience. That is the only sense in which morality presupposes absolute freedom. Morality grounds our conviction that we are free because we must ascribe absolute freedom to ourselves in order to understand ourselves as performing materially free actions in obedience to conscience and the moral law. If some people choose not to care about morality – that is, about material freedom – then as far as Fichte is concerned, that those people are not in fact free, so it would be pointless to try to demonstrate to them that they are. They have *freely* chosen (in the formal sense) not to be *free* (in the material sense).

Fichte does "summon" his readers to think freely, to perform the act of self-positing of which absolute freedom consists, and then follow the path of idealism that rests upon it (EE, p. 445; ZE, pp. 461–462). He "challenges" them to "exhibit the ethical law within [themselves]" (ZE, p. 466). But he acknowledges that they may choose not to heed this summons, and if they do not choose to do so, he has no moral argument to offer them for making a different choice. No doubt Fichte himself has a low opinion (as human beings) of those who acknowledge no morality at all, or who can accept only a version of morality that does not aspire to the heights (or, as some might prefer to say, the metaphysical extravagances) of a morality of absolute freedom; but he does not claim to have any argument to convince those people that they are absolutely free. That is why Fichte repeatedly issues the caveat that he cannot convince the confirmed dogmatist. Only those who freely choose to perform the acts he summons them to perform can come to be convinced.

> A single breath from a free human being is enough to blow their system away. But we cannot refute it *for them*. We do not write, speak or teach *for* them, for there is simply no way we could accommodate them. If we nevertheless continue to talk *about* them, we do this, not for their sake, but for others, in order to warn them against the errors of the former and to divert them from such hollow and meaningless babble. Our opponents should not feel themselves demeaned by this declaration. If they do feel themselves somehow belittled by our comments, they merely reveal their own bad conscience and place themselves publicly beneath us (ZE, p. 510).

Fichte argues that those who choose to be committed to morality (to a morality of absolute freedom based on a norm of self-sufficiency) are justified in the morally-based conviction that they are free. This justification is twofold: First, this conviction harmonizes with the unavoidable appearance that they are free, so it does not require them to regard this basic fact of consciousness as an illusion, which would, Fichte argues, undermine all confidence in what they think they know based on conscious experience. Second, once they have made the free choice to acknowledge the moral norm of self-sufficiency, they can be made to see that their conviction that they have made this choice does not cohere with the thought that the appearance of freedom is an illusion, so that accepting this appearance as truth is the only way to think of yourself once you have made this choice. The choice to recognize the norm of self-sufficiency thus provides a further rational ground for accepting as true the appearance that we are free, a ground that goes beyond that mere appearance itself.

Freedom vs. spiritual slavery. Fichte insists, however, that the idealists' conviction that they are free always remains a "faith" in the sense that there is nothing in the grounds for this conviction that dogmatists would have to acknowledge as providing *them* with a convincing reply to the thought that the appearance of freedom is only an illusion. From the dogmatist's standpoint, idealists merely choose to act in accordance with an appearance that cannot be demonstrated not to be illusory, and remain consistently committed to this illusion in their representation of their own actions. The internal coherence of the appearance of freedom and the idealist's choice to live according to a certain moral norm cannot be presented to anyone who has not already made this choice as a reason for making it, or for adopting the belief in freedom that it presupposes. Fichte thinks it cannot be otherwise: "Any communication of conviction by means of proof presupposes that both parties agree upon at least something. How then could the *Wissenschaftslehre* communicate itself to a dogmatist, since it *simply does not agree with him upon a single point* concerning the material of cognition, and thus there exists no common ground from which they could jointly proceed?" (ZE, p. 509)

We have seen that Fichte takes the appearance of freedom in our consciousness to be one advantage that the idealist has over the dogmatist. The second advantage Fichte claims that idealism has over dogmatism is that dogmatism "is quite unable to explain what it is supposed to explain, and this demonstrates its inadequacy" (EE, p. 435). What dogmatism needs to explain, Fichte thinks, is consciousness itself, the possibility of our representation of the objects or things that dogmatism takes to be primary, or even exclusively real. For Fichte, that consciousness is inseparable from self-consciousness, the absolute self-positing of the I, which is in turn a free act. To deny freedom, then, is to deny a transcendental condition for the possibility of experiencing the very things the dogmatist takes to be real, and commits the dogmatist to a transcendent metaphysical system based on a "thing in itself" that can never come before consciousness. Implicitly, of course, Fichte is also claiming that idealism, by contrast, can explain what it is supposed to explain: namely, how the same world of things is grounded in our experience of them – that is, how the objective world is made possible through the absolute self-positing of the I. But Fichte never completed his own system, so from this point of view, the advantage idealism is supposed to have over dogmatism would seem to evaporate, or at least it would be deferred until someone is able to complete the system Fichte projected. As a result, Fichte tends to see the conviction of freedom as something not to be demonstrated to those who don't believe in it, but as the object of a free faith requiring a choice that most dogmatists, on account of their defects of character, will never be able to make.

Fichte's position on free will is diametrically opposed to the Spinozist position he apparently held prior to his "conversion" to Kant's philosophy in 1790. But his attitude toward the differing stances on freedom of the will, and his perception of the relationship between opposing positions on it, remains strikingly similar to the attitudes and perceptions found in Spinoza (see especially S, *Ethics* V, P41S, P42S). Both philosophers see humanity as divided into those who act, and are free, and those who are passive, victims of their own slavish attitude of mind. Both philosophers offer the latter a path to freedom, but neither thinks many will take it, because they do not think it is easy for the free to communicate with the enslaved, nor for the enslaved even to want to escape their condition of spiritual servitude. For Fichte, this is because liberation requires a radical free choice, accomplishing an inner moral revolution; for Spinoza, it is because it requires a perfection of the intellect as difficult and rare as it is excellent. For Fichte, as for Spinoza, those self-condemned to slavery are difficult to reach because their condition of servitude itself holds them captive in a circle of illusion, cutting them off from the truth. If we want an accurate characterization of Fichte's attitude toward those who reject absolute freedom and the morality that goes with it, I think we should sooner describe it as "contempt" or "condescension" than as "blame" or "indignation". It has much in common with Spinoza's disdainful attitude toward those who are under various illusions about themselves and others, and who consequently do foolish and harmful things because they lack adequate ideas and are in bondage to irrational emotions.[10] In this way too, Fichte always remained a Spinozist.

---

[10]   See ZE, p. 499: [The dogmatist] has always sought refuge in an appeal to some sort of original being, even if this was nothing but a crude and formless matter. But idealism does away with this completely and leaves the dogmatist standing there naked and alone. To defend himself against such an attack, the dogmatist possesses no weapons beyond the attestation of his sincere displeasure, coupled with his assurance that he simply does not understand what he is expected to do and that he neither wishes nor is able to think of what is requested. We are quite happy to believe him when he assures us of this, and in turn we simply ask that he should also believe us when we insist that we, for our part, are quite able to think of our own system. If the dogmatist finds this to be too difficult as well, then we can refrain from making even this demand and can let him think whatever he pleases about this matter, for we have solemnly con-

Freedom as a presupposition of theoretical reason

Despite the apparently unbridgeable gulf between the opposed "faiths" of idealism and dogmatism, there is in Fichte one major line of argument that might be seen as having some traction with the dogmatist, even though Fichte himself does not seem disposed to think that a dogmatist might actually be convinced by such an argument. A crucial feature of Fichte's strategy in the *Wissenschaftslehre* of 1794 seems to have been to begin with a transcendental account of theoretical reason, with the result "that reason cannot even be theoretical if it is not practical" (GWL, p. 264). This in turn leads to:

> [T]he subordination of theory to the practical; for it follows that all theoretical laws are based on practical laws, or rather, since there can be only one of the latter, on one and the same law. [...] [Consequently,] there is a radical extirpation of that fatalism which rests on the assumption that our acting and willing are dependent on the system of our representations, in that it is here shown, on the contrary, that our system of representations depends on our drive and our will. [...] A drive of this sort would be one which absolutely gave birth to itself, an absolute drive, a drive for drive's sake. (If expressed as a law [...] it is a law for law's sake, an absolute law, or the categorical imperative – *You ought absolutely*) (GWL, pp. 294, 295, 327).

In developing this strategy, Fichte may be seen as following up a hint given by Kant in the Third Section of the *Groundwork*, when he attempts to argue that freedom must be ascribed to every rational being as a condition of its making theoretical judgments (GMS, p. 448). Neuhouser has described in some detail the working out of this strategy in the *Wissenschaftslehre* of 1794, and also explained how in the revised *Wissenschaftslehre* of 1797–1799, it gave way to the more direct appeal to the practical that we have just been examining (Neuhouser, 1990, pp. 41–65). Yet I think there remains something of Fichte's original intention of arguing regressively from the conditions of theoretical reason to freedom, in the form of Fichte's claim that the "proof" of freedom whose premises dogmatism lacks the power to grasp consists in the impossibility of explaining consciousness and representation objectively, as an effect of the causality of things (EE, pp. 432–433, 435–440).

Understanding and conviction. Another remnant of Fichte's original strategy lies in his claim that only the idealist is capable of being convinced (*überzeugt*) of his philosophy, while the dogmatist can never be: "Spinoza could not have

---

fessed on many occasions that we cannot force anyone to accept our system, since the acceptance of this system is something that depends upon freedom. – As I have said, the sole recourse left to the dogmatist is simply to assure us of his own sheer incapacity, which is a purely subjective matter.

been convinced of his own philosophy. He could only have *thought* of it; he could not have *believed* it" (ZE, p. 513). Conviction (*Überzeugung*), according to Fichte, always arises out of a condition of doubt, a condition of worry or concern (*Besorglichkeit*) in which "the imagination continues to waver between opposites" and ending with a "feeling of harmony" or "satisfaction", through which this wavering ceases, and "the power of the imagination is now bound or compelled, as it is in the case of everything real" (SL, p. 167). This "wavering of the imagination", according to Fichte, requires freedom, just as much as willing does (GWL, pp. 238–239; EE, p. 423; SL, pp. 67–68, 136). In this respect, the acquisition of "conviction" has freedom as its precondition in the same way as the acquisition of "understanding" (*Verstehen*) or "comprehension" (*Begreifen*):

> First of all – what does it mean to *understand* or *comprehend*? It means to *posit as fixed*, to *determine*, to *delimit*. I have comprehended an appearance if, through it, I have attained a complete cognitive whole that, with respect to all its parts, is grounded in itself; i.e. if each part is grounded or explained through all the others, and *vice versa*. Only in this way is it completed or delimited. – I have not comprehended something if I am still in the midst of explaining it, if my interpretation of it is still in a *state of wavering (Schweben)* and therefore not yet fixed; i.e. if I am still being led from one part of my cognition to the others. (I have not yet comprehended some contingent A, if I have not thought of a cause for A, and this means – since a particular kind of contingency must belong to A – if I have not thought of a particular cause for it) (GN, p. 77).

Here Fichte contrasts the state of *having understood or comprehended* with a temporally preceding state, in which one was still *coming to understand or to comprehend*. This preceding state is a hovering over or wavering (*Schweben*) between alternative possible judgments about what causes the object still to be comprehended, or (more generally) about how a cognitive whole relates to its constituent parts. Fichte seems to assume that for any fact to be theoretically understood or comprehended, there is a determinate cause, or grounding relation, which, when comprehended, will remove our sense of contingency from the object. Here the modal conceptions one might use in describing this contingency are merely *epistemic* modalities. For instance, first I have the thought: "It is *possible* that A is caused by X, but also possible that it is caused by Y". Then I come to think: "No: I see now that X *could not* have caused it, so it *must* have been caused by Y" – resulting in my comprehension of A as caused by Y. In this way, the possibilities regarding the object over which I hover, or between which I waver, are only epistemic possibilities: *For all I know*, A could have been caused by X or by Y. But once we comprehend A, it becomes *certain* what caused it, and so I can no longer judge otherwise than that Y caused it. My *judgment* then becomes *epistemically* necessary, even if the fact in question of what caused A is only a contingent fact. Dogmatism can perfectly well account for the fact that prior to arriving at understanding, comprehension or conviction, the mind "wavers" between these epistemic possibilities, regarding them as epistemically contingent. For the dogmatist, it can be causally necessitated that a given person remains confused or ignorant, hence in a state of epistemic contingency (or uncertainty) about many things. (This is in fact precisely the account Spinoza gives of this phenomenon at S, I, P33S1 and II, P44CS.)

The temporality of understanding. Yet there remains one crucial aspect of the wavering of imagination that cannot be accounted for in the same way: namely, the wavering of my mind itself, of which I am conscious prior to the act of comprehension, between the two alternative epistemic possibilities. In order to come to comprehension, I must entertain the two epistemic possibilities as possibilities (of some future fixing, determining or delimiting judgment) that are at this point in time still contingent in the sense that I must regard them as *open to me to judge.* Here I cannot regard the possibilities as merely epistemic, due only to my ignorance. I cannot regard my considering it contingent which of them I judge merely as a matter of my being ignorant of what my eventual judgment was already determined to be. The temporal process of coming to comprehend is possible only through a wavering at time t_1 between alternative possible judgments, and then my coming to fix or settle on one of them at a later time t_2. To regard the process as a genuine case of my coming to comprehend requires that both were really open to me to judge at t_1, in order that I may settle the matter by achieving comprehension at t_2. If instead I regard the matter as having already been settled or necessitated beforehand (unbeknownst to me) at t_1, that amounts to a denial that my judgment at t_2 came about precisely through the process of my (first) wavering between opposed epistemic possibilities and (then) settling, fixing, determining or delimiting the matter to one of them. Even where the possibilities are merely epistemic with reference to the object (for instance, the possible causes of A), the *possibilities of judging or fixing* that are open to me at t_1 must be more than epistemic. They must be real contingencies, capable of being settled by me, and at t_1 still open to my free agency to fix and determine later at t_2. This freedom, moreover, must be *absolute* in Fichte's sense: I must *be indeterminately* as questioner before I am later (self-)*determined* as judge. Or, in Sartrean terms: In order to judge at a time I must put myself *outside of* being: my *existence* as questioner must *precede my essence* as judge.[11]

---

[11] Sartre in fact closely follows Fichte in arguing that the question is the proof of freedom: "The questioner, by the very fact that he is questioning, posits himself as in a state of indetermination; *does not know* whether the reply will be affirmative or negative" (Sartre, 1956 a, p. 5). "It is essential that the questioner have the permanent possibility of dissociating himself from the causal series which constitutes being and which can produce only being. [...] He must be able to put himself *outside of* being" (Sartre, 1956 a, pp. 23–24).

Fichte thinks the process of transforming the wavering of imagination into the fixity of understanding is essential at every moment of time to our coming to the justified conviction of the reality of the material world around us. "Intuition", he says, is "fixed or stabilized by reason", so that an object can be considered one and the same in different determinations of it. Imagination then "wavers between conflicting directions", then through understanding "the transiency [of this wavering of imagination] is arrested, settled, as it were, or brought to a stand, and is rightly called *understanding*" (FW 1, pp. 232–233). Fichte cites certain philosophers (Salomon Maimon would seem to be among them) who have come to realize that ordinary understanding is a result of the exercise of imagination, but have been tempted by this to consider the entire process a deception (FW 1, pp. 227, 234). Fichte insists that they must be mistaken; for that which I must represent as necessary to successfully coming to understand cannot be represented as deception. That would make understanding itself a deception, which would be nonsense.

To be sure, it is always possible that some particular judgment (about the cause of A, or about the reality and the determinations of some object before me) was indeed pre-determined beforehand, by a process I did not understand, so that it did not after all come about by means of the wavering of my imagination and its fixation by understanding. But this is to exhibit this particular supposed act of coming to understand as a deception. If I represent my judgment as pre-determined, then I cannot, on pain of incoherence, also represent it as a genuine case of understanding or comprehension. This remains the case even if it resulted (even non-accidentally) in a *true* judgment about the cause of A. This is because it is a conceptual point about comprehension that the process of coming to comprehend must be essentially self-transparent: if it came about in such a way that the subject is essentially deceived about how it came about, then *understanding* or *comprehension* has not come about at all. A subject need not, of course, be conscious of every aspect of the process – for instance, of all the neuron-firings – that went into it. But the subject cannot be essentially self-opaque or in error about the normative-epistemic essentials of the process. And these include the real (not merely epistemic) contingency of the possibilities of judging that are open to me at t_1. If I were mistaken in believing at t_1 that my judging was genuinely contingent, dependent on the course of my thinking – that it was truly open to me at t_1 make any of several really possible judgments about the cause of A – then the judgment I do eventually make at t_2 about this cause could not possibly be a genuine case of my coming to understand or comprehend A.

Freedom and reason. Another way to think of it is this: to come to understand or comprehend is to come to judge something for a *good reason*, and to have one's judgment determined by that reason. A reason, however, has the peculiar property that although it may explain why I judge as I do, it does not do this by preventing me from judging otherwise or taking away from me the genuine possibility of judging otherwise. So a judgment made for reasons is always contingent, not merely epistemically, but really contingent. Reasons, in other words, even the best reasons, always leave us free to act against them. (Reasons, as Leibniz said, "incline without necessitating"). This is why the conspicuous truth that humans are the only irrational animals is grounded on the deeper truth that humans are the only rational animals.

Or again, we can also see it as a consequence of a point made earlier about acting on norms. Subjection to norms is just as essential to theoretical judgment or assent, hence to coming to understand or comprehend or be convinced, as it is to any other action. But it is only free acts that can be explained by their conformity to norms. To be aware of a norm as governing one's action, and to regard oneself as required to act (including: to judge) according to the norm, is therefore to presuppose that one is free in this acting (or judging): that the action (or judgment) is one of several really (not merely epistemically) possible acts (or judgments) and that it depends on me which of these possibilities I settle on or determine.

This is not like a case where something might appear to me to be one way, where I can know it is really another – as when the sun appears to move across the sky, but I know that it is really the earth turning on its axis, or the Müller-Lyer lines appear unequal but I know they are really equal. In these cases I am not rationally committed to assent to the "appearance", as I am rationally committed to assent to the claim that my understanding or conviction came about through a free judgment for reasons whenever I represent myself as coming to understand or be convinced. To suppose my acts of judging, understanding, comprehending, coming to be convinced for reasons, were all pre-determined beforehand is thus in effect to suppose that all such acts are illusory and self-deceptive. Unless I think of myself as having the capacity to judge for reasons between genuine possibilities, I must view the entirety of my epistemic life as self-opaque, a deception perpetrated on me (though necessarily with my own complicity) by external causes of which I am unaware.

Philosophers are routinely accused of overestimating the extent to which human beings act rationally. In view of the role irrationality (evil, weakness of will, sophistical rationalization, self-deception, self-opacity and the like) plays in the moral psychology of rationalist philosophers such as Descartes, Kant, and Spinoza, this charge seems as silly as it is ubiquitous. Some philosophers even like to toy with the thought that all our conscious processes involve self-opacity or deception. Nietzsche, post-modernists and neurophilosophers, for instance, sometimes enjoy titillating themselves with such thoughts.[12] As a more

---

[12]   In dreams, Nietzsche says, we often imagine a cause for a particular sensation (say, a far-off cannon shot we hear). The cannon shot appears to us later in the narrative of

recent neurophilosopher puts it: "Your conscious life is nothing but an elaborate post-hoc rationalization of things you really do for other reasons" (Ramachandran, 2004, p. 1).[13] The only point a philosopher like Fichte wants (or needs) to make here is that there is a *limit in principle* (on pain of incoherence) to the extent to which we can coherently represent *all* human thinking as self-opaque, deceptive or based on post-hoc rationalization. I cannot, for instance, represent my belief that all human thinking is self-opaque as a rational judgment to that effect if I include that very judgment within the scope of human thinking that suffers from self-opacity. Nietzsche, or a neurophilosopher, cannot suppose that the same deflationary accounts he gives of the mental lives of others applies to the acts of inquiry and discovery through which he has concluded that people act for reasons other than the ones of which they are conscious. To suppose this would be to discredit his own accounts of other people's mental lives.

How Spinoza avoids the incoherence. Spinoza does not belong to this species of philosophical incoherence, though he may face a different kind of problem. Spinoza holds, regarding certain privileged epistemic states which he calls "reason" and "intuition", that they involve comprehension of their own necessity (S, *Ethics* II, P40S, PP41–44). He dismisses as illusory all states involving "imagination", which (he agrees with Fichte) necessarily wavers between alternatives, representing its objects as contingent (S, *Ethics* II, P44CS). Spinoza might be quite correct in cases of understanding that have been settled in the past. Once I have seen clearly and distinctly that $2+3=5$, then as long as I retain the results of this insight as part of my beliefs, it will no longer be possible for me to believe that $2+3$ could equal any number other than 5. It is also true of many of our beliefs that they were not arrived at directly by such a process, but were acquired along with an entire web of beliefs which was arrived at through

the dream than its supposed cause, but in fact the representations produced by the state have been misunderstood as its causes. "In fact, we do the same thing when awake. [...] We want to have a reason for feeling this way or that, [and] we admit this fact only – become conscious of it only – when we have furnished some kind of motivation. [...] Thus originates a habitual acceptance of a particular causal interpretation, which, as a matter of fact, inhibits any investigation into the real cause – even precludes it" (Kaufmann, 1954, pp. 496–497).

13   Ramachandran offers this contemptuous dismissal of *your* conscious life (and mine), but what about *his own* conscious life? As Cathy Gere writes (she is reviewing Michael Gazzaniga's *Free Will and the Science of the Brain*, but she could be talking about almost any neuroscientist or neurophilosopher who ventures into this topic): "How is it that Gazzaniga, whose entire career has been based on the application of the scientific method, has so little regard for the workings of reason? With this denial he seems to claim rationality for himself while consigning the rest of us to automaton status" (Gere, 2011, p. 31).

temporal processes yet without each of them being acquired separately by such a process. Spinoza's position, therefore, might be coherent if reason and intuition are considered atemporally, as states in which the subject has always understood something, as it were, without ever needing to come to understand it. For then they might be necessitated in the same way as our standing conviction that $2+3=5$.

Spinoza also holds that time itself is a product of imagination (S, *Ethics* II, P44CS). Perhaps this implies that the temporal process of coming to understand presupposes the erroneous affirmation of real contingency, which is seen through once the object has been fixed through comprehension. Fichte's argument, however, proceeds from the premise that the temporality of our understanding is a transcendentally necessary condition of our experience of whatever we can ever understand, and is consequently real and undeniable. Nothing, in other words, has ever been understood except through a temporal process of coming to understand; freedom is a presupposition of this temporal process, and this is what Spinozist necessitarianism cannot account for: "All our consciousness commences with indeterminacy, for it commences with the power of the imagination, which is a hovering (*schwebendes*) power wavering (*schwankendes*) between opposites." (SL, p. 194) It is essential to our lives as temporal experiencers and knowers that we are confronted at every moment with the task of achieving some new understanding that presupposes first a wavering between alternatives and then a fixation on one of them.

Thus, instead of saying that Spinoza could never be convinced of his philosophy, Fichte might better have said that Spinoza could never have *come to be convinced* of it – adding, however, that *coming to be convinced* is, for a human subject, the only way of ever getting into the state of *being convinced*. Fichte might say that dogmatists might be convinced of their system, or comprehend the world in terms of it, if only they could accomplish this without ever having to *come to be* convinced or to comprehend. Perhaps this is how Spinoza's eternal God understands things, but it cannot apply to existing human beings, who are always in process of becoming.[14] Or perhaps it is the way Spinoza thinks we know things by the "second kind of knowledge" or "reason" – which is apparently the way the *Ethics* itself is being represented *more geometrico*. However, when Spinoza thinks of himself as knowing by the "third kind of knowledge" or "intuition", he supposes a spatio-temporally situated kind of knowing, where he directly perceives that the essence of a certain thing (for instance, of one of his own mental states) follows by common notions from an adequate idea of certain attributes of God (S, *Ethics* II, P40S2). Spinoza also

---

14   Except that Spinoza's God has no understanding (*intellectus*) at all, or if God can be said to have an understanding, it is no more like ours than Canis Major up in the night sky is like the little animal barking by our feet (S, *Ethics* I, P17C2S, cf. I, P31).

seems to think, however, that this third kind of knowledge can be achieved *sub specie aeternitatis*, so that what is known is not represented as having come to be intuited by an individual mind at a specific time (S, *Ethics* V, P22, P29). In his unfinished treatise *On the Improvement of the Intellect,* Spinoza reports that "the things I have been able to know by this kind of knowledge are as yet very few" (S, p. 238). We might regard even this as a wild exaggeration.

"Externalist justification". A notion of understanding without coming to understand might be what some epistemologists are trying to achieve in another way by adopting exclusively "externalist" theories of justification. These might be used to show how subjects can be justified in holding certain beliefs (hence perhaps in understanding or knowing them to be true), viewed entirely from an external perspective (hence perhaps not available to the knowing subject itself). Dogmatists might then be justified, in this externalist sense, in holding a view about themselves that could not be combined coherently with any account they could be in a position to give of how they arrived at this view, or came to be convinced of it, or came to think of themselves as justified in holding it. The problem with this, however, is that the judgments of the externalist episte-mologists themselves – their judgments about how people's convictions are justified – could in turn be coherently declared justified only by others, and never by these epistemologists themselves. We thus are offered a picture according to which people might have all kinds of justified convictions, or even scientific knowledge, but no one could be in a position to say that they do based on reasons they can claim as part of their own intellectual life. This is a picture it would be in principle impossible for you rationally to accept based on reasons or evidence available to you (since that would have to be "internal" justification). And that's a sufficient reason for any human being to reject this picture, even if it cannot be shown to be objectively false.

"The first-person standpoint". These reflections might provoke the objection that this argument could be valid only from a "first-person" standpoint, which might then be depicted as "subjective" in a way that would allow us to dismiss it as illusory. But of course the philosophers or scientists who engage in this act of dismissal would need to adopt a first-person stance on their own acts of this kind, and they could not then coherently demote *those* thoughts to the status of subjective illusions. In any case, it is simply not true that the presupposition of freedom involved in the attribution of understanding, comprehension, and conviction applies only to a first-person stance on our own mental lives. For we must equally represent any other person as free in this way if we propose to offer them reasons for any conviction and coherently suppose that they might be convinced by these reasons. By the same token, if we want to think, in the third-person, of still others as capable of being addressed in this way, and of coming to be convinced for reasons, we must presuppose that they are free as

well. There is no "purely objective" stance we can take on people that regards them as lacking freedom, unless we also cease to regard them as beings who can self-consciously *act*, or *interact* with others, or even (with comprehension) expect to *observe* others acting *for reasons*.[15]

Take the issue of free will itself. Suppose I am trying to decide what position is correct on this issue – Fichtean libertarianism, or some necessitarian position, whether Spinozist or soft-determinist. No matter how good the arguments on the necessitarian side of these disputes may be, the arguments always arrive on the scene too late. In order even to entertain them as rational arguments, I must already represent myself as having a variety of possible judgments open to me, in order to be capable of deciding the question at a time and according to reasons – in other words, I must already presuppose that necessitarianism is false. If I represent myself as coming to judge for reasons that my judgment is necessitated, then I thereby commit myself to the position that the judgment in question could not have been a judgment for reasons after all. *For me* that has to invalidate the necessitarian arguments (whatever their apparent merits) as possible rational grounds for my conviction.

In short: the necessitarian position cannot be coherently combined with the thought that I have come to be convinced of it for good reasons.[16] But exactly the same goes for my attempt to represent *you* as having adopted necessitarianism about yourself for good reasons, or *our* attempt to represent *some third person* as having done this. The problem is not that we take a first-person standpoint when we consider human agents (though of course we must do that, just as we must adopt the first-person standpoint when we consider *anything*), but rather that no one can ever coherently represent any conscious agent (any being that can and must take a first-person standpoint and act for reasons) merely as a causally necessitated mechanism. Fichte sees this point clearly:

---

[15]   Thus Gazzaniga may be on to something (and in agreement with Fichte) when he argues that freedom is a property of the way people interact (Gazzaniga, 2011, pp. 143–179). But he conforms to tedious compatibilist orthodoxy (and departs from Fichte) in seeing the issue solely as about "our social practices" of legal responsibility, blame and punishment. For Fichte, I-hood and rationality themselves belong only to beings who are "summoned" by others, so that a rational being can exist only insofar as there are many rational beings in communication with one another (GN, pp. 17–56; SL, pp. 218–225).

[16]   As Derek Parfit points out, radical skepticism about epistemic norms, although self-defeating in the way I have just pointed out, has been held by many recent philosophers: among them, Quine and the later Wittgenstein (Parfit, 2011, vol. 2, pp. 521–525). Such positions are content, for instance, to provide psychological accounts of our epistemic practices, while rejecting the very notion of a "normative epistemology" that might provide grounding for these psychological accounts. I think this shows that the position Fichte called "dogmatism", together with its self-defeating theoretical commitments, is still alive and well today, though now it usually goes by the name "naturalism".

The relationship between free beings is one of free interaction; it is by no means a relationship of mere causality operating through mechanical forces. [...] [In seeking to convince others] we begin with freedom, [...] and assume that they are free as well. To be sure, in presupposing the thoroughgoing validity of the mechanism of cause and effect, [the dogmatists] contradict themselves. What they say stands in contradiction to what they do; for to the extent that they *presuppose* mechanism, they at the same time elevate themselves above it. Their own act of thinking of this relationship is an act that lies outside the realm of mechanical determinism. Mechanism cannot grasp itself, precisely because it is mechanism. Only a free consciousness is able to grasp itself (ZE, pp. 509–510).

Why the conviction of freedom must remain a "faith". It is important to see, however, that the considerations just adduced do not show directly *that I am free*, or that my judgment ever actually selects, for good reasons, between genuinely contingent possibilities for judging. The above Fichtean arguments leave it still possible, considered abstractly in itself, that we never really come to understand or to judge for reasons at all, that all our supposed comprehension or understanding is always illusory. They show only that it belongs to the concept of coming to understand that it must involve freedom, and hence that we can never coherently represent ourselves – to ourselves, or to others – as coming to understand that we are not free (or, indeed as coming to understand anything at all, unless we are free). This is the most basic reason why Fichte holds that we can never finally prove that we are free, or that idealism can ultimately refute dogmatism, that the idealist position must be described as based on *faith*.

But this way of putting it, however, may also be misleading. The "faith" in question is not the least bit arbitrary, irrational, voluntary or even avoidable as long as we are thinking coherently about the world along with our own thoughts concerning it. There is no alternative to the conviction that we are free as long as we represent ourselves as understanding or comprehending anything, or having come to be convinced of anything at all through reasons. The necessary representation of ourselves as free involved in such self-representation is not a *psychological* necessity, something we "can't help thinking is so" (but from which a less frail or defective mind might be exempted). It is rather a *normative* necessity, arising as soon as I try coherently to combine my claim that I have come to understand with any representation of the process through which I have come to understand. Freedom is not so much proven as presupposed by all doubting, questioning, coming to be convinced, as a necessary condition of their occurrence.[17] Assent to this presupposition is therefore required if we represent ourselves or someone else as having engaged in these cognitive acts. Fichte observes that the task of deciding between alternatives for reasons is

---

[17]   "Anguish has not appeared to us as a *proof* of human freedom; the latter was given to us as the necessary condition for the question" (Sartre, 1956 a, p. 33).

continually our task as knowers or intelligences, simply because it is more fundamentally our task at every moment as agents – that is, as *willing* beings. For whenever we find ourselves in reflection, Fichte argues, we always find ourselves fundamentally as *will* (SL, pp. 18–23). It is the *willing* I or the "practical I" that is always the original I of self-consciousness (GN, pp. 20–23). And volition, along with the process of coming to understand or being convinced, is something we can coherently represent only as a conscious transition from indeterminacy to determinacy (SL, p. 137; cf. p. 79).

The traditional problem of free will

The traditional problem of free will, whatever position one may take on it, is the problem of reconciling human agency with our metaphysical conception of the world and how things work in it. Epicurus, who made the startling discovery of this problem around the beginning of the third century B.C., tried to solve it by the desperate act of postulating a "swerve" to the motion of the atoms that would allow for contingency, rationality, and accountability, and rescue us from the threat of fatalistic necessity. The reconciliation of freedom with our view of the objective world is equally the problem for naturalistic incompatibilists, such as Epicurus himself, and naturalistic compatibilists, who try to conceive of freedom in such a way that it can be fit more easily into the causal order of nature. The problem is not essentially different, however, from that of those incompatibilists who want to locate freedom among the faculties of Cartesian immaterial thinking substances or supernatural noumenal selves. For even their anti-naturalist picture is an attempt to make freedom *compatible* with our view of the world as a whole and the nature of the things or entities it contains.

We might be tempted to think Fichte belongs among those who seek such a supernaturalist solution. He does occasionally assert that that the failure of dogmatism and its "materialistic" conception of the world justifies us in claiming that as free agents we belong to an intelligible world (SL, p. 91; GGW, p. 181). But we misunderstand such remarks if we take them to refer to an attempt to explain freedom in terms of a theoretical metaphysics of noumena or things-in-themselves (such as Kant is often represented as doing).[18] Fichte's own conception of the "supersensible" is part of his philosophy of religion, whose status in relation to his ethics and transcendental philosophy is by no means obvious. But to take his claim that we are members of an intelligible world as asserting a transcendent metaphysics of supernatural entities cannot be correct, for this would be to transform Fichte's philosophy into a species of dogmatism.

---

[18]   That this is not really Kant's position, and in any case could not be a self-consistent Kantian position on freedom, is argued in Chapter 7 of Wood, 2008.

When Fichte claims that dogmatism is incapable of explaining the I in terms of "things", he means to exclude spiritual or supersensible as well as sensible "things".[19] For Fichte, the I is necessarily embodied in a natural, living body: the very idea of a non-physical, spiritual entity as the subject either of our thoughts or our free actions is incoherent and inconceivable. Whatever Fichte may be, he is not an incompatibilist-indeterminist who proposes to explain free action through a supernaturalist metaphysics postulating supersensible things-in-themselves.

Another possible stance on the traditional problem of free will (or indeed, on any philosophical problem), is not to solve it (either naturalistically or supernaturalistically), but rather to declare it *insoluble.* Philosophical problems can be treated this way either by being dismissed on some pretext or other as pseudo-problems, or by acknowledging them as permanent sources of dissatisfaction and perplexity that we have to learn to live with, however frustrating and humiliating this may be for us, as part of our human condition. The latter stance seems to be Kant's final word on the problems he explored in the Transcendental Dialectic (KrV, pp. A VII–VIII, A 293–298/B 349–355, A 338–340/B 396–398). When he rejects dogmatism as a system of philosophy, Fichte is in effect taking this Kantian position with regard to the traditional problem of free will. The only way freedom can (or needs to) be reconciled with our view of things is that its acceptance is a transcendental condition of the possibility of being conscious of an objective world, representing objects, or coming to convictions about them, or understanding or comprehending them. For the Fichtean idealist, freedom falls outside the objective world – not metaphysically, as if it belonged to some *other* world, but methodologically or transcendentally. Fichte's position, then is that the *insolubility* of the traditional problem of free will is a transcendental condition of the possibility not only of morality and agency, but even of our conscious experience of any objective world.

References

Breazeale, Daniel (ed.) (1988): *Fichte: Early Philosophical Writings*, Ithaca [= EW].
Fichte, Johann Gottlieb (1962 ff.): *J. G. Fichte-Gesamtausgabe*, ed. Reinhard Lauth and Hans Gliwitzky, Stuttgart [= FGA].
–   (1971): *Werke*, ed. I. H. Fichte, Berlin [= FW].
–   *Aphorismen über Religion und Deismus*, in: FW, vol. 5, pp. 1–8 [= ARD].
–   *Einige Vorlesungen über die Bestimmung des Gelehrten*, in: FW, vol. 6, pp. 291–346 [= VBG].

---

[19]   Don't forget that Fichte considers Berkeley a dogmatist rather than an idealist because Berkeley's system is based on the conception of mind or spirit as a kind of *immaterial substance* or *thing* (EE, p. 438).

– *Erste Einleitung in die Wissenschaftslehre*, in: FW, vol. 1, pp. 417–49 [= EE].
– *Grundlage des Naturrechts*, in: FW, vol. 3, pp. 1–385 [= GN].
– *Grundriß des Eigentümlichen der Wissenschaftslehre in Rücksicht auf das theoretische Vermögen*, in: FW, vol. 1, pp. 329–411 [= GEW].
– *System der Sittenlehre*, in: FW, vol. 4, pp. 1–365 [= SL].
– *Über Belebung und Erhöhung des reinen Interesse für Wahrheit*, in: FW, vol. 8, pp. 342–352 [= BEW].
– *Ueber den Grund unsers Glaubens an eine göttliche Weltregierung*, in FW, vol. 5, pp. 175–189 [= GGW].
– *Zweite Einleitung in die Wissenschaftslehre*, in: FW, vol. 1, pp. 451–518 [= ZE].
Gazzaniga, Michael (2011): *Who's in Charge? Free Will and the Science of the Brain*, New York.
Gere, Cathy (2011): "Hemispheric Disturbances", in: *The Nation*, December 5.
Ginet, Carl (1980): "The Conditional Analysis of Freedom", in: van Inwagen, Peter (ed.): *Time and Cause: Essays Presented to Richard Taylor*, Dordrecht, pp. 171–186.
Hegel, G. W. F. (1991): *Elements of the Philosophy of Right* (1821), ed. Wood, tr. Nisbet, Cambridge. Cited by paragraph (§).
Heidegger, Martin (1953): *Being and Time*, tr. Macquarrie, John and Robinson, Edward, New York.
Kant, Immanuel (1902 ff.): *Kants gesammelte Schriften*, ed. Königlich Preussischen Akademie der Wissenschaften, Berlin [= AA].
– *Kritik der reinen Vernunft*, in: AA, vols. 3–4 [= KrV].
– *Grundlegung zur Metaphysik der Sitten*, in: AA, vol. 4, pp. 385–464 [= GMS].
– *Kritik der praktischen Vernunft*, in: AA, vol. 5, pp. 1–164 [= KpV].
Kaufmann, Walter (ed.) (1954): *The Portable Nietzsche*, New York.
– (1956) *Existentialism from Dostoevsky to Sartre*, New York.
Neuhouser, Frederick (1990): *Fichte's Theory of Subjectivity*, New York.
Parfit, Derek (2011): *On What Matters*, Oxford.
Ramachandran, V. S. (2004): *A Brief Tour of Human Consciousness*, New York.
Sartre, Jean Paul (1956 a): *Being and Nothingness*, tr. Hazel Barnes, New York.
– (1956 b): "Existentialism is a Humanism", in: Kaufmann 1956, pp. 287–311.
– (1964): *Nausea*, tr. Lloyd Alexander, New York.
Schopenhauer, Arthur (1958): *World as Will and Representation*, tr. E. F. J. Payne, New York.
Spinoza, Benedict (1992): *Ethics, Treatise on the Emendation of the Intellect, and Selected Letters*, tr. Samuel Shirley, Indianapolis [= S].
Wood, Allen (2008): *Kantian Ethics*, New York.

Christian Klotz

Freiheit und Offenbarung. Über einen Aspekt des Verhältnisses zwischen Fichte und Schelling

When the exchange of letters between Fichte and Schelling ceased in 1802, it appeared as if their differences on the status of Naturphilosophie – and on the appropriate comprehension of the principle of philosophy – have become so large that they could not be overcome, and therefore, further discourse seemed impossible. Later polemic statements only confirmed that the divisiveness between both was irrevocably. On the other hand especially the later writings of Fichte and Schelling show, if considered from a completely different systematic point of view, the same philosophical venture: to deduce the essential concept of human freedom as an implication of the revelation of the Absolute, which is irrefutable, if you try to understand the Absolute as such. This venture is traceble both in Fichte's Anweisung zum seligen Leben (1806) and in Schelling's Freiheitsschrift (1809). This essay aims to discuss the relationship between Fichte and Schelling considering this aspect. It will be shown that Fichte and Schelling – although starting from a shared concept of revelation – define the concept of freedom differently. Their definitions can be characterized as a premoral and also as a moral concept of freedom. Up to this day their relation has not been sufficiently discussed.

Als der Briefwechsel zwischen Fichte und Schelling 1802 abbrach, war das Bewusstsein der Einigkeit, das beide Denker zunächst verbunden hatte, dem einer so tief greifenden Differenz gewichen, dass weiterer gedanklicher Austausch nicht mehr möglich schien. Schellings Projekt einer von der Transzendentalphilosophie unabhängigen Naturphilosophie, die vom Begriff eines objektiven Subjekt-Objekts ausgeht und das Ich als dessen höhere Potenz erweist, war mit Fichtes philosophischem Projekt offenbar unvereinbar, ja aus dessen Sicht nicht einmal als sinnvoll anzuerkennen. Spätere polemische Stellungnahmen bestätigen nur noch die Unwiderruflichkeit der Entzweiung. So begreift Schelling in seiner 1806 erschienenen, gemeinhin als „Anti-Fichte" bezeichneten Schrift auch die inzwischen gewandelte Fassung der fichteschen Wissenschaftslehre letztlich nur als eine weitere Bekräftigung der Konzeption der Natur als vernunftlose Mannigfaltigkeit und bloßes Hindernis freier Tätigkeit, die schon die frühe Wissenschaftslehre Fichtes kennzeichne.[1]

Sind also die Differenzen bezüglich des Naturbegriffs und die davon untrennbaren Unterschiede hinsichtlich des jeweils verfolgten philosophischen Projekts der einzige Gesichtspunkt, unter dem das Verhältnis zwischen Fichte

---

[1] S. Schelling, 1958, S. 595 ff.

und Schelling zu verstehen ist? In diesem Aufsatz soll der Versuch unternommen werden, sich von einer anderen Perspektive leiten zu lassen, um die Alternative zwischen fichteschem und schellingschem Denken zu verstehen – einer Perspektive, die sich gerade mit der Entwicklung im Denken Fichtes und Schellings nach dem Bruch 1802 abzeichnet. In Fichtes *Anweisung zum seligen Leben* von 1806 und Schellings *Freiheitsschrift* von 1809 – so meine für die folgende Untersuchung grundlegende These – lässt sich durchaus ein gemeinsames philosophisches Projekt erkennen. In beiden Theoriestücken spielt nämlich der Gedanke eine zentrale Rolle, dass das Absolute sich wesentlich offenbart, und dass seine Offenbarung sich im Menschen ereignet oder vollendet. Der Offenbarungsbegriff wird hier also jeweils eingeführt, um vom Gedanken des Absoluten her das menschliche Dasein zu erhellen. Dies unterscheidet den hier relevanten Offenbarungsgedanken von theologischen oder auch moraltheologischen Begriffen von Offenbarung, wie etwa dem vom frühen Fichte in seiner Schrift von 1792 noch vertretenen „kritischen" Offenbarungsbegriff.[2] In den genannten Schriften Fichtes und Schellings wird der Offenbarungsbegriff nun genauer in der Absicht herangezogen, die Freiheit als wesentliche Eigenschaft des Menschen zu erweisen und zu verstehen, worin diese eigentlich besteht. Im Folgenden sollen Fichtes *Anweisung* und Schellings *Freiheitsschrift* daher unter diesem Aspekt ins Verhältnis gesetzt werden: als unterschiedliche Ausführungen des Grundgedankens, dass der philosophisch zentrale Begriff der Freiheit des Menschen auf der Basis einer bestimmten Konzeption der Offenbarung des Absoluten zu explizieren ist.

Es soll hierbei gezeigt werden, dass Fichte und Schelling aufgrund unterschiedlicher Explikationen des Offenbarungsbegriffs zu verschiedenen Antworten auf die Frage gelangen, worin die für menschliches Dasein grundlegende Freiheit besteht. Der Konzeption der Freiheit als prä-volitiver Selbstbestimmung hinsichtlich der je eigenen „Weltansicht" (Fichte) steht der Begriff der Freiheit als Fähigkeit zum Guten und Bösen in einem ontologisch fundierten ethischen Sinn (Schelling) gegenüber. Dass eine solche Differenz hinsichtlich des Freiheitsbegriffs sich hier auftut, scheint mir ein bis heute kaum zureichend diskutierter Aspekt des Verhältnisses zwischen Fichte und Schelling zu sein. Es wird zu zeigen sein, dass beide Freiheitsbegriffe, obwohl sie ganz unterschiedliche Aspekte des menschlichen Daseins in den Mittelpunkt stellen, als solche durchaus systematisch vereinbar sind. Dies bedeutet freilich nicht, dass die in den hier zu betrachtenden Schriften von Fichte und Schelling hinsichtlich der menschlichen Freiheit vertretenen Positionen spannungslos ineinander gefügt werden können. Eine abschließende Betrachtung soll deutlich machen, dass in Fichtes *Anweisung* und Schellings *Freiheitsschrift* die Idee des je eigenen Selbst als Willenssubjekt in derart divergierender Weise interpretiert und bewertet

---

2   S. Fichte, 1998, bes. S. 33 ff.

wird, dass man von *alternativen* Ausführungen des idealistischen Projekts eines „Spinozismus der Freiheit" zu sprechen hat. Zuerst ist jedoch der jeweils vorliegende Zusammenhang zwischen Offenbarung des Absoluten und Freiheit des Menschen in den beiden Schriften Fichtes und Schellings deutlich zu machen.

1. Offenbarung, Weltansicht und Freiheit des Menschen in Fichtes *Anweisung zum seligen Leben*

Fichtes *Anweisung zum seligen Leben* setzt mit der Aufforderung ein, „das Sein" zu denken. Von diesem wird gesagt, dass es vollkommen durch sich und aus sich ist. Das Sein wird somit durch Attribute charakterisiert, die es als Absolutum kennzeichnen, und durch keine weiteren.[3] Für den Fortgang der *Anweisung* ist nun Fichtes hierüber hinausgehende Feststellung entscheidend, dass das Sein im definierten Sinn ganz in sich geschlossen und damit noch nicht „Dasein" ist, d. h. noch keine Äußerung seiner selbst im Sinne einer Manifestation oder „Offenbarung" seiner einschließt.[4] Fichte setzt in der *Anweisung* voraus, dass das Sein sich notwendig offenbart – wohl deshalb, weil es sonst kein „Leben", sondern nur statische Gleichheit mit sich selbst wäre. Die Offenbarung des Seins aber erfordert eine *Differenz* zwischen dem Sein und seiner Äußerung, die mit dem Sein als reinem Absolutum noch nicht gegeben ist. Diese Differenz ist freilich als innere Differenzierung des Seins zu verstehen, da die Offenbarung ja „Sichdarstellung" des Seins und insofern ein Verhältnis des Seins zu sich selbst ist.[5]

Die Frage, wie das Sein in seinem Dasein, d. h. die Offenbarung des Seins als solche verfasst sein muss, steht im Mittelpunkt des weiteren Gangs der *Anweisung*. Es ist diese Frage, die nach Fichte den Schlüssel zum Verständnis des menschlichen Bewusstseins bietet. Die Manifestation des Seins, so argumentiert Fichte hier, muss sich auf das Sein, wie es in sich ist, als Ausdruck seiner (als „Bild") beziehen. Sie muss somit einen auf das Sein bezogenen *repräsentationalen* Charakter besitzen. Fichte sagt daher, die Äußerung des Seins sei wesentlich „Wissen", oder „Bewußtsein" (nämlich des Seins).[6] Damit ist der Offenbarungsbegriff in einen direkten Zusammenhang mit dem Begriff des Bewusst-

---

[3]   S. AsL, S. 49. Der Ausgangspunkt der *Anweisung* entspricht hiermit dem Prinzip der späten Wissenschaftslehren Fichtes. Legt man die Wissenschaftslehre von 1804 (zweiter Vortrag) zugrunde, so kann man sagen, dass die Aufforderung, mit der die *Anweisung* einsetzt, den Leser auf den Standpunkt der „Vernunft- und Wahrheitslehre" versetzen soll, deren Grundgedanke eben der vom Sein als selbstgenügsamen Absolutum ist (s. Fichte, 1975, S. 160).

[4]   S. AsL, S. 50.

[5]   AsL, S. 73.

[6]   S. AsL, S. 50–52.

seins als repräsentierender Instanz gebracht. Das „Dasein" des Absoluten, sein Sich-Offenbaren, beginnt erst da, wo das Sein von einem Bewusstsein repräsentiert wird, in welcher Weise und mit welchem Grad von Explizitheit auch immer dies im einzelnen geschieht. Die Begriffe, in denen zu verstehen ist, wie das Absolute sich offenbart, sind folglich ausschließlich Begriffe von Bewusstseinsakten und ihren Inhalten, sofern diese – in mehr oder weniger transparenter Weise[7] – „Repräsentationen des Seins" sind.

Mit dem Gedanken, das Bewusstsein sei der Ort der notwendigen Offenbarung des Seins, ist freilich nur eine allgemeine Grundperspektive für die Erhellung des Bewusstseins vom Gedanken des Absoluten her eröffnet. Offenbar verstehen wir damit noch nicht, warum das Bewusstsein so ist, wie es ist – bezogen nämlich auf eine Mannigfaltigkeit von Gegenständen, die angeordnet sind im Raum und einem potenziell unendlichen Zeitfluss. Fichte sieht den Ursprung der für das Bewusstsein konstitutiven Mannigfaltigkeit in den Reflexionsprinzipien des Bewusstseins, denen zufolge im Wissen Bestimmtheit, damit aber auch Differenz und Vielheit gesetzt werden müssen. Das Bewusstsein kann also das eine Sein nur vermittels der Vorstellung einer Mannigfaltigkeit von Bestimmtheiten repräsentieren. Das Bestimmte in seiner Vielheit erscheint dem Wissen aber ursprünglich nicht als Produkt seiner selbst, sondern als vorhandene Welt. Die Welt ist sozusagen das im Bewusstsein gebrochene, vermannigfaltigte und vergegenständlichte Sein – und in diesem Sinn „Erscheinung" des Seins.[8]

Fichte vertritt die These, dass das „Dasein", d. h. die Offenbarung des Seins, wesentlich durch Freiheit gekennzeichnet ist. Für das Verständnis des hiermit ins Spiel gebrachten Freiheitsbegriffs ist es entscheidend, festzuhalten, dass Freiheit hier dem *Bewusstsein* als der das Sein vorstellenden Instanz zugesprochen wird. Freiheit im philosophisch grundlegenden Sinn ist in der *Anweisung* also wesentlich als eine Eigenschaft des vorstellenden Bewusstseins als solchen verstanden. Dementsprechend expliziert Fichte hier den Freiheitsbegriff unter Bezug auf die verschiedenen Weisen, in denen das Bewusstsein die Welt vorstellen kann, die er als „Weltansichten" bezeichnet. Von möglichen Ansichten der Welt ist dabei freilich in einem ganz eigentümlichen Sinn die Rede. Fichtes Grundgedanke ist hier, dass das Bewusstsein sich gleichsam einen Fokus gibt, indem es in Bezug auf das Mannigfaltige der Erscheinungen etwas als das „eigentlich Wahre" auszeichnet und anderes als unwesentlich erachtet. Würde es keinen Fokus setzen, so würde das Bewusstsein sich gleichsam in der Man-

---

[7] Dass Fichte nicht etwa die Selbsttransparenz des Bewusstseins unterstellt, wird deutlich, wenn er sagt, für das Bewusstsein könne sein eigener auf das Sein bezogener Bildcharakter verstellt und hinter „Schattenbildern" verborgen sein (s. AsL, S. 54).

[8] S. AsL, S. 63 ff. Vgl. die von Chr. Asmuth gegebene eingehende Darstellung der Konstitution des Bewusstseins in der *Anweisung* (Asmuth, 1999, S. 86 ff.).

nigfaltigkeit verlieren – und dies, wie Fichte unter Verwendung christlicher Metaphorik sagt, wäre der (geistige) „Tod". Dabei macht Fichte deutlich, dass die möglichen Ansichten der Welt nicht nur ein theoretisches Sich-Verhalten zur Welt bedeuten. Sie sind vielmehr wesentlich mit einem „Affekt" verbunden, d. h. mit einer bestimmten Weise, die Welt und das eigene Dasein zu erleben, die ihrerseits mit einer „Form des Lebens" verbunden ist.[9]

Inwiefern ist nun aber mit der Konzeption der dem Bewusstsein möglichen Weltansichten die Grundlage für einen Freiheitsbegriff gegeben? Indem das Bewusstsein eine Weltsicht annimmt, die im Gedanken eines „eigentlichen Wahren" ein Zentrum hat, erweist es sich als selbständig gegenüber der Mannigfaltigkeit der Erscheinungen. Statt diese Mannigfaltigkeit indifferent auf sich einströmen zu lassen, privilegiert es eine Instanz als die, der gegenüber alles andere nur unwesentlich oder Mittel zum Zweck ist. Von Freiheit wäre hier freilich noch nicht zu sprechen, wenn dies nicht wesentlich im Blick auf alternative Möglichkeiten geschehen würde, die Welt zentriert zu sehen. Nur unter dieser Bedingung ist die Annahme einer Weltansicht ein selbstbestimmter Akt, der eine Sichtweise in einem Raum von Möglichkeiten ergreift. Fichte nimmt an, dass es genau fünf grundlegend verschiedene Ansichten der Welt gibt, und bezeichnet deren Gesamtheit daher als die „Fünffachheit" des Bewusstseins.[10] Die im Hinblick auf den Freiheitsbegriff zentrale These in der *Anweisung* ist es, dass Freiheit „nur in Beziehung auf die angegebenen fünf Standpunkte des geistigen Lebens" besteht – sie ist „nichts mehr, denn die bloße Möglichkeit der Standpunkte des Lebens".[11]

Fichte führt damit einen Freiheitsbegriff ein, der sich auf den selbstbestimmten Charakter der Vorstellung des Seins bezieht, sofern diese sich als zentrierende Setzung eines eigentlich Wahren in Bezug auf das Mannigfaltige der Erscheinungen ausbildet. Der philosophisch grundlegende Freiheitsbegriff bezieht sich demnach auf den im Vorstellen der Welt angenommenen grundlegenden „Standpunkt", und nicht auf Handlungen oder die ihnen zugrunde liegenden Maximen. Dies ist offenbar in der *Anweisung* eine Konsequenz daraus, dass 1. Freiheit als Attribut des „Daseins" des Seins verstanden wird, und 2. das Dasein, d. h. die Offenbarung des Seins als *Vorstellung* des Seins aufgefasst wird. Unter diesen Annahmen ist Freiheit als Attribut des Vorstellens (der Ausbildung von „Weltansichten"), und nicht des Wollens oder Handelns zu fassen.

Dies wirft die Frage auf, welche Beziehung denn zwischen dem von Fichte als grundlegend angesetzten, auf Weltansichten bezogenen Freiheitssinn und

---

[9]   S. AsL, S. 107 ff. und 119.

[10]   S. AsL, S. 74 ff. Die systematische Grundlage der fünffachen Struktur der Weltansichten in der *Anweisung* ist im Prinzip der Fünffachheit zu sehen, wie es im zweiten Vortrag der Wissenschaftslehre 1804 aus der synthetischen Natur der Vernunft hergeleitet wird (s. Fichte, 1975, bes. S. 281 ff.).

[11]   AsL, S. 125.

dem Gedanken der Freiheit des Willens besteht. Man könnte hier die Auffassung vertreten, dass die Ausübung der Willensfreiheit die auf die Weltansichten bezogene Freiheit zur notwendigen Voraussetzung hat. Denn Entscheidungen und Zwecksetzungen werden innerhalb einer schon ergriffenen Lebensform vollzogen, setzen also die Aneignung einer Weltansicht immer schon voraus. Fichte geht aber noch einen Schritt weiter: Von der Weltansicht, die wir jeweils ergriffen haben, hängt es ab, ob wir uns überhaupt als mit Willensfreiheit begabte Akteure betrachten oder nicht. Denn diese Annahme ist der *Anweisung* zufolge nur ein Charakteristikum besonderer Weltansichten, keineswegs aber aller, die für uns möglich sind. Damit wird der Gedanke von sich als eigenständiger Akteur nicht mehr als eine universell gültige Voraussetzung gesehen, sondern als untergeordnetes Element besonderer Lebensformen. Diese These tritt im Gang der *Anweisung* derart in den Vordergrund, dass die fünffache Einteilung der möglichen Weltansichten schließlich von einer Zweiteilung überlagert wird, in der die Lebensformen unter dem Gesichtspunkt eingeteilt werden, ob sie das Selbstkonzept des als aus eigenem freien Willen handelnder Akteurs enthalten oder nicht.[12]

Im Rahmen der Zweiteilung stellen sich die ersten beiden Weltansichten im Sinne der fünffachen Einteilung – nämlich der auf die eigene Glückseligkeit zentrierte und der moralische Standpunkt – als durchaus verwandt dar, sofern sie wesentlich das Bild von sich als eigenständiger Akteur einschließen. Fichte bringt den Unterschied zwischen beiden Standpunkten zum Ausdruck, indem er die „materiale", d. h. als Fähigkeit zur Herstellung der eigenen Glückseligkeit definierte Freiheit vom „formalen" Freiheitssinn unterscheidet, der auf dem moralischen Standpunkt in Anspruch genommen wird.[13] Mit dem letzteren will Fichte ausdrücklich den im Sinne Kants verstandenen Standpunkt der Moralität in die Lehre der Lebensformen einbeziehen. Das in der *Anweisung* skizzierte Bild des moralischen Standpunkts verrät freilich zugleich in einigen Hinsichten eine Distanzierung Fichtes von Kants Verständnis des moralischen Standpunkts. Fichte beschreibt den moralischen Standpunkt in der *Anweisung* als ausschließlich an der Aufrechterhaltung des moralischen Selbstbilds, und damit an der Vermeidung von Selbstverachtung interessiert. Das Interesse gilt hier insofern nur dem, was durch eigenes Wollen auch gewährleistet werden kann.[14] Fichte folgert hieraus, dass der moralische Standpunkt unabhängig ist von der Hoffnung auf einen moralisch gerechten Weltzustand – auf das also, was Kant das „höchste Gut" nannte. Sofern die moralische Notwendigkeit solcher Hoffnung für Kant den inneren Zusammenhang zwischen moralischem Standpunkt und Religion herstellt, lehnt Fichte damit Kants Projekt einer „Moraltheologie"

---

[12]   S. AsL, bes. S. 126.
[13]   S. AsL, S. 128 ff.
[14]   S. AsL, S. 112 ff.

ab. So betont Fichte, der moralische Standpunkt könne nur durch „Inkonsequenz" zur Annahme eines Gottes kommen. Als angemessener Ausdruck des moralischen Standpunkts in seiner Selbstmacht gilt ihm stattdessen der goethesche „Prometheus".[15]

Indem es seinen Mittelpunkt im Gedanken des Gesetzes bzw. des durch das Gesetz ermöglichten intrinsischen Gutseins des Willens hat, ist das Bewusstsein aber noch weit entfernt davon, sich als Bild des Seins zu erfassen und damit in selbsttransparenter Weise dessen „Offenbarung" zu sein. Fichte konstruiert den Übergang zu diesem Standpunkt, der der Religion und der Philosophie zugeordnet wird, vermittels der „höheren Moralität", die vom moralischen Standpunkt im üblichen, vor allem aber im kantischen Sinn scharf abgesetzt wird. Die höhere Moralität zeichnet sich nämlich dadurch aus, dass hier der Gedanke von Freiheit im Sinne autonom-selbstbestimmten Wollens und Handelns gerade nicht mehr in Anspruch genommen ist.[16]

Ein zentrales Beispiel der höheren Moralität ist in der *Anweisung* der Standpunkt der künstlerischen Produktion.[17] Diese unterscheidet sich grundlegend vom Handeln des moralischen Subjekts, sofern sie nicht als eine vom eigenen Willen gesteuerte Tätigkeit zu verstehen ist. Man kann Fichtes Gedanken hier so formulieren, dass sich im künstlerischen Schaffen ein Produktionsprinzip Ausdruck gibt, das sich nicht als explizite Regel formulieren lässt und sich auch dem Künstler selbst nur im Produktionsprozess offenbart. Der eigentliche Akteur ist nicht der Künstler als Willenssubjekt, sondern ein sich in seinem Schaffen manifestierendes, implizites Produktionsgesetz. Fichte nimmt hier offenbar Elemente aus der von Kant in der *Kritik der Urteilskraft* formulierten Konzeption des Genies auf. Auch dort steht ja der Gedanke einer nicht explizit formulierbaren Regel im Mittelpunkt, die den künstlerischen Schaffensprozess steuert.[18] Fichte nimmt diesen Gedanken in der Weise auf, dass das implizite Produktionsprinzip zum eigentlichen Subjekt des Ausdrucksprozesses erklärt wird. Damit ist nun aber die Möglichkeit geschaffen, die durch die künstlerische Produktion exemplifizierte höhere Moralität mit dem Grundgedanken der Wissenschaftslehre in Verbindung zu bringen, dass das Bewusstsein wesentlich „Offenbarung", d. h. Vorstellung des Seins ist. In der Perspektive künstlerischen Schaffens wird sein Bild-Charakter für das Bewusstsein selbst manifest, indem die bewusste Produktion gar nicht mehr als freies regel- oder zweckgeleitetes Handeln, sondern als Sich-Ausdrücken eines impliziten Produktionsprinzips erscheint. Im religiösen und philosophischen Bewusstsein ist dieser

---

[15]   S. AsL, S. 116/17.
[16]   S. AsL, S. 80/81; S. 137 ff.
[17]   S. AsL, S. 139–42.
[18]   S. Kant, 1908, S. 307 ff. Fichte nimmt aus Kants Darstellung den (gleichbedeutenden) Ausdruck „Talent" auf, nicht explizit den des „Genies". Freilich spricht er von der Tugend als „Walten des Genius" (AsL, S. 145).

Gedanke zur Sicht allen Handelns und Geschehens als Ausdruck des für sich unexplizierbaren Absoluten gleichsam verallgemeinert.

Fichte drückt diesen Aspekt des religiösen und philosophischen Standpunkts in drastischen Worten aus, wenn er sagt, er erfordere die „Vernichtung" des Selbst. Und er beschreibt ihn als Überwindung und Preisgabe des Freiheitsgedankens.[19] Dies ist jedoch in seinem bestimmten, auf das moralische Freiheitsbewusstsein, und damit auf eine besondere „Weltansicht" bezogenen Sinn aufzufassen. Es wurde aber bereits deutlich, dass der in der *Anweisung* als philosophisch grundlegend angesetzte Freiheitsbegriff anderes meint als die kantische Akteursfreiheit – nämlich die Freiheit, eine der möglichen fokussierten Weltansichten anzunehmen. Angesichts der Tatsache, dass es verschiedene Möglichkeiten gibt, der Weltansicht ein Zentrum zu geben, muss diese Freiheit als eine unwiderrufliche Bedingung allen, auch des religiösen und philosophischen Bewusstseins gelten. Und so sagt Fichte auch, dass die so verstandene Freiheit selbst von Gott nicht aufgehoben werden könne. Denn der Gedanke dieser Freiheit ist nicht einer besonderen Weltansicht zugeordnet, sondern vorauszusetzen, wenn man überhaupt verstehen will, was es bedeutet, eine Weltansicht zu haben.[20]

2. Die aktuale Existenz Gottes in der Freiheit des Menschen: Schellings *Freiheitsschrift*

In seinem *Anti-Fichte* von 1806 stellt Schelling den Offenbarungsbegriff in den Mittelpunkt seiner Konzeption des Absoluten. Dies geschieht in der Absicht, den eigenen Begriff von Offenbarung gegen denjenigen abzusetzen, der bei Fichte – insbesondere in der *Anweisung* – leitend ist.[21] Schelling geht dabei davon aus, dass Gott qua lebendiges Sein nichts anderes ist als „Selbstoffenbarung". Diese findet aber in Gott als reiner Gleichheit mit sich noch gar nicht statt, sondern erfordert es, dass Gott zugleich innere Differenzierung, also „Vielheit" enthält. Das lebendige Sein Gottes ist somit durch den Gegensatz zwischen Eins-Sein und Vielheit gekennzeichnet, jedoch so, dass die Entgegengesetzten zugleich unauflösbar verbunden sind. Darin, das „Band" beider zu sein, d.h. als Eines nur in der Differenzierung wirklich zu sein, besteht eigentlich das Sein Gottes qua Selbstoffenbarung. Schelling betont, dass der Gegensatz „ebenso ursprünglich und wahr ist als die Einheit", da ohne ihn das lebendige Sein Gottes gar nicht zu denken sei.[22]

---

[19]   AsL, S. 130 u. 126.
[20]   S. AsL, S. 125.
[21]   S. Schelling, 1958, S. 648 ff.
[22]   Schelling, 1958, S. 646.

Damit ist die Offenbarung Gottes in einer Weise konzipiert, die die Vielheit zum ursprünglichen inneren Moment des Seins Gottes macht. Es ist diese Implikation, die dem Offenbarungsbegriff hier seine systematische Bedeutung gibt. Der Gedanke des Sich-Darstellens des Seins im vorstellenden und reflektierenden Bewusstsein hingegen spielt bei dieser Offenbarungskonzeption keine begrifflich tragende Rolle. Offenbarung ist bei Schelling nicht als Sich-Abbilden des absoluten Seins im Bewusstsein, sondern als Differenzierungsmoment im Sein Gottes gedacht. Schelling hat diese Differenz zur Konzeption Fichtes in seiner polemischen Schrift von 1806 ausdrücklich bemerkt.[23] Damit ist bereits in einer wichtigen Hinsicht der von dem Fichtes ganz verschiedene Offenbarungsbegriff vorgezeichnet, den Schelling später in der *Freiheitsschrift* einführen und als systematische Grundlage des Verständnisses von Freiheit einsetzen wird.

Auch dort geht Schelling von einer Dualität untrennbarer Momente in Gott aus, die für sein lebendiges Sein konstitutiv ist. Diese wird nun jedoch nicht mehr (wie im *Anti-Fichte*) durch die Begriffe von Einheit und Vielheit expliziert, sondern – bekanntlich – durch die Unterscheidung zwischen Gott als „Grund" von Existenz und Gott, sofern er „existiert". Damit erhält nun aber der Offenbarungsbegriff eine neue Auslegung. Unter dem Existenz-Aspekt Gottes versteht Schelling Gott in seiner „Idealität", d. h. als Einheitsprinzip.[24] Gott könnte aber nicht Einheit sein, wenn es in ihm nicht etwas gäbe, das als Vielheit aufgefasst und zur Einheit gebracht werden kann. Schelling bezeichnet diese Bedingung von Existenz als „Grund" der Existenz in Gott, womit offenbar kein kausaler Sinn zu verbinden ist, sondern eher der Gedanke einer *Schicht* Gottes, die es ihm ermöglicht, sich als Einheit zu artikulieren.[25] Der Grund-Schicht Gottes wird nun aber in der *Freiheitsschrift* ein ausgesprochen triebhaft-dynamischer Charakter zugesprochen. Schelling spricht von ihr daher auch typischerweise in Metaphern der Bewegtheit, so etwa, wenn er den Grund in Gott als „wogend wallend Meer" beschreibt.[26]

Die in der *Freiheitsschrift* eingeführte Konzeption des Grundes ist zu komplex, um hier in all ihren Aspekten betrachtet werden zu können. Es kann hier nur um eine Minimal-Interpretation gehen, die einige für den Offenbarungsgedanken in der *Freiheitsschrift* grundlegende Aspekte dieses Begriffs herausstellt. Geht man von der bereits bemerkten Rolle des Grundes als Bewegungs-Moment in Gott aus, so kann man Schellings Vergleich mit einer hinsichtlich ihres Wonach unbestimmten „Sehnsucht" zur näheren Charakterisierung des

---

23   S. Schelling, 1958, S. 653.
24   S. WmF, S. 80, wo Schelling allgemein das „Existierende" und das „Ideale" identifiziert.
25   Zur Interpretation der Grundes als Schicht vgl. Fuhrmans, 1964, bes. S. 144.
26   WmF, S. 33.

Grundes heranziehen.[27] Was Gott ursprünglich zur Offenbarung bewegt, ist eine volitive Schicht, die auf Realisierung aus ist, ohne ihr Wozu explizieren und bestimmen zu können. In diesem Sinn handelt es sich um eine *vor-rationale* volitive Schicht – in Schellings Worten: der Grund ist ein „Wille, in dem kein Verstand ist".[28] Dieser realisiert sich potenziell in einer komplexen Ordnung, die aber als solche nur hervortreten kann, sofern sein ursprünglich unartikulierter Inhalt expliziert wird. Der Grund ist insofern für sich noch „regellos"; er ist „Basis der Realität", aber für sich noch nicht realitätsfähig.[29] Die in ihm implizit beschlossene komplexe Einheit als solche zu begreifen und zu realisieren, dies ist wesentlich Tätigkeit Gottes, sofern er „ideell", d. h. Einheitsprinzip ist. Sofern er Idealität ist, die sich auf den Grund bezieht, bezeichnet Schelling Gott als „Verstand" – worin man eine nähere Charakterisierung Gottes hinsichtlich seiner Existenz zu sehen hat. Damit wird deutlich, dass „Grund" und „Existenz" untrennbare Aspekte Gottes sind: Ohne Gott, sofern er existiert, d. h. Verstand ist, bliebe der vor-rationale Impuls in Gott unartikuliert und regellos, so dass sein Inhalt gleichsam gestaltlos bliebe und nicht realisiert werden könnte; und ohne den Grund in ihm wäre Gott, sofern er existiert, d. h. ideell ist, ein Einheitsprinzip, das als solches leer bliebe, da es sich auf keine Vielheit beziehen könnte.

Dem Verstand als Attribut Gottes kommt in Schellings Darstellung eine Doppelfunktion zu, die für den der *Freiheitsschrift* eigentümlichen Offenbarungsbegriff von entscheidender Bedeutung ist. Sein erster Akt besteht darin, eine „reflexive Vorstellung" zu bilden, in der die ursprünglich unartikulierte Komplexität des vor-rationalen Impulses expliziert und als Einheit vorgestellt wird. Der Verstand begreift hierbei, welcher reale Einheitszusammenhang es ist, in dem die vor-rationale Antriebsschicht – der „Grund" in Gott – erfüllt werden kann. Schelling kann daher die reflexive Vorstellung des göttlichen Verstandes zugleich als urbildliche Vorstellung der *Welt* beschreiben, die dabei freilich erst als „mögliche" vorgestellt ist.[30] Sofern Gott den möglichen Weltzusammenhang vorstellt, auf dessen Realisierung er in ursprünglich impulshafter Weise aus ist, kann man nun aber von einem zielgerichteten Wollen sprechen, das

---

[27] S. WmF, S. 33 ff.

[28] WmF, S. 32. Schelling charakterisiert den Grund daher auch als „irrational" (WmF, S. 46). Damit ist jedoch nicht etwa gemeint, dass der Grund dem Verstand unzugänglich sei. Vielmehr versteht Schelling den Grund als wesentlich *potenziell* verstandesgemäß differenziert und vereinheitlicht, auch wenn er aus sich heraus nicht dazu befähigt ist, sich zu klarer Struktur zu bringen und sich seiner verstandesgemäßen Artikulation sogar widersetzt. Da der Ausdruck „irrational" leicht die hier irreführende Konnotation des nicht-rationalisierbaren mit sich führt, ziehe ich es vor, den Grund stattdessen als „vor-rational" zu charakterisieren.

[29] WmF, S. 32.

[30] S. WmF, S. 33 u. S. 70; vgl. S. 59 („zu der im göttlichen Verstande zuvor entworfenen Einheit des Weltganzen").

zunächst als „Wille zur Natur" zu charakterisieren ist.[31] Damit hat Schelling die Grundlage bereitet, um die Welt als Produkt eines willentlichen Schöpfungsakts zu denken, der einen zuvor als möglich gedachten Weltzusammenhang ins Dasein bringt. Auch die „wirkliche Schöpfung" wird von Schelling nun aber dem Verstand Gottes zugeordnet, der hierbei die im Grund noch unartikuliert beschlossenen Kräfte real scheidet und in verschiedenen Weisen vereinigt. Im Unterschied zur „Vorstellung" als seinem ersten Akt bezeichnet Schelling diese zweite Tätigkeit des göttlichen Verstandes als „Ein-Bildung", im Sinn eines Akts, der den im Grund zuvor nur implizit oder als Möglichkeit angelegten Einheitszusammenhang als aktual hervortreten lässt.[32]

Durch die Konzeption des ersten Verstandesakts Gottes wird der Vorstellungsbegriff bereits in einem gleichsam vor-weltlichen Zusammenhang eingeführt. Der göttliche Verstand stellt das „Wozu" seines vor-rationalen Antriebs reflexiv vor, und weiß damit bereits um den in ihm beschlossenen, obgleich noch nicht realisierten Einheitszusammenhang. Das Sich-Vorstellen Gottes ist aber noch nicht das eigentliche Offenbarungsgeschehen, das im Mittelpunkt der schellingschen Darstellung steht. Dieses ist vielmehr im realen Schöpfungsakt des Verstandes und dem durch ihn ermöglichten Weltzusammenhang situiert. In ihm stellt Gott sich nicht bloß vor, sondern manifestiert sich „als actu existierend".[33] Gott offenbart sich also nicht, indem er vorgestellt wird, sondern indem sich eine Realität gibt, die gerade außerhalb seines Sich-Vorstellens liegt. Damit ist bereits ein Punkt im Gedankengang der Freiheitsschrift erreicht, der eine grundlegende Differenz zu Fichtes Offenbarungskonzeption bemerken lässt. Doch bevor Schellings Offenbarungsbegriff zu dem Fichtes ins Verhältnis gesetzt wird, ist – in notgedrungen knapper Form – zu verdeutlichen, wie Schelling an diesen Offenbarungsbegriff einen Begriff der Freiheit des Menschen anschließt.

Schelling betrachtet es als wesentliche Aufgabe einer philosophischen Theorie der Freiheit, den Zusammenhang des Freiheitsbegriffs „mit dem Ganzen einer wissenschaftlichen Weltansicht" zu erhellen.[34] Dementsprechend steht der in der *Freiheitsschrift* eingeführte Begriff von Freiheit in einem engen Zusammenhang mit dem Verständnis der Natur, das sich im Ausgang vom Grundkonzept Gottes und der Offenbarung ergibt. Für dieses ist der Gedanke grundlegend, dass die Vielheit der Wesen in der Natur sich aus einer fortschreitenden Trennung und Vereinigung der im Grund noch unartikulierten treibenden Kräfte ergibt. In jedem Einzelnen lassen sich somit zwei Aspekte unterscheiden, die denen des Grundes und des Verstandes in Gott entsprechen: Zum einen sind

---

31   S. WmF, S. 35.
32   S. WmF, S. 34.
33   WmF, S. 36.
34   WmF, S. 9.

in ihm verschiedene Kräfte wirksam, die durch die Schöpfung aus dem Grund herausgehoben wurden und daher für sich den Charakter „blinder" Antriebe haben. Zum anderen sind diese in bestimmter, ihre Scheidung voraussetzender Weise zu einer Einheit organisiert. Anders gesagt besitzt jedes Wesen eine mehr oder weniger komplexe Trieb-Schicht – Schelling spricht von „blindem Willen"[35] –, und eine Einheit, in welche die Triebe eingebunden sind, so dass sie *ein* Wesen ausmachen. Im Hinblick darauf, dass sich Grade solcher Organisation unterscheiden lassen, in denen das im Grund beschlossene zunehmend geschieden wird, womit zugleich die jeweils erreichte Einheit zunehmende Komplexität aufweist, spricht Schelling von einer „stufenweisen" Entfaltung des Grundes durch den Verstand als reales Schöpfungsvermögen.[36] Dass der Grund in einer solchen Stufenordnung entfaltet wird, und nicht auf einen Schlag, erklärt Schelling aus einem „Widerstreben" des Grundes, der seinen vor-rationalen, impulshaft-blinden Charakter zu bewahren sucht und sich daher seiner Realisation in einem gegliederten Einheitszusammenhang gleichsam widersetzt. Die Stufenordnung ist also Ausdruck dessen, dass die Schöpfung eigentlich ein Kampf ist, in dem einer widerständigen, unorganisierten Triebschicht zunehmend die komplexe Einheit des Wirklichen abgerungen wird.[37]

Aufgrund ihres der Vereinheitlichung entgegenwirkenden Charakters erscheint die dem Grund abgewonnene Triebschicht als gleichsam „kontrahierendes" Prinzip, kraft dessen kein Wesen sich auf seine Position innerhalb des vom Verstand gestifteten allgemeinen Einheitszusammenhangs vollständig reduzieren lässt. In jedem Wesen sind Impulse wirksam, die sich aus diesem Zusammenhang nicht verstehen lassen und die in ihn widerstrebend eingefügt sind. Daher fasst Schelling die dem Grund entstammende Triebschicht auch als Prinzip der Vereinzelung und – in einem zunächst sehr allgemeinen Sinn – als Prinzip des „Eigenwillens" auf.[38] Die Einheit jedes Einzelnen, wie auch der Welt im Ganzen stellt sich damit als Werk eines ordnenden „Universalwillens" dar (wie Schelling den göttlichen Verstand auch bezeichnet), der sich eine an sich widerständige Mannigfaltigkeit unterordnet. Diese dramatisierte, vom Begriff der *creatio ex nihilo* weit entfernte Version des Schöpfungsgedankens stellt den

---

[35] WmF, S. 35.

[36] WmF, S. 34.

[37] Die Wurzel des Verständnisses der Schöpfung als Kampf entgegengesetzter Prinzipien kann in Schellings Umdeutung der kantischen Synthesislehre gesehen werden. Schon in der *Ich-Schrift* von 1795 hat Schelling die Synthesis als spannungsvolles Geschehen beschrieben, in dem das Subjekt gleichsam im Kampf mit der Vielheit der Bewusstseinsinhalte steht und gegen diese seine Identität zu erhalten strebt (s. Schelling, 1985, S. 97). Diese dramatisierende Auffassung der Synthesis ist in der *Freiheitsschrift* in das Bild der Trennungs- und Vereinigungstätigkeit des nun göttlichen Verstandes umgewandelt, wobei anstelle des identitätswidrigen sinnlichen Mannigfaltigen der widerständige Grund tritt.

[38] WmF, S. 34/35.

Rahmen dar, innerhalb dessen Schelling den Willen des Menschen und seine Freiheit lokalisiert.

Schellings Verständnis der Freiheit des Menschen ergibt sich in der *Freiheitsschrift* aus der Lokalisierung des Menschen innerhalb der Stufenordnung der Wesen, durch die der Grund in der Schöpfung entfaltet wird – wobei deren Funktion als Offenbarung Gottes eine entscheidende argumentative Rolle spielt. In der Ordnung der Geschöpfe, die durch zunehmende Entfaltung und Vereinheitlichung des Grundes bestimmt ist, erkennt Schelling dem Menschen die Stellung des Maximums zu. In ihm ist der Grund vollständig ausdifferenziert, d. h. der Mensch verfügt über eine maximal komplexe Schicht von vorrationalen (physischen und psychischen) „Kräften" und Antrieben. Zugleich aber besitzt er die Fähigkeit, dieser seiner Komplexität eine rationale Einheit aufzuerlegen, sowohl im Sinne interner Kohärenz als Einzelner, als auch im Sinne eines vernünftigen Sich-Verhaltens zu Anderen und der Natur im Ganzen. In diesem Sinn sagt Schelling, im Menschen sei „die ganze Macht des finstern Prinzips" und zugleich „die ganze Kraft des Lichts".[39] Aus diesem Menschenbild Schellings spricht sowohl die Anerkennung der nicht von vornherein rational geordneten Komplexität des Menschen, als auch der Glaube an seine Fähigkeit, in rationaler Weise eben diese Komplexität zu beherrschen und zu vereinheitlichen. Die maximale Differenzierung und Vereinheitlichung des vorrationalen Grundes, die sich im Menschen verwirklichen kann, ist nun aber nichts anderes als das Ziel der Schöpfung – das reale „Ebenbild" Gottes in der Welt. Denn rationale Entfaltung und Vereinheitlichung der ihm angehörenden vorgängigen Impuls-Schicht zu sein ist ja die wesentliche Bestimmung Gottes, sofern er „Grund" und „Existenz" zugleich ist – dies war der Ausgangsgedanke der *Freiheitsschrift*.

Die vollständige Durchdringung von Grund und Verstand, die Gott und der Mensch gemein haben, bezeichnet Schelling als *Geist*. Hierunter hat man also nichts anderes als die „Kongruenz" beider zu verstehen, die sich erst dann ergeben kann, wenn die im Grund beschlossenen Kräfte vollständig entfaltet und zu rationaler Einheit gebracht sind. Geist zu sein unterscheidet Gott und den Menschen von jedem bloßen Naturwesen, in dem die Kräfte des Grundes nur partiell entfaltet und vereinheitlicht sind. Er verleiht Gott und dem Menschen eine Mittelstellung zwischen Grund und Verstand, die Schelling sogar als Standpunkt der „Identität" bezeichnet. Doch ist der Mensch nicht in derselben Weise Geist, wie Gott. Er „ist Geist als ein selbstisches […] Wesen", d. h. als ein aus der Natur hervorgegangener, „in actu" existierender Einzelner.[40] Er übt seine Mittelstellung zwischen entfalteter vor-rationaler Triebschicht und Verstand somit in der Selbstmacht des von Gott unterschiedenen Einzelnen aus. Diese Diffe-

---

[39]   WmF, S. 35.
[40]   WmF, S. 36.

renz zwischen Gott und Mensch ist offenbar untrennbar von Schellings Offenbarungskonzeption – ohne sie, bemerkt Schelling, wäre „Gott als Geist [...] nicht offenbar".[41] Denn darin, dass die Einheit von Grund und Verstand „als actu existierend" manifestiert wird, besteht ja der Sinn der Schöpfung qua Offenbarung, die im Menschen zu ihrem eigentlichen Ziel kommt. Die Mittelstellung zwischen Grund und Verstand als aus der Natur herkommender Einzelner auszuüben bedeutet aber, die Rangordnung beider aus sich heraus festlegen zu können, ohne hierbei der für Gott wesentlichen Vormacht des differenzierenden und vereinigenden Verstandes gegenüber den „widerstrebenden" Kräften des Grundes folgen zu müssen. Als gott-ähnlicher Einzelner hat der Mensch somit die Fähigkeit, in seinem Denken und Handeln die ganze Ordnung von Grund und Verstand umzukehren, auf der die Schöpfung beruht. Er, und nur er, ist ein potenzieller Unordnungsfaktor in der Natur. Er kann den Verstand in den Dienst partikularer Antriebe stellen, die dann in ihrer Vereinzelung freigesetzt und zu letzten Antrieben seines Wollens werden, wobei der nun instrumentalisierte Verstand darauf ausgeht, ihnen das Ganze zu unterwerfen. Eine solche Umkehrung der Ordnung mag letztlich selbstzerstörerisch sein – Schelling vergleicht sie mit der Krankheit[42] –, aber sie kann eine eigene und die Ordnung des Ganzen in Frage stellende Kraft entfalten. Damit ist in Schellings Gedankengang der für die *Freiheitsschrift* grundlegende Begriff der menschlichen Freiheit als „Möglichkeit des Guten und des Bösen" erreicht.[43]

Der von Schelling hier eingeführte Freiheitsbegriff impliziert den Gedanken einer „ursprünglichen Unentschiedenheit" des Menschen.[44] Doch will Schelling damit nicht etwa die These verteidigen, dass gute oder böse Handlungen auf willkürlichen Einzelentscheidungen beruhen, die als solche von „zufälligen", d. h. nicht-verursachten Vorkommnissen ununterscheidbar wären. Um freies Handeln von zufälligen, zugleich aber auch von durch äußere Bedingungen in der Zeit determinierten Ereignissen zu unterscheiden, postuliert Schelling einen „intelligiblen" Charakter des Menschen, dessen innere Notwendigkeit zeitloser Grund der in der Zeit auftretenden Handlungen des Einzelnen sei. Die Tatsache, dass unser Handeln auf einer inneren Charakter-Notwendigkeit beruht, die durch Entscheidungen in der Zeit nicht mehr zu suspendieren ist, stellt nach Schelling aber nicht etwa die Zurechenbarkeit der Handlungen in Frage. Denn die gute oder böse Charakterbestimmtheit des Einzelnen soll ihrerseits Resultat einer selbstbestimmenden Handlung sein, die freilich als intelligible wesentlich vorreflexiv und immer schon vollzogen sei.[45] Schelling greift hier offenbar auf

<hr>

[41]   Ebd.
[42]   WmF, S. 38.
[43]   WmF, S. 36 u. S. 39.
[44]   WmF, S. 54.
[45]   S. WmF, S. 55 ff.

Kants Konzeption einer den Charakter des Menschen begründenden „intelligiblen Tat" zurück, um Selbstbestimmung und innere Notwendigkeit zusammenzubringen und so den Aporien des reinholdschen Willkürbegriffs zu entgehen.[46] Es ist jedoch fraglich, ob der Übergang in die Sphäre des Intelligiblen geeignet ist, den Gedanken der volitiven Selbstbestimmung verständlich zu machen. Denn auch hier erhebt sich die Frage, warum das nun als intelligibles „Urwollen" gefasste Wollen sich so bestimmt, wie es sich bestimmt – wobei wiederum die Differenz zwischen freiem Akt und zufälligem Vorkommnis sicherzustellen wäre. Durch die Konzeption der intelligiblen Selbstbestimmung werden also die Probleme, mit denen der Begriff des selbstbestimmten Wollens behaftet ist, womöglich nur verschoben, und nicht gelöst. Doch die Stärke und Originalität der *Freiheitsschrift* als Beitrag zum Verständnis des Freiheitsbegriffs besteht auch nicht darin, wie in ihr das „formelle Wesen" der Freiheit qua Selbstbestimmung gefasst wird, sondern in der durch sie gegebenen Erklärung des „realen Begriffs" der Freiheit, d. h. in der Konkretisierung und Lokalisierung des Gedankens der Freiheit des menschlichen Willens im Ganzen einer Welt- bzw. Naturkonzeption.[47]

3. Affinitäten und Differenzen im spekulativen Freiheitsverständnis Fichtes und Schellings

In den vorausgehenden Abschnitten wurde aus Fichtes religionsphilosophischer Hauptschrift und aus Schellings *Freiheitsschrift* der gedankliche Zusammenhang herausgehoben, der als Kern des jeweils vertretenen spekulativen Freiheitsverständnisses gelten kann. Es wurde deutlich, dass in beiden Theoriestücken der Offenbarungsbegriff für das intendierte Verständnis der menschlichen Freiheit auf der Grundlage des Gedankens vom Absoluten eine entscheidende Rolle spielt. Die Implikationen des Gedankens, dass das Absolute sich offenbaren muss, ermöglichen es jeweils, den Begriff des Absoluten für das philosophische Verständnis der Freiheit fruchtbar zu machen. Der Offenbarungsbegriff fungiert bei Fichte wie bei Schelling gleichsam als Wegweiser, der uns vom Gedanken des Absoluten zum philosophisch grundlegenden Begriff der menschlichen Freiheit führen soll.

Der auf diese Weise jeweils beschriebene gedankliche Weg fällt jedoch in beiden Schriften höchst unterschiedlich aus, und dies deshalb, weil der Offenbarungsbegriff selbst in ihnen unterschiedlich gefasst ist. In jedem Fall impliziert er die Differenz des Sich-Offenbarenden und dessen, worin dieses sich

---

⁴⁶ S. Kant, 1907, bes. S. 31. Vgl. hierzu Sturma, 1995, bes. S. 160 ff.
⁴⁷ Zur Unterscheidung zwischen formellem Wesen und realem Begriff der Freiheit, s. WmF, S. 25 u. S. 54.

offenbart, verstanden als eine innere Differenz im Absoluten selbst, sowie zugleich die Notwendigkeit des gedanklichen Übergangs vom ersten zum zweiten. Während das im Offenbarungsbegriff enthaltene Verhältnis bei Fichte das von „Sein" und (als vorstellend-reflektierendes Bewusstsein gefasstes) „Bild" ist, geht es bei Schellings Offenbarungsbegriff um das Verhältnis von Gott als „Potenz" und Gott als „Akt". Während Fichte die Offenbarung somit als Bewusstwerdung des Absoluten im Medium des reflektierend-vorstellenden Bewusstseins versteht, ist sie bei Schelling als eigentliche Realisierung Gottes gefasst, der erst hierin dazu kommt, „in actu" zu existieren. Aus dieser Differenz der jeweils leitenden Offenbarungsbegriffe ergibt sich eine grundlegende Differenz hinsichtlich des jeweils eingeführten Freiheitsbegriffs, der bei Fichte die Weise betrifft, in der das Absolute im Bewusstsein abgebildet wird, bei Schelling aber die Weise, in welcher der Mensch kraft seiner Stellung als Aktualisierung Gottes in der Welt existiert. So gelangt Fichte schließlich zum grundlegenden Konzept der Freiheit als Selbstbestimmung des Bewusstseins hinsichtlich der ihm möglichen „Weltansichten", Schelling aber zum Begriff der Freiheit als volitives Sich-Verhalten des Menschen zu „Grund" und „Licht" als den Bedingungen seines Daseins und der Schöpfung im Ganzen.

Dass die aus den Offenbarungsbegriffen Fichtes und Schellings resultierenden Freiheitsbegriffe höchst verschieden sind, bedeutet freilich nicht, dass sie als solche unvereinbar wären. Fichtes Freiheitsbegriff verweist auf einen Aspekt der menschlichen Selbstbestimmung, der jedem wie immer gearteten Selbstkonzept als Akteur vorgängig ist. Er beruht auf dem Gedanken, dass jedes praktische Selbstverständnis wesentlich zu einer Weltansicht gehört, in der etwas als wesentlich oder grundlegend ausgezeichnet wird und das insofern – wie dies hier ausgedrückt wurde – einen „Fokus" besitzt. Die Ausbildung einer zentrierten Weltsicht ist aber in mehr als nur einer Weise möglich (wobei Fichtes fünffache Systematisierung womöglich durch andere, differenziertere zu ersetzen ist). Es ist daher sinnvoll, von Freiheit nicht nur – und nicht einmal zuerst – im Sinne der Willensfreiheit zu sprechen, sondern in Bezug auf die Zentrierung der je eigenen Weltansicht, die wesentlich aktiver Vollzug und nie bloße Wirkung von Erfahrungen oder „Informationen" ist. Diese fichtesche Grundthese wird auch dadurch nicht entwertet, dass Fichte nur wenig Erhellendes darüber zu sagen hat, wie die Aneignung einer Weltansicht sich eigentlich vollzieht.[48] Nun lehnt Schelling zwar Fichtes Voraussetzung ab, dass Weltansichten als Vereinheitlichungen eines durch die Reflexion erzeugten Mannigfalten zu verstehen

---

[48] Insbesondere wird in Fichtes Darstellung nicht deutlich, inwiefern die Aneignung einer Weltansicht bzw. der Übergang von einer Weltansicht zu einer anderen rational sein, d. h. auf *Gründen* beruhen kann. Klar ist, dass Fichte keine rein intellektualistische Sicht der Aneignung von Weltansichten vertritt, sondern den „Affekten" (etwa der Selbstliebe) eine konstitutive Rolle hierbei zuerkennt (s. AsL, S. 127 ff.).

seien, das als solches noch jeder rationalen Einheit entbehrt. Er erkennt dem menschlichen Geist einen ursprünglichen epistemischen Kontakt mit einer unabhängigen und bereits vernünftig strukturierten Realität zu.[49] Doch die fichtesche Reflexion auf die Pluralität möglicher Weltansichten, wie auch die Lokalisierung des spekulativen Verständnisses der Welt als Offenbarung des Absoluten innerhalb des Raums möglicher Weltansichten, wird als solche von Schelling nicht kritisiert. So identifiziert Schelling sogar den religiösen Standpunkt, wie er innerhalb der fichteschen Fünffachheit auftritt, ohne Weiteres mit dem seiner Naturphilosophie.[50] Auch wenn in Schellings *Freiheitsschrift* die Reflexion auf den dort ausgeführten Standpunkt als besondere und höchste „Weltansicht" nicht ausgeführt wird, ist eine solche Reflexion mit der dort vertretenen Position somit durchaus kompatibel – damit aber auch ein Begriff von Freiheit, der sich auf die spontane Ausbildung und Aneignung von Weltansichten bezieht und der dem Begriff der Freiheit als Willensfreiheit noch vorgängig ist.

Dies bedeutet freilich nicht, dass die Freiheitsbegriffe Fichtes und Schellings spannungslos zusammengefügt werden können. In der Frage, welcher Status dem Gedanken der Freiheit des je eigenen Wollens in der Reflexion über die uns möglichen Weltansichten zuzuerkennen ist, tritt vielmehr eine tief greifende Differenz zwischen Fichte und Schelling zutage. Diese zeigt sich darin, wie die Überwindung des falschen Lebens jeweils verstanden wird, das bei Fichte mit dem Ausdruck der „Unseligkeit", bei Schelling dem des „Bösen" belegt ist. Dessen Kern wird von Fichte wie von Schelling darin gesehen, dass das je eigene Wollen in seiner Selbstmacht affirmiert und damit vom überindividuellen Wollen getrennt wird, in dem das Absolute sich in seiner Offenbarung Ausdruck gibt. Die Überwindung des unwahren Lebens erfordert dementsprechend in beiden Konzeptionen eine Selbstdistanzierung im Sinne der Ausbildung des Standpunkts eines nicht-partikular begründeten Wollens.

Wie bereits deutlich wurde, wird dieser Schritt von Fichte durch eine Analogie mit dem Standpunkt der Genieproduktion gedeutet, sofern diese in ihrer eigenen Perspektive nicht als durch eigenes Wollen bestimmte Handlung, sondern als Prozess der Manifestation eines überindividuellen, für sich freilich unexplizierbaren Prinzips verstanden ist. Fichte beschreibt den Übergang zur diesem Gedanken entsprechenden Sicht des eigenen Lebens als Eintritt in eine Lebensform, die derjenigen entgegengesetzt ist, welche durch das „Dasein eines Selbst" charakterisiert ist.[51] In diesem starken Verständnis der Selbstdistanzie-

---

[49]   S. *Anti-Fichte*, S. 670 ff.
[50]   S. *Anti-Fichte*, S. 679/80. Wenn Schelling gleich zu Beginn der *Freiheitsschrift* von einer „wissenschaftlichen *Weltansicht*" spricht, in deren Zusammenhang der Freiheitsbegriff gestellt werden solle, so mag die Verwendung dieses in Fichtes *Anweisung* zentralen Ausdrucks sogar ein implizites Fichte-Zitat sein (WmF, S. 9, m. H.).
[51]   S. AsL, S. 130.

rung ist die These vorausgesetzt, dass die Konzeption von sich als Einzelner, dessen selbstbestimmtes Wollen die eigenen Handlungen bestimmt, nichts anderes als ein Produkt der Reflexion darstellt, das nur relativ zu den ersten beiden Weltansichten Geltung besitzt, sich auf dem Standpunkt der höheren Moralität und Religion aber als Fiktion erweist.[52] Der Übergang zum überindividuell bestimmten Wollen wird von Fichte somit als Suspendierung des als bloßes Konstrukt interpretierten Gedankens vom Selbst als handlungsbestimmender Entscheidungsinstanz verstanden. Auf dem hierdurch ermöglichten Standpunkt verliert dann aber auch die Annahme des „Daseins" eines solchen Selbst ihren Sinn.

In Schellings Konzeption des Standpunkts verallgemeinerten Wollens wird dieses dagegen als immer noch wesentlich „selbstisch" verstanden, d. h. als je eigenes Wollen eines selbstbestimmten Einzelnen. Als aus der Natur herkommendes, auf der Basis einer vor-rationalen und widerständigen Triebschicht existierendes Wesen kann der Mensch in seinem Wollen nie den Standpunkt reiner Universalität einnehmen. Schellings Begriff der „Persönlichkeit" hat zu seinem Kern den Gedanken, dass menschliches (wie auch göttliches) Wollen wesentlich Wollen eines „Selbst" ist, das auf dem Grund als besondernder vorrationaler Schicht aufruht.[53] Die dem Menschen abverlangte Selbstdistanzierung kann für Schelling daher nicht in der Annullierung des Selbst als Fiktion bestehen. Das Bewusstsein, selbstbestimmter Einzelner zu sein, ist für Schelling ontologisch fundiert und daher gar nicht sinnvoll preiszugeben, auch nicht angesichts der Universalisierungsforderung.[54] Stattdessen soll der Mensch den „Eigenwillen" nicht zum „Selbstsein" erheben, d. h. er soll in einem Wollen, das wesentlich Selbstbestimmung eines Einzelnen ist, zugleich eine Distanz zur partikularisierenden Tendenz seiner Persönlichkeit aufbauen. Die Fähigkeit des Menschen, in einem solchen stets spannungsvollen Selbstverhältnis ein universalisiertes, auf die Einheit des (sozialen und natürlichen) Ganzen blickendes Wollen auszubilden, ist für Schelling definitiv begrenzt – die „Persönlichkeit und Selbstheit" des Menschen kann sich „nie zum vollkommenen Aktus erheben".[55]

---

[52] So sagt Fichte, dass das Bewusstsein der je eigenen Selbstbestimmung relativ zu den ersten beiden Standpunkten „ohne Täuschung" – da wesentliches Element der hier angenommenen Weltansicht – sei, während es auf dem höheren Standpunkt „nun allerdings trügen würde" (AsL, S. 126).

[53] S. WmF, S. 43.

[54] D. Sturma hat darauf hingewiesen, dass Schelling den Freiheitsbegriff nicht etwa moralphilosophisch begründet, sondern auf der Grundlage einer „Ontologie der Person" einführt (Sturma, 1995, S. 157) – wobei hinzuzufügen ist, dass Schellings Ontologie der Person ihrerseits Teil einer Ontologie alles Kreatürlichen ist, so dass die Freiheit des Menschen „in das Ganze einer wissenschaftlichen Weltansicht" eingefügt wird.

[55] WmF, S. 71.

Der Gedanke vom je eigenen Selbst als Willenssubjekt muss nach Fichte in der höchsten Weltansicht dem Bewusstsein des einen Willens weichen, der „alles in allem ist"[56], während er für Schelling eine ontologische Wahrheit darstellt, die vom Wesen des Menschen als der Gott „in actu" realisierenden Persönlichkeit untrennbar ist. Suspendierung der Selbst-Fiktion und möglichst weitgehende Universalisierung der zugleich unaufhebbar „selbstischen" Persönlichkeit sind somit die divergenten Konzepte der dem Menschen als Ort der Offenbarung des Absoluten abverlangten Selbst-Distanzierung, zu denen Fichte und Schelling schließlich gelangen. Stimmt man der Beschreibung des Projekts des Deutschen Idealismus als „Spinozismus der Freiheit" zu,[57] dann hat man hierin eine Differenz zwischen dem Denken Fichtes und Schellings zu sehen, die ein bereits mit dem Projekt des Idealismus unmittelbar aufgeworfenes Problem betrifft – die Frage nämlich, wie sich der in einem weiten Sinn „spinozistische" Gedanke des allumfassenden Absoluten als Ausgangsgedanke der Philosophie zum Bewusstsein unserer je eigenen volitiven Selbstbestimmung verhält. Fichte und Schelling sind auch in dieser Frage zu keiner einvernehmlichen Antwort gelangt. Damit dürfte aber auch deutlich geworden sein, dass der hier leitende Zusammenhang zwischen Freiheit und Offenbarung einen Aspekt darstellt, der in die Betrachtung einzubeziehen ist, wenn man das Verhältnis zwischen Fichte und Schelling in seiner Komplexität und in seiner gleichsam symptomatischen Bedeutung für das Verständnis der Grundfragen und -probleme des Deutschen Idealismus angemessen erfassen will.

Literatur

Asmuth, Christoph (1999): *Das Begreifen des Unbegreiflichen. Philosophie und Religion bei Johann Gottlieb Fichte 1800–1806*, Stuttgart-Bad Cannstatt.

Fichte, Johann Gottlieb (2001): *Die Anweisung zum seligen Leben, oder auch die Religionslehre*, hrsg. v. Verweyen, Hansjürgen, Hamburg. (Zitiert mit „AsL" unter Angabe der Seitenzahl.)

Fichte, Johann Gottlieb (1998): *Versuch einer Kritik aller Offenbarung*, hrsg. v. Verweyen, Hansjürgen, Hamburg.

Fichte, Johann Gottlieb (1975): *Die Wissenschaftslehre. Zweiter Vortrag im Jahre 1804*, hrsg. v. Lauth, Reinhard u. Widmann, Joachim, Hamburg.

Fuhrmans, Horst (1964): *Anmerkungen zur Freiheitsschrift*, in: Schelling, Friedrich Wilhelm Joseph: *Über das Wesen der menschlichen Freiheit*, Stuttgart, S. 139–180.

Henrich, Dieter (2003): *Between Kant and Hegel. Lectures on German Idealism*, Harvard.

---

[56]   AsL, S. 130.
[57]   S. Henrich, 2003, S. 73.

Kant, Immanuel (1907): *Die Religion innerhalb der Grenzen der bloßen Vernunft*, in: *Gesammelte Schriften Bd. 6*, hrsg. v. der Preussischen Akademie der Wissenschaften, Berlin, S. 3–202.

Kant, Immanuel (1908): *Kritik der Urteilskraft*, in: *Gesammelte Schriften Bd. 5*, hrsg. v. der Preussischen Akademie der Wissenschaften, Berlin, S. 167–485.

Schelling, Friedrich Wilhelm Joseph (2011): *Über das Wesen der menschlichen Freiheit*, hrsg. v. Buchheim, Thomas, Hamburg. (Zitiert mit „WmF" unter Angabe der Seitenzahl.)

Schelling, Friedrich Wilhelm Joseph (1958): *Darlegung des wahren Verhältnisses der Naturphilosophie zu der verbesserten Fichteschen Lehre*, in: *Schellings Werke Bd. 3*, hrsg. v. Schröter, Manfred, München (Nachdruck der Jubiläumsausgabe 1927), S. 595–720.

Schelling, Friedrich Wilhelm Joseph (1985): *Vom Ich als Princip der Philosophie oder über das Unbedingte im menschlichen Wissen*, in: *F.W.J. Schelling. Ausgewählte Werke Band 1*, Frankfurt (Nachdruck von *Friedrich Wilhelm Joseph Schellings Sämmtliche Werke Bd. 1*, hrsg. v. Schelling, K.F.A., Stuttgart), S. 151–244.

Sturma, Dieter (1995): „Präreflexive Freiheit und menschliche Selbstbestimmung (382–394)", in: Höffe, Otfried/Pieper, Annemarie (Hrsg.): *F.W.J. Schelling. Über das Wesen der menschlichen Freiheit*, Berlin, S. 149–172.

Michelle Kosch

Formal Freedom in Fichte's System of Ethics

Fichtes Darstellung der „Tätigkeit" besteht aus drei Teilen: Im Zentrum steht (1) seine Darlegung dessen, was es heißt, ein moralisch Handelnder zu sein (einen freien Willen in dem Sinne zu haben, wie er für die Zuschreibung von Verantwortung und die Adressierung moralischer Imperative erforderlich ist); (2) die Darstellung des konstituierenden Zwecks des moralischen Handelns (worin die materiale Unabhängigkeit oder Selbstgenügsamkeit der Vernunft besteht); und schließlich (3) die Darstellung der Verbindung beider (d. h. warum ein moralisch Handelnder materiale Selbstgenügsamkeit zu seinem Zweck machen sollte). Im folgenden Beitrag präsentiere ich eine Interpretation des ersten dieser drei Teile: Fichtes Darstellung der für moralisches Handeln notwendigen psychischen Vermögen oder der, wie er sie nennt, „formalen Freiheit".

I. Introduction

The chief interest in Fichte's account of moral agency lies, I believe, in the use to which he puts it in deriving a system of normative ethics and political philosophy in the Foundations of Natural Right (1797) and the System of Ethics (1798). Together these constitute a practical philosophy that is both recognizably Kantian in spirit and strikingly different from Kant's own in some of its chief substantive claims.

It is recognizably Kantian in its fundamental commitments about the relation between moral agency and moral norms. For Fichte, moral considerations always provide overriding reasons for action, and such reasons cannot fail to have (at least some) motivational force, and like Kant he bases those commitments on a more fundamental commitment to the autonomy of the free rational will: The free will is the source of its own norms, and morality is the constitutive end of free willing as such.

But Fichte's ethics is distinct from Kant's in deep and interesting ways. For example, whereas for Kant practical reason prescribes a procedural constraint (i.e., the categorical imperative test) on ends that are the product of prudential reasoning,[1] for Fichte practical reason directly prescribes a substantive end (i.e.,

---

[1]   I rely here on a reading of Kant that is controversial. I defend this interpretation in other work; I presuppose it here because I must presuppose something in order to draw the (I hope, clarifying) contrasts between Kant and Fichte that I will draw throughout the paper. Briefly, I believe that Kant's texts best support an interpretation on which the highest moral principle is a formal constraint (GMS, p. 400; cf. KpV,

the material self-sufficiency of rational agency wherever it occurs) (SL, pp. 59–60, 144–5, 149, 152–3, 209, 211–12, 275). The guiding thought behind his doctrine of duties is a non-welfarist form of consequentialism. Further disagreements with Kant follow, both in the account of moral deliberation and in the account of the moral worth of actions.[2]

I believe that some of these changes are salutary, and that Fichte's ethical project should interest anyone disposed to think of ethics in a broadly Kantian way. His doctrine of duties is less tortured than Kant's at some of the places at which Kant's is most tortured (chiefly the accounts of duties of beneficence[3] and self-improvement[4]). His account of the moral importance of scientific research and education, and a robust account of duties to future generations, go

---

pp. 21–29). We are obliged to embrace those among the ends offered by rational nature (collected under the categories happiness and perfection, or more generally humanity) that are embraceable given that and other formal constraints (MS, p. 395); one's own perfection and others' happiness are the most general categories of ends that survive that process (and so are obligatory ends) (Kant, MS, pp. 385–6). Some take Kant to present humanity as a substantive end in the second formulation of the categorical imperative in the Groundwork (and so deny that the highest moral principle is a formal one). On any reading Kant's account of obligatory ends will be distinct from Fichte's, both in their characterization and in their derivation. Some accounts of Kant will bring him closer to Fichte than others. But none of that affects the interpretation of Fichte I give here.

[2] To the recognizably Kantian requirement that the will of the agent be internally configured in the right way (cf. e.g., GMS, pp. 394, 397–9), Fichte adds a requirement that the action's actual consequences be such as to best promote the moral end (cf. SL, pp. 153–6).

[3] For Fichte, beneficence aims at promoting others' material self-sufficiency (their capacity to pursue ends in general) rather than their happiness. Some proponents of ethics in a Kantian spirit are already closer to the Fichtean picture than Kant's own here, justifying the (Kantian) duty to promote happiness on the grounds that this is an indirect way of supporting the development and exercise of others' agency. So for instance Herman argues that we are to attend to the well-being of others "because and insofar as it is in and through the pursuit of happiness that persons create and sustain themselves as agents. [...] agency-related needs are the object of aid [...]" (Herman, 2007, p. 228); "it is by means of our effect on the happiness of others that we tend to affect their rational condition and abilities" (ibid., p. 267). Compare also the account of "true needs" in Herman, 1993, pp. 55–7.

[4] Fichte's account of duties of self-improvement is quite straightforward, and these duties are exactly analogous to duties of beneficence. The problem with Kant's own account of duties of self-improvement is that her own perfection cannot be assumed to be an end any individual inevitably has, or else it would be ruled out as a duty by the same argument used to rule out the end of one's own happiness at MS, pp. 385–6; yet if it is only an end nature has for humans as a species (which is the view Kant seems to advance in the history essays – cf. e.g., "Idee zu einer allgemeinen Geschichte in weltbürgerlicher Absicht", pp. 18–22 and Kant, "Muthmaßlicher Anfang der Menschengeschichte" pp. 115–121) then no contradiction in willing can be derived from its generalized rejection; and there appears to be no third option.

beyond anything one sees in Kant or the Kantian literature. Finally, Fichte has a stronger basis than Kant on which to argue that some measure of socio-economic equality is a requirement of right.[5] On the whole Fichte's ethics seems to me a compelling way of working out what I take to be the core idea of the Kantian project: The idea that the fundamental moral value and the source of moral value is rational agency (and its exercise).[6]

We can divide Fichte's account of agency into three parts: the core account of what it is to be a moral agent (to have free will in the sense required to be morally responsible and an appropriate addressee of moral imperatives); the account of the constitutive end of moral agency (what reason's material independence or self-sufficiency amounts to); and the account of the connection between these two (that is, of why any moral agent must take material self-sufficiency as its end). What I would like to do in this paper is to present an interpretation of the first of these three parts: the core notion of moral agency, or what Fichte calls "formal freedom".

I will begin by presenting Fichte's general characterization of formal freedom, which has two main components (§ II). I will then examine what is involved in the second component and its conditions of possibility (§ III). I will conclude by examining some complications, and some consequences (positive or negative, depending on one's other commitments) of Fichte's view (§ IV).

II. Formal Freedom

The core notion of rational agency is something Fichte typically calls "formal freedom" (but often "freedom" unmodified). There are textual difficulties surrounding the term: in addition to using "formal freedom" to refer to moral agency, Fichte also uses it to refer to two further items. First, in both the System of Ethics and the Foundations of Natural Right (where this use predominates) he uses it to refer to a sphere of (mainly negative) protections on personal integrity and property. He argues that such protections are justified by the ways in which they further the exercise of free agency, but clearly what is at issue in formal freedom in this second sense is not a property of persons (free will) but a property of their situations (a set of action opportunities). Second, there are points in the System of Ethics (which I will discuss in § IV) at which Fichte appears to use the term "formal freedom" to refer to what is at most a com-

---

5   Pogge shows that Kant can mount at most a weak defense of egalitarian institutions (Pogge, 2002, pp. 153 ff.). Wood discusses Fichte's superiority on this score in chapter 11 of Wood, 2008.

6   Many moral philosophers who fall outside the "Kantian" rubric are sympathetic to a picture very like Fichte's. Sen's capabilities approach comes first to mind. See Sen, 1979, 1984, 1992, ch. 1–4, and 1999, ch. 1–4.

ponent of the core notion of moral agency as I will present it. I have chosen to use Fichte's term nonetheless, in part because it allows me to deal straightforwardly with the second textual difficulty; the use of "formal freedom" in these passages reflects a confusion that I would like to address head-on. But for now let me stipulate that where "formal freedom" occurs in this paper, it refers to moral agency (that is, free will in the sense required for an agent to be morally responsible and an appropriate addressee of moral imperatives).

Formal freedom, briefly stated, is the disposition to form intentions spontaneously on the basis of concepts of ends. To call it a disposition rather than a capacity or faculty is already to signal a departure from Kant. Fichte tells us that formal freedom is neither the activity of forming spontaneous intentions nor the mere capacity to do so, but the "tendency" to do so – a "tendency to determine itself absolutely, without any external impetus" (SL, p. 28; cf. 29, 30, 32, 37, 38).[7] For Kant the free will is a sort of causality or, alternatively, a faculty, and Fichte's conception fits well only the first of these characterizations.

Fichte's claim that that formal freedom requires spontaneity – "an absolutely free, conscious transition from indeterminacy to determination" (SL, p. 158) that is not explicable as the outcome of any sort of natural causality (SL, pp. 134–6; cf. 112, 158–9, 182) – recalls Kant's claim that the free will would have to involve transcendental freedom, "a causality [...] through which something happens without the cause of [that something] being itself determined according to necessary laws by a further antecedent cause – that is, an absolute spontaneity of the cause to begin, of itself, a series of appearances that [then] proceeds according to natural laws" (KrV, A 446/B 474).[8]

Kant thought such spontaneity to be empirically unobservable (also introspectively); and he recognized that the claim that we have freedom in this sense is philosophically controversial. But he thought spontaneity required for moral responsibility, and he thought our possession of it demonstrable from a practical point of view.[9]

Like Kant, Fichte emphasizes the free will's independence of determination by natural causes: "Every link in a natural chain is predetermined, whether by the law of mechanism or that of organism. [...] But what will occur in the I [...] is not predetermined and simply undeterminable. There is no law according to which free self-determinations follow and can be predicted, because these depend upon the determination of the intelligence, but this latter is as such simply free, pure activity" (SL, p. 134).[10] Fichte also agrees with Kant that only

---

7   All translations of Fichte are my own.
8   All translations of Kant are my own.
9   This is a condensed statement of a complex Kantian view that, moreover, evolved over time. For a more detailed discussion see Kosch, 2006 a, ch. 1.
10   Notice that natural causes are described as those operating according to the laws of "mechanism or organism". This points to a further disagreement with Kant (though

creatures displaying such independence are morally responsible, though his account of the connection between spontaneity and responsibility differs from Kant's. For Fichte, responsibility requires spontaneity, but only because responsibility requires thought, and spontaneity is one of the features that characterizes thought. (I will return to this difference in a moment.)

Because Fichte treats the transition from indeterminacy to (self-)determination as the object of introspective consciousness,[11] and because he treats the unpredictability of human behavior as (non-introspective) evidence that it involves some spontaneous causality, there is for him no special epistemological problem connected with it. He recognizes that the existence of such spontaneous causality is an object of philosophical controversy, but he sees that controversy as unsettle able by argument because informed by two incompatible basic assumptions. Those already committed to the universality of mechanistic causality ("dogmatists") will explain away the phenomenological and observational facts as illusions (SL, p. 25), but that explanation will appeal only to those who already deny the existence of free will. Those not so committed will take the facts at face value, but they likewise have no argument that will convince the others. One's stance on the spontaneity question is, according to Fichte, the object of a radical choice of philosophical disposition (SL, p. 26; cf. EE, pp. 429 ff.).[12]

not one directly relevant to the account of free will). On Fichte's view organisms (even non-human ones) are not mechanistically determined; their behavior must instead be understood in terms of a drive toward organization (of which self-preservation is a part) expressing itself both in their internal articulation and in their interactions with the environment (SL, p. 121). Kant's position in the Critique of the Power of Judgment was that we cannot comprehend how organisms could be produced by mechanistic causality (see KU, pp. 362–84); Fichte's position in the *Sittenlehre* appears to be that the activity of organisms cannot be the product of mechanistic causality (SL, pp. 110–15). Perhaps under Schelling's influence, he thinks of three types of causality as operating alongside one another in the world of experience: mechanistic causal laws govern inorganic nature, teleological principles govern organic nature, and laws of rational reflection govern rational agents. Both of the latter (teleological and rational) are normative, rather than (purely) descriptive. Those governing rational beings are, in addition, conscious and self-imposed (SL, p. 125), their operation mediated through concepts of ends.

11   For instance, he describes "consciousness of my indeterminacy" as "condition of the consciousness of my self-determination by free activity" (SL, p. 137).

12   Fichte is not committed, as Kant is, to the unknowable noumenal status of the free will, and so the Kantian caveat – that "that which, in relation to sensuous impulses, is entitled freedom may […] in relation to higher and more remote operating causes, be nature again" (KrV, A 803/B 831) – is not required. It has been laid to rest in the foundations of his transcendental philosophy, in the rejection of the Kantian thing in itself, which does away with any worries about intelligible determinism (cf. SL, pp. 17, 135–36, 160–61 and Neuhouser, 1990, pp. 120 ff.).

The characterization of formal freedom as spontaneity is a negative one: naturalistic explanations of human behavior are incomplete, and even phenomenological, consciousness of spontaneity is consciousness of being non-determined (SL, p. 137). But Fichte denies that unpredictability in the action of a cause suffices for attributing formal freedom to it (SL, p. 33). Spontaneity cannot exhaust the content of formal freedom; there must be a positive characterization as well (SL, pp. 36–8).

Fichte's positive characterization of formal freedom as a self-determination "through concepts" or "through thinking" (SL, pp. 35–8, 112) recalls Kant's description of practical freedom, the "capacity, through representations of that which itself is more remotely useful or harmful, to overcome the impressions on our sensible faculty of desire", and thus to escape determination by them (KrV, A 802/B 830; cf. A 534/B 562).

Kant thought of practical freedom as an empirically observable property that normal human adults have and animals lack.[13] He introduced it as a conception of freedom in principle compatible with determinism, and so philosophically uncontroversial. He also introduced it as the capacity that allows resistance to immediate inclination based on both moral and prudential reasons (KrV, A 802/B 830). His eventual conclusion that transcendental spontaneity is required for morally responsible agency made these claims inconsistent, since whatever is empirically observable must also be causally determined. This is surely one of the motivations for his later commitment to the inscrutability of moral character, and it rendered the project of giving an empirical account of how we can be morally motivated deeply problematic (KrV, A 551n/B 579n; cf. Rel., pp. 21n, 51).

The disposition to form representations of ends is, for Fichte as for Kant, what allows an agent to be motivated by something other than immediate inclination. Such ends can be moral, as when one "sets oneself an end that runs counter to all inclinations and is chosen nevertheless, from duty" (SL, p. 137). They can also be prudential: "I choose with full freedom of will, for I choose with consciousness of self-determination, [even in cases in which] I by no means sacrifice enjoyment to morality, but only to a different enjoyment" (SL, p. 162). Fichte even allows for a third kind of case with no Kantian correlate, that of a "heroic" character who is able to subordinate all other motivations to a blind and lawless (and so amoral) drive for self-sufficiency (SL, pp. 184–91).

Because Fichte lacked the Kantian commitments that would preclude empirical observation of a will to which spontaneous causality could be attributed,

---

[13] He contrasts the animal will, "which cannot be determined otherwise than through sensuous impulses, that is, pathologically", with the human will, which is not determined only by that which "immediately affects the senses" but can sometimes determine itself through reason (KrV, A 802/B 830; cf. A 534/B 562).

he could treat the free will as the object of straightforward empirical investigation. We can (and the moral philosopher is obliged to) give an empirical account of what is required to form concepts of ends and to resist immediate inclination in order to act on moral, prudential, or even "heroic" considerations. Moral agency is a complex psychological characteristic, involving component capacities whose production and maintenance requires the right sort of interaction with the right sort of human and natural environment. It is in the account of these components, and of their material conditions of possibility, that the raw materials of Fichte's doctrine of duties lie.

Although his commitment to spontaneity puts Fichte on the incompatibilist side of the free will debate, the resulting account reads very much like a compatibilist one. This is because his commitment to spontaneity is unlike that of the incompatibilist-on-the-street. For Fichte, responsibility is tied directly only to the disposition to form intentions based on concepts of ends, and spontaneity enters only because forming concepts of ends is an exercise of thought (and spontaneity is, for Fichte, the mark of the mental). An agent's actions are determined by his reasons as he sees them (as we see in the account of moral evil, which I will discuss in § IV); spontaneity enters at the level of seeing (or, occasionally, creating) the reasons. Saying that the will is spontaneous is for him therefore compatible with giving a full empirical explanation of both moral and immoral motivation.

III. Reflection

The formation of concepts of ends of all kinds relies on what Fichte calls "reflection". He uses this term to refer to two distinct capacities, interrelated but independently variable, which I will call minimal and evaluative reflection.

Reflection in the minimal sense involves taking oneself (especially one's actions, motives, and the connections between them) as an object of consideration. Fichte distinguishes two forms of self-consciousness: the sort of immediate conscious awareness one has of what one is doing (or planning or wanting), and the reflective self-consciousness of oneself-as-doing-this (or as-intending-to-do-this or as-having-this-desire). Reflection in the minimal sense is just the second of these two forms of self-consciousness, and Fichte calls this sort of self-scrutiny by both names: sometimes "self-consciousness" (SL, pp. 23, 29, 77, 89, 107, 161, 221), sometimes "reflecting" or "reflection" (SL, pp. 30–43 passim, 57, 73, 100, 109, 112, 124–6, 130–40 passim, 144, 147, 178).

At several points Fichte seems to claim that what becomes an object of reflection in the minimal sense comes, just in virtue of that, under the agent's control (SL, pp. 125, 135, 140–1, 178–80). But I do not think we can take these statements at face value. Reflective consciousness of some motive or capacity or deliberative pattern in oneself is surely necessary, but just as surely not sufficient, for controlling or correcting for it. We should read Fichte instead as claiming that, assuming that the other components of agency are in place, reflective consciousness suffices for control. As an example of what I take him to have in mind, take the case of an otherwise normal adult whose decisions are influenced by an unconscious bias. If at some point she becomes aware of having it (i.e., if the bias becomes the object of reflective self-consciousness), she thereby acquires responsibility for decisions influenced by it.[14]

As such cases demonstrate, reflection in this minimal sense admits of degrees: a person can be more or less reflective by taking more or less of her conduct, intentions, or motivational set as objects of consideration. Fichte describes spontaneous expansions of reflective self-consciousness, but his claim (to which I will return) that the level of moral cultivation possible for an individual depends on her social milieu (SL, p. 184) surely relies in part on the observation that many such expansions are the result of prompting by other agents.

Fichte also calls "reflection" an activity that clearly goes beyond reflective self-consciousness to encompass rational evaluation of the consistency of one's set of motivations, intentions, and beliefs about matters of fact (SL, pp. 111–131 passim, 159, 162, 165–72 passim, 185, 187, 191–2). Reflection in this evaluative sense requires minimal reflection, in that evaluating the appropriateness of actions, motives, and their connections requires having them in view in the first place. But evaluative reflection also involves beliefs about how the world is and might be made to be (i.e., beliefs about facts, general causal laws, and one's own causal capabilities); it also involves the application of a criterion of consistency to the conjunction of these beliefs and one's motivations and intentions. It involves, in other words, practical reasoning.[15]

Fichte's account of practical reasoning differs strikingly from Kant's. For Kant, moral reasoning involves the application of a procedural constraint (consistency with universal legislation in a kingdom of ends) to the pursuit of an end (one's own happiness) that is essentially agent-relative and that sets individual interests in opposition to one another. The technical-practical reasoning that produces the maxims upon which the categorical imperative test operates is purely calculative (i.e., means-ends or part-whole) reasoning aimed at ends subsidiary to the overarching end of happiness. For Fichte, by contrast, moral reasoning consists of the same maximizing calculative reasoning that, for Kant,

---

[14]   This should not be taken to suggest that Fichte is insensitive to the possibility of culpable ignorance (see, e.g., SL, p. 192).

[15]   We see this in Fichte's account of the origin of evaluative reflection. Rational beings have a drive toward independence, toward "absolute self-determination to activity of activity's sake" (SL, p. 131) rooted in "reason's tendency to determine itself purely through itself" (SL, p. 130). Reflection, Fichte tells us, is a manifestation of this higher drive and it is reflection in this broader evaluative sense that he has in mind (SL, pp. 130–1).

characterizes the prudential case only. It is distinguished only by the fact that its end is the specifically moral end (i.e., reason's material independence or self-sufficiency).[16] There is no additional step corresponding to the categorical imperative test because the moral end is agent-neutral from the outset and so cannot lead to the sort of collective self-undermining for which the categorical imperative test provides a corrective.

That he denies the existence of any substantive deontological principles is what I take Fichte to be saying when he says that morality determines practical deliberation (when it does) only by setting the end (SL, p. 166). The question for practical deliberation is what, for an agent in a determinate situation, progress toward this end requires – and the process of finding an answer to that question is just what it would be in any instance of theoretical reasoning.[17] This set of facts explains what would otherwise be a quite mysterious claim on Fichte's part: that all the reasoning involved in practical deliberation is "theoretical". What he means is that practical reasoning consists wholly in the sort of reasoning Kant calls "technical-practical" and sorts under the theoretical part of cognition.[18] In fact Fichte's assimilation of this sort of reasoning to Kantian reflecting judgment probably explains why he uses the term "reflection" to describe it (cf. KU, pp. 179 ff.; cf. AA 20, pp. 211 ff.). It is clear that Fichte means to signal his departure from Kant's account of practical reasoning in these passages.

Fichte thinks that all instances of practical reasoning aim at material independence or self-sufficiency in some sense, and that they differ only in how that end is conceived. Because rational beings are also natural beings, the end makes

---

[16]   Fichte defines the specifically moral end at SL, pp. 39–57 passim, 59–60, 144–5, 149, 152.

[17]   Fichte describes the phenomenology this way: the agent lets his theoretical faculties go their way until they hit upon something that produces a feeling of "cool approval" – a feeling just like the one that accompanies the discovery of the correct answer to any theoretical question, except that in this case we call the result "right" rather than "true" (SL, p. 167). Fichte does not say how we should understand the instrumental principle, which is usually thought of as a principle of practical, not theoretical, reason. But Kant's view of this is cloudy too: in the Groundwork, for instance, he calls it an analytic principle of practical reason; but the technical-practical reasoning he sorts under the theoretical part of cognition in the Critique of the Power of Judgment surely relies on it.

[18]   "All technical-practical rules (i.e., those of art and skill in general, and also of prudence, as a skill in having influence over human beings and their will), insofar as their principles rest on concepts, must be counted only as corollaries of theoretical philosophy. For they concern only the possibility of things according to concepts of nature, to which belong not only the means that can be found in nature, but even the will (as a faculty of desire, and so a natural faculty), insofar as it can be determined through natural incentives according to those rules" (KU, p. 172; cf. KU, p. 175 and AA 20, pp. 200–01; MS, pp. 217–18; and GMS, pp. 416 ff.).

itself felt as a drive.[19] Any organized product of nature has a drive to keep its parts together in something like the order in which they are already – a drive to self-preservation – out of which many subsidiary drives follow, including those that are strictly required for flourishing, but also including an inclination to pursue enjoyment for its own sake.[20] This "natural drive" is a configuration of a basic drive to self-determination, and since we are organized products of nature, we have it.

But rational and reflective beings are not constrained to the prompts of this natural drive. The basic drive to self-determination also has a pure form: what Fichte calls the "pure" drive (by which he seems to mean a drive to self-determination in a completely abstract and indeterminate form). The pure and the natural drives are united at the empirical level in what he calls the "ethical" or "mixed" drive (SL, pp. 151–2). Unlike the natural drive, the ethical drive is neutral with respect to person and time: it is directed not to the agent's independence in particular, but to the independence of rational will in general, and counsels sacrifices now for greater gains later. Unlike the pure drive, the ethical drive has concrete content, determined by the specific needs and capacities of a natural rational being in specific material and cultural circumstances and with a specific degree of reflective cultivation (and it is all of these together that dictate what progress toward self-sufficiency or independence will mean in a given case).

Like many, Fichte found the tension between moral and prudential considerations to have been too starkly drawn by Kant, and he emphasizes that there is no fundamental conflict between the pure drive and the natural drive (though of course there can be local conflicts). He also emphasizes the fine-grainedness of any given instance of practical reasoning.[21] This is not to deny the universal validity of the results of such reasoning, when they are correct. Anyone relevantly similarly situated should come to the same conclusion, and everyone should be able in principle to recognize the correctness of the conclusion. But the conclusion is universalizable when and because it is correct; its universalizability is not what makes it correct to begin with. Fichte emphasizes his

---

[19]   Fichte's drive-based moral psychology is a matter of some interest in its own right; I will constrain my discussion of it to what I need for my purposes here. For more discussion, see, e.g., Rohs, 1991 a; Rohs, 1991 b, pp. 104 ff.; and Wood, forthcoming.

[20]   The natural drive is discussed at SL, pp. 115 ff.; organization at SL, pp. 122–3; pleasure at SL, p. 129.

[21]   "The moral law, in relation to empirical human beings, has a determinate starting point (the determinate limitation in which the individual finds himself); it has a determinate (if never reachable) goal (absolute freedom from all limitation); and a completely determinate way through which it leads (the order of nature). Therefore for every determinate individual in a given situation there is something determinate that is required by duty – and this is what we can say the moral law demands in its application to [him]" (SL, p. 166).

disagreement with Kant here by explicitly demoting universalizability to heuristic rather than constitutive status.[22]

Calculative reasoning involves not only an end, but also beliefs about general causal laws and particular facts about an action situation, and an awareness of one's own status as a causally efficacious being.[23] In discussing cognitive attitudes and their role in practical reasoning, as he does at length in the second part of the System of Ethics, Fichte calls "Erkenntnisse" what I have just called "beliefs". Of course Fichte's German lacked a term corresponding to "belief" as now used in English-language philosophy; "Erkenntnis" is, for him, the default term for empirical belief. Still, we might sensibly ask: for Fichte, is an agent deliberatively rational to the extent that she operates correctly with the beliefs that she has, or does the truth of those beliefs also matter for her practical rationality? Not much about the wider project hangs on the answer to this question,[24] but I think a case can be made for the second alternative, and thus for the inclusion of some degree of theoretical knowledge among the conditions required for formal freedom.[25] And in fact Fichte often seems committed to theoretical

---

[22]   SL, pp. 233–4. Fichte sounds at this point like later consequentialists (e.g., Mill, Hare, Kagan, Parfit) who have sought in a similar way to bridge the apparent gap between consequentialist views and Kant's.

[23]   Beliefs about the nature of things are a condition of the possibility of setting ends that concern those things (SL, p. 103), and awareness of one's causal efficacy is a condition of the possibility of awareness of oneself as willing (SL, pp. 89–92). Fichte argues in § 1 of the Foundations of Natural Right that awareness of one's own causal efficacy is a condition of the possibility of self-consciousness (GN, pp. 17 ff.; cf. Neuhouser, 2001). What seems less controversial is that forming a conscious intention requires seeing the will as a causal force, and Fichte argues that for any given individual that is an empirical realization.

[24]   In particular, the answer to this question will not matter for that part of Fichte's ethical theory that concerns our duties to produce certain true beliefs, and refrain from producing false beliefs, in others. Those duties can be justified so long as Fichte is allowed the (reasonable) assumption that any deliberating agent has an interest, qua deliberating agent, in true relevant beliefs. Acquisition of these can be an end partially constitutive of rational deliberation even if having them is not itself a part of the concept of practical rationality.

[25]   Uncontroversially, there are epistemic conditions on moral responsibility: If I didn't know the gun was loaded (and it is not a case of culpable ignorance) I really can offer that as an excuse. To drive a wedge between conditions for responsibility and conditions for free will here requires an argument. But such an argument might not be so easy to make since, also uncontroversially, functional cognitive limitations (e.g., processing problems of sufficient severity) do undermine free will. We would need a justification for treating cognitive limitations that are not functional differently from functional limitations. But it is not clear what that would be. It seems clear that sufficiently deep ignorance (of the sort one might have, for example, in a social situation in a very foreign cultural milieu) can result in an inability to intend anything that would be remotely appropriate by one's own lights. It is not clear that we should say in those situations that the agent is free in forming intentions so long as she has some beliefs to operate with, however outrageously inappropriate those beliefs may be.

knowledge being essential not just for the freedom to do what one chooses, but for the capacity to choose freely to begin with (see, e.g., SL, pp. 66–75).

Fichte endorses a version of the distinction between basic and non-basic actions – in his terminology, things done by "immediate" and "mediated" causality (SL, pp. 98–9). The set of points at which one's will has immediate causal efficacy is one's body (in what is obviously a technical sense of that term).[26] All mediated causal efficacy is mediated through one's body; some is further mediated through interactions between external objects (as when one does something by setting some process in motion). An agent can intend to exercise mediated causal efficacy only by employing an understanding of the physical nature of and laws governing her body and the things on which it acts (SL, pp. 68, 70, 103, 109, 166–72 passim). At minimum, she needs to know what in her environment is contingent and so in principle alterable (SL, pp. 68–9). She also needs a determinate conception of her causal powers, and so a way of distinguishing between what she has herself brought about and what has simply happened (SL, p. 70). The more complex the projects she engages in, the more detailed the instrumental reasoning she engages in, and the more she needs to know about the physical world. This is why Fichte thinks some degree of causal knowledge of nature precedes reflection and, so, formal freedom. All drive-based behavior requires knowledge, and before one is a moral agent one is an effective causal agent (SL, pp. 101–110 passim).

This cognitive requirement for moral agency, and the dialectical interaction between knowledge and control of one's environment, will play a key role both in Fichte's political philosophy (as part of his justification for property rights) (GN, pp. 113–19) and in his ethics (as the justification for duties of truth-telling (SL, pp. 282–8, 290), truth-seeking (SL, p. 291), and collective support for a specialized class whose vocation is basic research (SL, p. 344)). It is in this cognitive requirement, and the use Fichte makes of it, that much of the very considerable interest in Fichte's ethics and political theory lies.

Like minimal reflection, evaluative reflection comes in degrees that vary based in part on social conditions. It relies on the demands made by others (e.g., the demand for consensus in cases of disagreement, which Fichte thinks we all must make and to which he thinks we all must submit) (SL, pp. 233–53 passim). It also relies on the example offered by others (and setting an example of morality is itself one of our moral duties, both in general (SL, pp. 313–25) and for those occupying the particular social roles of parent (SL, p. 338), and religious leader (SL, pp. 204, 352)).

---

[26] The set of points at which the will has immediate causality may be smaller (paralysis) or greater (some prostheses) than the set corresponding to the body in the ordinary biological sense.

Reflection has two further prerequisites that are not themselves components of it. About both it is clear that Fichte considers them necessary for moral agency. And about both I will have more to say in § IV, so I will describe them only briefly here. The first prerequisite is psychological. Fichte thinks that one cannot form an intention without some degree of deliberative effort, and so without the capacity for applying it one is not a moral agent. Since errors in practical reasoning result in part from a lack of such effort, I will discuss it at greater length in treating Fichte's account of moral evil in the next section. The second prerequisite is social. Fichte thinks that individuals become aware of their own capacity for free efficacy only as a result of interaction with other agents who make demands of them (GN, pp. 30–40).[27] From this Fichte concludes that if there are to be free agents at all, there must be more than one (GN, p. 39). I will discuss this claim further in treating the origin of reflective consciousness in the next section. The inclusion of evaluative reflection, and thus of some degree of deliberative rationality, as a component of formal freedom looks fairly uncontroversial. The capacity to refrain from what one's currently strongest inclination demands is contingent on having other, often temporally distant, ends whose fulfillment requires refraining from acting on this inclination. It is hard to see how we could have such ends without the exercise of evaluative reflection. And this also seems the best way to make sense of the many points at which Fichte seems to equate rationality and freedom.[28] But my characterization does raise three problems (one textual and two philosophical), to which I now turn.

IV. Three Complications

On occasion, Fichte describes reflection as a product of formal freedom. For an arbitrary instance of reflection this is not a problem for my account, since these are (or at least can be) formally free actions (and so themselves rely on prior instances of reflection). The textual problem arises in a passage in which Fichte describes the first awakening of reflective agency (SL, p. 179).[29]

The passage contains one of two apparently distinct stories that Fichte tells about the awakening of reflective agency. On the first, told in § 3 of the Foundations of Natural Right, an individual comes to self-awareness as a formally free being (that is, as a being able to form concepts of ends and able to choose in one

---

27   The argument is reiterated at SL, p. 178.

28   E.g.: "I posit myself as rational, therefore as free" (GN, p. 8). One can of course read this and other passages as asserting only that freedom is a necessary condition of rationality, or only that rationality is a sufficient condition of for freedom.

29   There are other troublesome passages. For example Fichte writes at SL, pp. 161–62 that one's awareness of one's capacity for formal freedom is what makes putting off fulfillment of immediate desires possible, and therefore makes reflection possible.

among many possible ways, GN, pp. 19–20) only as a result of norm-invoking, non-coercive interaction with another agent: a "summons".[30] The summoner recognizes in the summoned the potentiality of free agency,[31] and makes a demand upon the individual, "calling upon it to exercise its efficacy" (GN, p. 33). The summons is accompanied by the offer of a sphere of free activity: A set of action possibilities that is given, pre-formed, to the agent, who needs only to grasp one of them (GN, p. 41). What the summons conveys, then, is both a demand to exercise causal efficacy in accordance with a normative claim, and information about the action possibilities available and what they mean. It permits the appearance, at the same time, of some rudimentary reflective self-consciousness, some rudimentary practical reasoning, and a rudimentary form of end-oriented spontaneous action. The aim is to explain how a first free action – one taken without sophisticated reflective capacities already in place – is possible, and thereby to describe part of the actual moral development of children.[32]

On this first account of the awakening of reflective agency, a moral agent comes to be only by "being determined to be self-determining" by another moral agent (GN, p. 33). There are parts of the System of Ethics in which it appears we are being told the same story, and Fichte even refers the reader to the Foundations account (SL, p. 218). But there is also another story that appears in the System of Ethics, and this second account is the locus of the textual problem (SL, pp. 177 ff.). In it, Fichte describes a pre-reflective individual who acts "with freedom, indeed, in the formal sense of the word, but without consciousness of this its freedom" (SL, p. 178). He tells us that such a pre-reflective individual is free for an intelligence outside him, but "for himself – if he were anything for himself – is just an animal" (SL, p. 178).[33] And he tells us that such an individual's first reflection takes place in these circumstances as a purely spontaneous act, "through absolute freedom" (SL, p. 179). This agent is described as exercising the capacity for reflection for the first time as a result of an exercise of formal freedom.

This second story appears incompatible both with the summons account and with the account I have given of formal freedom. To make it compatible with the first, we might take it as a partial description of a situation that in fact involves a

---

[30] Fichte's idea of a summons is much discussed in the literature. A few examples (there are many more): Neuhouser, 2000; Honneth, 2001; Rohs, 1991 b, pp. 86 ff.; and Darwall, 2006, pp. 20 ff., 252 ff., et passim.

[31] The summoner recognizes the potentiality of free agency by the shape of the agent's body (GN, pp. 75–81).

[32] "The summons to free self-activity is what is called upbringing. All individuals must be brought up to be human beings, and would not become human beings otherwise" (GN, p. 39).

[33] By hypothesis he is not anything "for himself" because not self-conscious.

second agent and a summons; or we might take it to be a replacement of Fichte's earlier answer to the question of who the first summoner might have been (viz., God) (GN, pp. 39–40) with one in which reflection is something that just happens inexplicably and thereafter reproduces itself in the way described in Foundations § 3. But neither move would make this passage compatible with the account I have given of formal freedom: It seems clear that Fichte here uses "formal freedom" to refer to spontaneity alone.

I see no way to resolve this problem without sacrificing some part of the text. At this point we have already been told that spontaneity alone is not sufficient for formal freedom, which requires intentional action determined by the representation of an end. The representation of an end requires reflection, as does awareness of multiple possibilities and choice among them. And Fichte affirms these claims in this very passage: the pre-reflective individual is still in the grip of the unmodified natural drive, does not have a multiplicity of action possibilities, and is not a free intelligence (SL, p. 179).

Fichte's main concern in this passage is to emphasize that the actualization of the potential for reflection is not naturalistically explicable, but is something that must occur through spontaneity (SL, pp. 178–9; cf. SL, p. 132), and that even where it occurs in response to some external stimulus (like a summons) it is not caused by that stimulus (SL, p. 179; cf. SL, p. 125). We have already seen that reflection, since it involves thinking, involves spontaneity. But that does not entail that the first occurrence of reflection is itself the result of moral agency in the sense required for responsibility. And so, although Fichte uses "formal freedom" in this passage to describe what only spontaneity is, this should not lead us to conclude that for him spontaneity and formal freedom are equivalent.

So much for the textual problem. The second problem with taking evaluative reflection as partially constitutive of formal freedom is this: on Fichte's account, reflection (its domain, sophistication, procedural completeness) varies across the set of normal human adults. If reflection is a component of formal freedom, it follows that formal freedom will also vary. And if formal freedom is that in virtue of which we are morally responsible, then responsibility for action will, it seems, come in degrees.

There is no textual problem here, because this is in fact what Fichte wants to say. Every rational agent has, qua rational agent, the same capacity for formal freedom, but not every rational agent has developed that capacity to the same degree. This commitment is implicit in the discussion of the developmental psychology of freedom (SL, pp. 177 ff.), where Fichte distinguishes between the rational being "considered primordially", which has "everything that belongs to a rational being entire and without lack" and empirical individuals, who fall short of this ideal of agency to varying degrees (SL, pp. 177–8). What accounts for much of the variability, as we have seen, is variation in the agent's environment. There are some social and cultural circumstances in which agents' freedom is more highly cultivated, and in these circumstances agents are both more fully responsible for their actions and also able to become morally better than they could in other circumstances. "Through upbringing in the broadest sense – that is, through the general influence of society upon us – we are first cultivated in the use of our freedom. [...] If society were better, we would be too, even without individual merit. The possibility of individual merit is not thereby annulled; it simply begins at a higher level" (SL, p. 184). Not only does Fichte admit the possibility of degrees of responsibility varying with degrees of development in an agent's reflective capacities (SL, pp. 137, 178, 180); he also acknowledges duties arising out of the imperative to protect or promote other agents' "formal freedom" (where "formal freedom" seems to have the agency sense).[34]

In the end I find this consequence of Fichte's account unproblematic. It coincides with many ordinary intuitions: we often seem willing to admit a spectrum of degrees of moral responsibility among normal adults. It is also a feature of compatibilist accounts of free will that cash that notion out in terms of psychological capacities, and for the same reasons. I raise it as a problem only because it is a departure from the Kantian view, and does come with a cost that the Kantian view does not have. Kant accepted that an agent's circumstances can mitigate her responsibility for some actions; but he seemed committed to denying that moral agency itself can come in degrees.[35] He had good reason for that. If formal freedom is that in virtue of which we have a value beyond price – as for both Kant and Fichte it is – then to admit that it comes in degrees is to give up something of the fundamental Kantian equality of moral agents as such. Some might find that consequence hard to accept.[36]

---

[34]   These are not only episodic (refraining from actions – like deception – that might undermine responsibility for a single decision (SL, p. 283)); they are also more global (e.g., contributing to others' knowledge (SL, pp. 282–3, 290–91) or providing moral example and inspiration (SL, pp. 317–25)). And there are parallel self-regarding duties, appropriately describable as duties to increase the degree to which one can be responsible for what one does, by putting more energy into practical reflection (SL, pp. 155, 178, 180–85), correcting it by exposing it to criticism from other agents (SL, pp. 234–53 passim), and increasing the quantity and quality of one's theoretical knowledge (SL, p. 282).

[35]   For Kant's allowance of degrees of responsibility for individual actions, based on the circumstances of those actions, see, e.g., MS, p. 228. But Kant held that moral responsibility as an agent-characteristic is either absent or entire; there is no room in Kant's picture for an individual who, in a global sense, is a partially-responsible agent.

[36]   The cost is tied not simply to this account of formal freedom, but to Fichte's more general project of grounding political and moral duties in conditions of the possibility of agency. Fichte's argument for the moral importance of external limitations is what allows him to, e.g., give a more compelling account of intelligible property, and of the value of equality in its distribution, than any available to Kant. But Fichte's argument has, inevitably, this drawback as its flip side. (One can acknowledge the problem for Kant, while maintaining that the cost of Fichte's solution is too high. For a view like this see Shell, 1986, p. 156.)

The third problem is this: the inclusion of evaluative reflection (and so some degree of practical rationality) in the core notion of moral agency, coupled with Fichte's conviction that our (true) all-things-considered reasons are always our moral reasons, raises the worry that actions deficient in moral worth precisely thereby will be deficient in formal freedom. If that is true, then either we will be morally responsible only for morally correct actions, or the worse our actions are, the less we will be responsible for them (assuming what I think is correct, that both formal freedom and moral responsibility admit of degrees).

Again there is no textual problem here, since Fichte accepts this consequence. We see this in his account of moral error. He claims that agents always act on the best reasons they are aware of having, and since he agrees with Kant that moral reasons are the best reasons there are, he claims that agents always act on their moral duty to the extent that they are aware of it. It is "simply impossible and contradictory that someone might with distinct consciousness of what his duty is at the moment of action consciously decide not to do his duty" (SL, p. 191). What is possible – indeed, common – is that an agent's consciousness of his duty becomes obscured (SL, p. 192), or he acts without sufficient reflection, never acquiring an adequate consciousness of his duty in a given situation to begin with. Morally wrong actions are explicable, then, only by failures of practical reflection.

The characteristic failure of reflection is incompleteness, and the source of such failure, Fichte claims, is laziness about engaging fully in the process of practical deliberation that leads to conviction (SL, pp. 192–4, 199). This is why I have said that we should take deliberative energy or effort (where by that I mean simply the opposite of deliberative laziness) to be a precondition of formal freedom: the process Fichte describes as leading to error in moral reasoning must be identical to whatever process leads to error in any practical reasoning, because the sort of reasoning required is the same regardless of whether the end is the moral one or something short of that. If more deliberative effort results in more adequate (i.e., extensive, coherent) reflection, then such effort must also result in more formal freedom.

This means that the application of a determinate degree of effort to a given instance of deliberation cannot itself be an act of formal freedom on that very occasion. An agent can be blameworthy for her own degree of deliberative sloth only to the extent that it is the result of some past action of hers. But that action itself would be pro tanto irrational for that reason, and so have its source in a failure of practical deliberation, and so in deliberative laziness. The point is never reached at which an agent's level of deliberative energy is up to her. She is not fully responsible for her own immoral actions, but neither is she morally responsible for her own lack of moral responsibility.

This is exactly what Fichte tells us in discussing moral error: reflective laziness is not the result of a conscious policy; there is no maxim of letting consciousness of duty becomes obscured (SL, p. 193). It is, rather, the expression in us of a natural principle of inertia (SL, p. 199). We all start out thoughtless, as children, and are prone to revert to thoughtlessness out of habit. Virtue, by contrast, cannot become a habit.[37] And vice is typically not a state from which one can extract oneself on one's own.[38] The vicious are capable of the greater effort that virtue would require, but unaware of that capacity and incapable of spurring themselves to exercise it; the awareness of that capacity and the impetus to exercise it is the result of other agents' prodding.[39]

Fichte presents the section of the System of Ethics in which he discusses moral error as an account of radical evil in the Kantian sense (SL, pp. 198–9). That is a mischaracterization. On Fichte's account, vice is never chosen; it is the result of persistence in or reversion to the natural default state of unreflective behavior, in a social milieu in which it is possible to do better. Responsibility varies, then, with moral success: one is responsible for virtue to the extent that it is a result of the exercise of formal freedom, but one is not in the same way responsible for vice. Once again this is a consequence that might, depending on other commitments, be hard to accept.[40]

References

Darwall, Stephen (2006): *The Second-Person Standpoint*, Cambridge, MA.
Fichte, Johann Gottlieb (1971): *Werke*, ed. I.H. Fichte, Berlin [= FW].
– *Erste Einleitung in die Wissenschaftslehre*, in: *FW*, vol. 1, pp. 417–49 [= EE].
– *Grundlage des Naturrechts*, in: *FW*, vol 3, pp. 1–385[= GN].
– *System der Sittenlehre*, in: *FW*, vol. 4, pp. 1–365 [= SL].
Herman, Barbara (1993): *The Practice of Moral Judgment*, Cambridge, MA.
– (2007): *Moral Literacy*, Cambridge, MA.
Honneth, Axel (2001): "Die transzendentale Notwendigkeit der Intersubjektivität", in: Merle, Jean-Christophe (ed.): *Johann Gottlieb Fichte, Grundlage des Naturrechts*, Berlin, pp. 63–80.
Kant, Immanuel (1902 ff.): *Kants gesammelte Schriften Bds. III & IV*, ed. Königlich Preußische Akademie der Wissenschaften, Berlin [= AA].
– *Kritik der reinen Vernunft*, in: *AA*, vols. 3–4 [= KrV].

---

[37] "Practice and vigilance, standing guard over oneself must be continual; no one is certain of his morality even for a moment without continual strenuous effort" (SL, p. 193; cf. SL, pp. 199–204).

[38] The text is not clearly univocal here: there are points at which Fichte does seem to want to say one can spontaneously free oneself from thoughtlessness (e.g., at SL, p. 193).

[39] People have to "grasp themselves in their contemptibleness" and become disgusted, and this is one of the functions of positive religion (SL, pp. 204–5).

[40] This problem of the relation between formal freedom and morality is a descendant of a similar problem in Kant. I treat its Kantian form in Kosch, 2006 a and its Fichtean form in Kosch, 2006 b.

- "Idee zu einer allgemeinen Geschichte in weltbürgerlicher Absicht", in: *AA*, vol. 7, pp. 15–32.
- *Grundlegung zur Metaphysik der Sitten*, in: *AA*, vol. 4, pp. 385–464 [= GMS].
- "Muthmaßlicher Anfang der Menschengeschichte", in: AA, vol. 8, pp. 107–124.
- *Kritik der praktischen Vernunft*, in: *AA*, vol. 5, pp. 1–164 [= KpV].
- *Kritik der Urteilskraft*, in: *AA*, vol. 5, pp. 165–486 [= KU].
- *Metaphysik der Sitten*, in: *AA*, vol. 6, pp. 203–494 [= MS].
- *Die Religion innerhalb der Grenzen der bloßen Vernunft*, in: *AA*, vol. 6, pp. 1–202. [= Rel.]

Kosch, Michelle (2006 a): *Freedom and Reason in Kant, Schelling and Kierkegaard*, Oxford.
- (2006 b): "Kierkegaard's Ethicist: Fichte's role in Kierkegaard's construction of the ethical standpoint", in: *Archiv für Geschichte der Philosophie*, 88.2, pp. 261–295.

Neuhouser, Frederick (1990): *Fichte's Theory of Subjectivity*, New York.
- (2000): "Introduction", in: Neuhouser, Frederick (ed.): *J. G. Fichte, Foundations of Natural Right*, Cambridge, pp. vii–xxviii.
- (2001): "The Efficacy of the Rational Being", in: Merle, Jean-Christophe (ed.): *Johann Gottlieb Fichte, Grundlage des Naturrechts*, Berlin, pp. 39–49.

Pogge, Thomas (2002): "Is Kant's Rechtslehre a 'Comprehensive Liberalism'?", in: Timmons, Mark (ed.): *Kant's Metaphysics of Morals: Interpretive Essays*, Oxford, pp. 133–158.

Rohs, Peter (1991 a): "Der materiale Gehalt des Sittengesetzes nach Fichtes Sittenlehre", in: *Fichte-Studien*, 3, pp. 170–183.
- (1991 b): Johann Gottlieb Fichte, Munich.

Sen, Amartya (1979): "Utilitarianism and Welfarism", in: *The Journal of Philosophy*, 76.9, pp. 463–489.
- (1982): "Rights and Agency", in: *Philosophy & Public Affairs*, 11.1, pp. 3–39.
- (1985): "Well-being, Agency and Freedom: The Dewey Lectures 1984", in: The Journal of Philosophy, 82.4, pp. 169–221.
- (1992): *Inequality Reexamined*, Cambridge, MA.
- (1999): *Development as Freedom*, New York.

Shell, Susan Meld (1986): "What Kant and Fichte can teach us about human rights", in: Kennington, Richard (ed.): *The Philosophy of Immanuel Kant*, Washington, pp. 143–60.

Wood, Allen (2008): *Kantian Ethics*, Cambridge.
- (forthcoming): "Fichte: From Nature to Freedom (Sittenlehre §§ 9–13)", in: Merle, Jean-Christophe (ed.): *Johann Gottlieb Fichte, System der Sittenlehre*, Berlin.

Sebastian Schwenzfeuer

Der ontologische Begriff der Freiheit.
Über eine systematische Voraussetzung
von Schellings *Freiheitsschrift*

Schelling's Essay on human freedom *is based on different tenets developed in his* *philosophy of nature and identity. He assumes e.g. human freedom as a specifi-* *cation of a general, ontological freedom. Against Kant he defines philosophy as a* *science of the thing in itself that demonstrates freedom as the basis of all being. The* *paper investigates the possibility of Schelling's project and draws a line from his* Essay *back to the transcendental philosophy of Kant and Fichte and his own philo-* *sophy of absolute identity.*

Schelling setzt sich in seinen *Philosophischen Untersuchungen über das Wesen der menschlichen Freiheit* (1809) zum Ziel, den Begriff menschlicher Freiheit erstmals vor dem Hintergrund seiner Naturphilosophie zu explizieren. Wie er in der Vorrede zu dem Sammelband seiner Schriften, in dem die sogenannte *Freiheitsschrift* (als einzig neuer Text) erstmals veröffentlicht wurde,[1] festhält, gibt er damit zuerst den ideellen Teil seines Systems, abgerechnet die kurze 1804 veröffentlichte Abhandlung *Philosophie und Religion*, die er in einem für ihn seltenen Moment selbstkritischer Beurteilung als „undeutlich" (SW VII, S. 334) desavouiert. Gegen seine Gegner wie gleichermaßen gegen seine philosophi-schen Anhänger verwahrt er sich der Meinung, er habe zu den Themen der „Freiheit des Willens, Gut und Bös, Persönlichkeit usw." (SW VII, S. 334) bereits thetisch Stellung bezogen. Die Abhandlung von 1809 verspricht vor die-sem Hintergrund ein gewichtiges Wort in Sachen menschlicher Freiheit und die Rezeptionsgeschichte hat Schellings Text auf ihre Weise als einen Grundlagen-text idealistischen Denkens erwiesen.[2]

Im Folgenden soll *eine* entscheidende systematische Voraussetzung des schellingschen Freiheitskonzeptes analysiert werden. Der kurze Text ist, nicht zuletzt als (vermeintlich) ideeller Teil eines Gesamtsystems äußerst vorausset-zungsreich, und schon im Vorfeld sind hier gewichtige Prämissen investiert, ohne deren Verständnis der Ansatz der *Freiheitsschrift* insgesamt unverständlich bleiben muss. Insbesondere die naturphilosophischen Hintergrundannahmen der Ausführungen sind nur durch einige Bemühungen einsichtig zu machen.

---

[1] Vgl. SW VII, 333–335.
[2] Vgl. Hühn, 2010.

Zwar liegen die gegenwärtigen Diskussionen um die menschliche Freiheit im Zusammenhang der Frage nach der menschlichen Willensfreiheit, der Determiniertheit oder graduellen Indeterminiertheit menschlichen Handelns und Sich-Verhaltens keineswegs außerhalb des Horizontes der philosophischen Klassiker,[3] umgekehrt aber, und dies macht die fruchtbare hermeneutische Aneignung eigentlich schwierig, liegt Schellings eigener Ansatz zur menschlichen Freiheit, verglichen mit klassischen Positionen (wie etwas derjenigen Kants), weit außerhalb des üblicherweise Diskutierten. Prominent ist hierbei Schellings Ausgangspunkt in der *Freiheitsschrift*: die menschliche Freiheit als Artbegriff eines allgemeineren, ontologischen Gattungsbegriffs von Freiheit zu denken. Freiheit ist damit für sich noch gar nicht ein Charakteristikum des Menschen oder seines Willens. Schelling sieht seine Aufgabe im Text von 1809 primär darin, die differentia specifica des menschlichen Freiheitsbegriffs anzugeben. Bekanntlich besteht seine Antwort darin, die menschliche Freiheit als ein „Vermögen des Guten und des Bösen" (SW VII, S. 352) zu thematisieren.[4] Wie auch immer die inhaltliche Ausdeutung einer solchen Bestimmung aussehen mag, die hier nicht weiter betrachtet wird, ohne ein genaueres Verständnis dafür, dass es sich hierbei um eine Spezifikation eines zugrundliegenden allgemeineren Begriffes handelt, wird man Schellings Ansatz kaum etwas abgewinnen können. Es gilt, diesen Umstand dadurch transparent zu machen, dass die im Vorfeld der *Freiheitsschrift* getroffenen Entscheidungen, welche der Rede von einem allgemeinen, hier ontologisch genannten Freiheitsbegriff zugrunde liegen, insbesondere in Schellings Transzendental- und Identitätsphilosophie aufgespürt und auf ihren Sach- und Problemgehalt hin analysiert werden – kann es doch keineswegs als im Vorhinein ausgemacht und irgendwie als selbstverständlich gelten, dass Freiheit auch Eigenschaft oder Merkmal von Natur (im Sinne des nicht-menschlichen naturhaft Seienden) sei. Es soll im Folgenden diese zentrale Voraussetzung seiner Erörterung der menschlichen Freiheit in der Abhandlung von 1809 diskutiert werden.

1. Die Aufgabenstellung der *Freiheitsschrift* vor dem Hintergrund des Idealismus

Als Einstieg in diese Problematik des schellingschen Ansatzes eignet sich eine kurze Passage zu Beginn der *Freiheitsschrift*, in der Schelling Kants transzendentale Unterscheidung von den Dingen als Erscheinungen und den Dingen an sich aufnimmt.[5]

---

[3]   Vgl. beispielhaft aus der Vielzahl an Publikationen Fink, Rosenzweig, 2006; Pietrek, Buchheim, 2007; Beckermann, 2008.
[4]   Vgl. Buchheim, 1999; Hühn, 1998.
[5]   Vgl. Peetz, 1995, S. 130–163.

„Es wird aber immer merkwürdig bleiben, daß Kant, nachdem er zuerst Dinge an sich von Erscheinungen nur negativ, durch die Unabhängigkeit von der Zeit, unterschieden, nachher in den metaphysischen Erörterungen seiner Kritik der praktischen Vernunft Unabhängigkeit von der Zeit und Freiheit wirklich als correlate Begriffe behandelt hatte, nicht zu dem Gedanken fortging, diesen einzig möglichen positiven Begriff des An-sich auch auf die Dinge überzutragen, wodurch er sich unmittelbar zu einem höhern Standpunkt der Betrachtung und über die Negativität erhoben hätte, die der Charakter seiner theoretischen Philosophie ist" (SW VII, S. 352).

Die Merkwürdigkeit, die Schelling in Kants Ausführungen findet, fällt zunächst auf diesen selbst zurück: Vom kantischen Standpunkt aus gesehen verlangt Schelling Unmögliches, nämlich das Ansichsein des Seienden zu bestimmen. Noch vor der Frage, wieso Freiheit hier als Bestimmungsmerkmal eigentlich in Frage kommen sollte, ist zu klären, warum diese (positive) Bestimmung des Ansichseins in theoretischer Hinsicht für Schelling überhaupt denkbar ist, ignoriert er doch damit eines der zentralsten Resultate des kantischen Philosophierens und setzt sich dem Vorwurf, unkritisch Metaphysik zu treiben, unweigerlich aus. Nach Kant ist es ja, wie man weiß, unmöglich, dem Begriff des Ding an sich eine positive Bestimmung zu geben, gleichwohl in praktischer Absicht eine noumenale Bestimmung faktisch möglich ist.[6] Diese bleibt aber an die engen Bedingungen des praktischen Vernunftgebrauchs gebunden und erlaubt keinen Übergang zu metaphysischen Spekulationen in theoretischer Absicht.

Offenkundig teilt Schelling also nicht die Grundvoraussetzungen des kantischen Denkens, gleichwohl er zugleich an die kantische Terminologie anknüpft und den Begriff des Ansichseins übernimmt, wenn auch ganz anders wendet. Er gibt an dieser Stelle des Textes aber zugleich auch einen Hinweis darauf, in welcher Weise der Boden des kantischen Denkens verlassen wurde. Wenn er den „bloße[n] Idealismus" (SW VII, S. 352) für unfähig erklärt, „das Bestimmte der menschlichen Freiheit" gegenüber dem Gattungsbegriff der Freiheit aufzuzeigen, dann ist damit zumindest mitbehauptet, dass es dieser „bloße Idealismus" ist, der die kantischen Voraussetzungen hinter sich lässt und damit einen Freiheitsbegriff entwickelt, der über den Bereich menschlicher Praxis hinaus Anwendung findet. Diesen Schritt zu verstehen, ist für die *Freiheitsschrift* zentral, insofern Schelling ihn dort einfach voraussetzt und nur in einigen kurzen Bemerkungen zusammenfassend benennt, ohne aber dessen sachliche Relevanz noch einmal eigens zu entwickeln.

Zunächst muss bestimmt werden, worauf Schelling mit dem Ausdruck ‚bloßer Idealismus' referiert. Die Bestimmung des Ansichseins als Freiheit führt Schelling zunächst in einer komplementären Formel vor, wenn er das sogenannte „Urseyn" mit dem Wollen identifiziert. „Es gibt in der letzten und höchsten

---

[6]   Vgl. KpV, A 185–191.

Instanz gar kein anderes Seyn als Wollen. Wollen ist Urseyn" (SW VII, S. 350).
Als komplementär zur oben zitierten Bestimmung des Ansichseins als Freiheit
kann dieser Satz gelten, insofern das Ursein dem kantischen Ansichsein entspricht, wenn auch mit spezifisch anderen Konnotationen, und desweiteren der
Ausdruck ‚Wollen' auf den Begriff ‚Freiheit' zu beziehen ist. Beide Formeln
scheinen auf dasselbe abzuzielen, wenn Schelling damit gleichermaßen zu
beschreiben sucht, bis zu welchem „Punkt [...] die Philosophie zu unsrer Zeit
durch den Idealismus gehoben worden" (SW VII, S. 351) ist. Dem Idealismus
wird der Realismus gegenübergestellt, der mit der Person Spinozas verbunden
wird, eine Gegenüberstellung, die Schelling schon früh, etwa in den *Briefen
über Dogmatismus und Kritizismus* von 1795 vornimmt.[7] Demgegenüber wird
der Idealismus über seinen Inhalt, den Begriff der Freiheit, erläutert. Die Position Fichtes wird als Unterart des Idealismus, als „der subjektive [...] sich selbst
mißverstehende Idealismus" (SW VII, S. 351) charakterisiert. Sein (Selbst-)Miss-
verständnis liege laut Schelling darin, dass Fichte versäume zu zeigen, „daß
nicht allein die Ichheit alles, sondern auch umgekehrt alles Ichheit sey" (SW
VII, S. 351). Nichtsdestotrotz bleibt Fichtes Philosophie eine Form des Idealismus.

Zu zeigen, dass alles auch „Ichheit" sei, oder, wie er selbst explizierend
anführt: „Thätigkeit, Leben und Freiheit zum Grund habe"[8] (SW VII, S. 351),
dies scheint selbst eine Aufgabe des Idealismus zu sein, eines Idealismus freilich
von ganz anderer Art, verglichen mit dem fichteschen. Dieser Art von Idealismus, einen, so müsste man sagen: nicht-subjektiv, sondern wohl objektiv zu
nennenden Idealismus sei es gemäß Schelling vorbehalten, zu zeigen, dass das
Ursein Wollen oder komplementär dass das Ansichsein Freiheit ist. Schelling
setzt diesen seinerseits merkwürdigen Schritt, das Ansichsein (im Sinne Kants)
als Freiheit zu bestimmen, nur deswegen in der *Freiheitsschrift* voraus, weil er
seines Erachtens längst geleistet ist und auf ihn historisch verwiesen werden
kann. „Bis zu diesem Punkt ist die Philosophie zu unsrer Zeit durch den Idealismus gehoben worden: und erst bei diesem können wir eigentlich die Untersuchung unsres Gegenstandes aufnehmen" (SW VII, S. 350 f.). Die Funktion oder
Leistung dieses „bloßen" Idealismus bestehe also darin, das Ansichsein als
(nicht-menschliche) Freiheit erwiesen zu haben. Die Aufgabe der *Freiheitsschrift* liege dann darin, hiervon ausgehend die Spezifikation dieses Freiheitsbe-
griffes zum menschlichen Freiheitsbegriff anzugeben.

> „[W]enn Freiheit der positive Begriff des An-sich überhaupt ist, wird die Unter-
> suchung über menschliche Freiheit wieder ins Allgemeine zurückgeworfen, indem
> das Intelligible, auf welches sie allein gegründet worden, auch das Wesen der Dinge

---

[7]   Vgl. z. B. SW I, S. 302.
[8]   Diese Formulierung übernimmt Schelling von Friedrich Schlegel, vgl. Schlegel, 1975,
       S. 229.

an sich ist. Um also die specifische Differenz, d. h. eben das Bestimmte der menschlichen Freiheit, zu zeigen, reicht der bloße Idealismus nicht hin" (SW VII, S. 352).

Fraglich ist vor allem der erste, in der *Freiheitsschrift* nur vorausgesetzte Schritt. Selbst wenn die sachliche Stringenz dieses Schrittes zunächst offen bleiben muss, so ist Schellings Anknüpfen an den „bloßen" Idealismus sehr berechtigt. Macht man sich anhand der Gegenüberstellung seines Beweiszieles gegen das des fichteschen Idealismus klar, dass es sich hierbei nur um Schellings sogenannte Identitätsphilosophie handeln kann, dann wird dies deutlich. Schelling bestimmt nämlich die Position seiner Identitätsphilosophie in der *Darstellung meines Systems* von 1801, seiner ersten identitätsphilosophischen Schrift, so: „Der Standpunkt der Philosophie ist der Standpunkt der Vernunft, ihre Erkenntniß ist eine Erkenntniß der Dinge, wie sie *an sich*, d. h. wie sie in der Vernunft sind" (SW IV, S. 115, m. H.). Die Philosophie ist dann per definitionem eine Erkenntnis der Dinge an sich (bzw. des Ansichseins). Dies ist sowohl gegenüber dem „subjektiven" Idealismus Fichtes als auch gegenüber seiner eigenen ausgearbeiteten Transzendentalphilosophie (die im *System des transzendentalen Idealismus* vorliegt) ein markanter Unterschied. Dort wird das Ansichsein im Sinne eines Dinges an sich noch als unbestimmtes Gegenüber zum transzendentalen Ich entworfen, das ohne Wissen dieses Ich (d. h. in Schellings Terminologie: bewusstlos) von diesem produziert wird. Eigentlich ist das Ding an sich damit gar nichts anderes als Tätigkeit des Ich, ohne aber als solche gewusst zu werden. Schelling arbeitet nur auf seine Weise aus, was Fichte schon im zweiten Grundsatz der *Grundlage der gesammten Wissenschaftslehre* von 1794 als Gesetzsein des Nicht-Ich durch das Ich anspricht: die (durchaus kontraintuitive) Deutung des Anderen des Ich als Leistung dieses Ich.[9] Damit ist das Nicht-Ich zwar keinesfalls einfach Produkt dieses Ich, sonst wäre es gemäß der Logik dieser Überlegung Fichtes ja Ich, tritt aber auch nur im Rahmen der Setzungen dieses Ich auf (ist also in räumlicher Metaphorik gesprochen „im" Ich[10]). Das Nicht-Ich bzw. das Ding an sich in Schellings Transzendentalphilosophie[11] ist damit paradoxerweise zugleich Ich und auch nicht (das Paradoxe ergibt sich aber lediglich aus der sprachlichen Verkürzung).

Aber in einem noch bestimmteren, zweiten Sinne ist in Schellings Transzendentalphilosophie das gezeigt, was er 1809 auf die Formel bringt, dass „die Ichheit alles" (SW VII, S. 351) sei. Die schwierig zu deutende Relation zwischen Subjekt und Objekt, die nicht als Relation zweier Objekte zueinander missver-

---

[9] Vgl. Fichte, 1971, S. 101–103.
[10] Sehr deutlich in Fichte, 1971, S. 106.
[11] Vgl. Stolzenberg, 2003, S. 107, wo ein systematischer Unterschied zwischen Fichtes zweitem Grundsatz und der daran anschließenden Theorie des Anstoßes auf der einen Seite und Schellings Verständnis von Selbstbestimmung und Selbstbegrenzung des Ich auf der anderen Seite gesehen wird.

standen, sondern als Verwirklichung der Intention eines Subjektes, mithin Produktivität, interpretiert werden soll, führt noch zu einer weiteren Bestimmung, nämlich dass das Ich sich zu den Objekten verhalte, wie Sein zu Seiendem. „Man kann nämlich vom Ich nur deßwegen nicht sagen, daß es ist, weil es das *Seyn selbst* ist" (SW III, S. 375 f.). Damit ist die Asymmetrie zwischen Subjekt und Objekt ontologisch interpretiert. Dies ermöglicht es dann auch erst, das Produktionsverhältnis zwischen Subjekt und Objekt nicht als eine Objekt-Objekt-Relation misszuverstehen, wie es das Modell eines Artefakte herstellenden Handwerkers zunächst nahezulegen scheint.

Schellings eigene Ausarbeitung einer Transzendentalphilosophie muss demnach selbst unter den Begriff eines „subjektiven" Idealismus subsumiert werden, dessen insinuiertes Selbstmissverständnis im Falle Schellings wohl nur durch sein Projekt einer zur Transzendentalphilosophie parallelen Grundwissenschaft, seiner Naturphilosophie, zurückzuweisen wäre. Dies zu sehen, ist nicht unwichtig, insofern der 1809 dem Idealismus zugeschriebene Freiheitsbegriff nur in Schellings Transzendentalphilosophie und eben nicht in den identitätsphilosophischen Schriften ab 1801 ausgearbeitet ist. Der Begriff der Freiheit spielt etwa in der schon erwähnten *Darstellung meines Systems* (die Schelling später einmal im Rückblick als einzig authentische Ausarbeitung hat ansehen wollen – ein Urteil, dem man nicht zustimmen sollte) keine ersichtliche Rolle, gleichwohl Schelling der Identitätsphilosophie zuschreibt, den ontologischen Freiheitsbegriff entwickelt zu haben.

Es stellen sich hier zwei grundsätzliche Fragen, deren Beantwortung der Gegenstand des Folgenden bildet: 1. Wie kann die Identitätsphilosophie als eine Wissenschaft vom Ansichsein bestimmt werden? 2. Wie kann die Identitätsphilosophie zeigen, „daß alles Wirkliche (die Natur, die Welt der Dinge) Thätigkeit, Leben und Freiheit zum Grund habe" (SW VII, S. 351), gerade angesichts des Umstandes, dass diese Termini in ihr keine funktionale Rolle übernehmen?

2. Philosophie als Wissenschaft der Dinge an sich

Zunächst ist es hilfreich, die Bedeutung des Ausdruckes ‚Ding an sich' zu analysieren. Ausgehend davon, dass es sich hierbei nur um einen verkürzten Ausdruck handelt, der keine Art von Dingen spezifiziert (ansichseiende Dinge vs. nicht-ansichseiende Dinge), sondern um eine adverbiale Bestimmung, die eine Betrachtungsweise angibt, der Ausdruck also vollständig lautet ‚Dinge an sich selbst betrachtet'[12], liegt der Sinn dieser Redeweise zunächst darin, von den Relationen, die etwas zu etwas anderem hat, abzusehen. Etwas (ein Ding) an

---

[12]   Vgl. Prauss, 1974; Rang, 2000, S. 68–70; Mechtenberg, 2006.

sich betrachten heißt dann, es ohne solche Relationen zu betrachten und nur auf
das zu sehen, was ihm an sich oder wie Kant sagt „innerlich" (KrV, A 324)
zukommt. Diese Grundbedeutung ist noch ganz neutral gegenüber verschiedenen Verwendungskontexten, so kann Kant diese Bedeutung auch in einem ganz
empirischen Sinne verwenden, wenn er von der Rose spricht, wie sie an sich und
d. h. in dem spezifischen Kontext: wie sie unabhängig von den Farbwahrneh-
mungen verschiedener Betrachter ist.[13]

Der transzendentalphilosophische Gebrauch dieses Ausdruckes besteht darin,
eine bestimmte Relation auszuzeichnen, nämlich diejenige, die ein erkennendes
Subjekt zu einem erkannten (oder erkennbaren) Objekt hat. So würde in diesem
Zusammenhang die Dinge an sich zu betrachten heißen, sie ohne Relation auf
das erkennende Subjekt zu berücksichtigen. Dies ist nach Kant zwar möglich,
gar notwendig, aber inhaltlich nicht positiv erfüllbar, da mit dem Absehen vom
erkennenden Subjekt die Möglichkeit gegründeter (Erkenntnis-)Urteile aufhört.
Der Begriff eines Dinges an sich wird so zu einem rein negativen Begriff, insofern er nur dazu anhält, vom Beziehungsgrund auf das Subjekt abzusehen, ohne
aber auch schon positiv darüber etwas aussagen zu können, was nach dieser
Abstraktion eigentlich im Blick steht. Umgekehrt heißt dies, dass die Objekte
der Welt nur in ihrem Bezug zum Subjekt als inhaltlich gesättigte Objekte denkbar sind, wohingegen die Dinge an sich selbst betrachtet leer bleiben und als
bloßes Bezugsworauf aller sachhaltigen Urteile, als ein transzendentales X, fungieren.[14] In diesem Sinne erweisen sich die Objekte der Erfahrungserkenntnis
grundsätzlich als Erscheinungen dieses X, sofern sie als das Zugrundeliegende
(wenn auch unbestimmbare) gelten. Gehaltvoll wird der Unterschied zwischen
Dingen als Erscheinungen betrachtet und nicht als Erscheinungen, d. h. an ihnen
selbst betrachtet, durch den Nachweis, dass die Relation zwischen Subjekt und
Objekt für letztere konstitutiv ist. Die zweifache Konstitution der Erfahrungs-
gegenstände durch die Formen der Anschauung und ihre kategoriale Überfor-
mung des in diesen Formen gegebenen Inhaltes durch die Verstandesfunktionen
führt zu der Überlegung, dass die Gegenstände der Erfahrung insgesamt das
sind, was sie sind, durch ihren Bezug zu einem erkennenden Subjekt, da sie als
Erkennbare im Vorhinein den Formen der Anschauung gemäß sein müssen.

---

[13]   Vgl. KrV, A 30/B 45.

[14]   Vgl. KrV, A 250: „Alle unsere Vorstellungen werden in der Tat durch den Verstand auf
      irgend ein Object bezogen, und, da Erscheinungen nichts als Vorstellungen sind, so
      bezieht sie der Verstand auf ein Etwas als den Gegenstand der sinnlichen Anschauung:
      aber dieses Etwas ist in so fern nur das transscendentale Object. Dieses bedeutet aber
      ein Etwas = x, wovon wir gar nichts wissen, noch überhaupt, (nach der jetzigen Ein-
      richtung unseres Verstandes) wissen können, sondern, welches nur als ein Correlatum
      der Einheit der Apperception zur Einheit des Mannigfaltigen in der sinnlichen
      Anschauung dienen kann, vermittelst deren der Verstand dasselbe in den Begriff eines
      Gegenstandes vereinigt".

Schelling bestreitet nun diese Argumentationsstruktur, welche die transzendentalphilosophische Verwendung des Ausdruckes Ding an sich rechtfertigt, nicht intern, sondern greift eine ihrer Voraussetzungen an. Ähnlich wie Kant unterscheidet er nämlich in der Identitätsphilosophie zwischen Erscheinungen und Dingen an sich, die mit zwei Standpunkten der philosophischen Betrachtung, einem endlichen und einem unendlichen, einhergehen.[15] Gegenüber der Erkenntnis der Dinge als Erscheinungen positioniert er eine Form der Vernunfterkenntnis, welche die Dinge an sich, d. h. für Schelling die Dinge von Standpunkt des Absoluten aus erkennt. Vor dem Hintergrund der Semantik des Ausdruckes ‚an sich‘ kann dies nur dadurch geschehen, dass die Relation zwischen Subjekt und Objekt anders als in Kants transzendentaler Reflexion auf diese gefasst wird.

Schon Schellings Ausarbeitung seiner Transzendentalphilosophie (und hierin folgt er Fichtes Überlegungen) interpretiert die Subjekt-Objekt-Relation in anderer Weise als Kant, und zwar genau im Fokus auf das Problem des Ding an sich. Die vermeintliche Inkonsequenz in der Rede von einem Ding an sich[16] wird dadurch umgangen, dass ein Grundtheorem der kantischen Epistemologie, nämlich die Zweistämmigkeit der Erkenntnis, aufgegeben wird; der funktionale Unterschied zwischen Verstand und Sinnlichkeit, zwischen Denken und Anschauen, wird nivelliert, indem beides als verschiedene Ausprägungen derselben Ichtätigkeit gedeutet wird. Am deutlichsten wird dies in der Deduktion der Kategorien: Wo Kant die Deduktion der Kategorien (also ihre Rechtfertigung) und ihre Anwendung (in Form ihrer Schematisierung) unterscheiden muss, da

---

[15]   Vgl. z. B. folgenden Ausschnitt aus dem Dialog *Bruno*:
„*Bruno.* Jene Dinge also werden auch nichts unabhängig von diesem Wissen seyn.
Lucian. Durchaus nichts. Sie entstehen nur durch das Wissen und sind selbst dieses Wissen.
Bruno. Vortrefflich. Du siehst, wie wir in allen Punkten übereinstimmen. Die gesammte Erscheinungswelt ist also auch rein bloß aus dem Wissen für sich betrachtet zu begreifen.
Lucian. So verhält es sich.
Bruno. Aus welchem Wissen aber, aus einem solchen, welches an sich reell oder selbst bloß erscheinend ist?
Lucian. Nothwendig das letzte, wenn nämlich überhaupt das Entgegensetzen des endlichen Erkennens und des unendlichen und das Gleichsetzen desselben zur Erscheinung gehört“ (SW IV, S. 299).

[16]   Man hat darin eine Inkonsequenz Kants gesehen, etwa dass das Ding an sich die Sinne affizieren könne, was doch aber ein Fall von Kausalität bedeutet, also Anwendung einer Relationskategorie, die ja gerade für den Bereich des Ansichseins nicht zur Anwendung kommen soll. In Anbetracht dieser und ähnlicher Überlegungen kommt Friedrich Heinrich Jacobi 1787 zu seinem bekannten Diktum: „Ich muß gestehen, [...] [dass] ich darüber irre wurde, daß ich ohne jene Voraussetzung [das Ding an sich] in das System nicht hineinkommen, und mit jener nicht darin bleiben konnte“ (Jacobi, 1976, S. 304).

sind Schellings transzendentalphilosophische Deduktionen der Kategorien zugleich auch schon ihre Anwendung. Die kategorialen Setzungen des Subjektes sind immer schon auch ihre Geltung im Seienden. Daher erhält diese Art von Transzendentalphilosophie auch den merkwürdigen Anschein, als erzeuge sie ihre Gegenstände selbst und wie aus nichts, da es hier nicht zu einer Anwendung der Setzungen auf etwas kommt, sondern diese Setzungen dieses etwas schon selbst sind und in diesem Sinne die Objekte der Erfahrung durch das Subjekt „gesetzt" werden.

Es ist klar, dass dieser Schritt über Kant hinaus für Schellings Identitätsphilosophie wichtig bleibt, da die absolute Vernunfterkenntnis gerade auch auf der Indifferenz von Denken und Anschauen beruht. Gleichwohl ist damit das Eigentümliche der Identitätsphilosophie allein nicht zu fassen. Die Identitätsphilosophie kennzeichnet vielmehr, und das macht ihre besondere Stellung aus, dass sie eine Voraussetzung der Transzendentalphilosophie, sowohl in ihrer kantischen als auch fichteschen-schellingschen Variante, nicht teilt, nämlich die Voraussetzung, die Subjekt-Objekt-Relation als ein Wissen-für zu interpretieren und als Grund alles Wissens anzunehmen. Genauer meint dies die dreifache interne Relation des Wissens in einen Wissenden, sein Wissen und sein Gewusstes. Schellings Transzendentalphilosophie (gleich wie die fichtesche) macht davon Gebrauch, den Unterschied zwischen dem Wissenden und dem Wissen selbst aufzuheben und auf die Relation von Wissen und Gewusstem zu reduzieren.[17] Insofern das Ich reiner Akt des (Sich-)Wissens ist, ist es von seinem Wissen gar nicht verschieden, sondern dieses selbst. Es *hat* nicht nur Wissen, es *ist* es auch. Der darin angesetzte formale Unterschied ist aber nicht der zwischen dem Wissenden und seinem Wissen, sondern derjenige zwischen dem Wissen und dem Gewussten. Nur so lässt sich die Figur der Selbsterkenntnis und des Sich-Wissens im Selbstbewusstsein in Schellings Theorie sinnvoll interpretieren. Im Selbstbewusstsein liegt ein Wissensakt vor, der sich selbst zum Gegenstand hat. Schellings Identitätsphilosophie aber nivelliert darüber hinaus auch noch den Unterschied zwischen dem Wissen und seinem Gewussten. Es fragt sich, was dies heißen kann, wenn es in einem Wissen kein Gewusstes mehr gibt, scheint damit doch auf den ersten Blick gerade die Struktur von Wissen überhaupt aufgehoben, als im Wissen sich ein Subjekt mittels Vorstellungen, Begriffen und Urteilen intentional auf Sachverhalte bezieht, die im Falle der Wahrheit dieses Wissens Tatsachen sind.

Zunächst sei noch eine Reflexion über die Funktion dieser Überlegung zwischengeschaltet. Schelling gewinnt durch seine Bestimmung des Wissens als Indifferenz des Subjektiven und Objektiven die Möglichkeit, die für die Transzendentalphilosophie grundlegende Relation zwischen Subjekt und Objekt umzudenken und in einem damit das Wissen (sofern es durch diese Indifferenz

---

[17]   Vgl. Rang, 2000, S. 81 f.

bestimmt ist) als Wissen von den Dingen an sich zu begreifen. Dies ergibt sich einfach aus dem Sinn des Ausdruckes ‚an sich‘, der ‚nicht in Beziehung auf‘ bedeutet. Wird die in der Transzendentalphilosophie ausgezeichnete Relation zwischen Subjekt und Objekt als grundlegende aufgegeben (sie mag anderweitig eine Rolle spielen), dann wird auch die Unterscheidung zwischen den Dingen als Erscheinungen und den Dingen an sich hinfällig. Vorausgesetzt man kann dann immer noch sinnvoll von einem Wissen von etwas sprechen, dann wird dieses etwas, transzendental gesehen, an sich, d. h. ohne Bezug auf ein erkennendes Subjekt, betrachtet. Eine Philosophie, die ein solches Wissen entwickelt, wäre sinnvollerweise dann ein Wissen und als systematisch ausgearbeitete Disziplin eine Wissenschaft der Dinge an sich.

Dies hängt natürlich davon ab, dass man die Rede von der Indifferenz des Subjektiven und Objektiven sachhaltig ausdeuten kann. Schelling selbst bietet hierfür einige entscheidende Interpretationshilfen an. Er hebt nämlich selbst gelegentlich den fundamentalen Unterschied zwischen der Identitätsphilosophie und der Transzendentalphilosophie prägnant hervor, so schreibt er diesbezüglich 1804 in dem *System der gesammten Philosophie und Naturphilosophie insbesondere*: „Es gibt wahrhaft und an sich überall kein Subjekt, kein Ich, also auch kein Objekt, kein Nicht-Ich. Daß ich sage: ich weiß oder ich bin der Wissende, dieß ist schon das πρῶτον ποεῦδος. Ich weiß *nichts*, oder *mein* Wissen, insofern es wirklich *meines* ist, ist kein wahres Wissen. Nicht ich weiß, sondern nur das *All* weiß in mir, wenn das Wissen, das ich das meinige nenne, ein wirkliches, ein wahres Wissen ist" (SW VI, S. 140). Der Unterschied zwischen Identitäts- und Transzendentalphilosophie ist hier insofern pointiert benannt, als erstere auf der Erkenntnis aufbaut, Wissen sei Wissen des Alls (sowohl im Sinne des genitivus subjectivus als auch objectivus), letztere aber auf der Grundüberzeugung (kurz G), alles Wissen sei „mein Wissen" (genitivus subjectivus), die im Zitat als Grundirrtum abgewiesen wird. Offenbar ist Transzendentalphilosophie ohne eine solche Grundannahme weder inhaltlich noch methodisch möglich. Inhaltlich basiert sie auf dieser Grundannahme, weil ja (in der schellingschen Variante) gezeigt werden soll, dass alles Wissen auf dem Sich-Wissen des Subjektes beruht und durch dieses ermöglicht wird. Der strukturell damit zusammenhängende Sachverhalt ist, dass jedes Wissen (auch) als das Wissen eines Subjektes bestimmt werden muss und von diesem Subjekt als das seinige gewusst werden kann. Auch Kants Transzendentalphilosophie setzt dies voraus, insofern Wissen nur durch die ursprünglich-synthetische Einheit der Apperzeption möglich ist.[18] Diese besteht in der Möglichkeit, jedes Wissen als das Wissen, das ein Subjekt hat, identifizieren zu können.[19] Auf der Ebene der Urteile gesprochen bedeutet dies die Möglichkeit, zu jedem Urteil p den Satz „Ich weiß, dass p" zu

---

[18]   Vgl. KrV, B 131–136. Vgl. Seebaß, 1989; Bondeli, 2006.
[19]   Vgl. Cramer, 2003.

bilden. Zwar ist diese Möglichkeit nicht immer, sogar in den meisten Fällen der natürlichen Welteinstellung nicht realisiert, entscheidend ist aber Kants Rede von der Möglichkeit, die in jedem Fall eines Urteils p gegeben sein muss. Nur so kann, so Kants Überlegung, Wissen als ein einheitliches und zusammenhängendes Wissen und damit Wissen überhaupt möglich sein, andernfalls „würde etwas in mir vorgestellt werden, was gar nicht gedacht werden könnte" (KrV, B 131 f.).

Auch methodisch basiert die Transzendentalphilosophie auf der genannten Grundannahme G, dies spielt insbesondere in der fichteschen und schellingschen Variante eine tragende Rolle, wohingegen Kant die Transzendentalphilosophie zwar als Reflexionswissenschaft auf die Bedingungen der Möglichkeit von etwas etabliert, ohne dies aber in der Struktur der Subjektivität selbst gegründet sein zu lassen. Laut Schelling besteht aber das transzendentale Vorgehen darin, in jedem Schritt zugleich auf diesen zu reflektieren.[20] Diese Vorgehensweise eines beständigen Reflektierens ergibt sich aus dem Systemprinzip seiner Transzendentalphilosophie. Das Ich, das hier in einer bestimmten methodischen Extrapolation als Prinzip angesetzt wird, ist ja nichts anderes als ein beständiges Selbstreflektieren. Es ist das in dieser Reflexion auf sich als Reflektierenden sich konstituierende Wissen. Sofern es irgend möglich sein soll, diese Struktur als Prinzip eines Systems anzusetzen, dann ist das methodische Vorgehen für den Aufbau eines solchen Systems bereits vorgezeichnet. So ist das 1800 konstruierte System insgesamt gar nichts anderes als diese Selbstreflexion des Ich.

Was kann es nun heißen, das Wissen als das eines wissenden Subjektes (ausgedrückt mittels des Possessivpronomens ‚mein') als Grundirrtum zu verstehen und die Annahme G mithin als falschen Satz zu erweisen? Diese Frage stellt sich insbesondere für Schelling sehr nachdrücklich, nämlich angesichts der Tatsache, dass er, wie gesehen, selbst starken Gebrauch von dieser Grundannahme G in seiner Transzendentalphilosophie macht und diese sowohl inhaltlich als methodisch beansprucht. Das Verständnis dieses Punktes ist ein neuralgischer Punkt, insofern die Stellung und der Ansatz der Identitätsphilosophie davon abhängen. Die prominente Stelle in § 1 des *Systems der gesammten Philosophie* von 1804 unterstreicht dies überdeutlich. Auch schon im Text der *Darstellung meines Systems* von 1801 findet sich ein Analogon hierzu, wenn er dort, ebenfalls in § 1 fordert, dass „vom Denkenden abstrahirt werden" (SW IV, S. 114) muss. Dies bildet dort die Voraussetzung, um überhaupt den erörterten Begriff von Ver-

---

20   Vgl. SW III, 350 f.: „Im Philosophiren ist man nicht bloß das Objekt, sondern immer zugleich das Subjekt der Betrachtung. Zum Verstehen der Philosophie sind also zwei Bedingungen erforderlich, *erstens*, daß man in einer beständigen innern Thätigkeit, in einem beständigen Produciren jener ursprünglichen Handlungen der Intelligenz, *zweitens*, daß man in beständiger Reflexion auf dieses Produciren begriffen, mit Einem Wort, daß man immer zugleich das Angeschaute (Producirende) und das Anschauende sey".

nunft, Absolutem und philosophischer Erkenntnis zu verstehen. Die Konsequenz dieser von Schelling eingeforderten Abstraktion muss dann darin liegen, philosophisches Wissen als nicht-subjektives, absolutes Wissen zu verstehen. Zunächst ist es schwer zu sehen, was damit gemeint sein kann. ist doch auch die Grundannahme G keineswegs unplausibel, sondern es macht einen guten Sinn zu behaupten, jedes Wissen in Form eines Urteils p könne in den Satz „ich weiß/ denke, dass p" übergeführt werden. Es bezeugt dies ja nur, dass dieses Urteil von einem Urteilenden gefasst (und ausgesprochen) wird, der um sich als Urteilenden auch wissen kann. Die Form ‚ich denke, dass' ist es doch, die es ermöglicht, von dem Wissen als dem meinigen zu sprechen, das Possessivpronomen im Ausdruck ‚mein Wissen' bringt wohl eben diese Reflexion auf sich zum Ausdruck.[21]

Worauf Schellings Kritik an dieser Überlegung abzielt, ersieht man erst, wenn man eine weitere These mit heranzieht: „Jene Unterscheidung ist selbst schon ein Produkt unserer Subjektivität und sonach unserer Endlichkeit. Aber eben diese müssen uns im Philosophiren gänzlich verschwinden" (SW VI, S. 140). Diese These ist, wie der Kontext zeigt, offenbar eine Kritik an dem Unterschied von Subjekt und Objekt als Fundamentalunterschied. Diese Unterscheidung beruhe nämlich selber auf einer Voraussetzung, die unhinterfragt bleibe und in der Annahme besteht, dass ein jedes Wissen ein Attribut eines wissenden Subjektes sei, das dieses Wissen *hat*. Zunächst scheint dies kaum anderes zu sagen als die Kritik an der Annahme G, d. h. an dem Possessivverhältnis zwischen Subjekt und Wissen. Es zeigt aber erstens, dass schon die Reflexion auf das Wissen von weiteren Hintergrundannahmen geleitet ist, und zweitens nicht nur ein falscher Satz, sondern eine strukturelle Täuschung ist. Das macht auch erst die Rede von einem *Grund*irrtum wirklich verständlich, andernfalls es sich lediglich um eine falsche Aussage aufgrund unzutreffender Überlegungen handeln würde. Der strukturelle Irrtum besteht nach Schelling darin, das Wissen im Horizont der Subjektivität zu befragen. Die Reflexion kann ein Wissen nur deshalb auf ein wissendes Subjekt beziehen und damit die Grundannahme G behaupten, da dieses im Vorhinein schon erschlossen ist und als Bezugspunkt dieser Reflexion sich zur Verfügung stellt.[22] Gerade hier knüpft Schelling aber seine Einwände an.

Bedenkt man nämlich weiter, dass das Subjekt und dessen spezifische vorgängige Erschlossenheit bereits in Schellings Transzendentalphilosophie systematisch entwickelt wurde, dann wird seine Kritik an G auch weiter verständlich. Zwar befindet sich die Transzendentalphilosophie selber im Horizont der

---

[21]   Dies bringt das Possessivpronomen natürlich nur in diesem Zusammenhang zum Ausdruck, da klarerweise nicht jedes Possessivverhältnis auch schon ein Wissen um dieses impliziert.

[22]   Man erinnere sich hier etwa an Kants Rede vom „Anheften" des Verstandesgebrauchs an die ursprünglich-synthetische Einheit der Apperzeption, vgl. KrV, B 134, Anm.

Subjektivität, an die dort gegebenen Bestimmungen des Subjektes kann Schelling gleichwohl auch in der Identitätsphilosophie anschließen. Hier ist nur ein Punkt entscheidend: Gegenüber allen Vorstellungen eines zugrundeliegenden Substrates wird das Ich transzendental als reine Tätigkeit aufgewiesen, indem es als sich selbst Wissen in diesem Wissensakt bestimmt wird. Damit ist der Begriff des Subjektes von der Vorstellung eines irgendwie persistierenden Substrates abgelöst, es ist bloße Tätigkeit, die performativ ihre eigene Wirklichkeit hervorbringt. Das bedeutet aber für die strukturelle Analyse des Wissens, dass das Bezugsworauf der Reflexion über das Wissen, das ‚ich denke, dass‘, nicht einfach so zur Verfügung steht. Unter der Voraussetzung, dass Schellings transzendentaler Begriff des Subjektes sinnvoll ist, nämlich es als sich vollbringende Subjektivität zu deuten möglich ist (und wie er in transzendentalphilosophischer Absicht zu zeigen versucht: sogar notwendig ist), dann nimmt der Ausdruck ‚ich denke, dass‘ auch nicht auf ein bereits ursprünglich vorhandenes Selbstbewusstsein Bezug. Es referiert nicht auf das Subjekt, sondern bringt es in dieser Reflexion erst hervor.

In dieser Weise schließt Schellings Identitätsphilosophie an die Transzendentalphilosophie an, wenn auch in ersterer dieser Befund sehr anders interpretiert und bewertet wird. Er bedeutet nämlich identitätsphilosophisch gedacht, dass das Wissen zwar durch Reflexion auf das performativ erzeugte Subjekt bezogen werden kann, an sich aber jenseits dieser Reflexion steht und dem Subjekt vielmehr vorgängig ist. Statt dass das Subjekt das Wissen ermöglicht und ihm als dieser Ermöglichungsgrund vorausgeht, ist umgekehrt das Wissen selbst der Ermöglichungsgrund dieses Subjektes. Das Subjekt ist, das zeigt die transzendentale Reflexion gerade noch an, selber ein Produkt des Denkens. Damit erhält die von Kant festgehaltene Möglichkeit, alles Wissen (in Form von Urteilen) auf das Subjekt beziehen zu können, ein ganz anderes Aussehen, ohne dass dieses Theorem direkt aufgegeben würde. Es bedeutet nun die Möglichkeit, das Wissen irrtümlicherweise als dasjenige zu kennzeichnen, das ein Subjekt als Attribut hat. Die Bewertung fällt somit ganz anders aus: vom höchsten Punkt der transzendentalen Überlegung wird die Subjektreferenz zum Grundirrtum degradiert. Diese Subjektreferenz ist nach Schelling eben deshalb ein Irrtum, weil das Wissen an sich dem Subjekt vorgängig ist. Das Subjekt hat nicht Wissen, eher anders herum „hat“ das Wissen ein Subjekt. An der Ambiguität des letzteren Ausdruckes zeigt sich Schellings Überlegung sehr deutlich, kann man ihn doch auf zweierlei Weise verstehen: 1. Es gibt ein Subjekt, ein dem Wissen Zugrundeliegendes. 2. Das Wissen selbst ist das Zugrundeliegende und „hat“ das Subjekt als einen an ihm gesetzten Unterschied in sich. Da das Subjekt gemäß Schellings transzendentalphilosophischer Erörterung nur reiner Wissensakt ist, ist das Wissen ihm strukturell vorgängig.

Auf diese Weise entwickelt Schelling einen Begriff des Wissens, der subjektunabhängig ist und das nicht von einem Subjekt her, sondern umgekehrt letzteres vom Wissen her gedeutet wird. Dass dies zugleich elementare transzendentalphilosopische Einsichten in einem nachgerade hegelschen Sinne „aufhebt" (nämlich außer Geltung setzt und zugleich in anderer Form refomuliert), ermöglicht es, auch im Kontext der Identitätsphilosophie an Theoreme der Transzendentalphilosophie anzuknüpfen,[23] so auch an die Unterscheidung zwischen Erscheinungen und Dingen an sich, die ohne den transzendentalen Hintergrund keinen wirklichen Sinn hat.

Das von Schelling inaugurierte philosophische Wissen schreibt sich daher nicht mehr aus dem Unterschied zwischen Subjekt und Objekt als einer Fundamentaldifferenz her. Das heißt nicht, dass nicht zwischen Subjekt und Objekt unterschieden werden könnte und auch unterschieden wird. Es heißt aber, diesen Unterschied nicht als fundamental an- oder vorauszusetzen, sondern als interne Unterscheidung des Wissens in ihm selbst. Damit ist aber ein Weg eröffnet, das Wissen nicht mehr als „mein Wissen" zu verstehen und die Annahme G außer Kraft zu setzen. Ein solches Wissen hat dann keine, wie auch immer auszudeutende Relation von Subjekt und Objekt zugrundliegen und erfüllt in der Konsequenz auch nicht mehr die Voraussetzung, dieses Wissen als Wissen von Erscheinungen zu qualifizieren. Damit ist zumindest geklärt, inwiefern Schelling 1809 in der *Freiheitsschrift* wie selbstverständlich von einer Erkenntnis des Ansichseins (bzw.) des Urseins sprechen kann. Was zunächst aussieht wie ein Rückfall in vorkritische Metaphysik basiert der Sache nach auf einer Uminterpretation des transzendentalphilosophischen Ansatzes und einer Neubestimmung dessen, was ‚Wissen' heißt.[24]

3. Freiheit als Ansichsein

Damit dürfte der Sinn einer Betrachtung der Dinge an sich, von der Schelling spricht, zunächst gesichert sein. Es gilt nun im Anschluss, die zweite und ganz andere Frage zu klären, warum Schelling den Begriff der Freiheit als positive Bestimmung des Ansichseins verwenden kann. Die Ontologisierung der Freiheitskonzeption, die in der These (kurz S) besteht, „daß alles Wirkliche (die Natur, die Welt der Dinge) Thätigkeit, Leben und Freiheit zum Grund habe" (SW VII, S. 351), bedarf einer eigenen Rechtfertigung. Auch hier setzt Schelling in der *Freiheitsschrift* den Beweis dieser These voraus, insofern er dem Idealismus diesen Beweis zuschreibt, wenn er dabei auch deutlich macht, dass es sich hierbei nicht um den „subjektiven" Idealismus Fichtes allein und damit auch

---

23 Die damit einhergehende Ambiguität der Theoreme ist dem Verständnis der Identitätsphilosophie sicherlich nicht förderlich.

24 Eine ganz andere Frage ist dann, welchen Inhalt ein solches absolutes Wissen eigentlich hat. Innerhalb der Transzendentalphilosophie wird ja die Objektkonstitution im Wissen reflektiert, eine andere Interpretation des Wissens wird wohl auch Konsequenzen für die Struktur des darin Gewussten haben.

keineswegs allein um Schellings eigene Transzendentalphilosophie handelt. Vielmehr scheint die These von der Ontologisierung der Freiheit (S) formal nur die Umkehrung einer These des „subjektiven" Idealismus zu sein. Letztere bestehe in dem Satz (S*), dass „die Ichheit alles" (SW VII, S. 351) sei. S ist insofern die Umkehrung von S*, als S auch in der Form S´ ,alles ist Ichheit' angegeben wird. S´ und S sollen laut Schelling dasselbe besagen. Die inhaltliche Verbindung beider Formulierungen, S und S´, liegt wohl darin, dass der Ichheit „Tätigkeit, Leben und Freiheit" als deren wesentliche Prädikate zugesprochen werden und in der Umkehrung S dann als Prädikate von allem Wirklichen fungieren, sofern sie den Ausdruck ‚Ichheit' substituieren.

Zunächst sei die dem subjektiven Idealismus, d. h. Fichte, zugeschriebene These S* erörtert und zwar in ihrer erweiterten Formulierung[25] (‚Das Ich[26] qua Tätigkeit, Leben und Freiheit ist alles'). Hier ist es nicht sonderlich schwer, den Sinn dieser drei Prädikate anzugeben, um der Reihe nach vorzugehen: 1. Tätigkeit ist, wie oben bereits angeschnitten, keine Eigenschaft unter anderen, sondern bezeichnet die Seinsweise[27] der transzendentalen Subjektivität. Fichtes Rede von einer Tathandlung[28] könnte hier genauso angegeben werden, wie Schellings Bestimmung des Ich als eines Systemprinzips im *System des transzendentalen Idealismus*. „Das Ich ist reiner Akt, reines Thun" (SW III, S. 368) heißt es da lapidar. Damit ist von vornherein jede Vorstellung eines fixen Substrates abgehalten und die gesamte Transzendentalphilosophie in dieser Variante praktizistisch grundgelegt, was gegenüber der kantischen Variante eine massive Umdeutung darstellt. 2. Warum das Ich mit dem Prädikat ‚Leben' ausgezeichnet wird, ist vielleicht auf den ersten Blick weniger klar, da dieser Ausdruck etwa in Schellings Transzendentalphilosophie keine ersichtliche Funktion spielt.

---

[25] Vgl. SW VII, S. 351: „In der ersten Beziehung bemerken wir, daß es in dem zum System gebildeten Idealismus keineswegs hinreicht, zu behaupten, ‚daß Thätigkeit, Leben und Freiheit allein das wahrhaft Wirkliche seyen', womit auch der subjektive (sich selbst mißverstehende Idealismus Fichtes bestehen kann)".

[26] Man könnte sich fragen, ob ‚Ich' und ‚Ichheit' eigentlich synonym sind. Im betrachteten Kontext scheint mir ‚Ichheit' dasselbe zu heißen wie ‚transzendentales Ich'.

[27] Die Rede von Seinsweisen könnte anstößig scheinen, insofern sie als adverbiale Bestimmung des Prädikates ‚existieren' aufgefasst werden könnte, ‚existieren' aber nach moderner Lesart eine solche Bestimmung nicht erlaubt, sondern als Quantifikation über einem Gegenstandsbereich aufgefasst werden müsse (vgl. dazu klassisch Quine, 1963). Für den gegenwärtigen Zweck ist es ausreichend zu sagen, dass diese Redeweise nur so verstanden wird: Sofern das Ich existiert, kann es nur als reine Tätigkeit existieren. Auf das ‚existieren' kommt es hier gar nicht an, es könnte durch den Ausdruck ‚gedacht werden' ersetzt werden, so ersieht man, dass es sich hierbei um eine Eigenschaft des Ich handelt.

[28] Vgl. Fichte, 1971, S. 91: „Er [der unbedingte Grundsatz] soll diejenige *Thathandlung* ausdrücken, welche unter den empirischen Bestimmungen unseres Bewusstseyns nicht vorkommt, noch vorkommen kann, sondern vielmehr allem Bewusstseyn zum Grunde liegt, und allein es möglich macht".

Leben versteht er dort, ganz klassisch, als „Objekt [...], das ein inneres Princip der Bewegung in sich selbst hat" (SW III, S. 493). Diese Bestimmung gilt nun im eminentesten Sinne von dem transzendentalen Ich selbst, das ja nicht nur Tätigkeit überhaupt ist, sondern sein Bewegungsprinzip in einem innern Widerstreit antagonistischer Kräfte hat, „überhaupt trennt sich Inneres und Aeußeres im Ich, mit dieser Trennung ist ein Widerstreit im Ich gesetzt, der nur aus der Nothwendigkeit des Selbstbewußtseyns zu erklären ist" (SW III, S. 392). Von diesem Widerstreit heißt es weiter, dass er dem Ich notwendig sei. Dieser Streit der Kräfte ist das innere Bewegungsprinzip der schellingschen Transzendentalphilosophie, das Ich ist damit im Übrigen ähnlich konstruiert, wie der Organismus, der sich laut Schellings Ausführungen erst im und gegen den Andrang einer Außenwelt konstituiert.[29] 3. Das Prädikat ‚Freiheit' ist eng mit dem Begriff der Tätigkeit und dem Begriff des Lebens verbunden. Insofern das Ich als Tätigkeit selbstbewegt ist, ist es Selbsttätigkeit und d.h. Spontaneität. Diese Spontaneität des Ich ist es, die Schelling in der Transzendentalphilosophie von vornherein als dessen Freiheit ansetzt, anders als Kant etwa, der Freiheit als Autonomie in den Bereich praktischer Vernunftbestimmung zur Sittlichkeit setzt, ohne auch schon die spontanen Verstandeshandlungen, wie sie auch dem theoretischen Weltverhältnis zugrunde liegen, miteinzubeziehen.[30]

Es fragt sich, in welchem Sinne diese drei Bestimmungen umgekehrt als Prädikate von allem Wirklichen, also auch dem Seienden, das nicht im engeren Verständnis ein intentionales Subjekt ist, ausgesagt werden können. Es muss mit der Aussage S´, dass alles Ichheit sei, ein bestimmterer Sinn verbunden werden, als nur die Aussage, dass letztlich Subjekt und Objekt dasselbe seien. Gegen eine solche Ausdeutung seiner Identitätsphilosophie wehrt Schelling sich auch selber, indem er die Einheit des Subjektiven und Objektiven nicht als Einerleiheit verstanden wissen möchte.[31] Genauso wie die transzendentalphilosophische Position in der durchaus gehaltvollen These S* besteht, muss dem formal umgekehrten Satz ein solcher Inhalt zugewiesen werden können. Dies schließt auch die Möglichkeit aus, ihn lediglich als Konsequenz von S* darstellen zu wollen, etwas so, dass man das transzendentale Ich durch die genannten drei Prädikate bestimmt sein lässt, daran die Objekte durch das Ableitungsverhältnis, das zwischen ihnen und dem Subjekt besteht, in irgend einer Form teilhaben. Dies würde es nicht erlauben, wirklich von einer Umkehrung der Thesen zu sprechen, höchstens auf der sprachlichen Oberfläche mehr oder weniger präziser Ausdrucksweisen. Eine Umkehrung der Sache nach scheint aber vorzuliegen, wo sollte sonst das Fichte unterstellte Missverständnis liegen können?

---

[29] Vgl. Rang, 1988.
[30] Vgl. Prauss, 1983.
[31] Vgl. z.B. SW VII, S. 421 f.

Nun hat sich die Identitätsphilosophie schon oben als eine Art Umkehrung der Transzendentalphilosophie Kants, Fichtes und auch Schellings erwiesen. Insofern der reflektierende Bezug zwischen Wissen und Subjekt in dem Ausdruck ‚mein Wissen‘ bzw. ‚ich denke, dass‘ nun statt als Grundoperation als Grundirrtum verhandelt wird. Es ist zu vermuten, dass dieser Unterschied im Prinzipiellen mit den Formeln S, S´ und S* in der *Freiheitsschrift* direkt zusammenhängt. Dies würde bedeuten, dass es die Identitätsphilosophie ist, deren Kernthese in dem Satz S bzw. S´ besteht. Eine solche Überlegung hat nur die Schwierigkeit, die Ausdrücke „Tätigkeit, Leben und Freiheit" nicht unmittelbar als operative Termini in den identitätsphilosophischen Schriften zu finden. Es scheint geradezu, als ob diese erst mit der *Freiheitsschrift* selbst (wieder) in den Fokus rücken, anders als in der „statischen" All-Einheits-Metaphysik im Stile der Identitätsphilosophie. Eine solche Lesart hat nur eines entscheidend gegen sich: Schelling setzt die These S in der *Freiheitsschrift* voraus, muss demnach glauben können, diese bereits anderweitig erwiesen zu haben. Es steht kaum an zu glauben, er habe eine solch fundamentales Theorem nur hypothetisch angenommen oder dessen Beweis auf Später verschoben. Die *Freiheitsschrift* will je gerade vor dem Hintergrund des formellen und allgemeinen Begriffs der Freiheit (der eben in der These S besteht) den Begriff menschlicher Freiheit, als einen realen und lebendigen,[32] entwickeln.

Ein anderer wichtiger Rückverweis Schellings auf seine Identitätsphilosophie ist hier zu erwähnen. Die Formel ‚allem Wirklichen liegt X zugrunde‘ in der These S macht von einer Figur des Grundes Gebrauch, die Schelling wenig später im Text wiederum aus seiner Identitätsphilosophie herleitet. „Die Naturphilosophie unsrer Zeit hat zuerst in der Wissenschaft die Unterscheidung aufgestellt zwischen dem Wesen, sofern es existirt, und dem Wesen, sofern es bloß Grund von Existenz ist. Diese Unterscheidung ist so alt als die erste wissenschaftliche Darstellung derselben" (SW VII, S. 357). Die Naturphilosophie ist hierbei, wie aus den angegebenen Stellenverweisen und dem nicht gekennzeichneten, fast wörtlichen Zitat ersichtlich, klarerweise die Identitätsphilosophie selbst und der Name ‚Naturphilosophie‘ fungiert hier, wie auch an anderen Stellen,[33] als Redeweise pars pro toto. Die Identitätsphilosophie kann es allein sein, die den Ausdruck „Wollen ist Urseyn" (SW VII, S. 350), wenn schon nicht wörtlich ausgesprochen, so doch der Sache nach entwickelt haben muss. Nun spielt der Begriff des Wollens in den Schriften zwischen 1801 und 1806 kaum eine Rolle, schon gar keine prinzipielle, dennoch lässt sich Schellings Rückgriff in der *Freiheitsschrift* auf die Identitätsphilosophie gut verständlich machen und aufzeigen, inwiefern diese mit der These S zusammenhängt.

---

[32] Vgl. SW VII, S. 352.
[33] Vgl. insbesondere SW X, S. 99. In SW X, S. 107 rechtfertigt Schelling diesen Sprachgebrauch eigens.

Am einfachsten lässt sich dies anhand einiger Überlegungen Schellings von 1801, die Zeit des Übergangs von der transzendentalphilosophischen zur identitätsphilosophischen Phase, zeigen. In dem kleinen Aufsatz *Über den wahren Begriff der Naturphilosophie* gibt Schelling einige aufschlussreiche Reflexionen über seine eigene Transzendentalphilosophie, die einen Einblick gewähren in die sachlichen Gründe seiner philosophischen Neuausrichtung nach 1800.

> „Selbst in dem System des Idealismus mußte ich, um einen theoretischen Theil zu Stande zu bringen, das Ich aus seiner eignen Anschauung herausnehmen, von dem Subjektiven in der intellektuellen Anschauung abstrahiren – mit Einem Wort es als *Bewußtloses* setzen. – Aber das Ich, insofern es bewußtlos ist, ist nicht = Ich; denn Ich ist nur das Subjekt-Objekt, insofern es sich selbst als solches erkennt. Die Akte, welche dort als Akte des Ichs, also auch gleich in der höchsten Potenz aufgestellt wurden, sind eigentlich Akte des reinen Subjekt-Objekts, und sind *als* solche noch nicht *Empfindung*, *Anschauung* u.s.w., welches sie nur durch die Erhebung in das Bewußtseyn werden" (SW IV, S. 88).

Er spielt hier auf die „Geschichte des Selbstbewußtseyns" (SW III, S. 398) an, welche die Transzendentalphilosophie im Ganzen entwickelt und in mehreren Stufen, gemäß dem *System* von 1800 in der Abfolge von theoretischer und praktischer Philosophie, Teleologie und Ästhetik, darstellt.[34] Diese Etappen bilden verschiedene Schritte in der Ausbildung der im Prinzip der transzendentalen Subjektivität vorgezeichneten Struktur des Ich aus. Interessant ist nun die im Zitat herausgestellte Charakterisierung der theoretischen Philosophie. Die dort beschriebenen Handlungen (denn das Ich ist ja nichts anderes als ein Handeln) sind sämtlich bewusstlos. Dies ist denn auch ganz notwendig, insofern dort das Ich in denjenigen Handlungen vorgestellt wird, die ein Bewusstsein von etwas (auch von sich selbst) erst ermöglichen sollen und als basale Aufbaustufen nur in die wirkliche Erfahrung eingehen, ohne aber eigens und gesondert gewusst zu werden (wie etwa reine Empfindung und Sinnesdaten: man nimmt in konkreten Wahrnehmungen nicht Sinnesempfindungen, z.B. eine Rotempfindung, wahr, sondern etwas aufgrund von Sinnesdaten, z.B. etwas Rotes). Solche basalen Aufbaustufen sind nicht eigens thematisch und in diesem Sinne bewusstlos. Von daher ist es ganz konsequent, das Ich auf diesen Stufen insgesamt als bewusstlos zu bestimmen (erst im Zusammenhang der zweiten Epoche des dritten Hauptabschnittes werden Formen von Bewusstheit verhandelt).

Die entscheidende und überraschende Schlussfolgerung Schellings liegt aber darin, dass „das Ich, insofern es bewußtlos ist, nicht = Ich" (SW IV, S. 88) ist. Was ist das Ich dann? Die betrachteten Handlungen sind laut Schelling „Akte des reinen Subjekt-Objekts" (SW IV, S. 88). Der Ausdruck ‚Subjekt-Objekt‘ wird von Schelling auch dazu verwendet, das Ich selbst zu beschreiben. Das Spezifische liegt hier demnach in dem Adjektiv ‚rein‘, das den Terminus ‚Sub-

---

[34] Vgl. Claesges, 1974; Stolzenberg, 2003.

jekt-Objekt' gerade gegen das Bewusstsein diskriminiert. Schelling stellt das reine Subjekt-Objekt als das Prinzip der Naturphilosophie vor. Das reine Subjekt-Objekt ist demnach nur ein anderer Ausdruck für das, was Schelling als die hinter den empirischen Erscheinungen stehende schaffend-tätige Natur in Anlehnung an Spinoza als natura naturans begreift. In diesem Sinne ist es auch zu verstehen, wenn Schelling das reine Subjekt-Objekt mit der Natur gleichsetzt.[35]

Der Begriff einer natura naturans führt aber über den Horizont der Transzendentalphilosophie hinaus, keinem ist dies wohl deutlicher gewesen als Fichte, der sich, wie der Briefwechsel mit Schelling in der angesprochenen Zeit (1800–1801) dokumentiert, äußerst kritisch gegen Schellings naturphilosophische Ansätze verwehrt.[36] Der Kern der Auseinandersetzung liegt darin, dass Schellings Naturphilosophie ein eigenes und gegenüber der Transzendentalphilosophie anderes Prinzip beansprucht. Das reine Subjekt-Objekt ist kein Ich, sondern liegt diesem gewissermaßen als dessen Tiefenschicht noch zugrunde. Schelling deutet daher das Verhältnis der bewusstlosen Handlungen des reinen Subjekt-Objekts (bzw. des Ich im *System des transzendentalen Idealismus*) zu den bewussten Handlungen als Gründungsverhältnis und konstruiert damit ein Verhältnis, das im Kontext der Identitätsphilosophie im Modell der quantitativen Differenz und der Potenzierung beschrieben wird. Zentrale Theoreme von Schellings Naturphilosophie wären an diese im Umfeld der Transzendentalphilosophie gegebene Deutung der Tiefenstruktur des Subjektes anzubinden, etwa das Theorem, die Natur als Vorgeschichte des Menschen zu begreifen. Entscheidend für das hier erörterte Problem ist jetzt aber nur, zu sehen, dass das reine Subjekt-Objekt zwar kein Ich ist, aber dennoch, dies liegt der Kontext nahe, in Analogie zu dem Ich als Prinzip begriffen werden kann.[37] So ist es selber auch reine Tätigkeit, die frei aus sich heraus *„aus dem reinen Subjekt-Objekt das Subjekt-Objekt des Bewußtseyns entstehen"* (SW IV, S. 87) lässt. Ist das reine Subjekt-Objekt damit kein Ich, so ist es doch ichhaft.

Diese Überlegung entwickelt Schelling in seinen identitätsphilosophischen Schriften sehr sorgfältig unter dem Namen ‚absolute Identität' weiter und arbeitet die metaphysischen Implikationen und Voraussetzungen dieses Gedankens heraus.[38] Auffällig ist, dass er dabei bestimmte Vokabeln, etwa die in der *Freiheitsschrift* genannten, Tätigkeit, Leben und Freiheit, zu vermeiden sucht und

---

[35] „[D]enn durch jene Abstraktion gelange ich zum Begriff des reinen Subjekt-Objekts (= Natur), von welchem ich mich zum Subjekt-Objekt des Bewußtseyns (= Ich) erst erhebe" (SW IV, S. 86).

[36] Vgl. Fichte, Schelling, 1968, S. 105; dazu Hühn, 2005 und Jaeschke, Arndt, 2012, S. 343–361.

[37] Es ist diese Analogie, durch welche die Natur als ein Quasi-Subjekt erscheint, die Schellings Projekt einer Naturphilosophie mannigfacher Kritik ausgesetzt hat. Vgl. als Versuch einer sachlichen Rekonstruktion Schwenzfeuer, 2012.

[38] Vgl. Rang, 2000, insbes. S. 67–94.

stärker an spinozistische oder neuplatonische Ausdrucksweisen anknüpft (wie Substanz, Attribut, Eines, Identität). Dies darf aber keineswegs darüber hinwegtäuschen, dass Schelling Probleme zu lösen sucht, die erst im Kontext der Transzendentalphilosophie auffällig werden.

Soweit ist aber hinreichend entwickelt, worin die identitätsphilosophische Problemlage besteht, um den Rückverweis Schellings in der *Freiheitsschrift* angemessen zu verstehen. Die dem Idealismus zugeschriebene These S bezieht sich auf die im Begriff des reinen Subjekt-Objekts gefasste Überlegung einer Tiefenschicht des Subjektes. Ist dieses reine Subjekt-Objekt Prinzip alles naturhaft Seienden und selber von ichhafter Struktur (d. h. dem Ich bis auf dessen Selbstbewusstheit als einzelnes Ich analog), dann liegt allem naturhaft Seienden ein Prinzip zugrunde, das selbst durch die Prädikate Tätigkeit, Leben und Freiheit bestimmt werden kann. Tatsächlich liegt hier dann auch dasjenige Umkehrungsverhältnis vor, das Schelling in der *Freiheitsschrift* zwischen den Thesen S bzw. S´ und S* beansprucht. Als Prinzip alles naturhaft Seienden ist das reine Subjekt-Objekt ein ontologisches Prinzip, als Grundsatz formuliert ergibt sich in der Konsequenz genau die These S. Schelling kann demnach zurecht in der *Freiheitsschrift* auf den ontologischen Freiheitsbegriff rekurrieren, ohne ihn dort selbst zu beweisen, in dem 1801 gegebenen Begriff des reinen Subjekt-Objekts bzw. in der Folge unter dem Namen der absoluten Identität ist nämlich der Gedanke, dass „alles Wirkliche (die Natur, die Welt der Dinge) Thätigkeit, Leben und Freiheit zum Grund habe" (SW VII, 351) strukturell, wenn auch nicht wörtlich enthalten. Es zeigt sich, dass der ontologische Freiheitsbegriff keine bloß unplausible Hypostasierung des menschlichen ist, sondern eine Antwort auf Probleme der Transzendentalphilosophie darstellt.

Literatur

Beckermann, Ansgar (2008): *Gehirn, Ich, Freiheit. Neurowissenschaften und Menschenbild*, Paderborn.

Bondeli, Martin (2006): *Apperzeption und Erfahrung. Kants transzendentale Deduktion im Spannungsfeld der frühen Rezeption und Kritik*, Basel.

Buchheim, Thomas (1999): „Metaphysische Notwendigkeit des Bösen'. Über eine Zweideutigkeit in Heideggers Auslegung der Freiheitsschrift", in: Fehér, István M./ Jacobs, Wilhelm G. (Hrsg.): *Zeit und Freiheit. Schelling – Schopenhauer – Kierkegaard – Heidegger*, Budapest, S. 183–191.

Claesges, Ulrich (1974): *Geschichte des Selbstbewußtseins. Der Ursprung des spekulativen Problems in Fichtes Wissenschaftslehre von 1794–95*, Den Haag.

Cramer, Konrad (2003): „Kants ,Ich denke' und Fichtes ,Ich bin'", in: *Internationales Jahrbuch des Deutschen Idealismus/International Yearbook of German Idealism*, 1, S. 57–92.

Fichte, Johann Gottlieb/Schelling, Friedrich Wilhelm Joseph (1968): *Fichte – Schelling. Briefwechsel. Mit einer Einleitung von W. Schulz*, Frankfurt a. M.

Fichte, Johann Gottlieb (1971): *Grundlage der gesammten Wissenschaftslehre*, in: *Fichtes Werke, Bd. I*, hrsg. Fichte, Immanuel Hermann, Berlin (Nachdruck der Ausgabe von 1845 f.).

Fink, Helmut/Rosenzweig, Rainer (2006) (Hrsg.): *Freier Wille – frommer Wunsch?*, Paderborn.

Hühn, Lore (1998): „Die intelligible Tat. Zu einer Gemeinsamkeit Schellings und Schopenhauers“, in: Iber, Christian/Pocai, Romano (Hrsg.): *Selbstbesinnung der Moderne. Beiträge zur kritischen Hermeneutik ihrer Grundbegriffe*, Cuxhaven, S. 55–94.

Hühn, Lore (2005): „Die Verabschiedung des subjektivitätstheoretischen Paradigmas. Der Grunddissens zwischen Schelling und Fichte im Lichte ihres philosophischen Briefwechsels“, in: *Fichte-Studien*, 25, S. 93–111.

Hühn, Lore (2010): „Heidegger – Schelling im philosophischen Zwiegespräch. Der Versuch einer Einleitung“, in: Hühn, Lore/Jantzen, Jörg (Hrsg): *Heideggers Schelling-Seminar (1927/28). Die Protokolle von Martin Heideggers Seminar zu Schellings „Freiheitsschrift“ (1927/28) und die Akten des Internationalen Schelling-Tags 2006*, Stuttgart-Bad Cannstatt, S. 3–44.

Jacobi, Friedrich Heinrich (1976): *Beylage. Ueber den transcendentalen Idealismus*, in: *Werke, Bd. 2*, hrsg. Roth, Freidrich/Köppen, Friedrich, Darmstadt (Nachdruck der Ausgabe von 1815).

Jaeschke, Walter/Arndt, Andreas (2012): *Die Klassische Deutsche Philosophie nach Kant. Systeme der reinen Vernunft und ihre Kritik 1785–1845*, München.

Kant, Immanuel (1998): *Kritik der reinen Vernunft*, hrsg. Timmermann, Jens, Hamburg. (Zitiert mit „KrV“ und nach den Originalausgaben A und B.)

Kant, Immanuel (1968): *Kritik der praktischen Vernunft*, in: *Akademie-Textausgabe, Bd. V*, hrsg. Preußische Akademie der Wissenschaften, Berlin (Nachdruck der Ausgabe von 1908). (Zitiert mit „KpV“ und nach der Originalausgabe A.)

Mechtenberg, Lydia (2006): *Kants Neutralismus*, Paderborn.

Peetz, Siegbert (1995): *Die Freiheit im Wissen. Eine Untersuchung zu Schellings Konzept der Rationalität*, Frankfurt a. M.

Pietrek, Torsten/Buchheim, Thomas (2007) (Hrsg.): *Freiheit auf Basis von Natur?* Paderborn.

Prauss, Gerold (1974): *Kant und das Problem der Dinge an sich*, Bonn.

Prauss, Gerold (1983): *Kant über Freiheit als Autonomie*, Frankfurt a. M.

Quine, Willard Van Orman (1963): „On What There Is“, in: *From a Logical Point of View*, New York, S. 1–19.

Rang, Bernhard (1988): „Schellings Theorie des Lebens“, in: *Zeitschrift für Philosophische Forschung*, 42, S. 167–197.

Rang, Bernhard (2000): *Identität und Indifferenz. Eine Untersuchung zu Schellings Identitätsphilosophie*, Frankfurt a. M.

Schelling, Friedrich Wilhelm Joseph (1856): *Briefe über Dogmatismus und Kriticismus*, in: *Sämmtliche Werke, Bd. I*, hrsg. Schelling, Karl Friedrich August, Stuttgart. (Zitiert mit „SW“ und nach dem Band der angegebenen Ausgabe.)

Schelling, Friedrich Wilhelm Joseph (1857): *System des transscendentalen Idealismus*, in: *Sämmtliche Werke, Bd. III*, hrsg. Schelling, Karl Friedrich August, Stuttgart. (Zitiert mit „SW“ und nach dem Band der angegebenen Ausgabe.)

Schelling, Friedrich Wilhelm Joseph (1859 a): *Ueber den wahren Begriff der Naturphilosophie*, in: *Sämmtliche Werke, Bd. IV*. (Zitiert mit „SW“ und nach dem Band der angegebenen Ausgabe.)

Schelling, Friedrich Wilhelm Joseph (1859 b): *Darstellung meines Systems der Philosophie*, in: *Sämmtliche Werke, Bd. IV.* (Zitiert mit „SW" und nach dem Band der angegebenen Ausgabe.)

Schelling, Friedrich Wilhelm Joseph (1859 c): *Bruno, ein Gespräch*, in: *Sämmtliche Werke, Bd. IV.* (Zitiert mit „SW" und nach dem Band der angegebenen Ausgabe.)

Schelling, Friedrich Wilhelm Joseph (1860 a): *System der gesammten Philosophie und der Naturphilosophie insbesondere*, in: *Sämmtliche Werke, Bd. VI.* (Zitiert mit „SW" und nach dem Band der angegebenen Ausgabe.)

Schelling, Friedrich Wilhelm Joseph (1860 b): *Philosophische Untersuchungen über das Wesen der menschlichen Freiheit und die damit zusammenhängenden Gegenstände*, in: *Sämmtliche Werke, Bd. VII.* (Zitiert mit „SW" und nach dem Band der angegebenen Ausgabe.)

Schelling, Friedrich Wilhelm Joseph (1860 c): *Stuttgarter Privatvorlesungen*, in: *Sämmtliche Werke, Bd. VII.* (Zitiert mit „SW" und nach dem Band der angegebenen Ausgabe.)

Schelling, Friedrich Wilhelm Joseph (1861): *Zur Geschichte der neueren Philosophie*, in: *Sämmtliche Werke, Bd. X.* (Zitiert mit „SW" und nach dem Band der angegebenen Ausgabe.)

Schlegel, Friedrich Wilhelm (1975): *Über die Sprache und Weisheit der Indier*, in: *Kritische Friedrich-Schlegel-Ausgabe, Bd. VIII*, hrsg. Behler, Ernst, Paderborn, S. 105–433.

Schwenzfeuer, Sebastian (2012): *Natur und Subjekt. Die Grundlegung der schellingschen Naturphilosophie*, Freiburg.

Seebaß, Gottfried (1989): „Transzendentale Apperzeption", in: Funke, Gerhard/Seebohm, Thomas M. (Hrsg.): *Proceedings: Sixth International Kant Congress, Vol. 2*, Lanham, S. 323–339.

Stolzenberg, Jürgen (2003): „‚Geschichte des Selbstbewußtseins'. Reinhold – Fichte – Schelling", in: *Internationales Jahrbuch des Deutschen Idealismus/International Yearbook of German Idealism*, 1, S. 93–113.

Wayne Martin

Antinomies of Autonomy:
German Idealism and English Mental Health Law

Der derzeitige Zustand der Gesetze in England und Wales, die sich mit der psychischen Gesundheit befassen, weist eine Reihe systematischer Antinomien auf. Dies sollte nicht als ein Fehler in der Gesetzgebung angesehen werden. Diese Rechtsantinomien spiegeln vielmehr eine tiefer liegende antinomische Struktur wider, die dort wirksam ist, wo Pflegeberufe in einem weitgehend liberalen Rechtsumfeld praktiziert und reguliert werden. Anliegen dieses Beitrages ist es, diese antinomischen Strukturen zu identifizieren und zu prüfen, inwieweit die post-kantianische idealistische Tradition für eine Auseinandersetzung mit dieser Problematik argumentative Mittel zur Verfügung stellt.

§ 1: Kerrie's Antinomy

On the afternoon of 17 September, 2007, a 27-year old Norfolk woman called an ambulance and was transported to the accident and emergency ward at a local hospital. She had ingested approximately 350 ml of antifreeze. The main ingredient in antifreeze is ethylene glycol, a toxic substance; 350 ml is a potentially lethal dose. The indicated treatment for ethylene glycol poisoning is renal dialysis, which in this instance would almost certainly have saved the woman's life. But she refused to consent to treatment. Arriving at the emergency room, she presented a hand-written note in which she explained that she had drunk antifreeze in an attempt to end her life, and that she had come to hospital not to be saved, but in order that she might die comfortably, and not alone at home. Over the following hours she repeatedly refused all life-saving treatment. She died in the early hours of the morning of 19 September.

The woman's name was Kerrie Wooltorton. Her case came to public attention upon the publication of the Norfolk County Coroner's report, and has been a subject of controversy ever since. Much of the dispute has centered on the question of what the law dictates for a case of this sort, and in particular which legal framework is appropriate for navigating this tragic circumstance. Some have argued that the Wooltorton case should be approached by way of the *Mental Health Act* (MHA) of 1983. The MHA establishes the power to "section" mentally disordered individuals who are a danger to themselves or to others and to treat them involuntarily. Kerrie Wooltorton had been diagnosed with borderline personality disorder, and had a long history of self-harming behaviour; it is plain that she was a danger to herself. Accordingly, some have argued that she ought to have been sectioned and given life-saving treatment without her consent.

Others, including the Norfolk County Coroner, have taken a different view. They have viewed the Wooltorton case through the lens of the *Mental Capacity Act* of 2005 (MCA). The MCA is a new piece of legislation, rooted in a series of landmark court rulings in the 1990s. These court rulings, together with the statute that followed in their wake, are meant to ensure that competent adult patients have a right to refuse unwanted medical treatment. In one much-cited 1997 case, Justice Butler-Sloss ruled that an adult has "the absolute right to refuse medical treatment, for any reason, rational or irrational, or for no reason at all".[1] Butler-Sloss's formulation was itself adapted from a 1992 case in which Lord Donaldson wrote that "[the patient's right of choice] exists notwithstanding that the reasons for making that choice are rational, irrational, unknown or even non-existent".[2] But these rights are in one crucial respect conditional: an adult has the right to refuse treatment *if she has the mental capacity to do so*. Where capacity is lacking the rights of the patient must give way to forms of surrogate decision-making and duties of best-interest care.

The MCA defines the threshold concept of mental capacity as follows. A person has the capacity to make a decision for herself if she is able to "understand and retain" the information relevant to the decision, is able to "use or weigh" that information in reaching a decision, and is able to "communicate a choice". The Norfolk County Coroner and the medical personnel on hand at the hospital were unanimously in agreement that Kerrie Wooltorton satisfied this standard: she understood the diagnosis of ethylene glycol poisoning and the purpose of the proposed dialysis, she was able to "use and weigh" that information in reaching a decision, and she emphatically communicated her choice. Accordingly, they argued, she had a right to refuse treatment, even at the cost of her life. Moreover, to treat her without her consent would have amounted to a form of assault.

I propose to approach the case of Kerrie Wooltorton – and some other related cases – by making use of the notion of a legal antinomy. An antinomy is a distinctive form of contradiction; it comprises a pair of arguments, each sound, but yielding inconsistent conclusions. A body of law is antinomial insofar as it yields antinomies in this sense. The notion of an antinomy will of course be familiar to readers of this *Jahrbuch* from Kant's account of the dialectic of reason. Kant was concerned with antinomies of pure reason: the circumstance where reason itself leads us to contradictory conclusions; this was what Kant famously described as "the euthanasia of pure reason" (KrV, A 407/B 434). My use of the notion of an antinomy is indebted to Kant, but

---

[1]   *Re MB* [1997] EWCA Civ 3093.
[2]   *Re T* [1993] Fam. 95.

I shall not follow his lead slavishly. In particular, I am concerned here with antinomies of positive law rather than of pure reason, and I am concerned in particular with antinomies that yield contradictory *obligations*. Formally, the antinomies that concern me consist of a pair of sound arguments that together entail a conjunction of the form "S is obliged to φ and S is obliged to not-φ", where S is a person and φ is the name of a particular action. The Wooltorton case threatens to yield such an antinomy, where φ is the action of performing (or authorising) renal dialysis and S is the responsible medical officer on duty at the time of Wooltorton's hospital admission.

In what follows I shall argue that current mental health legislation in England and Wales exhibits systematic antinomial tensions. I show that these antinomial structures are not a quirk or defect of the legislation but are intrinsic to the reality that these laws seek to regulate. Throughout my aim will be to draw on the resources of the post-Kantian idealist tradition in trying to understand these antinomies and in thinking about how they can be managed. Before going further, however, I do need to be clear about one point. This essay is not an interpretation but an appropriation of German idealist texts. I operate at a considerable distance (some may say: a scandalous distance) from the historical texts themselves, and I am quite ready to adapt canonical doctrines where doing so serves my purposes. I take this liberty out of the conviction that the Kantian and post-Kantian tradition provides us with the most important sustained consideration of the significance of antinomial structures, and that certain lessons from that tradition can play an important role in clarifying and improving our current situation. If the result is in certain instances more like a crude cartoon than a finished portrait of the canonical heroes, that is a price I find worth paying.

§ 2: Two Unworkable Kantian Strategies

One of Kant's own strategies with the antinomies of pure reason was to identify a defect in the reasoning that generates the contradictory conclusions. Recall that this was Kant's tactic in diagnosing the first and second antinomies in *The Critique of Pure Reason*. An antinomy requires two *sound* arguments for contradictory conclusions; if one or the other of the pair is unsound then the antinomy is only apparent. We find a number of variants on this strategy in the literature that has grown up around the Kerrie Wooltorton case. At the coroner's inquest, several witnesses testified that Wooltorton was not suffering from a mental disorder of the sort that would warrant an MHA section.[3] Alter-

---

[3] The coroner reports: "Everyone was asked by me whether Kerrie was exhibiting any symptoms of a mental disorder or disability and the answer was very clearly in every case was no [...]" (Armstrong, 2009).

natively, one could claim that an MHA section provides only for involuntary treatment *of a mental disorder*, and that renal dialysis is not itself a treatment for a mental disorder. In either case the legal argument for compulsory treatment would be unsound. Others have argued that Wooltorton's psychological state left her unable to "use or weigh" the relevant information about her decision situation. If this is true then the argument for honoring her refusal would be unsound. It has also been argued that the MCA itself explicitly provides for blanket deference to the MHA in cases of conflict, so that no antinomial obligations can possibly arise.[4]

I do not myself find any of these defusing strategies conclusive. Consider the first two together. We have already seen that Wooltorton had been diagnosed with borderline personality disorder. That condition is the subject of much controversy in psychiatric circles, but it is listed in the authoritative manuals of psychological disorders, and self-harming behaviour is one of its chief manifestations. The courts have ruled that "treatment for a mental disorder" can include treatment for the physical consequences of harm that are the result of that disorder.[5] Under the circumstances, then, there is a strong prima facie case that § 3 of the MHA applies: Wooltorton suffered from a mental disorder of a nature or degree that warranted hospital treatment, and she was a danger to herself.

The claim that Wooltorton lacked capacity is much harder to gauge: a capacity assessment can require considerable professional skill, and that skill must be exercised in a face-to-face encounter with the patient who is being assessed. There are difficulties surrounding such assessments, to be sure, but it is striking that all those who encountered Wooltorton at the hospital were in agreement – and no one seems to have been in doubt – about her capacity when measured against the legal standard. Here it is crucial to note that the law explicitly recognizes that a person may suffer from a mental disorder and nonetheless be possessed of mental capacity.[6] One of the fundamental principles of the MCA approach is that capacity must be assessed with specific reference to the functional abilities of the individual in the face of the relevant decision; one cannot refute the legal presumption of capacity simply on the basis of a generic psychiatric diagnosis. What, finally, about the general claim as to the "trumping" precedence of the MHA? The legal issues here are complex, and for present purposes it is best not to get drawn too far into them. Suffice it to say that the deference of the MCA to the MHA is not wholesale; arguably the specific circumstances of the Wooltorton case fall outside its scope.[7]

---

[4]   Both these arguments were advanced by a pair of forensic psychiatrists commenting on the case in a letter to the *BMJ*: Bashir and Crawford, 2009, p. 988.
[5]   *B v Croydon HA* (aka *LB v Croydon* HA) CA [1995] 2 W.L.R. 294.
[6]   *Re C (Adult Refusal of Treatment)* [1994] 1 All ER 819.
[7]   The argument for trumping would have to turn on the provisions of MCA § 28. That section does in certain respects provide for deference to the MHA in cases of conflict.

Having said all that, there is nonetheless one sense in which the Wooltorton case falls short of a strict legal antinomy. Recall that the schema for a strict antinomy requires a conjunction of the form "S is obliged to φ and S is obliged to not-φ". In the Wooltorton case, we seem to fall short of such a conjunction, if only because the MCA generates *obligations* but the MHA establishes only *powers*. That is, the MCA *obliges* medical staff to respect a capacitous refusal; the MHA provides for the *power* to section but, strictly speaking, it does not *oblige* anyone to do so. If only in this way, the law avoids a flat-out contradiction. But while this is good for the law, it is not particularly helpful for the medical staff on the scene. It is natural to suppose that it is the duty of emergency room staff to use such powers as are available to them in order to save the lives of the patients in their care. To do otherwise is the basic form of negligence. So, if the MHA gives them the power to legally save Wooltorton's life, then there is considerable moral and professional pressure to exercise that power. In this sense, the combination of the MCA and the professional code of conduct would suffice to generate the obligation required for a strict antinomy.

I have argued so far that a Kantian "defusing" strategy does not suffice to show that Kerrie's Antinomy is merely apparent. If we are to get further, then we must dig deeper, and consider the source of the antinomial tension itself. Why does the law generate Kerrie's Antinomy? Is this simply an artifact of badly-worded legislation? Could the problems be solved, as some have argued, by a single unified statute?[8] I want to propose that the antinomial pressures exhibited by the Wooltorton case are in an important sense essential to the law, given its context and the form of relationship the law here seeks to regulate. In particular, I shall argue that a tendency toward antinomy is inevitable where the law regulates vocations of care in a broadly liberal legal environment.

One way to make this point is to consider the competing values that are at work in the respective statutes we have been considering. The primary value that informs the *Mental Health Act* is public health and safety. The modern MHA has its origins in Victorian legislation governing "Asylums, Lunatics and Madhouses". But its basic powers date back to the Vagrancy Act of 1774, which provided for the detention of those who are "furiously and dangerously mad".

It could accordingly be argued that honoring Wooltorton's refusal would in effect be a violation of § 28, if indeed Wooltorton's condition was such as to warrant an MHA section. But this claim might not withstand scrutiny. The relevant portion of the statute reads as follows: "Nothing in this Act authorises anyone (a) to give a patient medical treatment for mental disorder, or (b) to consent to a patient's being given medical treatment for mental disorder, if, at the time when it is proposed to treat the patient, his treatment is regulated by Part 4 of the *Mental Health Act*". But in the Wooltorton case the medical personnel did not "give a patient medical treatment"; they decided not to. So it is hard to see how their actions could be in violation of this section.

8   See Szmukler et al., 2010.

The modern statute has come a long way from those early beginnings (particularly in the strategies it adopts to insure against abuses), but in one crucial respect there is continuity: one of its basic aims is to protect public health and ensure public order. The MCA has a different normative priority. It finds its place in the tradition of human rights legislation and, as such, places special value on individual autonomy – the ability of individuals to make decisions for themselves. It is inevitable that these two values will come into conflict. Cases will arise in which a concern for public health points in one direction and the respect for autonomy points in another.

But there is a deeper source of the antinomial structures in this area of the law, and this pertains not so much to the values of the two statutory frameworks, but rather to the standpoint or perspective that each statute adopts toward the patient. Or, to put the point more exactly: the two legal frameworks each dictate a perspective that the care-provider must take up toward the potential care-recipient. Taken together these two standpoints in themselves generate antinomial tension. This is a point that requires elaboration.

Consider the circumstance of a psychiatric care-provider who is faced with the decision about whether to section a patient in order to provide involuntary care. Suppose that it is established that the individual suffers from a serious mental disorder and that there is appropriate treatment available that can only be provided in a hospital setting. But the patient does not consent. Should she be sectioned? In such circumstances everything comes to ride on the question of whether the individual in question is "a danger to self or others". How does one go about answering such a question? The first thing to notice is that this is a question about the future. The care-provider is tasked with making a prediction, based on the available information, about the future behaviour of the patient under a variety of possible circumstances. Care-providers are subject to intense public scrutiny if they get the prediction wrong. The crucial point for our purposes is that such a question is posed from what Strawson famously dubbed "the objective attitude".[9] The patient is a complex, partly dysfunctional biological mechanism that will be interacting causally with a complex environment. The task is to make an informed risk-assessment about the likely outcome of such interactions.

Consider now the standpoint prescribed by the MCA. Here the determinative question is not in any obvious way about the future; it is about the standing or status of a presently expressed intention. Here the psychiatric assessor is called upon to view the patient as an (actual or potential) agent. The critical question is, in effect, whether the presently expressed preferences are genuinely

---

[9]   Strawson, 1962.

an expression of the patient's free agency.[10] In this case, the perspective upon the patient is what Kant would call "practical" or "moral".

It is in the tension between these two standpoints, I submit, that we find an important source of Kerrie's Antinomy. If, in Kantian terms, we view Wooltorton "under the idea of freedom", then we treat her refusal as the manifestation of her free, self-determining choice. But when we view her instead through the prism of the MHA – "under the idea of probabilistic risk assessment", as it were – that same refusal shows up as simply one more symptom (effect) of Wooltorton's disorder (cause). Given the right sort of ancillary knowledge, we can extrapolate ahead to the further disastrous consequences to come. So which perspective should we adopt toward Wooltorton? Is she a suffering creature in the grip of a disorder that can be managed? Or is she a moral agent whose choices must be respected? The answer, of course, is *both*. It would be a fateful error to suppose that we can choose between these two perspectives. They both apply, and indeed the clinician is legally bound to take up both of them. The antinomial pressures that we find in the law reflect the antinomial pressures that result from the combination of these two perspectives.

If this much is correct then a second Kantian coping strategy suggests itself. We are not here in the domain of the mathematical antinomies, where the resolution lies in exposing a fallacy. We are rather in the domain of Kant's third antinomy, where the challenge is to accommodate two sound arguments, and to find room for both free agency and causal determination. Kant's own strategy for managing this challenge famously involves a form of dualism: both perspectives are legitimate, indeed requisite; the key is to confine each to its appropriate domain. One version of this dualism notoriously turns on the Kantian distinction between phenomena and noumena: considered as appearances our actions are determined; considered as noumena we are free. But we might also cast the dualism – this seems to have been a crucial part of Strawson's suggestion – as a dualism of theoretical and practical attitudes. Viewed from the theoretical standpoint, the patient's behaviour can be explained and (fallibly) predicted as so much causal output of a complex biological machine in a complex environment. Viewed practically we treat the patient's behaviour as the manifestation of autonomous agency. Freedom prevails from the latter standpoint; determinism (or probabilistic causation) from the former. As long as we do not mix or confuse the standpoints, the two descriptions of the patient need not contradict one another.

---

[10] This framing of the question of capacity can be found in judicial rulings in disputed cases. See for example *A Local Authority v Mrs A* [2010] EWHC 1549 Fam. In finding Mrs. A lacking in capacity, Mr. Justice Body writes: "I am satisfied that her decision not to continue taking contraception is not the product of her free will" (§ 73).

But these celebrated Kantian dualisms cannot help us with Kerrie's Antinomy. The problem is not that they introduce some rather heavy metaphysical baggage; set that concern aside for the moment. The more fundamental problem is that the clinical situation itself requires the clinician to adopt *both* these perspectives in the *same* medical encounter. This is the challenge of practicing the caring vocations in a liberal legal context that places a high value on the human rights of care-recipients. It is not open to the care-provider simply to see the patient as a "creature in need", nor can the care-provider somehow oscillate between one view of the patient as a rights-bearing person and another view of the same individual as a complex biological mechanism. The challenge is to occupy both perspectives at once without falling into antinomial contradiction.

§ 3: A Brief and Extravagant Fichtean Excursus

In looking for a way to meet this challenge, I propose to begin with what will undoubtedly seem an extravagant thought. Consider a framing of Kant's third antinomy in the sparse vocabulary of Fichte's *Wissenschaftslehre*. One the one hand (thesis) we find ourselves with what we might call the formula of autonomy: *the I determines itself*. On the other hand (antithesis), we have the principle of determination by something other: *the I is determined by the not-I*. For the Fichtean, we are committed to treating both of these principles as true, despite the obvious tension between them. The two principles are jointly constitutive of the status of finite rational subjectivity; they are both transcendental conditions on the possibility of judgement and action. The Fichtean seeks a resolution of the tension that avoids the Kantian dualisms: both principles must be true in the same world, in the same circumstance, from the same point of view. Can these requirements possibly be met?

This is where we come to the extravagant thought. Suppose it were the case that the not-I which determines the I were itself determined by the I. Imagine, if you will, that you are a kind of God: you have made the not-I exactly as you decided it should be, and you now allow yourself to be determined by the not-I you have made. There is, undoubtedly, something disturbingly solipsistic about such a thought. Nonetheless there would be, in such a circumstance, a certain kind of formal reconciliation of thesis and antithesis, determination-by-self and determination-by-other. For under such an extraordinary circumstance the I would indeed be determined by the not-I. We thus satisfy the requirements of determinism. But this deterministic moment would not itself compromise the freedom of the I, since the not-I that determines the I would itself be determined by the I. The circle is closed.

A Fichtean approach to the antinomy of freedom and determinism seeks to exploit this extravagant thought. It involves, first, a recognition of the permanent tension between thesis and antithesis. We finite beings will never find ourselves in the circumstances of the solitary god whom we have just described. But the Fichtean strategy for addressing that tension is ultimately not metaphysical but practical; it is a form of striving. The finite Fichtean subject *works* on the not-I, ever seeking to determine the world in accordance with its judgement as to how it ought to be. By remaking the world in this way, the gap between thesis and antithesis progressively closes: the I comes closer and closer to the point where self-determination and determination-by-other coincide.

I have described this Fichtean thought as extravagant. We might say that it combines Promethean ambition with Sisyphean absurdity. For of course the envisaged point of unity can never be obtained: in this sense Fichtean striving is unending. It is certainly not easy to see how such an extravagant thought could possibly be useful in finding our way through the all-too-concrete medico-juridical antinomies of the psychiatric clinic or accident and emergency ward. By definition the circumstances involve a state of affairs where things are *not* the way they ought to be. But might there nonetheless be some way in which a suitably domesticated variant of the extravagant Fichtean strategy might be put to use in taming the antinomies we have uncovered?

§ 4: Polly's Antinomy

On 30 March, 2009, Polly, aged 48, was involved in an automobile accident. She suffered a serious head injury and was taken unconscious to the hospital. Her medical condition was stabilized, but she did not regain consciousness. She was kept alive by life-supporting medical equipment which provided artificial nutrition and hydration. For the first few days in the hospital her breathing was supported by an artificial ventilator; subsequently a tracheostomy was performed, and she regained the ability to breathe on her own. Polly was unconscious for several months but then emerged into what is medically described as a "minimally conscious state".

Prior to her accident, Polly had been a fiercely independent woman. She led an adventurous life, travelling the world; her favorite pastimes included sailing and mountain-climbing. Her family describe her as someone who celebrated her physical strength and valued her independence. In cartoons and poems she described herself as a free spirit, someone who hated to be tied down or to be dependent on others; she wanted to be able to "fend for herself". In one of her notebooks she recorded that she imagines dying young while doing something exciting, that she does not want to be less able or to know that she is slowly going downhill. "Life is not measured by the number of breaths we take, but by the moments that take our breath away". Polly was also politically active, and (among other things) a persistent critic of medical paternalism, heroic medical measures, and the like. She even wrote a how-to pamphlet about advance decision-making, although she never completed a formal advance-decision document herself. Polly's family and friends agree that, given a choice, the Polly they knew would have preferred to die rather than survive in such a way as to be wholly dependent on care-providers, family, and the medical establishment.

Early on in the course of her care, members of Polly's family began to raise the question as to whether Polly would have wanted the sorts of life-preserving measures that were being provided to her. Would she have wanted to go through the ordeal of treatment and rehabilitation to achieve whatever degree of "recovery" might be possible? But the medical staff responsible for Polly's care were not prepared to countenance such questions. Their vocation is to save lives; several of them have vivid memories of patients who have emerged from a coma and gone on to regain some level of independence. From their perspective it seemed far too soon to give up on Polly. Over the course of two years following the accident, Polly's condition did marginally improve. Nonetheless she has been left with profound multiple mental and physical disabilities and is still dependent on artificial nutrition and hydration and round-the-clock assistance.

If Kerrie's Antinomy arose in the case of a patient who had capacity, Polly's Antinomy emerges in the case of a patient who lacks it. For at least as long as Polly was unconscious, and almost certainly long thereafter, Polly lacked the capacity to make treatment decisions for herself. In such circumstances the MCA requires someone else to make decisions on her behalf; call this "surrogate decision-making". The surrogate decision-maker might be a citizen providing first-aid at the scene of the accident; it might be the senior member of the paramedic team that arrives to provide assistance; later it might be the senior consultant in a brain trauma unit or a judge in the Court of Protection. So what should be the basis of such surrogate decisions? About this the law is also clear: surrogate decisions made on behalf of an incapacitous patient must be made *in the patient's best interest*. This is a familiar principle of medical ethics, the so-called principle of beneficence.

Earlier we considered the antinomial tension that arises because of the different values and perspectives that inform the MHA and the MCA. But we are now in a position to see that there is a tendency toward antinomy within the MCA itself. The tendency derives from the statute's commitment to two overarching principles: the principle of patient autonomy and the principle of beneficence. Both principles are deeply rooted: the former in the commitments of liberal law, the latter in the constitutive values of the vocations of care. But there are certainly circumstances where the two principles pull in opposite directions. In the terms of our schema, the principle of beneficence might yield an obligation to phi where the principle of autonomy would yield an obligation to not-φ. So how does the statute manage this threat of antinomy? Its crucial mechanism lies in its insistence on a bright line separating two circumstances. Under the law, any particular person at a particular time facing a particular decision *either has or lacks capacity*. For the capacitated patient, the principle of autonomy reigns supreme; for the incapacitous patient, the principle of beneficence takes priority.[11] By this contrivance the statute serves two principles without generating antinomial obligations.

But of course reality is not always so tidy. Naturally there will be grey areas and borderline cases; there will also be circumstances where capacity fluctuates. Suppose that Polly had been conscious and possessed capacity when the paramedics arrived at the accident scene. Under the law she would have the right to refuse treatment, even if the paramedics concluded that treatment was clearly in her best interest. But then Polly loses consciousness and capacity. What should the paramedic team do then? Here is a first circumstance where Polly's Antinomy makes itself felt. Should they honor her capacitous refusal and let her die by the roadside? Or, must they now act in accordance with their judgment as to her best interest, even if that means acting against her express wishes? If they decide to treat under the best-interest principle and Polly returns to consciousness during the treatment, should they once again desist if she demands that they do so? These questions defy easy answers precisely because of the antinomial tensions within the statute.

Polly herself did not possess capacity at the accident scene and the Emergency Services Team who responded did not have occasion to be troubled by antinomy. They carried out their vocation of care, doing what they could to stabilize Polly's condition and transporting her to the hospital. But as her care progresses, the antinomial tensions certainly make themselves felt. Is a tracheostomy in her best interest? What about a course of antibiotics to treat pneumonia? Polly is still unconscious and incapacitous, so surrogate decisions must be taken on her behalf. To the medical team the answers may seem obvious. Polly's best chances for survival and recovery require that she be weaned off the respirator, so the tracheostomy is a medical imperative. Without the antibiotics pneumonia could be fatal. It is only by helping Polly survive these immediate threats that the team will be able to assess her longer-term prospects for recovery. So an initial survey of best interests creates a prima facie obligation to make use of these medical interventions. On the other hand, the law explicitly requires that an assessment of Polly's best interests should take into account Polly's own past and current preferences, insofar as those are reasonably ascertainable. It also requires that Polly's family and others close to her be consulted and that reasonable efforts be taken to determine what Polly herself would have chosen under the circumstances. If this process is undertaken seriously, and the facts about Polly's character and values come to light, the medical team will certainly come to feel the pressure of the antithesis: if it becomes clear that Polly herself would have refused these treatments, then do we not have an obligation

---

[11]   This priority of the principle of beneficence is far from absolute. Among other things, it finds a limit in cases where an incapacitous patient has a legally valid and applicable advance directive. For present purposes I abstract from this complication.

to desist? Once again it is those who are involved in the vocations of care who most directly find themselves confronted with the antinomy.

Before leaving Polly, there is one further aspect of her antinomy which merits our attention, for once again it pertains to a difference in the perspective or point of view which the law prescribes. In the case of a refusal of treatment, the critical question under the law is whether the patient has capacity *at the material time* – i.e., at the time a decision needs to be made.[12] In practice, this can lead to a narrow, "time-slice" perspective on the potential care-recipient. An assessment of capacity focuses on "capacity-now"; an individual who is found to have capacity-now will accordingly have the right to make their own decision based on their *current* preferences and values. An experienced care-giver may well have reason to believe that this decision is one that the patient will later regret, but the liberal commitments of the law preclude paternalistic intervention on the basis of that assessment; a poor decision is not of itself evidence of incapacity. When it comes to a judgment of best-interest, by contrast, the requisite temporal perspective is quite different. A judgment of best interest is not a judgment about the interests of the present time-slice of the person; it is a judgement about that person as a whole, where the relevant whole is extended across a significant expanse of time. So, while respect for a capacitous decision tends to focus on the present moment, a best-interest assessment must somehow take in a view of a temporally extended totality.

§ 5: The Eve Standard

The extravagant speculative thought that we encountered in Fichte also finds a place in Hegel, albeit with a rather different inflection. Like Fichte, Hegel envisions a speculative reconciliation of self-determination and determination-by-other in a circumstance where the other is no longer something alien. Here is one of his formulations: *"For freedom it is necessary that we should feel no presence of something else which is not ourselves"*.[13] So formulated, Hegel's vision may well sound solipsistic – as if freedom requires that I be insulated from contact with anything or anyone else. But of course this is not at all Hegel's conclusion. The Hegelian variant on the Fichtean thought famously requires alterity (and indeed altercation!) in an intersubjective setting for freedom: self-determination is inextricably tied up with forms of determination by Others.

---

12   MCA, 2005, § 2, p. 1.

13   I take this formulation from Wallace's rather free translation of *Encyclopaedia* § 24, Zusatz 2 (Hegel, 1975, 8:39). Hegel's original reads as follows: *"Freiheit is nur da, wo kein Anderes für mich ist, das ich nicht selbst bin"* (Enz., p. 84).

The most famous intersubjective encounter in Hegel is of course the dialectic of master and slave, together with the struggle of life and death from which it originates. But both in his *Science of Logic* and in the *Philosophy of Right*, Hegel takes his initial orientation from a different intersubjective encounter: Adam's first encounter with Eve. Recall the story. God announces at Genesis 2:18 that Adam needs a "fitting partner" – or, as the King James has it, "a helper, meet for him". He proceeds to create all the wild beasts and birds, forming them out of the earth, and presenting them in turn to Adam. Adam gives names to each of them, but none are found to be a fitting partner. So far, all this is recounted; it is only when God creates Eve (out of Adam this time, rather than "out of the earth") that we finally hear Adam's first speech. "This at last is bone of my bone, flesh of my flesh. This one shall be called Woman, for from man was she taken" (Gen. 2:23).

For Hegel, the story of Eve inscribes a number of fundamental truths. It is, first, a story of *Anerkennung*. Adam *recognizes* Eve, and this recognition itself involves both a cognitive moment ("she is like me") and a normative moment ("she is *fitting*; she is appropriate for me"). In Adam's first speech the recognition is certainly not yet complete (among other things, Adam speaks *about* Eve, but he does not speak *to* her – nor she to him). Nonetheless we have from the outset the standard of recognition inscribed in the encounter with an Other. This in turn points to the second key concept Hegel extracts from the encounter in Eden: Adam's first speech expresses the basic logic of *Geist*. For Hegel, the concept of *Geist* essentially *is* the concept of an intersubjective collectivity which is constituted in relationships of recognition. Indeed in at least one place Hegel translates Adam's speech into his own preferred speculative idiom: "Just as Adam says to Eve: 'You are flesh of my flesh and bone of my bone', so does *Geist* say: 'This is *Geist* of my *Geist*, and its alien character has disappeared'" (PR § 4 Zusatz, p. 47). This "disappearance of an alien character" [*die Fremdheit ist verschwunden*] is crucial for the Hegelian strategy. The encounter with Eve involves an encounter not simply with a not-I, but with an Other that is not-other, a not-I that is both me and not-me.

These are riddling formulations, to be sure. But they reflect three underlying commitments of Hegel's project upon which I propose to draw. The first is what I shall call "the Eve Standard". Autonomous determination *can be* determination by another, as long as that other is an other whom I rightly recognize as appropriately not-other. So formulated, the Eve Standard is at best a schema. In particular, it calls for an elaboration of just what "rightly recognize" and "appropriately not-other" can mean, such that freedom is realized and preserved.

The second key point concerns contradiction. Hegel's articulation of the encounter with Eve is couched in forms that defy the principle of non-contradiction: Eve is both I and not-I, other and not-other; freedom requires alterity that has lost its alien character. We may well wonder whether and how these dialectical formulations might be tamed in a logic that honored consistency, but Hegel's stance is that the dialectic runs all the way down. And this itself, he claims, is a defining feature of *geistig* reality. Hegel: "What belongs to Nature is destroyed by contradiction, [...] but *Geist* has the power to preserve itself in contradiction" (Enz. § 382 Zusatz, 10:26–27). This is another lead worth pursuing. If *Geist* has the resources to absorb contradiction, might it have resources for managing antinomy as well?

These first two points are couched in the high-level abstractions of Hegel's logic, but they come closer to the ground in Hegel's strategy for considering how the Eve Standard might be satisfied in our own world. What would be the lived experience of the sort of self-determination-through-Others that Hegel has in mind? Central to Hegel's answer is the idea of a kind of ownership of the world – not in the sense of treating the world as my property, but of finding the world to be *my own*, in finding myself to be *at home* in it. In the *Encyclopaedia* Hegel introduces the notion of spirit (*Geist*) by explicitly linking this distinctive form of ownership with Adam's speech about Eve: "Therefore it [*der freie Geist*] is possessed of the confidence that in the world it will find its own self, that the world must be befriended to it, that, just as Adam said of Eve that she was flesh of his flesh, *Geist* has to seek in the world Reason of its own Reason" (*Enz.* § 440 Zusatz, p. 230).[14] To apply these Hegelian promptings seriously to our antinomies would be to consider how Eve's Standard might be met where the vocations of care are regulated in a broadly liberal legal environment. In such a circumstance where I am cared for beneficently by others whom I rightly recognize as appropriately not-other, in a world which I can find to be my own, paternalism and autonomy would coincide. Allow me one more story in order to try to make this schema plausible.

§ 6: "I made the decision on my own in the end"

John suffers from schizophrenia. He is in prison, awaiting trial on a criminal indictment.[15] In prison he refuses to accept treatment for his psychiatric condition. When he begins to develop de lusional symptoms, a MHA assessment is conducted. John is found to suffer from a mental disorder of a nature or degree

---

14   I have adapted Wallace's translation of this passage. Hegel's German reads as follows: "*Er besitzt daher die Zuversicht, daß er in der Welt sich selber finden werden, daß diese ihm befreundet sein müsse, daß, wie Adam von Eva sagt, sie sei Fleisch von seinem Fleische, so er in der Welt Vernunft von seiner eigenen Vernunft zu suchen habe*". Wallace uses "*reconciled*" to translate "*befreundet*" (Hegel, 1971, p. 179), but it is worth marking the difference between the sort of "friendship with the world" that Hegel invokes here and the reconciliation (*Versöhnung*) that is meant to be one of the deliverances of Hegelian philosophy.

15   I have discussed John in print elsewhere, in collaboration with Ryan Hickerson (Martin and Hickerson, forthcoming). For the case material regarding John, I am grateful to Beth Eastwood of the BBC.

to make hospital treatment appropriate; his condition is deemed to make him a danger to himself and to others. On the basis of this assessment he is sectioned for treatment under the MHA. He is transferred from prison to a secure ward in a National Health Service medical facility, where he receives involuntary treatment in the form of anti-psychotic medication. With treatment, John's schizophrenic symptoms are brought under control. But John also suffers from a physical ailment. He is a heavy smoker and in prison had begun to lose his speaking voice. In the hospital, tests show that he has advanced laryngeal cancer – cancer of the voice box. The indicated treatment is surgical removal of the voice box and the fitting of a speaking valve in John's throat.

Laryngeal cancer is not itself a mental disorder, so the proposed treatment is not covered by John's mental health section, nor indeed by the MHA. Surgical treatment for cancer would therefore require John's consent – if indeed John has the capacity to provide it. In consultation with his surgeon, John exhibits understanding of the diagnosis and the purpose of the treatment, and agrees to proceed with surgery. Back at the psychiatric ward, he discusses the situation with his care team and case worker. Plans are made for the surgery. But a few days later John's delusional symptoms return. He is now convinced that the proposed medical procedure is a conspiracy, and that the surgeon's specialty (commonly abbreviated as "ENT") is not "Ears, Nose and Throat", but "Electroneurotherapy", a fictional treatment that will kill him. He refuses to go ahead with the surgery.

By now we can recognize the tendency toward antinomy in such a circumstance. The care team's aim is to care for John, yet they are also committed to honoring John's rights as a patient. Should they treat John involuntarily in his own best interests? Should they desist in the face of his refusal? They know that in such circumstances the law requires a capacity assessment, but the outcome of such an assessment varies dramatically depending on the time they choose to conduct it. John's capacity fluctuates with his disorder, and perhaps also with his medication cycle, etc. In the end John decides to go ahead with the surgery. Reflecting back some time later, John sums up the episode in these words, spoken through his newly fitted valve: "The psychiatrist did say to me [that] someone else would have to make the decision because I was changing my mind. But I made the decision on my own in the end".[16]

Before considering the dialectical structure of John's case, it will be worth noting some of the events that unfolded *between* John's refusal and the final decision to proceed with the surgery. In the face of John's refusal, the care team undertook a number of steps. They consulted with John's family, and the family in turn with John. The surgeon, in consultation with the hospital's lawyers, drafted a letter, setting out John's condition and the medical options for treat-

---

[16]   BBC Radio 4 (2010).

ment, together with a frank summary of the likely outcomes of both treatment and non-treatment. They reviewed the letter with John, his family, and a case worker. The psychiatric team reviewed John's medication regimen and adjusted his dosage. John's decision came about through the mediation of these interventions.

In analyzing John's case, it is instructive to begin from his own retrospective assessment. It might be tempting to conclude that John's report is simply mistaken. From what *we* know of the case, it seems plain that John did *not* in fact make the decision *on his own*; a veritable army of Others helped him make it, and those Others played a significant role in *determining* what that decision turned out to be. Some of that determination came in the form of presenting him with information. But it also involved framing that information in ways designed to shape John's response to it; and it involved some quite direct manipulation of the neurochemistry of John's brain. In the sparse language of our dialectic: John was determined by the not-I.

So was John's retrospective report simply an error, perhaps even a delusion? Such a conclusion would be far too hasty. For one thing, John is well aware that other people played a significant role in enabling his decision. He is not *denying* their role in claiming the decision as his own. Yet despite the decisive role of others, John *experiences* his decision as his own; he *recognizes* it as his own, and it in turn is recognized as his decision. For in taking John's consent as valid, John's care team are recognizing John's ownership of the decision. So John's decision is determined by the other, yet it is also recognized as one that he made for himself. This is not an antinomy, but it is the sort of contradiction that the idealists claimed to find in *Geist*, and through which *Geist* is said to be able to endure.

If this is right – if John's case could be an instance of sustaining contradiction – then we want to know *how* it manages to do so. Let's try to tackle this question with reference to what Hegel taught us about Eve. According to the Eve Standard, John's self-determination is compatible with – indeed is made possible by – determination by others *insofar as John can rightly recognize those others as appropriately other*. And this in turn is to be assessed by considering whether and how John can find himself "at home" in a world that has "befriended" him. Of course Eve in John's circumstance is not any one person. A whole community of Others (an Otherhood?) played a critical role in determining his decision. And that community is by no means symmetrical or homogenous. It includes surgeons and psychiatrists but also case-workers and legal experts, friends and family. It ultimately includes, if only mediately, judges and courts, the BBC, and even you and me. In Hegel's vocabulary, it comprises the family, civil society, and the state. To apply the Eve Standard to John's circumstance would be to ask: is this Otherhood so constituted that John can rightly recognize it as appropriately other?

That is a big question, and it is not one that I can responsibly undertake to answer here. But it is worth singling out one feature of John's community that bears on our answer. That community somehow manages to bring together a number of quite different *perspectives* on John. Some in John's decision community are taking a view of John as a biochemical complex whose behaviour can be manipulated and indeed predicted with the tools of pharmaceutical medicine. Some are taking a view of John as a bearer of rights who must be respected; others view him primarily as a suffering individual in need of care. But there is also significant variation in the *temporal* perspective on John. The surgeon's perspective is focused on the growth of the cancer, which is increasingly threatening John's ability to breathe and could be fatal in a matter of days or weeks. Some members of the team are projecting ahead to the moment when John wakes up from the surgery. Will he complain at that point that he had been tricked or coerced into the surgery? The family is also projecting ahead, but with a longer view, trying to help John see that he still has much to live for, despite his current legal and medical troubles. But all this taking in of temporal complexity is not to the exclusion of the perspective where everything depends on the present moment. John's consent can only be legally taken if he possesses capacity *at the material time*. One could go on with this sort of analysis, but I hope the point is clear: John's Otherhood is a forum in which a whole array of divergent perspectives are held together in such a way that facilitates John's decision, and helps enable his retrospective ownership of it.

A final point to make about John's situation concerns not John himself, but the care-givers who played a role in John's world. The many practitioners of the vocations of care who came into contact with John at the material time of his decision encountered him with an orientation, we might even say an impulse, a habit (*hexis*) of beneficence. In their capacity as doctors, psychiatrists, social workers, even prison officers, an intrinsic aim of their vocation is to help John, to care for him, to act in such a way as to advance John's own interests. But this habit of beneficence does not hold sway unchecked. It is balanced and opposed by a duty, and presumably also a desire, to respect John's autonomy, his right of self-determination. That itself, we must hope, has become a habit of care too. In many circumstances of care, including John's, these two impulses/habits/reasons/motives pull in opposite directions. It is then all too easy to think of the tension between these two principles finitely, as a zero-sum game. Where the choice is vexed, one looks to the law for guidance. Which statute applies here? Which principle trumps the other? But in the logic of John's situation we find a possibility of holding the ensuing contradictions in such a way as to preserve both of these commitments.

§ 7: Applications

What remains is to consider whether and how this Hegelian schema might help us understand and navigate the antinomies from which we began. Before tackling this question directly, we must be careful to calibrate our expectations. No philosophical analysis or theoretical framework will make cases like those of Kerrie and Polly easy or happy; these are tragic hard cases in which any decision will be fraught and any outcome tinged with regrets. Moreover, it would be a mistake to expect any philosophical investigation of these questions of itself to provide "answers" to questions that must in the end be decisively influenced by subtle factors that can only be gathered "on the ground" in the clinical encounter and by empirical considerations about the populations to which Kerrie and Polly belong. The most we should expect of a philosophical analysis is that it might provide a framework within which such particular considerations can be taken into account.

But aside from these familiar general warnings, there is a further consideration that applies here. The main point that I have been trying to press is that antinomies like those of Kerrie and Polly are intrinsic to our current situation. No technical fix to the legislation – e.g., a better definition of "best interest" or an improved test for capacity – will make them go away. Indeed we can hypothesize that versions of Kerrie's and Polly's antinomies will arise in any jurisdiction which applies broadly liberal legal commitments in regulating the vocations of care. Accordingly, the last thing we should expect of our abstract Hegelian analysis is that it will show us that one side in the antinomial tension is the "right" one to endorse against the other. If the Hegelian analysis can nonetheless help orient our approach to the antinomies, it must be at a different level altogether, by providing a perspective from which we can acknowledge both thesis and antithesis, and by providing an orientation that can be put to work in navigating fields of practice that are characterized ineliminably by antinomial tension.

In approaching this task it is worth taking note of what we might think of as the *fractal* character of the antinomies that we have uncovered. Recall that in surveying the antinomial tensions we found a first instance in the tension between two competing statutes with overlapping jurisdictions: the MHA and the MCA. Looking more closely at the MCA, we found it to be organized around two leading concepts: the concept of capacity and the concept of best interests. Here again we found the ingredients for antinomy, insofar as the two leading concepts mapped onto different value structures and different perspectives on the patient. But then the antinomial tensions appeared again even within the narrower bounds of a best-interest assessment for a clearly incapacitous patient, as we found in the case of Polly's tracheostomy. Just as a fractal exhibits the same geometric pattern as one varies the scale, so in this domain of law and practice we find a systematic recurrence of a common antinomial structure at different layers within the overall body of mental health legislation. This suggests a strategy of analysis. Before tackling the individual antinomies by way of their legal and clinical particularities, we should consider first how we can manage the underlying tensions that are manifesting themselves in this fractal pattern where the law gets applied to hard cases.

If the antinomies that we have considered vary in their specifics, what they share is an underlying basic structure. This structure is best exhibited by focusing not so much on the *patients* involved but on the *care-givers* who find themselves confronted by those patients. For a care practitioner operating in a broadly liberal legal environment, the sphere of practice is fundamentally structured by two sets of impulses and two sets of duties. On the one hand there is an impulse of beneficence, and a corresponding duty to care for the patient in his or her best interest; on the other hand there is an impulse and a duty to respect the patient's autonomous decisions. While the legal and clinical particularities give different textures to the different cases, it is ultimately the potential for conflict between these two sets of impulses and duties that creates the potential for antinomy.

So what lessons can we apply from the Hegelian approach to these dialectical tensions? At one level, the lessons concern what we can broadly think of as *institutional design*. The antinomies we are considering do not manifest themselves in a vacuum, nor indeed can their significance be understood if we focus narrowly on the doctor-patient relationship as regulated by an abstract body of law. The circumstances of patients like Kerrie and Polly unfold within complex institutions populated by an array of diverse experts playing different roles in a common enterprise. Moreover, those institutions themselves exist in a broad social context in which families, civil society, and the State all play roles. The basic challenge for the Hegelian approach is to consider how this broader social (or *geistig*) context might be constituted so as to manage the contradictions that inevitably arise in particular cases. Is there some configuration of those institutions in which Kerrie and Polly found themselves that would be sufficiently robust as to allow their care-providers to do justice to *both* of their conflicting impulses and duties?

I cannot pretend to provide an adequate answer to this question here; my modest hope is that our articulation of what I have called Hegel's Eve Standard might provide a framework that can be used in tackling it. If our institutions of care can be designed in a way that meets the Eve Standard for particular patients, then there is an important sense in which both sides of the antinomial tension can be sustained. For where determination by an other takes the form of determination by a rightly recognized appropriate other, the opposed duties of care (for well-being) and respect (for autonomy) coincide.

This is a framework that we can apply more or less directly to the antinomy over Polly's tracheostomy. Here the care team has to make a best interest assessment on behalf of a plainly incapacitous patient, where authorization of the surgery creates the best available hope for Polly's survival and route to possible recovery, but would seem to involve acting contrary to what Polly herself would likely have chosen, and indeed in contravention of what the evidence suggests to be Polly's considered values and preferences. So what should the care team do? The Hegelian answer, if we can put the point rather paradoxically, is that they should take pause in order to *think about themselves*. How might *we*, as the decision-making body in this instance, so organize ourselves that we could be rightly recognized by Polly herself as an appropriate other, and hence could be experienced – if Polly herself were able to experience – as an Other whose determination is not an alien imposition? To some ears this may sound utopian, but it seems clear that this is an ideal that can be approximated to a greater or to a lesser extent. Consider the latter possibility first. Suppose that the medical team, in making their decision, considered only or primarily the statistical information about survival rates of patients in Polly's condition with or without a tracheostomy. Suppose that they reached their decision without meaningful consultation with Polly's family and without undertaking any serious inquiry to find out who Polly is and what she values. Suppose that Polly's family, when raising queries and objections about the propriety of Polly's treatment, were treated as "problem family members" and viewed as an obstruction to be managed rather than a source to be incorporated into the decision procedure. Suppose, finally, that the presiding consultant effectively takes the stance that there is no point in consultation with emotionally distraught people who know nothing of the medical factors that are decisive in the circumstances. Just to be clear: I do not mean here to allege that any of this actually happened in Polly's case. But if it had happened, then the Eve Standard would clearly not be met. Polly herself could never have recognized *this* community of decision as an appropriate other; she would rightly experience it as an alien other whose paternalistic intervention stripped her of all autonomy with respect to this critical medical intervention.

This may seem itself an odd way of expressing the point. After all, if Polly is already in a coma then has she not already lost all vestige of personal autonomy? My answer – if I may once again be allowed to court paradox – is "no". Polly may be unconscious but a pathway for respecting her autonomy remains open. For, suppose now that we replay the scene we have just rehearsed, but now play it out differently. Those who find themselves tasked with this decision now undertake to learn about Polly's values and preferences, and to consult with her family and friends. Suppose they now explicitly set out to constitute their Otherhood in such a way that Polly herself could have recognized it as her fitting Other, and *will* so recognize it retrospectively if indeed she emerges from her ordeal. Under such circumstances, I submit, Polly retains a significant form of autonomy even in her coma.

Here I must pause to consider a legal objection. It is common among jurists to distinguish between two opposed frameworks for best-interest decision-making. According to what is known as the "substituted standard", a best-interest decision is in effect an attempt to model the decision that the patient herself would have taken if she had been possessed of capacity at the material time when a decision has to be made. This is contrasted to an "objective" construal of the best-interest standard, which allows that patients are sometimes in error as to their own best interest.[17] It is easy to see that the two standards can diverge. A heroin addict who is lacking in capacity might well have opted for more heroin if he had been possessed of the capacity to make his own decision, but such a decision would not be in his best interest, objectively construed. Now in Polly's case, the governing legal authority is the MCA, which is commonly described as adopting an objective standard of best interests, rather than a substituted standard.[18] So it might be objected that the pathway I have just recommended contravenes the governing statute, to the extent that it allows itself to be decisively guided by what Polly herself *would* have decided, rather than by what is in fact in her best interest. To the extent that Polly's autonomy is respected, it is respected in contravention of law.

But the objection is based on a double mistake. There is a mistake, first, in adopting too stark an opposition between a substituted standard and an objective standard of best interests. For while it is true that current English law and judicial practice generally rejects a strictly substituted standard (which is often dismissed as "the American approach"), the "objective" standard of the MCA nonetheless incorporates a very strong degree of substituted reasoning in its prescribed procedure for determining objective best interest. Indeed the very first step in determining best interest is to undertake to discover what one can about the patient's own "values and preferences". The second mistake is to suppose that applying the Eve Standard will simply reproduce the outcome of the substituted standard. Polly's Others might end up making the decision that Polly herself would have made in the circumstances, but they will not always do so. An appropriate other will sometimes intervene in my life in order to override my current preferences in the service my own best interests. Such an intervention meets the Eve Standard insofar as I nonetheless can rightly recognize the intervening other as an appropriate other whose imposition is not in the end an imposition by an alien force.

Let's return, finally, to the hard case of Kerrie Wooltorton. Kerrie's Antinomy is not like Polly's in a number of important respects. Kerry's decision-making capacity is at least open to question, where Polly is obviously incapacitous. Kerrie is committing suicide, where Polly has been in an accident. Kerrie has a long and well-documented history of mental illness; Polly does not. But perhaps the most important difference is legal: Kerrie arguably falls under the jurisdiction of the MHA, a statute that places no particular value on the patient's autonomy, but is guided instead by the value of public health and public order. Can the approach we have taken with Polly's Antinomy also provide guidance in Kerrie's fundamentally different situation? I think that it can, at least to an extent. The reason for this comes back once again to the

---

[17]   See e.g., *Airedale NHS Trust v Bland* [1993] AC 789.
[18]   See e.g., *Re P* [2009] EWHC 163.

fundamental commonality that comes into view when we consider the basic structure *from the care-giver's perspective*. Despite the differences in the governing legal provisions, and despite the many important differences in the particular circumstances of the patients, the circumstance of the care-giver once again is structured by the now-familiar antinomial tensions: an impulse and duty to protect a vulnerable individual as against an impulse and duty to respect an autonomous person.

It is striking the extent to which the very considerable attention that has been paid to Kerrie's case has tended to focus on one of two sets of questions: questions about the details of Kerrie's medical history and condition, or questions about the provisions of the legal statute. In one way this may seem obvious: surely the problem here is to understand how the formal and abstract provisions of law apply to the concrete particularities of an individual patient. But if the analysis that I have offered here is correct, this focus has missed a crucial factor. If we are members of Kerrie's care team then we must not simply think about Kerrie and about the law; we must also think about ourselves. We should ask ourselves whether and how we can constitute ourselves as the sort of collective Other that meets the Eve Standard, such that when it comes to the point that we determine what happens with Kerrie's life, it is possible for Kerrie to recognize us as an other whose alien character has been overcome.

In applying this schema to Kerrie's Antinomy, however, we have to think differently about the scope and scale of the relevant Otherhood. In Polly's case it seems clear that family members form a core part of the relevant community of others. But if Kerrie's relationships with her family are fraught, or if indeed she is profoundly alienated from them, then their inclusion in the community of decision might well increase Kerrie's alienation from those who find themselves with the task of determining her fate. On the other hand, Kerrie's social worker, who can help the accident and emergency team understand the context and history of Kerrie's self-harming behaviour, might well play a critical role in coming closer to an arrangement that could satisfy the Eve Standard.

But all this might well seem to leave the main question unaddressed. After all, we began by providing an analysis of Kerrie's situation in terms of an antinomy of conflicting legal obligations. It is hard to see how restructuring the community of others at the hospital is of itself going to eliminate that antinomy, or tell us which of the two obligations to privilege. Make the Otherhood as Eve-ish as you want. At the end of the day Kerrie either receives the dialysis or she does not. In order to meet this objection, I suspect that we may have to undertake a massive shift in the scale of our account. Certainly this would be Hegel's own strategy. The community of others who are determining Kerrie's fate does not just comprise the hospital workers, or the hospital workers and their families, or the workers and the family and the social worker and the hospital's legal counsel. Ultimately it comes to comprise the whole relevant apparatus of civil society and the State as well. It implicates the legislators who adopted the relevant statutes and the judges who apply them and the Research Councils that provide funds for workshops to reflect about the dilemmas that ensue. The task Hegel sets himself in the *Philosophy of Right* is to describe a whole society that satisfies the Eve Standard.

I shall not here try to describe Hegel's solution to this large-scale problem. But it does seem to me that, for us, one element of the solution might be for such a society to adopt a range of overlapping and partly competing statutory arrangements that are applicable to a case like Kerrie's and are available to care-workers to deploy in the exercise of their vocation. If Kerrie finds herself in such a society, and if her local of decision community is constituted such that a choice among those statutory provisions is undertaken in a way that is itself guided by the Eve Standard, then Kerrie's Antinomy can be navigated – not in a way that avoids tragedy, but in way that satisfies both of the impulses and duties from which it ultimately arose.[19]

References

Armstrong, William (2009): *Inquest into the Death of Kerrie Wooltorton – Narrative Verdict* (HM Coroner Greater Norfolk District).

Bashir, Fareed and Crawford, Mike (2009): "Autonomy or life-saving treating for the mentally vulnerable?", in: *British Medical Journal*, 339, p. 988.

BBC Radio 4 (2010): "Mentally Ill and Refusing Surgery", *Inside the Ethics Committee*, Series 6, Episode 1 (London BBC/OU Co-Productions); originally broadcast 20 July, 2010. Transcript and recording downloaded from <http://www.bbc.co.uk/programmes/b00t1xsz> (August 1, 2010).

Hegel, G.W.F. (1970): *Werke*, ed. E. Moldenhauer and K.M. Michel, Frankfurt a. M. [= HW].

– *Enzyklopädie der philosophischen Wissenschaften* III: in HW, vols. 8–10 [= Enz].

– *Grundlinien der Philosophie des Rechts* in: HW, vol 7 [= PR].

Hegel, G.W.F. (1971): *Philosophy of Mind*, tr. W. Wallace, Oxford.

Hegel, G.W.F. (1975): *Logic*, tr. W. Wallace, Oxford.

---

[19]   This paper is dedicated to Polly and her Otherhood. Thanks are due to the Research Team of the Essex Autonomy Project (Fabian Freyenhagen, Tom O'Shea, Viv Ashley, Antal Szerletics and Rebecca Parsons), and to Gareth Owen, Keith Cooper, Beatrice Han-Pile, and Ryan Hickerson. Earlier versions of this paper were presented to workshops and conferences sponsored by the Wellcome Trust (*Coma, Consciousness and Brain Injury*), The Essex Centre for Psychoanalytic Studies (*Dependence, Independence, Interdependence*) and the Essex Autonomy Project (*Paternalism and Coercion*). I am grateful for the comments of participants at these events. Support for the research presented here was provided by the Arts and Humanities Research Council of Great Britain (AH/H001301/1: *Deciding for Oneself: Autonomous Judgement in History, Theory and Practice*).

Kant, Immanuel (1902 ff.): *Kritik der reinen Vernunft*, in: *Gesammelte Schriften Bde. III & IV*, ed. Königlich Preussische Akademie der Wissenschaften, Berlin [= KrV].

Martin, Wayne and Hickerson, Ryan (forthcoming): "Mental Capacity and the Applied Phenomenology of Judgement", in: *Phenomenology and the Cognitive Sciences*.

Strawson, Peter (1962): "Freedom and Resentment", in: *Proceedings of the British Academy*, 48, pp. 1–25.

Szmukler, George et al. (2010): "A Model Law Fusing Incapacity and Mental Health Legislation", in: *Journal of Mental Health Law*, 20, pp. 11–24.

Franz Knappik

Idealismus als Metaphysik der Freiheit: Hegel und Brandom

What is the metaphysical import of Hegel's views about freedom? The paper discusses a possible answer to this question that emerges from Robert Brandom's reading of Hegel. For Brandom, Hegel's idealism, and in particular his view that reality has a modally robust conceptual structure, accounts for the possibility of our thought being rationally, rather than just causally, constrained by reality. This constraint, in turn, is a necessary precondition of rational freedom. I argue that while the structure of this "rational constraint argument" does indeed apture an important aspect of Hegel's position, both its premises and its conclusions ought to be given a stronger reading than is suggested by Brandom. In particular, I contend that Hegel's views about the conceptual structure of reality amount to a full-blown realism about concepts, and that, for Hegel, our capacity to provide satisfactory explanations of experienced phenomena is a crucial element of freedom and rational constraint.

Ein wichtiges gemeinsames Anliegen Fichtes, Schellings und Hegels besteht darin, eine philosophische Position zu entwickeln, die den Begriff der Freiheit zu *dem* Schlüsselbegriff der Philosophie überhaupt macht. Im selben Jahr, 1795, in dem Fichte die Wissenschaftslehre als erstes „System der Freiheit" charakterisiert,[1] schreibt Schelling an Hegel, die Freiheit sei das „A und O aller Philosophie".[2] Hegel stimmt dem schon in seinem Antwortschreiben zu;[3] sein späteres enzyklopädisches System löst diesen Gedanken buchstäblich ein: Es beginnt mit der Untersuchung der „Gesetze, die [das Denken] sich selbst gibt, nicht schon *hat* und in sich vorfindet" (Enz. § 19 A), in der *Wissenschaft der Logik*, und es endet mit der Theorie des in vollkommener Weise freien „absoluten Geistes" in Kunst, Religion und Philosophie. Entsprechend erklärt Hegel, die „Aufgabe der Philosophie" sei „so lange nicht wahrhaft und immanent gelöst", als „die Freiheit nicht ihr Gegenstand und ihre Seele ist" (Enz. § 384 A).

Nun würde man von einer philosophischen Position, die dem Freiheitsbegriff eine zentrale Rolle zuweist, nicht zuletzt erwarten, dass sie eine detaillierte Theorie der metaphysischen Voraussetzungen von Freiheit bietet – dass sie also erklärt, wie die Welt beschaffen sein muss, damit es in ihr freie Wesen

---

[1]   Entwurf eines Briefs an Baggesen, in: *Briefe 1793–1795*, GA III, 2, S. 298.
[2]   Schelling an Hegel, 4.2.1795, in: *Briefe von und an Hegel*, Bd. 1, S. 22.
[3]   Hegel an Schelling, 16.4.1795, in: *Briefe von und an Hegel*, Bd. 1, S. 24.

geben kann. Für eine solche Klärung der metaphysischen Voraussetzungen von
Freiheit gibt die philosophische Tradition eine Reihe wichtiger Fragen vor: Wie
können Mentales und Physikalisches kausal interagieren? Sind Freiheit und
Determinismus miteinander vereinbar? Wenn ja, wie kann diese Vereinbarkeit
genauer erklärt werden? Wenn nein, ist Freiheit dennoch möglich – und wie?
Eine gründliche Behandlung dieser und verwandter Fragen dürfen wir von den
idealistischen Ansätzen zu einem „System der Freiheit" erst recht deshalb
erwarten, weil sie sowohl in Kants kritischer Philosophie als auch in der von
Jacobi initiierten Debatte über die Philosophie Spinozas – und somit in den beiden wichtigsten philosophischen Quellen für die Entstehung des Deutschen
Idealismus – eine zentrale Rolle spielen.[4]

Umso verwunderlicher ist es, dass bei Hegel die genannten Fragen zur
Metaphysik von Freiheit kaum jemals behandelt werden. Wenn Hegel denn einmal auf derartige Probleme zu sprechen kommt, dann tut er sie gewöhnlich als
belanglos ab – etwa, wenn er in seiner Erörterung des „freien Willens" in der
Einleitung zu den *Grundlinien der Philosophie des Rechts* beiläufig feststellt:
„In dem zur Zeit der *Wolffischen* Metaphysik vornehmlich geführten Streit, ob
der Wille wirklich frei oder ob das Wissen von seiner Freiheit nur eine Täuschung sei, war es die Willkür, die man vor Augen gehabt" (GPhR § 15 A).[5]
Gerade Hegel müsste es aber besser wissen – er müsste wissen, dass das Problem der Willensfreiheit vor ihm nicht nur zur Zeit der Schulmetaphysik, son-
dern zu fast allen Zeiten in der Philosophiegeschichte diskutiert und dass dabei
keineswegs Freiheit immer von vornherein auf bloße Willkür reduziert wurde. –
Gleichwohl scheint Hegel die Diskussion des Freiheitsbegriffs nicht etwa völlig
von metaphysischen Fragen entkoppeln zu wollen. Vielmehr gebraucht er den
Freiheitsbegriff häufig in Kontexten, in denen es um grundlegende ontologische
Strukturen der Wirklichkeit überhaupt geht. Insbesondere kennzeichnet er das
Kategoriensystem der „Logik des Begriffs", das geeignet sein soll, die Struktur
der Wirklichkeit als ganzer zu erfassen, als „Reich der Freiheit" (WdL, TW 6,
S. 238).[6] Dies legt nahe, dass Hegel zwar sehr wohl eine Theorie der metaphysi-

---

[4]   Vgl. hierzu u. a. Peetz, 1995, Teil II; di Giovanni, 2005, Kap. 4.

[5]   Vgl. daneben z.B. auch Enz. § 503 A; Enz. § 145 Z; s. dazu Pippin, 2008, S. 36 ff. –
   Nach der Deutung von Yeomans, 2012, Kap. 1 und passim, nimmt Hegel das klassische Problem der Willensfreiheit sehr wohl ernst und stellt es sogar in den Mittel
   „Selbstbestimmung" usw. in der *Logik* so direkt, wie Yeomans es tut, auf die Frage der
   Willensfreiheit bezogen werden können, weil die *Logik* ausdrücklich die Grundstruktur der *ganzen* Wirklichkeit zum Thema hat (z.B. WdL, TW 5, S. 61). Außerdem wird
   bei Yeomans die Möglichkeit von Wahlfreiheit zum zentralen Adäquatheitsmaßstab
   für die logischen Kategorien, was in direktem Widerspruch zu Hegels wichtigster
   methodologischer Kennzeichnung der *Logik* steht – nämlich der „Immanenz" ihrer
   gedanklichen Entwicklung, die keinen äußeren Maßstab zulässt (z.B. Enz. § 78 mit
   Anm., § 81 A).

[6]   Vgl. Enz. §§ 158, 159 A.

schen Implikationen von Freiheit formulieren will, dabei aber eine ganz andere Untersuchungsperspektive verfolgt, als sie sonst in diesem Bereich gängig ist. Es ist freilich alles andere als klar, wie diese alternative Perspektive genauer zu verstehen ist.

In diesem Beitrag beschäftige ich mich mit einer Interpretation von Hegels Theorie der metaphysischen Voraussetzungen von Freiheit, die in der jüngeren amerikanischen Hegel-Rezeption von John McDowell und Robert Brandom vorgeschlagen wurde. McDowells und Brandoms Deutungen relevanter Punkte bei Hegel können in Form eines Arguments zusammengefasst werden, das ich als *„rational constraint"*-Argument bezeichnen werde.[7] Diesem Argument zufolge besteht eine notwendige Bedingung für die Möglichkeit rationaler Freiheit darin, dass wir in unserer rationalen Tätigkeit nicht völlig ungebunden und willkürlich agieren, sondern uns an objektiven Gründen ausrichten – dass also die Wirklichkeit unser Denken *rational* (und nicht nur kausal) einschränkt. Eine solche rationale Einschränkung („rational constraint") ist aber nur möglich, so besagt das Argument weiter, wenn die Wirklichkeit bestimmte metaphysische Eigenschaften aufweist – wenn nämlich eine *ontologische Homogeneität* zwischen Geist und Welt besteht und die Wirklichkeit nicht jenseits, sondern *innerhalb* der Sphäre dessen lokalisiert ist, was *begrifflich strukturiert* ist. Die Thesen von der ontologischen Homogeneität zwischen Geist und Welt und der begrifflichen Strukturiertheit der Wirklichkeit machen für Brandom und McDowell Hegels *Idealismus* (oder zumindest einen wichtigen Teil davon) aus. Wenn diese Interpretation zutrifft, dann nimmt Hegel tatsächlich eine ganz andere Perspektive auf die Frage nach den metaphysischen Voraussetzungen von Freiheit ein, als es die gängigen Diskussionen über Willensfreiheit usw. tun: Um die Möglichkeit von Freiheit zu erklären, müssen wir demzufolge in erster Linie fragen, wie die Wirklichkeit beschaffen sein muss, um einen Maßstab für unsere *rationale Orientierung* zu bieten – und nicht, wie sie beschaffen sein muss, um unserer *kausalen Kontrolle* offenzustehen.

Während McDowell auf Grund seines quietistischen Philosophie-Verständnisses die Konklusionen des Arguments als triviale Aussagen deutet,[8] schreibt Brandom Hegel nicht-triviale metaphysische Thesen zu.[9] Im Folgenden werde ich mich daher auf Brandoms Interpretation konzentrieren und zum einen seine

---

[7] Zum Folgenden vgl. McDowell, 1996, S. 5 ff., S. 25 ff., S. 43 f.; zu Brandoms Version s. unten § 1.

[8] McDowell, 1996, S. 27. – Dass McDowell dennoch in diesem Zusammenhang Behauptungen aufstellt, die keineswegs unproblematisch sind, zeigt Willaschek, 2000.

[9] Auch Brandoms Position einschließlich seiner Hegel-Aneignung wird oft als rein semantische und pragmatische Analyse unserer sprachlichen Praktiken verstanden, die ohne metaphysische Festlegungen auskommen will; vgl. z. B. Kruck, 2003; Sans, 2004, S. 16 f., S. 226 ff., und Schnädelbach, 2004. Die metaphysische Dimension von Brandoms Position wird dagegen zu Recht von Habermas, 1999 hervorgehoben.

Deutung des Zusammenhangs von Idealismus und Freiheit bei Hegel diskutieren, zum anderen eine alternative Interpretation vorschlagen, die zwar in wichtigen Punkten an Brandom anknüpft, aber hinsichtlich der Hegel zugeschriebenen metaphysischen Festlegungen und des Freiheitsbegriffs wesentlich über sie hinausgeht: Hegel vertritt nach meiner Interpretation einen substantiellen metaphysischen Begriffsrealismus, demzufolge objektive Begriffe Erklärungsprinzipien der Einzelgegenstände sind, die sie instantiieren; dies steht in direktem Zusammenhang damit, dass für Hegel die Fähigkeit, Phänomene zu erklären und zu begreifen, ein zentrales Element rationaler Freiheit ist. – Ich gehe in vier Schritten vor: Zunächst rekonstruiere ich Brandoms Version des „rational constraint"-Arguments (§ 1), bespreche Einwände und führe Textevidenz bei Hegel an, die die Zuschreibung eines derartigen Arguments stützt (§ 2). Daran schließt sich eine kritische Diskussion von Brandoms Deutung des hegelschen Idealismus an, zu der ich eine Alternative präsentiere (§ 3). Hieraus ergibt sich auch eine andere Version des „rational constraint"-Arguments, die ihrerseits auf einem anderen Verständnis von Freiheit beruht (§ 4).

I. Brandom über Freiheit und Idealismus: Das „rational constraint"-Argument

In diesem Abschnitt präsentiere ich eine Version des „rational constraint"-Arguments, die zentrale Punkte von Brandoms Hegel-Deutung zusammenfasst. (Die Kritikpunkte, die ich in §§ 2 und 3 anführe, hängen nicht von dieser bestimmten Weise der Präsentation ab.)

1. Freiheit bei Kant und Hegel

Brandom deutet Hegels Freiheitsbegriff als eine Weiterentwicklung der kantischen Autonomiekonzeption von Freiheit. Den Grundgedanken kantischer Autonomie, an dem Hegel aus Brandoms Sicht festhält, charakterisiert er folgendermaßen:

> The difference between non-normative *compulsion* and normative *authority* is that we are genuinely *normatively* responsible only to what we *acknowledge as* authoritative. In this sense, only we can bind ourselves, in the sense that we are only *normatively* bound by the results of exercises of our freedom: (self-constitutive) *self-bindings,* commitments we have undertaken by acknowledging them (Brandom, 2009, S. 62 f.).

Gemäß der so verstandenen kantischen Position besteht ein konstitutiver Zusammenhang zwischen Freiheit, Selbst und rationalen Normen: Um frei zu sein, müssen wir uns an rationalen Normen ausrichten, ihnen also Autorität über unser Verhalten einräumen; durch diese Ausrichtung an Normen konstituieren wir ein Selbst mit konkreten theoretischen und praktischen Festlegungen (Überzeugungen, Absichten usw.).

Hierbei handelt es sich bereits um eine stark an Hegel angelehnte Interpretation von Kants Autonomiebegriff. Erstens klammert Brandom nämlich in seiner Wiedergabe den für Kant zentralen Gedanken aus, dass wir nur dann wirklich selbstbestimmt sind, wenn wir uns nicht einfach *irgendwelche* Normen auferlegen, sondern uns in der Wahl unserer Maximen – und damit in der Konstitution unseres praktischen Selbst – nach dem Sittengesetz richten. Nur dann gilt, dass wir nicht von externen Faktoren bestimmt werden, sondern wir uns selbst – kraft unserer Vernunftnatur – das Gesetz *sind*.[10] Für Hegel dagegen ist – wie für Brandom – die Ausrichtung am moralischen Gesetz *kein* Teil der Definition von Freiheit. (Das liegt allerdings nicht daran, dass es für Hegel gar keine normative Einschränkung unserer Selbstgesetzgebung gibt, sondern vielmehr daran, dass für Hegel Freiheit auf differenziertere und konkretere normative Vorgaben angewiesen ist, als sie das kantische Sittengesetz bereitstellt. Wir werden auf diesen Punkt, den Brandom in seiner Interpretation zu Unrecht vernachlässigt, in § 4 zurückkommen.)

Zweitens ist für Kant Autonomie das spezifische Kennzeichen der *praktischen* Vernunft.[11] Für Hegel dagegen sind *alle* Ausprägungen des Geistes Formen von Freiheit – der Geist *ist* nichts anderes als die „Bewegung selbst, von der Natur sich zu befreien" (*Fragment*, TW 11, S. 258). So schreibt Hegel insbesondere auch *epistemischen* Vermögen Formen von Freiheit zu. Dem schließt sich Brandom an, indem er die im obigen Zitat beschriebene Selbstbindung durch Normen als notwendige Bedingung *jeglicher* Rationalität auffasst.[12] Die Annahme, dass es auch epistemische Formen von Freiheit gibt, ist für unsere Thematik besonders wichtig: Denn der Gedanke einer für Freiheit erforderlichen rationalen Einschränkung unseres Denkens durch die Wirklichkeit, auf dem das „rational constraint"-Argument beruht, bezieht sich, wie wir gleich genauer

---

[10] So Kant in GMS, AA 4, S. 446 f. im Anschluss an Röm 2:14: „[W]as kann denn wohl die Freiheit des Willens sonst sein als Autonomie, d.i. die Eigenschaft des Willens, sich selbst ein Gesetz zu sein?".

[11] Auch Kant experimentiert an manchen Stellen mit einer Anwendung des Autonomie-Begriffs auf theoretische Kontexte, z.B. *Orientierung*, AA 8, S. 144 ff.; KU, AA 5, S. 294 f. Dabei geht es ihm aber offenbar – anders als im praktischen Bereich – nicht um eine konstitutive Bedingung für Rationalität, sondern nur um den „zweckmäßigen Gebrauch" (KU, AA 5, S. 295, Z. 7) unserer Vernunft. – Ferner behauptet Kant mehrfach, dass theoretische Vernunft transzendentale Freiheit erfordert (z.B. *Schulz-Rezension*, AA 8, S. 14). Es ist aber umstritten, ob dies die „offizielle" Position des kritischen Kant ist bzw. sein darf: vgl. u.a. Rosefeldt, 2000, Kap. 7; Düsing, 2002; Willaschek, 2010.

[12] Vgl. Brandom, 2009, S. 68 Fn. 4.

sehen werden, primär darauf, dass die Wirklichkeit den *Wahrheits*maßstab und die Quelle von *Gründen* für unsere *Überzeugungen* bildet.[13]

Für Brandom krankt nun Kants Freiheitsverständnis an einem wesentlichen Defizit, das Hegel in seiner Weiterentwicklung der kantischen Konzeption überwindet: Kant setzt nämlich voraus, dass es überhaupt Normen mit *bestimmtem begrifflichem Gehalt* gibt, an denen wir uns ausrichten können.[14] Dabei handelt es sich nach Brandom um eine dogmatische Annahme, an deren Stelle Hegel eine angemessenere *semantische* und *pragmatische* Theorie begrifflichen Gehalts setzt. – Die *semantische* Theorie der Struktur begrifflichen Gehalts, die Brandom Hegel zuschreibt, beruht auf dem Gedanken, dass das Kennzeichen begrifflichen Gehalts seine Artikulation durch Relationen materialer Inkompatibilität ist. Materiale Inkompatibilität besteht zwischen zwei Aussagen dann, wenn wir sie aufgrund der Bedeutung der in ihnen enthaltenen nicht-logischen Begriffe (also nicht lediglich auf Grund eines formalen Widerspruchs zwischen beiden Aussagen) nicht zugleich vertreten dürfen. Beispielsweise ist die Aussage „Dieser Gegenstand schmilzt bei 30° C" material inkompatibel mit der Aussage „Dieser Gegenstand ist aus Kupfer" (sofern beide auf denselben Gegenstand bezogen werden). Auf der Grundlage der Beziehung materialer Inkompatibilität lassen sich inferentielle Beziehungen definieren, wie sie die Grundlage der inferentialistischen Semantik in Brandoms Hauptwerk *Making it explicit* bilden: Die materiale Inferenz von p auf q ist genau dann zulässig, wenn alle Aussagen, die mit q inkompatibel sind, auch mit p inkompatibel sind.[15]

In seiner Rekonstruktion von Hegels *Pragmatik* der Selbstbestimmung durch begriffliche Normen vertritt Brandom hingegen die Auffassung, dass die Konstitution eines Selbst im Umgang mit begrifflichen Normen nur im Rahmen einer geteilten sozialen Praxis möglich ist, in der durch intersubjektive Anerkennungsprozesse begrifflicher Gehalt bestimmt wird. Frei sind wir in einer solchen Praxis dann, wenn unsere gegenseitigen Zuweisungen von Autorität und Verantwortung symmetrisch balanciert sind.[16] Hierfür sind neben synchronen auch diachrone Anerkennungsverhältnisse erforderlich; insbesondere müssen wir die Akteure vergangener Begriffsanwendungen anerkennen, indem wir retrospektiv eine rationale Rekonstruktion ihrer Begriffsanwendung formulieren. Dabei müssen wir die frühere Begriffsanwendung als Teil einer Entwicklung begreifen, die zum gegenwärtigen Stand des Begriffs- und Überzeugungssystems führt und damit einen Prozess der Bestimmung begrifflichen Gehalts bildet.[17]

---

[13] Weder Hegel noch Brandom interpretieren dabei epistemische Freiheit im Sinne eines problematischen doxastischen Voluntarismus; vielmehr entkoppeln beide Freiheit von Wille und Wahl. (Vgl. Brandom, 1994, S. 714 Fn. 18.)

[14] Vgl. Brandom, 2009, S. 66 f.

[15] Brandom, 2008 a, S. 121.

[16] Vgl. Brandom, 2009, S. 66 ff.

[17] Vgl. Brandom, 2002 b, S. 230 ff.; Brandom, 2009, S. 81 ff. Brandoms bevorzugtes Modell sind case-law-Systeme: In ihnen wird der Gehalt legaler Normen sukzessive

2. „Rational constraint"

Neben den wechselseitigen Einstellungen von Subjekten zueinander, in denen diese ihr Verhalten gegenseitig an Normen messen, müssen wir in diskursiven Praktiken auch der *Wirklichkeit* eine normative Rolle zuweisen, und zwar in zweifacher Weise: Erstens machen wir sie zum Maßstab und damit zur definitiven *Autorität* für die Wahrheit und Falschheit unserer Überzeugungen, denn in unseren Überzeugungen richten wir uns danach, wie die Wirklichkeit beschaffen ist.[18] Und zweitens zitieren wir Tatsachen als *Gründe* für unsere Überzeugungen und die auf ihnen basierenden Handlungen. In beiderlei Hinsicht müssen wir annehmen, dass die Wirklichkeit unser Überzeugungssystem rational und nicht nur kausal einschränkt.[19]

Damit etwas unsere Überzeugungen rational einschränken kann, muss es aber, so folgert Brandom weiter, selbst bestimmte ontologische Eigenschaften besitzen:

> [W]hat is represented must be intelligible as providing *reasons* for assessments of correctness and incorrectness of appearances or representings. [...] Giving reasons for undertaking a commitment [...] is endorsing a sample piece of reasoning, an inference, in which the premises provide good reasons for the commitment. It is to exhibit premises the endorsement of which entitles one to the conclusion. So the reasons, no less than what they are reasons for, must be conceptually articulated (Brandom, unveröffentlicht a, S. 11).

Damit die Wirklichkeit unser Denken im erläuterten Sinn rational einschränken kann – als Maßstab für die Wahrheit und als Quelle für die Rechtfertigung unserer Überzeugungen –, muss sie demnach selbst *begrifflich strukturiert* sein. Nur dann können wir nämlich Bestandteile der Wirklichkeit als Gründe für unsere Behauptungen zitieren: Denn als Grund können wir nur anführen, was der Inhalt einer Prämisse in einer Inferenz sein kann. (Das ist der zentrale Schritt im Argument, und er ist keineswegs unproblematisch; ich werde im nächsten Abschnitt hierauf zurückkommen.)

3. Begriffsrealismus und Idealismus

Was es bedeutet, begrifflich strukturiert zu sein, erklärt uns die oben zusammengefasste semantische Theorie begrifflichen Gehalts: Etwas ist demnach genau dann begrifflich strukturiert, wenn es durch Relationen des gegenseitigen Ausschlusses von miteinander material inkompatiblen Inhalten und, darauf auf-

---

durch Entscheidungen bestimmt, die durch Bezug auf als rational rekonstruierte Präzedenzfälle begründet werden. Für Diskussion vgl. Knappik, i. Ersch., Kap. 3.1.

[18] Brandom, 2009, S. 95.

[19] Brandom, unveröffentlicht a, S. 9. Vgl. Brandom, 2000, S. 163 ff.

bauend, durch materiale Implikationsbeziehungen artikuliert ist. „Begriffliche Struktur" in diesem Sinne ist etwas, das nicht nur den Inhalten unserer Überzeugungen, Behauptungen usw. zukommen kann, sondern das wir sinnvoll auch der objektiven Wirklichkeit zuschreiben können: Denn auch von Sachverhalten können wir sagen, dass sie einander ausschließen, einander implizieren usw.

Die These, dass die Wirklichkeit in diesem Sinne begrifflich strukturiert ist, bezeichnet Brandom als die These des „Begriffsrealismus":

(Begriffsrealismus) Die Wirklichkeit ist begrifflich strukturiert.[20]

Demnach sind Begriffe nicht nur psychologische oder linguistische Entitäten, die unser Denken und Sprechen artikulieren; vielmehr ist auch die von uns unabhängige Wirklichkeit durch Begriffe strukturiert. Nur wenn die These des Begriffsrealismus wahr ist – so Brandoms Version des „rational constraint"-Arguments –, kann die Wirklichkeit einen Wahrheitsmaßstab und eine Gründe-Quelle für unsere Überzeugungen bilden. Eine Wirklichkeit dagegen, die von der Sphäre subjektiven Begriffsgebrauchs ontologisch radikal geschieden ist, weil sie selbst nicht durch begriffliche Relationen artikuliert ist – wie in Brandoms Interpretation Kants Transzendentaler Idealismus –,[21] kann unser Denken nicht rational einschränken.

Brandom sieht in der These des Begriffsrealismus ein zentrales Element von Hegels Idealismus. Dies ist dann gerechtfertigt, wenn die folgende Definition von „Idealismus" angenommen wird:

(Idealismus) Alles, was es gibt, ist entweder selbst geistig oder von etwas Geistigem abhängig, und der Begriff der Abhängigkeit so weit gefasst wird, dass eine *semantische* Abhängigkeit ausreichend ist: Die vom Begriffsrealismus angenommene objektive begriffliche Struktur ist insofern von etwas Geistigem abhängig, als man den Begriff „begriffliche Struktur" nicht verstehen kann, wenn man nicht Begriffe aus dem Bereich des Geistigen (z. B. „Behauptung") versteht.[22]

---

[20]   Vgl. Brandom, 2002 a, S. 181; Brandom, 2009, S. 97 f.; Brandom, unveröffentlicht a, S. 16; Brandom, unveröffentlicht b, S. 29 f.

[21]   Vgl. Brandom, unveröffentlicht a, S. 7.

[22]   Vgl. Brandom, 2002 a, S. 194–196. (Brandoms Begriff für semantische Abhängigkeit ist „sense dependence"; die resultierende idealistische These bezeichnet er als „objektiven Idealismus".) – Die Hegel außerdem noch von Brandom zugeschriebene These des „Begriffsidealismus" („conceptual idealism"), nach der die Wechselbeziehung zwischen objektiven und subjektiven begrifflichen Strukturen in einem sozialen Prozess erzeugt wird (Brandom 2002 a, S. 385, Fn. 48, mit Verweis auf Brandom 2002 b), klammern wir für unsere Diskussion aus, weil sie die pragmatischen, nicht die metaphysischen Voraussetzungen für die Möglichkeit bestimmten begrifflichen Gehalts betrifft.

(Auf die Frage, inwieweit Hegel nicht auch Idealist in dem sehr viel stärkeren Sinn ist, der sich ergibt, wenn in der obigen Definition von „Idealismus" der Begriff der Abhängigkeit in einem ontologischen Sinn gelesen wird, werden wir in § 3 kurz zurückkommen.)

4. Modaler Realismus

Ein wesentliches Kennzeichen der objektiven begrifflichen Strukturen, die Brandom zufolge der hegelsche Begriffsrealismus annimmt, besteht darin, dass sie *modal robust* sind. Dies bedeutet, dass die objektiven begrifflichen Relationen, um die es hier geht, ein hohes Maß an Invarianz unter kontrafaktischen Umständen aufweisen. Dass z. B. der Sachverhalt „Die Flüssigkeit *x* ist Wasser" mit dem Sachverhalt „Die Flüssigkeit *x* ist undurchsichtig" inkompatibel ist, bedeutet nicht nur, dass sie de facto nicht gleichzeitig bestehen, sondern auch, dass sie unter allen anderen möglichen Umständen nicht zugleich bestehen würden, sofern dieselben Naturgesetze herrschen und relevante Ausschlussbedingungen nicht gegeben sind. Die Tatsachen bestehen in diesem Fall also nicht nur faktisch nicht zusammen, sie *können* nicht zusammen bestehen – materiale Inkompatibilität auf der Seite objektiver Tatsachen besteht in Inkompossibilität. Entsprechend sind auch Beziehungen der Implikation modal robust: Wenn der Sachverhalt A den Sachverhalt B material impliziert, bedeutet das nicht nur, dass de facto nicht A ohne B besteht – es bedeutet, dass B bestehen *muss*, wenn A besteht, dass also auch unter hinreichend vielen kontrafaktischen Umständen A nicht ohne B besteht. Materiale Implikation auf der Seite objektiver Tatsachen besteht also in *Nezessitation*.

Aus dieser Präzisierung des Begriffsrealismus folgt, dass es modale Sachverhalte gibt, die objektive Realität haben. Diese These bezeichnet Brandom als „modalen Realismus":[23]

(Modaler Realismus) Es gibt modale Sachverhalte.

In Brandoms Version besagt das „rational constraint"-Argument also, dass Freiheit als Autonomie nur unter der Voraussetzung möglich ist, dass die Wirklichkeit als Wahrheitsmaßstab und als Quelle für Gründe für unsere Überzeu-

---

[23] Vgl. Brandom, 2002 a, S. 181; Brandom, 2009, S. 98; Brandom, unveröffentlicht a, S. 16; Brandom, unveröffentlicht b, S. 21 ff. – Der modale Realismus in Brandoms Sinn ist von der viel spezifischeren Position zu unterscheiden, die David Lewis unter diesem Namen bekannt gemacht hat (es gibt mögliche Welten; diese sind maximale mereologische Summen aus raumzeitlich verbundenen Gegenständen; vgl. Lewis, 1986, S. 69 f.). Aus Brandoms modalem Realismus folgt weder, dass es mögliche Welten gibt, noch, dass sich modale auf nicht-modale Sachverhalte reduzieren lassen, wie Lewis meint (Lewis, 1986, S. 5 ff., Kap. 3). Vgl. unten § 3.

gungen dienen kann, und dass dies wiederum nur unter der Annahme von
Hegels Idealismus möglich ist, der insbesondere den Begriffsrealismus und den
modalen Realismus umfasst. – Den metaphysischen Gehalt von modalem Realismus und Begriffsrealismus in Brandoms Rekonstruktion werden wir in § 3
untersuchen. Zunächst betrachten wir das „rational constraint"-Argument in
sachlicher und exegetischer Hinsicht noch genauer.

II. Das „rational constraint"-Argument: Diskussion und Textevidenz

In diesem Abschnitt bespreche ich zwei Einwände gegen das eben präsentierte
Argument und führe anschließend Textevidenz dafür an, dass Hegel tatsächlich
Versionen der Aussagen vertritt, die Brandom ihm zuschreibt.

1. Ontologie von Gründen

Ein erster Einwand gegen das „rational constraint"-Argument richtet sich gegen die Behauptung, die Wirklichkeit müsse begrifflich strukturiert sein, weil
sie uns andernfalls keine Gründe für unsere Überzeugungen bieten könnte.
Betrachten wir der Einfachheit halber nur epistemische Gründe für Überzeugungen, die die nicht-mentale Wirklichkeit betreffen. Dann können wir das folgende Dilemma formulieren. Entweder sind alle Gründe Teil der nicht-mentalen Wirklichkeit, auf die sich unsere Überzeugungen beziehen, oder dem ist
nicht so. Wenn etwas ein Grund für eine Überzeugung über die nicht-mentale
Wirklichkeit sein kann, ohne selbst Teil dieser Wirklichkeit zu sein, dann folgt
aus der Natur unserer Gründe nichts über die ontologische Struktur der Welt.
Dies ist insbesondere dann der Fall, wenn Gründe – gemäß einer wichtigen
Position in der Debatte über die Ontologie von Gründen – mentale Zustände
sind, hier: Überzeugungen.[24] Also kann das „rational constraint"-Argument
nur gültig sein, wenn etwas Teil der nicht-mentalen Wirklichkeit (z. B. eine Tatsache) sein muss, um ein Grund für Überzeugungen über diese Wirklichkeit
sein zu können. In diesem Fall würde Brandom aber ohne weiteres Argument
eine bestimmte kontroverse Auffassung der Ontologie von Gründen voraussetzen. In beiden Fällen ist das „rational constraint"-Argument also für sich
genommen kein gutes Argument.

---

[24]   In Bezug auf epistemische Gründe vertritt diese Position u. a. Turri, 2009, dort auch
weitere Literatur. Zur analogen (und besser entwickelten) Debatte über Handlungsgründe vgl. z. B. Dancy, 2000; Bittner, 2005; Alvarez, 2010.

Um das „rational constraint"-Argument gegen diesen Einwand zu verteidigen, sollten wir zwischen zwei Fragen unterscheiden: erstens der Frage danach, welcher ontologischen Kategorie Gründe angehören, und zweitens der Frage danach, worauf die rechtfertigende Kraft von Gründen beruht. Unabhängig davon, welchen ontologischen Status Gründe besitzen, beruht ihre rechtfertigende Kraft auf inferentiellen Beziehungen zwischen Entitäten mit propositionaler Form: entweder zwischen dem Grund und dem Begründeten selbst, weil diese z. B. Propositionen, Sachverhalte oder Tatsachen sind; oder – in dem Fall, in dem Gründe mentale Zustände sind – zwischen dem *Inhalt* der Überzeugung, die den Grund ausmacht, und dem Inhalt der Überzeugung, die begründet wird. Selbst dann, wenn (gemäß dem ersten Horn des Dilemmas) Gründe tatsächlich mentale Zustände (wie Überzeugungen) sind, folgt daraus also noch nicht, dass die Möglichkeit von Rechtfertigung nichts über die ontologische Struktur der Wirklichkeit zeigt. Vielmehr scheinen in jedem Fall unsere Rechtfertigungen auf der Annahme zu beruhen, dass es Implikationsbeziehungen zwischen Sachverhalten von der Art „$p \rightarrow q$" gibt (z. B. „Wenn eine Flüssigkeit Lackmuspapier rot färbt, ist sie eine Säure"), auf Grund derer wir vom Konsequens überzeugt sein dürfen („Diese Flüssigkeit ist eine Säure"), wenn wir von der Antezedensbedingung überzeugt sind („Diese Flüssigkeit färbt Lackmuspapier rot"). Die Wirklichkeit bildet dann in *dem* Sinne die Quelle unserer Gründe, dass die Tatsachen, die zu ihr gehören, durch Implikationsbeziehungen verknüpft sind und es solche Beziehungen sind, auf die wir unsere Rechtfertigungen gründen. Brandom kann also für den Zweck des „rational constraint"-Arguments die Frage nach der Ontologie von Gründen offenlassen.

2. Status des Arguments

Der zweite Einwand besagt, dass das „rational constraint"-Argument bestenfalls einen Schluss darauf erlaubt, wie wir im Rahmen unserer diskursiven Praktiken die Wirklichkeit *konzipieren müssen* oder wie die Wirklichkeit beschaffen ist, *insofern* sie Gegenstand unserer Erkenntnis werden kann, nicht aber darauf, wie die Wirklichkeit *selbst* verfasst ist. Das „rational constraint"-Argument ist in Brandoms Version nämlich ein Argument, das implizite Voraussetzungen unserer epistemischen Praktiken explizit macht. Ein solches Argument kann allenfalls zeigen, dass bestimmte Auffassungen der Wirklichkeit rational oder nicht rational sind, weil sie mit unseren Praktiken vereinbar sind oder nicht; es kann aber nicht zeigen, dass bestimmte solche Auffassungen wahr oder falsch sind.[25]

---

[25] Ähnlich argumentieren in einem verwandten Kontext Pohl/Rosenhagen/Weber, 2008, S. 94.

Vor dem Hintergrund seiner eigenen Position in *Making it explicit* kann Brandom hierauf erwidern, dass der Einwand auf einer verfehlten Annahme beruht: der Annahme, wir könnten eine sinnvolle Unterscheidung zwischen der Wirklichkeit treffen, wie sie an sich beschaffen ist, und der Wirklichkeit, wie wir sie konzipieren müssen, um uns überhaupt in einer diskursiven Praxis auf sie beziehen zu können. Begriffe wie „Wirklichkeit" und „Tatsache" sind nämlich für Brandom *ebenso* semantisch abhängig von Begriffen, die geistige Phänomene bezeichnen, wie die Begriffe „objektive begriffliche Struktur", „Inkompatibilitätsbeziehung" usw.: „Wirklichkeit" kann in diesem Sinn z. B. als die Gesamtheit der Tatsachen definiert werden, wobei „Tatsache" wiederum als der „Inhalt einer wahren Aussage" definiert ist.[26] Die Wirklichkeit kann dann zwar sinnvoll von den Inhalten all unserer faktischen Überzeugungen als deren Korrektheitsmaßstab unterschieden werden – sie kann aber nicht sinnvoll von der „Wirklichkeit, wie wir sie konzipieren müssen, um uns überhaupt in einer diskursiven Praxis auf sie beziehen zu können" unterschieden werden.[27]

Während diese brandomsche Antwort darauf beruht, dass der Einwand des Skeptikers als unverständlich zurückgewiesen wird, nimmt Hegel selbst den Skeptiker sehr viel ernster. Insbesondere bietet die *Phänomenologie des Geistes* eine umfassende Auseinandersetzung mit skeptischen Positionen, deren Resultat die Überwindung des sogenannten „Gegensatzes des Bewusstseins" bildet: also des Gegensatzes zwischen einem Denken, das in seine bloß subjektive Sphäre eingeschlossen bleibt, und einer Wirklichkeit, die dem Denken kognitiv und praktisch nicht zugänglich ist.[28] Dem Freiheitsbegriff kommt hierbei keine tragende Rolle zu. Hegel glaubt also, aus Gründen, die vom „rational constraint"-Argument unabhängig sind, die Möglichkeit ausschließen zu können, die der skeptische Einwand gegen dieses Argument ins Feld führt.

3. Textevidenz

Als Beleg dafür, dass Hegel tatsächlich eine Version des „rational constraint"-Arguments vertritt, sei exemplarisch eine wichtige Passage aus dem „Vorbegriff" zur *Logik* in der Enzyklopädie angeführt. (Wir werden in den folgenden beiden Abschnitten sehen, dass Hegel die Prämissen und Konklusionen des Arguments wesentlich stärker interpretiert als Brandom; zunächst geht es nur

---

[26] Vgl. Brandom, 1994, S. 327 ff. – Dies gilt ungeachtet dessen, dass Begriffe wie „Wirklichkeit", „Gesamtheit der Tatsachen" usw. für Brandom notwendig vage bleiben: Brandom, 2008 a, S. 223 f.

[27] Dennoch kann jeder einzelne Vorschlag zur Identifikation dieser notwendigen Konzeption falsch sein.

[28] Vgl. z. B. PhG, TW 3, S. 72 (Skeptizismus) und WdL, TW 5, S. 42 (Gegensatz des Bewusstseins).

darum zu zeigen, dass Hegel *überhaupt* einen derartigen Zusammenhang annimmt.)

> Indem im Nachdenken ebensosehr die wahrhafte Natur zum Vorschein kommt, als dies Denken *meine* Tätigkeit ist, so ist jene ebensosehr das *Erzeugnis meines* Geistes, und zwar als denkenden Subjekts, Meiner nach meiner einfachen Allgemeinheit, als des schlechthin *bei sich seienden* Ichs, – oder meiner *Freiheit*. [...] Die Gedanken können nach diesen Bestimmungen *objektive* Gedanken genannt werden, worunter auch die Formen, die zunächst in der gewöhnlichen Logik betrachtet und nur für Formen *des bewußten* Denkens genommen zu werden pflegen, zu rechnen sind (Enz. §§ 23 f.).

Hegel betont hier zunächst, dass in unserer epistemischen Tätigkeit nicht etwa ein Gegensatz zwischen unserer Freiheit und der Bindung an den Maßstab besteht, den die Wirklichkeit (die „wahrhafte Natur" des Gegenstandes) ausmacht, sondern umgekehrt gerade dann, wenn wir in unserer Tätigkeit frei sind, die „wahrhafte Natur" des Gegenstands „zum Vorschein kommt". Subjektive Freiheit (der Gegenstand des Denkens als „*Erzeugnis meines* Geistes") und objektiver Gehalt unseres Denkens (das „zum Vorschein Kommen" der Wirklichkeit) bedingen einander demnach gegenseitig. Als Folgerung hieraus („nach diesen Bestimmungen") stellt Hegel anschließend die Behauptung auf, dass „Gedanken" nicht nur linguistische oder psychologische Entitäten sind, sondern die Wirklichkeit selbst durch „objektive Gedanken" strukturiert ist; wenn unser Erkennen gelingt, dann denken wir diejenigen Gedanken, die die Struktur der Wirklichkeit selbst ausmachen. Hegels Argumentation entspricht hier also genau dem „rational constraint"-Argument, das wir im Vorangegangenen betrachtet haben: Aus der Möglichkeit einer Form von Freiheit, die von der Ausrichtung an einem objektiven Maßstab nicht beschränkt, sondern durch sie erst ermöglicht wird, schließt Hegel auf eine ontologische Homogeneität zwischen Denken und Wirklichkeit. Statt von „objektiven Gedanken" spricht Hegel im Übrigen auch oft von „Begriff" oder „Begriffen", um die dem Geistigen homogene Struktur der Wirklichkeit zu kennzeichnen (hierauf werden wir im nächsten Abschnitt zurückkommen). Es ist also jedenfalls exegetisch korrekt, Hegel eine Auffassung zuzuschreiben, nach der die Wirklichkeit begrifflich strukturiert ist und dies wesentlich mit der Möglichkeit rationaler Freiheit zusammenhängt. Schließlich vertritt Hegel auch explizit eine realistische Theorie der *modalen* Dimension dieser begrifflichen Struktur: Er kritisiert nämlich ausdrücklich Kants antirealistische These, nach der die Modalität des Urteils lediglich eine Beziehung zwischen dem Urteilenden und dem Urteil ausdrückt, und rechnet modale Bestimmungen zu den objektiven Eigenschaften realer Gegenstände.[29]

---

[29] Enz. § 143 A, mit Einschränkung auf Notwendigkeit und Wirklichkeit; der Möglichkeit dagegen schreibt Hegel an dieser Stelle (ähnlich wie Spinoza: vgl. Ethik I, p. 33, sch. 1) einen bloß subjektiven Stellenwert zu.

III. Brandom vs. Hegel über Begriffsrealismus, Metaphysik und Freiheit

Brandoms Interpretation bietet plausible und fruchtbare Ansatzpunkte für das Verständnis des Zusammenhangs von Freiheit und Metaphysik bei Hegel, doch wird ihre Tragweite durch zusätzliche Annahmen Brandoms eingeschränkt, die mit wesentlichen Positionen Hegels konfligieren. Die relevanten Differenzen zwischen Brandoms Rekonstruktion und Hegels eigener Position betrachte ich im Folgenden, indem ich *erstens* Brandoms und Hegels Begriffsrealismus im Hinblick auf ihre unterschiedliche metaphysische Stärke vergleiche und *zweitens* die für diesen Unterschied verantwortliche Metaphysik-Skepsis Brandoms diskutiere, die ihrerseits auf einem bestimmten nicht-Hegelianischen Freiheitsverständnis beruht.

1. Hegels Idealismus, wie Brandom ihn rekonstruiert, beinhaltet – besonders in Form der These des Begriffsrealismus und des damit verbundenen modalen Realismus – substantielle metaphysische Festlegungen, weil er bestimmte metaphysische Optionen ausschließt, die nicht trivialerweise falsch sind: nämlich insbesondere a. die These, dass die Wirklichkeit keinerlei begriffliche Struktur aufweist (diese These schreibt Brandom Kant zu) und b. die These, dass es keine modalen Sachverhalte gibt und modale Aussagen keinen Wahrheitswert haben (modaler Eliminativismus). Dennoch ist der positive metaphysische Gehalt von Brandoms Version dieser hegelschen Positionen recht beschränkt, und dies steht im Gegensatz zu Hegels eigenen Ausführungen zu diesen Themen, der hier sehr viel spezifischere Aussagen zu machen scheint. Um diese Differenz möglichst genau formulieren zu können, müssen wir zwischen zwei verschiedenen Weisen unterscheiden, wie man die Aussage

(1) Die Wirklichkeit ist begrifflich strukturiert

und damit zusammenhängende Aussagen verstehen kann: nämlich einerseits als Spezifikation einer metaphysischen Funktion und andererseits als Identifikation des Trägers einer solchen Funktion. Wird die Aussage als Spezifikation einer metaphysischen Funktion verstanden, besagt sie, dass es *irgendetwas* gibt, das die Wirklichkeit begrifflich strukturiert, enthält aber keine genauere Identifikation oder Bestimmung derjenigen Entitäten, die diese Funktion ausüben. Da Brandom „begriffliche Struktur" durch modal robuste materiale Inkompatibilitätsbeziehungen definiert, kommen als Träger dieser Funktion diejenigen Arten von Entitäten in Frage, die Kandidaten für die ontologische Fundierung von modalen Tatsachen (hier speziell: Tatsachen darüber, ob Sachverhalte unter kontrafaktischen Bedingungen zusammen bestehen oder nicht) sind. Das sind zum einen intrinsisch modale Entitäten wie primitive modale Tatsachen, modale Propositionen, mögliche Welten (sofern ihre modalen Charakteristika als irreduzibel verstanden werden), Dispositionen, Essenzen, natürliche Arten, Naturgesetze u. a., und zum anderen Kandidaten, die selbst nicht modal sind und dazu dienen sollen, reduktive Theorien von Modalität zu formulieren: also insbesondere mögliche Welten in David Lewis' Sinn.[30] Entscheidend ist hier, dass Brandom *offenlässt*, welche dieser metaphysischen Arten die Funktion der begrifflichen Strukturierung der Wirklichkeit ausübt.

Wird dagegen (1) als Identifikation eines *Trägers* von metaphysischen Funktionen gelesen, dann handelt es sich dabei um eine wesentlich stärkere Aussage: nämlich die, dass die Struktur der Wirklichkeit gerade *nicht* durch Entitäten wie primitive modale Tatsachen, Dispositionen, mögliche Welten etc. festgelegt wird, sondern durch davon verschiedene *begriffliche* Entitäten. Es gibt nun sehr starke Textevidenz dafür, dass Hegel seinen Begriffsrealismus im zweiten, stärkeren Sinn verstanden haben will. Hegels Begriffsrealismus besagt demnach, dass die Wirklichkeit durch objektive *Begriffe* strukturiert wird; solche Begriffe sind für Hegel theoretisch wohlbestimmte Entitäten, nicht bloße Platzhalter. Dass dies Hegels Position ist, zeigen zahlreiche Stellen, an denen Hegel objektive Begriffe als metaphysische Erklärungsprinzipien beschreibt – und zwar als Prinzipien, die Erklärungen der Eigenschaften und des Verhaltens von Einzelgegenständen ermöglichen und die selbst Universalien sind, die immanent in ihren Instanzen existieren (ähnlich wie Aristoteles' „Zweite Ousia"). So erläutert Hegel etwa:

> Wenn es aber an dem ist, was vorhin angegeben worden und was sonst im allgemeinen zugestanden wird, daß die *Natur*, das eigentümliche *Wesen*, das wahrhaft *Bleibende* und *Substantielle* bei der Mannigfaltigkeit und Zufälligkeit des Erscheinens und der vorübergehenden Äußerung der *Begriff* der Sache, *das in ihr selbst Allgemeine* ist, wie jedes menschliche Individuum, [ob]zwar ein unendlich eigentümliches, das Prius aller seiner Eigentümlichkeit darin, *Mensch* zu sein, in sich hat, wie jedes einzelne Tier das Prius, *Tier* zu sein, so wäre nicht zu sagen, was, wenn diese Grundlage aus dem mit noch so vielfachen sonstigen Prädikaten Ausgerüsteten weggenommen würde, ob sie gleich wie die anderen ein Prädikat genannt werden kann, – was so ein Individuum noch sein sollte (WdL, TW 5, S. 26).

Der Begriff „Mensch" *ist* demnach eine bestimmte Entität, nämlich eine Universalie, die in einzelnen Menschen Realität hat und die „Natur", die „Grundlage" usw. dieser Individuen und ihrer besonderen weiteren Eigenschaften ausmacht. Welchem objektiven Begriff ein Individuum angehört, legt demnach fest, was das Individuum ist.[31] – Dass hegelsche Begriffe kraft dieses Stellenwerts

---

[30]   Vgl. oben Fn. 23 sowie allgemein Sider, 2003.

[31]   Für eine detailliertere Interpretation von Hegels Begriffsrealismus vgl. Knappik, i. Ersch., Kap. 5 und Knappik, unveröffentlicht; einen ähnlichen Ansatz vertreten u. a. Westphal, 1989, S. 141 ff.; Horstmann, 1990, S. 44 f.; Stern, 1990; deVries, 1991, S. 63 ff.

auch Erklärungsprinzipien bilden, geht aus einer weiteren Stelle besonders deutlich hervor. Von einer Erklärung, die eine einzelne Eigenschaft eines Gegenstandes isoliert als essentiell behandelt, schreibt Hegel dort: „[W]eil sie nicht den ganzen Umfang der Sache enthält, ist sie einseitiger Grund, deren die anderen besonderen Seiten wieder besondere haben und wovon keiner die Sache, welche ihre *Verknüpfung* ausmacht und sie alle enthält, erschöpft; keiner ist *zureichender* Grund, d. h. der Begriff" (WdL, TW 6, S. 109). Der Begriff als komplexer Zusammenhang spezifischer Eigenschaften macht demzufolge den *zureichenden Grund* – also: das Erklärungsprinzip – für die konkrete Beschaffenheit des Individuums aus. Der Begriff wäre aber kein *zureichender* Grund, wenn er nicht bestimmte Sachverhalte *notwendig* machen würde – z. B. macht die Instantiierung des Begriffs „Mensch" durch ein Individuum für Hegel notwendig, dass dieses Individuum denken kann. Objektive Begriffe in diesem Sinne sind also auch für die *modale* Dimension der Struktur der Wirklichkeit verantwortlich: Sie legen fest, wann Sachverhalte unter kontrafaktischen Umständen zusammen bestehen.

Hegels so verstandene Version des Begriffsrealismus ist offensichtlich eine wesentlich stärkere und spezifischere metaphysische These, als es der Begriffsrealismus in Brandoms Interpretation ist. Wohlgemerkt ist damit die metaphysische Dimension von Hegels Idealismus keineswegs erschöpft. Denn Hegel zufolge gibt es neben objektiven Begriffen im erläuterten Sinn auch noch *den* Begriff schlechthin als Metauniversalie, die durch einzelne („bestimmte") Begriffe instantiiert wird und die deren Eigenschaften erklärt, so wie bestimmte Begriffe die Eigenschaften von Einzelgegenständen erklären.[32] Insbesondere legt *der* Begriff fest, dass es eine Reihe von bestimmten Begriffen notwendigerweise *gibt,* und mithin auch, dass es Einzelgegenstände gibt, in denen diese Begriffe immanent existieren. In der folgenden Diskussion beschränken wir uns aber auf Hegels Metaphysik *bestimmter* Begriffe, denn sie ist derjenige Bestandteil von Hegels Idealismus, der am ehesten als Konklusion des „rational constraint"-Arguments verstanden und plausibel gemacht werden kann.

2. Dass Brandoms Rekonstruktion des hegelschen Begriffsrealismus in der erläuterten Weise wesentlich schwächer ist als das, was Hegel selbst ausdrücklich zur Metaphysik objektiver bestimmter Begriffe sagt, liegt in Brandoms Ansichten zu Hegels *Logik* und allgemeiner zum Stellenwert metaphysischer Aussagen begründet. Brandom selbst beschreibt den Unterschied zwischen Hegels spezifischen metaphysischen Thesen (z. B. über die Metaphysik bestimmter Begriffe) und den im Vergleich dazu viel unspezifischeren Thesen, die sich in seiner Rekonstruktion ergeben, wie folgt. Hegel ist laut Brandom der Ansicht, dass es

---

³² Vgl. z. B. WdL, TW 5, S. 30; *Beweise vom Dasein Gottes*, TW 17, S. 395 ff.

eine definitive Klasse logisch-metaphysischer Begriffe (die Kategorien der *Logik*) gibt, durch die erstens alle Aspekte unseres Redens über etwas adäquat explizit gemacht werden können und zweitens, vermittelt hierdurch, auch relevante Eigenschaften der Wirklichkeit qua Gegenstand unseres Diskurses erfasst werden können. Brandom dagegen bestreitet die Möglichkeit eines solchen abgeschlossenen logisch-metaphysischen Begriffssystems. Weil er (mit Benedetto Croce zu reden) in Hegels Annahme dieser Möglichkeit ein „totes", nicht ein „lebendiges" Element seiner Philosophie sieht, nimmt er sie nicht in seine rationale Rekonstruktion der hegelschen Position mit auf, sondern hält diesbezüglich nur an so allgemeinen Aussagen wie dem unspezifischen Begriffsrealismus fest.[33]

Da sich unsere empirischen Begriffe in ständiger Entwicklung befinden – nach Brandoms Hegel-Deutung *müssen* sie sich sogar endlos weiterentwickeln –,[34] kann es tatsächlich fragwürdig erscheinen, ob es ein definitives System von Begriffen geben kann, durch das wir alle impliziten Aspekte unseres Gebrauchs von empirischen Begriffen explizit machen können. Um Hegel gegen Brandom zu verteidigen, könnte man deshalb einwenden, dass Hegels logische Kategorien nicht oder zumindest nicht *nur* der expressiven Aufgabe dienen, die Brandom ihnen zuschreibt. Vielmehr sollen sie die *Grundstruktur* der Wirklichkeit und des Denkens erfassen und sind daher unabhängig von der kontinuierlichen Entwicklung unserer empirischen Begriffe.

Doch greift Brandoms Skepsis tiefer, denn er bestreitet auch, dass wir sinnvoll über die Grundstruktur der Wirklichkeit reden können – wie es Hegel u. a. mit seinen Aussagen zur Metaphysik objektiver Begriffe tut, die wir oben besprochen haben: „What sets off alarm bells for me in the ontological version [sc. einer Hegel-Deutung] is the notion of the true or ultimate structure of reality" (Brandom, 2008 b, S. 182). Das stärkste Argument, das Brandom für seine skeptische Position (und entsprechend für die Einschränkung des Begriffsrealismus auf die schwache, unspezifische Lesart) bietet, beruht auf dem pragmatistischen Gedanken, dass wir die Adäquatheit eines Vokabulars immer nur relativ zu einem bestimmten *Zweck* bewerten können, wobei die relevanten Zwecke vielfältig und feinkörnig individuiert sind. Ausgehend von logischen Vokabularen erläutert Brandom: „What is the right logic? Well, intuitionism is the right logic for the dimensions of inference that are made explicit by its vocabulary, *und so weiter*. And I think the same thing is true of logical vocabulary read more

---

[33] Brandom, 2005, S. 155 ff. – Die nach Brandom „zulässigen" metaphysischen Aussagen können dann als Aussagen über allgemeine Eigenschaften von Vokabularen verstanden werden, die notwendig dafür sind, dass solche Vokabulare überhaupt eine objektive Wirklichkeit repräsentieren können, die aber je ganz unterschiedlich realisiert sein können.

[34] Brandom, 2005, S. 139 ff.

broadly, so as to include the other kinds of things that Hegel (and, in a different tone of voice, I), would like to include. [...] The question is just ‚What can you use it to say?'" (Brandom, 2008 b, S. 183). In der modernen Logik ist es tatsächlich wenig sinnvoll, beispielsweise unter verschiedenen Konditionalen eines als das adäquateste, den objektiven begrifflichen Strukturen am ehesten entsprechende usw. privilegieren zu wollen. Für die weitere – und keineswegs selbstverständliche – These, dass dieser Punkt auch auf nicht-logische Vokabulare übertragen werden kann, argumentiert Brandom an anderer Stelle wie folgt. Die *Zwecke*, zu denen wir Vokabulare entwickeln und gebrauchen, sind nach Brandom selbst wesentlich davon abhängig, welche Vokabulare wir de facto verwenden – und zwar insbesondere davon, durch welche Vokabulare wir uns selbst beschreiben und interpretieren. Indem wir uns durch neue Vokabulare interpretieren, *transformieren* wir uns nämlich, so Brandom, und setzen uns dadurch auch neue Zwecke für den Gebrauch von Vokabularen – unter Umständen Zwecke, die wir zuvor gar nicht haben konnten, weil wir kein Vokabular hatten, in dem wir sie formulieren konnten.[35]

Dabei sind nicht nur die Möglichkeiten der weiteren Selbsttransformation durch neue Vokabulare und der entsprechenden Genese neuer spezifischer Zwecke unbegrenzt. Für Brandom kann auch nicht sinnvoll ein *übergreifendes*, generisches Ziel (wie kognitive Adäquatheit o. ä.) formuliert werden, das in den jeweiligen spezifischeren Zielen nur konkretisiert wird. Brandom deutet nämlich die Selbsttransformation und -entfaltung, die uns durch die Entwicklung von neuen Vokabularen möglich ist, als Ausprägung einer wichtigen Form von *Freiheit*, die er als „expressive Freiheit" bezeichnet. In der Konstruktion neuer Vokabulare und der Selbsttransformation, die damit einhergeht, verfolgen wir für Brandom nicht ein übergeordnetes Ziel, zu dem diese Vokabulare besser und weniger gut tauglich sein können, sondern die Vielfalt von Möglichkeiten des Selbstausdrucks ist für Brandom selbst intrinsisch wertvoll.[36] In Bezug auf philosophische Vokabulare schreibt Brandom etwa:

> [...] Hume, Kant, and Hegel himself have done their philosophical work well, and offered us candidate vocabularies whose adoption *makes* us into different sorts of beings. The lesson we should learn from studying their efforts is *not* a decision about who is *right*, but one concerning the importance of coming up with new, ever-more-interesting such vocabularies as candidates to identify with [...] (Brandom, 2009, S. 155).

---

[35]   Brandom übernimmt diesen Punkt von Richard Rorty: Brandom, 2000, S. 169.

[36]   Vgl. Brandom, 1979, S. 192 ff.; Brandom, 2005, S. 178 f., wo Brandom in unserer Fähigkeit zur freien Konstruktion neuer Vokabulare sogar unseren moralischen Wert begründet sieht; Brandom, 2009, S. 74 f. und Kap. 5. Zur Tradition eines derartigen Freiheitsverständnisses (z. B. Mill, Carnap, Rorty) vgl. Knappik, i. Ersch., Kap. 1.5 und 5.1.

Konkurrierende Begriffssysteme schaffen demnach ihre je eigenen besonderen Ausdrucksmöglichkeiten, die als Beitrag zu unserer expressiven Freiheit gesehen werden sollten, nicht als etwas, was an einem einheitlichen Maßstab gemessen werden könnte.

Für Brandom ergeben sich also nicht nur aus unserem Selbstverständnis als freie Wesen bestimmte metaphysische Konsequenzen, sondern umgekehrt liegt auch seiner *Einschränkung* der Möglichkeit von Metaphysik eine bestimmte Freiheitsauffassung zu Grunde. Dabei handelt es sich aber um ein Freiheitsverständnis, das mit demjenigen Hegels nicht in Einklang zu bringen ist. Denn es ist ein wesentlicher Aspekt von Hegels Freiheitstheorie, dass wir nur dann frei sind, wenn unser Denken und Handeln zumindest implizit auf ein bestimmtes, alternativloses Ziel hin ausgerichtet sind.[37] Dieses Ziel besteht in der vollständigen Realisierung von Freiheit, und das heißt für Hegel: in der vollständigen Entwicklung des Geistes, der in einer vernünftig geordneten Gesellschaft institutionelle Realität erhält und in Kunst, Religion und Philosophie ein umfassendes Bewusstsein seiner selbst und der Wirklichkeit als ganzer entwickelt.[38] Die Ausrichtung auf dieses Ziel schafft den normativen Rahmen für die freie Entfaltung individueller Anlagen und Bedürfnisse;[39] und speziell im Fall *epistemischer* Freiheit fordert der Objektivitätsanspruch des Denkens ein völliges Absehen von individuellen Bedürfnissen und Neigungen: Denn das Denken ist „dem Inhalte nach insofern nur wahrhaft [...], als es in die *Sache* vertieft ist und der Form nach nicht ein *besonderes* Sein oder Tun des Subjekts, sondern eben dies ist, daß das Bewußtsein sich als abstraktes Ich, als von *aller Partikularität* sonstiger Eigenschaften, Zustände usf. *befreites* verhält und nur das Allgemeine tut, in welchem es mit allen Individuen identisch ist" (Enz. § 23 A). Demnach müssen wir in unserem Denken diejenigen Begriffe und Vokabulare gebrauchen, die am ehesten geeignet sind, die „Sache" zu erfassen: Um bei Brandoms Beispiel aus der oben zitierten Passage zu bleiben, stellt sich für das epistemische Denken tatsächlich die Frage, ob Hume, Kant oder Hegel mit ihren Aussagen und mit den Begriffen, die sie entwickelt haben, recht haben oder nicht – die Verwendung bestimmter Vokabulare ist nicht einfach nur Sache unserer freien Selbstentfaltung und -transformation. Aus dieser Sicht kann die Entwicklung

---

[37] Dagegen gibt es im Fall der Entwicklungsprozesse, die wir nach Brandom in Bezug auf vergangene Begriffsanwendungen rational rekonstruieren müssen (vgl. oben § 1), erstens nicht *ein* alternativloses Ziel, und zweitens handelt es sich dabei stets um perspektivische Interpretationen aus der Sicht der jeweils gegenwärtigen Praxis, nicht um ein objektives Fortschrittsgeschehen wie bei Hegel.

[38] Vgl. z. B. GPhR § 27 (das im objektiven Geist entfaltete „vernünftige System" des Willens als Inhalt des freien Willens); Enz. § 469 A; § 484; § 550 A, TW 10, S. 352. Zu unserer *impliziten* Ausrichtung auf dieses Ziel vgl. u. a. *Philosophie der Geschichte*, TW 12, 40 ff.; Knappik, i. Ersch., Kap. 5.3.

[39] Vgl. z. B. GPhR § 258 A, TW 7, S. 399.

einer Vielfalt von Vokabularen, zwischen denen wir je nach gegebenem expressivem Ziel wählen können, allenfalls ein Mittel zum Zweck sein (etwa deshalb, weil wir ein Vokabular nur dann zuverlässig beurteilen können, wenn wir es mit Alternativen vergleichen können), nicht ein intrinsisches Gut.

Ähnlich wie Brandom in Bezug auf Kant die Orientierung am Sittengesetz als notwendige Bedingung für Autonomie ausklammert (s. o. § 1), blendet er also auch in seiner Hegel-Interpretation die Ausrichtung des Prozesses, in dem Freiheit verwirklicht wird, auf *ein* alternativloses, vernünftiges Ziel aus und interpretiert diesen Prozess stattdessen als prinzipiell offenes Geschehen. Hiermit hängt die Divergenz zwischen Brandoms und Hegels Verständnis des Begriffsrealismus, von der wir ausgegangen waren, direkt zusammen: Für Hegel besteht eine wesentliche Bedingung für eine vollständige Realisierung von Freiheit in der Verfügbarkeit eines privilegierten Begriffssystems, das die Wirklichkeit „an ihren Gelenkstellen schneidet" und ihre wirkliche begriffliche Struktur erfasst; für Brandom ist diese Art von Zielsetzung nicht sinnvoll, weshalb er nur die schwächere, unspezifische Lesart des Begriffsrealismus akzeptieren kann.

IV. Hegel über Freiheit und Verstehen

Das „rational constraint"-Argument, das wir in §§ 1 und 2 betrachtet haben, kann nur den Begriffsrealismus und den modalen Realismus in Brandoms schwacher, unspezifischer Lesart begründen, nicht auch in der stärkeren Version, die wir in § 3 Hegel zugeschrieben haben: Daraus, dass die Wirklichkeit den Wahrheitsmaßstab und die Gründe-Quelle für unsere Überzeugungen bildet, kann bestenfalls gefolgert werden, dass es *eine* begriffliche Struktur der Wirklichkeit gibt, aber nicht, dass eine bestimmte Art von Entitäten (wie Hegels objektive Begriffe) für diese Struktur verantwortlich ist. Wenn Hegel also eine Variante des „rational constraint"-Arguments vertritt, die zu einer viel stärkeren Konklusion führt als Brandoms Version, dann muss er auch stärkere Prämissen verwenden. In diesem Abschnitt schlage ich eine Interpretation dieser Prämissen vor. Dazu bespreche ich zunächst Hegels Verständnis der relevanten Art rationaler Einschränkung des Denkens durch die Wirklichkeit, dann seine Auffassung von Freiheit.

Diejenige Art von rationaler Einschränkung, die für Hegel – gemäß dem „rational constraint"-Argument – zum einen notwendig für rationale Freiheit ist und zum anderen eine idealistische Metaphysik in seinem Sinn impliziert, besteht darin, dass für Hegel die Wirklichkeit nicht nur den Maßstab für unsere Wahrheitsansprüche und die Quelle für unsere Rechtfertigungen bilden muss, sondern auch einen Gegenstand, der unserem *Verstehen* offensteht und Prinzipien für erfolgreiche Erklärungen enthält. Dabei liegt der Gedanke zu Grunde, dass wir in unserem Denken nur in dem Maße frei sind, als wir uns darin auf eine Wirklichkeit beziehen, von der wir einsehen können, warum sie so und nicht anders beschaffen ist. Facta bruta, die wir hinnehmen müssen, ohne sie begreifen zu können, sind demzufolge Einschränkungen unserer Freiheit; die Fähigkeit, Dinge *erklären* und *als notwendig begreifen* zu können, trägt hingegen zu unserer Freiheit bei. In einer Logik-Vorlesung Hegels heißt es dazu: „In der Existenz [sc. der Natur] ist [das] Feld der Notwendigkeit, aber indem wir die Natur begreifen, so sind wir darin frei" (*Vorlesungen über die Logik*, S. 174). Und allgemein schreibt Hegel, das „*Begreifen* eines Gegenstandes" bestehe

> in der Tat in nichts anderem, als daß Ich denselben sich zu *eigen* macht, ihn durchdringt und ihn in *seine eigene Form, d. i.* in die *Allgemeinheit,* welche unmittelbar *Bestimmtheit,* oder Bestimmtheit, welche unmittelbar Allgemeinheit ist, bringt. Der Gegenstand in der Anschauung oder auch in der Vorstellung ist noch ein *Äußerliches, Fremdes.* Durch das Begreifen wird das *Anundfürsichsein,* das er im Anschauen und Vorstellen hat, in ein *Gesetztsein* verwandelt; Ich durchdringt ihn *denkend.* [...] Wie er aber im Denken ist, so ist er *erst an und für sich;* wie er in der Anschauung oder Vorstellung ist, ist er *Erscheinung* [...]. Diese Objektivität hat der Gegenstand somit im *Begriffe* [...] (WdL, TW 6, S. 255).

Hegel beschreibt das Begreifen also als einen Prozess der *Aneignung* von etwas zunächst *Fremdem.* Diesen Aneignungsprozess des Begreifens charakterisiert Hegel an anderer Stelle auch so, dass wir dem Gegenstand die „Gestalt der *Freiheit*" geben und dabei das, was zunächst nur als kontingente Tatsache gegeben ist, als notwendig begreifen (Enz. § 12 A, TW 8, S. 58); auch die Rede vom „Gesetztsein" in der eben zitierten Passage kann so verstanden werden, dass wir den Gegenstand als ontologisch abhängig von einem anderen Faktor begreifen, der den Gegenstand und seine Beschaffenheit notwendig macht.

Der Kontext der zitierten Stelle zeigt zugleich, wie Hegels Rede von der „eigenen Form" des Ich bzw. der „Gestalt der Freiheit", die wir im Begreifen dem Gegenstand verleihen, zu deuten ist und wie Hegels Auffassung des „Begreifens" mit seiner Metaphysik bestimmter Begriffe zusammenhängt. Die Passage ist nämlich Teil einer Erläuterung der Metauniversalie *des* Begriffs schlechthin (vgl. oben, § 3), die Hegel hier als „Allgemeinheit, welche unmittelbar Bestimmtheit, oder Bestimmtheit, welche unmittelbar Allgemeinheit ist" charakterisiert. Hegel erklärt in diesem Kontext die Struktur des Begriffs an Hand von zwei Beispielen: erstens – in der zitierten Passage – einem Gegenstand, den wir begreifen, und zweitens dem Selbstbewusstsein. Am *Gegenstand* tritt die Struktur des Begriffs, die Einheit von Allgemeinheit und Bestimmtheit, dann zu Tage, wenn wir den Gegenstand mit seiner konkreten Beschaffenheit auf seinen Begriff zurückführen – also auf den objektiven bestimmten Begriff (vgl. oben § 3), den der Gegenstand instantiiert. In diesem Fall wird nämlich der intrinsische Zusammenhang sichtbar, der gemäß Hegels Begriffsrealismus zwischen der Seite der Allgemeinheit (der objektive Begriff als immanente Universalie) und der Seite der Bestimmtheit (der Einzelgegenstand als Instanz des Begriffs) besteht. Das *Selbstbewusstsein* weist dieselbe logische Struktur auf, denn auch für dieses ist es wesentlich, dass es zugleich einen allgemeinen Aspekt (das mit sich selbst identische Ich) und einen Aspekt der Bestimmtheit (die einzelnen mentalen Zustände, Episoden usw., die dem Ich angehören) besitzt. Auf Grund dieser Strukturgleichheit zwischen dem Selbstbewusstsein und dem Gegenstand qua Instanz eines objektiven Begriffs kann Hegel sagen, dass wir im Begreifen des Gegenstandes – also in dem Prozess, in dem wir die bestimmten Eigenschaften des Gegenstandes auf der Grundlage des objektiven Begriffs, den er instantiiert, verständlich machen – den Gegenstand in unsere eigene Form bringen und gerade dadurch die wahre Natur des Gegenstandes (den Gegenstand, wie er „an und für sich" ist, seine „Objektivität") erkennen.[40]

Warum aber steht *nur* eine Wirklichkeit, zu deren fundamentaler Struktur in Einzelgegenständen instantiierte objektive Begriffe gehören, unserem Verstehen offen – warum können nicht auch andere Entitäten und ontologische Strukturen (z. B. Naturgesetze, Dispositionen) als Grundlage erfolgreicher Erklärungen dienen und entsprechend unser Denken auf die relevante Art rational einschränken? Und: Warum ist die Fähigkeit, die Wirklichkeit auf die beschriebene Weise zu verstehen, eine notwendige Bedingung rationaler Freiheit? Hegel muss plausible Antworten auf diese Fragen bieten, damit der von ihm behauptete Zusammenhang zwischen Freiheit und Idealismus (insbesondere dem Begriffsrealismus im starken Sinn) einsichtig wird.

Eine auch nur annähernd vollständige Diskussion der für diese Fragen relevanten Kontexte bei Hegel würde den Rahmen dieses Beitrags bei weitem sprengen. Es scheint mir aber möglich zu sein, bei Hegel einen Gedankengang zu identifizieren, der zumindest im Ansatz eine Antwort auf beide Fragen bietet.[41] Wie schon erwähnt, schafft für Kant unsere Vernunftnatur, kraft derer wir durch das Sittengesetz gebunden sind, eine normative Anforderung, die wir erfüllen müssen, um autonom zu sein. Im Anschluss an Fichte[42] liest nun Hegel Kant so, dass dem kategorischen Imperativ im Theoretischen das Gebot der Widerspruchsfreiheit entspricht. Demzufolge besteht die normative Vorgabe für Autonomie-Freiheit für Kant (und Fichte) sowohl im Fall der theoretischen als auch der praktischen Vernunft in einer rein formalen Selbstidentität.[43] Hier setzt Hegels Kritik an. Im theoretischen wie im praktischen Bereich lässt das Gebot der Selbstidentität bzw. Widerspruchsfreiheit unser Verhalten in extre-

---

[40]   Die Tatsache, dass das Selbstbewusstsein und der begriffene Gegenstand dieselbe Struktur aufweisen, bedarf für Hegel ihrerseits einer Begründung; vgl. dazu unten Fn. 47.

[41]   Für eine ausführlichere Rekonstruktion vgl. Knappik, i. Ersch., Kap. 3 und 4.

[42]   Vgl. z. B. *Bestimmung des Gelehrten*, GA I, 3, S. 29 f.; *Ueber Belebung*, GA I, 3, S. 84.

[43]   Hegels Formalismus-Vorwurf wird oft als rein moralphilosophischer Punkt gelesen; doch führt Hegel (u. a. in Enz. §§ 42–60) zahlreiche Probleme, die er bei Kant in ganz unterschiedlichen Kontexten diagnostiziert, darauf zurück, dass bei Kant die (theoretische wie praktische) Vernunft auf die „*leere Identität* reduziert" wird (Enz. § 48 A).

mem Maße *normativ unterbestimmt*: Sowohl bezüglich der Verwendung bestimmter Begriffe bzw. der Akzeptanz bestimmter Überzeugungen als auch bezüglich der Entscheidung für bestimmte Projekte, Maximen und Handlungen werden sich stets unzählige relevante Kandidaten finden, die mit dem Gebot der Widerspruchsfreiheit in Einklang zu bringen sind. Da wir uns aber auf *bestimmte* Begriffe, Überzeugungen, Handlungsziele usw. festlegen müssen, um ein konkretes Selbst zu bilden, bleiben uns nur zwei Möglichkeiten, wie wir die resultierende normative Kluft überbrücken können: Entweder wählen wir willkürlich unter den verfügbaren Optionen, oder wir verhalten uns passiv und folgen der Option, die die stärkste motivationale Kraft auf uns ausübt. In beiden Fällen sind wir aber nicht selbstbestimmt, sondern durch zufällig gegebene Größen fremdbestimmt.[44] Dagegen benötigen wir für wirkliche Autonomie stärker bestimmte Normen, die uns zugleich nicht von außen vorgegeben sind, sondern in ähnlicher Weise notwendige Voraussetzungen vernünftiger Aktivität bilden wie Kants kategorischer Imperativ und das entsprechende Gebot der Widerspruchsfreiheit im Theoretischen. Vom freien Subjekt gilt hier allgemein, was Hegel in seiner Analyse der Struktur des freien Willens in der Einleitung der *Grundlinien der Philosophie des Rechts* ausführt: „[D]ie *Selbstbestimmung* des Ich" besteht darin, „in einem sich als das Negative seiner selbst, nämlich als *bestimmt, beschränkt* zu setzen und bei sich, d. i. in seiner *Identität mit sich* und Allgemeinheit zu bleiben, und in der Bestimmung, sich nur mit sich selbst zusammenzuschließen" (GPhR § 7). Die gesuchten Normen müssen es dem Subjekt daher ermöglichen, in der Auseinandersetzung mit mannigfaltigen Inhalten und der Konstitution eines Begriffs- und Überzeugungssystems „bei sich zu bleiben".

Innerhalb des Hegelschen Systems kann es nun als eine der zentralen Aufgaben der *Wissenschaft der Logik* verstanden werden, dieses Problem der normativen Unterbestimmtheit zu lösen – und zwar durch die Identifikation grundlegender begrifflicher Normen, die geeignet sind, eine zusätzliche normative Bestimmung zu leisten. Die *Logik* geht dabei von der einfachsten und unbestimmtesten Form rationaler Aktivität aus, nämlich dem Versuch, überhaupt nur *etwas* (in Hegels Terminologie: das unbestimmte „Sein" am Anfang der *Logik*) zu denken, und versucht, auf kontrollierte Weise die dabei implizit in Anspruch genommenen konkreteren normativen Voraussetzungen zu ermitteln – also gerade diejenigen begrifflichen Normen, die es dem Subjekt ermöglichen, in der Auseinandersetzung mit von ihm unterschiedenen Inhalten und der Konstitution eines konkreten Selbst „bei sich zu bleiben".

Dabei bieten die Kategorien der ersten beiden Bücher in der *Logik* (Seins- und Wesenslogik) insofern nur vorläufige Spezifikationen solcher Normen, als

---

44 Vgl. GPhR §§ 13 und 15, wo Hegel bezüglich des Willens beide Fälle nennt. Vgl. Patten, 1999, S. 48 ff.

sie selbst stets implizit auf weitere kategoriale Voraussetzungen verweisen und damit auf unkontrollierte Weise andere begriffliche Normen in Anspruch nehmen. Dieser Mangel an *semantischer* Transparenz hat zur Folge, dass diese Kategorien (zumindest für sich genommen) nicht in der Lage sind, die normativen Voraussetzungen für Selbstkonstitution zu schaffen: In ihrem Gebrauch bleiben wir nicht bei uns, sondern verlieren uns in unkontrollierten Übergängen. Besonders wichtig für unsere Fragestellung ist dabei ein bestimmter Aspekt dieses semantischen Defizits. Für Hegel schließt nämlich zumindest in vielen Fällen das semantische Defizit der Kategorien in Seins- und Wesenslogik ein *ontologisches* Defizit ein, das seinerseits zur Folge hat, dass Erklärungen, die wir mittels dieser Kategorien formulieren, zwangsläufig unvollständig und unbefriedigend sind. Um diesen Zusammenhang zu verstehen, betrachten wir einen einschlägigen Fall aus der Wesenslogik, nämlich die Kategorie des *Dings* mit realisierten dispositionalen *Eigenschaften* (WdL, TW 6, S. 129 ff.). Wenn wir einen Gegenstand als solches Ding interpretieren und dadurch seine besondere Beschaffenheit als Realisierung dispositionaler Eigenschaften erklären, dann legen wir uns damit in ontologischer Hinsicht nicht nur auf die Existenz dieses Einzelgegenstandes mit seinen Eigenschaften fest, sondern in impliziter und unkontrollierter Weise *auch* auf die Existenz weiterer Entitäten, von denen das Ding mit diesen Eigenschaften ontologisch abhängig ist: insbesondere darauf, dass es andere Dinge gibt, durch deren kausale Einwirkung die Realisierung der Dispositionen ausgelöst wurde (WdL, TW 6, S. 137), und darauf, dass es eine strukturelle Grundlage der dispositionalen Eigenschaften gibt („Materien", WdL, TW 6, S. 139). Dies sind Abhängigkeiten, die für die Erklärung des Gegenstandes mit seiner besonderen Beschaffenheit direkt relevant wären: Eine angemessene Erklärung des Explanandums müsste die fraglichen Faktoren *identifizieren* (z. B. angeben, welche strukturelle Grundlage für eine Disposition verantwortlich ist). Da unsere impliziten Festlegungen aber keine solchen Identifikationen leisten, sondern nur besagen, *dass* es weitere derartige Faktoren gibt, sind unsere Erklärungen, die auf Kategorien wie der des Dings mit (realisierten dispositionalen) Eigenschaften basieren, zwangsläufig unvollständig.

Die gesuchten kategorialen Bestimmungen, die dazu geeignet sind, rationale Selbstkonstitution zu ermöglichen, dürfen das genannte *semantische* Defizit und a fortiori auch das *ontologische* und *explanatorische* Defizit nicht aufweisen. Diese Bedingung erfüllt laut Hegel allein die Kategorie des *Begriffs* (also die logische Struktur, die die Metauniversalie *des* Begriffs schlechthin ausmacht) mitsamt den weiteren, in der „Logik des Begriffs" entwickelten kategorialen Bestimmungen, die sich aus ihr ergeben. Die Kategorie des „Begriffs" bietet dem Denken für Hegel eine normative Orientierung, die semantisch transparent ist; wenn das Denken sich durch die Bestimmungen des Begriffs leiten lässt, macht es keine unkontrollierten Übergänge mehr, sondern es „bleibt bei sich". Denn die logische Struktur des Begriffs besteht in der intrinsischen und expliziten Einheit eines *allgemeinen* und eines *besonderen* Aspektes; Hegel kennzeichnet diese Einheit ihrerseits als drittes Begriffsmoment, das der *Einzelheit*. Alle spezifischeren Begriffe, die diese logische Struktur ausprägen, sind daher so beschaffen, dass sie einen transparenten Zusammenhang (die Einheit, die das Moment der „Einzelheit" ausmacht) zwischen einem allgemeinen und einem besonderen Moment herstellen. Indem wir z. B. eine Konzeption eines bestimmten Begriffs (in Hegels Sinn) formulieren, spezifizieren wir einerseits eine Universalie als *allgemeinen* Faktor und andererseits Individuen mit *besonderen* Eigenschaften, die den Begriff instantiieren. Da der intrinsische Zusammenhang zwischen beiden Seiten durch die Struktur des Begriffs explizit gemacht wird, herrscht hier die semantische Transparenz, die bei den seins- und wesenslogischen Kategorien fehlt.[45] Insbesondere sind hier auch *ontologische* Transparenz und die Möglichkeit adäquater *Erklärungen* gegeben. Denn ontologisch legen wir uns dadurch, dass wir einen Gegenstand mit besonderen Eigenschaften als Instanz eines bestimmten Begriffs interpretieren, nur darauf fest, dass zwischen beiden eine wechselseitige ontologische Abhängigkeit besteht: Der Begriff ist verantwortlich für die besondere Beschaffenheit des Gegenstandes; umgekehrt verleiht erst der Gegenstand dem Begriff Realität. Diese wechselseitige ontologische Abhängigkeit bildet für Hegel eine explanatorisch (relativ) geschlossene Einheit: Da wir in dem Maß, wie die logische Struktur des Begriffs im Einzelfall ausgeprägt ist, die besonderen Eigenschaften des Gegenstandes auf der Grundlage des instantiierten bestimmten Begriffs erklären können, sind wir nicht zusätzlich auf die Annahme der Existenz anderer Faktoren festgelegt.[46]

Wegen ihrer semantischen – und damit auch ontologischen – Transparenz erlaubt es uns also nur die Kategorie des Begriffs (mitsamt den daraus folgenden weiteren Bestimmungen), in der Bezugnahme auf von uns verschiedene Inhalte „bei uns zu bleiben" und ein konkretes Selbst zu konstituieren. Demnach sind wir in unserer Auseinandersetzung mit heterogenen Inhalten *dann* frei, wenn wir sie in eine Gestalt bringen, in der sie explizit durch die logische Struktur des Begriffs artikuliert sind.[47] Im epistemischen Fall tun wir dies dadurch, dass wir

---

[45]   Hegel drückt dies in einer bekannten Formulierung so aus: „Die Notwendigkeit wird nicht dadurch zur *Freiheit*, daß sie verschwindet, sondern daß nur ihre noch *innere* Identität *manifestiert* wird [...]" (WdL, TW 6, S. 240).

[46]   In der endlichen Wirklichkeit besteht freilich nie *vollständige* explanatorische Geschlossenheit dieser Art. Hegel glaubt aber, dass auf der Grundlage der Metauniversalie des Begriffs schlechthin einerseits erklärt werden kann, warum grundlegende objektive Begriffe so und nicht anders bestimmt sind – dies hat v. a. die Philosophie mit ihrer Begründung der logischen und realphilosophischen Grundbegriffe zu leisten (vgl. z. B. Enz. § 12 A) –, und andererseits, warum es für viele Tatsachen selbst keine weitere Erklärung mehr gibt (vgl. Henrich, 1971; Kreines, 2008).

[47]   Hierauf baut auch Hegels Theorie des freien Willens mitsamt der Theorie über den zielgerichteten Prozess, in dem Freiheit in der sozialen Welt realisiert wird (vgl. oben § 3), auf: vgl. Patten, 1999, Kap. 3; Knappik, i. Ersch., Kap. 7. – Der einfachste Fall einer Anwendung der Kategorie des Begriffs besteht im *Selbstbezug des Ich*. Wie wir

Gegenstände als Instanzen objektiver bestimmter Begriffe interpretieren – dass
wir also (in mehr oder weniger umfassender Weise) die Gegenstände *begreifen*,
indem wir ihre besondere Beschaffenheit auf der Grundlage der relevanten
objektiven bestimmten Begriffe erklären.[48] Aus diesem Grunde erfordert epistemische Freiheit das Begreifen von Gegenständen durch die Anwendung der
Kategorie des Begriffs. Diese Anwendung und damit auch die durch sie ermög-
lichte rationale Selbstkonstitution sind ihrerseits nur möglich, wenn die Wirklichkeit selbst so durch die logische Struktur des Begriffs strukturiert ist, dass
sie aus Instanzen objektiver bestimmter Begriffe in Hegels Sinn besteht.[49]

Die beiden Fragen, die sich oben in Bezug auf Hegels Verständnis des Verhältnisses von Freiheit, Begreifen und der Metaphysik bestimmter Begriffe
ergeben hatten – warum muss die Wirklichkeit durch objektive Begriffe in
Hegels Sinn strukturiert sein, um unserem Verstehen offenzustehen; und warum ist ein solches Verstehen eine Bedingung für rationale Freiheit? –, können
wir also mit Hegel wie folgt beantworten: Rationale Freiheit erfordert eine normative Orientierung, die eine weder zufällige noch willkürliche Konstitution
eines „bei sich seienden" Subjekts ermöglicht; der „Begriff" bildet die normative Grundlage dieser Orientierung; wir strukturieren die Inhalte unseres Denkens durch die Form des Begriffs, indem wir sie begreifen; wir begreifen die
Inhalte unseres Denkens, indem wir die Gegenstände, auf die wir uns beziehen,
mit ihren besonderen Eigenschaften auf Grund der jeweils instantiierten objektiven Begriffe erklären; solche Erklärungen sind nur möglich, wenn die Wirklichkeit Prinzipien enthält, auf die wir diese Erklärungen gründen können

<hr>

gesehen haben, besteht für Hegel die Struktur des Selbstbewusstseins in einer intrinsischen Einheit zwischen einem besonderen Aspekt (das Ich als Reihe besonderer
Zustände, Episoden usw.) und einem allgemeinen Aspekt (das Ich als der Träger oder
Bezugspunkt dieser Zustände usw.). Wenn wir uns durch das Pronomen „ich" auf uns
selbst in dieser Doppelung von Aspekten beziehen, dann wenden wir damit für Hegel
in elementarer Weise die Kategorie des Begriffs an. (Vgl. insbesondere WdL, TW 6,
S. 253.) Hegel deutet entsprechend das Selbstbewusstsein auch als die einfachste Form
von Freiheit; vgl. z. B. Enz. § 20 A, TW 8, S. 75; § 424; GPhR § 5. – Der geschilderte
Zusammenhang erklärt ferner auch, warum für Hegel der begriffene Gegenstand dieselbe Form besitzt wie das Selbstbewusstsein und wir daher den Gegenstand durch
das Begreifen in unsere „eigene Form" bringen (s. o.).

[48] Die Philosophie setzt diesen Prozess fort, indem sie die bestimmten objektiven
Begriffe ihrerseits auf grundlegendere Begriffe bis hin zur Metauniversalie des Begriffs
schlechthin zurückführt: vgl. oben Fn. 46. Die verschiedenen epistemischen Fähigkeiten (Anschauung, Vorstellung usw.) deutet Hegel dabei als graduelle Ausprägungen
von Freiheit, die auf das Ziel des „begreifenden Erkennens" (z. B. Enz. § 2) ausgerichtet sind (Enz. § 445 A, TW 10, S. 242 f.).

[49] Hegels skizzierte Argumentation bietet uns zugleich auch einen Grund, warum wir
uns sicher sein können, dass dem so ist: Denn die Kategorie des Begriffs hat sich als
die einzige Kategorie erwiesen, deren Instanzen nicht zwangsläufig von etwas anderem ontologisch abhängig sind, und die deshalb einen berechtigten Anspruch auf
ontologische Fundamentalität erheben kann (zumindest, wenn Hegel auf Grund weiterer Argumente skeptische Szenarien ausschließen kann: s. o., § 2).

(Hegels Version des „rational constraint"), also wenn sie durch objektive Begriffe artikuliert ist. Hegel verfügt also tatsächlich über stärkere Prämissen für das „rational constraint"-Argument, die einen zumindest nicht prinzipiell abwegigen Begründungsansatz für seine stärkere Konklusion – die stärkere Lesart des Begriffsrealismus – bieten.

Fazit

Eingangs haben wir kurz gesehen, dass Hegel diejenigen Fragen, die gängigerweise in Bezug auf die metaphysischen Voraussetzungen von Freiheit gestellt werden – Fragen nach der Kompatibilität von Freiheit und Determinismus, nach der Notwendigkeit alternativer Möglichkeiten usw. – als unbedeutend oder irreführend (da auf einer Reduktion von Freiheit auf Willkür beruhend) betrachtet und stattdessen eine alternative Perspektive auf das Verhältnis von Freiheit und Metaphysik entwickelt. Ähnlich argumentiert Brandom,[50] dass die traditionelle Frage nach dem Verhältnis von Freiheit, alternativen Möglichkeiten und Determinismus falsch gestellt ist: Sie beruhe nämlich auf einer Verwechslung der für Freiheit allein relevanten deontischen Modalitäten mit alethischen Modalitäten (wie z. B. der alethischen Möglichkeit, anders gehandelt zu haben). Die von Brandom und Hegel verfolgten Fragestellungen und Argumentationen machen auf eine sonst vernachlässigte Art von metaphysischen Voraussetzungen für Freiheit aufmerksam. Die Hoffnung, dadurch den traditionellen Fragen der Kompatibilität usw. zu entkommen, ist aber trügerisch. Die metaphysischen Positionen, die bei Brandom und Hegel jeweils aus dem „rational constraint"-Argument resultieren, lösen die traditionellen Probleme nicht, und die Meinung, diese Probleme seien belanglos oder verfehlt, ist irrig. Selbst wenn nämlich Freiheit grundsätzlich vom Willen und der mit ihm verbundenen kausalen Spontaneität entkoppelt wird, wie dies in unterschiedlichen Formen sowohl bei Brandom als auch bei Hegel geschieht, können wir diese Freiheit nur unter der Annahme zuschreiben, dass bestimmte alternative Möglichkeiten (und zwar, pace Brandom, tatsächlich im alethisch-modalen Sinn) bestehen – dass z. B. eine Person mit einer irrationalen Überzeugung auch eine andere Überzeugung hätte bilden können. – Brandoms und Hegels originelle Perspektiven auf die Metaphysik der Freiheit bieten also keinen guten Grund dafür, dass wir die Frage nach alternativen Möglichkeiten und damit verwandte Fragen nicht mehr stellen sollten. Aber es ist sicher ein Fortschritt, wenn man sich klar macht, dass dies nicht die einzige Art von Fragen ist, die es sich auf diesem Gebiet zu stellen lohnt.[51]

---

[50]   Brandom, 2009, S. 58 f.
[51]   Mein herzlicher Dank gilt Erasmus Mayr für wertvolle Kommentare zu diesem Text sowie Axel Hutter und Robert Brandom für ihre Unterstützung im Rahmen der

Literatur

Alvarez, Maria (2010): *Kinds of Reasons: An Essay in the Philosophy of Action*, Oxford.

Bittner, Rüdiger (2005): *Aus Gründen Handeln*, Berlin/New York.

Brandom, Robert (1979): „Freedom and Constraint by Norms", in: *American Philosophical Quarterly*, 16, S. 187–196.

Brandom, Robert (1994): *Making it Explicit. Reasoning, Representing, and Discursive Commitment*, Cambridge (Mass.).

Brandom, Robert (2000): „Vocabularies of Pragmatism: Synthesizing Naturalism and Historicism", in: ders. (Hrsg.), *Rorty and His Critics*, Oxford, S. 156–183.

Brandom, Robert (2002 a): „Holism and Idealism in Hegel's *Phenomenology*", in: *Tales of the Mighty Dead. Historical Essays in the Metaphysics of Intentionality*, Cambridge (Mass.), S. 178–209.

Brandom, Robert (2002 b): „Some Pragmatist Themes in Hegel's Idealism", in: *Tales of the Mighty Dead*, S. 210–234.

Brandom, Robert (2005): „Sketch of a Program for a Critical Reading of Hegel. Comparing Empirical and Logical Concepts", in: *Internationales Jahrbuch des Deutschen Idealismus*, 3, S. 131–161.

Brandom, Robert (2008 a): *Between Saying and Doing: Towards an Analytic Pragmatism*, Oxford.

Brandom, Robert (2008 b): „Replies", in: Prien, Bernd/Schweikard, David (Hrsg.): *Robert Brandom: Analytic Pragmatist*, Frankfurt a. M., S. 163–194.

Brandom, Robert (2009): *Reason in Philosophy. Animating Ideas*, Cambridge (Mass.).

Brandom, Robert (unveröffentlicht a): „Knowing and Representing: Reading (between the lines of) Hegel's Introduction. Lecture One: Conceptual Realism and the Semantic Possibility of Knowledge", unveröffentlichter Entwurf, <http://www.pitt.edu/~brandom/downloads/KR1 CRSPK 11-5-29 a.doc> (26. 6. 2012).

Brandom, Robert (unveröffentlicht b): „Modal Expressivism and Modal Realism: Together Again", unveröffentlichter Entwurf, <http://www.pitt.edu/~brandom/downloads/MEMRTA 10-8-11 double-spaced b.doc> (26.6.2012).

Dancy, Jonathan (2000): *Practical Reality*, Oxford.

deVries, Willem (1991): „The Dialectic of Teleology", in: *Philosophical Topics*, 19, S. 51–70.

di Giovanni, George (2005): *Freedom and Religion in Kant and His Immediate Successors. The Vocation of Humankind, 1774–1800*, Cambridge.

Düsing, Klaus (2002): „Spontaneität und Freiheit in Kants praktischer Philosophie", in: ders.: *Subjektivität und Freiheit. Untersuchungen zum Idealismus von Kant bis Hegel*, Stuttgart-Bad Cannstatt, S. 211–235.

Fichte, Johann Gottlieb (1966 a): *Einige Vorlesungen über die Bestimmung des Gelehrten*, in: *Gesamtausgabe der Bayerischen Akademie der Wissenschaften*, Bd. I, 3, hrsg. Lauth, Reinhard/Jacob, Hans/Schottky, Richard, Stuttgart-Bad Cannstatt, S. 23–68. (Zitiert mit „*Bestimmung des Gelehrten*". *Gesamtausgabe* zitiert mit „GA" und Angabe von Reihe und Band.)

Dissertation (Knappik, i. Ersch.), auf der dieser Beitrag beruht. Außerdem danke ich Robert Brandom für die freundliche Erlaubnis, seine unveröffentlichten Entwürfe *Knowing and Representing* und *Modal Expressivism and Modal Realism* zu zitieren.

Fichte, Johann Gottlieb (1966 b): *Ueber Belebung und Erhöhung des reinen Interesse für Wahrheit*, in: GA I, 3, S. 83–90. (Zitiert mit *„Ueber Belebung"*.)

Fichte, Johann Gottlieb (1970): *Briefe 1793–1795*, in GA III, 2, hrsg. Gliwitzky, Hans/ Lauth, Reinhard/Jacob, Hans/Zahn, Manfred.

Habermas, Jürgen (1999): „Von Kant zu Hegel. Zu Brandoms Sprachpragmatik", in: ders.: *Wahrheit und Rechtfertigung. Philosophische Aufsätze*, Frankfurt a. M., S. 138–185.

Hegel, Georg Wilhelm Friedrich (1952): *Briefe von und an Hegel*, hrsg. Johannes Hoffmeister, 3 Bde., Hamburg.

Hegel, Georg Wilhelm Friedrich (2001): *Vorlesungen über die Logik, Berlin 1831. Nachgeschrieben von Karl Hegel*, hrsg. Udo Rameil, in: *Vorlesungen. Ausgewählte Nachschriften und Manuskripte*, Bd. 10, Hamburg. (Zitiert mit *„Vorlesungen über die Logik"*.)

Hegel, Georg Wilhelm Friedrich (1970 a): *Phänomenologie des Geistes*, in: *Werke in zwanzig Bänden. Theorie Werkausgabe*, hrsg. Michel, Karl Markus/Moldenhauer, Eva, Frankfurt a. M. 1970, Bd. 3. (*Phänomenologie des Geistes* zitiert mit „PhG". *Werke*, wo erforderlich, zitiert mit „TW" und Angabe des Bandes.)

Hegel, Georg Wilhelm Friedrich (1970 b): *Wissenschaft der Logik*, in: TW 5–6. (Zitiert mit „WdL".)

Hegel, Georg Wilhelm Friedrich (1970 c): *Grundlinien der Philosophie des Rechts*, in: TW 7. (Zitiert mit „GPhR" und Angabe der Paragraphenzahl.)

Hegel, Georg Wilhelm Friedrich (1970 d): *Enzyklopädie der philosophischen Wissenschaften*, in: TW 8–10. (Zitiert mit „Enz." und Angabe der Paragraphen-Zahl.)

Hegel, Georg Wilhelm Friedrich (1970 e): *Fragment zur Philosophie des Geistes*, in: TW 11, S. 517–550. (Zitiert mit *„Fragment"*.)

Hegel, Georg Wilhelm Friedrich (1970 f): *Vorlesungen über die Philosophie der Geschichte*, in: TW 12. (Zitiert mit *„Philosophie der Geschichte"*.)

Hegel, Georg Wilhelm Friedrich (1970 g): *Vorlesungen über die Beweise vom Dasein Gottes*, in: TW 17, S. 345–535. (Zitiert mit *„Beweise vom Dasein Gottes"*.)

Henrich, Dieter (1971): „Hegels Theorie über den Zufall", in: *Hegel im Kontext*, Frankfurt a. M., S. 158–186.

Horstmann, Rolf-Peter (1990): *Wahrheit aus dem Begriff. Eine Einführung in Hegel*, Frankfurt a. M.

Kant, Immanuel (1968 a): *Grundlegung zur Metaphysik der Sitten*, in: *Kants Werke. Akademie-Textausgabe*, Bd. 4, hrsg. Preussische Akademie der Wissenschaften, Berlin (Nachdruck der Ausgabe 1903), S. 385–464. (*Grundlegung* zitiert mit „GMS". *Kants Werke* zitiert mit „AA" und Angabe des Bandes.)

Kant, Immanuel (1968 b): *Kritik der Urtheilskraft*, in: AA 5, S. 165–486. (Zitiert mit „KU".)

Kant, Immanuel (1968 c): *Recension von Schulz's Versuch einer Anleitung zur Sittenlehre für alle Menschen, ohne Unterschied der Religion, nebst einem Anhange von den Todesstrafen*, in: AA 8, 9–14. (Zitiert mit *„Schulz-Rezension"*.)

Kant, Immanuel (1968 d): *Was heißt: Sich im Denken orientiren?*, in: AA 8, S. 131–148. (Zitiert mit *„Orientierung"*.)

Knappik, Franz (i. Ersch.): *Im Reich der Freiheit. Hegels Theorie autonomer Vernunft*, Berlin/New York.

Knappik, Franz (unveröffentlicht): „Towards a Reading of Hegel's ‚Concept': Concepthood, Comprehension, and Natural Kinds", Manuskript.

Kreines, James (2008): „Metaphysics without Pre-Critical Monism: Hegel on Lower-Level Natural Kinds and the Structure of Reality", in: *Bulletin of the Hegel Society of Great Britain*, 57/58, S. 48–70.

Kruck, Günter (2003): „Selbständigkeit und notwendige Vergewisserung. Hegels Urteilslehre im Vergleich zu Brandoms Verstehenstheorie", in: Koch, Anton Friedrich/Oberauer, Alexander/Utz, Konrad (Hrsg.): *Der Begriff als die Wahrheit. Zum Anspruch der Hegelschen „Subjektiven Logik"*, Paderborn u. a., S. 69–84.

Lewis, David (1986): *On the Plurality of Worlds*, Malden u. a.

McDowell, John (1996), *Mind and World. With a New Introduction*, Cambridge (Mass.)

Peetz, Siegbert (1995): *Die Freiheit im Wissen. Eine Untersuchung zu Schellings Konzept der Rationalität*, Frankfurt a. M.

Pippin, Robert (2008): *Hegel's Practical Philosophy. Rational Agency as Ethical Life*, Cambridge.

Patten, Allen (1999): *Hegel's Idea of Freedom*, Oxford.

Pohl, Michael/Rosenhagen, Raja/Weber, Arne M. (2008): „Realist and Idealist Interpretations of Brandom's Account of Objectivity", in: Prien, Bernd/Schweikard, David (Hrsg.): *Robert Brandom: Analytic Pragmatist*, Frankfurt a. M., S. 89–100.

Rosefeldt, Tobias (2000): *Das logische Ich. Kant über den Gehalt des Begriffes von sich selbst*, Berlin/Wien.

Sans, Georg (2004): *Die Realisierung des Begriffs. Eine Untersuchung zu Hegels Schlusslehre*, Berlin.

Schnädelbach, Herbert (2004): „Sozialpragmatischer Idealismus. Bemerkungen zu Robert B. Brandoms ‚Expressive Vernunft'", in: *Allgemeine Zeitschrift für Philosophie*, 29, S. 163–175.

Sider, Theodore (2003): „Reductive Theories of Modality", in: Loux, Michael J./Zimmermann, Dean W. (Hrsg.): *The Oxford Handbook of Metaphysics*, Oxford, S. 180–208.

Stern, Robert, Hegel (1990): *Kant and the Structure of the Object*, London.

Turri, John (2009): „The Ontology of Epistemic Reasons", in: *Noûs*, 43, S. 490–512.

Westphal, Kenneth (1989): *Hegel's Epistemological Realism*, Dordrecht.

Willaschek, Markus (2000): „On ‚The Unboundedness of the Conceptual'", in: Willaschek, Markus (Hrsg.): *John McDowell: Reason and Nature, Lecture and Colloquium in Münster 1999*, Münster, S. 35–40.

Willaschek, Markus (2010): „Die ‚Spontaneität des Erkenntnisses'. Über die Abhängigkeit der ‚Transzendentalen Analytik' von der Auflösung der Dritten Antinomie", in: Chotaš, Jiří/Karásek, Jindřich/Stolzenberg, Jürgen (Hrsg.): *Metaphysik und Kritik. Interpretationen zur „Transzendentalen Dialektik" der Kritik der reinen Vernunft*, Würzburg, S. 165–184.

Yeomans, Christopher (2012): *Freedom and Reflection: Hegel and the Logic of Agency*, Oxford.

Alex Neill/Sandy Shapshay

Moral and Aesthetic Freedom in Schopenhauer's Metaphysics

Schopenhauers negativer Befund hinsichtlich der conditio humana *wird bis zu einem gewissen Grad abgeschwächt durch seine Anerkennung der Möglichkeiten ästhetischer Erfahrung und der Verneinung des Willens zum Leben. Wie Schopenhauer indes selbst bemerkt, scheinen seine Ausführungen zu Letzterem unvereinbar mit seinem Determinismus zu sein. Wir behaupten nun, dass dies hinsichtlich seiner Darstellung des Ersteren nicht weniger der Fall ist. Nach einer kurzen Skizze des deterministischen Menschenbildes Schopenhauers diskutieren wir die Frage, ob der scheinbare Widerspruch dieses Menschenbildes mit seinen Ausführungen über die Verneinung des Willens zum Leben sowie über die ästhetische Erfahrung möglicherweise tatsächlich nur ein scheinbarer sein könnte – insofern sie nämlich als Spielarten rein passiver Erfahrung aufgefasst werden können. Wir behaupten aber, dass es in Schopenhauers Ausführungen Aspekte gibt, die in einer unaufgelösten Spannung zu seinem Determinismus bleiben. Tatsächlich entwirft Schopenhauer das Bild eines Menschen, für den letztlich sowohl ästhetische Erfahrung als auch die Verneinung des Willens schlicht unmöglich ist. Deshalb wenden wir uns Schopenhauers Begriff der ,transzendentalen' Freiheit zu und überlegen, wie man sich auf diese in einer Erklärung der Möglichkeit ästhetischer und asketischer Erfahrung berufen könnte. Schopenhauers eigene Begründung ist jedenfalls nicht überzeugend. Letztlich bleibt der seiner Konzeption von ästhetischer und asketischer Erfahrung inhärente Freiheitsbegriff gänzlich rätselhaft.*

I. Freedom and two paths to peace

The bleakness of Schopenhauer's notoriously pessimistic take on the human condition is mitigated to some extent by his recognition of two possibilities that he takes to be open, in one case to all of us, at least to some extent, and in the other to at least a few exceptional individuals. These possibilities are those of aesthetic experience, on the one hand, and of renunciation, or "denial of the will-to-live", on the other. In aesthetic experience, Schopenhauer says,

> all at once the peace, always sought but always escaping us on that first path of willing, comes to us of its own accord, and all is well with us. It is the painless State, prized by Epicurus as the highest good and as the state of the gods; for that moment we are relieved from the miserable pressure of the will. We celebrate the Sabbath of the penal servitude of willing; the wheel of Ixion stands still (WWR I, p. 196).[1]

---

[1] In some instances, for the sake of accuracy, we will utilize the newer translation of this volume by Judith Norman, Alistair Welchman and Christopher Janaway.

And with regard to renunciation,

> the man in whom the denial of the will-to-live has dawned, however poor, cheer-less and full of privation his state may be when looked at from outside, is full of inner cheerfulness and true heavenly peace. [...] [I]t is an unshakeable peace, a deep calm and inward serenity, a state that we cannot behold without the greatest longing [...] (WWR I, pp. 389–90).

In aesthetic experience, as he understands it, a subject "loses himself" in his contemplation of an object in such a way that "what is thus known is no longer the individual thing as such, but the *Idea*, the eternal form, the immediate objectivity of the will at this grade [of its manifestation in the phenomenal world]" (WWR I, p. 179). And for the denier of will, "knowledge of the whole, of the inner nature of the thing-in-itself", "present in a high degree of distinct-ness", "becomes the *quieter* of all and every willing" (WWR I, pp. 379, 378).

Implicit in these pictures of aesthetic and ascetic experience, it would appear, is a conception of the subject as a *free* subject. Consider, for example, Schopen-hauer's account of what he describes as "the transition that is possible, but to be regarded only as an exception" from ordinary experience to aesthetic experience. He writes:

> Raised up by the power of the mind [*die Kraft des Geistes*], we relinquish [*aufhört*] the ordinary way of considering things, and cease to follow under the guidance of the forms of the principle of sufficient reason merely their relations to one another, whose final goal is always the relation to our own will. Thus we no longer consider the where, the when, the why, and the whither in things, but simply and solely the *what*. Further, we do not let abstract thought, the concepts of reason, take posses-sion of our consciousness, but, instead of all this, devote [*hingiebt*] the whole power of our mind [*die ganze Macht seines Geistes*] to perception, sink ourselves completely therein, and let our whole consciousness be filled by the calm contem-plation of the natural object actually present, whether it be a landscape, a tree, a rock, a crag, a building, or anything else (WWR I, p. 178).

Schopenhauer's language here would seem to imply that the subject of aesthetic experience becomes such by virtue of a deliberate act that breaks the normal, conditioned course of experience: we "*do not let* abstract thought take posses-sion" of our minds, Schopenhauer says; we "*relinquish* the ordinary way of considering things". A few lines later, he suggests that "a knowing individual *raises himself* [...] to the pure subject of knowing" (ibid.); elsewhere, he suggests that in aesthetic contemplation "I *disregard*" and "*set aside*" the con-templated object's position in time and space (PP II, p. 417). These remarks suggest that in making the transition from ordinary to aesthetic experience the subject deliberately *chooses* to break free of the demands of his will and the grip of the principle of sufficient reason; to break free, that is, of what Schopenhauer elsewhere refers to as "the law of causation".

When he turns to ethics, Schopenhauer again appears to be working with a conception of the subject as essentially a free subject, one with the capacity to choose or decide whether to affirm or to deny the will-to-live. The latter option is modelled most clearly, he suggests, in certain works of tragedy, such as Calderón's *La vida es sueño* and Shakespeare's *Hamlet*, where we see that "the noblest men, after a long conflict and suffering, finally renounce for ever all the pleasures of life and the aims till then pursued so keenly, or cheerfully and willingly give up life itself" (WWR I, p. 253). "Willingly giving up" sounds very much like something that one wilfully decides to do. And Schopenhauer is clear that while such renunciation of the will-to-live, initiated by a subject's recognition of the "contradiction of the will-to-live with itself", is often accompanied by great personal suffering, renunciation "by no means results from suffering with the necessity of effect from cause; on the contrary, the will remains free" (WWR I, p. 395).

II. Schopenhauer's determinism

These remarks concerning the possibility of aesthetic experience and renunciation of the will-to-live are, on the face of it, in clear tension with the determinist position that Schopenhauer defends in the earlier sections of Book 4 of *The World as Will and Representation* and in his "Prize Essay on the Freedom of the Will". Indeed, Schopenhauer himself draws our attention to the tension, noting laconically that "[w]e might perhaps regard the whole of our discussion [...] of what I call the denial of the will [and, he might just as well have added, his discussion of aesthetic experience] as inconsistent with the previous explanation of necessity, that appertains just as much to motivation as to every other form of the principle of sufficient reason" (WWR I, p. 402).

In that "previous explanation", Schopenhauer grants that human beings may possess both physical and intellectual freedom, but he construes these in purely negative terms: in the case of physical freedom, it is freedom from material obstacles that would prevent one from doing what one wills; in the case of intellectual freedom, it is freedom from cognitive impairments, both internal (such as madness or intoxication) and external (such as deception or illusion grounded in extra-subjective factors). However, the key philosophical question for Schopenhauer is not whether I can *do* what I will, but rather whether I can *will* what I will (cf. FW, p. 6). In other words, is my will motivationally constrained such that I could not possibly will but in the manner that I do? This is the question of whether we are free in a moral sense, the question of whether human beings are endowed with *liberum arbitrium indifferentiae*, and this is the primary question he sets out to answer in his prize essay.

Schopenhauer's answer is that one is not free to choose what one wills. His grounds for this conclusion rest largely on his epistemological doctrine that the Principle of Sufficient Reason is the *a priori* form of all human experience. Accordingly, the natural world is universally causally determined. As he puts it, "all *changes* that occur in given objects in the real external world are therefore subject to the law of *causality*, and thus always occur as *necessary* and inevitable, whenever and wherever they occur. – To this law there can be no exception" (FW, pp. 24–25). The psychological realm is also entirely subject to the causal nexus: in this regard, the only difference between a rock and a rabbit, for example, is that the rabbit's behavior is governed by the causality of *motives* on the rabbit's nature. Schopenhauer defines "motivation" as "causality that passes through cognition" (FW, p. 27). Thus, given the nature of the rabbit, the presentation of a certain perception – say, that of a fox bounding toward it – provides a sufficient motive for the rabbit's flight, which follows with strict necessity.

The same holds true for human beings, though with two notable differences. First, unlike the rabbit's, the motives that operate in human psychology are typically presented in consciousness in conceptual and linguistic form. And second, Schopenhauer holds that, unlike rabbits, human beings have unique, individual characters, not just the character of their species. These differences notwithstanding, given the particular empirical character of a human being (empirical inasmuch as it is known *a posteriori*), if that human being is presented with certain motives, Schopenhauer holds, the resulting action follows with necessity.[2]

It is crucial to Schopenhauer's conception of the matter that for human beings, "the individual character is *inborn*; it is not a work of art or circumstances subject to chance, but that of nature herself" (FW, p. 46), and further, that individual character is *unchangeable*. He offers two *a priori* reasons in support of this position. First, given his view of the Principle of Sufficient Reason as the *a priori* form of our objective experience, any spontaneous action, one that actually *formed* character from nothing rather than one which *flowed from* a character, would constitute an "inexplicable miracle – an effect without a cause" (FW, p. 40); but the mind has no form for conceiving an effect without a cause, which is to say that the idea lacks real sense. This leaves open the possibility of modification of character through habituation in a manner that is not entirely spontaneous, but this option is foreclosed in Schopenhauer's thought by his second main reason for accepting determinism, namely, the *a priori* law that every *existentia* presupposes an *essentia*, that is, "everything that is must also be *something*, must have a definite essence" (FW, p. 51). Human beings, like everything else in nature, have essential qualities with which they are born.[3]

---

[2]   In principle, then, one could accurately predict a human being's actions, but in practice – given that one only comes to know a person's individual character, including one's own, through much experience, and that discerning the competing motives in a human being's consciousness is a complex business – this is likely to be difficult.

[3]   In addition, Schopenhauer offers a quasi-empirical reason for the inborn and unchangeable nature of the empirical character. By analogy with all other kinds of beings in nature, the empirical character of a human being must be like a force. Since forces of

Although Schopenhauer takes the empirical character to be fixed, individuals may learn through experience "what we want and what we can do" as well as "the dimensions and directions of our mental and physical abilities" and our "total strengths and weaknesses" (WWR^C I, p. 331). If a person acquires "knowledge of the invariable qualities of our own empirical character" then, he suggests, that person has developed "acquired character" [*den erworbenen Charakter*]. Schopenhauer's terminology here is infelicitous, we suggest, inasmuch as it suggests misleadingly that an individual can "acquire" a different character from her empirical one. What is really being "acquired" here is empirical *self-knowledge*. Schopenhauer's point is that a person may learn how most effectively – i.e., in a manner that is socially acceptable and in keeping with his physical and mental abilities – to achieve what he inevitably wills if he acquires empirical self-knowledge. To illustrate: imagine a heavy drinker, Bill, who has ruined his personal life by mistreating his family when drunk. In Schopenhauer's terms, one of Bill's empirical character traits is that he is "alcoholic". After hitting rock bottom, Bill joins Alcoholics Anonymous to work its twelve-step program. In doing so, he may come to recognise a fact about his empirical character, namely that he is *essentially* alcoholic. In Schopenhauer's terms, if he acquires such knowledge, he now has "acquired character". What this really amounts to, however, is the possibility of a difference in his behavior, on the basis of his acquired "empirical self-knowledge", despite the fact that his empirical character remains unchanged. Bill no longer believes that he can go to the bar and have "just one little drink". He realizes that this former belief of his is false and was perhaps all along, self-deceptive, and knows that, as soon as he puts himself in that situation, motives will act on his empirical character with the force of necessity, and he will arrive home drunk. Once he has "acquired empirical self-knowledge", however, he can refrain from putting himself in situations where he will be tempted to drink. He can consciously avoid bars and parties where alcohol is being served. He still wills the drink, and he wills to be a good father and husband too. By acquiring empirical self-knowledge, he can utilize his intellect to avoid the situations where he will, necessarily, drink – for he is essentially, alcoholic – as this behavior conflicts with what he also wills, namely, to have a happy family life.

---

nature are original and unchangeable, so too must be the empirical character (FW, pp. 49–50). Finally, Schopenhauer offers some pretty weak empirical reasons to bolster his case, writing that "[w]e can obtain confirmation of this truth from daily experience; but the most striking is obtained when after twenty or thirty years we meet an acquaintance again and soon spot in him precisely the same old tricks as before" (FW, p. 44). Also, we never trust anyone who has deceived us in the past and *mutatis mutandis* for those we have previously trusted.

III. Willing oneself into will-lessness?

On the basis of the thoughts outlined above – that human beings have inborn, unalterable empirical characters and that the law of causality operates with strict necessity in the psychological as well as the physical realm – Schopenhauer declares that "we have entirely suspended from human action all freedom and have recognised that such action is thoroughly subject to the strictest necessity [...]" (FW, p. 83). Our question, then, is this: How is this position consistent with Schopenhauer's characterization of the subject of aesthetic experience and of the person who renounces the will-to-live as apparently possessed of freedom?

Indeed, this question can be given a rather sharper focus: given that on Schopenhauer's view things can be experienced aesthetically only by a subject in whom individuality has been "abolished" (WWR I, p. 169), which is to say, by a subject in whom intellect has broken free of its service to the individual will, and hence is in a state of "will-lessness", the thought, illustrated in Section I above, that the transition into aesthetic experience depends on the subject's deliberate action implies that it is by an act of will that the intellect is freed from the service of the will. But given Schopenhauer's view of the nature of the relationship between intellect and will this looks to say the least problematic. He holds that the former is by nature subordinate to the latter in virtue of the fact that it "developed in that service, and indeed sprang from the will as the head springs from the trunk of the body [*Dem Dienste des Willens bleibt nun die Erkenntniß in der Regel immer unterworfen, wie sie ja zu diesem Dienste hervorgegangen ... ist*]" (WWR[C] I, p. 200). David Hamlyn, for example, suggests that it is "impossible to see" why or indeed how the will, so to speak, would let go of the intellect, that is, would in effect subvert *itself* (Hamlyn, 1980, pp. 109–110). And Paul Guyer, having construed Schopenhauer as holding that the transition from ordinary to aesthetic experience is "the consequence of an active, even violent adoption of a cognitive attitude by the individual mind", so that "we actively will [...] to free ourselves from the will", notes that there is "something unsettling" and "an air of paradox about Schopenhauer's account" (Guyer, 1996, p. 116).[4] But this, we suggest, understates the matter: The thought that the individual will subverts itself, which is what the thought that aesthetic experience is effected by an act of will on the part of the subject comes down to, is in Schopenhauerian terms not merely unsettling, but incoherent.

---

[4]   Guyer reads Schopenhauer as offering "a description of contemplation as the consequence of an active, even violent adoption of a cognitive attitude by the individual mind".

Schopenhauer himself, in a move that may seem at odds with his initial characterisation of aesthetic experience, insists that this is not his thought. "The change in the subject [of aesthetic experience]", he says in the second volume of *The World as Will and Representation*, "just because it consists in the elimination of all willing, cannot proceed from the will [*nicht vom Willen ausgehen*], and hence cannot be an act of arbitrary will [*kein Akt der Willkür*], in other words, cannot rest with us [*nicht in unserm Belieben stehen*]" (WWR II, p. 367) (translation modified). And he makes essentially the same point with regard to the denier of the will-to-live:

> Now since, as we have seen, that self-suppression of the will [*jene Selbstaufhebung des Willens*] comes from knowledge, but all knowledge and insight are such as are independent of free choice [*von der Willkür unabhängig ist*], that denial of willing, that entrance into freedom, is not to be forcibly arrived at by intention or design, but comes from the innermost relation of knowing and willing in man; hence it comes suddenly, as if flying in from without [*kommt daher plötzlich und wie von Außen angeflogen*] (WWR I, p. 404).

The "suddenly" in the last clause of this statement echoes something that should strike us as odd in the opening sentence of Schopenhauer's characterisation of aesthetic experience. "As we have said", he writes,

> the transition that is possible, but to be regarded as only an exception, from the common knowledge of particular things to knowledge of the Idea *takes place suddenly* [*plötzlich*], since knowledge tears itself free from the service of the will [*die Erkenntniß sich vom Dienste des Willens losreißt*] precisely by the subject's ceasing to be merely individual, and being now a pure will-less subject of knowledge (WWR I, p. 178) (emphasis provided).

In one sense of "sudden", the sense in which something that happens suddenly happens very quickly, or "all at once", this reference to the suddenness of the transition looks problematic. For one thing, it renders Schopenhauer's opening words ('As we have said') very puzzling, since nothing that he has said previously suggests that the transition is in this sense sudden, or indeed refers to the rapidity of the transition that takes place at all. Furthermore, the clause that follows, which seems to be supposed to explain why or how the transition is sudden, does no such thing, since nothing that Schopenhauer has said previously (or indeed anything he says in what follows) indicates that the "subject's ceasing to be merely individual" is an occurrence that takes place very quickly. His claim that the transition occurs suddenly thus starts to look at best unmotivated and at worst anomalous.

But this impression fades when we bear in mind that "suddenly" also has a rather different connotation of "happening very fast or all at once": to describe something as having happened suddenly in this sense is to say that it was unexpected. The German word that Schopenhauer uses is *"plötzlich"*, which also has the connotations both of happening quickly and unexpectedly. In English, indeed, the latter connotation is arguably primary: To describe an event as having occurred suddenly may or may not be to describe it as having taken place quickly, but it is always to describe it as having been unexpected. (Thus for example, we may say of someone that he died suddenly – i.e., unexpectedly – even though his dying was quite prolonged. But it is hard to imagine a correct use of "sudden" in which unexpectedness is not implied: if one says that someone one knew to have been suffering the final stages of a terminal illness died suddenly, one means that his death was unexpected at the time at which it occurred, even if it was in a more general sense expected.) And there is good reason, we suggest, to suppose that when Schopenhauer says that "the transition [...] from the common knowledge of particular things to knowledge of the Idea takes place suddenly" in the case of aesthetic experience, he is referring to the unexpectedness of the transition. For one thing, it fits well with his characterisation of the "denial of willing" as something that comes "as if flying in from without". For another, on this reading, Schopenhauer's claim in his initial characterisation of aesthetic experience – i.e., that this is something that he has said previously – is unproblematic: What he has said before, and says again in the clause that follows, is that the transition in question depends on the disappearance of individuality, on the intellect's becoming "free from the service of the will". And that is a change that will always be unexpected, in the sense that it will always represent a departure from what Schopenhauer has argued extensively to be the norm: "[F]or the most part, cognition always remains subordinated to the service of the [individual] will" (WWR^C I, p. 200).

Finally, and especially to the point just here, if Schopenhauer's claim is indeed that the transition into aesthetic experience or denial of the will-to-live is something that occurs unexpectedly, then it would be very odd if he supposes that transition to be something that we deliberately bring about through an act of will. It is significant that when we describe things as happening suddenly with regard to ourselves ("I was suddenly struck by the thought that ..." or "I suddenly realised that ...") the implication is that we are *passive* with respect to what has occurred; that it has the feel of something that has happened *to* us, rather than something that we have brought about. In short, we suggest, it is plausible to suppose that in describing the transition into aesthetic experience as occurring "suddenly" Schopenhauer's thought was that this transition, like that into "denial of willing", is unexpected in virtue of not being an effect that an agent deliberately tries to bring about, which is to say that it is not deliberately willed.

IV. Will-lessness and passivity: beauty and renunciation

Is there scope, then, despite Schopenhauer's characterisation of the transition from ordinary experience to aesthetic experience and denial of the will-to-live in such active terms, for seeing those transitions as something with respect to which the subject is essentially passive, as not dependent on any act of will, and hence as consistent with his determinism? Some of what he has to say about the experience of beauty suggests that there may be. When he first describes that experience, in Section 34 of WWR I, he characterizes it in active terms as involving a "transition" [*Uebergang*] brought about when cognition "tears itself free" from service to the will [*indem die Erkenntniß sich vom Dienste des Willens losreißt*] (WWR I, p. 178). But by Section 39, the experience of the beautiful is characterized as involving a much more passive-sounding "transport into a state of pure contemplative intuition" [*das Versetzen in den Zustand des reinen Anschauens*] that "occurs most easily when objects meet that state halfway" by "virtue of their intricate [...] clear and determinate form" (WWR^C I, p. 225). Beautiful objects, Schopenhauer holds, have an "obliging character" that "accommodates" the transition into a state of will-lessness in a perceiver; such objects "turn readily into representatives of their Ideas" inasmuch as the perception of them does not provoke activity of will. And when presented with such an object under certain conditions – roughly, conditions in which the demands of the will are not pressing – its "intricate [...] clear and determinate" form can become salient for a subject, bringing her to the point where she may be transported "into a state of pure contemplative intuition" (ibid.).

Schopenhauer's thought here is that under such conditions the subject "loses" her awareness of her individuality, and experiences beauty, because (a) the demands of the will are not pressing (the subject is not hungry, say, or afraid, or otherwise excited), (b) the object presented to consciousness does not present any direct motives to her will, and (c) the object is constituted in such a way that for a subject in these conditions the Idea that the object instantiates – its essential character, so to speak – is particularly accessible.[5] In short, although in experience of the beautiful a subject has certainly slipped out of the normal, conditioned, course of experience, no decision or choice or act of will on the subject's part is required to make that happen: all that is required is a certain sort of object and a relative calmness of will in the subject.

This picture of the experience of beauty as essentially something with respect to which the subject is passive is reflected in some of what Schopenhauer has to say about the possibility of renunciation, or denial of the will-to-live. The latter may be "attained", he maintains, via either of two pathways. On the first path, "that veil of Maya, the *principium individuationis*, is lifted from the eyes of a man to such an extent" (WWR I, p. 378) that "he knows the whole, comprehends its inner nature, and finds it involved in a constant passing away, a vain striving, an inward conflict, and a continual suffering" (WWR I, p. 379). This knowledge "becomes the *quieter* [*Quietiv*] of all and every willing" in him. And the quieting (Schopenhauer also describes it as "silencing" or "suppression" or

---

    (b) and (c) are in effect different ways of stating one and the same condition.

"breaking") of a person's individual will makes it possible for the person to "renounce" ("turn away from", "deny") the will-to-live, the "inner nature" not only of "his own phenomenon" but of phenomena in general (WWR I, p. 380).

The more common path to renunciation, however, lies via "the suffering personally felt, not the suffering merely known. [...] For only in the case of a few is mere knowledge sufficient to bring about the denial of the will, the knowledge namely that sees through the *principium individuationis*. [...] [I]n most cases the will must be broken [*gebrochen*] by the greatest personal suffering before its self-denial appears" (WWR I, p. 392). As these remarks set it out, then, the difference between the two paths to renunciation is as follows: on the first, *knowledge* leads to the quietening of the individual will, which makes denial of the will-to-live possible; on the second, *suffering* leads to the quietening of the individual will, which makes denial of the will-to-live possible.

We shall suggest below that this way of characterizing the difference between the two paths to renunciation is significantly misleading. But first, we should note that Schopenhauer's initial characterization of both paths looks consistent with the view that the experience of renunciation is one with respect to which the denier of the will-to-live is passive. Those who find themselves on the second pathway, after all, are unlikely to have brought their suffering on themselves, or at any rate, not in the sense that they have deliberately sought it out as a means to renunciation. Their suffering, that is, is something with respect to which such a person is passive; and if that suffering does indeed break her individual will, and if that does lead to her denial of the will-to-live in general (neither of which, as Schopenhauer sees it, are inevitable), neither of the latter depends on any decision of hers. Regarding the first pathway, the position is even clearer: on this, it is the acquisition of knowledge that leads to quieting of the individual will and allows denial of the will-to-live in general, and Schopenhauer is unequivocal in holding that "all knowledge and insight as such are independent of free choice", so that "denial of willing is not to be forcibly be arrived at by intention or design [...]" (WWR I, p. 404).[6] Whichever of the two paths it is arrived at by, then, the experience of renunciation may seem to be one with respect to which the subject is passive.

---

[6]   There is a complication with respect to Schopenhauer's apparent view that knowledge does not depend on choice, for he also says "the second path [...] leads to the denial of the will not, like the first, through the mere knowledge of the suffering of a whole world *which one acquires voluntarily* [*das man sich freiwillig aneignet*], but through the excessive pain felt in one's own person" (WWR I, p. 393) (emphasis provided). The implication in this passage is that it is only the second path that doesn't involve any volition at all; but this assertion conflicts with the idea that knowledge does not depend on free choice. Given Schopenhauer's repeated insistence on the independence of volition from the acquisition of knowledge of the essential nature of the world, we believe that Schopenhauer's invocation of "voluntarily acquired" knowledge of the inner nature of the world here is simply careless.

V. Will-lessness and agency: asceticism and sublimity

However, recognition of these considerations about the experience of beauty and the two pathways to renunciation, as Schopenhauer construes them, is not sufficient to dispel all worries about the tension between his determinism and his accounts of aesthetic experience and of denial of the will-to-live. It is true that the experience of beauty is, as he characterizes it, entirely passive. So too will be the experience of many of those who attain denial of the will-to-live via great personal suffering, which, although it "frequently produces complete resignation", Schopenhauer suggests, does so "often only at the approach of death" (WWR I, p. 392). (More on this in a moment.) But even if the experience of beauty is the most common kind of aesthetic experience, it is not the only kind; and even if the most common route to renunciation is one along which the denier of the will-to-live is carried passively, there is, as we have seen, more than one route to renunciation.

With regard to renunciation of the will-to-live attained via the first pathway, Schopenhauer makes the following point:

> we must not imagine that, after the denial of the will-to-live has once appeared through knowledge that has become a quieter of the will, such denial no longer wavers or falters. [...] On the contrary, it must always be achieved afresh by constant struggle. For as the body is the will itself [...] as phenomenon in the world as representation, that whole will-to-live exists potentially so long as the body lives, and is always striving to reach actuality and to burn afresh with all its intensity. We therefore find in the lives of saintly persons that peace and bliss we have described, only as the blossom resulting from the constant overcoming of the will; and we see the constant struggle with the will-to-live as the soil from which it shoots up. [...] Therefore we see also those who have once attained to denial of the will, strive with all their might to keep to this path by self-imposed renunciations of every kind, by a penitent and hard way of life, and by looking for what is disagreeable to them; all this in order to suppress the will that is constantly springing up afresh (WWR I, p. 391).

These remarks suggest that even if the initial transition into denial of the will-to-live is something with respect to which the subject is passive, maintaining this state requires "constant struggle", indeed a struggle "with all [one's] might". Schopenhauer goes on to give a series of examples that reinforce the idea that the ascetic path to renunciation is one that requires agency: Examples of ascetics who seek to mortify the flesh in various ways, illustrating, for example, that "the first step in asceticism" is "[v]oluntary and complete chastity", and that further steps include "voluntary and intentional poverty", fasting, and self-castigation (WWR I, p. 380).

It is worth noticing here that Schopenhauer's initial characterization of the difference between the two paths to denial of the will-to-live – which has it that on the first, knowledge leads to the quieting of the individual will, which makes denial of the will-to-live possible; whereas on the second, suffering leads to the quieting of the individual will, which makes denial of the will-to-live possible – is misleading. In fact, his view is that denial of the will-to-live *per se* depends on knowledge; the real difference between the two paths is that in the second, but not the first, that knowledge is acquired as a result of personal suffering. Thus, for example: "the denial of the will-to-live [...] always proceeds from that quieter of the will; and this is the knowledge of its inner conflict and its essential vanity, expressing themselves in the suffering of all that lives" (WWR I, p. 397). And: "[T]he approach of death and helplessness [...] are not absolutely necessary for such a purification through suffering. Even without them, the knowledge of the contradiction of the will-to-live with itself can, through great misfortune and suffering, violently force itself on us [...]" (WWR I, p. 394). Where imminent death is involved, presumably striving to "keep to this path" of denial will not be necessary; the experience of denial of the will-to-live in such cases, then, will be one to which the subject is entirely passive. But in other cases of "purification through suffering", maintenance of the denial of the will-to-live, no less than in cases where the requisite knowledge has been arrived at by a route other than that of personal suffering, will be need to be "achieved afresh by constant struggle".

The problem posed by the apparent willfullness of at least some cases of renunciation of the will-to-live is compounded when we recall that aesthetic experience comprises not only the experience of beauty but also that of the sublime. While beautiful objects accommodate the transition into the state of willlessness in a perceiver inasmuch as they do not provoke activity of will, Schopenhauer holds that sublime objects or states of affairs, by contrast, stand in "a hostile relation to the human will in general, as manifested in [...] the human body. They may be opposed to it, they may threaten it by their might that eliminates all resistance, or their immeasurable greatness may reduce it to nought" (WWR I, p. 201). Sublime objects and states of affairs, that is, are recognised by the subject as threatening in some sense, and that recognition is an impediment to transition into will-less contemplation of them. Despite this, Schopenhauer insists, such contemplation of the sublime is possible. However,

> with the sublime, that state of pure knowing is obtained first of all [*allererst*] by *a conscious* [*bewußtes*] *and violent tearing away* from the relations of the same object to the will which are recognized as unfavourable, by *a free exaltation, accompanied by consciousness, beyond the will* [*ein freies, von Bewußtseyn begleitetes Erheben über den Willen*] and the knowledge related to it. This exaltation must *not only be won* with consciousness, but *also be maintained*, and it is therefore accompanied by a constant recollection of the will, yet not of a single individual willing, such as fear or desire, but of human willing in general, in so far as it is expressed universally through its objectivity, the human body (WWR I, p. 202) (emphases provided).

Like most cases in which a person arrives at denial of the will-to-live, indeed all such cases in which denial is not closely followed by the person's death, experience of the sublime requires active sustenance or maintenance. But as Schopenhauer characterises it, experience of the sublime also requires active *initiation*, it is achieved by the subject's *violently tearing away* her attention from the threat posed by the object to her individual will (WWR I, p. 202). With respect to the sublime, if not to the beautiful, then, Guyer's suggestion that in Schopenhauer's view the transition from ordinary to aesthetic experience is "the consequence of an active, even violent adoption of a cognitive attitude by the individual mind", in which "we actively will [...] to free ourselves from the will", looks entirely accurate (Guyer, op. cit.). And Schopenhauer's insistence that this is not his view – "[t]he change in the subject [of aesthetic experience], just because it consists in the elimination of all willing, cannot proceed from the will" (WWR II, p. 367) – looks increasingly questionable.

At least part of the problem here, we suggest, lies in Schopenhauer's rhetoric.[7] His characterization of the difference between experience of the beautiful and experience of the sublime does indeed suggest that while the former is something that happens *to* us, the latter is something that we *bring about*: Again, in the experience of beauty it is the "quality of [the object] which facilitates knowledge of its Idea" that ("imperceptibly") "raises us to the will-free subject of knowing", while "with the sublime, that state of pure knowing is obtained first of all by a conscious and violent tearing away [...]" (WWR I, p. 202). But the phrase "first of all" [*allererst*] is crucial here: in fact the activity – the "violent tearing" – that Schopenhauer insists is essential to aesthetic experience of the sublime may be essential not as the efficient cause of that variety of experience, but rather as a condition of its possibility; not because it brings the experience about, but because it makes it possible for the experience to *happen to* the subject. A very plausible reading of Schopenhauer's thought on this, we suggest, is that in the experience of the sublime, just as in the experience of the beautiful, it is that quality of the object "which facilitates knowledge of its Idea" that effects the transition, that so to speak "pulls" the observer into will-lessness. In the case of beauty, this transition occurs easily, since beautiful objects do not provoke or arouse desire or emotion. Sublime objects, however, are perceived as in one way or another at least potentially a threat to the individual will; as such they are so to speak natural aggravators of desire and emotion, and these responses have to be in one way or another repressed or subdued if a transition to will-lessness is to be possible. That is, the subject must deliberately, by an act of will, in some sense disregard the perceived (if only as potential) threat. But to describe this in terms of the subject's "forcibly tear[ing] himself

---

[7]   For a fuller account of this interpretation of Schopenhauer's theory of the sublime, see Neill, 2012, pp. 206–218. For an interpretation that emphasizes the role of transcendental freedom in experience of the sublime, see Shapshay, forthcoming.

from his will", as Schopenhauer does at one point, is misleading, for disregarding the threatening aspect of the object cannot in itself produce will-lessness. Some of Schopenhauer's other ways of characterising the activity of the subject in this sort of context are less misleading, however: for example, "the beholder may not direct his attention to *this relation to his will* which is so pressing and hostile, but, although he perceives it and acknowledges it, he may consciously turn away from it" – that is, turn away from *that relation.* Again, "with the sublime, [will-lessness] is obtained first of all by a conscious and violent tearing away from *the relations of the same object to the will* which are recognised as unfavourable" – not a tearing away from the will itself, that is, but from concentration on the hostile relation that the object has to the will (WWR I, p. 201). We suggest, then, that Schopenhauer's thought is that aesthetic experience of the sublime is attained via a two-stage process, involving (first) an active disregarding of the threat posed by the object in question, which makes possible, though it does not in itself induce (second) a passive transition into will-lessness.

However, although this interpretation of his position defuses the concern that Schopenhauer's account of sublime experience contradicts his claim that one cannot directly will oneself into will-lessness, the more general worry that his accounts of sublime experience and of denial of the will-to-live are at odds with his determinism remains far from defused. For one thing, while we have addressed above the issue of how experience of the sublime is initiated, we have said nothing about how both that state, once attained, and the state of denial of the will-to-live, both of which are supposed to be states in which the individual will has in some sense been transcended, could depend on maintenance or sustenance, both of which, on the face of it, would seem to be very will-full. For another, nothing that we have said so far answers the question of how it is that the subject of sublime experience, if she really is the kind of slave to motives and will depicted in Schopenhauer's deterministic picture of human beings, is capable of actively disregarding the threat posed to her by the sublime object or state of affairs. And underlying both of these issues is a more fundamental worry, one that we have nudged against at several points above but not yet fully confronted. The fact is that Schopenhauer's deterministic picture of human beings – a picture, recall, that holds that we have unalterable empirical characters, that intellect is by nature subordinate to and in the service of the will, and that as a result causal laws are as necessarily operative in the psychological as they are in the physical realm – looks like a picture of a kind of being for whom aesthetic experience in general, let alone denial of the will, should simply be impossible. For as Schopenhauer construes both aesthetic experience and denial of the will, they are essentially states in which an individual's intellect has so to speak broken free of its service to that individual's will: they are, as he has it, *will-less.* Even if (as discussed in Section IV above) their occurrence need not depend on agency, then, a subject of these varieties of experience would no onger be the sort of slave to motives and will depicted in Schopenhauer's deterministic picture of human beings. In short, if aesthetic experience and denial of the will-to-live represent genuine possibilities in Schopenhauer's thought, then, his deterministic picture cannot be the end of the story.

VI. The Limits of Determinism

The bulk of Schopenhauer's prize essay on the freedom of the will is, as we indicated in Section II above, devoted to establishing the truth of determinism. In the essay's concluding section, however, he changes tack. Having "entirely removed all freedom of human action and recognised it as thoroughly subordinate to the strictest necessity", he suggests, he has taken us to "the point where we shall be able to understand *true moral freedom*, which is of a higher kind" (FW, p. 83). He goes on: "[F]or there is still a fact of consciousness which [...] I have so far entirely disregarded. This is the perfectly clear and certain feeling of *responsibility* for what we do, of *accountability* for our actions – a feeling that rests on the unshakable certainty that we ourselves are *the doers of our deeds*" (ibid.). In the last few pages of the essay, Schopenhauer suggests that the existence and indeed the character of "true moral freedom" can be inferred from this "fact of consciousness", allowing him to answer in the affirmative the question set by the Royal Norwegian Society of Sciences: "Can the freedom of the human will be proved from self-consciousness?"

The argument of these last few pages goes, in essence, as follows:

(1) We have an "unshakeable certainty that we ourselves are *the doers of our deeds*",

(2) This feeling is based on the recognition that with respect to any individual's action, "quite another action, indeed the action directly opposed to his own, was after all entirely possible and could have happened, *if only he had been another*",

(3) Thus, "the *responsibility* he is conscious of relates only provisionally and ostensibly to the deed, but fundamentally to his *character*; it is for *this* that he feels himself responsible",

(4) "And it is for *this* that others hold him responsible, as their judgment forsakes the deed at once in order to discover the qualities of the doer [...] their reproaches go back to his *character*". (In general, Schopenhauer suggests, "the epithets of moral badness [...] are predicates more of the *human being* than of actions. They are attached to the *character* [...]".)

(5) "Where *guilt* lies, there must *responsibility* lie also: and since the latter is the sole datum from which the conclusion to moral freedom is justified, *freedom* must also lie in the very same place, that is in the *character* of the human being – all the more so, as we have sufficiently convinced ourselves that it is not to be encountered directly in individual actions, whose occurrence, given the presupposition of the character, is strictly necessitated" (FW, p. 106).

At this point, Schopenhauer in effect faces a dilemma. On the one hand, he takes himself to have "disclosed" the fact that we are in some sense free, appealing to "data" that amount to "a fact of consciousness", and to have identified the "location" of that freedom in character. On the other hand, as he takes himself to have demonstrated earlier in the essay, "the character is inborn and unalterable". To escape the dilemma, he appeals to Kant's account of the relation between empirical and intelligible character:

> the empirical character, like the whole human being, is as an object of experience a mere appearance, hence tied to the forms of all appearance, to time, space and causality, and subordinate to their laws. On the other hand, the condition and basis of this whole appearance is the human being's *intelligible character* [...] which is independent of those forms [...] (FW, p. 86).[8]

It follows that to the intelligible character "there certainly also pertains absolute freedom, i.e. independence from the law of causality. [...] This freedom is, however, *transcendental* [...]". And in virtue of it "all deeds of the human being are his own work, however necessarily they issue from the empirical character upon its coincidence with motives [...]" (FW, p. 108).

The "intelligible character", we suggest, is in Schopenhauer's terms best understood as what he elsewhere describes as a "special Idea" (cf., e.g., WWR I, p. 158); that is to say, as a particular, indeed unique, mode of objectification of "the will as thing-in-itself" in an individual human being. As he puts it, the intelligible character "is the will as thing in itself, to the extent that it appears in a particular individual, to a particular degree" (WWR[C] I, pp. 315–316); "an extra-temporal and thus indivisible and unchanging act of will [*Willensakt*], whose appearance [...] is the empirical character" (WWR[C] I, p. 316). The freedom of the intelligible character, then, derives from – indeed, just *is* – the freedom of "the will as thing-in-itself", which is fundamentally a matter of independence of the forms of the Principle of Sufficient Reason, and hence of the law of causality. Freedom in this context, that is, is not to be construed in terms of freedom of action or decision, but rather in terms of the fact that no deterministic account of how or why an individual's intelligible character is as it is – that is, about how or why "the will as thing-in-itself" is objectified in just this way in this individual – is available. Given, then, that an individual's empirical character is as it is inasmuch as it is the manifestation in the phenomenal world of her intelligible character, and that there is no deterministic story to be told about why or how her intelligible character is as it is, then there can

---

8   Schopenhauer attests to his full adherence to Kant's distinction between the empirical and intelligible characters, and believes that this distinction grounds the "doctrine of the coexistence of freedom with necessity". Kant's doctrine, he suggests, affords "a thorough knowledge of the compatibility of human freedom with necessity" (FW, p. 73).

be no deterministic story – or at least none that points beyond the individual – about why her empirical character is as it is. It follows that although her actions are the result of the presentation of motives to her empirical character, and hence wholly empirically determined, there is no sense in which they are anything less than *hers*. And in this lies moral or transcendental freedom: the subject is indeed the doer of her deeds.

In Book IV of *The World as Will and Representation*, Schopenhauer appeals to just this latter notion of freedom in his discussion of the apparent tension between his determinism and his account of the possibility of denial of the will-to-live – a tension, as we have argued above, that is no less pressing with regard to his account of aesthetic experience.[9] We noted earlier that Schopenhauer is unembarrassed by this tension; as he says, "We might perhaps regard the whole of our discussion [...] of what I call the denial of the will as inconsistent with the previous explanation of necessity, that appertains just as much to motivation as to every other form of the principle of sufficient reason. [...] [*F*]*ar from suppressing this here, I call it to mind*" (WWR I, p. 402) (emphasis provided). He goes on:

> Now the contradiction between our assertions, on the one hand, of the necessity of the will's determinations through motives according to the character, and our assertions, on the other, of the possibility of the whole suppression of the will, whereby motives become powerless, is only the repetition in the reflection of philosophy of this *real* contradiction that arises from the direct encroachment of the freedom of the will-in-itself, knowing no necessity, on the necessity of its phenomenon (WWR I, p. 403).[10]

This remark echoes others that he has made in passing. Earlier, for example, he says that "[o]n [the denier of will] has dawned the knowledge in consequence of which [*in Folge welcher*] he gives up and denies that will-to-live that fills everything, and strives and strains in all. The freedom of this will first appears here in him alone, and by it his actions now become the very opposite of ordinary" (WWR I, p. 386). Again: "[I]n general, the denial of the will by no means results from suffering with the necessity of effect from cause; on the contrary, the will remains free. For here is just the one and only point where its freedom enters directly into the phenomenon [*in die Erscheinung eintritt*]" (WWR I, p. 395).

---

9   His failure to acknowledge this may simply be due to the fact that in WWR his account of the sublime comes before he has explicitly spelled out his determinist position.

10   Schopenhauer continues: "[B]ut the key to the reconciliation of these contradictions lies in the fact that the state in which the character is withdrawn from the power of motives does not proceed directly from the will, but from a changed form of knowledge" (ibid.). This restates the thought that we have discussed above, namely, that one cannot will oneself away from the will, but it does not help with the questions we listed at the end of the previous section.

Denial of the will-to-live, he repeats, "is the only act of its freedom to appear in the phenomenon" (WWR I, p. 398). And, finally:

> In truth, real freedom, in other words independence of the principle of sufficient reason, belongs to the will as thing-in-itself, not to its phenomenon, whose essential form is everywhere this principle of sufficient reason, the element of necessity. But the only case where that freedom can become immediately visible in the phenomenon [*unmittelbar in der Erscheinung sichtbar werden kann*] is the one where it makes an end of what appears [...]" (WWR I, p. 402).

The metaphors employed in these remarks, which have the freedom of the will as thing-in-itself "encroaching upon", "appearing in", "entering into", and "becoming immediately visible in" the phenomenon, are less than fully transparent. We might offer the following, very minimal, paraphrase: a denier of the will-to-live (or indeed a subject of aesthetic experience) is a subject in whom intellect has broken free of its servitude to the individual will, so that it is no longer restricted to knowledge governed by the forms of the Principle of Sufficient Reason; in such a case, intellect is free in just the sense that the will as thing-in-itself is free, i.e., unconstrained by the forms of the Principle of Sufficient Reason; in such a case, then, the freedom of the intellect mirrors the freedom of the will as thing-in-itself.

But this surely does not give us enough. What Schopenhauer owes us – what his invocation of the freedom of the will as thing-in-itself in this context promises – is an account of how the freedom of the will as thing-in-itself *explains* the possibility that the intellect of an individual may break free of its servitude to that individual's will in such a way that aesthetic and ascetic experience become available to her. The thought that when the intellect does break free of its service to the individual will it presents an image of the freedom of the will as thing-in-itself hardly amounts to that. Nor indeed does the thought that the intelligible character is morally or transcendentally free. As we argued above, this freedom amounts to no more than the fact that no deterministic story can be told about why the intelligible character is as it is; again, then, freedom here amounts simply to being unaccountable in terms of the Principle of Sufficient Reason, and not to anything that explains the capacity of the intellect to break free of its servitude to the individual will.

Some of what Schopenhauer says in this context does suggest that he has more in mind, and in particular that he takes the freedom of the will-in-itself not merely to be modeled in a person's denial of the will-to-live, but also to be what makes denial of the will-to-live possible. Thus, for example, he suggests that "the effect [i.e., the quieting of the will-to-live] of the quieter [i.e., of the relevant epistemic perspective] is ultimately an act of the freedom of the will [*die Wirkung des Quietivs doch zuletzt ein Freiheitsakt des Willens*]" (WWR I, p. 404). Taken at face value, this looks simply confused. Construed in one way, it calls to mind the idea that a person may freely will herself into will-lessness, an idea that, as we saw earlier, is not only of dubious coherence but one that

Schopenhauer himself explicitly rejects. Construed in another way, it suggests that the will considered as thing-in-itself is capable of action, which, given that the latter cannot be conceived in terms of the forms of the Principle of Sufficient Reason, is plainly misconceived. Construed more charitably, however, Schopenhauer's thought here may be that it is in some sense *because* the will-in-itself is free that it is possible for a subject to be free from determination by motive; that it is in some sense *because* the will-in-itself is independent of the Principle of Sufficient Reason that it is possible for a subject's intellect to break free of its service to the individual will.

In the end, however, all that Schopenhauer has to say along these lines amounts to no more than a suggestive hint. In the end, that is, he simply fails to deliver on the promise implicit in his appeal to the freedom of the will as thing-in-itself in the context of his discussion of the possibility of denial of the will-to-live. While he is quite clear that he takes the freeing of the intellect in an individual to be *evidence* of the freedom of the will as thing-in-itself, as we have indicated above, ultimately he offers nothing to explain how the latter may be related to the possibility of the former.

VII. Conclusion

Schopenhauer himself appears unembarrassed by what we have suggested here amounts to a significant lacuna in his account of the matters we have discussed above. We "can understand in what sense the admirable Malebranche could say: '*La liberté est un mystère*'", he suggests towards the end of his discussion: "*and he was right*" (WWR I, p. 404) (second emphasis provided). In the end, then, Schopenhauer seems content to leave unexplained and mysterious the relationship between the freedom of the will as thing-in-itself and the capacity in human beings for aesthetic experience and denial of the will-to-live.[11] There are a number of possible responses that one might have to this, including, doubtless non-exhaustively, the thoughts: (a) that as Schopenhauer's system has it, there just are points at which explanation comes to an end, and that this is one of them (this may or not count against the plausibility of his system, of course); (b) that there may be ways of explaining the human capacities for aesthetic experience and denial of the will-to-live in Schopenhauerian terms that do not depend on appeal to his conception of the freedom of the will as thing-in-

---

[11]   He quotes the same line at the end of the Prize Essay. This is by no means an unfamiliar move in Schopenhauer's work; consider for example his characterization of the identity of the subject of knowing with the subject of willing as the "miracle par excellence" (WWR I, pp. 102, 250–1), and his suggestion that it is "essentially impossible to demonstrate" his "explanation of the inner essence of music" (WWR I, pp. 257).

itself;[12] and (c) that there may be a way or ways of establishing the connection between what Schopenhauer takes to be the human capacities for aesthetic experience and denial of the will-to-live and his conception of the freedom of the will as thing-in-itself that we have failed to consider above. Our attempt in this essay to tease out at least some of the respects in which Schopenhauer's accounts of aesthetic experience and of denial of the will-to-live do and do not presuppose freedom in the subject of these varieties of experience, should, we hope, help in the determination of which of these thoughts is most fruitfully to be pursued.

References

Guyer, Paul (1996): "Pleasure and Knowledge in Schopenhauer's Aesthetics", in: Jacquette, Dale (ed.): *Schopenhauer, Philosophy and the Arts*, Cambridge, pp. 109–132.

Hamlyn, David (1980): *Schopenhauer*, New York.

Neill, Alex (2008): "Aesthetic Experience in Schopenhauer's Metaphysics of Will", in: *European Journal of Philosophy*, 16(2), pp. 179–193.

– (2012): "Schopenhauer on Tragedy and the Sublime", in: Vandenabeele, Bart (ed.): *Blackwell Companion to Schopenhauer*, Malden, MA, pp. 206–218.

Schopenhauer, Arthur (1966): *The World as Will and Representation*, vols. I–II, tr. Payne, E. F. J., New York [= WWR].

– (2001): *Parerga and Paralipomena*, vols. I–II, tr. Payne, E.F.J., Oxford [= PP].

– (2004): *Prize Essay on the Freedom of the Will*, tr. Payne, E.F.J., ed. Zöller, Günter, Cambridge [= FW].

– (2010): *The World as Will and Representation*, vol. I, tr. Janaway, Christopher, Norman, Judith, and Welchman, Alistair, Cambridge [= WWR^C].

Shapshay, Sandra (forthcoming): "Schopenhauer's Transformation of the Kantian Sublime", in: *Kantian Review*.

---

[12]   See, e.g., Neill 2008.

Hans Friedrich Fulda

Frei sein – in lebendiger Vernünftigkeit und unter objektiv-rechtlichen Normen

Für Ulrich Pothast in alter Freundschaft

Just as their counterparts in other languages, the German terms "befreien", "frei" and "Freiheit" have a lot of different meanings and are used in different contexts. In many contexts they are philosophically relevant and vital. This paper aims to show that amongst the classical writers of German idealism (if not amongst all philosophers) only Hegel developed an understanding of freedom based on the simple and true-to-life usage of these terms, an understanding that became essential for law. Hegel's definition helps to build a legal concept of freedom according to which legal norms do not constrain free will and action but stabilize them. At the same time it extends the state of freedom's scope to include all of humanity. After a brief look at the etymology of freedom (I) we will discuss Ulrich Pothast's concept of freedom as characterized by spirited reasonableness (II) and compare it to the relevant paragraphs of Hegel's philosophy of subjective Spirit (III). Based on the term of objective spirit, which according to Hegel is law, we will finally deduce a new and as yet unexplored meaning of 'state of freedom' in regard to legal norms (IV).

„Freiheit? Ein schönes Wort, wer's recht verstände! Was wollen sie für Freiheit? Was ist des Freiesten Freiheit? – Recht zu tun! – und daran wird sie der König nicht hindern". – Mit dieser den Niederländern insgesamt geltenden Replik leitet Herzog Alba die dramatische Wendung ein,[1] die er seinem Dialog mit *Egmont* (in Goethes gleichnamigem Trauerspiel) zu geben gedenkt. Der Dialog endet mit Egmonts Verhaftung und zieht die unverzügliche Hinrichtung nach sich, wodurch Egmont zum Freiheitshelden wird, nachdem er vorher in exemplarischer Weise frei gelebt hat. – Wenn man Albas Ausruf, mit der nötigen Philosophen-Naivität, als Aufforderung nimmt, sich um das rechte Verständnis des „schönen Worts" *Freiheit*, aber auch der mit ihm bezeichneten Sache zu bemühen, so orientiert man sich dafür wohl am besten zunächst am Adjektiv und Adverb „frei" und an dessen außerphilosophischen Verwendungen. Verweilen wir also einleitungsweise beim trivialen Gebrauch und dem normal-

---

[1] *Egmont. Ein Trauerspiel in fünf Aufzügen*, Vierter Aufzug, in: Goethe, Johann Wolfgang von (1994): *Goethes Werke Bd. 4*, Hamburger Ausgabe in 14 Bdn., hrsg. v. E. Trunz. 13., durchges. Aufl., München, S. 429.

sprachlichen „groszen zusammenhang", den das Wort „frei" dem Grimm'schen Wörterbuch zufolge im Deutschen hat, und nehmen wir zu den dort verzeichneten Wendungen gleich die wichtigsten Ausdrücke in den klassischen Sprachen hinzu, in denen sich die philosophischen Gedanken über Freiheit erstmals artikuliert haben! Aber befragen wir diese Wendungen und die großen philosophischen Texte aufs darin enthaltene Lebensbedeutsame hin, indem wir von alltäglich vertrauten Phänomenen in ihrer Relevanz für persönliches Verhalten und Erleben ausgehen!

I. Das Wort „frei" gemäß lexikalischer Auskunft

Wie uns die Wörterbücher belehren, kam das „Freisein" – sowohl in seiner Verbindung mit Vernünftigkeit als auch mit Rechtsnormen – *ursprünglich* zum Verständnis im *Zusammenleben* von Menschen. Seine Merkmale haben sich in Hervorhebung qualifizierter Zustände des Zusammenlebens herausgebildet. Das Wort „frei" (samt den Äquivalenten hierzu in anderen europäischen Sprachen) dürfte sogar primär zu einer Auszeichnung gedient haben, die auch rechtlicher Art war. Gleich dem lateinischen *ingenuus* qualifizierte es jemanden als Glied einer selbständig bestehenden Abstammungsgemeinschaft, dessen Kinder infolgedessen von Anfang an *liberi* sind. Und es qualifiziert die so Bezeichneten abgehoben von Fremden oder in anderer Weise nicht Dazugehörigen. Das macht eine ganze Reihe von Zügen des „groszen zusammenhangs" verständlich, in dem das Wort „frei" mit sprachlich eng verwandten Ausdrücken und den von ihnen bezeichneten Sachverhalten steht. Es zeigt z. B., was „frei" mit (jemanden) „freien" zu tun hat, und dass es wortgeschichtlich auch mit „froh" sowie „freuen" verwandt ist sowie bedeutungsverwandt mit „offen" und „offenstehend". Ferner: dass „frei" früh auch schon einen sozialen *status* bezeichnet: den Status des oder der Freien im Unterschied zu demjenigen des Knechts oder Sklaven. Mit Ablösung der tragenden Bedeutung, welche die Stammesgemeinschaft ursprünglich für die Einzelnen hatte, durch neue Institutionen (wie insbesondere diejenige der Stadt) geht die Auszeichnung „frei" auch auf diese Institutionen über und parallel dazu von Trägern des freien Status auf Mitglieder der neuen sozialen Gemeinschaft, d. h. auf diejenigen, die im vollen Sinn *Bürger* (politai, cives) sind. Mit der ständigen Bedrohung der Selbstherrschaft solcher Gemeinwesen wird „Freiheit" auch zu einem Kennzeichen für eine *gute*, sich stabil erhaltende politische *Ordnung*. Der Begriff solcher Freiheit bekommt zusätzliche Färbungen – die eine oder andere jeweils nach dem, was als für die Selbstherrschaft wesentlich erkannt wird und diese wirklich zu einer Selbst-Herrschaft macht.

Es versteht sich auch, dass es dabei naheliegt, der guten *Verfassung* eines solchen Gemeinwesens, die vor allem dessen Freiheit und die Freiheit der Mitglieder begründet, entsprechende Charakteristika des *erwachsenen Einzelnen*, sofern dieser frei ist, zuzuordnen; und es verwundert nicht, dass diese dann vorrangig Qualifikationen des erwachsenen Einzelnen in Bezug auf dessen Fähigkeiten und Befugnisse zu äußeren Handlungen sind – diejenigen Merkmale vor allem, über die uns die griechische praktische Philosophie belehrte: ἕκων (freiwillig), ἐξουσία (Vollmacht zu …, Verfügen über …), ἐφ' ἡμῖν bzw. ἐπ' αὐτῷ (dass es bei uns bzw. bei mir selbst steht, etwas zu tun oder zu unterlassen), προαίρεσις (das Vermögen oder die Festlegung darauf, etwas einem anderen vorzuziehen), βουλεύεσθαι (mit sich zu Rate gehen), βούλεσθαι (Wollen), αὐταρκὴς (selbstgenügsam), αὐτοκράτεια bzw. ἐγκράτεια (über sich selbst Verfügen, Selbstbeherrschung), αὐτονομία (Autonomie) und einige andere; sie alle jedoch, soweit es Sinn macht, mit ihren typischen Gegensätzen (von unfreiwillig bis Heteronomie) als demjenigen, was kennzeichnend für Unfreisein ist.

Bis heute ist das, was mit den positiven Ausdrücken bezeichnet wird, untrennbar von dem, was es für Menschen heißt, vernünftig zu sein; und es ist charakteristisch für Freiheitsverhältnisse, die zwischen Menschen bestehen. Es ist auch wohlverständlich, dass diese Qualifikationen einer freien Person oder ihrer sozial wichtigsten Äußerungen sowie Einstellungen besonders auffällig dann werden, wenn die Leistung und die Kraft der Gemeinwesen für den Einzelnen schwinden und andere Bindungen bedeutungsvoll oder sogar bedeutungsvoller werden als diejenige an eine Gemeinde, aus der man stammt. Wie aber kann das eine – die Leistung und Kraft des Gemeinwesens – sich im anderen – den in lebendiger Vernünftigkeit freien Personen – erhalten und das andere in jenem einen gedeihen? Diese Frage wird der Leitfaden sein, der die nächsten Abschnitte miteinander verbindet und am Ende hoffentlich ermöglicht, auf Herzog Albas eingangs zitierte Äußerung eine adäquate Antwort zu geben, – nicht aus dem Munde Egmonts, aber hoffentlich im Sinne Goethes.

II. „Frei sein" und lebendige Vernünftigkeit
(Pothast und Goethe)

Dass der Aufschluss über vernünftiges Freisein einer individuellen Person geschichtlich *aus* vergangener *sozialer* Realität des Zusammenlebens und deren Normierung an uns kam, also gewissermaßen *von außen her* erfolgte, heißt durchaus nicht, die Verständigung müsse nun bei dieser Realität halt machen und sich auf personale Eigenschaften beschränken, die sich direkt an ihr ablesen lassen, weil die Ausdrücke dafür nichts anderes bezeichnen als ein Stück von ihr im jeweiligen Individuum. Der bedeutungsgeschichtliche Tatbestand führt vielmehr vor eine grundsätzliche *Frage*: Können sich lebendige Vernünftigkeit und ein mit ihr verbundenes Freisein Einzelner in diesem Außenaspekt der lebendigen Person erschöpfen, wenn sie unsere innersten Überzeugungen befriedigen und unser Innerstes in diesem Äußeren voll zum Ausdruck kommen lassen sollen? Wohl kaum. Ist die Frage aber zu verneinen, so muss nach zusätzlichen Merkmalen für menschliches Freisein Ausschau gehalten werden. Zu solchen Merkmalen hat Ulrich Pothast vor einigen Jahren ein sehr verdienstvolles Buch veröffentlicht.[2] Schon im Titel kommt seine Haupttendenz zum Vorschein. Sie richtet sich mit Entschiedenheit gegen die Auffassung, Vernunft und Freiheit seien feste Qualitäten in einem jeden Menschen – womöglich sogar schon Qualitäten einer ihm zugeschriebenen Präexistenz. Polemisiert wird vornehmlich gegen die damit zusammenhängenden Abstraktionen, in denen Vernunft sowie Freiheit traditionellerweise gedacht werden. Das Buch wurde auch journalistisch gewürdigt.[3] Leider aber hat es dabei eine völlig abwegige, geringschätzige Kritik erfahren, während seine Haupttendenz keine Beachtung fand.[4]

Wie ich Ulrich Pothast verstehe, will er uns lehren, die obige Frage zu verneinen, weil wir Lebewesen sind, in denen alle jene schönen, an der geteilten Welt dann abzulesenden personalen Eigenschaften erst entstehen, wachsen und, so gut es geht, stabilisiert werden müssen, und weil aus diesem Grund für die Verneinung dieser Frage noch andere Qualifikationen für Freisein in lebendiger Vernünftigkeit ausgemacht werden müssen; noch andere als diejenigen, die in

---

[2]   Pothast, Ulrich (1998): *Lebendige Vernünftigkeit. Zur Vorbereitung eines menschenangemessenen Konzepts,* Frankfurt a. M. (im Folgenden zitiert als „*LV*" mit Seitenangabe).

[3]   In der Frankfurter Allgemeinen Zeitung vom 3.11.1998.

[4]   Der Verfasser der Rezension, Gustav Falke, wusste – an anderer Stelle – Substantielles über die Differenzen zu sagen, die Friedrich Heinrich Jacobi mit dem frühen Weimarer Goethe und Goethe mit Jacobi über den *Woldemar* hatte. Aber als Rezensent kann er es nicht lassen, sein Leder immer wieder über diesen einen Leisten zu schlagen. Unter Berufung auf Goethe und Hegel wendet er gegen Pothasts Thematisierung des – nicht immer schon versprachlichten – Spürens und gegen die Betonung von dessen Relevanz fürs Konzept lebendiger Vernünftigkeit sowie für deren Betätigung ein, so werde die Sprache von der Vernünftigkeit getrennt und die Vernunft aufs Rechnen verkürzt; damit aber müsse Pothast „alles Echte in einen unergründlichen und unverfügbaren Innengrund werfen. Dann" bestehe „die vernünftige Lebendigkeit nicht mehr darin, reflektierend und diskutierend eine menschliche Welt zu gestalten, sondern die Orakelsprüche des Inneren für letzte Entscheidungen zu nehmen. Das Nicht-anders-Können, sonst Zeichen von Unfreiheit", gelte „Pothast denn auch als Zeichen für eine intensive Stützung der Überzeugungen im spürend-körperlichen Leben". Auf diesem „Abweg nach innen" entspringe, „wie Jacobis ‚*Woldemar*' in Hegels Augen vorführt, eine ‚Quälerei der Reflexionen mit sich selbst und eine unendliche Empfindlichkeit in betreff auf alle übrigen' – kurz [es entspringe so]: die ganze Innerlichkeitskultur, die ja keineswegs erst vor dreißig Jahren erfunden wurde". Soweit Falke. Entsprechend süffisant lautet die Überschrift der Rezension: „Was drängst du denn so wunderlich, mein Herz?" Mit einer Zeile aus Schuberts *Winterreise* also macht sich der Rezensent pauschal über den Versuch lustig, Vernunft und Freiheit in lebendigen Personen individuiert und konkretisiert zu denken, ohne dass eins am anderen dabei Schaden nimmt.

der Tradition ihre Rolle gespielt und darin zu aporetischen metaphysischen Annahmen über einzelmenschliche Freiheit geführt haben. Dieser These ist, wie mir scheint, emphatisch zuzustimmen.[5]

Hiergegen Goethe zu bemühen, ist kurzschlüssig. Eher sollte man sich auf Gestalten seiner Dichtung als Kronzeugen berufen. Dazu ein paar Hinweise: Was immer der wirkliche Ritter mit der eisernen Hand für ein Verständnis von altdeutscher Ritterfreiheit gehabt haben mag – der Goethe'sche *Götz von Berlichingen* jedenfalls, dessen letzte, ersterbende Worte im gleichnamigen Drama „Freiheit! Freiheit!" sind,[6] weist damit auf eine düstere Zukunft – unsere Gegenwart – hin; auf eine Zeit nämlich, in der, wie er kurz zuvor sagte, dem Betrug „Freiheit gegeben" ist. Als Korrektiv dagegen verweist er mit seinen letzten Worten auf ein anderes, integres, persönliches Freisein, dessen Vorschein er selber lebte. – Nicht weniger, sondern in noch höherem Maß tut dies der Goethe'sche *Egmont*, der kein alt gewordenes Idol des Sturm und Drang mehr ist, sondern ein tragischer Held in seinen besten Jahren am Vorabend des unvermeidlich werdenden Freiheitskriegs seiner Nation. Das Drama ist endgültig 1787 konzipiert worden, also unmittelbar vor Beginn der Epoche revolutionä-

---

[5] Wer weniger flüchtig als der Journalist Falke zu Werk geht, sieht leicht, dass hier ein krasses Missverständnis waltet. Pothast hat sich mit Einwänden wie den umrissenen in seinem Buch selbst auseinandergesetzt. Er macht deutlich, dass es bei dem von ihm hervorgehobenen Spüren nur um ein die Entscheidungen individueller Personen *„von innen her stützendes ... Moment"* lebendiger Vernünftigkeit geht – ein Moment zudem, für das eine ganze Reihe von Merkmalen solcher zu berücksichtigen sind (vgl. LV, S. 183 ff., 258 ff., 266 f.). Ferner: Für das Wirken dieses Moments wird keineswegs Täuschungsunanfälligkeit behauptet (ebd., S. 193 ff.). Es soll die Erkundung weltlicher Sachverhalte durchaus nicht ersetzen, sondern kann sie allenfalls erleichtern (S. 205). Es muss schrittweise wirken, wenn es wirkt, und mit der Betonung dieses Moments wird nur etwas in den Vordergrund gestellt, ohne dessen Berücksichtigung wichtige Quellen von Vernunft verkümmerten (ebd., S. 225) und in der Vergangenheit verkümmert sind. Nicht aber soll von der durch dieses Moment ausgezeichneten Vernünftigkeit gesagt sein, ein Leben sei allein um ihrer willen, also privatistisch, zu führen, es komme nicht auf Bindungen an „(an Personen, Aufgaben, Gemeinschaften, vieles andere), die mehrheitlich um ihrer Inhalte willen eingegangen werden" (ebd., S. 235, 251). Es werden auch nicht die klassischen Mittel der Selbstvergewisserung abgewertet, die von Hegel und anderen bekräftigt wurden (S. 238), oder umsichtig überlegende Selbstprüfung (S. 247) oder die Anderen als Argumentationspartner sowie Prüfinstanzen für irrelevant erklärt (S. 243). In all diesen Hinsichten hat es Ulrich Pothast wahrlich nicht nötig, sich belehren zu lassen. Er hat dies alles selber betont. Für die Auffindung und Exemplifikation der Merkmale hingegen, um die es hier geht, hilft die Polemik gegen „Innerlichkeitskultur" nicht weiter, und der Verweis auf die mit anderen geteilte „Welt", in welcher das Selbst erst seine „Wirklichkeit" habe, ist schlicht borniert.

[6] *Götz von Berlichingen mit der eisernen Hand*, in: Goethe, Johann Wolfgang von (1994): *Goethes Werke Bd. 4*, Hamburger Ausgabe in 14 Bdn., hrsg. v. E. Trunz. 13., durchges. Aufl., München, S. 175.

rer europäischer Freiheitskämpfe. Nachdem dem Goethe'schen Egmont zu Bewusstsein gekommen ist, in welcher Verblendung durch die eigene dämonische Natur er selber gelebt hat und dass es darum sein Schicksal sein wird, nun, obwohl er – durch seinen Freund Wilhelm von Oranien – gewarnt war, als einer der ersten einer neuartigen, absolutistischen Unterdrückung zum Opfer zu fallen, fordert er die anderen zum ihre Güter schützenden Aufstand auf und geht dem eigenen Tod durch Exekution entgegen mit den Sätzen: „ich sterbe für die Freiheit, für die ich lebte und focht, und der ich mich jetzt leidend opfre"[7]. Das klingt nach pathetischem Bekenntnis zu bloß öffentlicher, äußerer Freiheit. Aber das „Beispiel", das er mit seinem Sterben nach eigenem, letztem Wort des Dramas gibt, ist nicht dasjenige eines beizeiten aufs Militärische setzenden politischen Helden. Dem hätte die φϱόνησις geboten, sich wie Wilhelm von Oranien, dessen Rat folgend, der drohenden Verhaftung durch den Militaristen Alba zu entziehen. Doch *die* Freiheit, die Egmont lebte und für die er nun sterben wird, geht nicht auf in politischen, ritterlichen und militärischen Tugenden. Aus ihrer Sicht erschien dem Egmont des Dramas der politische Stratege Wilhelm von Oranien „nicht ganz frei" – wie es heißt, als beide zur Besprechung der Frage zusammenkommen, ob es besser sei, als eingeladene Edle der Niederländer bei Alba, dem Abgesandten des Königs, zu erscheinen oder sich ihm vorsichtig zu entziehen und den Bruch mit dem Souverän so selbst zu verschulden. Egmont widersetzt sich Oraniens dringendem Rat, Alba fernzubleiben: am Ende jedoch nicht aus Sorglosigkeit, sondern aus dem lebendigen *Gespür*, dass es nicht zu seiner eigenen, freien Natur passen würde, das drohende Unheil durch misstrauische Vorwegnahme herbeizuführen: „– das ist ein fremder Tropfen in meinem Blute. Gute Natur, wirf ihn wieder heraus! Und von meiner Stirne die sinnenden Runzeln wegzubaden, gibt es ja wohl noch ein freundlich Mittel"[8]. Mit diesen Worten beendet Egmont seinen aufs Gespräch mit Oranien folgenden Monolog. Keine schlechte Verbalisierung eines lebendigen Spürens aus Nähe zu sich selbst! So nimmt das Schicksal seinen Lauf. Aber nicht Oranien, der überlegene politische Schachspieler und später erfolgreiche Freiheitskämpfer, sondern Egmont wird am Ende in einem Traumgesicht von der Freiheitsgöttin – welche die Gestalt seiner ihm seinetwegen in den Tod vorausgegangenen, aus dem einfachen Volk stammenden Geliebten hat – als Sieger mit einem Lorbeerkranz ausgezeichnet: als Held einer Freiheit, deren Vernünftigkeit lebendig ist und spürend betätigt wurde; also auch als Exempel eines *von uns* zu affirmierenden Freiseins – obwohl dies Freisein im dramatisch vorgeführten Fall mit (spezifisch moderner) tragischer Verblendung und einem erschütternden Schicksal verbunden war. Soviel zumindest ist mit Goethe gegen

---

[7] Ebd., S. 453.
[8] Ebd., S. 407.

den Rezensenten zugunsten von Ulrich Pothast zu sagen. Fazit: Freisein zusammen mit lebendiger Vernünftigkeit reduziert sich ebenso wenig wie diese Vernünftigkeit auf die äußere Wirklichkeit, in der beide zur Darstellung kommen; es muss nicht nur willentlich, sondern ebenso wie die lebendige Vernünftigkeit auch spürend betätigt werden.

III. „Frei sein" in Hegels Anthropologie – verglichen mit Ulrich Pothasts Auffassung

(a) Mit etwas mehr Aufwand als im Blick auf Goethe kann dieses Ergebnis auch unter Berufung auf Hegel bekräftigt werden. Die Bekräftigung ist in Hegels Anthropologie und Psychologie impliziert und wird sichtbar am Zusammenhang beider mit der hegelschen Philosophie des objektiven Geistes. Denn bei diesem Zusammenhang geht es nicht zuletzt auch um selbstbewusste menschliche Freiheit, die als Sitte „zur Natur geworden" ist.[9] – Die Verdeutlichung des Zusammenhangs würde verhindern helfen, dass man in die modernistische Falle tappt, ausgehend von vereinzeltem freiem Handeln zu reflektieren auf Willensfreiheit (bloß als Voraussetzung hierfür) und diese dann womöglich – wie in der nominalistischen Tradition und ihren philosophischen sowie theologischen Freiheitslehren – zu reduzieren auf bloße sogenannte freie Willkür (arbitrium liberum) und damit auf libertas indifferentiae, der man gleichwohl eine geheimnisvolle, all unserem Wissen über lebendige Naturwesen Hohn sprechende Macht zuschreibt, Ereignisse in unserem Organismus und von ihnen aus in der uns umgebenden Welt zu steuern. Doch auf diese lange Geschichte (oder gar ihre jüngsten Spottgeburten in der Debatte über Gehirnprozesse und Willensfreiheit) kann ich mich hier nicht einlassen. Ulrich Pothast hat sich davon bereits mit seiner *Unzulänglichkeit der Freiheitsbeweise* befreit,[10] wie auch – jedenfalls im Gefolge dieses Buchs – von der Annahme, ein konstitutiver Zusammenhang von Freiheit und Zurechenbarkeit oder auch Übelnehmenkönnen gebe uns nennenswerten Aufschluss darüber, was es heißt, auf menschliche Weise lebendig, vernünftig und frei zu sein. Auch hierin kann ich ihm nur beipflichten. Man sehe es mir also nach, wenn ich auf den Willkür- und Willensfreiheitsaspekt unseres Freiheitsverständnisses kaum eingehe. Er ist der Aspekt einer Freiheit, die sich, darunter zu einer Hauptsache gemacht, nur in Nebel auflösen kann.

---

9   Vgl. G. W. F. Hegel, *Encyclopädie der philosophischen Wissenschaften im Grundrisse*, Heidelberg ¹1817, ³1830, §§ 485; 513. (Zitiert als *Encyklopädie*, ¹1817 bzw. *Encyklopädie* unter Angabe des Paragraphen.)
10   Pothast, Ulrich (1980): *Die Unzulänglichkeit der Freiheitsbeweise. Zu einigen Lehrstücken aus der neueren Geschichte von Philosophie und Recht*, Frankfurt a. M.

Was mich im Folgenden, von Hegel angeregt, interessiert, ist menschliches Freisein unter Aspekten, bei deren Behauptung und Beschreibung ich mir der Übereinstimmung mit dem Autor Ulrich Pothast nicht mehr ganz so sicher bin wie im bisher Gesagten, wofür ich aber auf die Zustimmung meines Freundes Ulrich hoffe. Um klar zu machen, woher die Unsicherheit kommt, muss eine wichtige Unterscheidung im weiten Bereich akzeptabler Rede von Freisein berücksichtigt werden. Sie findet sich auch bei Pothast, aber ihre Glieder sind bei ihm nicht in gleich detaillierter Weise wie vieles andere besprochen. Ich meine die Unterscheidung zwischen dem mehr oder weniger *graduierten* Freisein einerseits, das auf Entstehen, Wachsen, Erhaltenbleiben und die Gefahren (sowie unvermeidlichen Prozesse) der Rückbildung hin zu betrachten ist, und andererseits einem nach der Richtung seiner Voraussetzungen hin zu bedenkenden *minimalen* Freisein sowie dem nach der Gegenrichtung eines maximalen Grades hin anzunehmenden, wenn auch nie endgültig erreichbaren Freisein als *letztem Ziel* wachsender Grade. Ulrich Pothast befasst sich vornehmlich mit dem erstgenannten, potentiell wachsenden, aber unfesten, oftmals also auch schrumpfenden Freisein. Und er befasst sich damit *vorrangig* in Bezug auf menschliches Handeln: An prominenter Stelle expliziert er dieses graduelle Freisein als die „Fähigkeit einer Person, dem von ihr selbst langfristig, von ihrer Überlegung und ihrem beruhigten Innengrund her für richtig Befundenen im Handeln nachzukommen" (LV, S. 263). Nahezu alles, was zu solchem Freisein und den Bedingungen sowie Merkmalen seiner Steigerung gesagt wird, leuchtet mir ein – insbesondere auch, dass solch graduelles Freisein nicht bestehen kann ohne lebendige Vernünftigkeit und dass sein Wachsen korreliert sowohl mit ihrer Steigerung als auch mit zunehmender, spürend betätigter Nähe der Person zu sich selbst. Was aber hat es mit *minimalem* Freisein auf sich, von dem das Wachsen seinen Ausgang nehmen muss? Und was mit Freisein als dem *maximalen*, worauf „reicheres Spüren" laut Auskunft des *Philosophisches Buches* „schließlich" ausgerichtet ist?[11] Hinsichtlich des minimalen sowie des maximalen Grades frage ich mich, ob die vornehmlich auf qualifizierte Fähigkeit zum Handeln abhebenden Charakterisierungen graduellen Freiseins nicht zu eng sind. Sie behalten, fürchte ich, grob gesagt einen praktizistischen touch oder genauer, mit einem Pothast'schen Ausdruck, eine „kognitiv-liberative" Beschränkung. Die scheint mir nicht voll zu lebendiger *Vernünftigkeit* zu passen und noch weniger zum weiten Horizont der Frage, was es heißt, auf menschliche Weise *lebendig* zu sein. Aber in beiden Richtungen, der aufs minimale wie der aufs maximale menschliche Freisein weisenden, knüpft sich hieran ein je spezifisches Verlangen nach Auskunft.

---

[11] Pothast, Ulrich (1988): *Philosophisches Buch. Schrift unter der aus der Entfernung leitenden Frage, was es heißt, auf menschliche Weise lebendig zu sein*, Frankfurt a. M., S. 430 (im Folgenden abgekürzt als „*PB*" mit Seitenangabe).

(b) In die Richtung auf korrelativen „Minimalbestand" (LV, S. 267) an Freisein und lebendiger Vernünftigkeit reflektiere ich nicht etwa, um daran einen markanten Unterschied zwischen uns Menschen und anderen Lebewesen festzumachen. Der Minimalbestand von beidem mag sich durchaus auch bei Lebewesen einer anderen (der unseren entsprechend verwandten) Gattung des Lebendigen finden. Ich frage danach, um herauszubekommen, ob wir nicht noch andere Dimensionen der Bestimmung von Freisein ausmachen können und auszeichnen müssen als die auf ein kognitiv-liberatives Mehr im Handelnkönnen angelegten, die dann doch wieder auf die drei „klassisch-idealistischen" Grundbestimmungen der Freiheit als Autonomie, Selbstbestimmung und Beisichselbstsein hinauslaufen. Und ich frage danach nicht zuletzt, weil Ulrich Pothast selbst dies im *Philosophischen Buch* nahegelegt hat (vgl. PB, S. 431 ff.). Vor allem hinsichtlich der Rolle, welche die *Kunst* im fraglichen Leben hat, werden dort nämlich Faktoren angesprochen, die zu Freisein und seiner Charakterisierung beitragen, sich aber nicht plausibel funktionalisiert und begrenzt denken lassen auf Freiwerden zum und im Handeln und theoretischen Erkennen. Das scheint mir darauf zu deuten, dass man bereits den *Minimalbestand* an Freisein inhaltlich reicher bestimmen muss, als es in beiden Büchern geschehen ist. Wenn ich recht sehe, erfahren wir über ihn in *Lebendige Vernünftigkeit* nur, dass er – außer dem korrelierten Minimum an lebendiger Vernünftigkeit und der charakterisierten, qualifizierten Fähigkeit einer Person zum Handeln – bei dieser Person noch das *Potential* einer Befreiung *von* „Druck und Zug" in der Spürenswirklichkeit einschließt und dadurch auch das Potential einer Befreiung *zu* spürend betätigter, sich vergrößernder Nähe zu sich selbst – einschließlich eines Potentials dazu, dass die Person frei wird *für* ein Mehr, dasjenige überhaupt zu sehen, was ihr und nur ihr gemäß ist, und es dann zu tun (LV, S. 101). Darüber hinaus spielt im *Philosophischen Buch* das sich frei bzw. freier *Fühlen*, die Realisierung der Potentiale als befreiend *Erleben* eine Rolle – außerdem aber ein unspezifizierter Hinweis auf *unverfügbare* Faktoren, durch deren Wirken ein lebendiges Individuum zu einem freien Handlungs*träger* wird (PB, S. 353). Ich möchte gerne wissen, welche Faktoren das paradigmatischerweise sind und was es auf sich hat mit ihrer *Affinität* zu Freisein oder gar mit ihrem Wirken im Freisein selbst.

Mindestens fünf solcher unverfügbaren Faktoren und freiheitsrelevanten Erstreckungen, in denen sie wirken, glaube ich unterscheiden zu können. Alle von ihnen zeichnen sich nicht nur dadurch aus, dass sich das Freisein in ihnen bereits an sehr elementaren Stadien der Entwicklung eines lebendigen Individuums ausmachen lässt, sondern auch dadurch, dass sich die Rede von Freisein und seinem Wachsen jeweils aus dem Gegensatz zu einem für Lebewesen unmittelbar evidenten *Zwang* oder einer infolge davon bestehenden *Bedrückung* oder einem *Hindernis* nahelegt.

1. Wir leben nicht nur empfindend, fühlend, vom Innengrund her spürend und in höher entwickelten kognitiv-liberativen geistigen Tätigkeiten. Wir *leben* –

viel elementarer – Zustände, zyklische Veränderungen und Prozesse der umgebenden Natur unmittelbar *mit*, wie schon Hegel lehrte;[12] und wir leben dabei gewisse dieser Zustände, Veränderungen, Prozesse als *belebend* mit, noch bevor wir die Umgebungsnatur *beseelt erleben* oder auch nur empfinden: z. B. den *freien* Himmel, das *Freie*, die *freie* Aussicht, den freien Fall, in welchem sich x (z. B. der Bungee-Springer) befindet, den *freien Lauf*, den etwas hat (z. B. die frei laufenden Hühner), aber auch den *freien Wuchs* z. B. eines alleinstehenden Baumes. Der Ausdruck „frei" und seine Abwandlungen sowie Verbindungen mit anderen Wörtern haben ihren Sinn in diesen Fällen nicht erst kraft einer Projektion oder Übertragung aus einem uns vom Erleben oder Fühlen her vertrauten Gegensatz zum Gebundenen, Bedrückenden, Verschlossenen, Verhangenen (wie ich früher dachte und sagte). Sie haben ihren Sinn aus dem, was es heißt, Freies in menschlich beseelter Natur *mit*zuleben, also damit selber ein Stückchen frei oder freier zu werden als wir es ohne solches Mitleben sind oder wären. Natürlicherweise lässt sich solches Freisein auch dadurch steigern, dass das Mitleben mit dem in der Umgebungsnatur Unfreien, Gedrückten, Verhangenen, Erzwungenen nicht in der selben Intensität erfolgt wie dasjenige mit dem Freien und Befreienden, – weil wir dahin gelangt sind, unsere mitlebende Kommunikation mit dem Gegenteil des um uns herum Belebenden, mit dem Bedrückenden also, zu dämpfen, ohne dass dem Mitleben mit dem Freien das gleiche widerfährt. Schon unter Bezugnahme auf so elementare Phänomene lässt sich an Beispielen verdeutlichen, *wie es ist*, ein freier Mensch zu sein oder freier als ein anderer. Allerdings wissen wir auch, dass sich solches Freisein in den Dienst besonders widerwärtiger, kalter Weisen von Unterdrückung nehmen lässt. Ich brauche mich dazu nur an die „Jungvolk"-Jahre unter den Nazis zu erinnern.

2. Eine andere Angelegenheit ist das – sympathetisch mit*erlebende* oder aus uns selbst kommende – Entstehen, Verlaufen, ineinander Übergehen und Vergehen von *Gefühlen*.[13] Auch unter ihnen gibt es bedrückende und befreiende; beim unbestimmt großen Umfang dessen, was alles Gefühl werden kann, mag es sogar Gefühle *von Freiheit* geben; und wer solche Gefühle der Befreiung oder gar Freiheit häufiger oder intensiver hat als ein anderer wird dadurch ein freierer Mensch als der andere sein oder werden. Aber da auch unsere Gefühle uns unverfügbar und nur indirekt beeinflussbar sind, werden oder sind wir auf eine gefühlsspezifische Weise, d. h. bezüglich der *Form* des Gefühls nur dadurch frei oder freier, dass wir außer der Sensibilität für besondere Gefühle und ihre je spezifische Prozessualität ein dauerhaft zum Freisein tendierendes *Selbstgefühl* aufbauen und es, ohne den natürlichen Verlauf der besonderen Gefühle zu deformieren, einigermaßen robust erhalten. Frei in seinem Gefühlsleben ist, sche-

---

[12] *Encyclopädie*, §§ 392 f.
[13] *Encyklopädie*, §§ 402–410.

matisch gesprochen, derjenige, der weder durch bedrückende Gefühle depressiv noch durch euphorische Gefühle manisch wird, sich aber auch nicht in irgendwelchen anderen Gefühlshaltungen als denen des Manisch-depressiven verhärtet und blockiert. Freier als zuvor oder als ein anderer ist derjenige, dem dies auch unter ungünstigeren Umständen und mit weniger Bändigung oder gar Unterdrückung seines Gefühlslebens gelingt.

3. Aber zu einem Minimum (und Wachstum) an freiem Empfindungs- und Gefühlsleben gehört nicht nur der vom jeweils Gelebten und Erlebten abhängige Wechsel an Gestimmtheiten, Erlebnissen und Gefühlen. Dieser Wechsel und die Nähe zu uns selbst, die sich in ihm herstellen lässt und so zu einem qualifizierten Freisein (im Sinn von Beisichselbstsein) führt, braucht und findet ein Gegenstück in Gewöhnungsprozessen und *Gewohnheiten*, die aus solchen Prozessen hervorgehen.[14] Andernfalls bliebe die Ökonomie eines auf den Innengrund zentrierten Lebens in fatalem Umfang instabil; und die Beschreibung solchen Lebens würde zu sehr auf universelle Fraglichkeit hin stilisiert, die gar nicht zu lebendigen Organismen passt. Gewohnheiten sind nicht zu haben ohne Abstumpfung von Erleben und sind weithin auch Ersatz fürs Spüren. Sie begrenzen es. Aber sie sind darum im Hinblick aufs Freisein nichts eo ipso Fragwürdiges. Im Gegenteil: Nur durch sie hindurch befreien wir uns vom trivialen, dumpf „gewöhnlichen“ Empfindungsleben und können uns so öffnen für subtilere Gefühlsinhalte (als die in der Beschreibung allzu dicht am Organischen hängenden), können Geschicklichkeiten und Fähigkeiten erwerben, ohne die noch nicht einmal irgendein freies Handeln denkbar wäre, geschweige denn ein aus beruhigtem Innengrund gesteuertes; also auch kein wachsendes Freisein. Nur Gewohnheitsbildungen machen die uns tragenden Gehalte zu einem persönlichen Besitz, der dann (unter zusätzlichen Voraussetzungen) die Zurechnung von Handlungen erlaubt. Sie gehören selbst schon zum Minimalbestand unseres Freiseins und tragen als solche auch zu dessen Steigerung bei – insbesondere dann, wenn sie nicht in üblen Gewohnheiten resultieren, sondern in denen, worin ein lebendiges Individuum auf gut entwickelte Weise bei sich selbst ist. Erst aufgrund von hinlänglich ausgebildeten Gewohnheiten und artspezifischen Geschicklichkeiten sind wir als schon erlebende Wesen noch vor eigentlichem Spüren auf minimale Weise frei, und lässt sich ein solcher Zustand evidentermaßen auch anderen Lebewesen zusprechen.

4. Hexis, d. h. Lebenshaltung durch zum Charakterzug ausgebildete Gewohnheiten, geht jedoch nicht nur in Handlungen und qualifizierte Fähigkeiten zu ihnen ein. Sie gehört auch zum Minimum an entwickelter Einheit des Inneren und Äußeren eines lebendigen Individuums: dass dessen Leiblichkeit in Gestalt, Bewegungsweise, Mimik und Gestik das Innere lebendig ausdrückt und durch Ausdrucksfähigkeit zum natürlichen Zeichen von Empfinden, Erle-

---

[14] Vgl. *Encyclopädie*, §§ 409 f.

ben und Sich-Fühlen, aber auch Gewohntsein macht. Auch in dieser ungehinderten Innen-Außen-Einheit, in der einer sich organspezifisch fühlt und zu fühlen gibt, also verhält, liegt ein unverfügbarer Bestandteil minimalen Freiseins.[15] Seine Entwicklung prägt sich exemplarisch aus und findet sich verbalisiert in einer „freien Miene", einem „freien Blick", „freien Gang", in „Freiheit des Betragens", „freiem Ton der Äußerungen", „Freiherzigkeit", „Freimut", „befreiendem Lachen" und vielen anderen anthropologischen Sachverhalten bzw. dazu gehörigen Wortbildungen mehr. Man müsste blind oder von Vorurteilen verblendet sein, nicht auch in solchen Manifestationen von Beseeltheit Exempla ebenso freier wie lebendiger Vernünftigkeit zu erkennen.

5. Unter den Faktoren minimalen und gleichwohl erworbenen sowie entwickelbaren Freiseins findet sich mindestens ein weiterer. Er steht im Gegensatz zu den beiden zuletzt genannten, habituellen und ist im Hinblick auf Kunst besonders wichtig. Kognitiv-liberative Aktivitäten und ihre Minimalvoraussetzungen an Freisein sind allemal auf Fürwahrhalten angewiesen, das sich seinerseits nur in *Kategorien* entwickeln kann: Kategorien für gegenständliche Inhalte des Empfindens, Wahrnehmens, Theoretisierens, technischen Realisierens und Ziele-Setzens. Die aber besitzen ziemlich hochgradige Stabilität und sind deren zu ihrer Funktion auch bedürftig. In der Kunst hingegen müssen wir uns – und sei es auch versuchsweise – vom kategorialen Netz unseres Fürwahr- (und -richtig-)Haltens auch *befreien* können. Aber dies „befreien" gilt nicht nur für die Kunst, wenngleich sie dafür exemplarisch ist. Es gehört schon überhaupt zu gestalterischer Produktivität und ästhetischer Sensitivität. Solches Freisein von Kategorien findet ja auch bereits bei simplem Wahrnehmen, Bekanntschaft haben und Vertraut werden mit was auch immer statt, wenn die entsprechende Einstellung in uns dominant wird. Es beschränkt sich auch nicht auf den Rahmen kognitiv-liberativer Entwicklung unserer Fähigkeiten. Denn es macht uns nach Pothast gerade *offen für anderes* als deren *Betätigungsweisen*: für andere Weisen, „da" zu sein für uns selbst und einer Welt gegenüber – ohne Festlegung auf die Richtung theoretischer *oder* praktischer Vernünftigkeit. Daher ist anzunehmen, dass es für dies Freisein auch einen (eigenen) Minimalbestand in uns gibt und dass von ihm aus das Selbst dahin gelangen kann, sich von seinen spezifischen Fürwahrhaltenszwängen sowie den sonstigen Regeln zur Erlangung empirischer Evidenz zu lösen. Aus der Perspektive unserer Disposition zu kognitiv-liberativer Entwicklung ist dieser Minimalbestand, und was sich aus ihm ergeben mag, freilich pejorativ zu beurteilen: als ein nur *privativer*, nämlich als freigemacht sein von allem, was uns objektiven Regeln unterwirft, wie von diesen Regeln selbst; als nur dem Privaten unserer Eigensphäre oder einem nicht-objektiv Allgemeinen überlassen sein, allen Gegenhalts in Objekten ledig und entsprechend verführbar. So erklärt sich die fundamentale *Ambivalenz* in

---

[15]   Vgl. *Encyclopädie*, §§ 411 f.

unserem normalsprachlichen Freiheitsverständnis, und so auch verstehen sich unsere häufigen Reden, in denen „frei" einen negativen Bewertungsakzent hat. Im Hinblick auf ästhetische Sensitivität aber und auf eine von ihrer Steigerung abhängige gestalterische Produktivität, woraus schließlich auch die Kunst hervorgeht, hat das entsprechende Minimum an Freisein seine eigene, spezifisch menschliche Vernünftigkeit und sein Potential zu weiterer Vernunftentwicklung. Es ist, kantisch gesprochen, Freisein *produktiver Einbildungskraft* und ihrer erscheinenden Produkte. Man sollte es weder allein für die Kunst gelten lassen noch im Minimalbestand eines Freiseins, das auf menschliche Weise lebendig und vernünftig ist, unterschlagen.

Soweit mein kleiner Beitrag zum großen Thema „Minimum von subjektivem, am lebendigen Individuum exemplifiziertem Freisein". Der Beitrag sollte zeigen, dass Freisein schon in seinem Minimalbestand *multidimensional* zu bestimmen ist und schwerlich zu reduzieren auf die traditionellen Hauptbegriffe „Beisichselbstsein" („Nähe zu sich selbst"), „Autonomie" und „Selbstbestimmtheit im Entscheiden und Handeln". Erst recht nicht ist es ausschließlich auf Handeln ausgerichtet.

(c) Wie aber verhält es sich mit Freisein als *Strebensziel*? Hierzu wenigstens, den vorliegenden Abschnitt abschließend, noch ein paar Bemerkungen, Fragen und Erwägungen: In Pothasts Buch *Lebendige Vernünftigkeit* sieht es so aus, als sei Freisein nur *eines* unter zahlreichen möglichen Zielen, wenngleich ein wichtiges (LV, S. 264). Über seinen vernünftigen Zusammenhang mit anderen Zielen oder die Zusammenhanglosigkeit zwischen ihm und ihnen wird indes kaum Auskunft gegeben. In den thematischen Grenzen des Buchs wäre die weitere Auskunft wohl auch schwer möglich. Im *Philosophischen Buch* hingegen findet sich, ein gut Stück darüber hinausgehend, dass das Wachsen lebendiger Vernünftigkeit nicht nur liberativ ist, sondern kombiniert mit wachsender Erkenntnis, also „kognitiv-liberativ". Ferner: dass das Freisein eine mit *gespürtem Glück* zusammengehende Möglichkeit fraglichen Lebens darstellt (PB, S. 357; vgl. auch S. 27 f.); dass die Richtung auf reicheres Spüren „schließlich auf Freisein" geht (PB, S. 430 ff.), dass aber die Weise, in welcher es jemandem durch *Kunst* gelingen kann, mehr *von* sich *für* sich zu sein, dem „kognitiv-liberativen Mehr" „an die Seite gestellt werden" mag, jedoch auch davon abgehoben werden muss (PB, S. 436, 446). Da beginnen Fragen, die, wie mir scheint, am Ende über Freisein in bloß individuell lebendiger Vernünftigkeit hinaus auch zu Freiheit unter objektiv-rechtlichen Normen führen müssen.

1. Gehen das kognitive und das liberative Moment im Ziel des Freiseins allemal Hand in Hand, oder gibt es nicht auch Möglichkeiten der Kollision zwischen den jeweils vom einen und vom anderen aus anzustrebenden Zielen? Wenn aber letzteres der Fall ist, wie man gewiss annehmen muss – was besagt das für den begrifflichen Gehalt und Rang von Freisein als Ziel? Mir scheint, es legt nahe, den Versuch einer inhaltlichen Bestimmung von Freiheit als *letztem Strebensziel* mit möglichst genauer Festlegung des Gewichts und der Anteile an

Wahrem und Gutem zu unterlassen und uns stattdessen ans absehbar Erreichbare zu halten, dabei aber – um praktisches Freisein zu optimieren – allemal dem bis dahin theoretisch erkennbar Wahren sowie Wahrscheinlichen Rechnung zu tragen. Das Optimum, um das es hier einzig gehen kann, ist also nicht ein nur objektiv letztes Strebensziel, das ausschließlich objektiv identifizierbar wäre, oder gar sein Erlangtsein. Es ist vielmehr die schon *gegenwärtig* zu identifizierende sowie erreichbar maximale Entwicklung und Freiheit unserer sowohl theoretisch wie praktisch (je spezifisch) erkennenden Intelligenz; als solche aber noch gar kein von jeweils „uns" unterschieden Objektives, sondern eine innerste, sowohl subjektive wie objektive Bestimmung unseres je eigenen Selbst, in der sich das theoretisch-kognitive und das praktisch-liberative Moment vereinigen und einander durchdringen.

2. Ein kognitiv-liberativ zu erstrebendes und dabei von störenden intellektualistischen Aspekten irgendwie bereinigtes Freisein als handelnd zu erreichendes Ziel mag beim Erreichen oder bei erfolgreichen Schritten der Annäherung an es sogar zusammengehen mit gespürtem *Glück*. Aber ist das allemal so – oder gibt es nicht auch hier Kollisionen zwischen der Befriedigung unseres Bedürfnisses, im Glück zu leben, und unserem Streben nach Freisein? Und wenn letzteres der Fall ist: was von beidem, Glück oder Freisein, verdient im Kollisionsfall den Vorrang? Zu lebendiger Vernünftigkeit dürfte es auch gehören, in solchen Zwangslagen von Fall zu Fall den voraussichtlich erträglichsten Kompromiss zwischen den kollidierenden Interessen zu suchen. Im Hinblick auf unsere theoretische sowie praktische Intelligenz und ihre Betätigung aber, von der nicht zuletzt unsere Einsicht in Forderungen des Rechts und der Gerechtigkeit sowie deren Erfüllung abhängt, besteht hier zweifellos ein Vorrang epistemisch sowie praktisch vernünftigen Freiseins vor irgendwelchen Forderungen des Wohls und des Glücks, ja, sogar vor jeglichem bloßen Erwägen solcher Forderungen. Das antike Konzept guten, erfüllten Lebens (εὖ ζῆν) ist selbst in Aristoteles' Analyse viel zu unscharf, um in sich klare Präferenzverhältnisse bezüglich des hier interessierenden Punktes erkennen zu lassen.

3. Eine ähnliche, wenngleich noch viel komplexere Beurteilung verdient wohl das Verhältnis zwischen einerseits Freisein, dessen Konzept Ergebnis der Überlegungen zu den beiden vorhergehenden Fragepunkten ist, und andererseits einem ihm an die Seite zu stellenden, in und durch *Kunst* möglichen Freisein: Hier scheint, was Freisein als Ziel angeht, auf den ersten Blick die Vereinbarkeit beider Konzepte eine klare Sache. Die Kunst setzt frei zu einem „Lebendigsein auf Versuch" (PB, S. 449 ff.), zu einem anderen Leben und Spüren als dem realiter mit all seinen Zwängen möglichen und zu verwirklichenden. Sie öffnet ein „Fenster zum Realen" (PB, S. 461 ff.). Was sie damit sichtbar oder spüren macht, hat als Ziel also neben der Verwirklichung anderer Ziele lebendiger Vernünftigkeit entweder keine Realisierungs-Chance oder eine, die neben der Verfolgung solcher Ziele besteht und deren Wahrnehmung dieser vorhergeht oder folgt. Soweit Realisierungschancen bestehen, greift ihr

Spürens-Ziel durch die Verwirklichung anderer Ziele sozusagen hindurch. Es steht also nicht nur am Anfang dieser Verwirklichung, sondern reicht in sie hinein und sogar über sie hinaus. Doch mögen beim Wahrnehmen der Chancen nicht auch Kollisionen bewusst werden? Zweifellos. Aber wenn sie entstehen: in welchem *Sinn* ist das aus produktiver Einbildungskraft kommende, in Kunst Gestalt annehmende Ziel dann eines von Freisein – und was entscheidet wie zwischen diesem Freisein und einem mit ihm konkurrierenden anderen? Was entscheidet über einen möglichen *Vorrang* des einen vor dem anderen? Wo kommen eventuelle Instanzen der Festlegung von Präferenz zwischen ihnen eigentlich her? Auch diese Fragen sind wichtig und verdienen sorgfältige Überlegung, wenn es um Freisein in lebendiger Vernünftigkeit geht. Im Hinblick auf den Zusammenhang solchen Freiseins mit objektiv-rechtlichen Normen aber haben sie offensichtlich keine Vordringlichkeit. Sie können also dahingestellt bleiben, wenn es nun erstmals eigens um diesen Zusammenhang zu tun ist.[16]

IV. „Frei sein" in Hegels Psychologie und Rechtsverständnis

Ebenso wie zum Minimum an Freisein lässt sich zu den obigen drei Fragepunkten mithilfe der angestellten Überlegungen die darin angedachte Fortsetzung der Pothast'schen Auskunft über Freisein ziemlich mühelos vorweg genommen finden in Hegels Philosophie des psychologisch differenzierten subjektiven Geistes.[17] Wie in dieser Philosophie gezeigt wird, ist der – vorerst nur direkt auf sich selbst bezogen thematisierte – Geist[18] einerseits *theoretische* Intelligenz. Als solche schließt er auch die für Kunst konstitutive, frei produktive Einbildungskraft in sich[19]; als ganze aber macht er vornehmlich die theoretisch-kognitive, synergetische Wirksamkeit aller zu ihr gehörigen Faktoren aus (wobei zu diesen Faktoren ein nicht nur der Form, sondern, wie am Ende erkennbar, auch dem Inhalte nach freies Denken gehört).[20] Andererseits hingegen ist der in direkter Beziehung auf sich thematisierte Geist *praktische* Intelligenz und in seiner Entwicklung durchaus als sich befreiend, mithin als „liberativ" tätig beschrieben. Beide – nur in begreifend erkennender Thematisierung aufein-

---

[16] Wenn der Zusammenhang auf eine systematisch zu entwickelnde Lehre vom objektiven Geist führt, müsste allerdings, was diese betrifft, zugestanden werden, dass es neben der darin abzuhandelnden, das Recht konstituierenden Objektivität – oder in weiterer Untersuchung spezieller Facetten an ihr – auch noch objektiv Geistiges geben muss, dessen Objektivität von der für das Recht konstitutiven grundverschieden ist.

[17] *Encyclopädie*, §§ 445–481.

[18] Dieser subjektive Geist ist als Geist überhaupt schon seinem Wesen nach Freiheit und manifestiert sich als solche in seiner Entwicklung (vgl. *Encyklopädie*, §§ 382 f.).

[19] *Encyklopädie*, §§ 456, 458A.

[20] *Encyklopädie*, §§ 446–468.

anderfolgenden – Wirksamkeiten, in denen sich das Wesen des Geistes als Freiheit manifestiert, vereinigen sich jedoch zum Konzept eines in Beziehung auf sich selbst *durch und durch freien* Geistes, der konkrete Einheit von theoretischer und praktischer Intelligenz ist.[21] Er steht also durchaus für das oben[22] umrissene und dabei vom Strebensziel ‚Glück‘ abgehobene Optimum erreichbaren, sowohl „kognitiven“ als „liberativen“ Freiseins.[23]

Wie aber soll solches Freisein unter objektiv-rechtlichen Normen unbeschädigt bestehen können oder sogar müssen; und wie gelangt man von der Einsicht in solches Freisein als eines, das aus lebendiger Vernünftigkeit kommt und besteht, auf überzeugende Weise zu einem *Verständnis von Recht*, das diesen Bedingungen wenigstens hinsichtlich seiner objektiven Normen mit deren fundamentalen Gehalten genügt? – Wenn ich Ulrich Pothast richtig verstehe, müsste er dazu feststellen: Gerade das in Beziehung auf sich selbst thematisierte, von seinem jeweiligen Innengrund gestützte, lebendig-vernünftige Freisein jedes einzelnen ist auch dann, wenn sich in ihm die theoretisch-kognitiven und die praktisch-liberativen Betätigungen auf die oben umrissene Weise vereinigen, *je individuell für sich* genommen noch viel zu *instabil*, als dass es sich und seine Tätigkeit ganz aus eigener Kraft in seiner Einheit erhalten könnte und in diese auch noch ein darauf abgestimmtes Wohl oder sogar ein angemessen temperiertes Glück zu integrieren vermöchte – ganz zu schweigen von den im dritten Fragepunkt zur Sprache gekommenen Faktoren, aus denen sich das ästhetische und für die Kunst wesentliche Freie nährt. Die Feststellung mag ihre Richtigkeit haben. Doch wie kann bei einer zusätzlichen Stützung oder Stabilisierung, die über den Innengrund hinausreicht, im Verhältnis zu ihm also eine „äußere“ ist, das lebendig-vernünftige Freisein davor bewahrt bleiben, dass es durch eben diese Stützung unvermeidlich eingeschränkt, beschädigt oder sogar in sein Gegenteil verkehrt wird? – Eine befriedigende Antwort auf diese Fragen können uns evidenterweise weder die institutionalistischen noch die kommunitaristischen, weder die utilitaristischen noch die pragmatistischen Ansätze der Rechtsphilosophie geben; genau genommen aber auch weder die abstrakt intersubjektivistischen (einschließlich der werttheoretischen) noch die ethizistischen. Denn wer das Recht und die Forderungen, die es verbindlich an einzelne richtet, ethizistisch begründet, der korrumpiert es ineins damit, dass er es lehrt; und wer in der Rechtsbegründung sowie Aufklärung über das Recht mit der Intersubjektivität beginnt, der kann *vor* der Thematisierung interpersonaler

---

[21] *Encyklopädie*, §§ 481 f.: Zum dahin führenden Gedankengang vergleiche man mit den §§ 476, 478, 480 die entsprechenden Einleitungsparagraphen in Hegel, G. W. F. (2009): *Grundlinien der Philosophie des Rechts*, (zitiert als *Grundlinien* unter Angabe des Paragraphen.), unter ihnen aber insbes. die §§ 10 f.; 15; 21–25; 26–28.

[22] Nämlich unter Fragepunkt 1 und 2.

[23] Vgl. damit Ulrich Pothasts Charakterisierung von „*Freisein als Ziel* partieller und nie vollkommener Selbstaneignung“ in PB, S. 356.

Rechtsbeziehungen keine rechtlichen Normen für Befugnisse und Pflichten auszeichnen, die je einzelne Menschen gemäß ihrer lebendigen Vernünftigkeit *sich selbst gegenüber* haben. Er wird auch schwerlich *in der Perspektive* praktischer Betätigung – oder auch philosophisch begreifenden Erkennens unserer Vernunft, die in allen Menschen eine und dieselbe ist – einsichtig machen können, dass das eigene Freisein, wenn sein Verhalten vernünftigen, objektiv-rechtlichen Normen entspricht, weder bei ihm selbst noch bei anderen das Freisein in lebendiger Vernünftigkeit verletzt. In der Lage dazu ist ja sogar genau genommen nicht einmal die kantische Rechtslehre, die – trotz eines entsprechenden, oberflächlichen Eindrucks[24] – durchaus nicht mit der Intersubjektivität „beginnt", da sie ihren Rechtsbegriff in subtiler Weise auf den „obersten Grundsatz der Sittenlehre" gründet.[25] Sie kann zwar von diesem obersten Grundsatz aus einen Begriff strikten, sich aller ethischen Beimischungen enthaltenden, allgemeinen Begriff des Rechts und seines Prinzips begründen Aber mit diesem Begriff und Prinzip ist weder die „lebendige" Vernünftigkeit des entsprechenden Rechts gesichert noch die Verbindlichkeit der Rechtspflichten gegen sich selbst (unter einem streng rechtlich zu verstehenden Imperativ „honeste vive") – und ist näher besehen nicht einmal das „auf dingliche Art persönliche Recht" in der Ehe, Familie und Hausgemeinschaft ableitbar als ein von allem Ethischen abstrahierendes, als das es behauptet wird. Auch die von Fichte ins Spiel gebrachte, zu Freiheit als Autonomie und Selbstbestimmung reinen Willens hinzutretende Freiheitsdimension ‚Beisichselbstsein' (oder in Pothasts Bezeichnung ‚Nähe zu sich selbst') stellt hier noch keine wirkliche Abhilfe dar, zumal sie bei Fichte mit einem früheren und späteren, beide Male aber höchst anfechtbaren Rechtsbegriff verbunden wird.[26]

Angesichts so enormer Schwierigkeiten einer aus Einsicht in die menschliche Vernunft geschöpften Rechtsphilosophie ist nur zu verständlich, dass Ulrich Pothast bislang keine Auskunft darüber gab, wie zu Freisein in lebendiger Vernünftigkeit auch das Recht wenigstens hinsichtlich seiner objektiven Normen gehört. Er hätte dazu vermutlich ein Stück weit auf Distanz gehen müssen zu seiner früh entwickelten Aversion gegen die allzu abstrakten Freiheitslehren des klassischen Deutschen Idealismus sowie Spinozas. Jedenfalls hätte er diese Begriffe nicht einfach beiseite lassen dürfen. Vielmehr wäre die Reflexion auf sie und auf ihre begrenzte Leistungsfähigkeit mit der Überlegung zu verbinden gewesen, wie sie zu ergänzen sind, um jenes Freisein zu denken, dessen es zu innerer Verbindung der herausgearbeiteten Freiseins-Bestimmun-

---

[24]   Nämlich von § B in *Metaphysische Anfangsgründe der Rechtslehre* (Königsberg 1797).

[25]   Allerdings ist die auf diesen Grund zurückgehende Begründung von Kant selbst nicht mehr ausgeführt worden (vgl. dazu meine Abhandlung *Notwendigkeit des Rechts unter Voraussetzung des Kategorischen Imperativs der Sittlichkeit.* In: *Jahrbuch für Recht und Ethik* (*Annual Review of Law and Ethics*) Bd. 6 (2006), S. 167–213.

[26]   Vgl. hierzu die soeben genannte Abhandlung, a. a. O. S. 177 f.; S. 186–188.

gen mit einem ihnen angemessenen und aus ihnen entspringenden Rechtsbegriff bedarf. Dazu im Folgenden noch einige an Hegel erinnernde Anregungen.

Wenn es richtig ist, dass das ebenso theoretisch-kognitive wie praktisch-liberative Freisein einer bisher nicht berücksichtigten *Stützung im Objektiven* bedarf, aber dieses Objektive dem stützenden Innengrund angemessen sein muss, so kann die fragliche Objektivität nicht irgendeine sein oder von irgendwoher kommen. Sie muss dem freien Geist und seiner ausgezeichnet lebendigen Vernünftigkeit selbst entstammen, muss die diesem Freisein *eigene* Objektivität sein und eine, die vom Freisein nicht nur in Anspruch genommen wird, weil zu seiner Stabilisierung „gebraucht"; vielmehr vor allem deswegen, weil sie aus seiner bzw. des freien Geistes weiterer Entwicklung selbstbestimmt „hervorgeht", sofern der Geist in dieser Entwicklung nun seine bloße Beziehung auf sich aus eigener, innerer Notwendigkeit des Begriffs überschreitet. Genau als solche hat Hegel die für uns nun relevante Objektivität zu Beginn seiner Philosophie des objektiven Geistes gedacht. Und keine andere Objektivität ist Hegel zufolge *das Recht* im allgemeinsten Sinne vernünftiger Rede von einem solchen.[27] Aber wie ist das zu verstehen?

Das *exemplarisch Freie* ist für Hegel nicht das rein-praktische Bewusstsein oder Selbstbewusstsein oder Ich oder Subjekt, sondern der *eine*, im unaufhaltsamen Überschreiten aller Grundbegriffe des Wirklichen konsequenterweise sich dem Denken aufdrängende, reine *Begriff*,[28] – und zwar in seiner ihm eigenen, ohne Wirklichkeitsvoraussetzung zu denkenden Entwicklungsdynamik. In dieser findet er sich zunächst zu Allgemeinheit, Besonderheit und Einzelheit differenziert und bestimmt deren Verhältnisse zueinander; dann *urteilt* er sich in Urteile (und in Urteilen) verschiedener Urteilsformen; und danach schließt er seine Allgemeinheit, Besonderheit und Einzelheit in verschiedenen Schlussweisen zusammen, vermittelt sie also miteinander und mit sich. Auch der Geist überhaupt, dessen Wesen, wie gesagt, selbst schon „die Freiheit" ist, durchläuft im Prozess seiner zunehmend wirksameren Manifestation[29] eine nicht zeitlich zu denkende Entwicklung, die zunächst den Geist überhaupt in seiner Beziehung auf sich selbst betrifft und als solche der Dynamik des einen Begriffs

---

[27]   In einer jüngsten, unter vielen Gesichtspunkten verdienstvollen, umfangreichen Publikation über Hegels *Grundlinien der Philosophie des Rechts* (Berlin 1821) ist leider dieser begriffliche Zusammenhang von Objektivität des Geistes und Recht unaufgehellt geblieben (vgl. K. Vieweg, *Das Denken der Freiheit. Hegels Grundlinien der Philosophie des Rechts.* München 2012, insbes S. 48–96).

[28]   Vgl. *Encyklopädie*, ¹1817, § 108: „Der Begriff ist das *Freye*, als die reine Negativität der Reflexion des Wesens in sich oder die *Macht* der Substanz, – und als die *Totalität* dieser Negativität, das *an und für sich bestimmte*"; ebd. ³1830, § 160: „Der Begriff ist das *Freie* als die *für sich seyende substantielle Macht* und ist *Totalität*, in dem *jedes* der Momente *das Ganze* ist, [...] so ist er in seiner Identität mit sich das *an und für sich bestimmte*".

[29]   *Encyklopädie*, ¹1817, § 382 f.

folgt. Zwar trägt diese Entwicklung, wie sie zunächst statthat, in ihrer zweitletzten Phase – derjenigen der praktischen Intelligenz – in sich auch eine konkretere Entwicklung vom besonderen Begriff des anfangs bloß *an sich* freien Willens zum *für sich* freien und dann im Verlauf von dessen *innerer* Objektivierung zur *Idee* des *an und für sich* freien Willens,[30] die allererst mit der letzten Phase der übergeordneten Begriffsentwicklung erreicht wird, – nämlich als diejenige des *freien Geistes*. Aber diese speziellere Entwicklung des besonderen Begriffs (freien Willens) über seine innere Objektivierung zu seiner Idee hindert nicht, sondern trägt gerade mit dazu bei, dass an ihrem Ende auch der Geist überhaupt in seiner zunächst innerbegrifflichen Entwicklung als freier Geist schließlich sich selber objektiviert, indem er – dem „Schluß der Notwendigkeit" gemäß – eine „Vermittlung durch Aufheben der Vermittlung" mit sich vollzieht und so zu einer neuen Unmittelbarkeit gelangt.[31] Aus dieser inneren, zum Begriff als solchem und seiner Dynamik gehörenden Notwendigkeit heraus also tut der freie Geist den Entwicklungsschritt, dessen sein Freisein zur Stabilisierung durch eigene Objektivierung bedarf. Und indem die neue Unmittelbarkeit, zu welcher der Geist qua Wille dabei gelangt, sich zugleich der Logik „freier Entlassung" der Idee[32] zum Realen verdankt, ist dieses objektiv-geistig Reale von so allgemeiner, aber begriffs- und damit freiseins-verträglicher Bestimmtheit, wie es ein unmittelbares „Dasein" für einen derart freien Willen – innerhalb oder außerhalb seiner selbst – überhaupt nur sein kann. Das Dasein, mit dem man es nun zu tun hat, ist also nicht bloße Objektivität überhaupt, wie z. B. diejenige eines Mechanismus,[33] sondern eine spezielle „Weise der Objectivirung des Begriffs".[34] – Wenn wir auch noch einsehen könnten, dass mit dem so gedachten Schritt zur Objektivität eben diese Objektivität als das Recht zu denken ist, so hätten wir im Ergebnis genau das, was wir suchen; und es bestünde eine gute Chance, darin auch zu erkennen, dass die objektiven Normen solchen Rechts das Freisein des freien Geistes nicht beeinträchtigen.[35]

Natürlich kann Recht, damit von ihm hier die Rede sein darf, „nicht nur als das beschränkt juristische Recht" zu nehmen sein[36] – sowohl im Sinn des „positiven" Rechts als auch im Sinn des vorkantischen „Naturrechts". Die Rede von

---

[30]   Vgl. *Encyklopädie*, §§ 476, 478, 481 sowie *Grundlinien*, §§ 10 f., 15, 21–25.

[31]   *Encyklopädie*, ¹1817, § 192.

[32]   Hier: der Idee des Willens als (an und für sich) freie Intelligenz. Vgl. *Encyklopädie*, §§ 481 f.

[33]   Vgl. *Encyklopädie*, §§ 194 f.

[34]   Vgl. Hegels eigenhändige Randbemerkung zu § 28 der *Grundlinien*, in: *Grundlinien der Philosophie des Rechts*. Bd. 14,2 Beilagen, S. 363.

[35]   Dass das Recht in seiner mehr oder weniger unvollkommenen *Befolgung*, *Ausübung* und *Pflege* zu einer solchen Beeinträchtigung führt, kann damit freilich nicht ausgeschlossen werden.

[36]   Vgl. *Encyklopädie*, § 486.

Recht, wenn sie denn berechtigt sein soll, kann auch nicht – wie bei Kant – hier sozusagen mit der Tür ins Haus fallen und den Inhalt philosophischer „Rechtslehre" gleich eingangs kennzeichnen als „Inbegriff der Gesetze, für welche eine äußere Gesetzgebung möglich ist"[37]. Es mag zwar sein, dass Recht, wie es nun zu denken ist und von Hegel bereits in allgemeinsten Bemerkungen über den objektiven Geist angekündigt wird,[38] im Gang der Entwicklung seines Begriffs nicht zuletzt als eines bestimmt werden muss, das Recht als „das *Gesetz*" ist.[39] Aber die Begrifflichkeit des Übergangs vom freien Geist (als noch bloß subjektivem) zum objektiven wirft dieses Rechtsverständnis gewiss nicht unmittelbar ab. Sie ermöglicht es glücklicherweise erst auf einem langen Weg zu ihm. Wohl aber kann von ihr aus – wenn man den Charakter des äußerlichen Daseins erwägt, mit dem man am Ende des Übergangs zum objektiven Geist zu tun bekommt – bereits Wichtiges gesagt werden, das für alles Recht grundlegend ist und den Gebrauch des Ausdrucks „Recht" hier schon ebenso gut rechtfertigt wie den Ausdruck „objektiver Geist". Das ist nun endlich zu zeigen.

Die wechselseitige Vermittlung des Allgemeinen, Besonderen und Einzelnen im Freisein eines durch und durch freien Geistes ist in ihrem letzten Stadium – der „Vermittlung durch Aufheben der Vermittlung" – so vollständig, dass jedes individuell Einzelne im innersten Komplex der sein Freisein als solches ausmachenden, *allgemeinen* Bestimmungen völlig übereinstimmt mit den anderen Einzelnen, was bei Mitberücksichtigung der Dimensionen des Glücks und des Ästhetischen freilich nicht möglich gewesen wäre. Diese Übereinstimmung aller individuell Einzelnen hinsichtlich ihres Freiseins „im allgemeinen" geht bei der Aufhebung von Vermittlung über auf deren Ergebnis, also ins äußere, freiseinsverträgliche Dasein seiner allgemeinen Bestimmungen. Zusätzlich zur inneren Bestimmung des Freiseins und zum ihr zugehörigen Zweck findet sich die entsprechende Allgemeinheit bei jedem Einzelnen also auch in seiner äußerlichen Objektivität als dem „Material" weiterer Bestimmung dessen, worin der an und für sich freie Wille sein vorgefundenes Dasein hat.[40] Ferner gehört zu diesem vorgefundenen Dasein in seiner bei allen Einzelnen übereinstimmenden Allgemeinheit auch, dass die Freiseins-Bestimmungen eines jeden für jeden sowohl in ihm selbst als auch in allen anderen einen *substantiellen* Zusammenhang bilden, der in jedem Einzelnen auch *erscheint*, sein *Anerkanntsein* findet und als *Macht* auftritt, als welche die Bestimmungen im Bewusstsein eines jeden *gelten*. Wie der Schluss der Vermittlung durch Aufheben der Vermittlung ein Schluss der Notwendigkeit ist, so hat auch sein Ergebnis, die vermittelte Unmittelbarkeit, den Charakter einer Notwendigkeit: derjenigen nämlich der Frei-

---

[37] Kant, *Metaphysische Anfangsgründe der Rechtslehre*, § A.
[38] *Encyklopädie*, §§ 485 f.
[39] *Encyklopädie*, §§ 529.
[40] Vgl. *Encyklopädie*, §§ 483 f.

seinsbestimmungen sowohl hinsichtlich ihres Zusammenhangs als auch in Bezug auf ihr Anerkanntsein seitens der Einzelnen – oder, mit anderen Worten, in Bezug auf „ihr Gelten im Bewußtsein".[41] Des Weiteren ist der Inhalt der objektiven Freiseinsbestimmungen nun „nur in der Form der Allgemeinheit".[42] Aber selbst das ist nicht alles: Infolge des Notwendigkeits-Charakters der Vermittlung, aus welcher die Freiseins-Bestimmungen zu ihrer Objektivität gekommen sind, machen sie in ihrem Zusammenhang, der ja nun ein *substantieller* ist, den *Grund* für jegliche Betätigung des Freiseins im äußeren, freiseinsverträglichen objektiven Dasein aus.

Cum grano salis kann man daher wohl sagen, dass wir es nun mit zweierlei freiem Willen zu tun haben: einerseits dem *subjektiv* an und für sich freien des subjektiven Geistes und andererseits dem *substantiellen* Willen als dem objektiven Gegenstück des ersteren, der sich zugleich als dessen innerster Kerngehalt manifestiert.[43] Wie es Reflexionsbestimmungen (nämlich z. B. die des Inneren und Äußeren sowie Oberen und Unteren) nun einmal an sich haben, relativ zu sein und sich ineinander zu verkehren oder ihre Positionen bei sich änderndem Kontext zu vertauschen, findet sich also der substanzielle Wille nicht nur exemplifiziert im äußeren Dasein (qua anderen Exemplaren lebendig-vernünftigen Freiseins), sondern auch in demjenigen, *dessen* „andere" diese Exempla sind und der für diese zum Bereich *ihrer* anderen gehört. Vor allem aber bekundet sich an dieser Stelle nun auch die Berechtigung der Rede von Recht: Der substantielle *Grund*, mit dem wir's hier zu tun haben, ist einer, *auf welchen* – als auf einen nicht nur äußeren, sondern zugleich inneren – jedes individuelle Exemplum an und für sich freien Willens *ein Recht hat*, das *vom Grund her* gehabt ist und ursprünglich auch zum Grund gehört: das Recht, welches dann sein „Gelten im Bewußtsein" eines jeden hat und darin Anspruch ist, von jedem gewürdigt und respektiert zu werden, aber auch sich selbst und jedem anderen Respekt zu zollen. Dieses Recht ist, obwohl selbst schon sehr komplex, sozusagen das Ur-Recht, das sowohl ist als auch gehabt wird; und ist für den subjektiven Willen nicht nur eine Befugnis, sondern infolge seines sowohl inneren wie äußeren Orts für jeden Einzelnen zugleich verpflichtend; und es gehört nicht nur zum subjektiv an und für sich freien Willen, sondern als Recht, das es *ist*, auch zu seinem substantiellen Grund; zu diesem aber vor allem auch als die *objektiv-rechtliche Norm*, unter der nicht nur der ihr entsprechende, an und für sich freie Wille, sondern ebenso wie er auch alles übrige, subjektive Wollen steht.

Wie sollte man vom Recht, sofern es derart objektive Norm ist, noch sagen können, dass es mit seinen fundamentalen normativen Gehalten das lebendig-

---

[41] Vgl. *Encyklopädie*, §§ 484 f.
[42] *Encyklopädie*, §§ 484 f.
[43] Vgl. *Encyklopädie*, §§ 485.

vernünftige Freisein beeinträchtige? Die Gehalte bilden ja gar keine Beschränkung des an und für sich freien Willens und sind sogar, genau genommen, nicht einmal beschränkend für die wirklich freie Willkür.[44] Vielmehr machen sie den innersten Grund des Freiseins aus. Zugleich aber erweitern sie dessen Aktionsradius in die äußeren Verhältnisse hinein. Als der Grund allen sich objektivierenden Freiseins hingegen fallen sie nicht wunderbarer Weise vom Himmel einer jenseitigen, „intelligiblen Welt" oder sind nur in dieser jenseitigen Welt wahrhaft „autonom". Sie sind so selbstgegeben und selbstbestimmt, wie es die übrigen Bestimmungen des Einen Begriffs des Geistes in diesem sind. Am Ende der Entwicklung des Begriffs objektiven Geistes werden sie sogar zu Normen, die Rechtsverhältnisse in der ganzen Menschenwelt bestimmen und damit auch deren weltgeschichtliche Entwicklung bis zur Hegelischen Gegenwart in groben Zügen begreiflich machen, so dass sie die Begreifenden davor bewahren können, sich bezüglich fundamentaler Überzeugungen von Recht und Unrecht bloß auf Sitte und Brauchtum oder die eigene kulturelle Tradition oder das geltende positive Recht berufen zu müssen, ohne dabei einen Grund geltend machen zu können, aus dem sich die eigene kulturelle Faktizität von bloß treu tradierter Unsitte unterscheidet. Wer im Gegensatz dazu begreift, der erkennt philosophisch seine eigene sittliche Bestimmtheit und ist sich darin gewiss, dass er diese auch ohne Philosophie als seine zweite – nämlich sittliche – Natur weiß, zugleich aber als „selbstbewußte Freiheit", die (begriffen im dritten Stadium der systematischen Entwicklung des Rechtsbegriffs) zu lebendig-vernünftiger Sitte geworden ist. Und er vermag sich die nähere Gestalt der Sittlichkeit solcher Sitte am Ende sogar als geschichtlich relative durchsichtig zu machen, ohne darüber in einen kulturalistischen Relativismus zu verfallen.[45]

Der lange Weg der der spekulativ begreifenden Rechtserkenntnis, der zum Stadium der Sittlichkeit führt, kann hier nicht mehr Station für Station durchschritten werden. Es sollte fürs noch Fehlende aber auch genügen, auf drei Besonderheiten aufmerksam zu machen, an denen sich die Eigenart des Wegs markant zu erkennen gibt:

1. Am Anfang der Erkenntnis scheint das Recht – unterm Titel ‚Das abstrakte Recht' – ganz wie in der Tradition des neueren Naturrechts bis zu Kant als dasjenige einer *Rechtsperson* in deren Außenbezug genommen zu werden: nur als Recht an äußeren Sachen, in vertraglichen Beziehungen zu anderen Rechtspersonen, in der Ahndung von Unrecht, das widerfährt. Sieht man näher zu, so zeigt sich jedoch, dass die Rechtsperson hier keineswegs nur in Beziehung auf das eine oder andere ihr Äußere (Sache, andere Person, anderer Umgang mit Recht) genommen wird, sondern gleich zu Beginn auch in ihrer lebendig-vernünftigen Rechtsbeziehung auf sich: in dieser nämlich hat sie

---

[44]   Vgl. *Grundlinien*, §§ 29 A.
[45]   Vgl. *Encyclopädie*, §§ 482 A, 485 f. und 513.

ebenso Rechts*pflichten* gegen sich selbst, wie sie auch eigentümliche Rechts-*befugnisse* sich selbst gegenüber besitzt.[46] Auch hierin bekundet sich das Recht mit seinen Normen als ein Freisein, als das es die älteren Rechtsphilosophien gar nicht gewürdigt hatten.

2. Ähnliches gilt von der aufs abstrakte Recht folgenden – ,Die Moralität' betitelten – Stufe der Begriffsentwicklung, auf welcher die Rechtsperson als Rechts*subjekt* bestimmt ist.[47] Dessen Willensbestimmungen nämlich – „inner-lich *als die seinigen gesetzt* und von ihm gewollt", während ihre „thätliche Aeußerung" mit entsprechender Freiheit rechtlich relevante *Handlung* ist – sind in der früheren Rechtsphilosophie ebenfalls zu kurz gekommen, obwohl gerade diese Freiheit nach Hegels Auffassung „vornehmlich .... im europä-ischen Sinn Freiheit" heißt:[48] die Willensbestimmtheit nämlich, die den un-schuldigen oder schuldhaften *Vorsatz*, die darüber hinaus auf Wohl oder Wehe gehende *Absicht* sowie die *das Gute* oder *das Böse* bezweckende Qualifikation bzw. Disqualifikation einer rechtlich normierten Handlung ausmacht.

3. Nur über die Verbindung mit diesen rechtlich relevanten, „moralischen" Aspekten der Handlung kommt es vom abstrakten (oder formellen) Recht aus zu *sittlich* bestimmtem Recht, in welches die Normen des abstrakten Rechts sowie der moralischen Handlungs-Aspekte – weiterhin normierend – integriert sind, so dass sie darin nach wie vor respektiert werden müssen. Allerdings gehören zum Recht, wie es die Sittlichkeit und ihre Komplexitätsstufen kenn-zeichnet, in zunehmendem Grade *auch kontingente Bestimmtheiten*, die sich nicht jeweils als vernunftnotwendige begreifen lassen. Wohl aber lässt sich an ihnen begreifen, dass ihre Kontingenzen den begreiflichen Normcharakteren nicht schaden, die sich nun – dem abstrakten Recht oder der sogenannten Mora-lität entstammend, zum Teil aber neu hinzukommend – im Kontext des Kontin-genten manifestieren. Die Kontingenzen betreffen vor allem auch Institutionali-sierungen, welche die Bestimmungen des abstrakten Rechts und der morali-schen Handlungsaspekte als integrale Bestandteile des gegenwärtig Sittlichen überall finden: in der institutionalisierten Gemeinschaft der Familie, in Institu-tionen der Wirtschaft, der Rechtspflege, der Sorge für soziale Wohlfahrt, der kommunalen Verbände und nicht zuletzt in den Institutionen des einzelnen, so oder so politisch verfassten Staats und seiner länderspezifischen Traditionen.

Wenn all dies in einem an der Idee der Freiheit orientierten Rechtsverständ-nis wie dem Hegelschen berücksichtigt ist, so lässt sich – stellvertretend für den Goethe'schen Egmont – nun auf Herzog Albas eingangs zitierte Behauptung – des Freiesten Freiheit sei es, Recht zu tun, woran der spanische König die Nie-derländer nicht hindern werde – philosophisch gelassen erwidern: „Ganz recht,

---

[46] Vgl. *Grundlinien*, §§ 41, 43, 47 f.; 57; 65–68; 70; *Encyclopädie*, §§ 488–490.
[47] *Encyclopädie*, §§ 503–512.
[48] *Encyklopädie*, §§ 503 f.

weil das Recht, dessen Forderungen zu befolgen sind, mitsamt den Befugnissen, die es gibt, nicht aus den Gewehrläufen kommt und schon gar nicht aus denen einer landesfremden Streitmacht, sondern aus dem innersten Grund des Frei-seins von Rechtspersonen in ihren privaten, gemeinschaftlichen, gesellschaft-lichen und politischen Verhältnissen, die in angestammter Sitte verankert sind. Wenn uns der König nicht hindern will, in diesem Sinne Recht zu tun: umso besser. Dann aber sollte er seine spanischen Truppen aus den Niederlanden unverzüglich wieder abziehen".

Literatur

Goethe, Johann Wolfgang von (1994): *Goethes Werke*. Hamburger Ausgabe in 14 Bdn., hrsg. v. E. Trunz, 13. durchges. Aufl., München.

Hegel, G.W.F. (1992): *Enzyklopädie der philosophischen Wissenschaften im Grund-risse (1830)*, in: *Gesammelte Werke Bd. 20*, in Verbindung mit der Deutschen For-schungsgemeinschaft hrsg. v.d. Rheinisch-Westfälischen Akademie der Wissen-schaften, hrsg. v. Wolfgang Bonsiepen, Hamburg. (Zitiert als *Encyklopädie* unter Angabe des Paragraphen.)

Hegel, G.W.F. (2000): *Enzyklopädie der philosophischen Wissenschaften im Grund-risse (1817)*, in: *Gesammelte Werke Bd. 13*, in Verbindung mit der Deutschen For-schungsgemeinschaft hrsg. v.d. Rheinisch-Westfälischen Akademie der Wissen-schaften, hrsg. v. Wolfgang Bonsiepen, Hamburg. (Zitiert als *Encyklopädie, [1]1817* unter Angabe des Paragraphen.)

Hegel, G.W.F. (2009): *Grundlinien der Philosophie des Rechts*, in: *Gesammelte Werke Bd. 14,1*, in Verbindung mit der Deutschen Forschungsgemeinschaft hrsg. v.d. Rheinisch-Westfälischen Akademie der Wissenschaften, hrsg. v. Wolfgang Bon-siepen, Hamburg. (Zitiert als *Grundlinien* unter Angabe des Paragraphen.)

Hegel, G.W.F. (2010): *Grundlinien der Philosophie des Rechts*, in: *Gesammelte Werke Bd. 14,2 Beilagen*, in Verbindung mit der Deutschen Forschungsgemeinschaft hrsg. v.d. Rheinisch-Westfälischen Akademie der Wissenschaften, hrsg. v. Wolf-gang Bonsiepen, Hamburg.

Kant, Immanuel (1969): *Metaphysische Anfangsgründe der Rechtslehre*, in: *Gesam-melte Schriften Bd. 6*, hrsg. Preussische Akademie der Wissenschaften, Berlin (Nachdruck der Ausgabe 1907).

Pothast, Ulrich (1980): *Die Unzulänglichkeit der Freiheitsbeweise. Zu einigen Lehr-stücken aus der neueren Geschichte von Philosophie und Recht*, Frankfurt a.M.

Pothast, Ulrich (1988): *Philosophisches Buch. Schrift unter der aus der Entfernung leitenden Frage, was es heißt, auf menschliche Weise lebendig zu sein*, Frank-furt a.M. (Zitiert mit „PB" unter Angabe der Seitenzahl.)

Pothast, Ulrich (1998): *Lebendige Vernünftigkeit. Zur Vorbereitung eines menschen-angemessenen Konzepts*, Frankfurt a.M. (Zitiert mit „LV" unter Angabe der Seitenzahl.)

II. Rezensionen

Thomas Kisser

Marco Giovanelli: *Reality and Negation – Kant's Principle of Anticipa-tions of Perception. An Investigation of its Impact on the Post-Kantian Debate.* Heidelberg u. a.: Springer, 2011, 252 S., ISBN 978-94-0070064-2 (= Studies in German Idealism; Bd. 11).

Der zweite Grundsatz der *Antizipationen der Wahrnehmung* (Im Weiteren: AdW) in der KrV, der das Konzept der Qualität auf die anschauliche Wirklich-keit bezieht und damit die Kategorien der Realität, der Negation und der Limi-tation entwickelt, spielt in der aktuellen Kant-Forschung keine prominente Rolle, wie man an Handbüchern und Kommentaren feststellen kann. Man sprach daher schon, wie Giovanelli erwähnt, von einem „vergessenen Prinzip" (S. xi). Im Idealismus kommt den Kategorien der Realität, der Negation und der Limitation oder Grenze jedoch eine enorme Bedeutung zu. Dies ist für Fichtes *Grundlage der gesammten Wissenschaftslehre* von 1794 ebenso offenkundig wie für Schellings Natur- und Identitätsphilosophie, wie auch für Hegels *Logik*. Alle idealistischen Philosophien geben den Kategorien der Qualität die erste Stelle in ihren systematischen Darstellungen. Im Neukantianismus wiederum, insbesondere bei Cohen, nehmen die AdW eine fundamentale Rolle für die Begründung der Wirklichkeit in Philosophie und Naturwissenschaft an. Welche sachlichen Kontinuitäten und Diskontinuitäten zeigen sich in dieser Tradition, die scheinbar so verdeckt beginnt? Dies ist die Frage Giovanellis. Nach einer Betrachtung des Theorems bei Kant bespricht Giovanelli dessen Rezeption bei Fichte, Schelling und Hegel, um dann dessen Wirkungsgeschichte in den nachidealistischen und neukantianischen Debatten des 19. und 20. Jahrhunderts zu verfolgen. Ein besonderer Schwerpunkt liegt auf Cohens Interpretation der intensiven Größe als erzeugender Größe, die sich auch als Interpretation Kants versteht und als solche bis in die zweite Hälfte des letzten Jahrhunderts wirkte. Giovanelli versucht damit zugleich die Historisierung als auch die Aktualisie-rung einer Fragestellung, die in den letzten Jahren aus dem Hauptstrom der Idealismusforschung eher verschwunden war.[1] Zupass kommt ihm dabei die Historisierung des Deutschen Idealismus, wie sie in den letzten Jahrzehnten u. a. im Umfeld der kritischen Editionen erarbeitet wurde und der wir insbeson-

---

[1]   Man vgl. etwa Horstmann, 2010. Aber auch in der Behandlung des Neukantianismus ist der Bezug auf die AdW nicht selbstverständlich, wie man bei Pollok, 2010, sieht. Etwas erstaunlich ist allerdings, dass ein Text sehr ähnlichen Zuschnitts, der aus-gehend von Kant über den Idealismus mit Schwerpunkt Fichte zu Cohen und Heidegger geht und dabei die Theorie der intensiven Größen zumindest teilweise ins Zentrum stellt, nämlich Vuillemin (1954), von Giovanelli nicht einmal im Literatur-verzeichnis erwähnt wird.

dere den Zugang zu den Naturphilosophien der Idealisten verdanken, denen auch Giovanelli seine Aufmerksamkeit widmet.

Die AdW (KrV, B 207 ff.) bilden den zweiten Grundsatz, der zeigt, dass Empfindungen notwendig einen Grad haben. Nach der Anschauung extensiver oder quantitativer Größen im Raum, die Kant im ersten Grundsatz behandelt, geht es hier um die intensiven Größen oder eben Grade, in denen wir Qualitäten in der Empfindung wahrnehmen, wie etwa warm oder kalt. Zwischen der ersten und der zweiten Auflage der KrV erfährt dieses Kapitel eine schon öfter (u. a. von Cohen und Heidegger) behandelte Neuformulierung. Dabei stellt sich nach Giovanelli die Frage „ob Empfindung einen Grad habe, wie die erste Auflage der KrV meint, oder die Realität, wie die zweite Auflage meint, oder beide. Im letzteren Falle müsste man fragen, ob Realität einen Grad habe, weil die Empfindung einen habe, oder ob umgekehrt, die Empfindung verschiedene Grade haben könne, weil das Reale, das dazu im Objekt korrespondiere, sich in Grade differenziere" (S. 18). Giovanellis Lösung des Problems liegt in der „untrennbaren Verbindung, die Kant zwischen Realität und Empfindung einsetzt: eine Verbindung, deren Ambiguität und Flüchtigkeit gerade in dieser Untrennbarkeit liege" (S. 19). Intensiv ist diese Größe, weil sie als Grad nicht aus Teilen zusammengesetzt ist wie die extensive, sondern als Einheit erfahren wird. Begrifflich bestimmte Realität hat dagegen keine Grade. Hier stehen sich die Gegensätze als Widerspruch entgegen: Etwas ist entweder A oder Nicht-A. Nur insofern Realität in der Empfindung erfahren wird, bilden deren Gegensätze, wie etwa warm und kalt, hell und dunkel, leicht und schwer, ein Kontinuum, das in Graden differenziert ist (S. 24 f.). „Die AdW setzen also den Übergang von Realität in metaphysischem Sinne zum Konzept phänomenaler Realität voraus" (S. 29). In diesem Konzept phänomenaler Realität zerbricht Kant die Einheit von Sein und Perfektion, die die ontologische Metaphysik bis in das leibnizsche System bewahrt hatte. Der Begriff eines realen Gegensatzes oder einer realen Negation war für die ontologische und rein begrifflich verfahrende Tradition in der Tat widersprüchlich, denn er ordnete einem Nichts einen Sachgehalt zu (S. 26 ff.), während die rein relationale Bestimmung Kants zwei Positivitäten in der Entgegensetzung vereint (S. 41 ff.). Diese Konzeption taucht das erste Mal in Kants *Versuch, den Begriff der negativen Größen in die Weltweisheit einzuführen* von 1763 auf. Darin unterscheidet er die logische Negation oder den Widerspruch von der Realrepugnanz. Während erstere eben bloß einen Widerspruch ergibt, vereint letztere zwei Kräfte in einem Subjekt und erzeugt ein Zero, d. h. einen bestimmten Zustand etwa der Ruhe oder Bewegung. Wendet man die Struktur der Intensität der AdW auf das Problem des Raumes und der Materie an, gelangt man zur Konzeption der sogenannten dynamischen Physik, die um 1800 für einige Jahre Naturwissenschaft und Naturphilosophie beherrschte. Materie wird darin nicht verstanden als unelastische Atome im Leeren, sondern als mehr oder weniger intensive Erfüllung des Raumes (S. 28 ff.). Die graduelle Unterschiedlichkeit ergibt sich aus der Verschränkung von Attraktions- und Repulsionskraft, die so die Materie bilden. An die Stelle „absoluter Raumerfülltheit und Leere als intrinsischer Eigenschaften von Atomen tritt die relative Erfülltheit oder Leere" (S. 35). Damit wird das eigentlich philosophische Problem der Physik, nämlich wie Veränderung als „Verbindung kontradiktorisch einander entgegengesetzter Bestimmungen im Dasein ein und desselben Dinges" (KrV, B 291) zu verstehen ist, lösbar. „Die Möglichkeit von Veränderung verlangt die Möglichkeit einer Form von Gegensatz, in der zwei Entgegengesetzte koexistieren können, ohne einen Widerspruch zu schaffen, und in dem Realität und Negation sich gegenseitig in einem Punkt der Indifferenz begrenzen" (S. 55). Daher müssen im Zero, wie bei einem Steinwurf im Umkehrpunkt von aufsteigender und fallender Bewegung, die Gegensätze ineinander übergehen. Das Zero wird also nicht als logischer Gegensatz zu Etwas, sondern als der geringste Grad an Realität einer Beschaffenheit bzw. Bewegung verstanden. Veränderung wird dadurch als quantitative Veränderung innerhalb derselben Qualität bestimmt und findet „nur der Größe nach" statt. Da der Grad beliebig gering werden kann, verbindet sich Kants Konzeption der Veränderung, sei es in der Subjektivität der Empfindung, sei es in der Objektivität der Materie, mit der Struktur infinitesimaler Größen und gibt damit der weiteren Entwicklung die Frage auf, wie genau dies zu verstehen ist. Denn für Kant bleibt die Einsicht in den Umschlag Privileg der Anschauung. Reine Begriffe stoßen beim Problem der Veränderung immer nur auf einen Widerspruch gegensätzlich bestimmter Zustände. Giovanelli entwickelt diese Konzeption klar und unter Einbeziehung des gesamten Werkes einschließlich des *opus postumum* und der Reflexionen Kants. Wie stellt sich nun in der nachkantischen Philosophie die Frage des Zero und des Gleichgewichts und des Themenkomplexes von Veränderung und Bewegung, in der die Problematik lauert, dass „Realität und Negation als positiv und negativ definiert sind, aber eben genau dadurch eine die andere annulliert" (S. 106). Wie lässt sich ein Konzept des Werdens fassen, das von einem rein logischen Standpunkt aus widersprüchlich bleibt und von einem realistischen Standpunkt aus Stabilität und Veränderung vereint?

Salomon Maimon und Lazarus Bendavid markieren die Wiederaufnahme der leibnizianischen Tradition an diesem historischen Punkt (S. 59–69), deren Pointe bei Giovanelli vielleicht etwas zu kurz kommt. Leibniz hatte ja die Problematik der Qualitäten aufgeworfen, nachdem Descartes die Materie allein durch die Extension definiert und auf diese reduktive Weise der Geometrie unterworfen hatte. Daher musste Leibniz das Problem der Qualitäten auch in der Mathematik formulieren und gelangte so zur Konzeption der *analysis situs* und des Infinitesimalkalküls, der im Kern ein Verhältnis von Größen, nämlich von Dreiecken hat, das sich als qualitatives Verhältnis, d. h. unabhängig von der Quantität der Dreiecke auch im Falle unendlicher Kleinheit, bewahrt und so das Tangentenproblem lösbar macht. Tatsächlich sind die Diskussionen der Idealisten und ihres Umfeldes wesentlich von der Aufnahme dieser Fragestellungen geprägt und die durchaus offene Erforschung dieser Konstellationen, die nicht nur die Naturphilosophien betrifft, kann von einem neukantianisch inspirierten Blick nur profitieren.

Wie bekannt, formuliert Fichte in der *Grundlage der gesammten Wissenschaftslehre* das Verhältnis von Ich und Nicht-Ich in den Termini der Realität, Negation und Limitation (S. 71–82). Fichte bringt so „durch die offenbar einfache Idee eines teilbaren Ich und Nicht-Ich den eigentlichen Kern der kritischen Philosophie zum Ausdruck" (S. 77). Dabei zeigt sich einerseits eine neue und theoretische Rolle der Qualität als „Urkategorie" (Zitat von Baumanns, S. 73), aus der die anderen Kategorien abgeleitet werden, andererseits schließt Fichtes Theorie der Empfindung an die AdW an. Giovanelli skizziert kurz die Konzeption der Einbildungskraft als Vermögen, die Gegensätze zu verbinden und bringt dabei das Zero als Nullgrad mit der sozusagen rein theoretischen Komponente bei Fichte in Verbindung (S. 77). Die Intensität markiert so den eigentlichen Charakter des Ich als Streben und Wollen. Schellings Lösung des Problems skizziert Giovanelli vor allem anhand von dessen Naturphilosophie. Ausführlicher stellt er die Konzeption der Dualität von Attraktions- und Repulsionskraft, wie sie nach Schelling die ganze Natur strukturiert, in der *Weltseele* von 1798 und im *Ersten Entwurf eines Systems der Natur* von 1799 dar (S. 82–109). Dabei weist er u. a. auf die quasiatomistische Lösung Schellings hin: Um das Ineinander der beiden Kräfte stabil zu machen, unterstellt Schelling der Natur „Hemmungspunkte", die nicht materiell sind, aber doch die sich unendlich ausdehnende Kraft binden, und so zu separaten Entitäten führen. In diesem Lichte erfährt auch Schellings Begriff des Absoluten als Indifferenz, wie er ab 1801 auftaucht, eine interessante Beleuchtung. Relativ große Aufmerksamkeit widmet Giovanelli Hegels Konzeption des Infinitesimalkalküls in den verschiedenen Fassungen der Logik, die auf die Theorie des Verhältnisses abstellen, denn der „Infintesimalkalkül bewahrt in der Entfernung der quantitativen Differenzen das wechselseitige Verhältnis der Größen" (S. 133). Dabei ergibt sich die Pointe, dass man „zum vollen Verständnis der philosophischen Bedeutung von Hegels Konzeption der Infinitesimalrechnung bedenken muss, dass die Bewahrung der Qualität im Verschwinden der Quantität als Antwort auf das [...] fundamentale Problem der Transzendentalphilosophie, das Problem des kontradiktorischen Gegensatzes in Werden und Wandel, verstanden werden muss" (S. 144). Hegel selbst bemerkt zu Beginn seiner *Logik*, dass die abstrakt logische Entgegensetzung von Sein und Nichts dieselbe ist, „die der Verstand gegen den Begriff braucht, den die höhere Analysis von den *unendlich-kleinen Größen* gibt. [...] Diese Größen sind als solche bestimmt worden, die *in ihrem Verschwinden sind*, nicht *vor* ihrem Verschwinden, denn alsdann sind sie endliche Größen; – nicht *nach* ihrem Verschwinden, denn alsdann sind sie nichts. Gegen diesen reinen Begriff ist eingewendet worden und *immer* wiederholt worden, daß solche Größen *entweder* Etwas seien *oder* Nichts, daß es keinen *Mittelzustand* [...] zwischen Sein und Nichtsein gebe" (Hegel, 1990,

S. 98). Hegel sieht bekanntlich seine der Theorie der Subjektivität überlegene Einsicht ganz allgemein darin, dass die Momente des Verhältnisses außerhalb des Verhältnisses nichts sind. Im Verhältnis, wie es auch in der höheren Analysis zu finden ist, zeigt sich die Identität von Identität und Differenz als wahrer Begriff des Unendlichen und mit dem, so Giovanelli, Hegel „über Schellings Konzept des Absoluten als rein quantitativer Indifferenz hinausgehen" kann (S. 148). Im Verschwinden der Größe wird die Negation, die das Quantum in Bezug auf die Qualität repräsentiert, wieder negiert und in dieser Negation der Negation verwandelt sich die schlechte Unendlichkeit der Quantität in die wahre und qualitative Unendlichkeit.

Giovanelli schließt sein Kapitel über die idealistische Philosophie mit einigen Sätzen über Herbart, der der Konzeption der reellen Negation widerspricht und in der Behauptung eines objektiven Seins des Negativen nur einen Widerspruch erkennen kann (S. 152 ff.). Negativität liegt für ihn nicht in den Dingen selbst, sondern nur in deren „zufälligen Ansichten" (S. 155). Oppositionen bestehen für Herbart nur in differenten Größen, nicht aber in Gegensätzen. Trendelenburg wirft Herbart wiederum vor, den Begriff der negativen Größen in den des Widerspruches bzw. der logischen Negation zurück zu verwandeln. Damit, so Trendelenburg, begeht er genau den umgekehrten Fehler wie Hegel und die Romantiker, die das Konzept der negativen Größen im puren Denken gesucht hatten, und damit die Kontradiktion in Kontrarietät verwandelt hatten. Trendelenburg stellt dem gegenüber die Anschauung der Bewegung als eigentlichen Übergang vom reinen Denken zur Erkenntnis der Wirklichkeit (S. 161 f.). Man sieht, die Problematik ersteht von Neuem auf. Damit geht Giovanelli zu seinem letzten Kapitel über, der Bedeutung der AdW im Neukantianismus. Dieser Übergang hat für Giovanelli auch eine hermeneutische Bedeutung: Denn stellte sich bisher das Problem der AdW im Lichte einer „metaphysischen Einheit", so kommt es jetzt unter die Ägide einer „logischen Einheit" im Sinne einer Theorie des wissenschaftlichen Erkennens (S. 164).

Cohens Logik der Erkenntnis wird von Giovanelli eingeführt in Absetzung der Diskussionen um die Psychophysik (S. 166–172), die ein reales Prinzip der Einheit von Bewusstsein und Materie in den Sinneseindrücken suchte. An dessen Stelle will Cohen eine neue Interpretation der AdW als methodisch zu sichernde Schnittstelle von Denken und Wirklichkeit setzen. Cohens Einsatz, die intensive Größe als Erzeugungsgröße zu verstehen, muss dabei als Antwort auf Versuche verstanden werden, die Kontinuität des Bewusstseins in der Kontinuität der Empfindung von Gegebenheiten zu sehen (S. 172 f.). So taucht das vermutlich grundlegendste neukantianische Denkmotiv auf: die kritische Analyse des Gegebenen auf seine Erzeugung hin. Diese Erzeugung kann aber keinesfalls in der Empfindung gefunden werden (S. 173 f.). Wie bekannt, richtet sich das Cohensche Denken auf den Ursprung, der sich in einem allgemeinen Begriff der Bewegung erklärt (S. 175). Giovanelli betont die Bedeutung der historischen Arbeit für Cohen, als Suche nach dem „Problem, das dieser Kalkül lösen sollte" (S. 185). Die Kernfrage der AdW ist in Cohens Interpretation der Übergang von der Geometrie zur Physik, der Wirklichkeit des Gegenstandes im eigentlichen Sinne. „Zu sagen, das Infinitesimale sei eine intensive Grösse", bedeute, das Infinitesimale als generierende Größe zu betrachten, „eine Entität, deren Grösse Null ist, aber in höherem oder geringerem Grade die Fähigkeit besitze, Grössen zu generieren". Der anschauliche Charakter dieser Erzeugungsgröße als „l'impeto, il talento, l'energia, il momento del discendere" (S. 189) beginnt zu verschwinden, wenn man sie auf die beschleunigte Bewegung anwendet und mit Leibniz im Kalkül findet. Dabei darf man Leibniz nicht so sehr als Mathematiker verstehen, sondern als Metaphysiker, der mittels der Zahl eine Konzeption der Wirklichkeit sucht, die sich nicht aus und in der Extension ergibt, sondern dieser als Inextensives vorausgeht (S. 190 ff.). Lasswitz wie auch Cassirer und Natorp werden diesen cohenschen Gedanken der Einheit von „Infinitesimalem, intensivem und der Kategorie der Realität" (S. 198) im Sinne einer Formulierung des Kraftbegriffs und einer Lehre von der Energie interpretieren (S. 194 ff.). In seiner Interpretation Kants kann sich Cohen auf dessen Definition des Momentes stützen, womit Kant den Grad der Realität bezeichnet, insofern dieser Ursache ist (S. 200 f.). Mit Kant gesprochen: „Die Große der Bewegung kommt auf Zeit und Raum an. Die Große der Geschwindigkeit (in einem Augenblick) ist die Größe des moments der Bewegung, wodurch nemlich ein Raum in einer Zeit kan zurückgelegt werden" (AA 18, S. 536; Refl. 4411). Die Reduktion auf den nichtextensiven Augenblick macht das Moment der Bewegung als erzeugende Größe und die extensive Bewegung in Raum und Zeit als erzeugte Größe sichtbar. Für Kant selbst war – wie schon bemerkt – Veränderung dabei noch eine schlechthin empirische Tatsache und als solche nur der Anschauung zugänglich. In der kantischen Inanspruchnahme der Empfindung sieht Cohen folgerichtig eher eine Verdunklung des Sachverhaltes der intensiven Größe im Sinne des Ursprungs, „von welchem alle extensive Grösse anhebt, in welchem sie ihr Fundament hat" (Cohen, 1914, S. 545; vgl. S. 200). Für Cohen ist der Konflikt zwischen apriorischem Begriff und empirischer Anschauung durch eine moderne Mathematik überwunden, die „das Konzept der Bewegung in sich aufgenommen und aus einem empirischen Begriff in eine wahre und eigentliche ideale Form verwandelt hat" (S. 203). Cohens Auffassung des Infinitesimalen als Erzeugungsgröße verwandelt sich bei Cassirer schließlich in den Begriff der Funktion, im Namen dessen Cassirer auch ein falsches Verständnis des Unendlich-Kleinen als Substanz zurückweist, ein Missverständnis, dem wohl auch Russell erlag (S. 207). Die Funktion als Beziehung von Größen wird nun von Cassirer als das Qualitative verstanden (S. 208 ff.). Damit zielt Cassirer jedoch auf eine umfassendere Charakterisierung des Idealismus der Mathematik als eine allgemeine „Analysis der Relationen", innerhalb derer der Infinitesimalkalkül nur noch als markantestes Beispiel verstanden wird (S. 210), ein Verständnis, das Cassirer schon in seinem Leibniz-Buch entwickelt und das seine Auffassung von Leibniz bestimmt

(S. 211). Ganz ähnlich wird Natorp den cohenschen Gedanken in Richtung einer reinen Relation entwickeln, die als generierende Größe den Relata vorhergeht. In seinen Schlusskapiteln sieht Giovanelli die AdW als Öffnung hin auf eine „ontologische" Interpretation Kants (Heimsoeth, Martin), in der dieser zumindest in eine engere Verbindung mit der vorkantischen Tradition gestellt wird.

Man sieht hoffentlich in dieser Paraphrase die Fruchtbarkeit der neukantianischen Perspektive für die Arbeit an den Texten des Idealismus. Leider öffnet Giovanelli diese Perspektive jedoch nicht wirklich auf neue Fragestellungen. So stellt sich doch erneut die Frage, warum Kant, anders als all seine Rezipienten, die Extension als kategorial primäre Form der Erfahrungswirklichkeit nimmt und der Intensität vorordnet. Eine genetische Fragestellung und Darstellung, die der Entwicklung der Negation von den vorkritischen Schriften in die KrV und in die Theorie der Physik hinein im Sinne einer neukantianisch inspirierten Geschichtsschreibung nachgegangen wäre, findet sich bei Giovanelli eigentlich nicht. Ganz unerwähnt bleibt Kants Konzept der „ungeselligen Geselligkeit", das offensichtlich für die soziale Welt das bedeutet, was die reelle Entgegensetzung von Attraktion und Repulsion für die natürliche. Enttäuschend bleibt vor allem der Fichteteil, wie Giovanelli selbst konzediert (S. 82). Offensichtlich liegt doch hier ein wahrhaft entscheidender Schritt der nachkantischen Philosophie, in der die Qualitätskategorien eine ganz neue Bedeutung und Funktion annehmen. Tatsächlich verdoppelt sich bei Fichte ja der Gedanke der Qualität und wird einerseits – und das ist so neu wie offensichtlich – zum Prinzip der Theoriebildung selbst, indem die Abfolge der Grundsätze damit konstruiert wird. Zum anderen behält der Gedanke der Qualität seine Funktion, die Theorie der Empfindung zu gestalten. Doch wie kommt Fichte dazu, die theoretische Funktion der Qualitätskategorien zu entwickeln? Mit einer Darstellung der *Grundlage* stellt sich dieses Problem erst und ist nicht gelöst. Diese Frage ist umso wichtiger, als auch Schelling und Hegel in der Folge den Primat der Qualität setzen. In diesen Zusammenhang gehört etwa die Diskussion zwischen Fichte und Schelling, die schließlich sogar zum Streit und zum Abbruch der Beziehung führt.[2] Die primäre Qualität, die die Quantitabilität ermöglicht, ist für Fichte, wie er im Briefwechsel mit Schelling und seit seiner *Darstellung der Wissenschaftslehre* von 1801 explizit formuliert, das Wissen selbst. Fichte wirft daher Schelling vor, die Qualitätskategorie im Rahmen der Naturphilosophie zu ontologisieren, und wie Schelling selbst ironisch formuliert „das Absolute zu quantifizieren". Diese Diskussion wird einer der entscheidenden Treibsätze der späten Wissenschaftslehren Fichtes, in der die Qualitätskategorie den Charakter der Gewissheit annimmt. Was auch immer sich für Fichte unter einem neukantianisch inspirierten Blick – und das heißt für die Funktion und Struktur der

---

[2]   Vgl. dazu Schelling, 2010, Bd. 1, S. 77 ff.

Qualitätskategorie – ergibt, mit einem einfachen Metaphysikvorwurf dürfte es nicht getan sein. Vielmehr sieht man, dass das Problem von Metaphysik oder Logik der Erkenntnis sich innerhalb der Geschichte des Idealismus stellt. Giovanelli belässt es in seiner Darstellung der fichteschen, aber auch der schellingschen Philosophie und all der anderen zahlreichen Positionen, die er behandelt, leider mit der Paraphrase einiger wichtiger Texte, vermag damit aber keine Konstellationen zu sehen und die Komplexität und Differenziertheit der Diskussionen zu erfassen. Zum Umfeld dieser Kontroverse zwischen Fichte und Schelling gehört etwa auch der Briefwechsel mit Eschenmayer, dessen Texte zwar von Giovanelli ebenfalls dargestellt werden, doch auch hier fehlt die Konstellation. In einem Brief vom 21.7.1801 wirft Eschenmayer Schelling vor, die Kategorie der Negation gar nicht ausreichend begründet zu haben, um eine innere Dualität der Kräfte annehmen zu können. Schelling, so Eschenmayer, fehle ein selbstständiger Begriff der Negation, wie ihn Fichte im zweiten Grundsatz der *Grundlage der Wissenschaftslehre* einführe (Schelling, 2010, S. 357ff.). Man sieht, wie einschlägig für Giovanellis Thema diese Kontroversen sind. Ein anderes Beispiel: Giovanelli stellt Schellings quasiatomistische Konzeption der Hemmungspunkte in der Natur von 1799 vor. Tatsächlich hatte Fichte in der Vorlesung der *Wissenschaftslehre nova methodo* 1798 den Begriff des Atoms für das Schema der Empfindung verwendet.

Mit Hegel scheint man nach Giovanelli gewissermaßen bei einer Lösung des Problems der Veränderung angekommen. Auch Hegels Konzept des Infinitesimalkalküls stellt Giovanelli ohne Rekurse auf konkrete Kontexte und Konstellationen dar, spricht allerdings von einer Metaphysizierung bei Hegel (S. 148), eine Kritik die bereits Cohen ausgesprochen hatte, der die Äußerungen Hegels zum Infinitesimalkalkül gar nicht erst diskutieren wollte (Cohen, 1968, § 84). Giovanelli zielt aber – ebenso wie Cohen – mit dem Begriff der Metaphysizierung nicht nur auf Hegel, sondern den ganzen Ablauf der idealistischen Philosophie, der so mit Hegel offensichtlich zu einem immanenten, wenn auch eben metaphysischen Ende gelangt. Giovanelli reproduziert also geradezu das völlig überholte Schema des Idealismus als Fortschritt von Fichte über Schelling zu Hegel. Leider bleibt so die Komplexität der Entwicklung des Idealismus – auch gegenüber dem Forschungsstand – bei Giovanelli deutlich unterbestimmt.

Man kann zwar nicht kritisieren, aber doch bedauern, dass Giovanelli die wohl bedeutendste zeitgenössische Position zum Problem der Intensität und der Qualität gar nicht mehr berührt. Die Wende zum Sein in und aus einer neukantianischen Tradition, wie sie nach Giovanelli bei Natorp schon anklingt, hat ihren prominentesten aktuellen Vertreter wohl in Gilles Deleuze. In *Differenz und Wiederholung* von 1968 geht Deleuze darauf aus, die Wesenlosigkeit der Negation zu zeigen und das Sein als Positivität und Mannigfaltigkeit, eben als ursprüngliche positive Differenz zu denken, die im – kantischen und idealistischen – Modus der Repräsentation verdeckt und „im Namen der Identität, der Analogie, des Gegensatzes und der Ähnlichkeit" (Deleuze, 1992, S. 180) ihrer

Kreativität beraubt wird. Deleuze nimmt mit seinem Projekt einer Umdrehung der Metaphysik hin zu der vergessenen und verdeckten reinen Intensität und Mannigfaltigkeit des Seins gewissermaßen den direkten Übergang vom Neukantianismus, der in Frankreich langlebiger als in Deutschland war, zur „Postmoderne". Dieses Konzept der Intensität als Differenz, die sich unter dem Titel der Wiederholung ursprünglich mit der Zeit verbindet, gehört so durchaus zum „Impact" der nachkantischen Philosophie. Man könnte sagen, Deleuze versucht, die kantianische Tradition auf die Intensität auf- und damit auch von ihr abprallen zu lassen. Abgesehen von der systematischen Kraft lassen sich hier auch wichtige Elemente einer Geschichte der Intensität und des Infinitesimalen finden, wie etwa die scotistische Univozität des Seins, die in der Kantforschung allenfalls von Anneliese Meier erwähnt wird (S. 22, Fn. 65), und mit der im Spätmittelalter eine neue Grundlage für das Konzept der Gradualität geschaffen wurde.[3] Interessant auch, dass bei Deleuze von allen Idealisten Schelling mit seinem Blick in die Tiefe des Ungrundes in der *Freiheitsschrift* von 1809 die positivste Erwähnung findet (Deleuze, 1992, S. 243). Hier soll nicht die These vertreten werden, dass Deleuzes Projekt „funktioniert", doch erkennt man den systematischen und historischen Reichtum von *Differenz und Wiederholung*, kann man durchaus von einem Anti-Cohen, dem originellen Versuch einer Logik des Seins als Kritik einer Logik der Repräsentation, sprechen, die den Zusammenhang dieser Diskussion neu konturiert und bereichert. Sichtbar wird dabei unter anderem, wie sehr sich auch die naturalistische Linie der neuzeitlichen Philosophie, wie etwa Spinoza oder Nietzsche sich an der Konzeption der Qualität und Intensität abarbeiten.

So bleibt eine Zwiespältigkeit gegenüber Giovanellis Arbeit. Einerseits hat Giovanelli im Ganzen einen souveränen Blick auf eine Geschichte geworfen, die nicht den Mainstream der heutigen Idealismusforschung ausmacht und diese inspirieren könnte. Obwohl dieser Blick sich als eine Übernahme der cohenschen Perspektive, die nicht wirklich geöffnet wird, erweist, bleibt Giovanellis Projekt und seine Textauswahl beeindruckend. Im Einzelnen vermag er jedoch seinen Plan kaum zu einer differenzierten Analyse und einem Erkenntnisgewinn auszugestalten. Die Interpretation des Deutschen Idealismus bleibt dabei als ganze problematisch. Giovanelli selbst konzediert häufig, dass er den Forschungsstand eher simplifizierend wiedergebe. Sein Ziel sei es gewesen, „to emphasize the themes and problems that recur in the detailed Marburg discussion concerning the Anticipations of Perception and that, in a radically different context, have played a central role in the entire history of german idealism"

---

[3] Vgl. dazu Deleuze, 1992, S. 59 ff. Einen Eindruck der Reichhaltigkeit des Buches gibt die kommentierte Bibliographie in der deutschen Ausgabe S. 380–393. Vgl. zur Wirkungsgeschichte des Scotismus auch auf Kant aus der neueren deutschen Forschung die bedeutende Arbeit von Honnefelder, 1990.

(S. 216). Man muss dem zustimmen, und kann hinzufügen, dass so, jedenfalls in Bezug auf die Marburger Schule, eine schöne Hinführung in die Problematik und die Texte entstanden ist. Der Forschungsstand wird dabei allerdings meistens eher vereinfacht wiedergegeben als erneuert.

Literatur

Cohen, Hermann (1914): *Logik der reinen Erkenntnis*, 2. verbesserte Aufl., Berlin.

Cohen, Hermann (1968): *Das Prinzip der Infinitesimalmethode und seine Geschichte. Ein Kapitel zur Grundlegung der Erkenntniskritik*, Frankfurt a. M. [Berlin [1]1883].

Deleuze, Gilles (1992): *Differenz und Wiederholung*, München [Paris [1]1968].

Hegel, G.W.F. (1990): *Wissenschaft der Logik. Lehre vom Sein. (1832)*, hg. von H.-J. Gawoll, Hamburg.

Honnefelder, Ludger (1990): *Scientia transcendens. Die formale Bestimmung der Seiendheit und Realität in der Metaphysik des Mittelalters und der Neuzeit. (Duns Scotus – Suárez – Wolff – Kant – Peirce)*, Hamburg.

Horstmann, Rolf-Peter (2010): „The Reception of the *Critique of Pure Reason* in German Idealism", in: Guyer, Paul (Hrsg.): *The Cambridge Companion to Kant's Critique of Pure Reason*, Cambridge, S. 329–345.

Kant, Immanuel: „*Versuch, den Begriff der negativen Größen in die Weltweisheit einzuführen*", in: *Gesammelte Schriften Bd. 2*, hrsg. von der Preussischen Akademie der Wissenschaften, Berlin, (Nachdruck der Ausgabe 1903). (Zitiert als *Gesammelte Schriften*), S. 165–202.

Kant, Immanuel (1973): *Kritik der reinen Vernunft*, in: *Gesammelte Schriften Bd. 4*, (Zitiert als „KrV" und nach den verschiedenen Auflagen als A und B.)

Pollok, Konstantin (2010): „The ‚Transcendental Method'. On the Reception oft he *Critique of Pure Reason* in Neo-Kantianism", in: Guyer, Paul (Hrsg.): *The Cambridge Companion to Kant's Critique of Pure Reason*, Cambridge, S. 346–379.

Schelling, F.W.J. (2010): *Briefe 1800–1802*, Historisch-Kritische Ausgabe hg. im Auftrag der Bayerischen Akademie der Wissenschaften, Reihe III: Briefe. Bd. 3 in 2 Teilbänden, hrsg. von Thomas Kisser, Stuttgart-Bad Cannstatt.

Vuillemin, Jules (1954): *L' Héritage Kantien et la Révolution Copernicienne*, Paris.

Michael Morris

Karl Leonhard Reinhold: *Ueber das Fundament des philosophischen Wissens nebst einigen Erläuterungen über die Theorie des Vorstellungsvermögens*, in: Bondeli, Martin (Hrsg.): *Gesammelte Schriften, Kommentierte Ausgabe*, Basel: Schwabe Verlag, 2011, Bd. 4, CV+252 S., ISBN 978-3-7965-2601-5.

Martin Bondeli's new edition of this short but seminal work surpasses the previous Meiner Verlag edition of 1978 in two respects. First, it includes A. W. Rehberg and J. C. Schwab's negative reviews of Reinhold's previous work, the first volume of the *Beiträge*. According to Reinhold these reviews, particularly that of Rehberg, provided the primary impetus for the reflections, revisions, and innovations developed in the *Fundament*. Additionally, this edition also includes J. B. Erhard's and F. K. Forberg's defense of Reinhold's philosophy against the objections raised in these highly critical reviews. When it was first published in 1791, the *Fundament* included these contributions from Erhard and Forberg, and thus the new edition restores the text to its original form.

Secondly, in contrast to the previous edition of 1978, this one comes with meticulous annotation and an extensive introduction. Bondeli's superb scholarship highlights the specific innovations of the *Fundament*, locating them within the significant but often subtle trajectory of Reinhold's philosophical development. Drawing upon his extensive knowledge of the period, Bondeli further situates these innovations within the context of the complex debates that surrounded them, considering the contribution of many largely forgotten thinkers such as J. A. Eberhard, G. G. Fülleborn, G. E. Schulze, J. F. Flatt, K. H. Heydenreich, L. H. Jakob, J. Baggesen, C. C. E. Schmid, J. G. Buhle, S. Maimon, and many others. The significance of these surrounding debates becomes evident once we consider Reinhold's conception of philosophy as a collective enterprise. Reinhold frequently encouraged his students to develop, articulate, and defend his project, to treat it as a common enterprise, and he closely followed the responses and criticisms of his philosophical opponents. Accordingly, when tracing the subtle transformations that distinguish the programmatic position of the *Fundament* from those developed in the works that preceded and followed it, we must often attend to these broad and frequently neglected debates. In this matter, Bondeli's significant editorial contributions prove both superlative and indispensable.

The inclusion of Rehberg's review provides the reader with an excellent entrée into the central themes of the *Fundament*. This review poses the central challenges that Reinhold seeks to address in the text, and it develops a sharp and polemical distinction between the methodological approaches and philosophical intentions of Kant's critical philosophy, on the one hand, and Reinhold's professed attempts to build upon and complete that philosophy on the other. In the "Introduction", Bondeli emphasizes the significant and even visceral impact that this review had upon Reinhold. According to Forberg's memoirs, the review apparently left Reinhold dejected and despondent. On the evening he first received it, Reinhold spoke with "an usually subdued voice and tears filled his eyes" (p. XII). Sometime later, however, in a letter to Jens Baggsen, Reinhold cast this review in a somewhat more positive light, portraying it as the inspiration for the intellectual efforts that produced the *Fundament* (ibid.).

Rehberg's review of the *Beiträge* also provides us with a helpful reminder of the political intentions that guided Reinhold's philosophical project. It thereby suggests a partial answer to the central question we face when considering Reinhold's philosophy: Namely, why did Reinhold so adamantly insist that philosophy must be deduced from a single, self-evident, and universally acknowledged first principle? Towards the beginning of his review, Rehberg notes:

> In the introduction to the second and fifth essay, he [Reinhold] provides a spirited account of the value of a universally recognized principle of human knowledge. According to this account, the clear knowledge of human rights, and thus also [good] legislation and the welfare of states, depends upon it. This claim is all too evidently and completely related to the spirit of a fundamental but one-sided philosophy of politics, which appears to be attaining great influence [i.e. in France], and whose content and implications are far too important for this reviewer to ignore (p. 130).

While the contemporary reader of the *Beiträge* may be forgiven for failing to recognize the work's somewhat indirect allusions to the politics of the French Revolution, the initial readers of this text could hardly overlook these and their bold philosophical implications. Reinhold clearly perceived his completion of Kant's philosophical revolution as nothing less than the *sine qua non* for any successful resolution to the legislative debates and violent conflicts that attended the revolution in France, a position he elaborated on numerous occasions. As he insists in his essay, "Ueber die Teutschen Beurtheilung der französischen Revolution", the successful conclusion of the French Revolution depended upon both *the indisputable disambiguation of the concepts* and *the irrefutable deduction of the principles* contained in the "Declaration of the Rights of Man". This, in turn, depended upon the discovery of some self-evident, universally acknowledged, and wholly univocal first principle of philosophy, one that might serve as the basis for natural right, morality, and all other branches of theoretical and practical knowledge.

Against this background, we can begin to see how the sometimes virulent debates about the esoteric aspects of Reinhold's theoretical philosophy tended to function as semi-covert disagreements about the potential role of philosophy, reason, theory and universal rights with the domain of politics. Indeed, two years after writing his critical review of Reinhold's *Beiträge*, Rehberg published a two-volume critique of the French Revolution, his *Untersuchungen über die französische Revolution*, a work that develops certain themes already suggested in his earlier critique of Reinhold's philosophy. Similarly, after defending Reinhold against Rehberg's criticisms, J. B. Erhard went on to write a pro-revolutionary work, his 1795 *Ueber das Recht des Volks zu einer Revolution*. We find further evidence for the omnipresence of debates about revolutionary politics in a remark that Forberg made to Reinhold. In light of the numerous negative reviews of the first volume of the *Beiträge*, Forberg suggested that perhaps Reinhold should write a book on the French Revolution, since the interests of the day seemed to turn increasingly away from more abstract theoretical questions and towards the more spectacular events unfolding in France (LV, p. 31). Despite Forberg's advice, Reinhold pursued his own strategy in dealing with the intellectual trends and political events of his day: he sought to convince his contemporaries that the solution for political problems lay somewhere in the apparently abstruse realm of Kantian philosophy.

After the passage quoted above, Rehberg provides a brief discussion of the shortcomings of excessively theoretical approaches to politics, and he then turns to develop more specific objections to Reinhold's theoretical philosophy, particularly to Reinhold's proposed deduction of Kantian philosophy from a single, self-evident principle: the so-called "principle of consciousness" or "*Satz des Bewusstseins*". As Reinhold construed it, Kant's philosophy provides an account of the three fundamental capacities involved in the generation of knowledge. Specifically, Kant's philosophy considers *sensibility*, *understanding*, and *reason* as the three cognitive capacities that respectively generate *intuitions*, *concepts*, and *ideas*. While Reinhold acknowledges the basic adequacy of Kant's account, he nonetheless insists that Kant fails to fix the meaning of his concepts in a manner that precludes all ambiguities and potential misunderstandings, that his essentially transcendental or regressive argumentative strategy can only convince those who have already accepted his conception of experience, and that a complete account of the various domains of philosophical knowledge, including natural right, necessitates further inquiries into the root structures of representation and volition, inquiries still more profound and penetrating than those provided by Kant.

To remedy these defects, Reinhold suggests that we consider the general nature of representation as articulated in the principle of consciousness. When Kant elaborates the nature of intuitions, concepts, and ideas, he treats these fundamental kinds of representation in their specificity, but he never articulates the more general features that constitute representation as such. It is only with Reinhold's discovery of the principle of consciousness, itself grounded in the universal "fact of consciousness", that the most general structures of representation emerge with clarity and self-evidence. The principle of consciousness states: "In consciousness, the representation is *distinguished from* and *related to* the subject and the object by the subject" (p. 50). Reinhold holds that the truth and meaning of this principle are self-evident, and that it provides the basis for definitively establishing the truth and meaning of Kant's various statements concerning the nature and limits of each particular kind of representation.

In considering the aspirations of this bold philosophical project, Rehberg develops three particularly salient lines of criticism. First, he insists that Reinhold's principle of consciousness presents a mere definition, and he thus accuses Reinhold of transforming philosophy into an essentially analytical enterprise, one that audaciously sets out from the definition of a single concept. He further argues that this procedure transforms philosophy into an arbitrary enterprise. He holds that, with regard to concepts, synthesis always precedes analysis. In other words, when we analyze a concept, we can only discover those predicates that we ourselves have placed in it. Therefore, unless we can assume the *necessity* of some prior synthesis, our analysis of a concept reveals nothing but certain contingent or arbitrary characteristics included within that concept, those characteristics attached to the concept through the predilections of a particular philosopher or the conventions of standard usage (pp. 131–2).

While the structure and flow of the *Fundament* derive from Reinhold's consideration of the history of modern philosophy – the work begins with the initial opposition between Locke's empiricism and Leibniz's rationalism, moves to the skeptical challenges raised by Hume and Crusius, and finally turns to the preliminary solution proffered by Kant and the more permanent one suggested by Reinhold – we can nonetheless see how the issues raised by Rehberg's first criticism emerge again and again as a *leitmotif* and central preoccupation of the text. For instance, Reinhold's discussion of Crusius treats the limitations of conceptual analysis and the principle of contradiction at great length. Following Crusius, Reinhold suggests that analysis, which proceeds via the principle of contradiction, produces truths that are only *conditionally* necessary. If certain predicates are *already* included in the concept, then the principle of contradiction allows us to demonstrate the truth and necessity of the judgment that expresses the relation of the predicate to the subject. In such cases, the real issue does not turn on the process of analysis itself. Instead, it involves the justification for a particular, pre-analytic construal of a given concept (p. 30).

In these terms, Reinhold considers the debate about the judgment "everything that arises has a cause". At the level of conceptual analysis, this debate remains irresolvable, since the various parties in the debate have different conceptions of the central concept – i.e., "arising" or "*Entstehen*". One party comes to the debate assuming that everything that arises is an effect, and it therefore concludes that everything that arises has a cause. In other words, this party begins by thinking the concept of "arising" as one that includes that of "effect", and their analysis, proceeding via the principle of contradiction, simply articulates and confirms what they already thought. By contrast, the other party in the debate has a different conception of "arising" and therefore comes to a different conclusion. Thus the real issue does not rest upon analysis; rather, it concerns the existence of some ground or reason [*Grund*] for the pre-analytical inclusion of the predicate "effect" in the concept "arising" (pp. 31–2). Reinhold illustrates this same point by considering the judgment, "a circle is round". The unconditional necessity of this judgment rests upon some relation between the concept "circle" and the intuition with which this concept is indivisibly [*unzertrennlich*] bound, and it is this intuition – or, more accurately, the construction of this concept in intuition – that provides the reason or ground for the inclusion of the predicate "round" in the concept "circle" (pp. 32–3).

Shortly after he lays out these issues in his discussion of Crusius, Reinhold then turns to address Rehberg's criticism that (a) the principle of consciousness is a definition, and that, therefore, (b) Reinhold transforms philosophy into a wholly analytical and thus arbitrary enterprise. In response, Reinhold makes two points. First, he emphatically states that the principle of consciousness does not present the definition of representation, but rather it presents the principle from which the definition of representation can first be determined in a necessary and non-arbitrary way. In other words, the principle of consciousness supplies the reason or ground for the non-arbitrary determination of the concept of representation. In turn, the principle of consciousness "expresses" [*ausdrücken*] a fact, the so-called "fact of consciousness" which itself provides the ground or reason for the particular features of the principle of consciousness (p. 51).

This response raises an obvious question. Namely: How can a "fact" ground a necessary synthesis? On the standard construal, facts are given by empirical experience, and experience cannot ground necessary judgments. In other words, *a posteriori* judgments are not necessary, and thus Reinhold's attempt to ground the first principle of philosophy in a fact appears both peculiar and highly problematic. Although Reinhold does not directly address this issue, he at least suggests an answer at one point, when he states that the fact of consciousness "cannot be further analyzed [*zergliedert*] or reduced into simpler features" (p. 52). This fact is "determined through itself insofar as the concepts, which it exhibits, can only be explained through it" (ibid.). The fact of consciousness thus has a unique character. On the one hand, it has a complex structure, the structure expressed in the principle of consciousness. Accordingly, the fact itself is not strictly or merely simple. At the same time, however, these features or structures do not have a wholly independent existence or intrinsic nature that can be conceived in isolation from one another. We cannot understand or conceive the various structural features of the fact of consciousness – i.e., both the representation's *distinction from* and *relation to* the subject and the object – in isolation from the unified totality of these structures in the fact of consciousness itself. If a "fact" can indeed have this kind of holistic structure, then the relations united within it are *necessarily* united. In other words, they cannot exist in isolation from one another, and they cannot exist in some alternative combination.

Rehberg's second line of criticism seems to pose a more serious challenge, one to which Reinhold does not have an apt response. Reinhold's project seeks to provide an account of the general features of representation as a means for establishing and articulating the specific features of intuitions, concepts, and ideas, which are the three specific kinds of representation. In other words, intuitions, concepts, and ideas are three *species* in the *genus* of representation. Reinhold frequently employs the language of genus and species in describing the relationship between his account of representation and Kant's discussion of intuitions, concepts, and ideas. If this language accurately reflects Reinhold's proposal to deduce and clarify Kant's philosophy on the basis of a general account of representation, then the enterprise seems hopelessly confused, since the general features of a genus do not allow us to determine the specific features of the various kinds that fall under it (p. 132). For instance, from the general concept of humanity we cannot deduce the particular features that distinguish humanity into two sexes. Similarly, starting out from the general concept of an animal, we cannot determine the specific features that distinguish vertebrates from invertebrates, or mammals from coldblooded animals.

Of course, Fichte, Schelling, and Hegel would later develop dialectical forms of argument and special conceptions of logic that were specifically intended to facilitate deductive procedures that proceeded from the generic to the specific, from the universal to the particular. These later and more radical developments notwithstanding, Rehberg correctly insists upon the prima facie implausibility of this argumentative strategy. In response to Rehberg's challenge, Reinhold appears to acquiesce, falling back upon a position that severely mitigates the more radical aspirations of his philosophical foundationalism. Specifically, he introduces a host of additional "facts of consciousness", one for each of the particular forms of representation. While Reinhold's initial "fact of consciousness" was to ground the principle of consciousness and provide a basis for elaborating the general features of representation, he now maintains that a full account of the *specific* features of intuitions, concepts, and ideas requires us to consult new and more specific facts of consciousness (p. 63). Unfortunately, Reinhold's occasional remarks in the *Fundament* provide little that would fill out this *ad hoc* response to Rehberg's challenge.

Rehberg's third line of criticism points out the significant differences between Reinhold's and Kant's philosophical approaches, and it highlights the problems that Reinhold's emphasis upon the most general features of representation causes, at least when viewed in light of his commitment to both the thing-in-itself and the Kantian postulates. These doctrines assume that concepts and ideas are not *intrinsically* restricted to the phenomenal realm of spatiotemporal experience (pp. 137–8). If these idealistic limitations attached to our basics concepts as such, merely in virtue of their status as concepts, then we could neither coherently nor meaningfully entertain the hypothetical application of these concepts to objects that exist beyond the restricted forms of human experience. Thus, for instance, if some intrinsic feature of our concepts of substance and causality precluded their application to objects beyond human experience, then Kant's rational faith in God, as a substance that transcends space and time, becomes a patent absurdity, and the same conclusion must be drawn concerning his discussions of the thing-in-itself, which exists beyond experience but nonetheless plays some causal role in the generation of it.

Of course, our cognitive application of these basic concepts *is* limited to the objects given in space and time, to objects which are therefore phenomenal, but this limitation derives from the distinctive ways that objects must be given *to us*. The limitations that beset our cognitive use of these concepts derive from the relationship of these concepts to the distinctive forms of human sensibility, not from any general features of these concepts as such. In a sense, Kant's entire strategy depends upon the looseness of fit in the relation between sensibility, understanding, and reason. This means that the categories of the understanding and the ideas of reason are not essentially linked to the forms of intuition that characterize human sensibility. It also means that the idealistic conclusions of Kant's philosophy only emerge from the contingent relationship between these three faculties. By contrast, Reinhold seeks to establish the ideality of human cognition at the level of representation as such, and thus his argument necessarily implies the ideality of *all* forms of human representation, including our concepts and ideas (pp. 137–8).

While Reinhold does not address this third line of criticism, Erhard provides a partial response, insisting that Reinhold's strategy in no way precludes the existence of some non-human intellect, whose radically different forms of representation do not place idealistic limitations on its cognition. Erhard further suggests that, just like Kant, Reinhold too restricts the focus of his discussion to the particular features of human cognition (p. 92). However, even though Reinhold's philosophy may allow for the possibility of some non-human and non-restricted form of cognition, this form of cognition, and its related modes of representation, will be *wholly* different from ours, and we can have no conception of what its concepts or ideas might be like. By contrast, Kant can cogently entertain the existence of a form of cognition that shares our concepts but applies them under different conditions. This is fully coherent and possible, since the categories of our understanding do not, as such, come with any idealistic restrictions.

Rehberg's criticisms and Reinhold's responses exhibit the peculiar status of the *Fundament*, a text that presents a moment of extreme tension in the developmental trajectory of German Idealism. While still revealing the Kantian origins of this movement, the text already suggests the more exotic and radical developments to come. Thus the apparently empirical and peculiarly holistic nature of Reinhold's fact [*Tatsache*] of consciousness leads directly to Fichte's attempt to ground philosophy in some fundamental act [*Tathandlung*] that is constitutive for all experience as such. Similarly, Rehberg's second criticism highlights the difficulties involved in deriving the distinctive features of the species from the common characteristics of the genus. This attempt to deduce the particular from the universal finds its ultimate expression in Hegel's dialectical and intrinsically dynamic account of the concept (*Begriff*), in his repeated criticisms of abstract universals, and in his attempt, in the *Science of Logic*, to "deduce" philosophy from the most general concept of all, the concept of being. Finally, Reinhold's emphasis on representation and systematic necessity raises significant difficulties for the Kantian postulates and the doctrine of the thing-in-itself, difficulties reflected in Fichte and Hegel's rejection of the transcendence involved in Kant's particular version of idealism.

References

Forberg, Friedrich Karl (1840): *Lebenslauf eines Verschollenen*, Hildburghausen und Meiningen [= LV].

Reinhold, Karl Leonhard (1793): "Ueber die Teutschen Beurtheilung der französischen Revolution", in: *Der neue Teutsche Merkur*, Bd. I, S. 387–424.

Reinhold, Karl Leonhard (1978): *Über das Fundament des philosophischen Wissens*, ed. Wolfgang H. Schrader, Hamburg.

Rainer Schäfer

Paul Redding: *Analytic Philosophy and the Return of Hegelian Thought*. Cambridge: Cambridge Univ. Press, 2007, 252 S., ISBN 978-0-521-87272-0.

Reddings Buch hat das folgende Programm: Das erste Kapitel (S. 21–55) zeichnet anhand der Philosophie von McDowell den Weg der analytischen Philosophie über Sellars' Kritik am „Mythos des Gegebenen" zurück zu Hegel. Im ersten Kapitel steht der „Mythos des Gegebenen" in epistemischer Hinsicht im Mittelpunkt; im zweiten Kapitel geht es um den „Mythos des Gegebenen" in logischer Hinsicht. Redding führt aus, dass Hegels Idee einer Identität von Geist und Welt in McDowells Anverwandlung und Modifikation zu der These verarbeitet wird, dass die Erfahrung einen komplett begrifflichen Gehalt habe; welches mit Sellars über Sellars hinausgeht. – In Parenthese sei darauf hingewiesen, dass diese Art der Kant/Hegel-Deutung schon vor hundert Jahren zahlreiche Neukantianer vertreten haben; dies führte zu einem begrifflich dominierten Wissensbegriff, der den genuinen und nichtbegrifflichen Anteil der sinnlichen Anschauung an der Erfahrung, den Kant so eindrücklich betont, vergisst. Redding weist daher zu Recht darauf hin, dass in der Anschauung gegebene Singularität von der Partikularität zu unterscheiden ist, die in einem Urteil zu Wissen verarbeitet werden kann. – Das an Sellars orientierte Hauptargument McDowells besagt, dass das, was in die Erfahrung hineingenommen werden kann, nicht aus unbegrifflichen Singularitäten, einem bloß perzeptuell gegebenen x hingenommen werden kann; das richtet sich natürlich gegen Grundlagen des Empirismus. Unbegriffliche Singularitäten gäben eben keine Bestimmtheit her. Radikaler als Sellars betont McDowell die Ungebundenheit des logischen Raums der Gründe, der also nicht aus Anschauungssingularitäten schon eine Ordnungsregel vorgezeichnet bekommen kann. Das Erfahrene bestehe vielmehr aus einem immer schon konzeptualisierten so oder so beschaffenen Dies-da; ein nichtbegrifflicher Inhalt des Wissens ist eine epistemische Verwirrung. Nach Redding liegt in diesem Zug McDowells eine Ab- und Rückkehr vom logischen Atomismus/Empirismus à la Russell zu Aristoteles; Erfahrbares muss gegenüber der kategorialen Form einer prôtê ousia offen sein. Redding betont hier Nähen und Auseinandersetzungen McDowells zu/mit Gareth Evans und Strawson.

Das zweite Kapitel (S. 56–84) verfolgt den gedanklichen Weg von Sellars zu Hegel im Werk von Brandom anhand des Motivs des „Mythos des Gegebenen" in logischer Hinsicht. Auch hier werden kantische Aspekte hervorgehoben. Der begriffliche Gehalt des Wissens wird hierbei bekanntlich holistisch, expressivistisch und inferentiell bestimmt. Der Inhalt einer Vorstellung wird durch Zuordnungen zu akzeptablen Inferenzen bestimmt, über die Zuordnungen entscheidet normativ geordnetes Verhalten. Brandoms Hegelianismus besteht in dem rationalistischen Verständnis von Sprachspielen der Zuschreibung und Rechtfertigung von Wissen. Daraus folgt ein Pragmatismus, der sich aus der nachpositivistischen Phase der analytischen Philosophie speist und sich von Quine, Davidson und Rorty anregen lässt. Redding zeigt auf, dass man mit Brandom den Mythos logischer und perzeptueller Gegebenheit auf Russell zurückzuführen hat. Der Autor geht von der These aus, dass um die 19. Jahrhundertwende, also zu Beginn der analytischen Tradition, Moores und Russels generelle Verurteilung des Idealismus als eines durch fehlerhafte Logik und absurde Metaphysik irregeleiteten Standpunktes dazu führte, dass eine ernsthafte Auseinandersetzung mit Hegel (und den anderen Idealisten) im angloamerikanischen Raum nicht stattfand, sich dies aber mittlerweile durch Philosophen wie McDowell und Brandom geändert hat. Hegel machte nach Russell die Voraussetzung, die universelle logische Geltung der Subjekt-Prädikat-Relation des kategorischen Urteils habe auch ontologische Valenz, und er kombiniere das mit einem Monismus, die ganze Welt sei eine einzige subjektive Substanz. Hiermit setze Hegel a) unkritisch die traditionelle Logik und b) einen abstrusen Subjektivismus voraus, welches alle Idealisten machten. – Das erscheint dem Rezensenten als eine abstruse Melange aus Versatzstücken von Aristoteles, Spinoza, Leibniz, plus ein wenig Kant und Hegel; zusammengerührt mag das den Idealismus Bradleys – Russells Lehrer – ergeben, aber nichts, dem die genannten großen Denker hätten zustimmen können, und auch nichts, das einem argumentierenden Idealismus auch nur entfernt ähnlich sieht. Redding (S. 8) sieht hierin natürlich zu Recht eine Idealismus-Karikatur Russels, die leider lange Zeit ernst genommen wurde. Insofern ist interessant, dass sich die antiidealistische Haltung zu Beginn der analytischen Philosophie an einem Pappkameraden entzündete; Redding verweist auf Durkheims These, dass zur Bildung von Gruppenidentitäten solche Missverständnisse sehr hilfreich sind und natürlich auch kulturelle Prägungen der Mitglieder spiegeln. –

Die quantifikatorische, die propositionale Logik und insbesondere die Prädikatenlogik erster Stufe wurde von der analytischen Tradition als „neue" Logik gesehen, u. a. aus den Arbeiten Freges extrapoliert und gegen die verfehlte „alte", klassisch-aristotelische Logik abgesetzt. Daneben konzipiert Russell eine pluralistische Ontologie, die neben Raum und Zeit als realen Entitäten, und Materie, die sich aus Elementarteilchen zusammensetzt, auch Universalien in einem realistischen platonischen Ideenhimmel enthält. Analog sieht Moore die wissensunabhängigen Fakten – z.B. Propositionen, die die Welt konstituieren –, gegenüber dem Geist, der versucht, jene Distanz mittels Sätzen zu überbrücken. Geist und Welt sind durch das Erkennen von Urteilen in Kontakt zu bringen. Dies soll den kantischen Subjektivismus vermeiden. Die Probleme dieses Ansatzes führen Moore dann zu seiner Verbindung aus Common sense und Empirismus und auch bei Russell bleiben Reste des Empirismus.

Von diesen Formen und Dogmen des Empirismus hat sich die analytische Philosophie bekanntlich durch die Studien von Sellars („Mythos des Gegebenen", „Raum der Gründe") und eine gründliche Frege-Rezeption (bes. Freges Kontextprinzip) befreit. Diese sellarsschen und fregeschen Motive sind meiner Meinung nach ein wohl verstandener Kantianismus, der nicht mit jener Kant-Karikatur zu verwechseln ist. Wenn Kant einerseits lehrt, „Anschauungen ohne Begriffe sind blind" und andererseits mit der Kategoriendeduktion der B-Auflage in der *KrV* zeigt, dass Anschauungen immer schon unter Kategorien kontextuell stehen (d. h. in synthetischen Urteilen vorkommen), dann erledigt dies den „Mythos des Gegebenen" und zeigt auch im Sinne von Sellars auf, dass sich der logische Raum des Gebens und Nehmens von Gründen nicht im Reich des Empirischen finden lässt; das kann auch nach Kant schon deswegen nicht sein, weil die Kategorien dieselben Einheiten sind, die auch die logischen Urteilsfunktionen bilden. Schon Kants Urteilstheorie impliziert das fregesche Kontextprinzip. Jedenfalls geht nach Redding für Brandom wie für McDowell der Weg zu Hegel über und durch Kant. Dies ist ein Kant, dem durch Hegel die Flügel um eine einseitig apriorische Reinheit, eine abgesonderte transzendentale Sphäre gestutzt wurden, wodurch die Geschichte als Ort der Realisation von Begrifflichem und von Gründen aufgewertet wurde. Das genuin kantische Thema, die Weise zu bestimmen, wie der Geist dem begegnenden Mannigfaltigen begriffliche Rahmen gibt und es damit für den Raum der Gründe aufnahmefähig macht, ist ein Kreuzungspunkt der Theorien von Sellars, Brandom und McDowell mit Kant und Hegel. Die Lektüre von Hegel als einem sehr genauen Kantianer zeichnet natürlich auch die Untersuchungen von Pippin aus.

Drittes und viertes Kapitel (S. 85–114 und S. 115–144) beschäftigen sich mit Kant und Hegel selbst sowie mit der Frage, ob McDowell und Brandom mit ihren sellarsschen Lesarten jene beiden tatsächlich treffen. Im dritten Kapitel werden solche Aspekte von Kants Transzendentalphilosophie hervorgehoben, die ihn zum Vorläufer der logischen Revolution machten, die die analytische Philosophie hervorbrachte. Bei Kant mischen sich nach Redding Aspekte, die bereits auf Frege vorausweisen mit solchen einer überkommenen aristotelischen Logik (syllogistische Konzeption der Interferenz, Begriffslogik etc.). Z.B. findet Redding den Gedanken der modernen Logik, dass eine Klasse mit nur einem Element nicht mit dem einen Element selbst identifiziert werden darf, in Kants transzendentallogischer Unterscheidung von einzelnen/singulären und besonderen/partikulären Urteilen vorgeprägt. Hegel wende sich dann mit seiner Theorie der bestimmten Negation gerade gegen jene rückwärtsgewandten Aspekte der Logik (und der transzendentalen Logik) bei Kant. So weise Hegels Theorie der bestimmten Negation weiter in die moderne Logik. Sowohl McDowells Konzept der Begrifflichkeit erfahrungsmäßigen Gehalts als auch der Inferentialismus Brandoms haben ihre geistige Wurzel in Hegels Wendung der bestimmten Negation gegen die traditionelle Logik.

Das fünfte Kapitel (S. 145–174) beschäftigt sich wieder mit McDowell und zwar mit Fragen der Vereinbarkeit von praktischer und theoretischer Vernunft in der phronesis sowie mit der logischen Grammatik der Evaluation von Gründen. Die Rückkehr des aristotelischen Konzepts der phronesis wird vom frühen McDowell in den Rahmen eines modernen Pragmatismus integriert. Die phronesis als Einheit von Theorie und Praxis erkennt Redding im sechsten Kapitel (S. 175–199) in Kants Theorie des ästhetischen Urteils wieder. Das ästhetische Urteil sei für Hegels eigene Urteilstheorie entscheidend gewesen (S. 175 ff., 19 u. ö.) und habe wesentlich dazu beigetragen, dass Hegel in seiner Logik eine inferentialistische Theorie des Urteils entwickelt habe; in dieser Weise deutet Redding Hegels Aufhebung des Urteils in den Schluss. Das erscheint dem Rezensenten problematisch, weil einerseits das ästhetische Urteil nicht gerade eine beleuchtete Rolle in Hegels Urteilstheorie spielt – es gelingt Redding auch nicht, das am Text zu belegen – und es andererseits nicht moderne Inferentialität ist, in die sich das Urteil in Hegels Logik aufhebt, sondern gerade in die aristotelische Syllogismuslehre, die allerdings, wie auch das Urteil, in Hegels Sicht als verständiges Denken zu kritisieren ist. Redding muss hier eine neuartige Lesart der aristotelischen Syllogistik unterbringen, die den Syllogismus als eine nichtformale Inferenz zur besten Erklärung deutet und so den Bogen zur Thematik einer logischen Grammatik der Evaluation von Gründen schlägt. Es wäre noch zu klären, wieso ausgerechnet das ästhetische Urteil von Kant Inferentialismus ermöglichen soll, ist es doch nach Kant gerade dadurch ausgezeichnet, dass es nicht auf den Begriff gebracht werden darf, weil sonst das freie Spiel der Vermögen aufgehoben und es zum theoretischen Urteil mit Einsatz von Kategorien geworden wäre.

Die beiden letzten Kapitel (S. 200–219 und S. 220–236) sind der Thematik gewidmet, die Hegel in den Augen der analytischen Philosophen lange Zeit ganz unmittelbar diskreditiert hat, nämlich seine sympathisierende Haltung zum Widerspruch. Das Nichtwiderspruchsprinzip aufzuheben war ein so absurdes Foul gegen das Denken und Argumentieren, dass jeder ordentliche Analytiker spätestens an dieser Stelle die rote Karte ziehen und Hegel aus dem Spiel nehmen musste. Derzeit applaudiert Graham Priest aus der Ecke der nicht-klassischen, parakonsistenten Logik diesem Spielzug Hegels (man kann vielleicht bezweifeln, ob sich Hegel in dieser Ecke so wohl oder gut verstanden gefühlt hätte, weil er eigentlich nicht einfach den Widerspruch – neben den Wahrheitswerten wahr und falsch – toleriert; sondern ihn vielmehr als einfach einheitlichen Ursprung allen wahren Denkens und als selbst auch wahr ansieht; man kann sich meiner Meinung nach fragen, ob Hegel nicht nur eine drei- oder nochmehrwertige Logik abgelehnt hätte, sondern nicht auch schon die zweiwertige Logik: Es gibt nur einen einzigen Wahrheitswert, nämlich wahr, falsch ist kein in der Logik vorkommender „Wahrheits"wert, wer logisch denkt, denkt Wahres, wer Falsches denkt, denkt nicht logisch; das heißt natürlich nicht, dass einzelne Gedankeninhalte unvollständig sein können und daher ihr Wahrheitsgehalt eine dialektische Weiterführung fordert; Unvollständigkeit eines Gedankens macht ihn aber nicht falsch, sondern ergänzungsbedürftig). Redding versucht zu zeigen, dass Hegels ablehnendes Verhältnis zum Nichtwiderspruch komplex ist und ein konsequentes Resultat seines kognitiven Kontextualismus einerseits und der bestimmten Negation klassischer Begriffslogik andererseits. Hegel untersuche das Gesetz der Widerspruchsfreiheit hinsichtlich basaler ontologischer Bestimmungen von Objekten, die für unser Denken normativ sind. Nach Hegels kritischer Untersuchung zeige sich, dass solche ontologischen Bestimmungen kontextsensitiv sind und somit einem Kontextwechsel unterliegen. Sowohl die Denk- als auch die Objektbestimmungen wechseln mit dem Kontext. Diese Art des Kontextwechsels sei für Hegel der positive Sinn des Widerspruchs und gipfele in der Ansicht, alles sei widersprüchlich. – Der Rezensent ist sich nicht ganz sicher, ob damit nicht zuviel bewiesen wurde, weil sich bei Hegel Widersprüche auch in höhere Einheiten aufheben und nicht einfach bestehen bleiben. – Jedenfalls steckt hierin ein gewisses Problem der Rekonstruktion Reddings, denn bei ihm klingt es stellenweise so, als seien einerseits die Objekte dem dialektisch-widersprüchlichen Wandel unterworfen und ebenso auf der anderen Seite unsere Kognitionen. Das ist aber meiner Meinung nach ein unterschwelliger (cartesianischer) Dualismus, den Hegel so nicht mitgemacht hätte, oft genug betont Redding an anderen Stellen zu Recht und mit Verweis auf Brandom die Identität von Denken und Sein bei Hegel; dann können es aber nicht zwei parallele Widersprüche sein, sondern es waltet derselbe Widerspruch im Denken wie im Sein, weil Denken Sein ist. Jedenfalls darf man einem Denkkontextualismus nicht einen Objektkontextualismus gegenüberstellen. Auf diese Weise ist von vornherein verhindert, dass eine Inkonzinnität auftritt, die Redding zu Recht bei allen von Sellars inspirierten hegelianischen Philosophen ausmacht, nämlich den Versuch, Hegel vor einer metaphysischen Weltdeutung zu bewahren, die impliziert, dass es eine Charakteristik der realen Welt selbst ist, dass sie sowie auch alle ihre Objekte widersprüchlich sind. Redding sieht zu Recht, dass Hegel dies durchaus gesagt hätte, man darf schließlich nicht „zuviel Zärtlichkeit für die Endlichkeit der Welt" aufbringen, aber er argumentiert (an einigen Stellen) immer noch aus einer problematischen dualistischen Grundhaltung heraus.

Hegels „metaphysischste" Voraussetzung der Notwendigkeit einer Versubjektivierung der „unendlichen Substanz" wird von Redding als seine Vermeidungsstrategie einer noch viel problematischeren metaphysischen Voraussetzung verstanden. Dabei handelt es sich um die Zurückweisung des „metaphysischen Positivismus", Reddings Bezeichnung für den Platonismus. Der metaphysische Positivismus ist der ontologische Begleiter des epistemischen „Mythos des Gegebenen". Hegels Subjektivierungsstrategie wird als durchgeführter kritischer Kantianismus gedeutet, der sich gegen ontologischen Dogmatismus wendet. Dabei kritisiere Hegel die Metaphysik nicht in abstrakter Weise, sondern hebe sie durch die bestimmte Negation zu einem neuartigen Typus auf. – Für kontinentale Hegel- und Idealismusforscher ist das nicht neu, denn diese Thematik wurde vielfach verhandelt und Hegels Typus der antidogmatischen Metaphysik ist z. B. als eine darstellende Kritik oder als kritische Darstellung schon in den 70er Jahren des letzten Jahrhunderts rekonstruiert worden. Redding hätte vielleicht auch noch thematisieren können, dass es nun mit der neuartigen Logik, wie sie im Ausgang von Frege konzipiert wird, auch eine gewisse Schieflage gibt, denn Frege ist Platoniker. Hier gibt es also gerade den „Mythos des Gegebenen" in logischer Hinsicht, was einen ontologischen Mythos des Gegebenen impliziert. Gegen diesen wenden sich, wie Redding ja zu Recht herausgearbeitet hatte, Kant und Hegel. Wie also bekommt man die notwendige Subjektivierung mit dem Fregianismus zusammen? –

Insgesamt kann man das Fazit ziehen, dass Redding Hegel sehr nah an Kant heranrückt und vielleicht die eine oder andere beide trennende Kritik Hegels an Kant schärfer betont werden kann. Sicherlich stehen mit McDowell und Brandom die beiden analytischen Denker, die sich am intensivsten mit Hegel beschäftigen und ihn auch am intensivsten in ihr eigenes Denken umverwandeln, zu Recht im Zentrum des Buches. Intensiver kann man aber auch Denker mit ausgeprägter Antipathie gegen Idealismus und Hegel wie Quine oder Davidson untersuchen, also solche Analytiker die sicherlich ein höheres Niveau als Russell haben. Diese kommen bei Redding natürlich auch vor, aber nicht in eigenständiger Würdigung, mehr am Rande. In einer Fußnote deutet Redding an, er hätte auch über Kripke den Neohegelianismus analytischer Denker aufweisen können. Wie sieht es mit eigenen Studien zu Putnam und Rorty aus? Ist vielleicht Rortys Neopragmatismus mit Vorliebe für Kontingenz, Ironie und Solidarität die sinnvolle doppelte Negation des Geschichtlichen gegenüber Brandoms rationalistisch-optimistischem Geschichtspragmatismus? Hat man eigentlich Hegels Antipragmatismus wirklich verstanden, wenn man nach seiner Lektüre Pragmatiker ist? Bekanntlich werden die Sellars folgenden Denker oft als postanalytische Philosophen bezeichnet, diese Trennung innerhalb der analytischen Philosophie in Traditionalisten und Postanalytiker hätte auch stärker betont und vielleicht sogar philosophisch produktiv weitergedacht werden können: Die postanalytische Bewegung nach Sellars mit Brandom und McDowell als bestimmte Negation der analytischen Philosophie?! Über die mit einer doppelten Negation auch wieder hinauszugehen ist?! Nach der lohnenden Lektüre von Reddings elaboriertem und kenntnisreichem Buch wird einem jedenfalls klar, dass ein hegelisch-analytisches Symphilosophieren möglich ist und dass Hegel gegen einige gegenwärtige Philosophen, die hinter dem Niveau von Brandom und McDowell zurück bleiben möchten, eingewendet hätte, dass sie zu wenig Vertrauen in Kraft und Virtualität des Gedankens haben.

Richard Crouter

Peter Grove: *Deutungen des Subjekts Schleiermachers Philosophie der Religion*. Berlin & New York: Walter de Gruyter, 2004, pp. xii + 658, ISBN: 3-11-018224-6.

Peter Grove's impressive study, which originated as a Danish dissertation and corresponds to a German habilitation, must be ranked among the most thorough investigations of Schleiermacher's philosophy of religion published during the last decade. Indeed, the book continues to attract readers as a virtual "archaeology of the mind" of the philosopher-theologian. Grove effectively combines historical-genetic explanation of Schleiermacher's key ideas with a systematic conceptual analysis of pivotal texts, both early and late. If the German is often difficult and occasionally tedious for non-native speakers, this is inherent in the terrain. Grove's study confirms the tendency of recent studies of classical German philosophy (e.g., Dieter Henrich's) that soften the lines that are typically drawn between idealism and post-idealism, thus bringing out a higher degree of continuity. The book deserves careful study by anyone who remains puzzled by the question of how Schleiermacher fits into the emerging picture of German idealism and early romanticism and where the lines are to be drawn between what is common to the era of Kant and Fichte and what, if anything, is innovative in Schleiermacher's discourse regarding religion, meta-physics, and self-consciousness. Its 600 pages cover not just the well-known books published in Schleiermacher's lifetime, the *Reden* and the *Glaubenslehre*, but appeal directly to philosophical ethics as a crucial link in the deployment of ideas in the later works, including the dialectics.

Grove critically and constructively engages Schleiermacher discussions in Germany of the last thirty years. Issue is taken, in varying degrees, with aspects of the work of Günter Meckenstock, Eilert Herms, and Falk Wagner, while the author's predilections and interpretative moves are informed by recent work by Andreas Arndt on the impact of Friedrich Schlegel and by Ulrich Barth and Konrad Cramer on Schleiermacher's theory of subjectivity. Apart from Julia Lamm's study of Schleiermacher and Spinoza, English-language work is not within the author's purview. Yet, the sweep of Grove's treatment leaves few issues centrally related to Schleiermacher untouched and, for this reason, deserves to be brought into conversation with English-language work by Andrew Dole, David Klemm, Jacqueline Mariña, and Wayne Proudfoot, among others.

The book's two main parts follow an introduction, which formulates the questions behind the study and conveys the design of the argument. The first of these main parts, "Presuppositions" traces Schleiermacher's original philo-sophical context in the early 1790s when he encounters Kant amid the Spino-zistic revival in Germany and continues on to consider the period from 1796 to 1803, where the practice of Friedrich Schlegel's *symphilosophieren* provides an implicit metaphysic and sense of transcendence as early romantic facets of Schleiermacher's teaching. Schleiermacher thus puts his own intellectual stamp on the legacy of Kant and Fichte. These early choices, so Grove argues, remain intact even as the problems they raise are transposed to other sets of ideas and new intellectual proposals.

A second, larger part of the book gets into the heart of Schleiermacher's early and mature legacy under the heading, "Formation of Theories". Part II has three sections that analyze and track the movement of the theologian-philosopher's ideas. Although a review can hardly capture the nuances of Grove's argument, a sketch of the contours of this "theory formation" can suggest the author's main points.

Section II.A rehearses prior research on the 1799 *Reden* and gives a close reading of the concept of religion as arising from an "intuition of the universe" and "feeling" and as implying a pre-reflective unity between the universe and human being that is lost when intuition becomes separated from feeling. Close examination of a scheme of thought that can name the universe as "the infinite", "the world spirit", "the whole", or even as a personal God shows how the text conceals its appeal to a "higher realism" and "implicit metaphysic" in which a problematized "idea of God" is taken as an "interpretation of the universe" (pp. 358–67). As a result, the *Reden*'s implicit metaphysic is independent of the religious consciousness; religious consciousness is dependent upon metaphysics, not the reverse (p. 370). In section II.B (pp. 373–430) Grove takes up Schleiermacher's philosophical ethics in his post-1804 work, especially the *Brouillon zur Ethik* of 1805/06, which follows the largely critical *Grundlinien einer Kritik der bisherigen Sittenlehre* of 1803. Moving to a more properly philosophical topic, the section examines the role played by "intuition" and "feeling" as well as "self-consciousness" in the theory of knowledge and ethics. The choice of themes is not incidental or arbitrary; by proceeding in this way, Grove is able to show the ongoing philosophical centrality of ideas that are closely associated with two more strictly theological contexts: the *Reden* and the *Glaubenslehre*. This move allows Grove to point to an underlying thematic continuity that enables him to set aside, at least in this study, the thorny problem of conceptual editorial changes that take place in the second and third editions of the *Reden*.

In II.C (pp. 433–612), arguably the heart of Peter Grove's book, a large final section examines religion and metaphysics in the late work, specifically in the *Dialektik* and the *Glaubenslehre*. Rather than rehearse details, a reviewer can perhaps best convey certain of the author's chief claims: (1) that theory depends upon pre-theory; (2) that thematizing subjectivity, whether innovative or not, leads to a self-consistent modest metaphysics that complements the specific claims of religious consciousness; (3) that Schleiermacher develops two distinct (early, and then later) versions of the philosophy of religion, each of which has certain strengths and potential weaknesses.

(1) Schleiermacher's view that theory proceeds from pre-theoretical thought is evident, beginning with the early *symphilosophieren* undertaken with Friedrich Schlegel. Though the idea assumes various forms in his work, Schleiermacher dismisses the idea of deriving the whole of philosophy from a single principle and building up a system of philosophy on the basis of a thesis that is contained in such a principle. His thinking rests on a conceptual openness, as seen in the introductions to the various lectures on dialectics. For him philosophy is necessarily defined individually, must have the form of infinite approximation, and cannot be taught directly as a science. The transcendental part of the dialectics teaches that the concept of subjectivity does not yield a final way of thinking about foundations; rather, subjectivity is accorded the status of something relative, which points to the absolute. Similarly, concepts of the absolute as the results of Schleiermacher's metaphysics are conclusive (*Schlußbetrachtungen*) only as presuppositions and as problematical concepts or ideas that are, as it were, not yet filled in.

(2) On Grove's reading, Schleiermacher's thematizing of subjectivity via the concept of immediate self-consciousness has often been interpreted in opposite ways: (a) as merely a further variant of a widespread circular, and thus erroneous, explanation of a consciously-aware self-relatedness and (b) as an original proposal, which rises above this error and resolves problems in which the most important theoreticians of classical German philosophy – above all Kant and Fichte – were also allegedly engaged.

Grove holds that both these views are inadequate. He maintains that the concept of immediate self-consciousness consistently and appropriately draws upon Schleiermacher's presuppositions regarding the theory of consciousness. The theologian-philosopher's conception of self-consciousness is more subtle and differentiated than is presented in much current research, even if Schleiermacher's concept of immediate self-consciousness may not actually be innovative. Since he draws significantly from elements in the theory of subjectivity that he shares with contemporaries, his contribution to this field of inquiry should not be overestimated. Yet his concept of feeling as a form of concrete subjectivity through which the subject relates to others and to the world does have elements of originality. For Grove, Schleiermacher's definition of religious subjectivity deepens our understanding of subjectivity. Schleiermacher's contribution consists in his resolute insistence that our clearest self-consciousness always includes a moment of impenetrability or opaqueness, such that, even in our highest self-activity and freedom, we only find ourselves in a provisional state of certainty. Here I take Grove to mean that for Schleiermacher we can never attain a secure concept of the absolute as undifferentiated objective reality, but only as a necessary presupposition. Readers of *Deutungen* will doubtless continue to debate how, whether, and the degree to which this philosophical underpinning can serve the felt needs of religious faith.

Though it is implied more than secured, having a foundation matters, and its corollaries translate into recognizably theistic accounts of the human condition. Grove's Schleiermacher presents human subjectivity as essentially not sufficient. As free, knowledge-seeking beings we are never all-powerful and transparent in our self-relatedness, but are driven beyond ourselves to interpret our lack of self-transparency and to regard the incomprehensible world as resting on a transcendent ground. In varying ways the point has been present since the outset of Schleiermacher's assault on pre-critical, rational metaphysics.

(3) In the end, Grove sees Schleiermacher as developing two distinct versions of his philosophy of religion, each with its characteristic strengths and weaknesses. In the first, Schleiermacher develops the concept of the religious consciousness that dominates the first edition of the *Reden*, where an "intuition of the universe" is bound up with feeling. This is, however, a shortened formula for the idea that religion is an "intuition of the individual as a presentation of the universe". This "as" expresses the idea of a pre-predicative, pre-reflective interpretation, which religion takes as referring to everything individual and finite. Grove acknowledges that some interpreters prefer this line to Schleiermacher's subsequent formulations, but argues that the weakness of this position consists in its limited ability to give an adequate theoretical account of the s ubject of the religious consciousness.

The second version of Schleiermacher's philosophy of religion draws from two different theoretical contexts within his late work. Together these form a conception which taken as a whole must be judged as superior to the way religion is conceived in the *Reden*. Its foundation in the theory of subjectivity and in the metaphysical underpinnings of a philosophy of religion contains a potential that has not yet been exhausted. In this mature theory a more robust analysis of "feeling" in the *Glaubenslehre* and the *Dialektik* allows Schleiermacher to explicate the concept of religion more strictly within a theory of subjectivity. (Here Grove adeptly combines analysis of the more expansive and consequential first edition of the *Glaubenslehre* with relevant passages from the second . Similarly, he draws from several versions of the *Dialektik*, while having frequent recourse to the 1822 formulations). This move leads to an interpretative moment, which is not restricted to the original form of the concept of religion. Feeling and self-consciousness present no epistemic relation of the subject to something else, though they are themselves determined through a grounding relationship such that, when the "religious consciousness" is taken as "feeling", other finite things and the world can be perceived. As a result, one no longer needs to claim that the religious consciousness only perceives immediately. Instead one can here speak more pointedly about interpreting human selfhood reflectively, i.e., in relation to the entities of the world. In this manner the idea of self-consciousness is first properly located within the dialectic, explicates its nature as pre-theoretical, and in this sense conceives of itself as a modest metaphysics.

In the end, how might one sum up Grove's overall argument? First and foremost, the book is an achievement of the first order. Its readers are treated to a sustained close reading of Schleiermacher that takes full advantage of the *Kritische Gesamtausgabe*. Historical and textual discriminations are integrated into a tough-minded systematic analysis of the theologian-philosopher's various claims. Footnotes are replete with supporting evidence, occasional barbs, and argumentative asides. All of this yields large gains for readers, even where one might take issue with the author.

Second, a general hermeneutical point: the seriousness of Schleiermacher as philosopher should no longer be in doubt. Even if Schleiermacher remains largely unrecognized within the canon of mainstream philosophy – which is the case – the translator of Plato is scarcely an amateur, interloper, or dilettante in philosophical matters. If it is today out of fashion to think philosophically in defense of religion, then this may only be a reflection of our dominant secular habits of mind. Grove acknowledges that doubts can be raised about Schleiermacher's originality. He believes such doubts are warranted for his aesthetics and also for his hermeneutics, in the sense of a specific discipline. Grove's contention that the philosopher's dialectics are more innovative than the hermeneutics will drive readers to plunge ahead, if they have not done so already, with study of the relevant volumes of the *Kritische Gesamtausgabe* I.10.1 and 10.2. When Grove claims further that the *one* discipline where Schleiermacher's achievement must be judged as outstanding lies in the "philosophy of religion", he uses the familiar intellectual tag not in a technical sense, or one that might apply to Anglo-American analytic treatments, but in order to refer to serious philosophical reflection of any sort regarding metaphysics and religion.

Third, Grove makes an impressive case that Schleiermacher's various claims regarding the idea of God rest upon a differentiated, carefully articulated theory. Beginning with the *Reden,* Schleiermacher's thought moves away from pre-critical philosophical theology. The theory's constructive proposal grasps the origin of the idea of God through two different modes of interpreting the subject. (Hence the use of a plural in Grove's title: *Deutungen des Subjekts.*) Part of the theory reconstructs the formation of the religious idea of God. In the *Reden* this is initially understood as a pre-reflective interpretation of the idea of the universe that is presupposed in the religious interpretation. Subsequently, however, the idea of God is bound to the religious consciousness more foundationally by reconstructing its origin in human life while being grasped as a reflexive interpretation of the religious consciousness. This second part of the theory is developed in the metaphysics of the dialectic. It proceeds not from subjective but from objective consciousness and conceives of God as a necessary presupposition. With reference to how we understand ourselves and the world, God is presented two ways, to speak metaphorically, both as anchor and as source, i.e., as the transcendent ground of all knowing and being and also as the "Whence" of subjectivity and thereby also of the entire world.

Fourth, as Grove reads the late Schleiermacher, the two poles of metaphysics and religion are not equivalent pursuits, but are nonetheless seen as complementary. The theory, shaped as a reconstruction of the origin of the idea of God in conscious life, has a dual thesis regarding the validity and the content of this idea. The idea of God claims universal metaphysical validity, but it is at the same time indefinite. As grasped by religion the idea of God is, of course, definite, even if this awareness remains only subjective. The universally grounded metaphysical idea of God still warrants the truth of this claim. Schleiermacher's manner of treating metaphysics and religion in his early as well as in his late work thus does not succumb to the critique of mixing metaphysics and religion. It includes a way of locating each, while pinpointing their divergence. The theoretical explication of religion and its interpretation needs metaphysics in order to give a suitable account of the idea of God. At the same time, Schleiermacher's main thesis also obtains – if one extends the line and includes the concrete dimension of community, which also distinguishes religion from metaphysics – that metaphysics alone is incapable of sustaining an interpretation of life in a thoroughly binding manner.

Autoren/Authors

Richard Crouter, Prof., John M. and Elizabeth W. Musser Professor of Religious Studies, Emeritus, Department of Religion, Leighton Hall, Third Floor, Carleton College, One North College Street, Northfield, MN, 55057 USA

Hans Friedrich Fulda, Prof. Dr., Albert-Ueberle-Str. 24, 69120 Heidelberg

Pierre Keller, Prof., Department of Philosophy, Humanities & Social Sciences Building, 900 University Avenue, University of California – Riverside, Riverside, CA 92521 USA

Thomas Kisser, Dr., Schellingstr. 63, 80799 München

Heiner F. Klemme, Prof. Dr., Johannes Gutenberg-Universität, Philosophie der Neuzeit, 55099 Mainz

Christian Klotz, Prof. Dr., Universidade Federal de Goiás (UFG), Faculdade de Filosofia, Campus Samambaia, Caixa Postal 131, 74001-970 Goiânia (GO), Brasilien

Franz, Knappik, Dr. des., Humboldt-Universität zu Berlin, Institut für Philosophie, Unter den Linden 6, 10099 Berlin

Michelle Kosch, Prof., Department of Philosophy, 218 Goldwin Smith Hall, Cornell University, Ithaca, New York 14853-3201 USA

Charles Larmore, Prof., W. Duncan MacMillan Family Professor in the Humanities, Department of Philosophy, Box 1918, Brown University, Providence RI 02912 USA

Wayne Martin, Prof., School of Philosophy and Art History, University of Essex, Wivenhoe Park, Essex, CO4 3SQ UK

Michael Morris, Prof., Philosophy Department, University of South Florida, 4202 East Fowler Avenue, FAO226, Tampa, FL 33620 USA

Alex Neill, Dr., Department of Philosophy, Humanities Building, University of Southampton, Avenue Campus, Highfield, Southampton SO17 1BF UK

Rocco Porcheddu, Dr., Taeitusstr. 15a, 50678 Köln

Rainer Schäfer, Dr., Philosophisches Seminar der Universität Heidelberg, Schulgasse 6, 69117 Heidelberg

Sebastian Schwenzfeuer, Universität Freiburg, Philosophisches Seminar, Werthmannplatz, 79085 Freiburg

Sandy Shapshay, Prof., Department of Philosophy, Indiana University, 026 Sycamore Hall, 1033 E. Third Street, Bloomington, IN 47401 USA

Allen Wood, Prof., Ruth Norman Halls Professor of Philosophy, Department of Philosophy, Indiana University, 026 Sycamore Hall, 1033 E. Third Street, Bloomington, IN 47401 USA

Hinweis an die Verlage / Letter to Publishers

Wir möchten alle Verlage bitten, uns auf Neuerscheinungen aufmerksam zu machen, in denen der *Deutsche Idealismus* thematisch ist. Es kann sich dabei sowohl um vergleichende Arbeiten zu Autoren und Themen des Deutschen Idealismus handeln wie auch um Beiträge zu einzelnen Autoren oder systematischen Themen. Für Rezensionsexemplare sind wir dankbar. Dabei sollten englischsprachige Exemplare bitte an die deutsche Adresse, deutschsprachige Exemplare bitte an die amerikanische Adresse geschickt werden. Arbeiten in anderen Sprachen senden Sie bitte ebenfalls an die deutsche Adresse.

We would like to ask publishing houses to inform us of new materials appearing which relate to the theme of *German Idealism*. Comparative works on author and themes of German Idealism or contributions on individual authors and themes are welcome. We are thankful for review copies. Please send copies in English to the German address and copies in German to the American address. Works in other languages we ask to be sent to the German address as well.

Prof. Dr. Karl Ameriks, University of Notre Dame, Department of Philosophy, 100 Malloy Hall, Notre Dame, Indiana 46556, USA

Prof. Dr. Jürgen Stolzenberg, Seminar für Philosophie, Martin-Luther-Universität Halle-Wittenberg, Schleiermacherstr. 1, 06114 Halle (Saale), Germany